W9-CFX-532

God designed Scripture to speak to us, to speak to you and to me, to speak to each of us—daily and deeply. We often don't hear from God daily or deeply because we are afraid to listen to the sacred questions God's Word provokes in us as we read. Instead of listening to those sacred questions, we too easily skirt and suppress and slide away from the deep questions the Bible provokes. But Kellye Fabian designs this book with pastoral sensitivity and theological depth to permit those questions, then to listen to those questions, and finally to seek answers by listening to what God is saying in his ever-new-and-fresh Word. *Sacred Questions* is designed to promote sacred faith seeking sacred understanding.

SCOT MCKNIGHT, Julius R. Mantey Chair of New Testament, Northern Seminary

Kellye has been a friend for years, and I've had the privilege of being guided by both her questions and her prayers many times in those years. Kellye's intelligence and depth and creativity shine through every page, and I'm so delighted that her gentle and wise questions and prayers have now been captured in a format that will allow so many people to experience their transformative power.

SHAUNA NIEQUIST, author of five books, including *Present over Perfect* and *Savor*

A significant crisis in contemporary Christianity is our difficulty relating Scripture to life. What we lack isn't information but integration. Kellye Fabian knows the power of good questions. They invite honesty, wonder, and a loving response to what is most real. If you have the courage to ask the questions in this book, it will change your life.

MARK SCANDRETTE, director of ReIMAGINE: A Center for Integral Christian Practice; author of *Free, Practicing the Way of Jesus,* and *Belonging and Becoming*

Kellye's love of the Bible and spiritual disciplines shines bright everywhere she goes—including here!

MARGARET FEINBERG, author of *Taste and See*

Each morning for the past four years, Kellye Fabian's devotions have been feeding my soul, reminding me how to slow down, guiding me into prayer with the Father, and helping me walk deeply with Jesus and receive all that the Holy Spirit has for me. When you dive into *Sacred Questions*, come expecting to be pastored and empowered, guided and equipped through the use of Scripture, story, prayer, and reflection on how to live your one and only life in response to our great God.

STEVE CARTER, speaker, author of *This Invitational Life*

When a smart woman chases after the Lord, a book like this is born. Kellye ushers us right into the throne room, with grace and humble confidence. This book is a lifetime companion.

TRICIA LOTT WILLIFORD, author of *You Can Do This*

Sacred Questions is unique in the "devotional" space. Where many devotionals leave you pondering the words of the author, *Sacred Questions* leaves you pondering God's Word—and God himself. Kellye Fabian is a masterful guide who takes you into God's presence, then gracefully removes herself and leaves you alone with your Father.

KEITH FERRIN, author, speaker, biblical storyteller

I've always been drawn to reflective people who ask probing questions, which is why I fell in love with *Sacred Questions* immediately. Kellye Fabian is a seasoned and trusted guide for anyone who wants to enter a holy dialogue with God that will transform them from the inside out.

STEVE WIENS, pastor, author of *Beginnings* and *Whole*

The questions we ask define our future. Like large doors swinging on small hinges, the questions we ask unlock new journeys, holy conviction, and unexpected destiny. Kellye Fabian has a unique gift with the most perceptive and illuminating questions. In her book *Sacred Questions*, Kellye will gently guide you on a journey that will inevitably lead you to new doors of discovery.

DARREN WHITEHEAD, DMin, senior pastor of Church of the City and author of *Holy Roar* (coauthored with Chris Tomlin)

SACRED
QUESTIONS

{KELLYE FABIAN}

A Transformative Journey through the Bible

A *NavPress* resource published in alliance
with Tyndale House Publishers, Inc.

TO SISTER FLORENCE,
you saw my gift for writing.

TO MY SWEET JAMIE,
you're the Rory to my Lorelai.

TO STEVE,
your love heals me.

NavPress is the publishing ministry of The Navigators, an international Christian organization and leader in personal spiritual development. NavPress is committed to helping people grow spiritually and enjoy lives of meaning and hope through personal and group resources that are biblically rooted, culturally relevant, and highly practical.

For more information, visit www.NavPress.com.

Sacred Questions: A Transformative Journey through the Bible

Copyright © 2018 by Kellye Fabian. All rights reserved.

A NavPress resource published in alliance with Tyndale House Publishers, Inc.

NAVPRESS is a registered trademark of NavPress, The Navigators, Colorado Springs, CO. The NAVPRESS logo is a trademark of NavPress, The Navigators. *TYNDALE* is a registered trademark of Tyndale House Publishers, Inc. Absence of ® in connection with marks of NavPress or other parties does not indicate an absence of registration of those marks.

The Team: Don Pape, Publisher; Caitlyn Carlson, Acquisitions Editor; Cara Iverson, Copy Editor; Jennifer Ghionzoli, Designer

Cover and interior images are the property of their respective copyright holders, and all rights are reserved. Dove © Prixel Creative/Lightstock; Holy Week icons © Joe Cavazos/Lightstock; lamb © Schroeder Creations/Lightstock; circle © Charli's Web/Creative Market; photo of oil painting © LEKS illustrations/Creative Market.

Author photograph copyright © 2016 by New Branch Films. All rights reserved.

The author is represented by the Christopher Ferebee Agency, www.christopherferebee.com.

Some of content in this book was previously published in the Willow Creek Devotional Series by Kellye Fabian. Used with permission.

Unless otherwise indicated, all Scripture quotations are taken from the *Holy Bible*, New Living Translation, copyright © 1996, 2004, 2015 by Tyndale House Foundation. Used by permission of Tyndale House Publishers, Inc., Carol Stream, Illinois 60188. All rights reserved. Scripture quotations marked MSG are taken from *THE MESSAGE*, copyright © 1993, 1994, 1995, 1996, 2000, 2001, 2002 by Eugene H. Peterson. Used by permission of NavPress. All rights reserved. Represented by Tyndale House Publishers, Inc. Scripture quotations marked NIV are taken from the Holy Bible, *New International Version,*® *NIV.*® Copyright © 1973, 1978, 1984, 2011 by Biblica, Inc.® Used by permission. All rights reserved worldwide.

Some of the anecdotal illustrations in this book are true to life and are included with the permission of the persons involved. All other illustrations are composites of real situations, and any resemblance to people living or dead is purely coincidental.

For information about special discounts for bulk purchases, please contact Tyndale House Publishers at csresponse@tyndale.com, or call 1-800-323-9400.

Cataloging-in-Publication Data is available.

ISBN 978-1-63146-928-2

Printed in the United States of America

24	23	22	21	20	19	18
7	6	5	4	3	2	1

Contents

Introduction

Be patient toward all that is unsolved in your heart.
RAINER MARIA RILKE

God's Word has not done its complete work until it evokes an answer from us.
EUGENE PETERSON

MY SPIRITUAL JOURNEY began with a question: "Why don't I have faith?"

I wrote those words in my brand-new Bible in 2005, right in the middle of what I now call "the dark years." "Why don't I have faith?" was not an intellectual question; it was a cry for help.

Of course, from an outsider's perspective, my life probably looked fine. I was a successful trial lawyer at a firm in Chicago. I owned a house and car. I flew first class all over the country. I drank the best wine. I had all the things that defined a "successful life." But on the inside—in my heart and mind—I was a mess. Just a couple of years earlier, I had gotten divorced. My heart was broken—not because of anything my husband had done, but because I just didn't know who I was or what my life was supposed to be about. I had a beautiful daughter, and I loved her more than I thought possible. But those years were filled with loneliness and emptiness. I was on a desperate (and often destructive) search to discover who I was and if I was worthy of being loved.

Perhaps because I had spent years asking questions as a lawyer, my first thought about faith was a question. I couldn't shake that thought after reading Romans 12:3: "By the grace given me I say to every one of you: Do not think of yourself more highly than you ought, but rather think of yourself with sober judgment, in accordance with the faith God has distributed to each of you" (NIV). If the Bible was true (and at that point I didn't know if it was) and God had given each person some amount of faith, why hadn't I received any?

Without knowing it, my question began what would become the most transformative spiritual practice of my life: asking questions as I read the Bible and sitting with those questions in God's presence, not as a way to receive answers but as a way to be changed. In other words, in that first question, I wasn't really seeking an answer to why I didn't have faith. I was seeking to know God, to believe him, and to trust him—to *have* faith.

As I reflect back, I can see that God has used this practice of asking questions to show me who he is, allow me to see myself more clearly, break patterns of sin, grow in forgiveness and love, and join his work in the world. Most days, I'm walking around with a question in my heart and mind that arose during my time reading Scripture that morning. For example, *Why did that verse cause such anxiety in me? What's getting in the way of my forgiving that person? Why did those words stand out so much when I read them? What people and practices in my life help me live with more joy and patience?*

I want to invite you into this daily practice of asking sacred questions. It has been transformative and life giving for me, and I think it can be for you, too. Asking sacred questions opens a holy dialogue with the loving, ever-present God who is at once holding all things together and dwelling within us. Instead of doing all the talking, we learn how to listen for what God is saying. We all long for space to hear him, to allow ourselves to receive his love, and yet we often either fail to make the time or are unsure how to do it (and maybe a little of both). Jesus calls us to come to him in our weariness, with our burned-out selves and broken hearts. He calls to us in our greatest triumphs and most devastating mistakes. Yet in our busyness, our brokenness, our pain, or even in just the fullness of life, we resist this invitation. We forget that he desires us to remain in him, and we forget to turn to him. We forget we are in a relationship. We forget that it is in God that we live and move and have our being.

My prayer is that this book will help you respond to Jesus' invitation over the next year—that you can enter into a holy space in which you become attuned to his voice as he encourages, loves, trains, comforts, heals, challenges, and transforms you. And I pray that responding to his invitation allows you to draw closer to him and live every day with your heart and eyes lifted to him, and your hands outstretched to the world.

HOW TO USE THIS BOOK

The book is divided into twelve primary sections (and one each for Christmas and Easter), each covering a topic that shapes our relationships with God, ourselves, and others. In the broadest sense, the book will lead you on an intentional journey of transformation from the inside out.

The first four topics—responding to Jesus' invitations, opening to God's love, knowing the one you follow, and finding your identity in Christ—are meant to ground your heart, mind, and soul in the truth that in Christ, you are unendingly loved and unshakably secure.

The next two topics—abiding in God in a world of distractions and being formed by what's true—begin the outward movement, as you will confront the things that try to dislodge you from the truth that you are loved and secure. These sections help you learn to rest in God even as the world tosses you around.

The next five topics—loving like Jesus, opening your eyes to the Kingdom of God, aligning with the Holy Spirit, lamenting your pain and the pain of the world, and worshiping God for the beauty of creation—turn your eyes, ears, and heart outward to join in the redemptive work God is doing in the world.

Finally, in the last primary section—for the sake of others—you will allow your life to speak and reflect your relationship with Jesus, doing good in the world with the Holy Spirit's help and inviting others into the life Jesus has granted you.

The sections vary in length, each including seven to fifty-six days of daily practices. My recommendation is to start at the beginning and take this formative one-year journey. But if a particular topic resonates deeply with your current season, you can engage the sections in whatever order you choose.

THE DAILY PRACTICE

Reading the Scripture is vital for transformation as you walk through this book. The words of God are not study material but food for your soul. Read slowly, savoring the words as if they were coming from the mouth of a close friend or spouse. You may be tempted from time to time to skip the Scripture and go straight to the questions. Of course, any engagement with God matters, so be gracious to yourself. But no human words carry the transformative power of God's words. Although the questions in each section are provocative and compelling, they are transformative only if the power of the Holy Spirit carries them into your heart. So if you are short on time or attention on a particular day, just read the Scripture and trust that even if you are distracted or uninterested, God will continue to work in you.

The Scripture each day is taken from the New Living Translation, but you can use whatever version of the Bible you are most comfortable with and in whatever form best suits you. Maybe you need a physical Bible on your lap, or perhaps you prefer to use an app or website such as YouVersion or BibleGateway. In most sections, the Scripture reading is followed by a short paragraph designed to increase understanding of the context of the verses or to highlight a particular aspect of the passage.

Asking sacred questions each day is meant to help you reflect on what God revealed as you read. Examine your thoughts, attitudes, and actions in his presence and with his guidance. The questions are meant not to merely increase your biblical knowledge but to reveal the state of your soul, allowing you to partner with God as he shapes, heals, and transforms you.

Finally, prayer is a vital component of each daily practice. Spend time opening yourself to God's guidance, thanking him, asking him to transform you in the ways you need and to send you out into the world as an embodiment of his love and grace.

A WAY TO BEGIN

Perhaps you have been walking with God for a long time and know exactly how to bring your body, mind, and heart into awareness of his loving presence. Wonderful! In that case, let your holy conversation begin! If you're not sure how to dive in or you're looking for a new approach, here's a guide.

Place

Find one place where you can sit every day and seek to hear from God. Maybe it's your favorite chair or spot on the couch. Maybe it's the train on your way to work. Or maybe it's a plastic chair at a coffee shop. What matters is that, as much as possible, you go to the same location each day. You will find that this consistency will allow you to be more open and less distracted. You will spend less energy adjusting to the environment and have more brain space to engage with God. In Luke 22:39, we learn that it was usual for Jesus to go to the Mount of Olives to pray. Jesus practiced going to a particular place to meet with God.

Posture

Approach your daily practice with an open heart and open hands. So often we read the Bible with an agenda. This isn't necessarily a bad thing, but this should not be the *only* way we read the Bible. When we do this, we are seeking to impose our plans or are looking for specific information.

A slight shift in your posture and approach can lead to much more than answers and information. As you sit down to reflect on the Scriptures each day, open your hands. Showing with our bodies an openness to God's agenda and his desire for us, we are more likely to experience transformation.

Plan

Before you begin this book, decide how you will read through it. Will you begin with the first section and read straight through, or will you start with a segment that feels relevant to a particular struggle you're navigating? Each daily practice should take about twenty minutes. You can always spend more time on a certain daily practice depending on how deeply you allow yourself to engage the sacred questions. Of course, you don't need to be overly rigid if you feel God leading you elsewhere, but it's good to have a plan so you're spending more time reading and reflecting and less time deciding what to read.

Presence

Our lives are filled with distractions, and some of us find it a challenge to be fully present with another person. Our smartphones have become appendages, so we are constantly tempted to be somewhere other than where we are. If you can, allow yourself to be fully attentive to God and expectant about encountering his presence. This may end up being the most challenging aspect of engaging in this daily practice. How do you stay present, and what do you do when you get distracted? Here are four helpful tips:

1. **Harness your phone.** If you'll be tempted to check Facebook, your email, the weather, or your calendar, put your phone in another room and silence your ringer.
2. **Set a timer** to ring when your allotted daily practice session is almost up. This allows you to be fully present in your daily practice without having to keep checking the clock.
3. **Download distracting thoughts.** Keep a note card next to you, and when tasks and to-dos flood your mind, write them down so you can return to them later.
4. **Re-center yourself.** If you notice that your mind has run away and you're no longer present, simply re-center yourself by speaking the opening prayer for the day or another short prayer that helps return your attention to God.

Pen and Paper

When we seek to focus our minds, hearts, and bodies, remembering we are in God's loving presence, God will speak love and grace and truth into our hearts. He will remind us who he is; he will remind us who we are in Christ. He will illuminate in our hearts and lives the things that do not reflect Christlikeness. He will begin to soften us toward others, friends and enemies alike. He will transform our desires to match his. He will heal us, guide us, and invite us into his restorative work in the world.

But this is a slow process. You can go days without feeling a particular revelation or change in the moment. For this reason, I highly recommend keeping a pen and paper nearby so you can write down and reflect on whatever insights and thoughts you have as you journey through this book. Often we don't notice the slight, slow shifts in our souls and ways of thinking except in retrospect. So write in your Bible, in this book, in your journal—whatever works best for you and allows you to return to your notes later and see how God has worked. Try to stay in touch with how you're feeling as you read and reflect and pray.

A BLESSING

Now, as you begin, may you know the presence of the Holy Spirit in your every breath, the lavish love your heavenly Father has for you as you are, and the peace of the Lord Jesus Christ, the one for whom all things were created and in whom all things hold together.

Invited

Responding to Jesus' Invitations

IN ONE OF my most vivid memories, I stand with my younger sister in front of the fish tank in our room and say, "We're on our own now. We have to take care of ourselves." I was ten. My mom had just gotten remarried, and we had moved from a house in southwest Michigan to a high-rise across the lake. We were separated from our dad and stepmom and ushered into a new life. My stepdad was a quadriplegic, and it became clear to me that our lives, and particularly my mom's life, now centered around him.

The funny thing about this memory is that I'm not certain it actually happened. I do have a younger sister, and we did have a fish tank. But I don't know if I said those words. I only know that I had a deep sense early in my life of being on my own.

My sense of aloneness only increased as I grew up. I became convinced that life was an individual sport, like golf. I would have to fight my way to importance and value. I couldn't rely on other people; I had to carve my own path.

I learned what it meant to be responsible, independent, and self-sufficient. Those aren't bad qualities in and of themselves, but for whatever reason, I didn't simultaneously feel the counterbalance of childhood whimsy, the ability to depend on others, or the sense that if I reached out, someone would be there. Over time I learned how to stay safe and keep secrets, to not let anything about my inner world—my desires, struggles, doubts, loneliness, worries—show. This way of living led me to isolation—a refusal to allow other people into my experiences, my thoughts, or my heart. Ultimately, it made me struggle to receive love.

The fortress around my heart grew impassable. But in the midst of the most destructive, desperate years of my life, I became aware of a kind of beckoning deep in my soul. Slowly my ears began to open, and eventually I received the invitation of Jesus: "Come to me. Come to me. Come to me and I will give you rest." In response, I gave him my life. And as the psalmist said, "He lifted me out of the slimy pit, out of the mud and mire; he set my feet on a rock and gave me a firm place to stand. He put a new song in my mouth, a hymn of praise to our God" (Psalm 40:2-3, NIV). The fortress walls came crumbling down and love flooded in.

Jesus' invitations have continued since I received and responded to that first one. He invites each of us in personal and profound ways throughout our lives. So it only makes sense that we begin this transformational journey through the Bible by immersing ourselves in his life-changing, life-giving invitations. Over the next fifteen days, we will begin to understand how to respond to Jesus' invitations with our minds, hearts, and bodies.

DAY 1

COME TO ME

a prayer to open

Here I am, Lord. Quiet my mind. Open my heart. Give me ears to hear your invitation and the faith to respond.

READ MATTHEW 11:25-30

At that time Jesus prayed this prayer: "O Father, Lord of heaven and earth, thank you for hiding these things from those who think themselves wise and clever, and for revealing them to the childlike. Yes, Father, it pleased you to do it this way!

"My Father has entrusted everything to me. No one truly knows the Son except the Father, and no one truly knows the Father except the Son and those to whom the Son chooses to reveal him."

Then Jesus said, "Come to me, all of you who are weary and carry heavy burdens, and I will give you rest. Take my yoke upon you. Let me teach you, because I am humble and gentle at heart, and you will find rest for your souls. For my yoke is easy to bear, and the burden I give you is light."

REFLECT

In this passage, we read Jesus' most fundamental invitation. "Come to me," he says, and we cannot help but exhale. We are weary of our own struggles, the brokenness of the world, the painful relationships in our lives. We are burdened by our drive to achieve, by unmet expectations, by the wounds we carry with us. The sins of our pasts and the pain we have caused haunt us, and we long to be free. Aware of what pulls at our hearts, Jesus invites us not to believe doctrines or abide by rules but to find in him the rest we have been longing for.

- As you read today's passage, what words of Jesus stood out to you the most? Why do you think those particular words caught your attention?

- Read the passage again slowly. Which of your burdens or struggles come to mind? Where are you longing for rest? What invitation do you sense Jesus extending to you through this passage with respect to that particular longing?

- Do you know someone who seems burdened or weary? Seek God's guidance as to how you might share Jesus' invitation with that person or be a channel of the rest he offers.

SACRED QUESTIONS

Loving God, thank you for this invitation that my soul longs for so deeply. Give me the courage and faith to say yes and move toward Jesus. Help me see what weighs on my heart and causes me to live in the ways of hurry and worry instead of peace and freedom. Teach me to walk with you and to show others, by the way I live, what it means to be yours. Amen.

DAY 2

COME AND SEE

a prayer to open

Here I am, Lord. Quiet my mind. Open my heart.
Give me ears to hear your invitation and the faith to respond.

READ JOHN 1:35-39

The following day John was again standing with two of his disciples. As Jesus walked by, John looked at him and declared, "Look! There is the Lamb of God!" When John's two disciples heard this, they followed Jesus.

Jesus looked around and saw them following. "What do you want?" he asked them.

They replied, "Rabbi" (which means "Teacher"), "where are you staying?"

"Come and see," he said.

REFLECT

"Come and see." Jesus offered this invitation in response to the question "Where are you staying?" But he seemed to have much more in mind than simply showing his disciples his lodging. As we continue reading, we understand what he was really saying: "If you want to know who I am, just follow along. See what I do, how I respond to others, how I love." Jesus didn't demand blind allegiance. He didn't ensure that those he encountered had the right beliefs or behaviors first. He invited them to walk with him and watch his interactions. He invited them to draw their own conclusions. And this invitation sparked such curiosity and expectancy that fishermen dropped their nets, and tax collectors gave up their profits to follow.

- What do you think Jesus was seeking to communicate to each person he approached?

- Read today's passage again slowly. What invitation do you sense Jesus extending to you through this passage? What does he want you to come and see about him right now?

- Do you know someone who doesn't have a relationship with Jesus? Seek God's guidance and wisdom as to how you might be able to extend an invitation to "come and see" so that person can learn more about Jesus.

Invited

•

Loving God, thank you for the simple invitation to come and see, to experience your goodness and love. Give me eyes to see where I've gotten off track or forgotten what's true about Jesus and the life and love he offers. Call me again and again to come and see. Grant me the courage and words to extend this invitation to the people in my life who are longing for more and only need someone to pique their curiosity and invite them. Amen.

FOLLOW ME

a prayer to open

Here I am, Lord. Quiet my mind. Open my heart.
Give me ears to hear your invitation and the faith to respond.

READ LUKE 9:57-62

As they were walking along, someone said to Jesus, "I will follow you wherever you go."

But Jesus replied, "Foxes have dens to live in, and birds have nests, but the Son of Man has no place even to lay his head."

He said to another person, "Come, follow me."

The man agreed, but he said, "Lord, first let me return home and bury my father."

But Jesus told him, "Let the spiritually dead bury their own dead! Your duty is to go and preach about the Kingdom of God."

Another said, "Yes, Lord, I will follow you, but first let me say good-bye to my family."

But Jesus told him, "Anyone who puts a hand to the plow and then looks back is not fit for the Kingdom of God."

REFLECT

Our world offers many leaders, causes, and trends to follow. But Jesus says, "Follow *me*."[1] This seems an easier invitation for those who lived when he walked the earth—they could, quite literally, follow Jesus and watch how he loved, healed, forgave, and shared about the Kingdom of God. Yet even with Jesus physically present and calling to them, many still could not say yes. Responding to Jesus' invitation to follow will always mean saying no to other responsibilities and desires. We will want to say, "I will follow you, but first let me . . ." Jesus asks us to say, "Yes, Lord, I will follow you," and trust that our competing obligations and wants will find their proper place.

- What emotions and reactions stir in you as you read Jesus' response to each person in today's passage?

- Consider the primary places in which your day-to-day life happens—your home, workplace, church, or neighborhood. What does it mean to follow Jesus in each of those places? What kinds of relationships, obligations, and desires tend to distract you from Jesus' call to follow him?

- Read today's passage again slowly. What invitation do you sense Jesus extending to you through this passage?

Loving God, thank you for Jesus' invitation to follow. As best I know how, I say yes. My heart wants to follow, but give me the faith, the courage, and the strength to trust that as I do, you will help me love the people you've placed in my life well, do the work you've given me with faithfulness, and serve with compassion those you've called me to serve. When distractions come and obligations threaten to pull me away from you, call me back and remind me to follow. Amen.

DAY 4

BELIEVE

a prayer to open

Here I am, Lord. Quiet my mind. Open my heart.
Give me ears to hear your invitation and the faith to respond.

READ MATTHEW 9:18-31

The leader of a synagogue came and knelt before [Jesus]. "My daughter has just died," he said, "but you can bring her back to life again if you just come and lay your hand on her."

So Jesus and his disciples got up and went with him. Just then a woman who had suffered for twelve years with constant bleeding came up behind him. She touched the fringe of his robe, for she thought, "If I can just touch his robe, I will be healed."

Jesus turned around, and when he saw her he said, "Daughter, be encouraged! Your faith has made you well." And the woman was healed. . . .

When Jesus arrived at the official's home, he saw the noisy crowd and heard the funeral music. "Get out!" he told them. "The girl isn't dead; she's only asleep." But the crowd laughed at him. . . . Jesus went in and took the girl by the hand, and she stood up! The report of this miracle swept through the entire countryside.

After Jesus left the girl's home, two blind men followed along behind him, shouting, "Son of David, have mercy on us!" . . .

Jesus asked them, "Do you believe I can make you see?"

"Yes, Lord," they told him, "we do."

Then he touched their eyes and said, "Because of your faith, it will happen." Then their eyes were opened, and they could see! Jesus sternly warned them, "Don't tell anyone about this." But instead, they went out and spread his fame all over the region.

REFLECT

In today's passage, we see Jesus perform three stunning miracles: healing a chronically sick woman, raising a dead girl to life, and restoring the sight of two blind men. But Matthew reports these miracles so matter-of-factly and quickly that we are apt to miss their significance. Through miracles, Jesus implicitly invited people to believe that he was the one God had promised to send to his people—the Messiah and King who would save and restore. And if Jesus was the Messiah-King, then God had kept his promises, and God's Kingdom had arrived. Jesus is still inviting us to believe he is the one who saves, heals, and restores.

- Imagine being present to witness one of the miracles we read about in today's passage. What do you see around you? What words and noises do you hear? What do you feel as Jesus acts to bring restoration? What does Jesus want you to believe about him in that moment?

Invited •

5

- Read today's passage again slowly. What invitation do you sense Jesus extending to you? What is he asking you to believe?

- Do you have friends or family members who say they are Christians but seem unsure or unclear about who Jesus is? Seek God's guidance as to how you might be able to extend them an invitation to believe.

DAY 5

BE BORN AGAIN

a prayer to open Here I am, Lord. Quiet my mind. Open my heart. Give me ears to hear your invitation and the faith to respond.

READ JOHN 3:1-15

There was a man named Nicodemus, a Jewish religious leader who was a Pharisee. After dark one evening, he came to speak with Jesus. "Rabbi," he said, "we all know that God has sent you to teach us. Your miraculous signs are evidence that God is with you."

Jesus replied, "I tell you the truth, unless you are born again, you cannot see the Kingdom of God."

"What do you mean?" exclaimed Nicodemus. "How can an old man go back into his mother's womb and be born again?"

Jesus replied, "I assure you, no one can enter the Kingdom of God without being born of water and the Spirit. Humans can reproduce only human life, but the Holy Spirit gives birth to spiritual life. So don't be surprised when I say, 'You must be born again.' The wind blows wherever it wants. Just as you can hear the wind but can't tell where it comes from or where it is going, so you can't explain how people are born of the Spirit."

"How are these things possible?" Nicodemus asked.

Jesus replied, "You are a respected Jewish teacher, and yet you don't understand these things? I assure you, we tell you what we know and have seen, and yet you won't believe our testimony. But if you don't believe me when I tell you about earthly things, how can you possibly believe if I tell you about heavenly things? No one has ever gone to heaven and returned. But the Son of Man has come down from heaven. And as Moses lifted up the bronze snake on a pole in the wilderness, so the Son of Man must be lifted up, so that everyone who believes in him will have eternal life.

REFLECT

Nicodemus, a leader among the Jewish religious authorities, came to Jesus at night, obviously not wanting to be seen for fear of what his friends and fellow teachers might think. But something about Jesus caused Nicodemus to ask questions, and to Nicodemus's surprise, he learned that Jesus was not asking anyone to add another religious task to their daily routine as a way to earn God's favor; rather,

Jesus was inviting people to receive a new life altogether—one that would allow access to the Kingdom of God.

- What does your new life in Jesus look like? How has it been different from the old? What parts of the old life are you still holding on to?

- Read today's passage again slowly. What invitation related to new life do you sense Jesus extending to you?

- Do you know a "Nicodemus"—someone who seems to have it all together but is longing for something more, something deeper? Seek God's guidance as to how you might be able to invite that person to receive new life in Christ.

RESPOND_____

Loving God, thank you for this invitation to be born again and receive new life. You placed in me a desire for more than money, power, success, and stuff. You created me with a longing to know you and to be a part of your Kingdom, where love, mercy, and peace reign. Help me continue to embrace the new life you've given me. And give me eyes to see those who are longing for more so I can extend your invitation. Amen.

DAY 6

BE SEEN

a prayer to open

Here I am, Lord. Quiet my mind. Open my heart.
Give me ears to hear your invitation and the faith to respond.

READ JOHN 20:11-29 _____

Mary was standing outside the tomb crying, and as she wept, she stooped and looked in. She saw two white-robed angels, one sitting at the head and the other at the foot of the place where the body of Jesus had been lying. "Dear woman, why are you crying?" the angels asked her.

"Because they have taken away my Lord," she replied, "and I don't know where they have put him."

She turned to leave and saw someone standing there. It was Jesus, but she didn't recognize him. "Dear woman, why are you crying?" Jesus asked her. "Who are you looking for?"

She thought he was the gardener. "Sir," she said, "if you have taken him away, tell me where you have put him, and I will go and get him."

"Mary!" Jesus said.

She turned to him and cried out, "Rabboni!" (which is Hebrew for "Teacher").

"Don't cling to me," Jesus said, "for I haven't yet ascended to the Father. But go find my brothers and tell them, 'I am ascending to my Father and your Father, to my God and your God.'"

Mary Magdalene found the disciples and told them, "I have seen the Lord!" Then she gave them his message.

That Sunday evening the disciples were meeting behind locked doors because they were afraid of the Jewish leaders. Suddenly, Jesus was standing there among them! "Peace be with you," he said. As he spoke, he showed them the wounds in his hands and his side. They were filled with joy! . . . Again he said, "Peace be with you. As the Father has sent me, so I am sending you." Then he breathed on them and said, "Receive the Holy Spirit. If you forgive anyone's sins, they are forgiven. If you do not forgive them, they are not forgiven."

One of the twelve disciples, Thomas . . . , was not with the others when Jesus came. They told him, "We have seen the Lord!"

But he replied, "I won't believe it unless I see the nail wounds in his hands, put my fingers into them, and place my hand into the wound in his side." . . .

Later the disciples were together again, and this time Thomas was with them. The doors were locked; but suddenly, as before, Jesus was standing among them. "Peace be with you," he said. Then he said to Thomas, "Put your finger here, and look at my hands. Put your hand into the wound in my side. Don't be faithless any longer. Believe!"

"My Lord and my God!" Thomas exclaimed.

Then Jesus told him, "You believe because you have seen me. Blessed are those who believe without seeing me."

REFLECT

Jesus' words in today's passage are so personal and intimate, spoken to meet the exact need he saw in each person. To Mary, who somehow didn't recognize him in her despair, he spoke her name, gently making his presence known with a single word. To the disciples fearing for their lives, Jesus spoke peace and gave them the Holy Spirit by his very breath. Jesus called the disbelieving Thomas close and extended his wounds for Thomas to feel.

- When you first decided to believe in Jesus, what need was he meeting in you (for example, your need for grace, purpose, belonging)?

- Read today's passage again slowly. What invitation about being seen do you sense Jesus extending to you?

- Who do you know who thinks they are too needy or have too many doubts to be loved by Jesus right now? Seek God's guidance as to how you might be able to invite them to be met by Christ in the midst of their need.

RESPOND

Loving God, thank you for the invitation to be seen, truly seen, in all my need. Thank you that you speak words right into the insecurity and burdens I carry. I bring my needs to you now and pray that you would whisper words that only you know will bring comfort. Help me to be someone who sees others with your eyes and offers words of grace, healing, and hope. Amen.

DAY 7

BE KNOWN AND ACCEPTED

a prayer to open   Here I am, Lord. Quiet my mind. Open my heart.
Give me ears to hear your invitation and the faith to respond.

READ JOHN 4:1-30

Jesus knew the Pharisees had heard that he was baptizing and making more disciples than John. . . . So he left Judea and returned to Galilee. . . .

Eventually he came to the Samaritan village of Sychar. . . . Jacob's well was there; and Jesus, tired from the long walk, sat wearily beside the well about noontime. Soon a Samaritan woman came to draw water, and Jesus said to her, "Please give me a drink."

He was alone at the time because his disciples had gone into the village to buy some food.

The woman was surprised, for Jews refuse to have anything to do with Samaritans. She said to Jesus, "You are a Jew, and I am a Samaritan woman. Why are you asking me for a drink?"

Jesus replied, "If you only knew the gift God has for you and who you are speaking to, you would ask me, and I would give you living water."

"But sir, you don't have a rope or a bucket," she said, "and this well is very deep. Where would you get this living water?" . . .

Jesus replied, "Anyone who drinks this water will soon become thirsty again. But those who drink the water I give will never be thirsty again. It becomes a fresh, bubbling spring within them, giving them eternal life."

"Please, sir," the woman said, "give me this water! Then I'll never be thirsty again, and I won't have to come here to get water."

"Go and get your husband," Jesus told her.

"I don't have a husband," the woman replied.

Jesus said, "You're right! You don't have a husband—for you have had five husbands, and you aren't even married to the man you're living with now. You certainly spoke the truth!"

"Sir," the woman said, "you must be a prophet. So tell me, why is it that you Jews insist that Jerusalem is the only place of worship, while we Samaritans claim it is here at Mount Gerizim, where our ancestors worshiped?"

Jesus replied, "Believe me, dear woman, the time is coming when it will no longer matter whether you worship the Father on this mountain or in Jerusalem. You Samaritans know very little about the one you worship, while we Jews know all about him, for salvation comes through the Jews. But the time is coming—indeed it's here now—when true worshipers will worship the Father in spirit and in truth. The Father is looking for those who will worship him that way. For God is Spirit, so those who worship him must worship in spirit and in truth."

The woman said, "I know the Messiah is coming— the one who is called Christ. When he comes, he will explain everything to us."

Then Jesus told her, "I AM the Messiah!"

Just then his disciples came back. They were shocked to find him talking to a woman, but none of them had the nerve to ask, "What do you want with her?" or "Why are you talking to her?" The woman left her water jar beside the well and ran back to the village, telling everyone, "Come and see a man who told me everything I ever did! Could he possibly be the Messiah?" So the people came streaming from the village to see him.

REFLECT

This passage is multilayered and touches on many different theological issues, but as we focus on Jesus' invitations, it's hard not to notice his unique one to the Samaritan woman: to be truly known. What stunned this woman—and caused her to share her experience with her entire town—was not that a Jewish man offered her living water to end her thirst or that he claimed to be the long-awaited Messiah. What astounded her was that he knew it all—every darkness of her heart and every thought that had crossed her mind—and yet loved her and invited her to drink.

- Jesus stayed with the Samaritans for two days, and many came to believe in him as the Savior (see John 4:40-41). Based on what we have read so far about Jesus, what do you imagine he said to the Samaritans that caused them to believe? What might his invitation to them have been?

- Read today's passage again slowly. What invitation related to being fully known and accepted do you sense Jesus extending to you?

- Who do you know who seems ashamed of current or past experiences and might think they could never be loved if really known? Seek God's guidance as to how you might be able to extend to that person an invitation to be fully known and accepted by Christ.

Loving God, thank you for the invitation to be fully known and accepted. At times, I have a nagging sense that if I were truly known—all the things I've done and thought and said, all my fears and failures—no one could accept me. But you already know and see all that is inside me—my mind, heart, and soul—and yet you call to me still, inviting me to receive your love and promising to renew my mind, transform my heart, and restore my soul. Thank you. Amen.

DAY 8

BE HEALED

a prayer to open
Here I am, Lord. Quiet my mind. Open my heart.
Give me ears to hear your invitation and the faith to respond.

READ JOHN 5:2-15

Inside [Jerusalem], near the Sheep Gate, was the pool of Bethesda, with five covered porches. Crowds of sick people—blind, lame, or paralyzed—lay on the porches. One of the men lying there had been sick for thirty-eight years. When Jesus saw him and knew he had been ill for a long time, he asked him, "Would you like to get well?"

"I can't, sir," the sick man said, "for I have no one to put me into the pool when the water bubbles up." . . .

Jesus told him, "Stand up, pick up your mat, and walk!"

Instantly, the man was healed! He rolled up his sleeping mat and began walking! But this miracle happened on the Sabbath, so the Jewish leaders objected. They said to the man who was cured, "You can't work on the Sabbath! The law doesn't allow you to carry that sleeping mat!"

But he replied, "The man who healed me told me, 'Pick up your mat and walk.'"

"Who said such a thing as that?" they demanded.

The man didn't know, for Jesus had disappeared into the crowd. But afterward Jesus found him in the Temple and told him, "Now you are well; so stop sinning, or something even worse may happen to you." Then the man went and told the Jewish leaders that it was Jesus who had healed him.

REFLECT

Imagine lying by a pool for years, waiting to be healed but feeling edged out each time. Now imagine that a man arrives, speaks a few words—and suddenly you can walk for the first time in thirty-eight years. What's fascinating is that Jesus suggests the man's sin was the cause of his illness and the man had a role to play in staying healthy after being healed. In other words, Jesus issued a two-part invitation: receive healing *and* turn away from sin. We shouldn't interpret this to mean that every physical ailment is a result of sin (Jesus debunked that theory in John 9:1-3); however, Jesus *is* inviting us to receive the healing he offers and turn from destructive behaviors and attitudes.

• Why do you think Jesus asked the man whether he wanted to get well?

• Read today's passage again slowly. What invitation related to receiving healing do you sense Jesus extending to you? What is Jesus inviting you to turn away from?

- Who in your life is addicted to something destructive (a substance, a behavior, a relationship)? Seek God's guidance as to how you might be able to invite that person to receive the healing Jesus offers.

RESPOND

Loving God, thank you for the invitation to be healed. Please continue to heal my hurts and bind up my wounds. Show me my part to play to remain healthy, inside and out, and to be transformed by your love. And help me remember that others are hurting too. May I be gentle in my interactions so your healing may be known in me and through me. Amen.

DAY 9

BE FREE

a prayer to open

Here I am, Lord. Quiet my mind. Open my heart.
Give me ears to hear your invitation and the faith to respond.

READ JOHN 8:3-11

The teachers of religious law and the Pharisees brought [to Jesus] a woman who had been caught in the act of adultery. They put her in front of the crowd.

"Teacher," they said to Jesus, "this woman was caught in the act of adultery. The law of Moses says to stone her. What do you say?"

They were trying to trap him into saying something they could use against him, but Jesus stooped down and wrote in the dust with his finger. They kept demanding an answer, so he stood up again and said, "All right, but let the one who has never sinned throw the first stone!" Then he stooped down again and wrote in the dust.

When the accusers heard this, they slipped away one by one . . . until only Jesus was left in the middle of the crowd with the woman. Then Jesus stood up again and said to the woman, "Where are your accusers? Didn't even one of them condemn you?"

"No, Lord," she said.

And Jesus said, "Neither do I. Go and sin no more."

REFLECT

Jesus' interaction with this woman provides an example of what he brought into the world: grace and truth. Jesus extended grace to the woman, but he also called her to live in truth by leaving her life of sin. He wanted her to be free, no longer enslaved to sin. Jesus extends this invitation today, calling us to receive his grace and forgiveness. He doesn't stop there, though; he also invites us to turn from sin and be free.

- What sins in your past do you condemn yourself for even though Christ does not condemn you? When you put your faith in Christ, those sins were fully

Invited

forgiven. Imagine Jesus sitting next to you and speaking these words to you: "I do not condemn you. I have forgiven you. You are free." Ask God to help you receive Jesus' words.

• Read this passage again slowly. What invitation related to turning away from sin do you sense Jesus extending to you?

• Who in your life do you find yourself quietly criticizing or condemning? Seek God's guidance about how you might be able to extend Jesus' love and grace to that person.

RESPOND

Loving God, thank you for your grace and the invitation to be free. Thank you for calling me to live in truth. Illuminate the ways I subtly criticize my family, my friends, my coworkers, and even strangers while ignoring the darkness and sin inside me. Give me eyes to see those who desperately need your grace and the reminder that you love them. Use me to be your ambassador of grace and freedom. Amen.

DAY 10

RECEIVE LIFE TO THE FULL

a prayer to open

Here I am, Lord. Quiet my mind. Open my heart.
Give me ears to hear your invitation and the faith to respond.

READ JOHN 10:7-18

[Jesus said,] "I tell you the truth, I am the gate for the sheep. All who came before me were thieves and robbers. But the true sheep did not listen to them. Yes, I am the gate. Those who come in through me will be saved. They will come and go freely and will find good pastures. The thief's purpose is to steal and kill and destroy. My purpose is to give them a rich and satisfying life.

"I am the good shepherd. The good shepherd sacrifices his life for the sheep. A hired hand will run when he sees a wolf coming. He will abandon the sheep because they don't belong to him and he isn't their shepherd. And so the wolf attacks them and scatters the flock. The hired hand runs away because he's working only for the money and doesn't really care about the sheep.

"I am the good shepherd; I know my own sheep, and they know me, just as my Father knows me and I know the Father. So I sacrifice my life for the sheep. I have other sheep, too, that are not in this sheepfold. I must bring them also. They will listen to my voice, and there will be one flock with one shepherd.

"The Father loves me because I sacrifice my life so I may take it back again. No one can take my life from me. I sacrifice it voluntarily. For I have the authority to lay it down when I want to and also to take it up again. For this is what my Father has commanded."

REFLECT

"I have come that they may have life, and have it to the full" (verse 10, NIV). Something deep within us says yes when we hear this. Yes, we want this life to the full. Yes, we long for more than the mundane and routine. We want to love well, get messy, and be free. What stops us? What holds us back?

When we fill our lives with busyness and refuse to quiet ourselves in God's presence, we close our ears to his voice, we forget we are his, and we lose our way. But Jesus says that the only way to have life to the full is to remain close to him, so close that we can hear and know his voice.

- Reflect on the times you have felt most alive. How would you describe those times to a friend? How would you describe your life now? Is there a gap between "life to the full" and what you're currently experiencing? How would you describe that gap?

- Read today's passage again slowly. What invitation related to experiencing life to the full do you sense Jesus extending to you?

- Do you know someone who seems to think their life is empty or without meaning? Seek God's guidance as to how you might invite that person to experience life to the full in Christ.

RESPOND_____

Loving God, thank you for the invitation to experience life to the full. I say yes. Help me receive this life you offer. Show me how to stay close, so close that I can hear your voice. Give me the courage to slow my mind and quiet myself in your presence. When I stray, call me back to you and help me remember I am yours. Remind me that life to the full has love at the center. May my life reflect your love. Amen.

RECEIVE ETERNAL LIFE

a prayer to open   Here I am, Lord. Quiet my mind. Open my heart.
Give me ears to hear your invitation and the faith to respond.

READ JOHN 6:35-51 _____

Jesus replied, "I am the bread of life. Whoever comes to me will never be hungry again. Whoever believes in me will never be thirsty. But you haven't believed in me even though you have seen me. However, those the Father has given me will come to me, and I will never reject them. For I have come down from heaven to do the will of God who sent me, not to do my own will. And this is the will of God, that I should not lose even one of all those he has given me, but that I should raise them up at the last day. For it is my Father's will that all who see his Son and believe in him should have eternal life. I will raise them up at the last day. . . .

"No one can come to me unless the Father who sent me draws them . . . and at the last day I will raise them up. As it is written in the Scriptures, 'They will all be taught by God.' Everyone who listens to the Father and learns from him comes to me. (Not that anyone has ever seen the Father; only I, who was sent from God, have seen him.)

"I tell you the truth, anyone who believes has eternal life. Yes, I am the bread of life! Your ancestors ate manna in the wilderness, but they all died. Anyone who eats the bread from heaven, however, will never die. I am the living bread that came down from heaven. Anyone who eats this bread will live forever; and this bread, which I will offer so the world may live, is my flesh."

REFLECT _____

"Anyone who eats this bread will live forever." Just as Jesus offers life here and now—to the full—he also offers life forever. Though we die, we will be raised up and given new bodies and new life in God's presence for eternity. But this life is extended to us only in Jesus—and in the sacrifice of his very body. No other person or experience sustains, overcomes, and resurrects. All else that we might be tempted to trust in fades and disappoints.

- What fears do you have about death or what happens after death? When do those anxious thoughts or feelings most often arise in you?

- Read this passage again slowly. What invitation related to receiving eternal life do you sense Jesus extending to you?

- Do you know someone who lives with fear about death? Seek God's guidance as to how you might invite them to receive the eternal life Christ offers.

RESPOND _____

Loving God, thank you for the invitation into eternal life. Thank you that in Jesus, I don't need to fear death or condemnation but can look forward with hope and anticipation to the day I will be raised to life and live in your Kingdom forever. Guide me through times of fear and doubt, comforting me with what is to come. Allow the hope I have in you to seep out in my words, actions, and countenance so that others can see you in me. Amen.

DAY 12

BRING ME WHAT YOU HAVE

a prayer to open Here I am, Lord. Quiet my mind. Open my heart. Give me ears to hear your invitation and the faith to respond.

READ MATTHEW 14:13-21 _____

[Jesus] left in a boat to a remote area to be alone. But the crowds heard where he was headed and followed on foot from many towns. Jesus saw the huge crowd as he stepped from the boat, and he had compassion on them and healed their sick.

That evening the disciples came to him and said, "This is a remote place, and it's already getting late. Send the crowds away so they can go to the villages and buy food for themselves."

But Jesus said, "That isn't necessary—you feed them."

"But we have only five loaves of bread and two fish!" they answered.

"Bring them here," he said. Then he told the people to sit down on the grass. Jesus took the five loaves and two fish, looked up toward heaven, and blessed them. Then, breaking the loaves into pieces, he gave the bread to the disciples, who distributed it to the people. They all ate as much as they wanted, and afterward, the disciples picked up twelve baskets of leftovers. About 5,000 men were fed that day, in addition to all the women and children!

We tend to spend our thoughts and energy seeking after more—more money, more prestige, more responsibility, more love, more education. Of course, these "mores" are not necessarily unhealthy or destructive. But rarely do we ask, *What might God do with what I have right now?* Some of this stems from feeling inadequate, especially when we compare ourselves to others. Or perhaps we are unwilling to open our hands to give God what we see as ours. Maybe we lack imagination and belief about what he can and desires to do: multiply what we have to display his goodness, bless those around us, and increase our faith. Jesus did not fault his disciples and the crowd for having little. Instead, he said, "Bring me what you have, and I will show you that in my hands, your little is extravagant surplus."

- What would you offer in response to Jesus' invitation to bring him what you have? What qualities, strengths, weaknesses, skills, doubts, and possessions are yours to offer? Which things are you holding back, or what feels too insignificant or unformed for you to bring forward?

- Read this passage again slowly. What invitation related to offering whatever you have do you sense Jesus extending to you?

- Do you know someone who—whether because they feel inadequate, struggle with confidence, or even lack imagination—needs encouragement to bring whatever they have to Jesus for his use? Seek God's guidance as to how you might invite that person to bring forward what can be multiplied in Jesus' hands.

Loving God, thank you for the invitation to bring all I am and have to you. Give me the strength to turn away from the temptation to constantly seek after more and instead take stock of all you have given me. And as best I know how, I offer it to you. Use me and what I have to display your goodness, bless those around me, and increase my trust in you. Open my eyes to the gifts of others so I can remind them that whatever they have can be multiplied in your hands. Amen.

LOVE AS I HAVE LOVED

a prayer to open　　　Here I am, Lord. Quiet my mind. Open my heart.
Give me ears to hear your invitation and the faith to respond.

READ JOHN 13:12-35

After washing their feet, he . . . asked, "Do you understand what I was doing? You call me 'Teacher' and 'Lord,' and you are right, because that's what I am. And since I, your Lord and Teacher, have washed your feet, you ought to wash each other's feet. I have given you an example to follow. Do as I have done to you. I tell you the truth, slaves are not greater than their master. Nor is the messenger more important than the one who sends the message. Now that you know these things, God will bless you for doing them." . . .

Jesus said, "The time has come for the Son of Man to enter into his glory, and God will be glorified because of him. And since God receives glory because of the Son, he will give his own glory to the Son, and he will do so at once. Dear children, I will be with you only a little longer. And as I told the Jewish leaders, you will search for me, but you can't come where I am going. So now I am giving you a new commandment: Love each other. Just as I have loved you, you should love each other. Your love for one another will prove to the world that you are my disciples."

REFLECT

Jesus did what no other rabbi of his day would have done. In fact, the task of washing feet was reserved for non-Jewish servants. Jesus' act had theological significance: It symbolized the washing of sin that Jesus would accomplish through his death. But he was also setting an example of how his disciples should love and serve one another. Everyone would know who they followed by the love they showed. This is still true today.

- Look back on the past week. How well did you love the people around you? Where did you sense stinginess or a lack of generosity in your response to others?

- Read this passage again slowly. What invitation related to loving and serving as Jesus did do you sense he is extending to you?

- Do you know someone who is in a season of difficulty or pain? Seek God's guidance as to how you might love that person through words and actions.

RESPOND

Loving God, thank you for the invitation to love and serve. I want the way I love my family, my friends, my coworkers, my neighbors, and even strangers to show that I am a follower of Jesus. Bring to my attention the areas in which I am stingy with love or lacking in generosity, and grow in me a desire to serve as a way to demonstrate your love and draw people to you. Amen.

REMAIN IN ME

a prayer to open

Here I am, Lord. Quiet my mind. Open my heart.
Give me ears to hear your invitation and the faith to respond.

READ JOHN 15:1-27

I am the true grapevine, and my Father is the gardener. He cuts off every branch of mine that doesn't produce fruit, and he prunes the branches that do bear fruit so they will produce even more. You have already been pruned and purified by the message I have given you. Remain in me, and I will remain in you. For a branch cannot produce fruit if it is severed from the vine, and you cannot be fruitful unless you remain in me.

Yes, I am the vine; you are the branches. Those who remain in me, and I in them, will produce much fruit. For apart from me you can do nothing. Anyone who does not remain in me is thrown away like a useless branch and withers. Such branches are gathered into a pile to be burned. But if you remain in me and my words remain in you, you may ask for anything you want, and it will be granted! When you produce much fruit, you are my true disciples. This brings great glory to my Father.

I have loved you even as the Father has loved me. Remain in my love. When you obey my commandments, you remain in my love, just as I obey my Father's commandments and remain in his love. I have told you these things so that you will be filled with my joy. Yes, your joy will overflow! This is my commandment: Love each other in the same way I have loved you. There is no greater love than to lay down one's life for one's friends. You are my friends if you do what I command. I no longer call you slaves, because a master doesn't confide in his slaves. Now you are my friends, since I have told you everything the Father told me. You didn't choose me. I chose you. I appointed you to go and produce lasting fruit, so that the Father will give you whatever you ask for, using my name. This is my command: Love each other.

If the world hates you, remember that it hated me first. The world would love you as one of its own if you belonged to it, but you are no longer part of the world. I chose you to come out of the world, so it hates you. Do you remember what I told you? "A slave is not greater than the master." Since they persecuted me, naturally they will persecute you. And if they had listened to me, they would listen to you. They will do all this to you because of me, for they have rejected the one who sent me. They would not be guilty if I had not come and spoken to them. But now they have no excuse for their sin. Anyone who hates me also hates my Father. If I hadn't done such miraculous signs among them that no one else could do, they would not be guilty. But as it is, they have seen everything I did, yet they still hate me and my Father. This fulfills what is written in their Scriptures: "They hated me without cause."

But I will send you the Advocate—the Spirit of truth. He will come to you from the Father and will testify all about me. And you must also testify about me because you have been with me from the beginning of my ministry.

REFLECT

Jesus used the image of a vine and its branches to help his disciples better understand his relationship to the Father, his disciples' relationship to him, and their relationship to the world. Jesus continues to invite us to stay connected to him as a branch stays connected to the vine, taking all its nutrients and strength from the vine. In doing so, we are empowered to bear fruit—to love as Jesus calls us to. If we separate ourselves from Jesus, we end up incapable of loving others and keeping his commands.

- Have there been times when you have felt disconnected from God? What caused that disconnection?

Invited

•

- Read this passage again slowly. What invitation related to staying connected to Jesus do you sense he is extending to you?

- Do you know someone who is feeling disconnected from God? Seek God's guidance as to how you might be able to invite that person back into a connection with Christ.

RESPOND

Loving God, thank you for the invitation to stay connected to Jesus as the source of my love and strength. There are times I get caught up in the busyness of life and the calls of this culture and drift off, away from the vine. Help me keep my eyes fixed on you and the things you care about so I can glorify you by the fruit I bear. May people come to know your love by looking at my life. Amen.

GO INTO THE WORLD!

a prayer to open   Here I am, Lord.   Quiet my mind.   Open my heart.
Give me ears to hear your invitation and the faith to respond.

READ JOHN 20:19-23

That Sunday evening the disciples were meeting behind locked doors because they were afraid of the Jewish leaders. Suddenly, Jesus was standing there among them! "Peace be with you," he said. As he spoke, he showed them the wounds in his hands and his side. They were filled with joy when they saw the Lord! Again he said, "Peace be with you. As the Father has sent me, so I am sending you." Then he breathed on them and said, "Receive the Holy Spirit. If you forgive anyone's sins, they are forgiven. If you do not forgive them, they are not forgiven."

REFLECT

One of the greatest temptations in our world today is to consider our relationships with Jesus private—to believe that we have been invited for only our sake. We may be inclined to focus on the fact that we are saved and destined for heaven and can therefore live out the rest of our days without fear. Although these things *are* true, they are not the whole story. As we have seen by studying Jesus' many invitations, he invites us so we can go into the world and invite others. When Jesus rose from the dead, he visited his disciples and extended one final invitation to them—an invitation to extend his invitation of life to the rest of the world (Matthew 28:19). Not only that, but Jesus spoke his peace over them and breathed his Spirit on them so they could extend the invitation without fear, in his power, and with his love.

- What are the biggest barriers or distractions that keep you from extending Jesus' invitation to life? What are the practices or environments that make it more likely for you to do so?

- Read this passage again slowly. What invitation related to carrying Jesus' invitation to life into the world do you sense him extending to you?

- Reflect on the places that you frequent. Seek God's guidance as to how, in those environments, you might extend Jesus' invitation to life.

RESPOND

Loving God, thank you for the invitation to go into the world and extend the invitation of life in Christ. Please help me know how and where to do that. I need your Spirit to fill me with courage and peace and love. I need eyes that see the world as you do: full of redemptive potential, longing to know you more, and desperate for wholeness. Let my life be an invitation, an example of the life you offer. Amen.

Surrendered

Opening to God's Love

ONE YEAR WHEN my daughter was in middle school, for a short-lived and precious season I had the opportunity to pick her up from school every day. Each day, as I got in the very long car line and put the car in park, an overwhelming sense of anticipation overtook me.

When the bell rang at 2:41 p.m., kids poured out of the doors. Some came out in groups, pushing and laughing. Some walked out alone. Still others came out in pairs, having seemingly deep conversations. My girl was always one of the last to exit. But when she did, it took all I had in me not to roll down the window and yell, "There's mine! There's my girl! Here I am, honey!" (I didn't do that, of course, but just know that it was a strong temptation.) I'd see her pink backpack, nearly bigger than her whole body, and her slight smile of recognition when she saw me. She'd heft her heavy bag onto the car floor and slide into the seat.

There wasn't one day that I didn't feel overcome by love for her during these pickup times. I wanted to know everything about her day: who said what to whom at lunch, what made her laugh, what her teacher said about this or that, how gym class went. I wanted to hear about when she felt sad or if her feelings got hurt or whether she was disappointed about a test score. I wanted to know and hear and see all of it. My first instinct—no matter her day—was to reach out to her and hug her and provide reassurance. Nothing could make me not love her, not want to reach out and comfort her, or not want what was best for her. Nothing in me wanted to withhold or punish or yell. My love for her was (and is) unshakable.

Nothing has helped me understand more about God's love than that one year picking my daughter up from school. What I realized was that as sure as my love for my daughter was, God's love had to be infinitely more. And if that was true, couldn't I trust that I had nothing to fear by surrendering more and more of my life to God? After all, if I, in all my humanness, could so thoroughly and joyfully and unconditionally love my daughter, how much more must the Creator and Sustainer of all things thoroughly, joyfully, and unconditionally love me? What if the way I wanted to know every single detail about my daughter's heart is a window into God's stance toward me? And what if his first inclination toward me—his instinctive move—when I share my joys and worries or confess my worst sins is not a distant head nod or disappointment and anger but rather a desire to pull me near, say all is well, and assure me of his unending love? What if that was true?

The hardest thing for most of us to grasp is that we are so loved by God. Yes, Jesus invites us to come to him, but to live in his love—to really believe it so it permeates our lives—is another matter altogether. We all have been broken by people who have loved us and by our own sinfulness and pride. We are overcome by fear and worry. And we fall into busyness and fail to open space to hear from the God who loves us. Receiving his love isn't something most of us can just decide to do. So we have to present ourselves to God over and over and ask him to remind us of how he loves us and how he sees us. Knowing his love isn't an intellectual exercise; we must sit and listen to his voice, surrendering ourselves to his love.

For the next thirty days, we will read Scriptures and practice the ancient discipline *lectio divina* (divine reading) to remind us who God is and what his love looks like and means. The first five days center us on Jesus, on who God has revealed himself to be. If we start anywhere else, we will get off track. We'll spend days six through ten filling our hearts and minds with the truth of how God loves us and with all he has done to demonstrate that love. Next we will sit with those parts of ourselves that act as a barrier to God's love, such as fear, pride, worry, busyness, sin, and pain. And then we'll end where we began: focusing our eyes on the person and character of God.

WHO IS GOD?

DAY 1

THE VISIBLE IMAGE OF GOD

Wherever you are, remember you are in God's loving presence. Close your eyes to dismiss any distractions. Open your hands as a way of doing with your body what you long for your heart and soul to do. Breathe in deeply and out slowly to relax your mind and your heart.

a prayer to open

Open me to your love, Lord.
In your great mercy, open me to your love.

READ COLOSSIANS 1:15-20

Christ is the visible image of the invisible God.
    He existed before anything was created and is
        supreme over all creation,
for through him God created everything
    in the heavenly realms and on earth.

He made the things we can see
    and the things we can't see—
such as thrones, kingdoms, rulers, and
    authorities in the unseen world.

Everything was created through him and for
   him.
He existed before anything else,
   and he holds all creation together.
Christ is also the head of the church,
   which is his body.
He is the beginning,
   supreme over all who rise from the dead.

So he is first in everything.
For God in all his fullness
   was pleased to live in Christ,
and through him God reconciled
   everything to himself.
He made peace with everything in heaven and
   on earth
by means of Christ's blood on the cross.

REFLECT _____

Lectio Divina #1

Read today's passage slowly and out loud. Pay attention to the word or phrase that stands out to you.

• What do you sense God is saying to you through that word or phrase? Take a minute to listen.

Lectio Divina #2

Read today's passage a second time, again slowly and out loud. Listen for what invitation God may be extending to you through the word or phrase you identified.

• How does the word or phrase apply to your life right now? Take a minute to listen.

Lectio Divina #3

Read today's passage for a third time, and then enter into a conversation with God. Remember that you are in his loving presence. Present your questions, concerns, resistance, and repentance.

• What image of God do you hold that is different from your image of Jesus?

• How does Jesus as the visible image of God influence how you view God and his love?

A PRAYER TO CLOSE_____

Loving God, thank you for pouring out your love to me and for me and in me.
Thank you for loving me. I am yours. Amen and amen.

REVEALED

Wherever you are, remember you are in God's loving presence. Close your eyes to dismiss any distractions. Open your hands as a way of doing with your body what you long for your heart and soul to do. Breathe in deeply and out slowly to relax your mind and your heart.

a prayer to open

Open me to your love, Lord.
In your great mercy, open me to your love.

READ JOHN 1:1-18

In the beginning the Word already existed.
  The Word was with God,
  and the Word was God.
He existed in the beginning with God.
God created everything through him,
  and nothing was created except through him.
The Word gave life to everything that was created,
  and his life brought light to everyone.
The light shines in the darkness,
  and the darkness can never extinguish it.

God sent a man, John the Baptist, to tell about the light so that everyone might believe because of his testimony. John himself was not the light; he was simply a witness to tell about the light. The one who is the true light, who gives light to everyone, was coming into the world.

He came into the very world he created, but the world didn't recognize him. He came to his own people, and even they rejected him. But to all who believed him and accepted him, he gave the right to become children of God. They are reborn—not with a physical birth resulting from human passion or plan, but a birth that comes from God.

So the Word became human and made his home among us. He was full of unfailing love and faithfulness. And we have seen his glory, the glory of the Father's one and only Son.

John testified about him when he shouted to the crowds, "This is the one I was talking about when I said, 'Someone is coming after me who is far greater than I am, for he existed long before me.'"

From his abundance we have all received one gracious blessing after another. For the law was given through Moses, but God's unfailing love and faithfulness came through Jesus Christ. No one has ever seen God. But the unique One, who is himself God, is near to the Father's heart. He has revealed God to us.

REFLECT

Lectio Divina #1

Read today's passage slowly and out loud. Pay attention to the word or phrase that stands out to you.

• What do you sense God is saying to you through that word or phrase? Take a minute to listen.

Lectio Divina #2

Read today's passage a second time, again slowly and out loud. Listen for what invitation God may be extending to you through the word or phrase you identified.

• How does the word or phrase apply to your life right now? Take a minute to listen.

Lectio Divina #3

Read today's passage for a third time. Enter into a conversation with God. Remember that you are in his loving presence. Present your questions, concerns, resistance, and repentance.

- What does Jesus reveal to you about who God is?
- What does Jesus reveal about God's love for you?

A PRAYER TO CLOSE

Loving God, thank you for pouring out your love to me and for me and in me.
Thank you for loving me. I am yours. Amen and amen.

DAY 3

THROUGH HIS SON

Wherever you are, remember you are in God's loving presence. Close your eyes to dismiss any distractions. Open your hands as a way of doing with your body what you long for your heart and soul to do. Breathe in deeply and out slowly to relax your mind and your heart.

a prayer to open

Open me to your love, Lord.
In your great mercy, open me to your love.

READ HEBREWS 1:1-4

Long ago God spoke many times and in many ways to our ancestors through the prophets. And now in these final days, he has spoken to us through his Son. God promised everything to the Son as an inheritance, and through the Son he created the universe. The Son radiates God's own glory and expresses the very character of God, and he sustains everything by the mighty power of his command. When he had cleansed us from our sins, he sat down in the place of honor at the right hand of the majestic God in heaven. This shows that the Son is far greater than the angels, just as the name God gave him is greater than their names.

REFLECT

Lectio Divina #1

Read today's passage slowly and out loud. Pay attention to the word or phrase that stands out to you.

- What do you sense God is saying to you through that word or phrase? Take a minute to listen.

Lectio Divina #2

Read today's passage a second time, again slowly and out loud. Listen for what invitation God may be extending to you through the word or phrase you identified.

• How does the word or phrase apply to your life right now? Take a minute to listen.

Lectio Divina #3

Read today's passage for a third time, and then enter into a conversation with God. Remember that you are in his loving presence. Present your questions, concerns, resistance, and repentance.

• What does God tell you about his character through Jesus?

• What is God saying to you through Jesus about who he is?

A PRAYER TO CLOSE

Loving God, thank you for pouring out your love to me and for me and in me. Thank you for loving me. I am yours. Amen and amen.

DAY 4

THOUGH HE WAS GOD

Wherever you are, remember you are in God's loving presence. Close your eyes to dismiss any distractions. Open your hands as a way of doing with your body what you long for your heart and soul to do. Breathe in deeply and out slowly to relax your mind and your heart.

---

a prayer to open

Open me to your love, Lord.
In your great mercy, open me to your love

READ PHILIPPIANS 2:1-11

Is there any encouragement from belonging to Christ? Any comfort from his love? Any fellowship together in the Spirit? Are your hearts tender and compassionate? Then make me truly happy by agreeing wholeheartedly with each other, loving one another, and working together with one mind and purpose.

Don't be selfish; don't try to impress others. Be humble, thinking of others as better than yourselves. Don't look out only for your own interests, but take an interest in others, too.

You must have the same attitude that Christ Jesus had.

Though he was God,
    he did not think of equality with God
    as something to cling to.
Instead, he gave up his divine privileges;
    he took the humble position of a slave
    and was born as a human being.
When he appeared in human form,
    he humbled himself in obedience to God
    and died a criminal's death on a cross.

Therefore, God elevated him to the place of
  highest honor
and gave him the name above all other
  names,
that at the name of Jesus every knee should
  bow,

in heaven and on earth and under the earth,
and every tongue declare that Jesus Christ is
  Lord,
to the glory of God the Father.

REFLECT

Lectio Divina #1

Read today's passage slowly and out loud. Pay attention to the word or phrase that stands out to you.

- What do you sense God is saying to you through that word or phrase? Take a minute to listen.

Lectio Divina #2

Read today's passage a second time, again slowly and out loud. Listen for what invitation God may be extending to you through the word or phrase you identified.

- How does the word or phrase apply to your life right now? Take a minute to listen.

Lectio Divina #3

Read today's passage for a third time, and then enter into a conversation with God. Remember that you are in his loving presence. Present your questions, concerns, resistance, and repentance.

- What do these depictions of Jesus tell you about God's character?
- What do you sense God saying to you about who he is?

A PRAYER TO CLOSE

Loving God, thank you for pouring out your love to me and for me and in me.
Thank you for loving me. I am yours. Amen and amen.

DAY 5

ALL THE FULLNESS

Wherever you are, remember you are in God's loving presence. Close your eyes to dismiss any distractions. Open your hands as a way of doing with your body what you long for your heart and soul to do. Breathe in deeply and out slowly to relax your mind and your heart.

a prayer to open

Open me to your love, Lord.
In your great mercy, open me to your love.

READ COLOSSIANS 2:6-10

Just as you accepted Christ Jesus as your Lord, you must continue to follow him. Let your roots grow down into him, and let your lives be built on him. Then your faith will grow strong in the truth you were taught, and you will overflow with thankfulness.

Don't let anyone capture you with empty philosophies and high-sounding nonsense that come from human thinking and from the spiritual powers of this world, rather than from Christ. For in Christ lives all the fullness of God in a human body. So you also are complete through your union with Christ, who is the head over every ruler and authority.

REFLECT

Lectio Divina #1

Read today's passage slowly and out loud. Pay attention to the word or phrase that stands out to you.

• What do you sense God is saying to you through that word or phrase? Take a minute to listen.

Lectio Divina #2

Read today's passage a second time, again slowly and out loud. Listen for what invitation God may be extending to you through the word or phrase you identified.

• How does the word or phrase apply to your life right now? Take a minute to listen.

Lectio Divina #3

Read today's passage for a third time, and then enter into a conversation with God. Remember that you are in his loving presence. Present your questions, concerns, resistance, and repentance.

• What would allowing your roots to grow down into Christ look like for you?

• How does knowing that all the fullness of God lives in Christ affect your understanding of God's love?

A PRAYER TO CLOSE

Loving God, thank you for pouring out your love to me and for me and in me. Thank you for loving me. I am yours. Amen and amen.

GOD IS LOVE

Wherever you are, remember you are in God's loving presence. Close your eyes to dismiss any distractions. Open your hands as a way of doing with your body what you long for your heart and soul to do. Breathe in deeply and out slowly to relax your mind and your heart.

a prayer to open

Open me to your love, Lord.
In your great mercy, open me to your love.

READ 1 JOHN 4:7-21

Dear friends, let us continue to love one another, for love comes from God. Anyone who loves is a child of God and knows God. But anyone who does not love does not know God, for God is love.

God showed how much he loved us by sending his one and only Son into the world so that we might have eternal life through him. This is real love—not that we loved God, but that he loved us and sent his Son as a sacrifice to take away our sins.

Dear friends, since God loved us that much, we surely ought to love each other. No one has ever seen God. But if we love each other, God lives in us, and his love is brought to full expression in us.

And God has given us his Spirit as proof that we live in him and he in us. Furthermore, we have seen with our own eyes and now testify that the Father sent his Son to be the Savior of the world. All who declare that Jesus is the Son of God have God living in them, and they live in God. We know how much

God loves us, and we have put our trust in his love.

God is love, and all who live in love live in God, and God lives in them. And as we live in God, our love grows more perfect. So we will not be afraid on the day of judgment, but we can face him with confidence because we live like Jesus here in this world.

Such love has no fear, because perfect love expels all fear. If we are afraid, it is for fear of punishment, and this shows that we have not fully experienced his perfect love. We love each other because he loved us first.

If someone says, "I love God," but hates a fellow believer, that person is a liar; for if we don't love people we can see, how can we love God, whom we cannot see? And he has given us this command: Those who love God must also love their fellow believers.

REFLECT

Lectio Divina #1

Read today's passage slowly and out loud. Pay attention to the word or phrase that stands out to you.

• What do you sense God is saying to you through that word or phrase? Take a minute to listen.

Lectio Divina #2

Read today's passage a second time, again slowly and out loud. Listen for what invitation God may be extending to you through the word or phrase you identified.

• How does the word or phrase apply to your life right now? Take a minute to listen.

Lectio Divina #3

Read today's passage for a third time, and then enter into a conversation with God. Remember that you are in his loving presence. Present your questions, concerns, resistance, and repentance.

• What truth about his love is God calling you to surrender to through today's passage?

• What resistance do you feel to his call?

A PRAYER TO CLOSE

Loving God, thank you for pouring out your love to me and for me and in me. Thank you for loving me. I am yours. Amen and amen.

HOW DEARLY GOD LOVES US

Wherever you are, remember you are in God's loving presence. Close your eyes to dismiss any distractions. Open your hands as a way of doing with your body what you long for your heart and soul to do. Breathe in deeply and out slowly to relax your mind and your heart.

a prayer to open

Open me to your love, Lord.
In your great mercy, open me to your love.

READ ROMANS 5:1-8

Since we have been made right in God's sight by faith, we have peace with God because of what Jesus Christ our Lord has done for us. Because of our faith, Christ has brought us into this place of undeserved privilege where we now stand, and we confidently and joyfully look forward to sharing God's glory.

We can rejoice, too, when we run into problems and trials, for we know that they help us develop endurance. And endurance develops strength of character, and character strengthens our confident hope of salvation. And this hope will not lead to disappointment. For we know how dearly God loves us, because he has given us the Holy Spirit to fill our hearts with his love.

When we were utterly helpless, Christ came at just

the right time and died for us sinners. Now, most people would not be willing to die for an upright person, though someone might perhaps be willing to die for a person who is especially good. But God showed his great love for us by sending Christ to die for us while we were still sinners.

REFLECT _____

Lectio Divina #1

Read today's passage slowly and out loud. Pay attention to the word or phrase that stands out to you.

• What do you sense God is saying to you through that word or phrase? Take a minute to listen.

Lectio Divina #2

Read today's passage a second time, again slowly and out loud. Listen for what invitation God may be extending to you through the word or phrase you identified.

• How does the word or phrase apply to your life right now? Take a minute to listen.

Lectio Divina #3

Read today's passage for a third time, and then enter into a conversation with God. Remember that you are in his loving presence. Present your questions, concerns, resistance, and repentance.

• What truth about his love is God calling you to believe through today's passage?

• What resistance do you feel to his call?

A PRAYER TO CLOSE_____

Loving God, thank you for pouring out your love to me and for me and in me. Thank you for loving me. I am yours. Amen and amen.

DAY 8

NOTHING CAN SEPARATE US

Wherever you are, remember you are in God's loving presence. Close your eyes to dismiss any distractions. Open your hands as a way of doing with your body what you long for your heart and soul to do. Breathe in deeply and out slowly to relax your mind and your heart.

Surrendered

•

31

a prayer to open

Open me to your love, Lord.
In your great mercy, open me to your love.

READ ROMANS 8:31-39

What shall we say about such wonderful things as these? If God is for us, who can ever be against us? Since he did not spare even his own Son but gave him up for us all, won't he also give us everything else? Who dares accuse us whom God has chosen for his own? No one—for God himself has given us right standing with himself. Who then will condemn us? No one—for Christ Jesus died for us and was raised to life for us, and he is sitting in the place of honor at God's right hand, pleading for us.

Can anything ever separate us from Christ's love? Does it mean he no longer loves us if we have trouble or calamity, or are persecuted, or hungry, or destitute, or in danger, or threatened with death? . . . No, despite all these things, overwhelming victory is ours through Christ, who loved us.

And I am convinced that nothing can ever separate us from God's love. Neither death nor life, neither angels nor demons, neither our fears for today nor our worries about tomorrow—not even the powers of hell can separate us from God's love. No power in the sky above or in the earth below—indeed, nothing in all creation will ever be able to separate us from the love of God that is revealed in Christ Jesus our Lord.

REFLECT

Lectio Divina #1

Read today's passage slowly and out loud. Pay attention to the word or phrase that stands out to you.

- What do you sense God is saying to you through that word or phrase? Take a minute to listen.

Lectio Divina #2

Read today's passage a second time, again slowly and out loud. Listen for what invitation God may be extending to you through the word or phrase you identified.

- How does the word or phrase apply to your life right now? Take a minute to listen.

Lectio Divina #3

Read today's passage for a third time, and then enter into a conversation with God. Remember that you are in his loving presence. Present your questions, concerns, resistance, and repentance.

- What truth about his love is God calling you to receive through today's passage?

- What resistance do you feel to his call?

A PRAYER TO CLOSE

Loving God, thank you for pouring out your love to me and for me and in me. Thank you for loving me. I am yours. Amen and amen.

SEE HOW OUR FATHER LOVES US

Wherever you are, remember you are in God's loving presence. Close your eyes to dismiss any distractions. Open your hands as a way of doing with your body what you long for your heart and soul to do. Breathe in deeply and out slowly to relax your mind and your heart.

a prayer to open

Open me to your love, Lord.
In your great mercy, open me to your love.

READ 1 JOHN 3:1-3

See how very much our Father loves us, for he calls us his children, and that is what we are! But the people who belong to this world don't recognize that we are God's children because they don't know him. Dear friends, we are already God's children, but he has not yet shown us what we will be like when Christ appears. But we do know that we will be like him, for we will see him as he really is. And all who have this eager expectation will keep themselves pure, just as he is pure.

REFLECT

Lectio Divina #1

Read today's passage slowly and out loud. Pay attention to the word or phrase that stands out to you.

- What do you sense God is saying to you through that word or phrase? Take a minute to listen.

Lectio Divina #2

Read today's passage a second time, again slowly and out loud. Listen for what invitation God may be extending to you through the word or phrase you identified.

- How does the word or phrase apply to your life right now? Take a minute to listen.

Lectio Divina #3

Read today's passage for a third time, and then enter into a conversation with God. Remember that you are in his loving presence. Present your questions, concerns, resistance, and repentance.

- What truth about his love is God calling you to trust through today's passage?
- What resistance do you feel to his call?

Surrendered

Loving God, thank you for pouring out your love to me and for me and in me.
Thank you for loving me. I am yours. Amen and amen.

DAY 10

ROOTS THAT GROW DOWN

Wherever you are, remember you are in God's loving presence. Close your eyes to dismiss any distractions. Open your hands as a way of doing with your body what you long for your heart and soul to do. Breathe in deeply and out slowly to relax your mind and your heart.

a prayer to open

Open me to your love, Lord.
In your great mercy, open me to your love.

READ EPHESIANS 3:14-20

I fall to my knees and pray to the Father, the Creator of everything in heaven and on earth. I pray that from his glorious, unlimited resources he will empower you with inner strength through his Spirit. Then Christ will make his home in your hearts as you trust in him. Your roots will grow down into God's love and keep you strong. And may you have the power to understand, as all God's people should, how wide, how long, how high, and how deep his love is. May you experience the love of Christ, though it is too great to understand fully. Then you will be made complete with all the fullness of life and power that comes from God.

Now all glory to God, who is able, through his mighty power at work within us, to accomplish infinitely more than we might ask or think.

REFLECT

Lectio Divina #1

Read today's passage slowly and out loud. Pay attention to the word or phrase that stands out to you.

• What do you sense God is saying to you through that word or phrase? Take a minute to listen.

Lectio Divina #2

Read today's passage a second time, again slowly and out loud. Listen for what invitation God may be extending to you through the word or phrase you identified.

• How does the word or phrase apply to your life right now? Take a minute to listen.

Read today's passage for a third time, and then enter into a conversation with God. Remember that you are in his loving presence. Present your questions, concerns, resistance, and repentance.

- What truth about his love is God calling you to allow yourself to be filled with through today's passage?

- What resistance do you feel to his call?

A PRAYER TO CLOSE_____

Loving God, thank you for pouring out your love to me and for me and in me. Thank you for loving me. I am yours. Amen and amen.

READ JOHN 1.35-39 _____   **FEAR**

RECEIVE GOD'S SPIRIT

Wherever you are, remember you are in God's loving presence. Close your eyes to dismiss any distractions. Open your hands as a way of doing with your body what you long for your heart and soul to do. Breathe in deeply and out slowly to relax your mind and your heart.

a prayer to open

Open me to your love, Lord.
In your great mercy, open me to your love.

READ ROMANS 8:15-17 _____

So you have not received a spirit that makes you fearful slaves. Instead, you received God's Spirit when he adopted you as his own children. Now we call him, "Abba, Father." For his Spirit joins with our spirit to affirm that we are God's children. And since we are his children, . . . together with Christ we are heirs of God's glory. But if we are to share his glory, we must also share his suffering.

REFLECT _____

Lectio Divina #1

Read today's passage slowly and out loud. Pay attention to the word or phrase that stands out to you.

- What do you sense God is saying to you through that word or phrase? Take a minute to listen.

Lectio Divina #2

Read today's passage a second time, again slowly and out loud. Listen for what invitation God may be extending to you through the word or phrase you identified.

- How does the word or phrase apply to your life right now? Take a minute to listen.

Lectio Divina #3

Read today's passage for a third time, and then enter into a conversation with God. Remember that you are in his loving presence. Present your questions, concerns, resistance, and repentance.

- What fear might be preventing you from opening more fully to God's love?
- What is God saying to you about that fear? Listen.

A PRAYER TO CLOSE

Loving God, thank you for pouring out your love to me and for me and in me. Thank you for loving me. I am yours. Amen and amen.

DAY 12

WITH YOU

Wherever you are, remember you are in God's loving presence. Close your eyes to dismiss any distractions. Open your hands as a way of doing with your body what you long for your heart and soul to do. Breathe in deeply and out slowly to relax your mind and your heart.

a prayer to open

Open me to your love, Lord.
In your great mercy, open me to your love.

READ ISAIAH 41:8-14

But as for you, Israel my servant,
    Jacob my chosen one,
    descended from Abraham my friend,
I have called you back from the ends of the
        earth,
    saying, "You are my servant."
For I have chosen you
    and will not throw you away.
Don't be afraid, for I am with you.
    Don't be discouraged, for I am your God.
I will strengthen you and help you.
    I will hold you up with my victorious right hand.

See, all your angry enemies lie there,
    confused and humiliated. . . .
You will look in vain
    for those who tried to conquer you.
Those who attack you
    will come to nothing.
For I hold you by your right hand—
    I, the LORD your God.
And I say to you,
    "Don't be afraid. I am here to help you. . . .
I am the LORD, your Redeemer.
    I am the Holy One of Israel."

Lectio Divina #1

Read today's passage slowly and out loud. Pay attention to the word or phrase that stands out to you.

• What do you sense God is saying to you through that word or phrase? Take a minute to listen.

Lectio Divina #2

Read today's passage a second time, again slowly and out loud. Listen for what invitation God may be extending to you through the word or phrase you identified.

• How does the word or phrase apply to your life right now? Take a minute to listen.

Lectio Divina #3

Read today's passage for a third time, and then enter into a conversation with God. Remember that you are in his loving presence. Present your questions, concerns, resistance, and repentance.

• What does God want you to remember in the midst of fear?
• What particular fear is he inviting you to release?

A PRAYER TO CLOSE

Loving God, thank you for pouring out your love to me and for me and in me.
Thank you for loving me. I am yours. Amen and amen.

DAY 13

UNAFRAID

Wherever you are, remember you are in God's loving presence. Close your eyes to dismiss any distractions. Open your hands as a way of doing with your body what you long for your heart and soul to do. Breathe in deeply and out slowly to relax your mind and your heart.

a prayer to open

Open me to your love, Lord.
In your great mercy, open me to your love.

Surrendered

The LORD is my light and my salvation—
so why should I be afraid?
The LORD is my fortress, protecting me from
danger,
so why should I tremble?
When evil people come to devour me,
when my enemies and foes attack me,
they will stumble and fall.
Though a mighty army surrounds me,
my heart will not be afraid.
Even if I am attacked,
I will remain confident.
The one thing I ask of the LORD—

the thing I seek most—
is to live in the house of the LORD all the days of
my life,
delighting in the LORD's perfections
and meditating in his Temple.
For he will conceal me there when troubles come;
he will hide me in his sanctuary.
He will place me out of reach on a high rock.
Then I will hold my head high
above my enemies who surround me.
At his sanctuary I will offer sacrifices with shouts
of joy,
singing and praising the LORD with music.

REFLECT

Lectio Divina #1

Read today's passage slowly and out loud. Pay attention to the word or phrase that stands out to you.

- What do you sense God is saying to you through that word or phrase? Take a minute to listen.

Lectio Divina #2

Read today's passage a second time, again slowly and out loud. Listen for what invitation God may be extending to you through the word or phrase you identified.

- How does the word or phrase apply to your life right now? Take a minute to listen.

Lectio Divina #3

Read today's passage for a third time, and then enter into a conversation with God. Remember that you are in his loving presence. Present your questions, concerns, resistance, and repentance.

- What promises of God can you hold on to in the midst of fear?
- What do those promises reveal about his love?

A PRAYER TO CLOSE

Loving God, thank you for pouring out your love to me and for me and in me.
Thank you for loving me. I am yours. Amen and amen.

NEVER ABANDONED

Wherever you are, remember you are in God's loving presence. Close your eyes to dismiss any distractions. Open your hands as a way of doing with your body what you long for your heart and soul to do. Breathe in deeply and out slowly to relax your mind and your heart.

a prayer to open

Open me to your love, Lord.
In your great mercy, open me to your love.

READ HEBREWS 13:5-6

Don't love money; be satisfied with what you have. For God has said,

"I will never fail you.
I will never abandon you."

So we can say with confidence,

"The LORD is my helper,
so I will have no fear.
What can mere people do to me?"

REFLECT

Lectio Divina #1

Read today's passage slowly and out loud. Pay attention to the word or phrase that stands out to you.

• What do you sense God is saying to you through that word or phrase? Take a minute to listen.

Lectio Divina #2

Read today's passage a second time, again slowly and out loud. Listen for what invitation God may be extending to you through the word or phrase you identified.

• How does the word or phrase apply to your life right now? Take a minute to listen.

Lectio Divina #3

Read today's passage for a third time, and then enter into a conversation with God. Remember that you are in his loving presence. Present your questions, concerns, resistance, and repentance.

• What fears do you have regarding money?
• What is God saying to you about your money fears? Listen.

A PRAYER TO CLOSE

Loving God, thank you for pouring out your love to me and for me and in me.
Thank you for loving me. I am yours. Amen and amen.

NO FEAR

Wherever you are, remember you are in God's loving presence. Close your eyes to dismiss any distractions. Open your hands as a way of doing with your body what you long for your heart and soul to do. Breathe in deeply and out slowly to relax your mind and your heart.

a prayer to open

Open me to your love, Lord.
In your great mercy, open me to your love.

READ 2 TIMOTHY 1:6-10

Fan into flames the spiritual gift God gave you when I laid my hands on you. For God has not given us a spirit of fear and timidity, but of power, love, and self-discipline.

So never be ashamed to tell others about our Lord. And don't be ashamed of me, either, even though I'm in prison for him. With the strength God gives you, be ready to suffer with me for the sake of the Good News. For God saved us and called us to live a holy life. He did this, not because we deserved it, but because that was his plan from before the beginning of time—to show us his grace through Christ Jesus. And now he has made all of this plain to us by the appearing of Christ Jesus, our Savior. He broke the power of death and illuminated the way to life and immortality through the Good News.

REFLECT

Lectio Divina #1

Read today's passage slowly and out loud. Pay attention to the word or phrase that stands out to you.

• What do you sense God is saying to you through that word or phrase? Take a minute to listen.

Lectio Divina #2

Read today's passage a second time, again slowly and out loud. Listen for what invitation God may be extending to you through the word or phrase you identified.

• How does the word or phrase apply to your life right now? Take a minute to listen.

Lectio Divina #3

Read today's passage for a third time, and then enter into a conversation with God. Remember that you are in his loving presence. Present your questions, concerns, resistance, and repentance.

• How might power, love, and self-discipline help you overcome fear?

- What do you sense God wants to show you about yourself in the midst of fear?

A PRAYER TO CLOSE

Loving God, thank you for pouring out your love to me and for me and in me.
Thank you for loving me. I am yours. Amen and amen.

BANISHING PRIDE

HUMBLE YOURSELF

Wherever you are, remember you are in God's loving presence. Close your eyes to dismiss any distractions. Open your hands as a way of doing with your body what you long for your heart and soul to do. Breathe in deeply and out slowly to relax your mind and your heart.

a prayer to open

> Open me to your love, Lord.
> In your great mercy, open me to your love.

READ JAMES 4:6-10

He gives grace generously. As the Scriptures say,

> "God opposes the proud
> but gives grace to the humble."

So humble yourselves before God. Resist the devil, and he will flee from you. Come close to God, and God will come close to you. Wash your hands, you sinners; purify your hearts, for your loyalty is divided between God and the world. Let there be tears for what you have done. Let there be sorrow and deep grief. Let there be sadness instead of laughter, and gloom instead of joy. Humble yourselves before the Lord, and he will lift you up in honor.

REFLECT

Lectio Divina #1

Read today's passage slowly and out loud. Pay attention to the word or phrase that stands out to you.

- What do you sense God is saying to you through that word or phrase? Take a minute to listen.

Lectio Divina #2

Read today's passage a second time, again slowly and out loud. Listen for what invitation God may be extending to you through the word or phrase you identified.

Surrendered

•

41

- How does the word or phrase apply to your life right now? Take a minute to listen.

Lectio Divina #3

Read today's passage for a third time, and then enter into a conversation with God. Remember that you are in his loving presence. Present your questions, concerns, resistance, and repentance.

- Where do you sense that pride might be preventing you from opening to God's love?
- Where is God calling you to exercise humility?

A PRAYER TO CLOSE

Loving God, thank you for pouring out your love to me and for me and in me.
Thank you for loving me. I am yours. Amen and amen.

DAY 17

BURDENS

Wherever you are, remember you are in God's loving presence. Close your eyes to dismiss any distractions. Open your hands as a way of doing with your body what you long for your heart and soul to do. Breathe in deeply and out slowly to relax your mind and your heart.

a prayer to open

Open me to your love, Lord.
In your great mercy, open me to your love.

READ GALATIANS 6:2-5

Share each other's burdens, and in this way obey the law of Christ. If you think you are too important to help someone, you are only fooling yourself. You are not that important.

Pay careful attention to your own work, for then you will get the satisfaction of a job well done, and you won't need to compare yourself to anyone else. For we are each responsible for our own conduct.

REFLECT

Lectio Divina #1

Read today's passage slowly and out loud. Pay attention to the word or phrase that stands out to you.

- What do you sense God is saying to you through that word or phrase? Take a minute to listen.

Lectio Divina #2

Read today's passage a second time, again slowly and out loud. Listen for what invitation God may be extending to you through the word or phrase you identified.

- How does the word or phrase apply to your life right now? Take a minute to listen.

Lectio Divina #3

Read today's passage for a third time, and then enter into a conversation with God. Remember that you are in his loving presence. Present your questions, concerns, resistance, and repentance.

- How might pride be closing off your ability to surrender to God's love?
- Where is God calling you to be a servant of others?

A PRAYER TO CLOSE

Loving God, thank you for pouring out your love to me and for me and in me.
Thank you for loving me. I am yours. Amen and amen.

WORRY

DAY 18

YOUR FATHER KNOWS

Wherever you are, remember you are in God's loving presence. Close your eyes to dismiss any distractions. Open your hands as a way of doing with your body what you long for your heart and soul to do. Breathe in deeply and out slowly to relax your mind and your heart.

a prayer to open   Open me to your love, Lord.
In your great mercy, open me to your love.

READ MATTHEW 6:25-34

That is why I tell you not to worry about everyday life—whether you have enough food and drink, or enough clothes to wear. Isn't life more than food, and your body more than clothing? Look at the birds. They don't plant or harvest or store food in barns, for your heavenly Father feeds them. And aren't you far more valuable to him than they are? Can all your worries add a single moment to your life?

And why worry about your clothing? Look at the lilies of the field and how they grow. They don't work or make their clothing, yet Solomon in all his glory was not dressed as beautifully as they are. And if God cares so wonderfully for wildflowers that are here today and thrown into the fire tomorrow, he will certainly care for you. Why do you have so little faith?

So don't worry about these things, saying, "What will we eat? What will we drink? What will we wear?" These things dominate the thoughts of unbelievers, but your heavenly Father already knows all your needs. Seek the Kingdom of God above all else, and live righteously, and he will give you everything you need.

So don't worry about tomorrow, for tomorrow will bring its own worries. Today's trouble is enough for today.

REFLECT_____

Lectio Divina #1

Read today's passage slowly and out loud. Pay attention to the word or phrase that stands out to you.

- What do you sense God is saying to you through that word or phrase? Take a minute to listen.

Lectio Divina #2

Read today's passage a second time, again slowly and out loud. Listen for what invitation God may be extending to you through the word or phrase you identified.

- How does the word or phrase apply to your life right now? Take a minute to listen.

Lectio Divina #3

Read today's passage for a third time, and then enter into a conversation with God. Remember that you are in his loving presence. Present your questions, concerns, resistance, and repentance.

- What worries are preventing you from opening more fully to God's love?
- What is God saying to you about your worries?

A PRAYER TO CLOSE_____

Loving God, thank you for pouring out your love to me and for me and in me. Thank you for loving me. I am yours. Amen and amen.

PRAY

Wherever you are, remember you are in God's loving presence. Close your eyes to dismiss any distractions. Open your hands as a way of doing with your body what you long for your heart and soul to do. Breathe in deeply and out slowly to relax your mind and your heart.

a prayer to open

Open me to your love, Lord.
In your great mercy, open me to your love.

READ PHILIPPIANS 4:6-7

Don't worry about anything; instead, pray about everything. Tell God what you need, and thank him for all he has done. Then you will experience God's peace, which exceeds anything we can understand. His peace will guard your hearts and minds as you live in Christ Jesus.

REFLECT

Lectio Divina #1

Read today's passage slowly and out loud. Pay attention to the word or phrase that stands out to you.

• What do you sense God is saying to you through that word or phrase? Take a minute to listen.

Lectio Divina #2

Read today's passage a second time, again slowly and out loud. Listen for what invitation God may be extending to you through the word or phrase you identified.

• How does the word or phrase apply to your life right now? Take a minute to listen.

Lectio Divina #3

Read today's passage for a third time, and then enter into a conversation with God. Remember that you are in his loving presence. Present your questions, concerns, resistance, and repentance.

• What do you need from God? What can you thank him for?
• How might gratitude help you overcome your worries?

A PRAYER TO CLOSE

Loving God, thank you for pouring out your love to me and for me and in me. Thank you for loving me. I am yours. Amen and amen.

WORRIES AND CARES

Wherever you are, remember you are in God's loving presence. Close your eyes to dismiss any distractions. Open your hands as a way of doing with your body what you long for your heart and soul to do. Breathe in deeply and out slowly to relax your mind and your heart.

a prayer to open

Open me to your love, Lord.
In your great mercy, open me to your love.

READ 1 PETER 5:6-9

Humble yourselves under the mighty power of God, and at the right time he will lift you up in honor. Give all your worries and cares to God, for he cares about you.

Stay alert! Watch out for your great enemy, the devil. He prowls around like a roaring lion, looking for someone to devour. Stand firm against him, and be strong in your faith. Remember that your family of believers all over the world is going through the same kind of suffering you are.

REFLECT

Lectio Divina #1

Read today's passage slowly and out loud. Pay attention to the word or phrase that stands out to you.

- What do you sense God is saying to you through that word or phrase? Take a minute to listen.

Lectio Divina #2

Read today's passage a second time, again slowly and out loud. Listen for what invitation God may be extending to you through the word or phrase you identified.

- How does the word or phrase apply to your life right now? Take a minute to listen.

Lectio Divina #3

Read today's passage for a third time, and then enter into a conversation with God. Remember that you are in his loving presence. Present your questions, concerns, resistance, and repentance.

- What worries can you give to God? How will you do that?
- Who could hear your worries and provide perspective?

Loving God, thank you for pouring out your love to me and for me and in me. Thank you for loving me. I am yours. Amen and amen.

BUSYNESS

DAY 21

AT HIS FEET

Wherever you are, remember you are in God's loving presence. Close your eyes to dismiss any distractions. Open your hands as a way of doing with your body what you long for your heart and soul to do. Breathe in deeply and out slowly to relax your mind and your heart.

a prayer to open

Open me to your love, Lord.
In your great mercy, open me to your love.

READ LUKE 10:38-42 _____

Jesus and the disciples . . . came to a certain village where a woman named Martha welcomed him into her home. Her sister, Mary, sat at the Lord's feet, listening to what he taught. But Martha was distracted by the big dinner she was preparing. She came to Jesus and said, "Lord, doesn't it seem unfair to you that my sister just sits here while I do all the work? Tell her to come and help me."

But the Lord said to her, "My dear Martha, you are worried and upset over all these details! There is only one thing worth being concerned about. Mary has discovered it, and it will not be taken away from her."

REFLECT_____

Lectio Divina #1

Read today's passage slowly and out loud. Pay attention to the word or phrase that stands out to you.

• What do you sense God is saying to you through that word or phrase? Take a minute to listen.

Lectio Divina #2

Read today's passage a second time, again slowly and out loud. Listen for what invitation God may be extending to you through the word or phrase you identified.

• How does the word or phrase apply to your life right now? Take a minute to listen.

Surrendered

•

Lectio Divina #3

Read today's passage for a third time, and then enter into a conversation with God. Remember that you are in his loving presence. Present your questions, concerns, resistance, and repentance.

- How is busyness getting in the way of your opening more fully to God's love?
- What is God saying to you about your busyness?

A PRAYER TO CLOSE_____

Loving God, thank you for pouring out your love to me and for me and in me.
Thank you for loving me. I am yours. Amen and amen.

DAY 22

REMAIN

Wherever you are, remember you are in God's loving presence. Close your eyes to dismiss any distractions. Open your hands as a way of doing with your body what you long for your heart and soul to do. Breathe in deeply and out slowly to relax your mind and your heart.

a prayer to open

Open me to your love, Lord.
In your great mercy, open me to your love.

READ JOHN 15:1-11_____

I am the true grapevine, and my Father is the gardener. He cuts off every branch of mine that doesn't produce fruit, and he prunes the branches that do bear fruit so they will produce even more. . . . Remain in me, and I will remain in you. For . . . you cannot be fruitful unless you remain in me.

Yes, I am the vine; you are the branches. Those who remain in me, and I in them, will produce much fruit. For apart from me you can do nothing. Anyone who does not remain in me is thrown away like a useless branch and withers. Such branches are gathered into a pile to be burned. But if you remain in me and my words remain in you, you may ask for anything you want, and it will be granted! When you produce much fruit, you are my true disciples. This brings great glory to my Father.

I have loved you even as the Father has loved me. Remain in my love. When you obey my commandments, you remain in my love, just as I obey my Father's commandments and remain in his love. I have told you these things so that you will be filled with my joy. Yes, your joy will overflow!

REFLECT_____

Lectio Divina #1

Read today's passage slowly and out loud. Pay attention to the word or phrase that stands out to you.

- What do you sense God is saying to you through that word or phrase? Take a minute to listen.

Lectio Divina #2

Read today's passage a second time, again slowly and out loud. Listen for what invitation God may be extending to you through the word or phrase you identified.

- How does the word or phrase apply to your life right now? Take a minute to listen.

Lectio Divina #3

Read today's passage for a third time, and then enter into a conversation with God. Remember that you are in his loving presence. Present your questions, concerns, resistance, and repentance.

- What most often keeps you from spending time with Jesus?
- What is God saying to you about how you spend your time?

A PRAYER TO CLOSE_____

Loving God, thank you for pouring out your love to me and for me and in me.
Thank you for loving me. I am yours. Amen and amen.

CONFESSING SIN

WASH ME CLEAN

Wherever you are, remember you are in God's loving presence. Close your eyes to dismiss any distractions. Open your hands as a way of doing with your body what you long for your heart and soul to do. Breathe in deeply and out slowly to relax your mind and your heart.

a prayer to open   Open me to your love, Lord.
                        In your great mercy, open me to your love.

READ PSALM 51:1-11_____

Have mercy on me, O God,   Wash me clean from my guilt.
    because of your unfailing love.   Purify me from my sin.
Because of your great compassion,   For I recognize my rebellion;
    blot out the stain of my sins.   it haunts me day and night.

Against you, and you alone, have I sinned;
I have done what is evil in your sight.
You will be proved right in what you say,
and your judgment against me is just.
For I was born a sinner—
yes, from the moment my mother
conceived me.
But you desire honesty from the womb,
teaching me wisdom even there.
Purify me from my sins, and I will be clean;
wash me, and I will be whiter than snow.
Oh, give me back my joy again;
you have broken me—
now let me rejoice.
Don't keep looking at my sins.
Remove the stain of my guilt.
Create in me a clean heart, O God.
Renew a loyal spirit within me.
Do not banish me from your presence,
and don't take your Holy Spirit from me.

REFLECT

Lectio Divina #1

Read today's passage slowly and out loud. Pay attention to the word or phrase that stands out to you.

- What do you sense God is saying to you through that word or phrase? Take a minute to listen.

Lectio Divina #2

Read today's passage a second time, again slowly and out loud. Listen for what invitation God may be extending to you through the word or phrase you identified.

- How does the word or phrase apply to your life right now? Take a minute to listen.

Lectio Divina #3

Read today's passage for a third time, and then enter into a conversation with God. Remember that you are in his loving presence. Present your questions, concerns, resistance, and repentance.

- What sins from your past are keeping you from opening more fully to God's love?
- What is God saying to you about those sins? Listen.

A PRAYER TO CLOSE

Loving God, thank you for pouring out your love to me and for me and in me.
Thank you for loving me. I am yours. Amen and amen.

YOU FORGAVE ME

Wherever you are, remember you are in God's loving presence. Close your eyes to dismiss any distractions. Open your hands as a way of doing with your body what you long for your heart and soul to do. Breathe in deeply and out slowly to relax your mind and your heart.

a prayer to open

Open me to your love, Lord.
In your great mercy, open me to your love.

READ PSALM 32

Oh, what joy for those
   whose disobedience is forgiven,
   whose sin is put out of sight!
Yes, what joy for those
   whose record the LORD has cleared of guilt,
   whose lives are lived in complete honesty!
When I refused to confess my sin,
   my body wasted away,
   and I groaned all day long.
Day and night your hand of discipline was
    heavy on me.
   My strength evaporated like water in the
    summer heat.
Finally, I confessed all my sins to you
   and stopped trying to hide my guilt.
I said to myself, "I will confess my rebellion to
   the LORD."
   And you forgave me! All my guilt is gone.

Therefore, let all the godly pray to you while
    there is still time,
   that they may not drown in the floodwaters of
    judgment.
For you are my hiding place;
   you protect me from trouble.
   You surround me with songs of victory.
The LORD says, "I will guide you along the best
    pathway for your life.
   I will advise you and watch over you.
Do not be like a senseless horse or mule
   that needs a bit and bridle to keep it under
    control."
Many sorrows come to the wicked,
   but unfailing love surrounds those who trust
    the LORD.
So rejoice in the LORD and be glad, all you who
   obey him!
   Shout for joy, all you whose hearts are pure!

REFLECT

Lectio Divina #1

Read today's passage slowly and out loud. Pay attention to the word or phrase that stands out to you.

• What do you sense God is saying to you through that word or phrase? Take a minute to listen.

Lectio Divina #2

Read today's passage a second time, again slowly and out loud. Listen for what invitation God may be extending to you through the word or phrase you identified.

• How does the word or phrase apply to your life right now? Take a minute to listen.

Lectio Divina #3

Read today's passage for a third time, and then enter into a conversation with God. Remember that you are in his loving presence. Present your questions, concerns, resistance, and repentance.

- What sin or guilt might be keeping you from opening more fully to God's love?

- What is God saying to you about trusting him to fully forgive you?

A PRAYER TO CLOSE

Loving God, thank you for pouring out your love to me and for me and in me. Thank you for loving me. I am yours. Amen and amen.

DAY 25

FAITHFUL TO FORGIVE

Wherever you are, remember you are in God's loving presence. Close your eyes to dismiss any distractions. Open your hands as a way of doing with your body what you long for your heart and soul to do. Breathe in deeply and out slowly to relax your mind and your heart.

a prayer to open

Open me to your love, Lord.
In your great mercy, open me to your love.

READ 1 JOHN 1:5-10

God is light, and there is no darkness in him at all. So we are lying if we say we have fellowship with God but go on living in spiritual darkness; we are not practicing the truth. But if we are living in the light, as God is in the light, then we have fellowship with each other, and the blood of Jesus, his Son, cleanses us from all sin.

If we claim we have no sin, we are only fooling ourselves and not living in the truth. But if we confess our sins to him, he is faithful and just to forgive us our sins and to cleanse us from all wickedness. If we claim we have not sinned, we are calling God a liar and showing that his word has no place in our hearts.

REFLECT

Lectio Divina #1

Read today's passage slowly and out loud. Pay attention to the word or phrase that stands out to you.

- What do you sense God is saying to you through that word or phrase? Take a minute to listen.

Lectio Divina #2

Read today's passage a second time, again slowly and out loud. Listen for what invitation God may be extending to you through the word or phrase you identified.

- How does the word or phrase apply to your life right now? Take a minute to listen.

Lectio Divina #3

Read today's passage for a third time, and then enter into a conversation with God. Remember that you are in his loving presence. Present your questions, concerns, resistance, and repentance.

- Where do you need to more fully receive God's forgiveness?
- What is God saying to you about the fullness and finality of his forgiveness?

A PRAYER TO CLOSE

Loving God, thank you for pouring out your love to me and for me and in me. Thank you for loving me. I am yours. Amen and amen.

PAIN AND SUFFERING

DAY 26

I HAVE OVERCOME THE WORLD

Wherever you are, remember you are in God's loving presence. Close your eyes to dismiss any distractions. Open your hands as a way of doing with your body what you long for your heart and soul to do. Breathe in deeply and out slowly to relax your mind and your heart.

a prayer to open

Open me to your love, Lord.
In your great mercy, open me to your love.

READ JOHN 16:29-33

Then his disciples said, "At last you are speaking plainly. . . . Now we understand that you know everything, and there's no need to question you. From this we believe that you came from God."

Jesus asked, "Do you finally believe? But the time is coming—indeed it's here now—when you will be scattered, each one going his own way, leaving me alone. Yet I am not alone because the Father is with me. I have told you all this so that you may have peace in me. Here on earth you will have many trials and sorrows. But take heart, because I have overcome the world."

Lectio Divina #1

Read today's passage slowly and out loud. Pay attention to the word or phrase that stands out to you.

• What do you sense God is saying to you through that word or phrase? Take a minute to listen.

Lectio Divina #2

Read today's passage a second time, again slowly and out loud. Listen for what invitation God may be extending to you through the word or phrase you identified.

• How does the word or phrase apply to your life right now? Take a minute to listen.

Lectio Divina #3

Read today's passage for a third time, and then enter into a conversation with God. Remember that you are in his loving presence. Present your questions, concerns, resistance, and repentance.

• How are your trials and sorrows keeping you from opening more fully to God's love?

• What is God saying to you about the trials and sorrows you've experienced?

A PRAYER TO CLOSE

Loving God, thank you for pouring out your love to me and for me and in me.
Thank you for loving me. I am yours. Amen and amen.

DAY 27

RELEASED

Wherever you are, remember you are in God's loving presence. Close your eyes to dismiss any distractions. Open your hands as a way of doing with your body what you long for your heart and soul to do. Breathe in deeply and out slowly to relax your mind and your heart.

a prayer to open

Open me to your love, Lord.
In your great mercy, open me to your love.

What we suffer now is nothing compared to the glory he will reveal to us later. For all creation is waiting eagerly for that future day when God will reveal who his children really are. . . . All creation was subjected to God's curse. But with eager hope, the creation looks forward to the day when it will join God's children in glorious freedom from death and decay. For we know that all creation has been groaning as in the pains of childbirth right up to the present time. And we believers also groan, even though we have the Holy Spirit within us as a foretaste of future glory, for we long for our bodies to be released from sin and suffering. We, too, wait with eager hope for the day when God will give us our full rights as his adopted children, including the new bodies he has promised us. We were given this hope when we were saved. (If we already have something, we don't need to hope for it. But if we look forward to something we don't yet have, we must wait patiently and confidently.)

And the Holy Spirit helps us in our weakness. For example, we don't know what God wants us to pray for. But the Holy Spirit prays for us with groanings that cannot be expressed in words. And the Father who knows all hearts knows what the Spirit is saying, for the Spirit pleads for us believers in harmony with God's own will. And we know that God causes everything to work together for the good of those who love God and are called according to his purpose for them. For God knew his people in advance, and he chose them to become like his Son. . . . And having chosen them, he called them to come to him. And having called them, he gave them right standing with himself. And having given them right standing, he gave them his glory.

REFLECT

Lectio Divina #1

Read today's passage slowly and out loud. Pay attention to the word or phrase that stands out to you.

- What do you sense God is saying to you through that word or phrase? Take a minute to listen.

Lectio Divina #2

Read today's passage a second time, again slowly and out loud. Listen for what invitation God may be extending to you through the word or phrase you identified.

- How does the word or phrase apply to your life right now? Take a minute to listen.

Lectio Divina #3

Read today's passage for a third time, and then enter into a conversation with God. Remember that you are in his loving presence. Present your questions, concerns, resistance, and repentance.

- How does your understanding of the suffering in the world get in the way of your opening more fully to God's love?
- What is God saying to you about the suffering you see?

A PRAYER TO CLOSE

Loving God, thank you for pouring out your love to me and for me and in me.
Thank you for loving me. I am yours. Amen and amen.

FOREVER

Wherever you are, remember you are in God's loving presence. Close your eyes to dismiss any distractions. Open your hands as a way of doing with your body what you long for your heart and soul to do. Breathe in deeply and out slowly to relax your mind and your heart.

a prayer to open

Open me to your love, Lord.
In your great mercy, open me to your love.

READ PSALM 136

Give thanks to the LORD, for he is good!
His faithful love endures forever.
Give thanks to the God of gods.
His faithful love endures forever.
Give thanks to the Lord of lords.
His faithful love endures forever.
Give thanks to him who alone does mighty miracles.
His faithful love endures forever.
Give thanks to him who made the heavens so skillfully.
His faithful love endures forever.
Give thanks to him who placed the earth among the waters.
His faithful love endures forever.
Give thanks to him who made the heavenly lights—
His faithful love endures forever.
the sun to rule the day,
His faithful love endures forever.
and the moon and stars to rule the night.
His faithful love endures forever.
Give thanks to him who killed the firstborn of Egypt.
His faithful love endures forever.
He brought Israel out of Egypt.
His faithful love endures forever.
He acted with a strong hand and powerful arm.
His faithful love endures forever.

Give thanks to him who parted the Red Sea.
His faithful love endures forever.
He led Israel safely through,
His faithful love endures forever.
but he hurled Pharaoh and his army into the Red Sea.
His faithful love endures forever.
Give thanks to him who led his people through the wilderness.
His faithful love endures forever.
Give thanks to him who struck down mighty kings.
His faithful love endures forever.
He killed powerful kings—
His faithful love endures forever. . . .
God gave the land of these kings as an inheritance—
His faithful love endures forever.
a special possession to his servant Israel.
His faithful love endures forever.
He remembered us in our weakness.
His faithful love endures forever.
He saved us from our enemies.
His faithful love endures forever.
He gives food to every living thing.
His faithful love endures forever.
Give thanks to the God of heaven.
His faithful love endures forever.

Lectio Divina #1

Read today's passage slowly and out loud. Pay attention to the word or phrase that stands out to you.

- What do you sense God is saying to you through that word or phrase? Take a minute to listen.

Lectio Divina #2

Read today's passage a second time, again slowly and out loud. Listen for what invitation God may be extending to you through the word or phrase you identified.

- How does the word or phrase apply to your life right now? Take a minute to listen.

Lectio Divina #3

Read today's passage for a third time, and then enter into a conversation with God. Remember that you are in his loving presence. Present your questions, concerns, resistance, and repentance.

- What truth from Psalm 136 does God want you to hold on to?
- What of God's actions in your life might you add to this prayer, followed by "his faithful love endures forever"?

A PRAYER TO CLOSE

Loving God, thank you for pouring out your love to me and for me and in me. Thank you for loving me. I am yours. Amen and amen.

DAY 29

UNFAILING LOVE

Wherever you are, remember you are in God's loving presence. Close your eyes to dismiss any distractions. Open your hands as a way of doing with your body what you long for your heart and soul to do. Breathe in deeply and out slowly to relax your mind and your heart.

a prayer to open   Open me to your love, Lord.
                    In your great mercy, open me to your love.

Surrendered

Shout with joy to the LORD, all the earth!
Worship the LORD with gladness.
Come before him, singing with joy.
Acknowledge that the LORD is God!
He made us, and we are his.
We are his people, the sheep of his pasture.
Enter his gates with thanksgiving;
go into his courts with praise.
Give thanks to him and praise his name.
For the LORD is good.
His unfailing love continues forever,
and his faithfulness continues to each
generation.

REFLECT _____

Lectio Divina #1

Read today's passage slowly and out loud. Pay attention to the word or phrase that stands out to you.

- What do you sense God is saying to you through that word or phrase? Take a minute to listen.

Lectio Divina #2

Read today's passage a second time, again slowly and out loud. Listen for what invitation God may be extending to you through the word or phrase you identified.

- How does the word or phrase apply to your life right now? Take a minute to listen.

Lectio Divina #3

Read today's passage for a third time, and then enter into a conversation with God. Remember that you are in his loving presence. Present your questions, concerns, resistance, and repentance.

- What truth from Psalm 100 does God want you to hold on to?
- Where do you see his goodness right now?

A PRAYER TO CLOSE _____

Loving God, thank you for pouring out your love to me and for me and in me. Thank you for loving me. I am yours. Amen and amen.

CHRIST IS THE VISIBLE IMAGE OF GOD

Wherever you are, remember you are in God's loving presence. Close your eyes to dismiss any distractions. Open your hands as a way of doing with your body what you long for your heart and soul to do. Breathe in deeply and out slowly to relax your mind and your heart.

a prayer to open

Open me to your love, Lord.
In your great mercy, open me to your love.

READ COLOSSIANS 1:15-20

Christ is the visible image of the invisible God.
  He existed before anything was created and is
    supreme over all creation,
for through him God created everything
  in the heavenly realms and on earth.
He made the things we can see
  and the things we can't see—
such as thrones, kingdoms, rulers, and
    authorities in the unseen world.
  Everything was created through him and for
    him.
He existed before anything else,
  and he holds all creation together.

Christ is also the head of the church,
  which is his body.
He is the beginning,
  supreme over all who rise from the dead.
  So he is first in everything.
For God in all his fullness
  was pleased to live in Christ,
and through him God reconciled
  everything to himself.
He made peace with everything in heaven and
    on earth
  by means of Christ's blood on the cross.

REFLECT

Lectio Divina #1

Read today's passage slowly and out loud. Pay attention to the word or phrase that stands out to you.

• What do you sense God is saying to you through that word or phrase? Take a minute to listen.

Lectio Divina #2

Read today's passage a second time, again slowly and out loud. Listen for what invitation God may be extending to you through the word or phrase you identified.

• How does the word or phrase apply to your life right now? Take a minute to listen.

Lectio Divina #3

Read today's passage for a third time, and then enter into a conversation with God. Remember that you are in his loving presence. Present your questions, concerns, resistance, and repentance.

- In the last thirty days, how has God shaped your image of him as loving?
- In what way have you been able to surrender more to his love?
- What practices might you carry forward to help you live more fully in his love?

A PRAYER TO CLOSE

Loving God, thank you for pouring out your love to me and for me and in me. Thank you for loving me. I am yours. Amen and amen.

Revealed

Knowing the One You Follow

IN 2011 I went to South Africa and met a guy named Mike. He and his wife led an outreach called Dumpsite Ministry in Johannesburg. Every Saturday morning, they made meals and drinks for people who lived on a trash dump. The families lived in one-room shelters built with wood, metal, and plastic scraps that barely held together. Most of the shelters had no furniture, and the floors were dirt. There was no water, electricity, or plumbing. The people were largely unemployed, and many were sick.

On the day I tagged along with Mike, we carried over food in black crates and big buckets of lemonade by truck. When we arrived, about sixty women and children awaited us. Mike preached a short sermon to those gathered while the rest of us unloaded and passed out the food and drinks. Then things got interesting.

I noticed that a line had begun to form off to one side. "That's the line for prayer and healing," someone told me. This caught my attention. I walked over just as Mike took his position at the front. As each person approached, he spoke their name. He listened to their request, reached out to touch their arm or forehead, and prayed. He also recorded each and every person's prayer request in his cell phone so he could continue praying for them. The sun was hot and there was no shade, yet Mike patiently worked his way through the line. A woman beside me said that people had come to Mike and been healed. I had no reason to believe otherwise as I watched this beautiful outpouring of love and faith.

Next, Mike began to walk through the dump itself. People began to rush out of their shelters, calling to him. He interacted with everyone as we walked. The joy on the faces I saw belied their horrific circumstances. As Mike engaged with each person, you would have thought he'd run into wealthy businesspeople who could support his ministry. These people were kings in Mike's eyes, deserving of his attention and care.

One man walked up, wavering on his feet. His skin was covered in open sores caused by HIV. Mike put his arm around the man, asked him how he was feeling, and told him he needed to see the doctor. The man lamented to Mike that he had no way to get to the doctor. In response, Mike told him he'd come back later and take him there. Just like that.

As we continued on, a woman approached, greeted Mike, and then sang a song of praise to God for him. A man walked over and told Mike his roof was leaking. Mike assured him he had nails in his truck that would fix the leak.

This must have been what it was like to walk with Jesus. Christ had a body and walked among living, hurting, sick people. He had hands, eyes, feet, and ears. In fact, he still does! People sought Jesus out not because he represented something but because he looked at them, listened to them, healed them with his hands, and spoke to them with his mouth.

Too often in our Western culture, we have disembodied Jesus, turning him into a mere idea. But he is a person with hands and feet and a beating heart and active mind. We have to (and we get to) know who we follow. Jesus is not distant, floating off in the sky somewhere. He is not a white-bearded Santa look-alike; he is Jesus, a person. In Jesus, all the fullness of God lives in bodily form (Colossians 2:9). Jesus is revealed to us in part by people like Mike, but to really know Jesus we must immerse ourselves in his life—how he talked to sinners, touched the sick, healed the broken, freed the prisoners, taught his followers, and loved the world. For thirty days we will journey through the Gospel of Luke and discover what Jesus' key interactions, experiences, and teachings reveal to us about who God is—because we cannot know God absent from what Jesus did in his body on this earth.

TRUTH REVEALED

a prayer to open

Open my eyes and help me to see you.
Open my heart and help me to know you.
Jesus, my Lord and my God.

READ LUKE 1:1-25

Many people have set out to write accounts about the events that have been fulfilled among us. They used the eyewitness reports circulating among us from the early disciples. Having carefully investigated everything from the beginning, I also have decided to write an accurate account for you, most honorable Theophilus, so you can be certain of the truth of everything you were taught.

When Herod was king of Judea, there was a Jewish priest named Zechariah. . . . Zechariah and [his wife] Elizabeth were righteous in God's eyes, careful to obey all of the Lord's commandments and regulations. They had no children because Elizabeth was unable to conceive, and they were both very old.

One day Zechariah was serving God in the Temple, for his order was on duty that week. As was the custom of the priests, he was chosen by lot to enter the sanctuary of the Lord and burn incense. . . .

While Zechariah was in the sanctuary, an angel of the Lord appeared to him. . . . Zechariah was shaken and overwhelmed with fear when he saw him. But the angel said, "Don't be afraid, Zechariah! God has heard your prayer. Your wife, Elizabeth, will give you a son, and you are to name him John. You will have great joy and gladness, and many will rejoice at his birth, for he will be great in the eyes of the Lord. He must never touch wine or other alcoholic drinks. He will be filled with the Holy Spirit, even before his birth. And he will turn many Israelites to the Lord their God. He will be a man with the spirit and power of Elijah. He will prepare the people for the coming of the Lord. He will turn the hearts of the fathers to their children, and he will cause those who are rebellious to accept the wisdom of the godly."

Zechariah said to the angel, "How can I be sure this will happen? I'm an old man now, and my wife is also well along in years."

Then the angel said, "I am Gabriel! I stand in the very presence of God. It was he who sent me to bring you this good news! But now, since you didn't believe what I said, you will be silent and unable to speak until the child is born. For my words will certainly be fulfilled at the proper time."

Meanwhile, the people were waiting for Zechariah to come out of the sanctuary, wondering why he was taking so long. When he finally did come out, he couldn't speak to them. Then they realized from his gestures and his silence that he must have seen a vision. . . .

Soon afterward his wife, Elizabeth, became pregnant and went into seclusion for five months. "How kind the Lord is!" she exclaimed. "He has taken away my disgrace of having no children."

REFLECT _____

Tempted as we are to jump right into the story of Jesus, we must pause and consider Luke's opening lines, which ground us firmly in the reality that this is no made-up story. Jesus' birth, life, death, and resurrection were events that could be carefully investigated. Luke conducted interviews with eyewitnesses—people who saw, heard, and touched Jesus himself. Some probably saw Jesus from afar or gathered to hear him on hillsides. Others likely ate meals with him, walked alongside him, and felt his touch on their shoulders. Something unbelievable had happened, and Luke sought to preserve the facts, the teachings, the miracles, and the truth that a new chapter of history had begun in Jesus Christ. May Luke's account reveal to us, by the power of the Holy Spirit, the certainty about who Jesus, our God and Savior, is.

- How does Luke's statement that he "carefully investigated everything from the beginning" influence your view of the rest of what he says?

- As you begin your journey through the book of Luke, what do you desire for God to show you about who Jesus is?

- What does today's passage reveal to you about the coming Jesus?

RESPOND _____

Father, thank you for your saving grace and my new life in Jesus Christ! Allow me to encounter you and gain understanding of your presence as I read Luke's account of Jesus' life, death, and resurrection. Give me ears to hear your words to me, strengthen my faith, and transform my desires so I can better follow your ways. Amen.

THE LORD'S SERVANT

a prayer to open

Open my eyes and help me to see you.
Open my heart and help me to know you.
Jesus, my Lord and my God.

READ LUKE 1:26-56

In the sixth month of Elizabeth's pregnancy, God sent the angel Gabriel to Nazareth, a village in Galilee, to a virgin named Mary. She was engaged to be married to a man named Joseph, a descendant of King David. Gabriel appeared to her and said, "Greetings, favored woman! The Lord is with you!"

Confused and disturbed, Mary tried to think what the angel could mean. "Don't be afraid, Mary," the angel told her, "for you have found favor with God! You will conceive and give birth to a son, and you will name him Jesus. He will be very great and will be called the Son of the Most High. The Lord God will give him the throne of his ancestor David. And he will reign over Israel forever; his Kingdom will never end!"

Mary asked the angel, "But how can this happen? I am a virgin."

The angel replied, "The Holy Spirit will come upon you, and the power of the Most High will overshadow you. So the baby to be born will be holy, and he will be called the Son of God. What's more, your relative Elizabeth has become pregnant in her old age! . . . For the word of God will never fail."

Mary responded, "I am the Lord's servant. May everything you have said about me come true." And then the angel left her.

A few days later Mary hurried . . . to the town where Zechariah lived. . . . At the sound of Mary's greeting, Elizabeth's child leaped within her, and Elizabeth was filled with the Holy Spirit.

Elizabeth gave a glad cry and exclaimed to Mary, "God has blessed you above all women, and your child is blessed. Why am I so honored, that the mother of my Lord should visit me? When I heard your greeting, the baby in my womb jumped for joy. You are blessed because you believed that the Lord would do what he said."

Mary responded,

"Oh, how my soul praises the Lord.
How my spirit rejoices in God my Savior!
For he took notice of his lowly servant girl,
and from now on all generations will call me blessed.
For the Mighty One is holy,
and he has done great things for me.
He shows mercy from generation to generation
to all who fear him.
His mighty arm has done tremendous things!
He has scattered the proud and haughty ones.
He has brought down princes from their thrones
and exalted the humble.
He has filled the hungry with good things
and sent the rich away with empty hands.
He has helped his servant Israel
and remembered to be merciful.
For he made this promise to our ancestors,
to Abraham and his children forever."

Mary stayed with Elizabeth about three months and then went back to her own home.

REFLECT

As many times as we might read this story, it still stuns. What could it possibly have been like for this girl to hear that she would bear the Messiah her people had so long awaited? She had been chosen and set apart. We know by Mary's immediate response to Gabriel and her beautiful song that she understood the weight of responsibility she had been given, yet she leaned in, allowed her faith to lead her, and committed herself to the unknown.

- Reread Mary's response to Gabriel, as well as her response to Elizabeth. What do her words reveal about her?

- Elizabeth said to Mary, "You are blessed because you believed that the Lord would do what he said" (verse 45). What promises from God do you need his help to believe?

- What does today's passage reveal to you about the coming Jesus?

RESPOND

Father, help me to believe your words, those you speak in Scripture and those you whisper into my heart. When I doubt you, your goodness, your love, and your presence, remind me of the ways you have blessed me, loved me, and revealed yourself to me. Help me respond to you as Mary did. After all, I too am your servant, and I pray that the words you speak to me are fulfilled, whether they seem impossible, difficult to believe, or contrary to my desires. Amen.

DAY 3

GLORY IN THE HIGHEST!

a prayer to open

Open my eyes and help me to see you.
Open my heart and help me to know you.
Jesus, my Lord and my God.

READ LUKE 2:1-21

At that time the Roman emperor, Augustus, decreed that a census should be taken throughout the Roman Empire.... All returned to their own ancestral towns to register for this census. And because Joseph was a descendant of King David, he had to go to Bethlehem in Judea.... He took with him Mary, to whom he was engaged, who was now expecting a child.

And while they were there, the time came for her baby to be born. She gave birth to her firstborn son. She wrapped him snugly in strips of cloth and laid him in a manger, because there was no lodging available for them.

That night there were shepherds staying in the fields nearby, guarding their flocks of sheep. Suddenly, an angel of the Lord appeared among them, and the radiance of the Lord's glory surrounded them. They were terrified, but the angel reassured them. "Don't be afraid!" he said. "I bring you good news that will bring great joy to all people. The Savior—yes, the Messiah, the Lord—has been born today in Bethlehem, the city of David! And you will recognize him by this sign: You will find a baby wrapped snugly in strips of cloth, lying in a manger."

Suddenly, the angel was joined by a vast host of others—the armies of heaven—praising God and saying,

"Glory to God in highest heaven,
and peace on earth to those with whom God is pleased."

When the angels had returned to heaven, the shepherds said to each other, "Let's go to Bethlehem! Let's see this thing that has happened, which the Lord has told us about."

They hurried to the village and found Mary and Joseph. And there was the baby, lying in the manger. After seeing him, the shepherds told everyone what had happened. . . . All who heard the shepherds' story were astonished, but Mary kept all these things in her heart and thought about them often. The shepherds went back to their flocks, glorifying and praising God for all they had heard and seen. It was just as the angel had told them.

Eight days later, when the baby was circumcised, he was named Jesus, the name given him by the angel even before he was conceived.

In this passage, we see the wonder and awe of those on earth and those in heaven. No one could experience the birth of Jesus and remain unmoved. Even the heavens erupted in praise! No other moment in history has held such glory, love, and goodness. Jesus had arrived, and so too had the Kingdom of God. Sin and death were in their final hours, and the old order of things would begin to bend to God's will. An eternal revolution had begun in a small body in a small town.

- What do you think Mary and Joseph thought about as they walked the eighty miles to Bethlehem, knowing that the coming child was the Messiah? What fears, doubts, or joys would have come to mind?

- When and how did you first come to realize your need for a Savior? How did you feel, and what did you do?

- What does today's passage reveal to you about Jesus?

RESPOND

Father, thank you that this story is not a fairy tale but that it happened in a real place, during a real time. Help me remember that Jesus was born into the very world I live in, with the same sun and moon and stars. Help me keep in mind that Jesus is not a concept, a set of rules, a made-up character but rather the one who came to save sinners like me. When your glory is revealed, let me be the first to sing, "Glory to God in the highest!" and stand in awe. Let this not just be a refrain I sing but a life I live. Amen.

DAY 4

MY EYES HAVE SEEN

a prayer to open

Open my eyes and help me to see you.
Open my heart and help me to know you.
Jesus, my Lord and my God.

READ LUKE 2:23-52

The law of the Lord says, "If a woman's first child is a boy, he must be dedicated to the LORD." So they offered the sacrifice required in the law of the Lord. . . .

At that time there was a man in Jerusalem named Simeon. He was righteous and devout and was eagerly waiting for the Messiah to come and rescue Israel. The Holy Spirit was upon him and had revealed to him that he would not die until he had seen the Lord's Messiah. That day the Spirit led him to the Temple. So when Mary and Joseph came to present the baby Jesus to the Lord as the law required, Simeon was there. He took the child in his arms and praised God, saying,

"Sovereign Lord, now let your servant die in peace,
  as you have promised.
I have seen your salvation,
  which you have prepared for all people.
He is a light to reveal God to the nations,
  and he is the glory of your people Israel!"

Jesus' parents were amazed. . . . Then Simeon blessed them, and he said to Mary, the baby's mother, "This child is destined to cause many in Israel to fall, and many others to rise. He has been sent as a sign from God, but many will oppose him. As a result, the deepest thoughts of many hearts will be revealed. And a sword will pierce your very soul."

Anna, a prophet, was also there in the Temple. . . . She never left the Temple but stayed there day and night, worshiping God with fasting and prayer. She came along just as Simeon was talking with Mary and Joseph, and she began praising God. She talked about the child to everyone who had been waiting expectantly for God to rescue Jerusalem. . . .

They returned home to Nazareth. . . . There the child grew up healthy and strong. He was filled with wisdom, and God's favor was on him. . . .

When Jesus was twelve years old, they attended the [Passover] festival as usual. After the celebration . . . they started home to Nazareth, but Jesus stayed behind in Jerusalem. His parents . . . assumed he was among the other travelers. But when he didn't show up that evening, they started looking for him. . . .

When they couldn't find him, they went back to Jerusalem to search for him there. Three days later they finally discovered him in the Temple, sitting among the religious teachers, listening to them and asking questions. All who heard him were amazed at his understanding and his answers.

His parents didn't know what to think. "Son," his mother said to him, "why have you done this to us? Your father and I have been frantic, searching for you everywhere."

"But why did you need to search?" he asked. "Didn't you know that I must be in my Father's house?" But they didn't understand what he meant.

Then he returned to Nazareth with them and was obedient to them. And his mother stored all these things in her heart.

Jesus grew in wisdom and in stature and in favor with God and all the people.

REFLECT

After Mary and Joseph dedicated Jesus to God at the Temple, Jesus "grew up healthy and strong [and] filled with wisdom" (verse 40). We next see Jesus in the Temple courts, this time at age twelve. It's hard not to focus on Mary and Joseph's anxiety in seemingly misplacing Jesus—imagine the pressure they felt as the parents of the Savior of the world! But when we look closely, we see both Jesus' deep connection to God the Father early in his life and the uncertainty and mystery in which his parents lived as he grew.

- What would it have been like for Mary and Joseph to hear prophetic words about their baby son or to find their twelve-year-old among the teachers in the Temple?

- Where are you experiencing more uncertainty than usual? What do you sense God inviting you to know or do?

- What does today's passage reveal to you about Jesus?

RESPOND

Father, thank you for the new life you have granted me in Jesus Christ. Allow me to experience your presence today and help me demonstrate your goodness and grace to those I encounter. Give me peace and patience in uncertainty and the ability to trust that I am in your hands, carried by your love. Shape my desires so I can better follow your ways this day. Amen.

Revealed

FREEDOM FOR THE PRISONERS

a prayer to open

Open my eyes and help me to see you.
Open my heart and help me to know you.
Jesus, my Lord and my God.

READ LUKE 4:1-22

[Jesus] was led by the Spirit in the wilderness, where he was tempted by the devil for forty days. Jesus ate nothing all that time and became very hungry.

Then the devil said to him, "If you are the Son of God, tell this stone to become a loaf of bread."

But Jesus told him, "No! The Scriptures say, 'People do not live by bread alone.'"

Then the devil took him up and revealed to him all the kingdoms of the world in a moment of time. "I will give you the glory of these kingdoms and authority over them," the devil said, "because they are mine to give to anyone I please. I will give it all to you if you will worship me."

Jesus replied, "The Scriptures say,

'You must worship the LORD your God
and serve only him.'"

Then the devil took him to Jerusalem, to the highest point of the Temple, and said, "If you are the Son of God, jump off! For the Scriptures say,

'He will order his angels to protect and guard
you.
And they will hold you up with their hands
so you won't even hurt your foot on a
stone.'"

Jesus responded, "The Scriptures also say, 'You

must not test the LORD your God.'"

When the devil had finished tempting Jesus, he left him until the next opportunity came.

Then Jesus returned to Galilee, filled with the Holy Spirit's power. Reports about him spread quickly through the whole region. He taught regularly in their synagogues and was praised by everyone.

When he came to the village of Nazareth . . . he went as usual to the synagogue on the Sabbath and stood up to read the Scriptures. The scroll of Isaiah the prophet was handed to him. He unrolled the scroll and found the place where this was written:

"The Spirit of the LORD is upon me,
    for he has anointed me to bring Good News
        to the poor.
He has sent me to proclaim that captives will
        be released,
    that the blind will see,
that the oppressed will be set free,
    and that the time of the LORD's favor has
        come." . . .

Then he began to speak to them. "The Scripture you've just heard has been fulfilled this very day!"

Everyone spoke well of him and was amazed by the gracious words that came from his lips. "How can this be?" they asked. "Isn't this Joseph's son?"

REFLECT

We see two stunning pictures of Jesus in today's passage. First, he faces down Satan, the enemy of the human race and the father of lies. Then Jesus stands up in a synagogue—the very center of first-century Jewish life—and declares himself the fulfillment of a prophecy made hundreds of years earlier. Imagine standing in that synagogue, a Jewish person who had heard about the coming Messiah since birth and whose family had been awaiting this coming Savior for hundreds of years. What would you have been thinking and feeling?

• What would it have been like for the people to listen to Jesus read from the prophet Isaiah and hear him say that he was the fulfillment of that Scripture?

• What might it mean for you when you are in the midst of your greatest temptations—those things that threaten your freedom, cause you to distance yourself from God, and convince you to seek your own desires above all else—that Jesus overcame Satan?

• What does today's passage reveal to you about Jesus?

RESPOND_____

Father, thank you for Jesus. Thank you that by him and through him I am able to have freedom, forgiveness, and purpose. This old life, the one I seek to leave behind, is full of sin and selfishness. Help me, Lord, in the midst of my temptations and doubts to keep my eyes fixed on you. Help me, by your grace, to stand on your words and promises in the face of those things that threaten to turn me away from you, seduce me into seeking my own glory, or cherish what fulfills a temporary need. Amen.

DAY 6

MIRACLES THAT ASTONISH

a prayer to open

Open my eyes and help me to see you.
Open my heart and help me to know you.
Jesus, my Lord and my God.

READ LUKE 5:1-16 _____

One day as Jesus was preaching on the shore of the Sea of Galilee, great crowds pressed in on him to listen to the word of God. He noticed two empty boats at the water's edge. . . . Stepping into one of the boats, Jesus asked Simon, its owner, to push it out into the water. . . . [He] taught the crowds from there.

When he had finished speaking, he said to Simon, "Now go out where it is deeper, and let down your nets to catch some fish."

"Master," Simon replied, "we worked hard all last night and didn't catch a thing. But if you say so, I'll let the nets down again." And this time their nets were so full of fish they began to tear! A shout for help brought their partners in the other boat, and soon both boats were filled with fish and on the verge of sinking.

When Simon Peter realized what had happened, he fell to his knees before Jesus and said, "Oh, Lord, please leave me—I'm such a sinful man." For he was awestruck by the number of fish they had caught,

as were the others with him. . . .

Jesus replied to Simon, "Don't be afraid! From now on you'll be fishing for people!" And as soon as they landed, they left everything and followed Jesus.

In one of the villages, Jesus met a man with an advanced case of leprosy. When the man saw Jesus, he bowed with his face to the ground, begging to be healed. "Lord," he said, "if you are willing, you can heal me and make me clean."

Jesus reached out and touched him. "I am willing," he said. "Be healed!" And instantly the leprosy disappeared. Then Jesus instructed him not to tell anyone what had happened. He said, "Go to the priest and let him examine you. Take along the offering required in the law of Moses for those who have been healed of leprosy. This will be a public testimony that you have been cleansed."

But despite Jesus' instructions, the report of his power spread even faster, and vast crowds came to hear him preach and to be healed of their diseases. But Jesus often withdrew to the wilderness for prayer.

The miracles in this passage tend to steal our attention, but it's interesting to shift our focus to the way Simon Peter and the man with leprosy respond to Jesus. In experiencing Jesus' power over nature, Simon seems to discover something not only about himself but about Jesus, too. And although we don't see it as clearly in the text, we can assume that because news spread about Jesus quickly, the man with leprosy didn't hold his tongue about what he'd experienced. Do we respond with this same kind of humility and awe to what we see God do?

- What do the responses to Jesus' miracles bring to light about Simon Peter and the man with leprosy?

- Simon, James, and John pulled their boats ashore, left everything, and followed Jesus. What behaviors, attitudes, or relationships is Jesus calling you to leave to follow him?

- What does today's passage reveal to you about Jesus?

RESPOND

Father, thank you for calling me to follow Jesus and giving me the courage to say yes. I long to leave the destructive behaviors and attitudes that keep me from following after you wholeheartedly. Give me eyes to see your miracles in the world, whether it's the transformation of a life or the healing of a heart, and let me be someone who cannot keep quiet but must shout from the mountaintops about your goodness and healing. Amen.

DAY 7

HEALED AND FORGIVEN

a prayer to open

Open my eyes and help me to see you.
Open my heart and help me to know you.
Jesus, my Lord and my God.

READ LUKE 5:17-32

One day while Jesus was teaching, some Pharisees and teachers of religious law were sitting nearby. . . . And the Lord's healing power was strongly with Jesus.

Some men came carrying a paralyzed man on a sleeping mat. They tried to take him inside to Jesus, but they couldn't reach him because of the crowd. So they went up to the roof and took off some tiles. Then they lowered the sick man on his mat down into the crowd, right in front of Jesus. Seeing their

faith, Jesus said to the man, "Young man, your sins are forgiven."

But the Pharisees and teachers of religious law said to themselves, "Who does he think he is? That's blasphemy! Only God can forgive sins!"

Jesus knew what they were thinking, so he asked them, "Why do you question this in your hearts? Is it easier to say 'Your sins are forgiven,' or 'Stand up and walk'? So I will prove to you that the Son of Man has the authority on earth to forgive sins." Then

Jesus turned to the paralyzed man and said, "Stand up, pick up your mat, and go home!"

And immediately, as everyone watched, the man jumped up, picked up his mat, and went home praising God. Everyone was gripped with great wonder and awe, and they praised God, exclaiming, "We have seen amazing things today!"

Later, as Jesus left the town, he saw a tax collector named Levi sitting at his tax collector's booth. "Follow me and be my disciple," Jesus said to him. So Levi got up, left everything, and followed him.

Later, Levi held a banquet in his home with Jesus as the guest of honor. Many of Levi's fellow tax collectors and other guests also ate with them. But the Pharisees and their teachers of religious law complained bitterly to Jesus' disciples, "Why do you eat and drink with such scum?"

Jesus answered them, "Healthy people don't need a doctor—sick people do. I have come to call not those who think they are righteous, but those who know they are sinners and need to repent."

REFLECT

The Pharisees made up the largest sect within Judaism and controlled the synagogues. They were skeptical of Jesus because they believed that the Messiah would come in power like a military leader and reject those who failed to keep the Law. So when Jesus claimed to be able to do things that only God could do, the Pharisees accused him of blasphemy. And when Jesus came near to sinners—eating, walking, and spending time with them—they concluded he could not be their Savior.

- How did each of those present respond when Jesus healed and forgave the paralyzed man?

- Tax collectors, sinners, and the physically unclean or sick were the outcasts of Jesus' day, yet it was with these people that Jesus spent his time. Who are the outcasts of our day, and what kind of response do they stir in you?

- What does today's passage reveal to you about Jesus?

RESPOND

Father, thank you for your power and desire to heal and forgive. In moments of great doubt and discouragement, I forget to seek your presence and to call out your name. Increase my faith and plant in me a desire to seek out the untouchables, invite the outcasts, and share your grace with sinners. Mold my heart to look more like Jesus' heart, and my hands to serve those who believe they are beyond your reach. Amen.

DAY 8

CALLED TO LOVE

a prayer to open

Open my eyes and help me to see you.
Open my heart and help me to know you.
Jesus, my Lord and my God.

[Jesus said,] "Love your enemies! Do good to those who hate you. Bless those who curse you. Pray for those who hurt you. If someone slaps you on one cheek, offer the other cheek also. If someone demands your coat, offer your shirt also. Give to anyone who asks; and when things are taken away from you, don't try to get them back. Do to others as you would like them to do to you.

"If you love only those who love you, why should you get credit for that? Even sinners love those who love them! And if you do good only to those who do good to you, why should you get credit? Even sinners do that much! And if you lend money only to those who can repay you, why should you get credit? Even sinners will lend to other sinners for a full return.

"Love your enemies! Do good to them. Lend to them without expecting to be repaid. Then your reward from heaven will be very great, and you will truly be acting as children of the Most High, for he is kind to those who are unthankful and wicked. You must be compassionate, just as your Father is compassionate.

"Do not judge others, and you will not be judged. Do not condemn others, or it will all come back against you. Forgive others, and you will be forgiven. Give, and you will receive. Your gift will return to you in full—pressed down, shaken together to make room for more, running over, and poured into your lap. The amount you give will determine the amount you get back. . . .

"And why worry about a speck in your friend's eye when you have a log in your own? How can you think of saying, 'Friend, let me help you get rid of that speck in your eye,' when you can't see past the log in your own eye? Hypocrite! First get rid of the log in your own eye; then you will see well enough to deal with the speck in your friend's eye."

REFLECT

Oh that we could live out these words of Jesus more often! What would our world look like? Our families and communities? Our churches and workplaces? In our culture, it has become the norm to criticize and condemn people based on any number of opinions or attitudes. Rarely do we find respectful dialogue and debate. And the growing divisiveness weighs on our souls and infects our hearts. Jesus knows what happens when we give in to judgmentalism and condemnation. He calls us to take a different road: one of forgiveness, self-reflection, goodness, blessing, love, and generosity.

• Where did you experience the most resistance as you read this passage? Did any person come to mind? What did you hear Jesus calling you to pray or do for that person?

• In what ways have you contributed to divisiveness? What do you need to confess to God? What relationships do you need to seek to repair?

• What does today's passage reveal to you about Jesus?

RESPOND

Father, thank you for these words from Jesus. My heart can be so full of thoughts of revenge, judgment, and self-righteousness. Help me look inward and see what you want to transform for your honor and glory. Give me a generous spirit toward others, especially my enemies and those I judge and condemn by my words or thoughts. Create in me a heart that only ever loves, blesses, forgives, and extends mercy. Amen.

DEMONSTRATING GREAT FAITH

a prayer to open

Open my eyes and help me to see you.
Open my heart and help me to know you.
Jesus, my Lord and my God.

READ LUKE 7:2-17

The highly valued slave of a Roman officer was sick and near death. When the officer heard about Jesus, he sent some respected Jewish elders to ask him to come and heal his slave. . . . "If anyone deserves your help, he does," they said, "for he loves the Jewish people and even built a synagogue for us."

So Jesus went with them. But just before they arrived at the house, the officer sent some friends to say, "Lord, don't trouble yourself by coming to my home, for I am not worthy of such an honor. I am not even worthy to come and meet you. Just say the word from where you are, and my servant will be healed. I know this because I am under the authority of my superior officers, and I have authority over my soldiers. I only need to say, 'Go,' and they go, or 'Come,' and they come. And if I say to my slaves, 'Do this,' they do it."

When Jesus heard this, he was amazed. Turning to the crowd that was following him, he said, "I tell you, I haven't seen faith like this in all Israel!" And when the officer's friends returned to his house, they found the slave completely healed.

Soon afterward Jesus went with his disciples to the village of Nain, and a large crowd followed him. A funeral procession was coming out. . . . The young man who had died was a widow's only son, and a large crowd from the village was with her. When the Lord saw her, his heart overflowed with compassion. "Don't cry!" he said. Then he walked over to the coffin and touched it, and the bearers stopped. "Young man," he said, "I tell you, get up." Then the dead boy sat up and began to talk! And Jesus gave him back to his mother.

Great fear swept the crowd, and they praised God, saying, "A mighty prophet has risen among us," and "God has visited his people today." And the news about Jesus spread throughout Judea and the surrounding countryside.

REFLECT

Many of us spend a great deal of time in our prayers asking God for the things we need, and of course Jesus does tell us to do that (see Matthew 7:7-11). But how much time do we spend seeking the healing, restoration, forgiveness, and wholeness of others? In these stories, we see the love the Roman officer had for his servant, and the love the mother had for her son. We see this centurion exercise his faith on behalf of the servant. And we see Jesus respond to the heartbroken mother by restoring life to her son.

- On whose behalf can you exercise your faith—however little or much that may be? (Maybe it's someone who is struggling with faith, has fallen away from God, or has not yet come to know Jesus.) What would that look like?

- Where do you need your trust in God increased? How might you not only pray for his help but also take one step in faith?

- What does today's passage reveal to you about Jesus?

Revealed

•

Father, increase my faith and expand my ability to trust even when I'm groping blindly for any evidence of you. So often I long to see you, to sense you, to hear from you. But, Lord, help me believe even when I am overcome with sadness and heartbreak. Keep my heart attached to you in the dark and through the doubt. Cast away all fear and remind me of your sustaining, unending love. Amen.

DAY 10

COME AS YOU ARE

a prayer to open

Open my eyes and help me to see you.
Open my heart and help me to know you.
Jesus, my Lord and my God.

READ LUKE 7:36-50

One of the Pharisees asked Jesus to have dinner with him. . . . When a certain immoral woman from that city heard he was eating there, she brought a beautiful alabaster jar filled with expensive perfume. Then she knelt behind him at his feet, weeping. Her tears fell on his feet, and she wiped them off with her hair. Then she kept kissing his feet and putting perfume on them.

When the Pharisee who had invited him saw this, he said to himself, "If this man were a prophet, he would know what kind of woman is touching him. She's a sinner!"

Then Jesus answered his thoughts. "Simon," he said to the Pharisee, "I have something to say to you."

"Go ahead, Teacher," Simon replied.

Then Jesus told him this story: "A man loaned money to two people—500 pieces of silver to one and 50 pieces to the other. But neither of them could repay him, so he kindly forgave them both, canceling their debts. Who do you suppose loved him more after that?"

Simon answered, "I suppose the one for whom he canceled the larger debt."

"That's right," Jesus said. Then he turned to the woman and said to Simon, . . . "When I entered your home, you didn't offer me water to wash the dust from my feet, but she has washed them with her tears and wiped them with her hair. You didn't greet me with a kiss, but from the time I first came in, she has not stopped kissing my feet. You neglected the courtesy of olive oil to anoint my head, but she has anointed my feet with rare perfume.

"I tell you, her sins—and they are many—have been forgiven, so she has shown me much love. But a person who is forgiven little shows only little love." Then Jesus said to the woman, "Your sins are forgiven."

The men at the table said among themselves, "Who is this man, that he goes around forgiving sins?"

And Jesus said to the woman, "Your faith has saved you; go in peace."

REFLECT

What a scene this is: a woman cast out, known to the whole town as a sinner, fallen to her knees and weeping in devotion to Jesus Christ. The Pharisee's discomfort is palpable. Indeed, to have dinner with a Pharisee, you had to meet certain standards of cleanliness. Sinners were not welcome, so it was scandalous for the sinful woman to even step foot into Simon's home. But Jesus' standards are different. He doesn't say to seek him out only once we've gotten it all together; his invitation is to come to him as we are and he will make us clean.

- Think of a time when you felt exposed and unworthy. What caused those feelings? How did Jesus respond?

- Who can you extend Jesus' invitation to this week? Is there someone you know who's trying to clean up to become worthy? Who believes they're too far gone, unredeemable? Ask God to give you an opportunity to share the good news that they are invited now, as is.

- What does today's passage reveal to you about Jesus?

RESPOND_____

Father, thank you for your forgiveness and mercy. I am just like the woman in this passage: sinful, unworthy, and desperate for healing. You know every dark thought and secret sin, but you have taken me in and called me your beloved child anyway. Help me see with your eyes of love every person you place in my path so I am able to extend a caring word or touch to the outcasts, the sin-filled, and the unworthy. Amen.

A PERSEVERING HEART

a prayer to open

Open my eyes and help me to see you.
Open my heart and help me to know you.
Jesus, my Lord and my God.

READ LUKE 8:4-15 _____

One day Jesus told a story . . . : "A farmer went out to plant his seed. As he scattered it across his field, some seed fell on a footpath, where it was stepped on, and the birds ate it. Other seed fell among rocks. It began to grow, but the plant soon wilted and died for lack of moisture. Other seed fell among thorns that grew up with it and choked out the tender plants. Still other seed fell on fertile soil. This seed grew and produced a crop that was a hundred times as much as had been planted!" When he had said this, he called out, "Anyone with ears to hear should listen and understand."

His disciples asked him what this parable meant. He replied, "You are permitted to understand the secrets of the Kingdom of God. But I use parables to teach the others so that the Scriptures might be fulfilled:

'When they look, they won't really see.
When they hear, they won't understand.'

"This is the meaning of the parable: The seed is God's word. The seeds that fell on the footpath represent those who hear the message, only to have the devil come and take it away from their hearts and prevent them from believing and being saved. The seeds on the rocky soil represent those who hear the message and receive it with joy. But since they don't have deep roots, they believe for a while, then they fall away when they face temptation. The seeds that fell among the thorns represent those who hear the message, but all too quickly the message is crowded out by the cares and riches and pleasures of this life. And so they never grow into maturity. And the seeds that fell on the good soil represent honest, good-hearted people who hear God's word, cling to it, and patiently produce a huge harvest."

We all want to be those who hear and retain God's Word, and we all long to act out of noble and good hearts. But, as Jesus says, all kinds of things get in the way: testing and temptation, worry, money, pleasures, evil, and the lack of a good foundation. How do we overcome these barriers and receive and act on God's Word? Only by staying connected to Jesus, acknowledging him as Lord and King and obeying his command to love, can we receive God's Word and act out his purposes. Otherwise, we are lost and easily pulled away by the things of this world.

- Reflect on the four types of people Jesus refers to. Where do you see yourself?

- What are the worries, riches, and pleasures that might threaten your desire and faith to follow Jesus?

- What does today's passage reveal to you about Jesus?

Father, thank you for opening my heart to you and allowing me to receive your message of grace and forgiveness. Please protect me through storms and preserve my faith. Lord, if my faith begins to falter or get choked out, please intervene, pull me back, and place people in my life to speak truth to me. I long to persevere and stand firm so that I can be a part of expanding your Kingdom and demonstrating your love to the ends of the earth. Amen.

DAY 12

THE SON OF GOD

a prayer to open

Open my eyes and help me to see you.
Open my heart and help me to know you.
Jesus, my Lord and my God.

One day Jesus left the crowds to pray alone. Only his disciples were with him, and he asked them, "Who do people say I am?"

"Well," they replied, "some say John the Baptist, some say Elijah, and others say you are one of the other ancient prophets risen from the dead."

Then he asked them, "But who do you say I am?"

Peter replied, "You are the Messiah sent from God!"

Jesus warned his disciples not to tell anyone who he was. "The Son of Man must suffer many terrible things," he said. "He will be rejected by the elders, the leading priests, and the teachers of religious law. He will be killed, but on the third day he will be raised from the dead."

Then he said to the crowd, "If any of you wants to be my follower, you must give up your own way, take up your cross daily, and follow me. If you try to hang on to your life, you will lose it. But if you give up your life for my sake, you will save it. And what do you benefit if you gain the whole world but are yourself lost or destroyed? If anyone is ashamed of me and my message, the Son of Man will be ashamed of that person when he returns in his glory and in the glory of the Father and the holy angels. I tell you the truth, some standing here right now will not die before they see the Kingdom of God."

About eight days later Jesus took Peter, John, and James up on a mountain to pray. And as he was praying, the appearance of his face was transformed, and his clothes became dazzling white. Suddenly, two men, Moses and Elijah, appeared and began talking with Jesus. They were glorious to see. And they were speaking about his exodus from this world, which was about to be fulfilled in Jerusalem.

Peter and the others had fallen asleep. When they woke up, they saw Jesus' glory and the two men standing with him. As Moses and Elijah were starting to leave, Peter, not even knowing what he was saying, blurted out, "Master, it's wonderful for us to be here! Let's make three shelters as memorials—one for you, one for Moses, and one for Elijah." But even as he was saying this, a cloud overshadowed them, and terror gripped them as the cloud covered them.

Then a voice from the cloud said, "This is my Son, my Chosen One. Listen to him."

REFLECT

"Who do you say I am?" This is a question Jesus asks each of us. When we decide to follow Jesus, we are saying something about who we believe him to be. Initially we might say he is our rescuer or redeemer. Over time we might say he is our healer and our comforter. Sometimes our actions might say something different from our words. Perhaps our lips say that Jesus is our Lord, but our conduct reflects that money, fame, or lust is. No matter how many times we get off track, Jesus always calls to us and invites us back to follow him.

- Take a moment to reflect on how you would answer Jesus' question "Who do you say I am?" How do your thoughts and actions align with your belief about who Jesus is?

- What threatens to take your attention and devotion away from Jesus? What daily practices or routines might help you protect against that happening?

- What does today's passage reveal to you about Jesus?

RESPOND

Father, thank you for saving me and inviting me into a new life with you through Jesus. I don't ever want to take this gift for granted or lose sight of the lengths you went through to show your love for me. Give me the courage and the words to share what I know to be true about Jesus and how he has transformed my heart and my life. Give me strength to reject anything that pulls me away from you, and remind me that nothing can separate me from your love. Amen.

GO AND DO LIKEWISE

a prayer to open

Open my eyes and help me to see you.
Open my heart and help me to know you.
Jesus, my Lord and my God.

READ LUKE 10:25-37

One day an expert in religious law stood up to test Jesus by asking him this question: "Teacher, what should I do to inherit eternal life?"

Jesus replied, "What does the law of Moses say? How do you read it?"

The man answered, "'You must love the LORD your God with all your heart, all your soul, all your strength, and all your mind.' And, 'Love your neighbor as yourself.'"

"Right!" Jesus told him. "Do this and you will live!"

The man wanted to justify his actions, so he asked Jesus, "And who is my neighbor?"

Jesus replied with a story: "A Jewish man was traveling from Jerusalem down to Jericho, and he was attacked by bandits. They stripped him of his clothes, beat him up, and left him half dead beside the road.

"By chance a priest came along. But when he saw the man lying there, he crossed to the other side of the road and passed him by. A Temple assistant walked over and looked at him lying there, but he also passed by on the other side.

"Then a despised Samaritan came along, and when he saw the man, he felt compassion for him. Going over to him, the Samaritan soothed his wounds with olive oil and wine and bandaged them. Then he put the man on his own donkey and took him to an inn, where he took care of him. The next day he handed the innkeeper two silver coins, telling him, 'Take care of this man. If his bill runs higher than this, I'll pay you the next time I'm here.'

"Now which of these three would you say was a neighbor to the man who was attacked by bandits?" Jesus asked.

The man replied, "The one who showed him mercy."

Then Jesus said, "Yes, now go and do the same."

REFLECT

We all are tempted to find loopholes—ways of more easily and comfortably following Jesus' commands. "Love your neighbor," Scripture tells us, and we want to know who that means, exactly—surely not everyone! Or we want to know how far this love should go or what it must entail. We want to set boundaries so we can love in ways that don't cost us too much or make us feel uncomfortable. But Jesus says that love is expansive, extensive, and expensive. And there is no better story to illustrate these truths about love than the story of the Good Samaritan. Who must we love? Even your enemy, Jesus says. What does love look like? Inconvenient, costly, and intentional, Jesus says.

- When you hear the word *neighbor*, who comes to mind? How is your definition of that word expanded by Jesus' teaching in this parable?

- Who are the people—whether in your community, your country, or the world—you have a hard time extending mercy to? How is Jesus calling you to respond to those people?

- What does today's passage reveal to you about Jesus?

Father, forgive me for walking away from, turning my back on, and closing my eyes to those who need mercy and care the most. Clean out the dark corners of my heart where so much judgment, hatred, and contempt lurk. Banish all fear and free my mind from distractions that call me to lesser ways and lesser loves. Take my hands and feet, Lord, and use them to demonstrate your love in this world. Amen.

DAY 14

TEACH US TO PRAY

a prayer to open

Open my eyes and help me to see you.
Open my heart and help me to know you.
Jesus, my Lord and my God.

READ LUKE 11:1-13

One of his disciples came to him and said, "Lord, teach us to pray, just as John taught his disciples." Jesus said, "This is how you should pray:

'Father, may your name be kept holy.
May your Kingdom come soon.
Give us each day the food we need,
and forgive us our sins,
as we forgive those who sin against us.
And don't let us yield to temptation.'"

Then, teaching them more about prayer, he used this story: "Suppose you went to a friend's house at midnight, wanting to borrow three loaves of bread. You say to him, 'A friend of mine has just arrived for a visit, and I have nothing for him to eat.' And suppose he calls out from his bedroom, 'Don't bother me. The door is locked for the night, and my family and I are all in bed. I can't help you.' But I tell you this—though he won't do it for friendship's sake, if you keep knocking long enough, he will get up and give you whatever you need because of your shameless persistence.

"And so I tell you, keep on asking, and you will receive what you ask for. Keep on seeking, and you will find. Keep on knocking, and the door will be opened to you. For everyone who asks, receives. Everyone who seeks, finds. And to everyone who knocks, the door will be opened.

"You fathers—if your children ask for a fish, do you give them a snake instead? Or if they ask for an egg, do you give them a scorpion? Of course not! So if you sinful people know how to give good gifts to your children, how much more will your heavenly Father give the Holy Spirit to those who ask him."

REFLECT

This prayer Jesus teaches his disciples is historically referred to as the Lord's Prayer or the "Our Father." When reading this passage, we probably focus on the actual prayer and tend to skip over the story Jesus tells afterward. Jesus seems to be telling his disciples that although it is important what we pray, it is more important to know the one to whom we are praying. Our Father longs to pour out blessing on us, answer our deepest desires, and commune with us. He is not the annoyed, judgmental neighbor who won't lend food in a time of need unless you badger him enough that he gives in. So Jesus is telling us to pray to our Father knowing that he loves us, is for us, and desires to bless us.

- What do you notice about the prayer Jesus teaches his disciples? What's included that surprises you? What's not included that you thought would be?

- What is the image of God you've had in your mind as you've prayed? (Is it the true Father who loves you, or a distorted image that needs to be corrected?)

- What does today's passage reveal to you about Jesus?

RESPOND

Father, may your name, your very essence, be held holy and in the highest regard. May your Kingdom come here on earth as it already exists in heaven. Provide me this day with what I need to extend your Kingdom and love your people. Forgive me all my wrongdoings, omissions, and mistakes, just as I will forgive others who hurt, betray, or fail to love me. Lead me through and out of every temptation so that I may remain steadfast and strong in my faith and service to you. Amen.

SEEK HIS KINGDOM

a prayer to open

Open my eyes and help me to see you.
Open my heart and help me to know you.
Jesus, my Lord and my God.

READ LUKE 12:22-34

Jesus said, "That is why I tell you not to worry about everyday life—whether you have enough food to eat or enough clothes to wear. For life is more than food, and your body more than clothing. Look at the ravens. They don't plant or harvest or store food in barns, for God feeds them. And you are far more valuable to him than any birds! Can all your worries add a single moment to your life? And if worry can't accomplish a little thing like that, what's the use of worrying over bigger things?

"Look at the lilies and how they grow. They don't work or make their clothing, yet Solomon in all his glory was not dressed as beautifully as they are. And if God cares so wonderfully for flowers that are here today and thrown into the fire tomorrow,

he will certainly care for you. Why do you have so little faith?

"And don't be concerned about what to eat and what to drink. Don't worry about such things. These things dominate the thoughts of unbelievers all over the world, but your Father already knows your needs. Seek the Kingdom of God above all else, and he will give you everything you need.

"So don't be afraid. . . . For it gives your Father great happiness to give you the Kingdom.

"Sell your possessions and give to those in need. This will store up treasure for you in heaven! And the purses of heaven never get old or develop holes. Your treasure will be safe; no thief can steal it and no moth can destroy it. Wherever your treasure is, there the desires of your heart will also be."

REFLECT

"Can all your worries add a single moment to your life?" (verse 25). If only we could fully live into this truth! So many of us can be overcome by fear. We worry about what will happen many steps out into the future. And all the while, God is whispering, *Be present. Notice me where you are.* We spend so much time reflecting on past mistakes and daydreaming about potential future problems. Jesus tells us to keep our eyes focused on God's Kingdom and know that he will provide us with all we need.

• In this passage, what promises did Jesus make about God's care for you?

• What do you worry about most? How might you release this worry into God's hands this week through prayer and by speaking his promises in this passage to yourself?

• What does today's passage reveal to you about Jesus?

RESPOND

O Father, you are the maker of all things, yet you know even my smallest need and most hidden concern. You know the time I spend spinning with worry. Would you, by your grace, build my trust and allow me to see a glimpse of your Kingdom in every moment, every face, every joy, and every trial? Please help me hold on to the things that last, the things of your Kingdom, and let go of all things that fade and fail and rot. Amen.

DAY 16

ACT IN LOVE

a prayer to open

Open my eyes and help me to see you.
Open my heart and help me to know you.
Jesus, my Lord and my God.

READ LUKE 14:1-14

One Sabbath day Jesus went to eat dinner in the home of a leader of the Pharisees. . . . There was a man there whose arms and legs were swollen. Jesus asked the Pharisees and experts in religious law, "Is it permitted in the law to heal people on the Sabbath day, or not?" When they refused to answer, Jesus touched the sick man and healed him and sent him away. Then he turned to them and said, "Which of you doesn't work on the Sabbath? If your son or your cow falls into a pit, don't you rush to get him out?" Again they could not answer.

When Jesus noticed that all who had come to the dinner were trying to sit in the seats of honor . . . he gave them this advice: "When you are invited to a wedding feast, don't sit in the seat of honor. What if someone who is more distinguished than you has also been invited? The host will come and say, 'Give this person your seat.' Then you will be embarrassed, and you will have to take whatever seat is left at the foot of the table!

"Instead, take the lowest place at the foot of the table. Then when your host sees you, he will come and say, 'Friend, we have a better place for you!' Then you will be honored in front of all the other guests. For those who exalt themselves will be humbled, and those who humble themselves will be exalted."

Then he turned to his host. "When you put on a luncheon or a banquet," he said, "don't invite your friends, brothers, relatives, and rich neighbors. For

Revealed

•

81

they will invite you back, and that will be your only reward. Instead, invite the poor, the crippled, the lame, and the blind. Then at the resurrection of the righteous, God will reward you for inviting those who could not repay you."

REFLECT

In our culture, we have been shaped to desire the best seats, the most comfortable spots, and the places and spaces saved for the honorable. We'd rather take selfies with famous people than with the forgotten, we'd rather be at a table near the powerful than in a soup kitchen with the homeless, and we'd rather be sitting with the respected than standing next to the outcasts. But Jesus shows us a different way. He calls us to the unimportant, the disrespected, the end of the line, and the middle seat. He calls us out of ourselves and into the lives of others.

- Look at each of the three scenarios in this passage. What is the common theme?

- As you consider Jesus' teachings in this passage—to love when it is inconvenient, put others before yourself, reach out to the outcasts—which one is hardest for you to follow and why?

- What does today's passage reveal to you about Jesus?

RESPOND

Father, forgive me. I am so much more likely to act in love when it is convenient and suits my own agenda. I am forever seeking the place of honor and wanting to be exalted, whether overtly or in subtle ways. I spend more time trying to prove my worth than pointing people to you. Dispel my desire to be honored and approved of by others. Mold and change my heart so that, for your sake, I see others first, act on their behalf at every opportunity, and reach out to the lonely and forgotten. Amen.

DAY 17

THE LOST ARE FOUND!

a prayer to open

Open my eyes and help me to see you.
Open my heart and help me to know you.
Jesus, my Lord and my God.

READ LUKE 15:1-10

Tax collectors and other notorious sinners often came to listen to Jesus teach. This made the Pharisees and teachers of religious law complain that he was associating with such sinful people. . . .

So Jesus told them this story: "If a man has a hundred sheep and one of them gets lost, what will he do? Won't he leave the ninety-nine others in the wilderness and go to search for the one that is lost until he finds it? And when he has found it, he will joyfully carry it home on his shoulders. When he arrives, he will call together his friends and neighbors, saying, 'Rejoice with me because I have found my lost sheep.' In the same way, there is more joy in heaven over one lost sinner who repents and returns to God than over ninety-nine others who are righteous and haven't strayed away!

"Or suppose a woman has ten silver coins and loses one. Won't she light a lamp and sweep the entire house and search carefully until she finds it? And when she finds it, she will call in her friends and neighbors and say, 'Rejoice with me because I have found my lost coin.' In the same way, there is joy in the presence of God's angels when even one sinner repents."

REFLECT

Have you ever noticed how much kids love to play hide-and-seek? Didn't you? Remember how excited you felt when you were found? You were supposed to discover the best hiding place, but what a thrill it was to be found! We all hide from God. And it's for all kinds of reasons: shame, guilt, rebellion, fear. But if we sit still enough, in the quiet, we discover that what we really want—our deepest desire—is to be sought out, found, picked up, and returned to the God who loves us and wants to make us whole. What's amazing is that he is thrilled to find us. All of heaven rejoices when he finds us where we are and says, "There you are! Come with me!"

- What would you turn over heaven and earth to find if you lost it? Describe the emotion that stirs when you think about God searching for you and rejoicing over you in this way.

- How is he inviting you to be part of his mission to search for the lost and rejoice over the found?

- What does today's passage reveal to you about Jesus?

RESPOND

Father, thank you for finding me! I'm sure I would have called off the search, figured the lost could never be found. After all, I endlessly turned away from you, rejected your ways, and closed my eyes to you. But you, Lord, never stopped and never gave up. You pursued me without ceasing. You gently called to me again and again, even as I chased after sin. You put people in my path to show me your love. Would you use me now as you pursue others? Put me in someone's path and allow me to show your love. Amen.

A GOOD AND GRACIOUS FATHER

a prayer to open

Open my eyes and help me to see you.
Open my heart and help me to know you.
Jesus, my Lord and my God.

Jesus [said,] "A man had two sons. The younger son told his father, 'I want my share of your estate now before you die.' So his father agreed to divide his wealth between his sons.

"A few days later this younger son packed all his belongings and moved to a distant land, and there he wasted all his money in wild living. . . . A great famine swept over the land, and he began to starve. He persuaded a local farmer to hire him, and the man sent him into his fields to feed the pigs. The young man became so hungry that even the pods he was feeding the pigs looked good to him. . . .

"When he finally came to his senses, he said to himself, 'At home even the hired servants have food enough to spare, and here I am dying of hunger! I will go home to my father and say, "Father, I have sinned against both heaven and you, and I am no longer worthy of being called your son. Please take me on as a hired servant."'

"So he returned home to his father. And while he was still a long way off, his father saw him coming. Filled with love and compassion, he ran to his son, embraced him, and kissed him. His son said to him, 'Father, I have sinned against both heaven and you, and I am no longer worthy of being called your son.'

"But his father said to the servants, 'Quick! Bring the finest robe in the house and put it on him. Get a ring for his finger and sandals for his feet. And kill the calf we have been fattening. We must celebrate with a feast, for this son of mine was dead and has now returned to life. He was lost, but now he is found.' So the party began.

"Meanwhile, the older son was in the fields working. When he returned home, he heard music and dancing in the house, and he asked one of the servants what was going on. 'Your brother is back,' he was told, 'and your father has killed the fattened calf. We are celebrating because of his safe return.'

"The older brother was angry and wouldn't go in. His father came out and begged him, but he replied, 'All these years I've slaved for you and never once refused to do a single thing you told me to. And in all that time you never gave me even one young goat for a feast with my friends. Yet when this son of yours comes back . . . you celebrate by killing the fattened calf!'

"His father said to him, 'Look, dear son, you have always stayed by me, and everything I have is yours. We had to celebrate this happy day. For your brother was dead and has come back to life! He was lost, but now he is found!'"

REFLECT

This is a story many of us know so well that we skip over words and perhaps don't pay attention as we're scanning through. Oh, but does it ever get old to see the father run to his wayward son? Imagine what it would have been like for the onlookers! Did they think something else would happen—an argument or a public shaming? Or did they know that running to his son was exactly what the father would do? Had they seen him around the house, in the yard, with his other son and the neighbors—gracious, good, forgiving, gentle, and joyous? The parable of the Prodigal Son is an amazing story of the way God welcomes the lost back home. But it's also a compelling reminder about who God is: a gracious, good, forgiving, gentle, and joyous Father. Of course he runs to us!

- What ultimately drove the son to return to his father's home? Reflect on what hunger drove you to turn to God.

- What desires in you remain unfulfilled as you seek to follow Jesus?

- What does today's passage reveal to you about Jesus?

RESPOND

Father, thank you for only ever running toward me and welcoming me home. I was so lost and so confused. I was seduced by the world and all it promised and offered. But nothing ever satisfied or lasted. I was left with a deep hunger for something more, something permanent. As you begin to transform me and open my eyes to your presence and Kingdom, I could burst with gratitude. Please continue to guide me into your love. Amen.

A GOD-FIRST LIFE

a prayer to open

Open my eyes and help me to see you.
Open my heart and help me to know you.
Jesus, my Lord and my God.

READ LUKE 18:18-30

Once a religious leader asked Jesus this question: "Good Teacher, what should I do to inherit eternal life?"

"Why do you call me good?" Jesus asked him. "Only God is truly good. But to answer your question, you know the commandments: 'You must not commit adultery. You must not murder. You must not steal. You must not testify falsely. Honor your father and mother.'"

The man replied, "I've obeyed all these commandments since I was young."

When Jesus heard his answer, he said, "There is still one thing you haven't done. Sell all your possessions and give the money to the poor, and you will have treasure in heaven. Then come, follow me."

But when the man heard this he became very sad, for he was very rich.

When Jesus saw this, he said, "How hard it is for the rich to enter the Kingdom of God! In fact, it is easier for a camel to go through the eye of a needle than for a rich person to enter the Kingdom of God!"

Those who heard this said, "Then who in the world can be saved?"

He replied, "What is impossible for people is possible with God."

Peter said, "We've left our homes to follow you."

"Yes," Jesus replied, "and I assure you that everyone who has given up house or wife or brothers or parents or children, for the sake of the Kingdom of God, will be repaid many times over in this life, and will have eternal life in the world to come."

REFLECT

God asks all of us to let go of, or turn from, whatever gets in the way of our relationships with him. We tend to make gods out of people or possessions, robbing God of his rightful place in our lives and ourselves of richness and joy. The rich ruler seems to have placed his ultimate trust in his possessions, so much so that he decided he couldn't give them up at Jesus' call. Money can have this effect. Some of us, though, put too much of our ultimate hope in other people—perhaps our spouses or parents or children, or maybe authority figures or leaders. Placing our ultimate hope in anything or any person other than God will result in a lesser life. Putting God at the center of our lives and trusting more of ourselves to him, on the other hand, means life abundant—life with purpose.

• Look at Jesus' words in this passage. What kinds of emotions or resistance do they stir in you? Ask for God's guidance as you sort through whatever is stirred.

- If others were to look through your monthly expenditures and calendar, what would they conclude you treasure most? Is there anything you feel God calling you to relinquish?
- What does today's passage reveal to you about Jesus?

RESPOND

Father, I want my loyalty to be to you above all else. I grip other things and relationships so tightly, as if I could control them and they could sustain me fully and forever. But, Lord, I know that only you can fill my heart and satisfy my soul. And I know that it is only by your grace and through your Spirit that I can love the family and friends you have given me. Show me what is taking your place in my heart, and give me the ability to release it to you. Continue to guide me. Amen.

DAY 20

THE KING

a prayer to open

Open my eyes and help me to see you.
Open my heart and help me to know you.
Jesus, my Lord and my God.

READ LUKE 19:29-46

As [Jesus] came to the towns of Bethphage and Bethany . . . he sent two disciples ahead. "Go into that village over there," he told them. "As you enter it, you will see a young donkey tied there that no one has ever ridden. Untie it and bring it here. If anyone asks, 'Why are you untying that colt?' just say, 'The Lord needs it.'"

So they went and found the colt, just as Jesus had said. And sure enough, as they were untying it, the owners asked them, "Why are you untying that colt?"

And the disciples simply replied, "The Lord needs it." So they brought the colt to Jesus and threw their garments over it for him to ride on.

As he rode along, the crowds spread out their garments on the road ahead of him. . . . All of his followers began to shout and sing as they walked along, praising God for all the wonderful miracles they had seen.

"Blessings on the King who comes in the name of the LORD!

Peace in heaven, and glory in highest heaven!"

But some of the Pharisees among the crowd said, "Teacher, rebuke your followers for saying things like that!"

He replied, "If they kept quiet, the stones along the road would burst into cheers!"

But as he came closer to Jerusalem and saw the city ahead, he began to weep. "How I wish today that you of all people would understand the way to peace. But now it is too late, and peace is hidden from your eyes. Before long your enemies will build ramparts against your walls and encircle you and close in on you from every side. They will crush you into the ground, and your children with you. Your enemies will not leave a single stone in place, because you did not recognize it when God visited you."

Then Jesus entered the Temple and began to drive out the people selling animals for sacrifices. He said to them, "The Scriptures declare, 'My Temple will be a house of prayer,' but you have turned it into a den of thieves."

What a difference a week makes! In this passage, we read of crowds cheering and celebrating the coming of God to Jerusalem to save his people. Yet just a few days later, these same crowds would be jeering and calling for the brutal murder of Jesus on the cross. And as we see in Jesus' words, he knew what was coming. Despite this, he continued to teach and proclaim the Kingdom of God to his final breath.

- Imagine yourself watching as Jesus entered Jerusalem on a colt. Would you have been among those welcoming him or among those rebuking and scoffing at those who did?

- Jesus told his disciples that they would find a colt in a particular place and would be asked a particular question when they went to untie it. His disciples believed him, and they found things to be just as Jesus had said. Is there something you are having a hard time believing to be true about God or your own identity as his child? How might you pray about that issue?

- What does today's passage reveal to you about Jesus?

RESPOND _____

Father, my heart is pulled in two different directions as I read about Jesus entering Jerusalem for the last time: overwhelming grief for his suffering, and unending gratitude that this suffering saved me. I am so thankful that you opened my eyes to your presence, called me out of my fear and cynicism, and welcomed me as your child. I want to be someone who hangs on your every word and prompting of my spirit. Keep me close to you. I am yours. Amen.

DAY 21

SO THEY PREPARED

a prayer to open

Open my eyes and help me to see you.
Open my heart and help me to know you.
Jesus, my Lord and my God.

READ LUKE 22:1-13 _____

Passover . . . was approaching. The leading priests and teachers of religious law were plotting how to kill Jesus, but they were afraid of the people's reaction.

Then Satan entered into Judas Iscariot, who was one of the twelve disciples, and he went to the leading priests and captains of the Temple guard to discuss the best way to betray Jesus to them. They were delighted, and they promised to give him money. So he agreed and began looking for an opportunity to betray Jesus. . . .

Now the Festival of Unleavened Bread arrived. . . . Jesus sent Peter and John ahead and said, "Go and prepare the Passover meal, so we can eat it together."

"Where do you want us to prepare it?" they asked him.

He replied, "As soon as you enter Jerusalem, a man carrying a pitcher of water will meet you. Follow him. At the house he enters, say to the owner, 'The

Teacher asks: Where is the guest room where I can eat the Passover meal with my disciples?' He will take you upstairs to a large room that is already set up. That is where you should prepare our meal." They went off to the city and found everything just as Jesus had said.

REFLECT _____

Passover, or the Feast of Unleavened Bread, is an annual Jewish festival that commemorates the night that God sent the last of ten plagues on the Egyptians, who held the Israelites as slaves. As a final way to convince the pharaoh of Egypt to release the Israelites, God struck down every firstborn Egyptian. The Israelites were spared from this plague and the judgment that came with it by placing the blood of a slaughtered lamb on the doorframe of their homes as a sign of their faithfulness to God. Passover pointed to Jesus, who became the ultimate Passover lamb: the one sacrificed to liberate us from our slavery to sin.

- How do you think the disciples reacted when they found Jesus' predictions about the location of the colt (from yesterday's reading) and the availability of the room for Passover to be correct? How might this have bolstered their faith?

- Have you betrayed a spouse, family member, or friend in some way? What led you to do it? How did you feel once you'd done it?

- What does today's passage reveal to you about Jesus?

RESPOND _____

Father, thank you for the ultimate Passover lamb, Jesus. Thank you for sparing me the punishment for my sins, which seem to outnumber the stars in the sky. Thank you that your grace is enough to cover them all and that through Jesus I am cleansed and freed. Thank you for the constant reminders of your presence that increase my faith and deepen my knowledge of and love for you. Forgive me for the ways I have betrayed you and the people I love. Repair the hearts I've torn and the wounds I've opened. Amen.

SERVANT, FORGIVER, AND FRIEND

a prayer to open

Open my eyes and help me to see you.
Open my heart and help me to know you.
Jesus, my Lord and my God.

Jesus said, "I have been very eager to eat this Passover meal with you before my suffering begins. For I tell you now that I won't eat this meal again until its meaning is fulfilled in the Kingdom of God."

Then he took a cup of wine and gave thanks to God for it. Then he said, "Take this and share it among yourselves. For I will not drink wine again until the Kingdom of God has come."

He took some bread and gave thanks to God for it. Then he broke it in pieces and gave it to the disciples, saying, "This is my body, which is given for you. Do this in remembrance of me."

After supper he took another cup of wine and said, "This cup is the new covenant between God and his people—an agreement confirmed with my blood, which is poured out as a sacrifice for you.

"But here at this table, sitting among us as a friend, is the man who will betray me. For it has been determined that the Son of Man must die. But what sorrow awaits the one who betrays him." The disciples began to ask each other which of them would ever do such a thing.

Then they began to argue among themselves about who would be the greatest among them. Jesus told them, . . . "Those who are the greatest among you should take the lowest rank, and the leader should be like a servant. Who is more important, the one who sits at the table or the one who serves? The one who sits at the table, of course. But not here! For I am among you as one who serves.

"You have stayed with me in my time of trial. And just as my Father has granted me a Kingdom, I now grant you the right to eat and drink at my table in my Kingdom. . . .

"Simon, Simon, Satan has asked to sift each of you like wheat. But I have pleaded in prayer for you, Simon, that your faith should not fail. So when you have repented and turned to me again, strengthen your brothers."

Peter said, "Lord, I am ready to go to prison with you, and even to die with you."

But Jesus said, "Peter, let me tell you something. Before the rooster crows tomorrow morning, you will deny three times that you even know me."

REFLECT

Few of us get to plan our last meal. And who knows whether we'd really want to! But Jesus knew what awaited him and exactly how he wanted his last meal to go. He had important instructions to give his friends that would continue to be followed thousands of years later. He knew he would suffer, die, rise from the dead, and ascend again into heaven to be with the Father. And he knew that his followers throughout time would need something to practice to remember him, his love for them, and what he'd done for them. So "he took bread, gave thanks and broke it, and gave it to them, saying, 'This is my body given for you; do this in remembrance of me'" (verse 19, NIV). Then "he took the cup, saying, 'This cup is the new covenant in my blood, which is poured out for you'" (verse 20, NIV). A few breaths later, he reminded his disciples of their duty to serve as he did. In his last hours, Jesus wanted his body, his blood, the new covenant, and his servanthood to be remembered.

- Look again at Jesus' words. Identify the promises and instructions he gave his disciples.

- Who do you have authority over? How does the way you exercise that authority compare to Jesus' instructions about how his followers are to wield it? What changes might you make to model Jesus' way?

- What does today's passage reveal to you about Jesus?

Revealed

•

Father, this passage makes my heart heavy as I think about what it must have been like for Jesus this last night before his gruesome death. How must it have been to have his betrayer sitting at the table, sharing the bread and the wine? What must he have been feeling as he looked into the faces of his friends and watched the sun set and darkness grow? Give me a heart to receive Jesus' last promises and instructions to his disciples. Show me how to be a servant, a forgiver, and a friend. Amen.

DAY 23

STRENGTH IN SUFFERING

a prayer to open

Open my eyes and help me to see you.
Open my heart and help me to know you.
Jesus, my Lord and my God.

READ LUKE 22:39-53

Then, accompanied by the disciples, Jesus left the upstairs room and went as usual to the Mount of Olives. There he told them, "Pray that you will not give in to temptation."

He walked away . . . and knelt down and prayed, "Father, if you are willing, please take this cup of suffering away from me. Yet I want your will to be done, not mine." Then an angel from heaven appeared and strengthened him. He prayed more fervently, and he was in such agony of spirit that his sweat fell to the ground like great drops of blood.

At last he stood up again and returned to the disciples, only to find them asleep. . . . "Why are you sleeping?" he asked them. "Get up and pray, so that you will not give in to temptation."

But even as Jesus said this, a crowd approached, led by Judas. . . . Judas walked over to Jesus to greet him with a kiss. But Jesus said, "Judas, would you betray the Son of Man with a kiss?"

When the other disciples saw what was about to happen, they exclaimed, "Lord, should we fight? We brought the swords!" And one of them struck at the high priest's slave, slashing off his right ear.

But Jesus said, "No more of this." And he touched the man's ear and healed him.

Then Jesus spoke to the leading priests, the captains of the Temple guard, and the elders who had come for him. "Am I some dangerous revolutionary," he asked, "that you come with swords and clubs to arrest me? Why didn't you arrest me in the Temple? I was there every day. But this is your moment, the time when the power of darkness reigns."

REFLECT

This is a hard scene for us to really enter into, maybe because we've read it many times, or perhaps because the agony Jesus suffers over what he knows is coming is too much for our hearts to bear. Either way, this is a place to pause and reflect on the identity and character of the one we follow. What allowed Jesus to keep walking ahead? From where did he draw the strength and courage to lay down his life for the sake of the world?

• Focus on the first two paragraphs of this passage. Where was Jesus? How often had he been there? Who was with him? What was his posture? What was his prayer? What one word would you use to describe the scene?

- Consider the ways you or someone you love is currently suffering. Is there anything in this passage that gives you consolation or hope in the midst of that anguish?

- What does today's passage reveal to you about Jesus?

RESPOND

Father, I don't know quite how to respond as I consider the suffering Jesus endured for the love of a world that would betray him openly, come after him with swords, and publicly humiliate and kill him. What compassion you must feel as tears of anguish fall down my face, knowing as you do the agony of betrayal, heartache, and physical pain. Remind me of your presence, and strengthen me in seasons of suffering. Allow me to bring your grace and healing to others in the midst of their suffering. Amen.

DAY 24

FROM JESUS' LIPS

a prayer to open

Open my eyes and help me to see you.
Open my heart and help me to know you.
Jesus, my Lord and my God.

READ LUKE 22:54-70

So they arrested him and led him to the high priest's home. And Peter followed at a distance. The guards lit a fire in the middle of the courtyard and sat around it, and Peter joined them there. A servant girl noticed him in the firelight and . . . said, "This man was one of Jesus' followers!"

But Peter denied it. "Woman," he said, "I don't even know him!"

After a while someone else looked at him and said, "You must be one of them!"

"No, man, I'm not!" Peter retorted.

About an hour later someone else insisted, "This must be one of them, because he is a Galilean, too."

But Peter said, "Man, I don't know what you are talking about." And immediately, while he was still speaking, the rooster crowed.

At that moment the Lord turned and looked at Peter. Suddenly, the Lord's words flashed through Peter's mind: "Before the rooster crows tomorrow morning, you will deny three times that you even know me." And Peter left the courtyard, weeping bitterly.

The guards in charge of Jesus began mocking and beating him. They blindfolded him and said, "Prophesy to us! Who hit you that time?" . . .

At daybreak all the elders of the people assembled. . . . Jesus was led before this high council, and they said, "Tell us, are you the Messiah?"

But he replied, "If I tell you, you won't believe me. And if I ask you a question, you won't answer. But from now on the Son of Man will be seated in the place of power at God's right hand."

They all shouted, "So, are you claiming to be the Son of God?"

And he replied, "You say that I am."

Such a human response Peter gives when asked about his connections to Jesus. Of course, we'd like to read of a courageous, faith-filled, trusting disciple who stood up for Jesus in the face of death. But instead we get Peter—so bold later in his life, but here afraid and human. Whatever motivated Peter, we get a clearer image of who Jesus is, based on what he predicted would happen with Peter and on his testimony before the high priests and teachers of the law.

- Why do you think Peter denied knowing Jesus?
- Are there situations in which you downplay your commitment to Jesus or avoid the topic? Why are you afraid to share or make known your faith?
- What does today's passage reveal to you about Jesus?

RESPOND

Father, I need courage. It is easy to raise my hands in praise, call on your name, and share stories about your redemption and presence with others who follow you. But I can shrink back in fear when faced with sharing my faith or acknowledging my allegiance to you with non-Christians, especially my family and friends. Give me the courage today to speak your name and share the story of your forgiveness, grace, and transforming love in my life. Let people say of me that I am one of yours. Amen.

DAY 25

KING OF THE JEWS

a prayer to open

Open my eyes and help me to see you.
Open my heart and help me to know you.
Jesus, my Lord and my God.

READ LUKE 23:1-24

The entire council took Jesus to Pilate, the Roman governor. They began to state their case: "This man has been leading our people astray by telling them not to pay their taxes to the Roman government and by claiming he is the Messiah, a king."

So Pilate asked him, "Are you the king of the Jews?"

Jesus replied, "You have said it."

Pilate . . . said, "I find nothing wrong with this man!"

Then they became insistent. "But he is causing riots by his teaching wherever he goes." . . .

Pilate sent [Jesus] to Herod Antipas, because Galilee was under Herod's jurisdiction, and Herod happened to be in Jerusalem at the time.

Herod was delighted at the opportunity to see Jesus, because he had heard about him and had been hoping . . . to see him perform a miracle. He asked Jesus question after question, but Jesus refused to answer. Meanwhile, the leading priests and the teachers of religious law stood there shouting their accusations. Then Herod and his soldiers began mocking and ridiculing Jesus. Finally, they put a royal robe on him and sent him back to Pilate. . . .

Then Pilate called together the leading priests and other religious leaders, along with the people, and he announced his verdict. "You brought this man to me, accusing him of leading a revolt. I have examined him thoroughly . . . and find him innocent. . . . Nothing this man has done calls for the death penalty. So I will have him flogged, and then I will release him."

Then a mighty roar rose from the crowd, and with one voice they shouted, "Kill him, and release Barabbas to us!" (Barabbas was in prison for taking part in an insurrection in Jerusalem against the government, and for murder.) Pilate argued with them, because he wanted to release Jesus. But they kept shouting, "Crucify him! Crucify him!"

For the third time he demanded, "Why? What crime has he committed? I have found no reason to sentence him to death. So I will have him flogged, and then I will release him."

But the mob shouted louder and louder, demanding that Jesus be crucified, and their voices prevailed. So Pilate sentenced Jesus to die as they demanded.

REFLECT

Crowds calling for crucifixion. Religious leaders providing false testimony. Government officials making decisions to appease the masses and protect themselves. And the king of the Jews, the Son of God, stood silent in the midst of chaos. He refused to quiet the crowds, defend himself against the fake charges, or dissuade the wrong decisions. He had come to proclaim and introduce a new day—a new Kingdom. That meant facing the worst kind of suffering in order to defeat the values of the worldly kingdom—sin and death—once and for all.

- Review the words said to Jesus and the ways the government or religious leaders sought to humiliate him. What must Jesus have been feeling as he experienced all that is reported in this passage?

- Have you ever been publicly humiliated or accused of something you didn't do? What reaction did you have, and what scars do you still carry from that incident?

- What does today's passage reveal to you about Jesus?

RESPOND

Father, as I imagine the screaming crowds, the mocking, and the sneering laughter as Jesus stood before his people and government leaders, I feel heartsick. He took all this on himself willingly, this humiliation and degradation. For me. For love. Please help this truth sink into my heart. The only response I can think of, Lord, is to say thank you and hold out my hands for your use in this world. Let my every word and action today reflect my gratitude that Jesus suffered such great humiliation for me and for this world that you made and love. Amen.

FATHER, FORGIVE THEM

a prayer to open

Open my eyes and help me to see you.
Open my heart and help me to know you.
Jesus, my Lord and my God.

READ LUKE 23:32-43

Two others, both criminals, were led out to be executed with him. When they came to a place called The Skull, they nailed him to the cross. And the criminals were also crucified—one on his right and one on his left.

Jesus said, "Father, forgive them, for they don't know what they are doing." And the soldiers gambled for his clothes by throwing dice.

The crowd watched and the leaders scoffed. "He saved others," they said, "let him save himself if he is really God's Messiah, the Chosen One." The soldiers mocked him, too, by offering him a drink of sour wine. They called out to him, "If you are the King of the Jews, save yourself!" A sign was fastened above him with these words: "This is the King of the Jews."

One of the criminals hanging beside him scoffed, "So you're the Messiah, are you? Prove it by saving yourself—and us, too, while you're at it!"

But the other criminal protested, "Don't you fear God even when you have been sentenced to die? We deserve to die for our crimes, but this man hasn't done anything wrong." Then he said, "Jesus, remember me when you come into your Kingdom."

And Jesus replied, "I assure you, today you will be with me in paradise."

REFLECT

What better picture is there of a worthy Savior than Jesus in the last moments of his life? Even as soldiers drive nails through his wrists and feet, the gathered crowd and rulers sneer at and jeer him, the soldiers mock him, and a criminal insults him, he forgives. He forgives! Even though we turn away, deny him, and rebel against his will and ways, he forgives.

- Imagine being one of Jesus' followers as he walked to his crucifixion and was nailed to the cross, his arms spread and his body bleeding. What thoughts would have been going through your mind? How would your faith in him have been affected?

- What is the worst thing anyone has ever done to you? Have you forgiven that person? If so, what was the process you went through? If not, what is one step you could take toward forgiveness?

- What does today's passage reveal to you about Jesus?

RESPOND

Father, thank you for the incredible outpouring of love and forgiveness of Jesus on the cross. I cannot comprehend the heart and courage it would have required. Yet you call me to love and forgive as Jesus did. Please fill me with your power and strength so I can extend love to those I find hard to love and forgive, even the one who has hurt me the deepest. Give me the courage to act not as the world acts—with anger, vengeance, and separation—but as Jesus would act in this world. Amen.

HE BREATHED HIS LAST

a prayer to open

Open my eyes and help me to see you.
Open my heart and help me to know you.
Jesus, my Lord and my God.

READ LUKE 23:46-56

Then Jesus shouted, "Father, I entrust my spirit into your hands!" And with those words he breathed his last.

When the Roman officer overseeing the execution saw what had happened, he worshiped God and said, "Surely this man was innocent." And when all the crowd that came to see the crucifixion saw what had happened, they went home in deep sorrow. But Jesus' friends, including the women who had followed him from Galilee, stood at a distance watching.

Now there was a good and righteous man named Joseph. He was a member of the Jewish high council, but he had not agreed with the decision and actions of the other religious leaders. . . . He was waiting for the Kingdom of God to come. He went to Pilate and asked for Jesus' body. Then he took the body down from the cross and wrapped it in a long sheet of linen cloth and laid it in a new tomb. . . . This was done late on Friday afternoon . . . as the Sabbath was about to begin. . . .

The women from Galilee followed and saw the tomb where his body was placed. Then they went home and prepared spices and ointments to anoint his body. But by the time they were finished the Sabbath had begun, so they rested as required by the law.

REFLECT

This darkest of days must have overwhelmed all those who had placed their hope in Jesus. Imagine having walked and eaten with him, believing he had come to put all wrong things right, and then seeing him breathe his last. Generations and generations of hope had been laid on Jesus' shoulders, but now his healing hands were dead. Did the disciples start to remember during this time the words Jesus had spoken? He said he'd never leave them. He said he'd have to suffer. He said he would be raised again. He hadn't ever lied to them, so maybe there was still hope.

- Look through this passage and identify the role of each person or group mentioned. What do you know about the people gathered in the area of Jesus' crucifixion?

- What is the darkest day you have experienced? Who gathered around you and tended to you during that time? Is there someone you know who needs to be cared for right now? How might you reach out to that person in love?

- What does today's passage reveal to you about Jesus?

RESPOND

Father, there is such darkness in this world. Every day holds seemingly unending stories of violence, hatred, anger, and apathy. I want to be someone who tends to the hurting and lonely, who runs to the places of darkness to bring light and hope. Give me a heart attuned to the needs of those in pain, hands that comfort, and words that speak the truth of your presence and love. And in my moments and seasons of darkness, Lord, surround me with tender souls and loving arms. Amen.

Revealed

•

HE HAS RISEN

a prayer to open

Open my eyes and help me to see you.
Open my heart and help me to know you.
Jesus, my Lord and my God.

READ LUKE 24:1-12

Very early on Sunday morning the women went to the tomb, taking the spices they had prepared. They found that the stone had been rolled away from the entrance. So they went in, but they didn't find the body of the Lord Jesus. As they stood there puzzled, two men suddenly appeared to them, clothed in dazzling robes.

The women were terrified and bowed with their faces to the ground. Then the men asked, "Why are you looking among the dead for someone who is alive? He isn't here! He is risen from the dead! Remember what he told you back in Galilee, that the Son of Man must be betrayed into the hands of sinful men and be crucified, and that he would rise again on the third day." . . .

So they rushed back from the tomb to tell his eleven disciples—and everyone else—what had happened. It was Mary Magdalene, Joanna, Mary the mother of James, and several other women who told the apostles what had happened. But the story sounded like nonsense to the men, so they didn't believe it. However, Peter jumped up and ran to the tomb to look. Stooping, he peered in and saw the empty linen wrappings; then he went home again, wondering what had happened.

REFLECT

He said he would rise, and he did. A new day had dawned—one where life prevails over death. In God's Kingdom, death doesn't get its way. But how odd it must have been for Jesus' mother, Mary Magdalene, and Joanna to hear, "He isn't here! He is risen" (verse 6). All the hope that had been dashed when Jesus died on the cross must have rushed back in a single moment. He had risen from the dead, just as he said he would. Unprecedented! Unheard of! He had risen from the dead!

- What would the women have been thinking and feeling as they walked from their homes to the tomb? When they first saw that Jesus' body was not there? When they heard the news that Jesus had risen? When they were reminded of Jesus' words that he would rise again?

- Although Jesus told his disciples several times that he would be killed and rise again (see Luke 9:21-22; 18:31-33; John 2:18-22), they did not understand and were filled with confusion and doubt when his body was not in the tomb. As you read about Jesus' resurrection, what doubts and questions arise in you? How is your faith affected?

- What does today's passage reveal to you about Jesus?

RESPOND

Father, thank you for the truth of the resurrection and for the fulfillment of all your promises in Jesus! Thank you for the reminder that Jesus rose from the grave amidst people who, like me, were filled with doubt, questions, and skepticism. Lord, fill my heart with faith and hope. Remind me that you bring life out of death and that in Jesus, you have raised me to life, adopted me into your family as a beloved child, and given me the gift of your Holy Spirit to guide and empower me to love. Amen.

THEIR EYES WERE OPENED

a prayer to open

Open my eyes and help me to see you.
Open my heart and help me to know you.
Jesus, my Lord and my God.

READ LUKE 24:13-35

That same day two of Jesus' followers were walking to the village of Emmaus. . . . As they walked along they were talking about everything that had happened. . . . Jesus himself suddenly came and began walking with them. But God kept them from recognizing him.

He asked them, "What are you discussing so intently as you walk along?"

They stopped short, sadness written across their faces. Then one of them, Cleopas, replied, "You must be the only person in Jerusalem who hasn't heard about all the things that have happened there the last few days."

"What things?" Jesus asked.

"The things that happened to Jesus, the man from Nazareth," they said. "He was a prophet who did powerful miracles, and he was a mighty teacher in the eyes of God and all the people. But our leading priests and other religious leaders handed him over to be condemned to death, and they crucified him. We had hoped he was the Messiah who had come to rescue Israel. This all happened three days ago.

"Then some women from our group of his followers were at his tomb early this morning, and they came back with an amazing report. They said his body was missing, and they had seen angels who told them Jesus is alive! Some of our men ran out to see, and sure enough, his body was gone." . . .

Then Jesus said to them, "You foolish people! You find it so hard to believe all that the prophets wrote in the Scriptures. Wasn't it clearly predicted that the Messiah would have to suffer all these things before entering his glory?" Then Jesus took them through the writings of Moses and all the prophets, explaining from all the Scriptures the things concerning himself.

By this time they were nearing Emmaus. . . . They begged him, "Stay the night with us, since it is getting late." So he went home with them. As they sat down to eat, he took the bread and blessed it. Then he broke it and gave it to them. Suddenly, their eyes were opened, and they recognized him. And at that moment he disappeared!

They said to each other, "Didn't our hearts burn within us as he talked with us on the road and explained the Scriptures to us?" And within the hour they were on their way back to Jerusalem. There they found the eleven disciples and the others who had gathered with them. . . .

Then the two from Emmaus told their story of how Jesus had appeared to them as they were walking along the road.

REFLECT

The disciples who walked on the road to Emmaus with Jesus didn't recognize him until he reenacted the Last Supper with them. And there in that moment, their eyes were opened. Yet they realized that their hearts recognized him first before their eyes, when he explained what the Scriptures said about him. Only in retrospect did they realize they'd known it was him all along.

Revealed

•

- Why did Jesus' breaking of the bread and giving thanks open the eyes of his followers and allow them to recognize him?

- Look back on the major events in your life, whether good or bad. Do you see evidence you weren't aware of at the time of God's presence in the people who surrounded you or in the circumstances? Where do you see evidence of God's presence in your current season of life?

- What does today's passage reveal to you about Jesus?

RESPOND

Father, open my eyes to you! I long to be aware of your presence in every moment and interaction. It is in you that I have my very being, yet I fail to recognize you, I forget you, and I even turn away from clear evidence of your presence. Help me live with open eyes, seeing you in the laughter and tears of strangers and friends, experiencing you in the power of a summer storm and the grace of a sunset, and praising you for your vast and intricate creation. Open my eyes, Lord! Amen.

DAY 30

YOU ARE WITNESSES

a prayer to open

Open my eyes and help me to see you.
Open my heart and help me to know you.
Jesus, my Lord and my God.

READ LUKE 24:36-52

Jesus himself was suddenly standing there among them. "Peace be with you," he said. But the whole group was startled and frightened, thinking they were seeing a ghost!

"Why are you frightened?" he asked. "Why are your hearts filled with doubt? Look at my hands. Look at my feet. You can see that it's really me. Touch me and make sure that I am not a ghost, because ghosts don't have bodies, as you see that I do." As he spoke, he showed them his hands and his feet.

Still they stood there in disbelief, filled with joy and wonder. Then he asked them, "Do you have anything here to eat?" They gave him a piece of broiled fish, and he ate it as they watched.

Then he said, "When I was with you before, I told you that everything written about me in the law of Moses and the prophets and in the Psalms must be fulfilled." Then he opened their minds to understand the Scriptures. And he said, "Yes, it was written long ago that the Messiah would suffer and die and rise from the dead on the third day. It was also written that this message would be proclaimed in the authority of his name to all the nations, beginning in Jerusalem: 'There is forgiveness of sins for all who repent.' You are witnesses of all these things.

"And now I will send the Holy Spirit, just as my Father promised. But stay here in the city until the Holy Spirit comes and fills you with power from heaven."

Then Jesus led them to Bethany, and lifting his hands to heaven, he blessed them. While he was blessing them, he left them and was taken up to heaven. So they worshiped him and then returned to Jerusalem filled with great joy.

Luke's account ends with Jesus being taken up to heaven. Before Jesus went, he ensured that the disciples knew three specific truths. First, he was no mere spirit—he rose from the dead in his body, and that mattered because of what it said about what awaited all humans. Second, he showed them he had fulfilled the Scriptures, proving he indeed was the Messiah they had been waiting for and he had come to inaugurate the Kingdom of God. Third, he instructed them to be his witnesses to the world. He had equipped them to do just that, and they would soon be empowered by the Holy Spirit to do what was beyond their ability alone. How might our lives be changed if we reminded ourselves of these same three truths regularly?

- Why do you think it was important to Jesus for his disciples to touch him and see him eat something? How do you think this influenced the way the disciples later shared what they had experienced?
- What does today's passage reveal to you about Jesus?
- What are two or three truths God has revealed to you about Jesus through the book of Luke? What has become solidified in your heart? What are you still wrestling to understand or believe?

RESPOND

Father, thank you for speaking to me through the Scriptures and for the ways you have grown my faith and understanding. Thank you for the moments I have encountered you and become more aware of your presence. Please continue to open my eyes to the truth of who you've revealed yourself to be in Jesus. May your will be done in and through me. Amen.

Rooted

Finding Your Identity in Christ

I GREW UP in a secular home in Chicago. Although we celebrated Christmas and Easter, to us those holidays really just meant Christmas trees, presents, and painted eggs. We didn't go to church or pray or read the Bible. I went to a Catholic grade school and high school but didn't really understand or engage in what was taught.

In my family, the unspoken goal was to get the best education, get the best job, get married, have kids, make as much money as possible, and have the ability to be financially secure. If these particular goals were met, I would be "a success." So from a young age, whether consciously or not, I set out to be a success in the way my family and our culture defined it.

I finished high school, got my bachelor's degree, got married, went to law school, and graduated first in my class. A month after graduating from law school I had a daughter, and a month later I took and passed the bar exam. Not long after that I started my first real job at the top law firm in the country. So far so good. I was getting closer and closer to being a success. But it didn't stop there. As a first-year lawyer, I worked eighty hours a week, was a mom to a new baby, and traveled all over the United States. I had achieved everything I'd set out to achieve—and I was twenty-seven years old.

But then three things happened: My daughter was diagnosed with epilepsy, my husband had a very significant and radical surgery and almost died, and my marriage fell apart and ended in divorce. These three things happened over a period of eighteen months. And none of them fell within the vision I had created for success or measured up to the life I had anticipated.

Somehow I figured I just needed to work harder and achieve more to get things back on track, so for about five years, I worked more hours and traveled more miles. I drank more, stayed out later, and began dating successful men I met on airplanes and at work meetings. Within those five years, I moved five times. I changed jobs. I bought more books, traveled farther and farther away. I was so lost. I didn't know what I actually enjoyed doing, what defined me, who loved me, where I belonged, what I believed. I didn't know how to stop climbing and striving and trying, and I didn't know what the goal was or where the path was leading. All I saw when I looked ahead was more indulgence, more travel, less satisfaction, and less clarity. My vision of myself was blurry, my soul was empty, and my heart ached more than it loved.

At some point I realized that none of the stuff I had surrounded myself with meant anything. And because everything about who I was, my value as a person, my identity, was tied to all these things, a wave of embarrassment and hopelessness crashed over me. If all this stuff was worthless, then I too was worthless. Without a full understanding of who exactly I was calling out to or what I was asking for, I wrote this poem:

My Plea

Oh, God! Where are you?
Why can't I see you?
Why can't I feel you?
Please, God, hear me!
Have you ever seen me?
Will you ever see me?
Will I ever feel you?
Where are you, oh God?
Why do others see you wherever they go?
Why do I see you nowhere?
Why are my eyes closed to you?
Have you been here?
Was it you, God,
Who created the light of my life,
My blue-eyed angel? It had to be you.
Are you testing me and I'm failing?
What happens if I fail forever?
What happens when I'm standing at your gates
And I see you for the very first time?
Will you let me in, or forsake me because I
Could not and cannot find you?
I'm trying . . . or am I?
What takes control of me so that I am blind to you?
Greed? Vanity? Lust? Self-indulgence?
I have never known you, and I'm
So sorry this did not occur to me until now.
Have you abandoned me? Have I lost you?
I will continue searching; please forgive me.
Oh, God! Please, please find me,
Because I cannot find you.

For three more years, I muddled along, wrestling with my identity. Then in November 2008, a friend of mine told me about a church that had been very impactful in his life. Although I resisted initially—after all, I hadn't been to church in at least fifteen years—I eventually decided to try it out. On my first visit, I cried throughout the entire service and had the deep sense that I never wanted to leave. Something had happened. I went for several weeks in a row and read the book of Luke. Then, on December 20, 2008, knowing only that God had reached out to me, I prayed to receive his saving grace.

I didn't know that a new identity awaited me, but slowly I began to understand that my value did not rest in the things I had, the places I traveled, or the men I dated. I began to see that my identity actually had nothing to do with what I could achieve. It was based on who I belonged to. And now I am seeking with every breath to live into my identity in Christ. I have to remind myself constantly, because I forget, I get caught up in the things of this world, I become afraid, I stumble. I have to ask in the quiet moments, *Who am I? Who do you, God, say that I am? Tell me again. Remind me.*

The Bible is full of reminders about who we are. God knows how much we need it. We have fickle, fearful hearts, so he has given us a source to come back to again and again when we forget. I don't know what your identity story is or where you get tripped up or seek to be other than God's beloved, but for the next twenty-eight days, we will journey through the book of Ephesians, a letter about identity. It is the apostle Paul's message to those asking the question I have wrestled with so much of my life: "Who am I?" No matter where you are on your spiritual journey or how you've wrestled with identity in your life, Paul will remind you who you are. And as he does, you can be rooted again and again in your true identity in Jesus Christ.

IN CHRIST

10/14

a prayer to open

Here I am, Lord. Remind me who I am.
I am loved. I am known. I belong to you.

READ EPHESIANS 1:3-4

All praise to God, the Father of our Lord Jesus Christ, who has blessed us with every spiritual blessing in the heavenly realms because we are united with Christ. Even before he made the world, God loved us and chose us in Christ to be holy and without fault in his eyes.

REFLECT

The most significant piece of who we are as followers of Jesus is that we are in Christ. Many other things are true about us, as we will see on our journey through Paul's letter. But the most fundamental of all is that we are in Christ. So often we say and hear that Christ is in us, and indeed, this is true. Far more, however, Scripture speaks of the fact that we are in Christ. In him we find our identity, our true love, our life, our freedom, our power to overcome, our ability to endure, and ultimately our eternal life. At the center of our relationship with God the Father is our identity in Christ the Son. If we could wake up every day and be reminded that we are in Christ, though we would still suffer and groan and sin, we might begin to live into the reality of who we are.

- In what kinds of things have you placed your identity—a job, money, a relationship, a position, pain, an experience? What have you allowed to define you?

- Reflect for a few moments on what it means for your actual, walking-around life that you are in Christ. In other words, how might this reality begin to shape how you are in the world?

- Take a moment to quiet yourself in God's loving presence. Ask him to open your eyes and heart to the ways he wants you to live more fully into your fundamental identity in Christ. What did God bring to mind?

RESPOND

Father, I lift my hands to you! Thank you that the truest thing about me is that I am in Christ, fully and finally. I need not be defined by what I do or my past experiences or pain or sin. My identity is in Christ and sustained by him. Thank you for this life and your blessing. Help me remember that I am in your hands and have been since before I took my first breath. Keep my perspective wide, letting me see the work you are doing in me and in the world. May your praise always be on my lips. Allow me to live this day in you. Amen.

ADOPTED AND FREED

a prayer to open

Here I am, Lord. Remind me who I am.
I am loved. I am known. I belong to you.

READ EPHESIANS 1:5-8

God decided in advance to adopt us into his own family by bringing us to himself through Jesus Christ. This is what he wanted to do, and it gave him great pleasure. So we praise God for the glorious grace he has poured out on us who belong to his dear Son. He is so rich in kindness and grace that he purchased our freedom with the blood of his Son and forgave our sins. He has showered his kindness on us, along with all wisdom and understanding.

REFLECT

In the Roman world in which Paul wrote this letter, unwanted babies were often left by their families to die or be enslaved. Some of these slaves would have been in and around Ephesus, hearing Paul's words that through Christ they had been adopted and freed, lavished with grace, showered with kindness. We may not have been actually abandoned or physically enslaved, but we have been lost and enslaved by sin. Through Jesus and by God's grace, we have been scooped up, brought into God's family, and released from our captivity to sin. We are adopted and we are free. In Christ that is our identity.

- Consider the various words and phrases that describe God's character and action toward you: *great pleasure, glorious grace, poured out, rich in kindness and grace, purchased, forgave.* What do these words mean about who you are in his eyes?

- Reflect on the words *adopted* and *freed.* If you really lived into the truth that you are God's beloved daughter or son and that you are free, what would change in the way you talk to yourself; interact with people in your family, at work, and in your community; and share your faith with others?

- Take a moment to quiet yourself in God's loving presence. Ask him to open your eyes and heart to the ways he wants you to live more fully into the truth that in Christ, you have been adopted into God's family and freed from the captivity of sin. What did God bring to mind?

RESPOND

Father, thank you for your love that pours out of you, not reluctantly but freely, abundantly, unreservedly. And for your grace, Father, which you have lavished upon me, withholding not a single drop. Thank you that it is your pleasure and will to forgive—to redeem and to adopt me as your beloved child! How it is that you could love me this much I may never know, but I pray that today your grace and forgiveness would infuse my every thought, word, and act. Amen.

Rooted

UNDER CHRIST

10/18

a prayer to open

Here I am, Lord. Remind me who I am.
I am loved. I am known. I belong to you.

READ EPHESIANS 1:9-11

God has now revealed to us his mysterious will regarding Christ—which is to fulfill his own good plan. And this is the plan: At the right time he will bring everything together under the authority of Christ—everything in heaven and on earth. Furthermore, because we are united with Christ, we have received an inheritance from God, for he chose us in advance, and he makes everything work out according to his plan.

REFLECT

What is God doing in the world, through the church, and in our lives? Through Christ, Paul said, we know. History is not hurtling toward some unknown end or progressing without design and intention. Rather, God is bringing everything in heaven and on earth together under the authority of Christ. All the warring and violent, broken and dysfunctional, hurting and desperate pieces within this world—and, indeed, within us—are being brought together under the authority of Christ. *Everything* in heaven. *Everything* on earth. Everything in your house, at your work, in your community, in your mind and heart. Everything.

- Where in your life can you see significant change since you have been following Jesus? What has changed? How would you describe that change to a friend?

- What in yourself do you currently long to have brought under the authority of Christ? Is it a thought pattern, a desire, a compulsion? Ask God to help you open the place where that particular issue is lodged and allow it to be brought under the authority of Christ.

- Take a moment to quiet yourself in God's loving presence. Ask him to open your eyes and heart to the ways he wants you to live more fully into the truth that you, having put your trust in Jesus, have placed yourself under the authority of Christ. What did God bring to mind?

RESPOND

Father, thank you for revealing your will to unify all things under the authority of Jesus Christ. I know all the parts of me that rebel against you in big and small ways. Help me submit those parts to you so you may transform them. Open my eyes to see the way you are working in the midst of the disunity and conflict in my life and in the world. I pray, Father, that I would be an instrument of your peace and unity, that I would be someone who ushers your Kingdom into the torn-apart places, and that you would use me to reveal Christ, the hope of glory. Amen.

SACRED QUESTIONS

CHRIST'S OWN

10-19

a prayer to open

Here I am, Lord. Remind me who I am.
I am loved. I am known. I belong to you.

READ EPHESIANS 1:12-14

God's purpose was that we Jews who were the first to trust in Christ would bring praise and glory to God. And now you Gentiles have also heard the truth, the Good News that God saves you. And when you believed in Christ, he identified you as his own by giving you the Holy Spirit, whom he promised long ago. The Spirit is God's guarantee that he will give us the inheritance he promised and that he has purchased us to be his own people. He did this so we would praise and glorify him.

REFLECT

What a sweeping and mysterious event Paul describes! A promise God made to Abraham to bless all the nations through his descendants (see Genesis 12:1-3) had come true in and through Jesus. Before Jesus, only the Jewish people had relationships with God, but when God came into the world to be with us, a new day began: All people could now be included in that unique relationship. We are included the moment we believe. When we put our trust in Christ, we become his own and receive the gift of the Holy Spirit as evidence that we belong to him. We no longer need to struggle with those needling questions that plague so many of us for so long: "Who am I? Who do I belong to?" We can instead rest in the truth that we belong to Christ. Fundamentally, before all else, we are loved by him, we are included in him, and we belong to him.

- What emotions do you feel when you read that the moment you believed, you were identified as Christ's own? Consider what it might mean for the way you interact with your family or colleagues or those you struggle to love if your whole being believed that you belong to Christ.

- List some truths and qualities you know to be true about Christ. What does it mean to be included in him and called his own?

- Take a moment to quiet yourself in God's loving presence. Ask him to open your eyes and heart to the ways he wants you to live more fully into the truth that you are Christ's own. What did God bring to mind?

RESPOND

Father, thank you for including me in Christ. How this works is a mystery, and I cannot claim to fully understand it. But I receive it, Lord, with a humble, grateful heart. I feel small and incapable of all you are calling me to: to love fully and unconditionally, pursue reconciliation and peace, reach out to the oppressed and lonely, share the good news of your Kingdom and love, and walk in your ways and truth. Empower me by your Spirit, whom you have placed inside me, to remember who I am and live the life to which you are calling me. Amen.

Rooted

•

10-20

CONFIDENT IN HOPE

a prayer to open

Here I am, Lord. Remind me who I am.
I am loved. I am known. I belong to you.

READ EPHESIANS 1:15-18

Ever since I first heard of your strong faith in the Lord Jesus and your love for God's people everywhere, I have not stopped thanking God for you. I pray for you constantly, asking God, the glorious Father of our Lord Jesus Christ, to give you spiritual wisdom and insight so that you might grow in your knowledge of God. I pray that your hearts will be flooded with light so that you can understand the confident hope he has given to those he called—his holy people who are his rich and glorious inheritance.

REFLECT

To come to know God better and to grasp who we are in Christ, we need more than books to read and truths to believe. We need special wisdom and insight from God. Of course, learning things about him requires intellect, a good memory, and perhaps motivation. But to *know* him requires something altogether different: attentiveness, humility, curiosity, willingness, and space. When we begin to open space in our hearts and minds, we are flooded with understanding. The hope that God has given us—of resurrection, renewal, restoration in and through Christ—breaks into our present and becomes a reality that we can hold on to with confidence.

- Consider the individual in your life you know best. With that person in mind, how would you explain the difference between knowing things about that person and knowing that person?

- Reflect on your daily and weekly routines. How are you doing at opening space to allow God to flood your heart and mind with wisdom and insight about him? What differences do you see in your spirit and relationships when you do make space?

- Take a moment to quiet yourself in God's loving presence. Ask him to open your eyes and heart to the ways he wants you to live more fully into the truth that he has given you a confident hope you need not fear—his promise of resurrection, renewal, and restoration of all things. What did God bring to mind?

RESPOND

Oh, Father, my heart longs for you. I want to know you better every single moment of each day. Please give me wisdom and revelation of who you are and how you love. Please give me power when I am weak and incapable of overcoming obstacles. Please enlighten my heart with the hope to which you have called me. And bring to mind someone in my life who needs encouragement so I can share your Word and love. Amen.

10-24

EMPOWERED

a prayer to open

Here I am, Lord. Remind me who I am.
I am loved. I am known. I belong to you.

READ EPHESIANS 1:19-23

I also pray that you will understand the incredible greatness of God's power for us who believe him. This is the same mighty power that raised Christ from the dead and seated him in the place of honor at God's right hand in the heavenly realms. Now he is far above any ruler or authority or power or leader or anything else—not only in this world but also in the world to come. God has put all things under the authority of Christ and has made him head over all things for the benefit of the church. And the church is his body; it is made full and complete by Christ, who fills all things everywhere with himself.

REFLECT

The power of God is active today in and for us who believe in Jesus. And although most of us would assent to this truth, we don't live as though it's true. We are more likely to feel overpowered than empowered. We are more likely to act out of fear than wholehearted love. We are more likely to act with caution and rationality than with bold faith. What would it mean to live as though the power of God is a force at work in the world, in our hearts, and in the church? What would it mean for us to know that on our own we can't love our enemies, forgive those who hurt us, or resist all that tempts us away from centering our lives on Christ but that with and in the present, active power of God, we can do these things and more? What if our eyes were open to the truth that Christ fills all things everywhere with himself?

- In what area of your life do you feel powerless? Perhaps it's a sin pattern or temptation, a fear, certain circumstances, or a past experience or hurt. What would need to happen for you to overcome whatever you identified? For example, does a desire need to be changed or transformed? Do you need peace or courage? Do you need the ability to forgive where you've been unable to so far?

- How might you invite the power of God—the same power that raised Jesus from the dead and that is available to you through Christ—into wherever you are currently struggling? What bold prayer would you pray if you believed in the presence of this power?

- Take a moment to quiet yourself in God's loving presence. Ask him to open your eyes and heart to the ways he wants you to live more fully into the truth that you have been empowered by the same mighty power that raised Christ from the dead and seated him at God's right hand. What did God bring to mind?

Rooted

•

Father, thank you for the breadth of the truth in this passage. Thank you that Jesus rules over all authorities and powers. Remind me of this when I drift into believing that politicians and governments have final authority. Open my eyes to your reign and your presence here on earth through the body of Christ, his church. Empower me, Father, to overcome all fear and temptation so I can be free to love and live for your name and glory. Strengthen my heart and mind so I can extend your grace and love to a thirsty soul today. Use me for your purposes with your strength to make your love known. Amen.

DAY 7

CHANGED 10-24

a prayer to open

Here I am, Lord. Remind me who I am.
I am loved. I am known. I belong to you.

READ EPHESIANS 2:1-3

Once you were dead because of your disobedience and your many sins. You used to live in sin, just like the rest of the world, obeying the devil—the commander of the powers in the unseen world. He is the spirit at work in the hearts of those who refuse to obey God. All of us used to live that way, following the passionate desires and inclinations of our sinful nature. By our very nature we were subject to God's anger, just like everyone else.

REFLECT

Simply by virtue of being a follower of Jesus, each of us has an old self: who we were before we knew Jesus and committed our lives to him. During Paul's day, there was, of course, no such thing as a lifelong Christian. Everyone was what today we might call a convert, so most, if not all, of the people to whom Paul was writing could clearly identify the difference between their old and new selves.

This is not necessarily true with us today. Although this is changing, we live in a world in which the Christian story has been built into our common language and experience. Many people consider themselves to have been Christians from a very young age and don't necessarily have clearly identifiable old selves and new selves, at least not in the way Paul described it to the Ephesians. But regardless, we can all point to moments or seasons when transformation happened, when the new life Jesus Christ offers swept over us and we recognized the ways we had been in rebellion against God.

- Reflect on when you were confronted with your rebellion against God and his ways. How had you been following the passionate desires and inclinations of your sinful nature? What caused you to see your rebellion?

- Identify one way your life in Christ looks different from how your life looked before you were confronted with your rebellious, worldly ways. In what areas does your life still look more like the old self than like the self in Christ? What attitudes or behaviors do you long to see transformed?

• Take a moment to quiet yourself in God's loving presence. Ask him to open your eyes and heart to the ways he wants you to live more fully into the truth that you have a new self in Jesus Christ. What did God bring to mind?

RESPOND

Oh, Father, thank you for rescuing me from my own rebellion in chasing after the things of this world, sometimes so obvious and sometimes subtle and ruinous. Thank you for showing me a new way—a way that truly satisfies the longing in my soul and restlessness of my spirit. So many things in this world seduce me away from you. They seem to carry a promise of happiness and security and belonging. But they disappoint and draw me into deeper discontent. I need a constant flow of your love and grace. On my own I drift away, pulled to temporary pleasures. Let my life be a reminder to others that you transform individual hearts, there is hope, and there is a lasting love. Amen.

DAY 8

LOVED

a prayer to open

Here I am, Lord. Remind me who I am.
I am loved. I am known. I belong to you.

READ EPHESIANS 2:3-5

All of us used to live that way, following the passionate desires and inclinations of our sinful nature. By our very nature we were subject to God's anger, just like everyone else.

But God is so rich in mercy, and he loved us so much, that even though we were dead because of our sins, he gave us life when he raised Christ from the dead. (It is only by God's grace that you have been saved!)

REFLECT

"But God . . ." This phrase appears dozens of times throughout the Bible. "You intended to harm me, *but God* intended it all for good," Joseph told his brothers who had sold him into slavery (Genesis 50:20).[2] "My health may fail, and my spirit may grow weak, *but God* remains the strength of my heart; he is mine forever," the psalmist reminded himself (Psalm 73:26).[3] "With the help of lawless Gentiles, you nailed him to a cross and killed him. *But God* released him from the horrors of death and raised him back to life, for death could not keep him in its grip," Peter preached in his first sermon (Acts 2:23-24).[4] God has always acted and is always acting in contrast to death and darkness. He brings goodness, strength, life, and love. We can be sure that where we see darkness, death, and despair, the phrase

"But God . . ." can be used. Darkness seems to settle over us, but God brings light. Death seems to overcome us, but God brings life. Despair seems to overtake us, but God brings hope. We are subject to our worldly desires and the pull of our sinful natures, leading us toward death. But God, who is love, brings us out of death and into life because he loves us so richly and deeply.

- Read Paul's words again, but this time replace the plural pronouns (the *us* and *we*) with personal pronouns (*I* and *me*). What stirs in you when you read the passage this way? Where do you feel resistance? Relief? Uncertainty?

- Reflect on a "But God . . ." experience you have had. What happened? How did you feel? What did God do? How did you experience the truth of being loved by him?

- Take a moment to quiet yourself in God's loving presence. Ask him to open your eyes and heart to the ways he wants you to live more fully into the truth that you are loved fully and unendingly by the Creator of all things, the God of the universe. What did he bring to mind?

RESPOND

Father, how you love us! How you love me! Your love and your mercy are beyond my comprehension. I don't have the words to express my gratitude for your saving grace, but I want my life to be my thanks. Your love, expressed by your mercy and grace, has changed everything—everything in the world, everything in my life. What could I do but give you all that I am in return! I give you my heart, my eyes, my hands, my words, my thoughts, and my desires. Receive them, Lord, and use them for your glory and purposes. Amen.

DAY 9

WITH CHRIST

a prayer to open

Here I am, Lord. Remind me who I am. I am loved. I am known. I belong to you.

READ EPHESIANS 2:6-7

For he raised us from the dead along with Christ and seated us with him in the heavenly realms because we are united with Christ Jesus. So God can point to us in all future ages as examples of the incredible wealth of his grace and kindness toward us, as shown in all he has done for us who are united with Christ Jesus.

REFLECT

What is true of Jesus has become true of us. Though we walk the earth, we are united with Christ, who has been resurrected and seated at the right hand of the

Father. Though we may feel dead and be tempted by parts of our old lives or the desires of our old selves, we are, in actuality, united with, tied to, incorporated by, wrapped up in the resurrected Christ himself. And all this is not just for some future day but for this day, today. We are not waiting for bodily resurrection (although that will happen too); we can experience resurrection now. We need not sleepwalk through our lives, waiting for heaven; resurrection power and life has begun. Of course, as Paul repeatedly reminded, this isn't a result of our goodness or a product of the good things we have done but is because of God's unthinkable kindness and grace.

- Reflect on a time in which you were essentially sleepwalking, living in a kind of dull reality instead of in the light and truth of resurrection. How would you describe that time in your life? What awakened you?

- What does a life lived in the reality of union with Christ Jesus look like today? What would your life look like if you could fully grasp and live into this reality? What would change about your current attitudes or behaviors?

- Take a moment to quiet yourself in God's loving presence. Ask him to open your eyes and heart to the ways he wants you to live more fully into the truth that you have been united with the resurrected Christ. What did God bring to mind?

RESPOND_____

Father, your grace is beyond my comprehension. It is not what I deserve or what I ever could have imagined for myself. Lord, I receive it. What do I have to fear, clothed in your grace as I am? How can I maintain a single regret of my past since you have raised me up in Christ Jesus to demonstrate the reach of your grace? Awaken me! Help me be a carrier of your grace—someone who spreads it, speaks it, and lives in the reality of it so others can't help but want to receive it themselves. Bless you, Lord. Amen.

DAY 10

11-4

CREATED ANEW

a prayer to open

Here I am, Lord. Remind me who I am.
I am loved. I am known. I belong to you.

READ EPHESIANS 2:8-10 _____

God saved you by his grace when you believed. And you can't take credit for this; it is a gift from God. Salvation is not a reward for the good things we have done, so none of us can boast about it.

For we are God's masterpiece. He has created us anew in Christ Jesus, so we can do the good things he planned for us long ago.

We have been saved by God's grace and created anew. Saved because God loves us. Created anew to participate with him in his restoration and reconciliation of all things. How often we grasp on to the being-saved part but forget or fail to step into our new role as partners with God. We haven't been saved to just go to heaven one day but to fulfill a purpose on earth—a purpose that contributes to the work the Creator of all things is doing in our families, our communities, our countries. We have been saved for the sake of others, for the sake of the world. Before we believed and were saved, we already had a purpose; it just couldn't be fulfilled. Our selfishness and sinfulness prevented us. But then something changed when the enormity and reality of grace sank in. Our eyes were opened, and new life began to emerge.

- What events, circumstances, and wounds of your past seem to follow you around and prevent you from embracing the truth that God has created you anew in Christ Jesus? As you reflect on whatever you identified, what do you sense God inviting you to do?

- If you could really embrace the truth that you have been created anew so that you can do good things God planned for you to do, how would your life be different? Where would you have increased strength and courage? To whom would you extend more patience and grace? Where would you sense less fear and anxiety?

- Take a moment to quiet yourself in God's loving presence. Ask him to open your eyes and heart to the ways he wants you to live more fully into the truth that you have been created anew in Christ Jesus. What did God bring to mind?

RESPOND

Father, this gift of grace brings me to my knees. I hardly understand a love that remains so consistent and unbending as to extend this gift in light of all the ways I have ignored, resisted, rejected, and dishonored you. But your grace is broad and deep, more so than any transgression. There is no place you will not follow me to pour out your grace. There is no moment in which you will decide to abandon your pursuit of me. Remind me of the truth that you have created me anew, and send me out to do the good you have prepared for me to do. Amen.

BROUGHT NEAR

a prayer to open

Here I am, Lord. Remind me who I am.
I am loved. I am known. I belong to you.

READ EPHESIANS 2:13-18

But now you have been united with Christ Jesus. Once you were far away from God, but now you have been brought near to him through the blood of Christ.

For Christ himself has brought peace to us. He united Jews and Gentiles into one people when, in his own body on the cross, he broke down the wall of hostility that separated us. He did this by ending the system of law with its commandments and regulations. He made peace between Jews and Gentiles by creating in himself one new people from the two groups. Together as one body, Christ reconciled both groups to God by means of his death on the cross, and our hostility toward each other was put to death.

He brought this Good News of peace to you Gentiles who were far away from him, and peace to the Jews who were near. Now all of us can come to the Father through the same Holy Spirit because of what Christ has done for us.

REFLECT

Often we think of God as residing somewhere far away—up in the sky or beyond the farthest universe—where we have no access. But he is closer than we could imagine, filling our lungs, sustaining our breaths, experiencing our sorrow, and sourcing our joy. He is that near. Jesus has made it so. Jesus brought peace, quieting our rebellion against God, hushing our innate desires to turn toward lesser gods for fulfillment and purpose, and stilling the deep longing in our souls to be known and loved. A peace that passes understanding. A peace that defies that state of the world. A peace that cannot be found in the absence of God. We have been brought near, and nothing can separate us from God's love.

- Reflect on the idea of God seeking you out and bringing you near him. What comes to mind as you reflect? What image might help you remember your closeness when circumstances threaten to distract or overwhelm you or when doubt about God's love for you creeps into your heart and mind?

- What does it look like for Jesus to be your peace in your walking-around life—when you get cut off in traffic, face difficult news, are triggered by a harsh comment, or feel anxious about money?

- Take a moment to quiet yourself in God's loving presence. Ask him to open your eyes and heart to the ways he wants you to live more fully into the truth that you have been brought near to him through the blood of Christ. What did God bring to mind?

Father, thank you for seeking me out and bringing me near. Help me live every moment in the peace of knowing that you are closer than I can grasp, sustaining my every breath. I am so often on edge and irritated by the insignificant. I can be plagued by anxiety and driven by fear. Help me live out the reality of having been brought near to you and held near by you. May Jesus Christ be at the center of my being and my relationships so my soul is settled and my love without restraint. Continue molding me into a peacemaker so I may live in a way that demonstrates your presence in my life and in the world. Amen.

DAY 12

JOINED TOGETHER IN CHRIST

a prayer to open

Here I am, Lord. Remind me who I am.
I am loved. I am known. I belong to you.

READ EPHESIANS 2:19-22

So now you Gentiles are no longer strangers and foreigners. You are citizens along with all of God's holy people. You are members of God's family. Together, we are his house, built on the foundation of the apostles and the prophets. And the cornerstone is Christ Jesus himself. We are carefully joined together in him, becoming a holy temple for the Lord. Through him you Gentiles are also being made part of this dwelling where God lives by his Spirit.

REFLECT

Our Western world holds individualism and independence among its highest values. And these values have shaped not only our culture but also the church. Indeed, although we are around other people, much of our experience in church is centered on individual encounters, individual prayers, individual worship, and individual learning and application. Even our communal places, such as small groups, mainly focus on individual spiritual growth. But Paul reminds us that life in Christ is not an individual endeavor. Not only have we been joined together with God through Christ, but we have been joined together with all believers in Christ, forming a holy temple where God dwells. We are citizens of a common people. We are members of one family.

- Reflect on your daily, weekly, and monthly spiritual practices. How many of them are individualized? How many are communal? What communal practices do you engage in on a regular basis? What do those particular practices form in you?

- Consider the practices of confession, discernment, forgiveness, reconciliation, and mutual submission. What do these practices look like when practiced alone? What do they look like when practiced in community?

- Take a moment to quiet yourself in God's loving presence. Ask him to open your eyes and heart to the ways he wants you to live more fully into the truth that you have been joined together with all other believers in Christ. What did God bring to mind?

RESPOND

Father, thank you for welcoming me into your family through Christ and joining me together with those who love you. As a stranger, I felt lost, unsure, full of doubt. Thank you for giving me the gift of belonging, security, and faith. Remind me that this is not a life to be lived alone or at a safe distance from other believers. Show me what it means to truly live in communion with others—to confess, discern, forgive, and submit one to another. Allow me to be present to others in suffering, joy, and the mundane. And may your Kingdom come in and through your church. Amen.

DAY 13

n-9

ACCESS TO GOD'S PRESENCE

a prayer to open

Here I am, Lord. Remind me who I am.
I am loved. I am known. I belong to you.

READ EPHESIANS 3:2-13

[I am] assuming, by the way, that you know God gave me the special responsibility of extending his grace to you Gentiles. As I briefly wrote earlier, God himself revealed his mysterious plan to me. As you read what I have written, you will understand my insight into this plan regarding Christ. God did not reveal it to previous generations, but now by his Spirit he has revealed it to his holy apostles and prophets.

And this is God's plan: Both Gentiles and Jews who believe the Good News share equally in the riches inherited by God's children. Both are part of the same body, and both enjoy the promise of blessings because they belong to Christ Jesus. By God's grace and mighty power, I have been given the privilege of serving him by spreading this Good News.

Though I am the least deserving of all God's people, he graciously gave me the privilege of telling the Gentiles about the endless treasures available to them in Christ. I was chosen to explain to everyone this mysterious plan that God, the Creator of all things, had kept secret from the beginning.

God's purpose in all this was to use the church to display his wisdom in its rich variety to all the unseen rulers and authorities in the heavenly places. This was his eternal plan, which he carried out through Christ Jesus our Lord.

Because of Christ and our faith in him, we can now come boldly and confidently into God's presence. So please don't lose heart because of my trials here. I am suffering for you, so you should feel honored.

REFLECT

There is something quite stunning about the notion that we can, because of our faith in Jesus Christ, confidently enter into God's presence. He is the holy Creator and Sustainer of all things. When Isaiah saw the Lord, he nearly collapsed under the weight of his own sinfulness (Isaiah 6). When Jesus filled Peter's nets with a miraculous number of fish, Peter fell to his knees, suddenly aware of his sinfulness

Rooted

•

(Luke 5:1-11). And each of us has experienced the unbearable heaviness of our sin at various points in our lives. We too cannot help but recognize our shortcomings and propensity to act selfishly and without love. We too would be tempted to curl up and hide from our holy God or cower with fear in his presence. But Paul says that because we are in Christ, we have nothing to fear, no unworthiness to overcome. We have been made clean, washed white, and raised up—so much so that we can enter into God's presence with boldness.

- Reflect on a season when you were more aware than usual of your sinfulness. What in particular was happening during that time? How did you experience God's presence during that season?

- When you close your eyes and imagine being in God's presence, what do you picture? What feelings arise in you? What words do you long to say? What does your body desire to do?

- Take a moment to quiet yourself in God's loving presence. Ask him to open your eyes and heart to the ways he wants you to live more fully into the truth that because of your faith in Christ, you can confidently enter into God's presence. What did God bring to mind?

RESPOND

Father, thank you for Jesus. Thank you for opening a way. Thank you that I can come into your presence and you see me with eyes of love, the eyes of a perfect Father. Help me live in the truth of your unending love and grace. Give me the faith and courage to come before you with my whole life—my desires, wounds, joys, gifts, and weaknesses. Remind me that I am yours, that every part of me is yours. And may I be a carrier of this incredible news of grace so others can come to know that Jesus has granted anyone who says yes access to the Creator and Sustainer of all things. Amen.

ROOTED IN LOVE 11-13

a prayer to open

Here I am, Lord. Remind me who I am.
I am loved. I am known. I belong to you.

READ EPHESIANS 3:14-19

When I think of all this, I fall to my knees and pray to the Father, the Creator of everything in heaven and on earth. I pray that from his glorious, unlimited resources he will empower you with inner strength through his Spirit. Then Christ will make his home in your hearts as you trust in him. Your roots will grow down into God's love and keep you strong. And may you have the power to understand, as all God's people should, how wide, how long, how high, and how deep his love is. May you experience the love of Christ, though it is too great to understand fully. Then you will be made complete with all the fullness of life and power that comes from God.

When we are rooted in God's love, we are strong. Storms and trials may shake us, but they will not cause us to fall; we are rooted deeply in life-giving soil. But when we allow ourselves to be distracted or seek to root ourselves in temporary success, the affirmation of others, or the rightness of our own opinions, we begin to weaken. The force of God's love no longer empowers us, because we've distanced ourselves from the source of our power and ability to bring love into the world. How do we stay rooted? We remind ourselves of Christ's life, death, and resurrection; we set aside time to rest in God's presence so he can remind us, heal us, and hold us; we gather with other Christians and experience the presence of Christ and his love in community; and we pray that God will open us more and more to grasp his love as much as we are able.

- Reflect on a time you felt overwhelmed by God's love. What caused you to recognize his love so clearly? What practices help you return to the experience of his love in a similar way?

- Ask God to call your attention to someone who needs this prayer (Ephesians 3:14-19) spoken over them this week. Who did you think of? How might you pray this prayer over that person in a meaningful way?

- Take a moment to quiet yourself in God's loving presence. Ask him to open your eyes and heart to the ways he wants you to live more fully into the truth that you are rooted in his love. What did God bring to mind?

RESPOND

Father, help me grasp the fullness of your love. When I doubt my worth, when I distrust your care, and when I turn my eyes away from you, keep me rooted and rested in your love. Your love covers all, never leaves or leaks, and binds me to you forever. Let me be a light of your love, a carrier, a dispenser. Let no one leave my presence without knowing that your love remains and guides and leads and heals. All else fades and fails. Amen.

DAY 15

11-15

BEING TRANSFORMED

a prayer to open

Here I am, Lord. Remind me who I am.
I am loved. I am known. I belong to you.

READ EPHESIANS 3:14-21

When I think of all this, I fall to my knees and pray to the Father, the Creator of everything in heaven and on earth. I pray that from his glorious, unlimited resources he will empower you with inner strength through his Spirit. Then Christ will make his home in your hearts as you trust in him. Your roots will grow down into God's love and keep you strong. And may you have the power to understand, as all God's people should, how wide, how long, how high, and how deep his love is. May you experience the love of Christ, though it is too great to understand fully. Then you will be made complete with all the fullness of life and power that comes from God.

Now all glory to God, who is able, through his mighty power at work within us, to accomplish infinitely more than we might ask or think. Glory to him in the church and in Christ Jesus through all generations forever and ever! Amen.

REFLECT

God is at work within us. He did not come to earth, save us, and decide to leave us as we are, stuck in our old, dying selves. He is working to transform everything that distorts and destroys. He is restoring and reconciling all things to himself through Jesus—right now. This includes our hearts, minds, bodies, and souls. Nothing is left as is. Every shattered heart, open wound, selfish part, and broken relationship is being transformed, healed, and restored. Even now. And what we can imagine God is doing in and through us pales in comparison to what he's actually doing.

- Reflect on the prayers you bring to God each day. What do they reflect about your belief in his power to transform?

- What hurt, disappointment, betrayal, brokenness, compulsion, addiction, or hang-up in your life seems beyond restoration? Spend a few minutes bringing whatever you identified into God's presence—boldly and confidently—for restoration and healing. What is your prayer? What do you long for God to do? Who can you ask to join you in your prayer?

- Take a moment to quiet yourself in God's loving presence. Ask him to open your eyes and heart to the ways he wants you to live more fully into the truth that his power is at work within you to transform and restore you. What did he bring to mind?

RESPOND

Father, my view of you is too narrow, my imagination too small. Your ways are so beyond what I am capable of dreaming up. Yet I tend to think of you as having only a little more perspective than I do, a little more love than I do, and a little more capacity than I do. Forgive me. Forgive me for drawing a box around you in my own mind and heart, as if this could contain you. Remind me of your majesty, greatness, and work in every part of me to heal, restore, reconcile, and make whole. Keep transforming me. Amen.

CALLED BY GOD

11-14

a prayer to open

Here I am, Lord. Remind me who I am.
I am loved. I am known. I belong to you.

READ EPHESIANS 4:1-4 _____

Therefore I, a prisoner for serving the Lord, beg you to lead a life worthy of your calling, for you have been called by God. Always be humble and gentle. Be patient with each other, making allowance for each other's faults because of your love. Make every effort to keep yourselves united in the Spirit, binding yourselves together with peace. For there is one body and one Spirit, just as you have been called to one glorious hope for the future.

REFLECT _____

When we think of calling, we usually think of vocation. Paul seemed to mean something different: that every person who is in Christ has been called to represent God in this world. Whatever else we might be called to do in this world, we are first and foremost called to be representatives of Christ to a world longing for healing, peace, reconciliation, and wholeness. To lead a life worthy of that calling means not only to live differently from what we see modeled in the world but also to live differently from what comes naturally. It requires no effort for us to be selfish, prideful, defensive, and short tempered. But to be humble, gentle, and patient? To live united and at peace with others? This requires a choice to partner with the Holy Spirit's transformative work in us, discipline, and a community that tells us the truth.

• Consider the circumstances in the last week in which you have not exercised humility, gentleness, or patience. What were you experiencing in those circumstances? What invitation from God do you sense arising out of what you experienced? What might need to be transformed? Surrendered? Released?

• What spiritual practices help you grow in humility, gentleness, and patience? What situations or relationships tend to undermine these qualities?

• Take a moment to quiet yourself in God's loving presence. Ask him to open your eyes and heart to the ways he wants you to live more fully into the truth that he has called you to be Christ's representative in the world. What did God bring to mind?

RESPOND _____

Father, forgive me for my impatience, my pride, and my irritation with others. I need your help. I know I am at my worst when I am tired, overwhelmed, or rushed. I cannot drum up the energy or ability to extend grace, peace, or love when I have not spent time with you, studying your Word, seeking your guidance, and abiding in your presence. I want only to reflect Jesus to the people I meet. Guide me into your presence by your grace so I may be filled. Amen.

Rooted

GIFTED BY GOD *11-17*

READ EPHESIANS 4:5-16

There is one Lord, one faith, one baptism, one God and Father of all, who is over all, in all, and living through all.

However, he has given each one of us a special gift through the generosity of Christ. That is why the Scriptures say,

"When he ascended to the heights,
he led a crowd of captives
and gave gifts to his people."

Notice that it says "he ascended." This clearly means that Christ also descended to our lowly world. And the same one who descended is the one who ascended higher than all the heavens, so that he might fill the entire universe with himself.

Now these are the gifts Christ gave to the church: the apostles, the prophets, the evangelists, and the pastors and teachers. Their responsibility is to equip God's people to do his work and build up the church, the body of Christ. This will continue until we all come to such unity in our faith and knowledge of God's Son that we will be mature in the Lord, measuring up to the full and complete standard of Christ.

Then we will no longer be immature like children. We won't be tossed and blown about by every wind of new teaching. We will not be influenced when people try to trick us with lies so clever they sound like the truth. Instead, we will speak the truth in love, growing in every way more and more like Christ, who is the head of his body, the church. He makes the whole body fit together perfectly. As each part does its own special work, it helps the other parts grow, so that the whole body is healthy and growing and full of love.

REFLECT

God has given us each a special gift so we can help others grow to be more like Christ, but we often think of certain gifts as more important. For example, we see the preacher teaching the crowds and it's hard not to think that a teaching gift holds a higher position on the gifts hierarchy than the gifts we have. But Paul frequently made clear that every gift matters (see Romans 12:4-8; 1 Corinthians 12). Without every gift, the body of Christ does not work, is not healthy, and fails to grow. And it's not just a select few who have received gifts; every follower of Jesus has been given special gifts that can help others grow to be more like Christ, full of love.

- What special gifts has God given you through the generosity of Christ? In a spirit of gratitude (as opposed to shame, guilt, or comparison with others), review the past year and the ways you have used your gifts to help others grow in Christlikeness. Whose life has God touched or transformed through you?

- In your current season of life, how is God inviting you to use the gifts he has given you? What resistance or reservations do you feel about this?

- Take a moment to quiet yourself in God's loving presence. Ask him to open your eyes and heart to the ways he wants you to live more fully into the truth that he has blessed you with special gifts to help others grow in Christlikeness. What did he bring to mind?

RESPOND_____

Father, thank you for the special gifts you have given me to use to help others grow in Christlikeness. Forgive me for the times I have diminished my gifts or deemed them to be insignificant or unhelpful. Grow my gratitude and appreciation for the way you've made me, and forgive me for degrading the gifts of others whether in thought, word, or action. I want to be someone who lifts up others, encourages them to grow in love, and allows them to see how much you cherish them. Open my eyes to see where to use what you've so generously given me. Amen.

CREATED TO BE LIKE GOD 11-20

a prayer to open

Here I am, Lord. Remind me who I am.
I am loved. I am known. I belong to you.

READ EPHESIANS 4:17-28_____

With the Lord's authority I say this: Live no longer as the Gentiles do, for they are hopelessly confused. Their minds are full of darkness; they wander far from the life God gives because they have closed their minds and hardened their hearts against him. They have no sense of shame. They live for lustful pleasure and eagerly practice every kind of impurity.

But that isn't what you learned about Christ. Since you have heard about Jesus and have learned the truth that comes from him, throw off your old sinful nature and your former way of life, which is corrupted by lust and deception. Instead, let the Spirit renew your thoughts and attitudes. Put on your new nature, created to be like God—truly righteous and holy.

So stop telling lies. Let us tell our neighbors the truth, for we are all parts of the same body. And "don't sin by letting anger control you." Don't let the sun go down while you are still angry, for anger gives a foothold to the devil.

If you are a thief, quit stealing. Instead, use your hands for good hard work, and then give generously to others in need.

REFLECT _____

The old self and the new self are concepts Paul returned to again and again in his letter to the Ephesians. He knew the pull our old habits, routines, and sins have on us and how tempted we are to return to our former ways. In times of stress, chaos, or pain, we fall back to what is familiar. What we see modeled around us, our emotions, and all the experiences that have shaped us over the course of our lives can drag us away from the life God gives. And so, when we find ourselves engaged in habits that reflect our old lives, the solution is to stop and take a path that reflects our new selves in Christ. To do this, we must open ourselves to the Holy Spirit

Rooted

•

to renew our thoughts and attitudes. This is the daily discipline of surrendering our minds and hearts to God and asking him to make our thoughts and attitudes reflect his. Over time, as we throw off the old and surrender ourselves to the work of the Spirit, we begin to reflect God to the world, just as we were created to do.

- Paul mentioned lying, anger, and stealing as examples of behaviors in which the old self engages. What attitudes or behaviors act as warning signs that you've slipped into your old self? What do you currently do when these attitudes or behaviors show themselves? What trusted family member or friend might help you identify and turn from these attitudes and behaviors?

- What spiritual practices, relationships, and activities help you open yourself to the Holy Spirit so your thoughts and attitudes can be renewed? How might you incorporate those practices, relationships, and activities more into your daily life?

- Take a moment to quiet yourself in God's loving presence. Ask him to open your eyes and heart to the ways he wants you to live more fully into the truth that he has created you to reflect his attitudes and thoughts to the world. What did he bring to mind?

RESPOND

Father, thank you for the grace and strength you offer so I can turn from falsehood, darkness, and anger and live into the life you came to give in Jesus. I long to live fully and freely in the new, redeemed, restored self. Help me by your Spirit and in your mercy to put on the new self each day and surrender every thought, attitude, and action to your transformative, loving work. When I am tempted to fall back on the familiar, show me the way back to you. Open my eyes and humble my heart so I return to your ways. Remind me that I was created to be like you, as hard as that is to comprehend. Nothing can separate me from your love. Amen.

DAY 19

SAVED *11-22*

a prayer to open

Here I am, Lord. Remind me who I am. I am loved. I am known. I belong to you.

READ EPHESIANS 4:29–5:2

Don't use foul or abusive language. Let everything you say be good and helpful, so that your words will be an encouragement to those who hear them.

And do not bring sorrow to God's Holy Spirit by the way you live. Remember, he has identified you

as his own, guaranteeing that you will be saved on the day of redemption.

Get rid of all bitterness, rage, anger, harsh words, and slander, as well as all types of evil behavior. Instead, be kind to each other, tenderhearted, forgiving one another, just as God through Christ has forgiven you.

Imitate God, therefore, in everything you do, because you are his dear children. Live a life filled with love, following the example of Christ. He loved us and offered himself as a sacrifice for us, a pleasing aroma to God.

Now that we are saved, we have been enabled to live in a way we couldn't before. Imagine using only words that are good, helpful, and encouraging to others. Or imagine having no bitterness or anger—never lashing out with harsh words or slander. Imagine being only kind, tenderhearted, and forgiving. Is that possible? What if the natural outcome of recognizing we are saved—really letting it sink into the depths of our minds and hearts—was kindness and goodness in everything we did? If we believed we were saved, eternally secure, forever and endlessly loved, we would have no need for fear, no reason to be angry or bitter when our egos felt threatened, and no desire to withhold forgiveness when hurt. Something in us would soften, our hearts would be open yet not afraid, and we could extend compassion to others, seeing them through the eyes of Christ.

- Reflect on the last time you lashed out at someone (whether in thought, word, or action). What caused you to react the way you did? What was triggering the way you were feeling?

- Which of the attitudes and behaviors that Paul mentioned—abusive language, bitterness, rage, anger, harsh words, slander—do you sense God inviting you to examine in your life? What is the invitation?

- Take a moment to quiet yourself in God's loving presence. Ask him to open your eyes and heart to the ways he wants you to live more fully into the truth that you are saved, eternally secure, forever and endlessly loved. What did he bring to mind?

RESPOND

Father, in my everyday life, help me remember that I am saved, secure, eternally loved. How easily I forget! Fill me with your grace and power to live in the way of love. Open opportunities for me to extend kindness, compassion, and forgiveness, and give me the courage to take them. I desire to be someone who builds up others, encouraging them and cheering for them instead of being envious or resentful. I long to be pure in my speech and free from bitterness or anger. Help me to be generous and forgiving, as you are. Let my life, words, and thoughts be pleasing to you. Amen.

A PERSON OF LIGHT

a prayer to open

Here I am, Lord. Remind me who I am.
I am loved. I am known. I belong to you.

READ EPHESIANS 5:3-14

Let there be no sexual immorality, impurity, or greed among you. Such sins have no place among God's people. Obscene stories, foolish talk, and coarse jokes—these are not for you. Instead, let there be thankfulness to God. You can be sure that no immoral, impure, or greedy person will inherit the Kingdom of Christ and of God. For a greedy person is an idolater, worshiping the things of this world.

Don't be fooled by those who try to excuse these sins, for the anger of God will fall on all who disobey him. Don't participate in the things these people do. For once you were full of darkness, but now you have light from the Lord. So live as people of light!

For this light within you produces only what is good and right and true.

Carefully determine what pleases the Lord. Take no part in the worthless deeds of evil and darkness; instead, expose them. It is shameful even to talk about the things that ungodly people do in secret. But their evil intentions will be exposed when the light shines on them, for the light makes everything visible. This is why it is said,

> "Awake, O sleeper,
> rise up from the dead,
> and Christ will give you light."

REFLECT

We may have once believed that certain behaviors and attitudes were acceptable or justified for one reason or another. Perhaps they made us feel satisfied, happy, or successful. Maybe certain ways of acting made us feel in control and powerful or smart and worthy of the praise of others. But now that our eyes are opened and light has been poured out in us, we see that these behaviors and attitudes are shrouded in darkness and destroy the good that God seeks to build in us and accomplish through us. This Scripture calls us to live into who we actually are: people of light. We know that living into our identity as people of light is easier said than done, as we are constantly pulled into darkness by our own hearts, our circumstances, the evil one, and sometimes the people around us. Yet as we surrender ourselves, piece by piece, over the course of our lives, the light dispels the darkness and we naturally produce what is good and right and true.

- Consider how Paul contrasted impurity, greed, obscenity, and coarse joking with thanksgiving. What do you think he was getting at by doing this?

- Are there occasions in which you engage in the things Paul spoke about? What catalyzes your engagement in them? Insecurity, anger, unmet desire, doubt? What might God be inviting you to as you consider thankfulness instead?

- Take a moment to quiet yourself in God's loving presence. Ask him to open your eyes and heart to the ways he wants you to live more fully into the truth that you have light from the Lord within you and can live as a person of light. What did God bring to mind?

Father, thank you for new life, second chances, and your unending grace. I can slip so easily into those things that have no home in me, the things that come from darkness and cause destruction. I pray that you would continue to transform my heart and mind. Let words of thanksgiving always be on my tongue so I see your work, your holiness, and your goodness and am reminded that you have set me apart for your purposes. May others see your light in me and be drawn into your love. Amen.

DAY 21

ABLE TO CHOOSE   11-27

a prayer to open   Here I am, Lord. Remind me who I am.
                                      I am loved. I am known. I belong to you.

READ EPHESIANS 5:15-20

So be careful how you live. Don't live like fools, but like those who are wise. Make the most of every opportunity in these evil days. Don't act thoughtlessly, but understand what the Lord wants you to do. Don't be drunk with wine, because that will ruin your life. Instead, be filled with the Holy Spirit, singing psalms and hymns and spiritual songs among yourselves, and making music to the Lord in your hearts. And give thanks for everything to God the Father in the name of our Lord Jesus Christ.

REFLECT

Even as God has gifted us in so many ways when we put our trust in Christ, we still have a choice: We can live into our identity in Christ and access the power and love and presence of God; or we can continue in our old ways, living like fools and acting without intention and thought, closing ourselves off to the Spirit, and walking through life without gratitude, feeling entitled. Living with intention—fixing our eyes on the hope we have in Jesus, directing our minds to what is good and noble, treating our bodies as temples of God, loving others with patience and self-sacrifice—requires effort and surrender. Although it is true that as we grow and mature, we become the kinds of people who can live this way, we don't just slide into a life of love. We have to practice. And we do this by refraining from certain things—such as acting thoughtlessly and foolishly and getting drunk—and by engaging in other things—making the most of the opportunities we are given, listening for God's words to us, singing songs in worship, and giving thanks. The good news is that the Holy Spirit will empower us in all of these things.

- What are the activities and thoughts you engage in that help you cope with the difficulties in your life but prevent you from being attuned to the Holy Spirit?

Rooted

•

- What are the thoughts and activities you need to refrain from in order to live more into your identity in Christ? What are the thoughts and activities you need to engage in more in order to fully live into your identity in Christ?

- Take a moment to quiet yourself in God's loving presence. Ask him to open your eyes and heart to the ways he wants you to lean into the truth that you have a choice about how to live and that the Holy Spirit will empower you. What did God bring to mind?

RESPOND

Father, fill my soul to overflowing with your Spirit. Allow me to see with your eyes, listen with your ears, and love with your heart. I pray that your words—the psalms, hymns, and songs of your Spirit—would be on my tongue, quick to spill onto others to bless and encourage them. Let my heart always be giving you thanks and praise for the breath you have given and the opportunities to share your love. Help me to live into my identity in Christ and put in the effort it takes to grow and live according to your loving ways. Where I fail, turn me back to you and set me on the right path. Amen.

DAY 22

SUBMITTED

a prayer to open

Here I am, Lord. Remind me who I am. I am loved. I am known. I belong to you.

READ EPHESIANS 5:21-33

And further, submit to one another out of reverence for Christ.

For wives, this means submit to your husbands as to the Lord. For a husband is the head of his wife as Christ is the head of the church. He is the Savior of his body, the church. As the church submits to Christ, so you wives should submit to your husbands in everything.

For husbands, this means love your wives, just as Christ loved the church. He gave up his life for her to make her holy and clean, washed by the cleansing of God's word. He did this to present her to himself as a glorious church without a spot or wrinkle or any other blemish. Instead, she will be holy and without fault. In the same way, husbands ought to love their wives as they love their own bodies. For a man who loves his wife actually shows love for himself. No one hates his own body but feeds and cares for it, just as Christ cares for the church. And we are members of his body.

As the Scriptures say, "A man leaves his father and mother and is joined to his wife, and the two are united into one." This is a great mystery, but it is an illustration of the way Christ and the church are one. So again I say, each man must love his wife as he loves himself, and the wife must respect her husband.

REFLECT

Submitted is a word we don't like in our culture. It carries a sense of "less than," a surrender of ourselves. We are apt to be told, "Rise up! Take the lead! Strive for importance!" We want to be at the top of the heap, the front of the line, the most prestigious place at the table. And Paul said something quite different. Of course, this idea of submitting to one another is not Paul's; it is Jesus'. We see it in Jesus' words ("Even the Son of Man came not to be served but to serve others, and to give his life as a ransom for many" [Mark 10:45]), but we see it more powerfully in his actions: coming to earth in human form, serving those he came into contact with, refusing to be made king by human hands, washing his disciples' feet, and laying down his life for the sake of the world. Paul described Jesus' actions this way in Philippians 2:5-8:

You must have the same attitude that Christ Jesus had.

> Though he was God,
> he did not think of equality with God
> as something to cling to.

Instead, he gave up his divine privileges;
he took the humble position of a slave
and was born as a human being.
When he appeared in human form,
he humbled himself in obedience to God
and died a criminal's death on a cross.

- In what context is it most difficult for you to think about submitting to someone else (for example, at work or in your family)? Why is it difficult?

- Reflect on any resistance you feel when you read Paul's words in this passage. Where is the resistance coming from? What, if anything, shifts in you as you read the Philippians passage about Jesus (2:5-8)?

- Take a moment to quiet yourself in God's loving presence. Ask him to open your eyes and heart to the ways he wants you to submit to others in your life out of reverence for Christ. Who did God bring to mind?

RESPOND

Father, thank you for showing me, through Jesus, how to submit and how to love. Help me demonstrate the humility Jesus taught and modeled. Encourage me to release my need to be first, best, and right. Give me the courage to build up, encourage, and enliven others. Give me eyes to see each person I meet today with your love and mercy. Convict my heart when I seek my own glory, credit, and honor. May all I do be for your glory and honor, and may you heal and correct my failures and faults. Amen.

DAY 23

11-29

ABLE TO HONOR

a prayer to open

Here I am, Lord. Remind me who I am.
I am loved. I am known. I belong to you.

READ EPHESIANS 6:1-4

Children, obey your parents because you belong to the Lord, for this is the right thing to do.

"Honor your father and mother." This is the first commandment with a promise: If you honor your father and mother, "things will go well for you, and you will have a long life on the earth."

Fathers, do not provoke your children to anger by the way you treat them. Rather, bring them up with the discipline and instruction that comes from the Lord.

REFLECT

Few commandments carry as much angst with them as "honor your father and mother." Parents can hurt us, disappoint us, leave us, ignore us, and dishonor us. Perhaps we know only one of our parents or lost one or both too soon. Whatever our situation, honoring our parents is complicated and changes over the course of our lives. As little children, we learn to obey our parents through discipline. As teenagers, most of us experiment with disobedience, seeing how far we can push the limits of our parents' rules. As young adults, we differentiate ourselves and learn to live apart from our parents, while trying to visit for family gatherings. As parents ourselves, we need our parents to help us grow into the parents we want to be. And then as our parents grow old, our responsibility to care for them increases and they need more from us than we need from them. Sometimes honoring them is easy, but more often it's one of the hardest jobs we have because our parents are flawed—and so are we.

The difficulty we have in honoring our parents must be why Paul included it here at the end of his letter to the Ephesians, just after instructing his listeners to submit to one another in love. The only way we can consistently carry out this command is by the power of the Holy Spirit in us as changed, empowered, and rooted Christ followers.

- Why do you think God places such high value on honoring our parents?
- What does it look like to honor your father in light of who he is, your family dynamics, and how God has equipped you? What does it look like to honor your mother in light of who she is, your family dynamics, and how God has equipped you?
- Take a moment to quiet yourself in God's loving presence. Ask him to open your eyes and heart to the ways he wants you to honor your father and mother (or their legacy). What did he bring to mind?

RESPOND

Father, you know my story and my struggle. You know the ways my parents have loved me, the ways they have disappointed and hurt me, and the ways I have honored and dishonored them. Lord, help me view them through your eyes, as your children whom you love. Help me see that they are human and carry with them hurt and pain that I may never know or understand. I forgive their trespasses and hold them in your glorious light. By your grace, give me the privilege of honoring them in your name. Amen.

11-30

A SERVANT OF CHRIST

a prayer to open

Here I am, Lord. Remind me who I am.
I am loved. I am known. I belong to you.

READ EPHESIANS 6:5-9

Slaves, obey your earthly masters with deep respect and fear. Serve them sincerely as you would serve Christ. Try to please them all the time, not just when they are watching you. As slaves of Christ, do the will of God with all your heart. Work with enthusiasm, as though you were working for the Lord rather than for people. Remember that the Lord will reward each one of us for the good we do, whether we are slaves or free.

Masters, treat your slaves in the same way. Don't threaten them; remember, you both have the same Master in heaven, and he has no favorites.

REFLECT

This passage can be hard for us to read in our modern world. It has been misused during the course of history to justify slavery and oppress Christians and non-Christians alike. What place does it have here in Paul's letter about identity in Christ? The first paragraph makes us so uncomfortable that we often miss or underestimate the revolutionary statement Paul was making about masters: "Masters, treat your slaves in the same way. . . . [God] has no favorites" (verse 9). This would have been shocking to anyone reading or hearing Paul's letter in the first century. His point was that whatever our social, political, and economic status on earth, we are all equal in God's eyes. Paul was using an image that would have been common in his day to illuminate the relationship we have with Christ. We no longer have to roam around this world alone without a purpose, being driven here and there by our own desires and longings. Rather, we belong to someone. But not just anyone: We belong to the King, who sees us not as his property but as his beloved children he protects, provides for, and guides into lives of abundance.

- Most of us tend to consciously or subconsciously classify or rank people based on their social, political, or economic status. Reflect on a time you have done this. What impact did doing so have on your view of the person involved?

- What does it look like to be a servant of Christ where you work (whether at home, at an office, on a community board, or elsewhere)? What do you sense God inviting you to adjust in what you currently do?

- Take a moment to quiet yourself in God's loving presence. Ask him to open your eyes and heart to the ways he wants you to lean into the security of knowing you belong to him. What did he bring to mind?

Rooted

Father, thank you for loving me and calling me yours. Open my eyes to the ways I am thinking of myself more highly than others or failing to recognize your image in each person I encounter. I am your servant and long to serve you wherever I find myself: at home, at work, in my community, in my church. Empower me by your Holy Spirit so I can see what I do as service to you and not get wrapped up in trying to get the approval of others. May I find myself anchored in the truth of being your treasured child, created to love and be loved by you. Amen.

DAY 25

STRONG IN THE LORD

a prayer to open

Here I am, Lord. Remind me who I am.
I am loved. I am known. I belong to you.

READ EPHESIANS 6:10-12

A final word: Be strong in the Lord and in his mighty power. Put on all of God's armor so that you will be able to stand firm against all strategies of the devil. For we are not fighting against flesh-and-blood enemies, but against evil rulers and authorities of the unseen world, against mighty powers in this dark world, and against evil spirits in the heavenly places.

REFLECT

Having reminded the followers of Jesus in Ephesus of their identity in Christ and instructed them about what that identity means, Paul made them aware of one last critical detail: They were in a spiritual battle. *We* are in a spiritual battle. Evil powers and spirits are out to destroy and diminish the gospel message and those who carry it. Of course, this is no surprise to God. He has given us what we need to resist any evil schemes of the devil. Our job is to remember what is true and stand in it to the end. We have God's righteousness, truth, salvation, and peace in Jesus Christ; we have God's power by the Holy Spirit; and we have the faith God has given us. In Christ and with Christ and through Christ, we are safe, powerful, and strong.

- What questions and fears arise in you when you read Paul's words about our struggle against the powers of this dark world and forces of evil in the heavenly places?

- How would you describe being strong in the Lord? What does that mean? Have you experienced times when you could describe yourself as strong in the Lord or times when you have been weak? What has been the difference?

- Take a moment to quiet yourself in God's loving presence. Ask him to open your eyes and heart to the ways he wants you to be strong in him, rely on who you are in Christ, and stand firm. What did God bring to mind?

Father, protect me in this struggle against evil. There are days I look around and it seems that evil has taken over, causing me to sometimes fall into despair. Help me remember the truth, power, and peace you offer to fend off the devil's schemes to invade my mind and heart. Keep me focused on you, your ways, and your Word so I can overcome and persevere in times of trouble and temptation. And, Lord, give me eyes to recognize your goodness and your Kingdom. Amen.

DAY 26

PREPARED

a prayer to open

Here I am, Lord. Remind me who I am.
I am loved. I am known. I belong to you.

READ EPHESIANS 6:13-15

Put on every piece of God's armor so you will be able to resist the enemy in the time of evil. Then after the battle you will still be standing firm. Stand your ground, putting on the belt of truth and the body armor of God's righteousness. For shoes, put on the peace that comes from the Good News so that you will be fully prepared.

REFLECT

Like the Ephesians, we are in the midst of a battle, and we can remain strong and stand firm in the face of that battle if we put on every piece of God's armor. Paul's word choice could mean either the armor God himself wears (see Isaiah 59:17) or the armor he has and will supply to his beloved children for their protection. This passage speaks about three specific pieces of armor: the belt of truth, the body armor of righteousness, and shoes of peace. A belt keeps body armor in place. The body armor protects the heart and lungs. The shoes prevent being disabled by shards, spikes, or stones in the ground. Without these three pieces of armor, we are not only exposed and vulnerable but also unable to carry the message of the gospel. Imagine if our bodies were protected by the armor of our own righteousness, full of holes and made of aluminum foil! Imagine if the belt that held that armor on was the half-truths and lies upon which so many of us have built our reputations or self-image! Imagine if our shoes were those of angry aggressors wanting to fight and destroy instead of spreading the good news about the life and light of Jesus! Thankfully, God gives us something far better, something that allows us to withstand any attack.

- In what area of your life do you sense the devil scheming or strategizing against you?
- Which of the three pieces of armor that Paul mentioned—truth, God's

righteousness, and peace—do you need to be intentional about putting on right now? (For example, do you sense you are wavering on what's true? Or are you seeking to rely on your own goodness or righteousness? Or is what you bring forth into the world something less than the gospel of peace?)

- Take a moment to quiet yourself in God's loving presence. Ask him to open your eyes and heart to the ways he wants you to become aware of the spiritual battles you are facing and rely on his armor to protect and prepare you. What did he bring to mind?

RESPOND_____

Father, I need your truth, righteousness, and readiness. On my own, I fall down at even the slightest challenge. Please remind me of who I am in Christ and of my righteousness in your sight through him. Fear holds me back and prevents me from being ready to share the gospel, flee from the devil's schemes, and stand for peace when all else cries for vengeance. I need your truth; I need your righteousness; I need your readiness. May it be so.

EQUIPPED

a prayer to open

Here I am, Lord. Remind me who I am. I am loved. I am known. I belong to you.

READ EPHESIANS 6:16-18_____

In addition to all of these, hold up the shield of faith to stop the fiery arrows of the devil. Put on salvation as your helmet, and take the sword of the Spirit, which is the word of God.

Pray in the Spirit at all times and on every occasion. Stay alert and be persistent in your prayers for all believers everywhere.

REFLECT_____

For the past three days, we have read about the ways God has equipped us as followers of Jesus to withstand Satan's schemes to seduce our hearts away from God and question our own security in Jesus. In addition to a belt, body armor, and shoes, we are also equipped with a shield of faith, a helmet of salvation, and the sword of the Spirit. We can learn how to use some of these tools by looking at Jesus. When he was taken into the wilderness and tempted by Satan, Jesus used a shield of faith and the sword of the Spirit. He responded to each of Satan's three temptations by speaking the Word of God aloud (see Matthew 4:3-10). Not only that, but he also exercised faith by believing God's Word over Satan's promises and lies. Amazingly, we are equipped to ward off Satan's lies and promises and can access the power of the Holy Spirit through prayer, if only we would stay alert!

- Reflect on your greatest temptation (for example, engaging in destructive or sinful conduct; not loving in the ways Jesus calls; or not believing what God has revealed as true about you, himself, or others). When you give in to that particular temptation, what are you not believing about either what God has said or what he has revealed about himself?

- What kinds of activities, attitudes, and relationships prevent you from being alert and able to pray?

- Take a moment to quiet yourself in God's loving presence. Ask him to open your eyes and heart to the ways he wants you to see and utilize the tools he has equipped you with to grow your trust in him. What did he bring to mind?

RESPOND_____

Father, thank you for this rich reminder that through Christ, you have equipped me with faith, salvation, and your Word. I don't always live as if I am armed with these things. Sometimes I feel vulnerable, afraid, unsure, and alone. Sink this image and these words into my heart and mind so I wake up in the morning trusting fully that there is no reason to hold back my love. You have set me free and given me all I need to love as you do and stand firm to the end. Amen.

DAY 28

WHO YOU ARE

a prayer to open

Here I am, Lord. Remind me who I am.
I am loved. I am known. I belong to you.

READ EPHESIANS 2:1-10_____

Once you were dead because of your disobedience and your many sins. You used to live in sin, just like the rest of the world, obeying the devil—the commander of the powers in the unseen world. He is the spirit at work in the hearts of those who refuse to obey God. All of us used to live that way, following the passionate desires and inclinations of our sinful nature. By our very nature we were subject to God's anger, just like everyone else.

But God is so rich in mercy, and he loved us so much, that even though we were dead because of our sins, he gave us life when he raised Christ from the dead. (It is only by God's grace that you have been saved!) For he raised us from the dead along with Christ and seated us with him in the heavenly realms because we are united with Christ Jesus. So God can point to us in all future ages as examples of the incredible wealth of his grace and kindness toward us, as shown in all he has done for us who are united with Christ Jesus.

God saved you by his grace when you believed. And you can't take credit for this; it is a gift from God. Salvation is not a reward for the good things we have done, so none of us can boast about it. For we are God's masterpiece. He has created us anew in Christ Jesus, so we can do the good things he planned for us long ago.

What a rich, compelling, and encouraging passage of Scripture! These words belong on our walls, as our screen savers, on the inside of our eyelids, and in the very depths of our souls. We once had reason to be afraid, dead as we were in our sins and held captive to our own desires and inclinations. But that isn't us anymore. We are not slaves to sin. We are not destined for death. We are not purposeless. We are

- in Christ
- adopted
- under Christ
- Christ's own
- confident in hope
- empowered
- changed
- loved
- with Christ
- created anew
- brought near
- joined together with others in Christ

- granted access to God's presence
- rooted in love
- being transformed
- called by God
- gifted by God
- created to be like God
- saved
- people of light
- able to choose
- submitted to others
- strong in the Lord
- prepared
- equipped

This is who we are. This is who you are.

- As you read through the preceding list, what stirs in your heart and soul? Which of the descriptors can you easily receive? Which of the descriptors give rise to resistance or just don't seem true of you? Which of the descriptors do you need to hang on your wall, tape to your bathroom mirror, or have tattooed on your heart?

- Reflect on the past twenty-eight days, which you've spent responding to whatever God raised within you about your identity. What stands out? What has been his most consistent message or invitation to you?

- Take a moment to quiet yourself in God's loving presence. Ask him to open your eyes and heart to the one truth about who you are in Christ that he wants you to take with you even as you complete this part of the journey. Write down whatever God brings to mind.

RESPOND_____

Father, I read through this list and see in black and white what I know you say is true of me both in the words of Scripture and by your actions. Can it be? Help me embrace the truth of who I am in you and step fully into that truth so I can be and do what you've called me to in this world. When I get stuck or waylaid, pull me back to you. Remind me who I am. Remind me that I am yours. I am yours. Amen.

WHEN I WAS thirteen or fourteen, I got braces. My teeth weren't crooked, really, but apparently my teeth and jaw had some structural issues that could cause problems later. I don't remember the braces themselves ever being too bad, but I still have nightmares about the headgear I was supposed to wear at bedtime. This metal device hooked into the fasteners on my top teeth and then stayed fixed to my face with a strap that wrapped around the back of my neck. Nearly thirty years later, I can still feel the pain I experienced when putting the headgear on. The idea was that as I slept, the pressure exerted would restructure my mouth in a way that I'd allegedly be grateful for when I grew up.

Other than the extreme awkwardness of sleeping with a metal arc around my face, I never felt the movement that was happening in my mouth. I couldn't look in the mirror day by day and see a difference. But a year later, my orthodontist said I was done with the procedure and no longer needed to torture myself. The transformation had happened. I could see that a few teeth that had been turning inward or sideways had straightened out, and years later I wouldn't have problems as my wisdom teeth came in and I finished growing.

This basically explains my relationship with Scripture, too—although that transformation process is still ongoing. At times what God does through Scripture is just as painful—although not physically—as that headgear. Most of the time, though, I don't notice the restructuring that's happening on a daily basis. But some significant transformation has happened over my years reading the Bible, and that is why I keep coming back to it day after day, year after year. God is using his Word to prepare me to live now and in his Kingdom forever.

My typical day starts when my alarm sounds at 5:28 a.m. I put my contacts in so I can see more than dark shapes and shadows, feed the dog and let her outside, turn the coffee on, and light a favorite candle. Then I curl up in my living room chair under a blanket and sit in the quiet, looking out the back window. Most days I sit for about ten minutes and try to remember that God is present with me, Jesus is Lord of all, and I am known and loved. The first words I usually speak are "Thank you for . . ." And then I grab my Bible off the table to my right and turn to whatever I'm in the midst of reading.

I use several different tools to help my reading: a one-year-through-the-Bible plan, some favorite devotional books, the lectionary. Or I will read through a particular book in the Bible and focus on one part each morning. I usually read Scripture for about ten to fifteen minutes, pausing now and then to savor it, sometimes reading it aloud if my eyes are glazing over the text. Sometimes I'll write out the text if it's especially powerful or meaningful to me that morning. During this time, I don't look at commentaries or study materials. I don't try to figure out what the Greek or Hebrew words might have meant. I simply soak in the words and allow God to use them in me. In certain seasons, I will then write a prayer or poem in my journal; in others, I will take a few deep breaths and turn to whatever is next in my day. I don't have a revelation every time. Some days I have to push through distraction, boredom, and stress. Other days I feel deeply connected to God, and a flash of insight into him or myself will come.

This is a practice I can't live without. Grounding myself in God's presence every day through Scripture is the only way I can be okay in the world. When I go a few days without this sacred time, I am short tempered, tired, more prone to sadness and despair, easily distracted and tempted, and incapable of loving the way I desire. Even in this hyperconnected world of social media, I feel more disconnected from my family and friends and coworkers when I am less connected to God.

King David—whom God described as "a man after my own heart" (Acts 13:22)—is an example of someone whose heart was devoted to God. He obviously didn't have Facebook and Twitter to distract him, but he had plenty of other battles on his hands. So in this thirty-day section, we will enter into David's life to learn what a heart and life look like when they are truly grounded in God's presence. How did David respond to such things as betrayal, criticism, temptation, and fear? His story, told in a sprawling narrative in the Old Testament, draws us in and reminds us who God is and what a heart surrendered to him looks like.

WE WANT A KING!

12-14

a prayer to open   My Lord, my God, show me your heart. Ground me in your presence.
Draw me near and hold me close.

READ 1 SAMUEL 8:4-22

Finally, all the elders of Israel met at Ramah to discuss the matter with Samuel. "Look," they told him, "you are now old, and your sons are not like you. Give us a king to judge us like all the other nations have."

Samuel was displeased with their request and went to the LORD for guidance. "Do everything they say to you," the LORD replied, "for they are rejecting me, not you. They don't want me to be their king any longer. Ever since I brought them from Egypt they have continually abandoned me and followed other gods. And now they are giving you the same treatment. Do as they ask, but solemnly warn them about the way a king will reign over them."

So Samuel passed on the LORD's warning to the people who were asking him for a king. "This is how a king will reign over you," Samuel said. "The king will draft your sons. . . . Some will be generals and captains in his army, some will be forced to plow in his fields and harvest his crops, and some will make his weapons and chariot equipment. The king will take your daughters from you and force them to cook and bake and make perfumes for him. He will take away the best of your fields and vineyards and olive groves and give them to his own officials. . . . He will take your male and female slaves and demand the finest of your cattle and donkeys for his own use. He will demand a tenth of your flocks, and you will be his slaves. When that day comes, you will beg for relief from this king you are demanding, but then the LORD will not help you."

But the people refused to listen. . . . "Even so, we still want a king," they said. "We want to be like the nations around us. Our king will judge us and lead us into battle."

So Samuel repeated to the LORD what the people had said, and the LORD replied, "Do as they say, and give them a king."

REFLECT

Today's passage begins with the Israelites—who had been governed for hundreds of years by God-appointed judges and led most recently by the prophet Samuel—demanding that they be governed instead by a king as the nations that surrounded them were. Imagine what it must have been like for Samuel, after leading the Israelites faithfully for his entire life, to hear their demand that he be replaced and they be governed like the pagan nations. God brought Samuel comfort in the midst of this difficult time, though, reminding him that it was God the Israelites were rejecting, not Samuel.

- What motivated the Israelites to ask for a human king? Why did they want to be like "all the other nations" (verse 5)? In what ways are you seeking to be like other people?

- Review God's response to Samuel in verses 7-9. In what ways have you been rejected by family, friends, or coworkers for doing the right thing or deciding to follow God's ways? How might God comfort you in those moments?

- What things in this world most often tempt you to turn away from him?

Grounded

•

139

Father, help me embrace your plans for my life. I am so tempted to turn to the ways of this world instead of placing my full trust in you, your timing, and your wisdom. I long for you to be the King and Lord of my every thought, word, and action. Please give me the courage to walk in your ways even in the face of insult or rejection. May your will be done in me. Amen.

DAY 2

A NEW KING   12-18

a prayer to open   My Lord, my God, show me your heart. Ground me in your presence. Draw me near and hold me close.

READ 1 SAMUEL 9:2-10:24

Saul was the most handsome man in Israel—head and shoulders taller than anyone else in the land.

One day [Saul's father's] donkeys strayed away, and he told Saul, "Take a servant with you, and go look for the donkeys." So Saul took one of the servants . . . but they couldn't find the donkeys anywhere. . . .

Saul said to his servant, "Let's go home. By now my father will be more worried about us than about the donkeys!"

But the servant said, "I've just thought of something! There is a man of God who lives here in this town. He is held in high honor by all the people because everything he says comes true. . . . Perhaps he can tell us which way to go."

"But we don't have anything to offer him," Saul replied. "Even our food is gone, and we don't have a thing to give him."

"Well," the servant said, "I have one small silver piece. We can at least offer it to the man of God and see what happens!" . . .

"All right," Saul agreed, "let's try it!" . . .

As they were climbing the hill to the town, they met some young women coming out to draw water. So Saul and his servant asked, "Is the seer here today?"

"Yes," they replied. . . . "He has just arrived to take part in a public sacrifice up at the place of worship. Hurry and catch him before he goes up there to eat." . . .

So they entered the town, and as they passed through the gates, Samuel was coming out toward them to go up to the place of worship.

Now the LORD had told Samuel the previous day, "About this time tomorrow I will send you a man

from the land of Benjamin. Anoint him to be the leader of my people, Israel. He will rescue them from the Philistines, for I have looked down on my people in mercy and have heard their cry."

When Samuel saw Saul, the LORD said, "That's the man I told you about! He will rule my people."

Just then Saul approached Samuel at the gateway and asked, "Can you please tell me where the seer's house is?"

"I am the seer!" Samuel replied. "Go up to the place of worship ahead of me. . . . In the morning I'll tell you what you want to know and send you on your way. And don't worry about those donkeys that were lost three days ago, for they have been found. And I am here to tell you that you and your family are the focus of all Israel's hopes."

Saul replied, "But I'm only from the tribe of Benjamin, the smallest tribe in Israel, and my family is the least important of all the families of that tribe! Why are you talking like this to me?" . . .

When they came down from the place of worship and returned to town, Samuel took Saul up to the roof of the house and prepared a bed for him there. At daybreak the next morning, Samuel called to Saul, "Get up! It's time you were on your way." So Saul got ready, and he and Samuel left the house together. When they reached the edge of town, Samuel told Saul to send his servant on ahead. After the servant was gone, Samuel said, "Stay here, for I have received a special message for you from God." . . .

Then Samuel took a flask of olive oil and poured it over Saul's head. He kissed Saul and said, "I am doing this because the LORD has appointed you to be the ruler over Israel, his special possession." . . .

Later Samuel called all the people of Israel to meet before the LORD. . . . And he said, "This is what the LORD, the God of Israel, has declared: I brought you from Egypt and rescued you from the Egyptians and from all of the nations that were oppressing you. But though I have rescued you from your misery and distress, you have rejected your God today and have said, 'No, we want a king instead!' Now, therefore, present yourselves before the LORD by tribes and clans."

So Samuel brought all the tribes of Israel before the LORD, and the tribe of Benjamin was chosen by lot. Then he brought each family of the tribe of Benjamin before the LORD, and the family of the Matrites was chosen. And finally Saul son of Kish was chosen from among them. But when they looked for him, he had disappeared! So they asked the LORD, "Where is he?"

And the LORD replied, "He is hiding among the baggage." So they found him and brought him out, and he stood head and shoulders above anyone else.

Then Samuel said to all the people, "This is the man the LORD has chosen as your king. No one in all Israel is like him!"

And all the people shouted, "Long live the king!"

REFLECT

What a remarkable thing it is to see how God orchestrated this first meeting between Saul and Samuel! The day before Saul went out looking for his father's lost donkeys, God was already speaking to Samuel about this young man God had chosen to be Israel's first human king. We are told that Saul was tall and handsome, as the kings of the surrounding nations would have been, but when he was called forward to receive the approval of the people, he cowered in fear. Nevertheless, the Israelites affirmed him as king and began an era in which God's people pursued the heart of the world instead of the heart of God. Don't we know this path well?

- What might Saul's state of mind and emotions have been as he wandered around looking for his father's donkeys, continuing to get farther and farther away from his home, and then encountering Samuel, who anointed him the first king over God's people?

- When have you felt lost and unsure of the way to go? Where have you seen God's presence or orchestration of circumstances?

- When have you rejected God or his ways in order to pursue something that was popular or would make you more like the world? What was motivating you? Where did you see God in the midst of that time?

RESPOND

Father, I know there have been times when I have treated you as the Israelite people did, rejecting and turning away from you. Show me the ways I'm chasing after the things of the world and seeking to look more like "all the other nations" instead of attaching my heart to you and the things you long to do in and through me to accomplish your purposes. Help me remain focused on you. Amen.

REJECTED AS KING   12-19

a prayer to open   My Lord, my God, show me your heart. Ground me in your presence.
Draw me near and hold me close.

READ 1 SAMUEL 15:1-29

One day Samuel said to Saul, "It was the LORD who told me to anoint you as king of his people, Israel. . . . This is what the LORD of Heaven's Armies has declared: I have decided to settle accounts with the nation of Amalek for opposing Israel when they came from Egypt. Now go and completely destroy the entire Amalekite nation—men, women, children, babies, cattle, sheep, goats, camels, and donkeys."

So Saul mobilized his army at Telaim. . . . Then Saul and his army went to a town of the Amalekites and lay in wait in the valley. . . .

Then Saul slaughtered the Amalekites. . . . He captured Agag, the Amalekite king, but completely destroyed everyone else. Saul and his men spared Agag's life and kept the best of the sheep and goats, the cattle, the fat calves, and the lambs—everything, in fact, that appealed to them. . . .

Then the LORD said to Samuel, "I am sorry that I ever made Saul king, for he has not been loyal to me and has refused to obey my command." Samuel was so deeply moved when he heard this that he cried out to the LORD all night.

Early the next morning Samuel went to find Saul. . . . When Samuel finally found him, Saul greeted him cheerfully. "May the LORD bless you," he said. "I have carried out the LORD's command!"

"Then what is all the bleating of sheep and goats and the lowing of cattle I hear?" Samuel demanded.

"It's true that the army spared the best of the sheep, goats, and cattle," Saul admitted. "But they are going to sacrifice them to the LORD your God. We have destroyed everything else."

Then Samuel said to Saul, "Stop! Listen to what the LORD told me last night!"

"What did he tell you?" Saul asked.

And Samuel told him, "Although you may think little of yourself, are you not the leader of the tribes of Israel? The LORD has anointed you king

of Israel. And the LORD sent you on a mission and told you, 'Go and completely destroy the sinners, the Amalekites, until they are all dead.' Why haven't you obeyed the LORD? Why did you rush for the plunder and do what was evil in the LORD's sight?"

"But I did obey the LORD," Saul insisted. "I carried out the mission he gave me. I brought back King Agag, but I destroyed everyone else. Then my troops brought in the best of the sheep, goats, cattle, and plunder to sacrifice to the LORD your God in Gilgal."

But Samuel replied,

"What is more pleasing to the LORD:
your burnt offerings and sacrifices
or your obedience to his voice?
Listen! Obedience is better than sacrifice,
and submission is better than offering the
fat of rams.
Rebellion is as sinful as witchcraft,
and stubbornness as bad as worshiping idols.
So because you have rejected the command
of the LORD,
he has rejected you as king."

Then Saul admitted to Samuel, "Yes, I have sinned. I have disobeyed your instructions and the LORD's command, for I was afraid of the people and did what they demanded. But now, please forgive my sin and come back with me so that I may worship the LORD."

But Samuel replied, "I will not go back with you! Since you have rejected the LORD's command, he has rejected you as king of Israel."

As Samuel turned to go, Saul tried to hold him back and tore the hem of his robe. And Samuel said to him, "The LORD has torn the kingdom of Israel from you today and has given it to someone else— one who is better than you. And he who is the Glory of Israel will not lie, nor will he change his mind, for he is not human that he should change his mind!"

REFLECT

It's hard not to cringe as we see Samuel confronting Saul for disobeying God's clear instruction to destroy completely the Amalekites, a people who rejected God, opposed the Israelites, and generally terrorized other nations. Saul tried to rationalize his disobedience by blaming his soldiers and redefining God's command. His attempt at repentance fell on deaf ears because what he really cared about was saving face with the people, not being restored to relationship with God. We are not strangers to this strategy. When we disobey God, whether knowingly or not, our first response is rarely repentance. We want to defend and deflect out of pride or fear or simple stubbornness.

- What do you notice about Saul's response when Samuel calls him out on his failure to obey God's command? When has someone called you out on a failure to obey God? How did that feel?

- Why is obedience to God's Word and ways important?

- Reflect on a time when you have disregarded God's ways—whether intentionally or not—and then sought to rationalize your conduct by defending yourself or deflecting blame. What do you think was motivating you? What do you think God desires in these circumstances?

RESPOND_____

Father, thank you for being a loving Father and providing a way to you through Jesus Christ despite all my disobedience and waywardness. Help me to follow you, and remind me that your Word and ways lead to life. Illuminate my disobedience or partial obedience, and by your grace, turn me back to you. Amen.

DAY 4

THIS IS THE ONE

a prayer to open   My Lord, my God, show me your heart. Ground me in your presence.
Draw me near and hold me close.

READ 1 SAMUEL 16:1-23 _____

Now the LORD said to Samuel, "You have mourned long enough for Saul. I have rejected him as king of Israel, so fill your flask with olive oil and go to Bethlehem. Find a man named Jesse who lives there, for I have selected one of his sons to be my king."

But Samuel asked, "How can I do that? If Saul hears about it, he will kill me."

"Take a heifer with you," the LORD replied, "and say that you have come to make a sacrifice to the LORD. Invite Jesse to the sacrifice, and I will show you which of his sons to anoint for me."

So Samuel did as the LORD instructed. When he arrived at Bethlehem, the elders of the town came trembling to meet him. "What's wrong?" they asked.

"Do you come in peace?"

"Yes," Samuel replied. "I have come to sacrifice to the LORD. Purify yourselves and come with me to the sacrifice." . . .

When they arrived, Samuel took one look at Eliab and thought, "Surely this is the LORD's anointed!"

But the LORD said to Samuel, "Don't judge by his appearance or height, for I have rejected him. The LORD doesn't see things the way you see them. People judge by outward appearance, but the LORD looks at the heart."

Then Jesse told his son Abinadab to step forward and walk in front of Samuel. But Samuel said, "This is not the one the LORD has chosen." Next Jesse summoned Shimea, but Samuel said, "Neither is this the one the LORD has chosen." In the same way all seven of Jesse's sons were presented to Samuel. But Samuel said to Jesse, "The LORD has not chosen any of these." Then Samuel asked, "Are these all the sons you have?"

"There is still the youngest," Jesse replied. "But he's out in the fields watching the sheep and goats."

"Send for him at once," Samuel said. "We will not sit down to eat until he arrives."

So Jesse sent for him. He was dark and handsome, with beautiful eyes.

And the LORD said, "This is the one; anoint him."

So as David stood there among his brothers, Samuel . . . anointed David with [olive] oil. And the Spirit of the LORD came powerfully upon David from that day on. . . .

Now the Spirit of the LORD had left Saul, and the LORD sent a tormenting spirit that filled him with depression and fear.

Some of Saul's servants said to him, "A tormenting spirit from God is troubling you. Let us find a good musician to play the harp whenever the tormenting spirit troubles you." . . .

"All right," Saul said. "Find me someone who plays well, and bring him here."

One of the servants said to Saul, "One of Jesse's sons from Bethlehem is a talented harp player. Not only that—he is a brave warrior, a man of war, and has good judgment. He is also a fine-looking young man, and the LORD is with him."

So Saul sent messengers to Jesse to say, "Send me your son David, the shepherd." Jesse responded by sending David to Saul. . . .

So David went to Saul and began serving him. Saul loved David very much, and David became his armor bearer. . . . Whenever the tormenting spirit from God troubled Saul, David would play the harp. Then Saul would feel better, and the tormenting spirit would go away.

REFLECT _____

In this passage, we meet David for the first time. He was the youngest of eight sons, and from the outside he looked far less kingly than any of his brothers. But God didn't look at his appearance or external attributes; he looked at the state of his heart and spoke these incredible words: "This is the one" (verse 12). David would become the standard against which all other kings and rulers in Israel's future would be measured. But as we'll see as we read on, David was not perfect. He made life-altering mistakes and life-ending choices. But there was something unique about his heart toward God that made him stand out and become a chosen instrument in God's hands for God's purposes.

- Identify all the characteristics used to describe David in this passage. Which ones stand out most?

- Who do you know that you would describe as having a heart for God? What causes you to describe them that way?

- What areas of your own heart seem misaligned with God? What is your prayer with respect to these particular areas?

RESPOND _____

Father, I long to be a person like David with a heart that beats for you. Examine the very depths of my soul and replace any darkness with your light, and any hatred with your love. Remove any stinginess or anger. Point out the ways I do not honor you with my thoughts. Transform my heart so that it is open and responsive to your Spirit. And use me to bring your love into the world. Amen.

IN THE NAME OF THE LORD 12-21

a prayer to open   My Lord, my God, show me your heart. Ground me in your presence.
Draw me near and hold me close.

READ 1 SAMUEL 17:32-53

"Don't worry about this Philistine," David told Saul. "I'll go fight him!"

"Don't be ridiculous!" Saul replied. "There's no way you can fight this Philistine and possibly win! You're only a boy, and he's been a man of war since his youth."

But David persisted. "I have been taking care of my father's sheep and goats," he said. "When a lion or a bear comes to steal a lamb from the flock, I go after it with a club and rescue the lamb from its mouth. . . . I have done this to both lions and bears, and I'll do it to this pagan Philistine, too, for he has defied the armies of the living God! The LORD who rescued me from the claws of the lion and the bear will rescue me from this Philistine!"

Saul finally consented. "All right, go ahead," he said. "And may the LORD be with you!"

Then Saul gave David his own armor. . . . David put it on, strapped the sword over it, and took a step or two to see what it was like, for he had never worn such things before.

"I can't go in these," he protested to Saul. "I'm not used to them." So David took them off again. He picked up five smooth stones from a stream and put them into his shepherd's bag. Then, armed only with his shepherd's staff and sling, he started across the valley to fight the Philistine.

Goliath walked out toward David with his shield bearer ahead of him, sneering in contempt. . . . "Am I a dog," he roared at David, "that you come at me with a stick? . . . Come over here, and I'll give your flesh to the birds and wild animals!" . . .

David replied to the Philistine, "You come to me with sword, spear, and javelin, but I come to you in the name of the LORD of Heaven's Armies—the God of the armies of Israel, whom you have defied. Today the LORD will conquer you, and I will kill you and cut off your head. And then I will give the dead bodies of your men to the birds and wild animals, and the whole world will know that there is a God in Israel! And everyone assembled here will know that the LORD rescues his people, but not with sword and spear. This is the LORD's battle, and he will give you to us!"

As Goliath moved closer to attack, David quickly ran out to meet him. Reaching into his shepherd's bag and taking out a stone, he hurled it with his sling and hit the Philistine in the forehead. . . . Goliath stumbled and fell face down on the ground.

So David triumphed over the Philistine with only a sling and a stone. . . . Then David ran over and pulled Goliath's sword from its sheath. David used it to kill him and cut off his head.

When the Philistines saw that their champion was dead, they turned and ran. Then the men of Israel and Judah gave a great shout of triumph and rushed after the Philistines. . . . The bodies of the dead and wounded Philistines were strewn all along the road. . . . Then the Israelite army returned and plundered the deserted Philistine camp.

REFLECT

Most of us have heard this story many times: A young shepherd boy slays the giant Goliath with a mere slingshot! We've learned to cheer on the underdog and be courageous in the face of insurmountable obstacles. But a closer look at this passage gives us a glimpse of the heart God saw in David. David's profound faith in God compelled him to take on Goliath when even Saul—the tall, handsome, and fully armored king—was paralyzed with fear. And God reveals his presence and power through his faithful servant David.

• What do you see in David that motivated him to defeat Goliath?

Grounded

•

- What is one obstacle you're currently facing? What role does your faith in God play as you consider overcoming or pushing through that obstacle?
- How do you typically respond to fear?

RESPOND

Father, grow my faith in you so I can act boldly and bravely. Help me remember your presence and provision in my life. Remind me, in the midst of fear, of your faithfulness and love. Give me eyes to see your hand at work in the world and the wisdom to rely on your strength instead of my own. And may my heart remain attached to you in victory and defeat. Amen.

DAY 6

THE LORD WAS WITH DAVID 12^{-22}

a prayer to open   My Lord, my God, show me your heart. Ground me in your presence. Draw me near and hold me close.

READ 1 SAMUEL 18:1-15

After David had finished talking with Saul, he met Jonathan, the king's son. There was an immediate bond between them, for Jonathan loved David. . . . And Jonathan made a solemn pact with David, because he loved him as he loved himself. . . .

Whatever Saul asked David to do, David did it successfully. So Saul made him a commander over the men of war, an appointment that was welcomed by the people and Saul's officers alike.

When the victorious Israelite army was returning home after David had killed the Philistine, women from all the towns of Israel came out to meet King Saul. They sang and danced for joy with tambourines and cymbals. This was their song:

"Saul has killed his thousands,
and David his ten thousands!"

This made Saul very angry. "What's this?" he said. "They credit David with ten thousands and me with only thousands. Next they'll be making him their king!" So from that time on Saul kept a jealous eye on David.

The very next day a tormenting spirit from God overwhelmed Saul, and he began to rave in his house like a madman. David was playing the harp, as he did each day. But Saul had a spear in his hand, and he suddenly hurled it at David, intending to pin him to the wall. But David escaped him twice.

Saul was then afraid of David, for the LORD was with David and had turned away from Saul. Finally, Saul sent him away and appointed him commander over 1,000 men, and David faithfully led his troops into battle.

David continued to succeed in everything he did, for the LORD was with him. When Saul recognized this, he became even more afraid of him.

REFLECT

David experienced the favor of God after stepping forward in faith to defeat Goliath. He won the loyalty, trust, and love of not only the Israelites but also Saul's own son and heir, Jonathan. Saul, on the other hand, descended into anger, jealousy, and fear and was overtaken by "a tormenting spirit from God" (verse 10) as a result of his disobedience. As the story continues, we will see the devastating impact fear and jealousy can have on a human heart. But in David we will see how love and trust in God act as powerful antidotes for fear and move us toward hope.

- What was at the heart of Saul's jealousy toward David?

- In what areas do you struggle with anger or jealousy? What fear underlies those feelings?

- Is there any anger, jealousy, or fear currently taking up space in your heart? What is one step you can take toward releasing those feelings?

RESPOND

Father, thank you for every blessing you have poured into my life. Help me release any fear that hides in my heart and triggers anger and jealousy. Heal the wounds that have created this fear and hindered my ability to follow you fully. Give me the courage to love generously and with a heart that believes the best about others. Lead me into hope and life. Amen.

DAY 7

A JEALOUS HEART n-23

a prayer to open   My Lord, my God, show me your heart. Ground me in your presence. Draw me near and hold me close.

READ 1 SAMUEL 18:17-29

One day Saul said to David, "I am ready to give you my older daughter, Merab, as your wife. But first you must prove yourself to be a real warrior by fighting the LORD's battles." For Saul thought, "I'll send him out against the Philistines and let them kill him rather than doing it myself."

"Who am I, and what is my family in Israel that I should be the king's son-in-law?" David exclaimed. "My father's family is nothing!" . . .

In the meantime, Saul's daughter Michal had fallen in love with David, and Saul was delighted when he heard about it. "Here's another chance to see him killed by the Philistines!" Saul said to himself. But to David he said, "Today you have a second chance to become my son-in-law!"

Then Saul told his men to say to David, "The king really likes you, and so do we. Why don't you accept the king's offer and become his son-in-law?"

When Saul's men said these things to David, he replied, "How can a poor man from a humble family afford the bride price for the daughter of a king?"

When Saul's men reported this back to the king, he told them, "Tell David that all I want for the bride price is 100 Philistine foreskins! Vengeance on my enemies is all I really want." But what Saul had in mind was that David would be killed in the fight.

David was delighted to accept the offer. . . . He and his men went out and killed 200 Philistines. Then David fulfilled the king's requirement by presenting all their foreskins to him. So Saul gave his daughter Michal to David to be his wife.

When Saul realized that the LORD was with David and how much his daughter Michal loved him, Saul became even more afraid of him.

REFLECT

As David's stature among God's people grew and he became more and more successful, Saul became obsessed with getting rid of him. Imagine the state of Saul's heart and mind as he devised schemes and manipulated his own family in order to eliminate his perceived enemy. Jealousy did to Saul what it so often does to us: It eats away at our hearts, affects our ability to reason, and eventually destroys us because of the way it influences our view of others.

- Based on Saul's actions and statements in this passage, what words would you use to describe the state of his heart?

- What words would you use to describe David based on today's Scripture?

- What happens in your relationship with God when you're preoccupied with vengeful or angry thoughts? How does he respond to you in the midst of your anger?

RESPOND

Father, I am so grateful that you see into the depths of my heart and that nothing is hidden from you. You know the ways I become preoccupied with negative thoughts. You know my envy, my lack of generosity, my fear. Forgive me, and please remind me of your unending love and your desire to transform my heart so that each day I grow into the person you made me to be. Amen.

DAY 8

DELIVER ME!   12-24

a prayer to open   My Lord, my God, show me your heart. Ground me in your presence. Draw me near and hold me close.

READ PSALM 59

Rescue me from my enemies, O God.
  Protect me from those who have come to
    destroy me....
They have set an ambush for me.
  Fierce enemies are out there waiting, LORD,
    though I have not sinned or offended them.
I have done nothing wrong,
  yet they prepare to attack me.
  Wake up! See what is happening and help
    me!
O LORD God of Heaven's Armies, the God of
    Israel,
  wake up and punish those hostile nations.
  Show no mercy to wicked traitors....
Listen to the filth that comes from their mouths;
  their words cut like swords.
  "After all, who can hear us?" they sneer.
But LORD, you laugh at them.
  You scoff at all the hostile nations.
You are my strength; I wait for you to rescue me,
  for you, O God, are my fortress.
In his unfailing love, my God will stand
    with me.

He will let me look down in triumph on all my
    enemies.
Don't kill them, for my people soon forget such
    lessons;
  stagger them with your power, and bring
    them to their knees,
  O Lord our shield.
Because of the sinful things they say,
  because of the evil that is on their lips,
let them be captured by their pride,
  their curses, and their lies.
Destroy them in your anger!
  Wipe them out completely!
Then the whole world will know
  that God reigns in Israel....
But as for me, I will sing about your power.
  Each morning I will sing with joy about your
    unfailing love.
For you have been my refuge,
  a place of safety when I am in distress.
O my Strength, to you I sing praises,
  for you, O God, are my refuge,
  the God who shows me unfailing love.

David wrote Psalm 59 during the time Saul was attempting to have him killed. David's prayer is directed less against Saul as a personal enemy and more against the enemies of God. By attempting to kill David, God's appointed king and progenitor of the coming Messiah, Saul was trying to thwart God's purposes. There seems no end to the ways we humans seek to thwart God's purposes, from the unseen sins we practice in our hearts and minds (such as deception, hatred, and lust) to the spectacular demonstrations of evil we experience in mass shootings and acts of terror. We all long to be delivered from the enemies of love and righteousness.

- What do you notice about God through reading this passage?

- When have you been accused of something you didn't do? What were your thoughts during that time? What kinds of conversations did you have with God?

- What does it mean for God to be your strength during times of trouble? What would it look like in your life?

RESPOND

Father, thank you for sending Jesus to rescue us from our sin and take on the wrath we deserve. Thank you that I can live in freedom and that you have promised to transform me into the likeness of Christ over the course of my life because I have received your gift of grace. My heart is open to your love. May your will be done. Amen.

DAY 9

FEAR REIGNITED $12-27$

a prayer to open   My Lord, my God, show me your heart. Ground me in your presence. Draw me near and hold me close.

READ 1 SAMUEL 19:1-18

Saul now urged his servants and his son Jonathan to assassinate David. But Jonathan, because of his strong affection for David, told him what his father was planning. "Tomorrow morning," he warned him, "you must find a hiding place out in the fields. I'll ask my father to go out there with me, and I'll talk to him about you. Then I'll tell you everything I can find out."

The next morning Jonathan spoke with his father about David, saying many good things about him. "The king must not sin against his servant David,"

Jonathan said. "He's never done anything to harm you. He has always helped you in any way he could. Have you forgotten about the time he risked his life to kill the Philistine giant and how the LORD brought a great victory to all Israel as a result? . . . Why should you murder an innocent man like David?" . . .

So Saul listened to Jonathan and vowed, "As surely as the LORD lives, David will not be killed."

Afterward Jonathan called David and told him what had happened. Then he brought David to Saul, and David served in the court as before. ·

War broke out again after that, and David led his troops against the Philistines. He attacked them with such fury that they all ran away.

But one day when Saul was sitting at home, with spear in hand, the tormenting spirit from the LORD suddenly came upon him again. As David played his harp, Saul hurled his spear at David. But David dodged out of the way, and leaving the spear stuck in the wall, he fled and escaped into the night.

Then Saul sent troops to watch David's house. They were told to kill David when he came out the next morning. But Michal, David's wife, warned him, "If you don't escape tonight, you will be dead by morning." So she helped him climb out through a window, and he fled and escaped. . . .

When the troops came to arrest David, she told them he was sick and couldn't get out of bed.

But Saul sent the troops back to get David. He ordered, "Bring him to me in his bed so I can kill him!" But when they came to carry David out, they discovered that it was only an idol in the bed with a cushion of goat's hair at its head.

"Why have you betrayed me like this and let my enemy escape?" Saul demanded of Michal.

"I had to," Michal replied. "He threatened to kill me if I didn't help him."

So David escaped and went to Ramah to see Samuel, and he told him all that Saul had done to him.

REFLECT_____

Saul's obsession with getting rid of David seems to have affected everyone around him, causing them to lie and manipulate their circumstances. Deception became the primary mode of operation for Saul's daughter Michal and his son Jonathan. But given Saul's persistence, authority, and ability to order David's death, it's hard to see what choice they had if they wanted to protect David. Fear drives us to become paranoid, skeptical, and self-protective. We alienate those around us and close our hearts to God's work. When we are overtaken by fear, may we remember the truth of his presence and provision.

- What reignited Saul's desire to kill David after Jonathan reconciled the two men and Saul took an oath that David would not be put to death?

- Reflect on a time you lied or manipulated a situation in order to protect someone else. How did that situation make you feel?

- How have you acted in a way that may have led others to lie or engage in unkind or sinful conduct? How do you feel about that situation now? What do you need to confess to God?

RESPOND_____

Father, thank you for the reminder in this passage of how much my conduct and attitudes can influence those around me. I pray that when I am tempted to lie or act in ways that are contrary to your will, you would bring the truth to my mind and heart. I pray that I would be attuned to your Spirit in the midst of difficult circumstances. By your grace, help me see and take the steps necessary to eradicate any conduct or attitudes that tempt any of my family, friends, or coworkers to sin. Amen.

A TRUSTED FRIEND 12-27

a prayer to open   My Lord, my God, show me your heart.   Ground me in your presence.
Draw me near and hold me close.

READ 1 SAMUEL 20:1-23

David now fled . . . and found Jonathan. "What have I done?" he exclaimed. "What is my crime? How have I offended your father that he is so determined to kill me?"

"That's not true!" Jonathan protested. "You're not going to die. He always tells me everything he's going to do, even the little things. I know my father wouldn't hide something like this from me. It just isn't so!"

Then David took an oath before Jonathan and said, "Your father knows perfectly well about our friendship, so he has said to himself, 'I won't tell Jonathan—why should I hurt him?' But I swear to you that I am only a step away from death!" . . .

"Tell me what I can do to help you," Jonathan exclaimed.

David replied, "Tomorrow we celebrate the new moon festival. I've always eaten with the king on this occasion, but tomorrow I'll hide in the field and stay there until the evening of the third day. If your father asks where I am, tell him I asked permission to go home to Bethlehem. . . . If he says, 'Fine!' you will know all is well. But if he is angry and loses his temper, you will know he is determined to kill me. Show me this loyalty as my sworn friend—for we made a solemn pact before the LORD—or kill me yourself if I have sinned against your father. But please don't betray me to him!"

"Never!" Jonathan exclaimed. "You know that if I had the slightest notion my father was planning to kill you, I would tell you at once."

Then David asked, "How will I know whether or not your father is angry?"

"Come out to the field with me," Jonathan replied. And they went out there together. Then Jonathan told David, "I promise by the LORD, the God of Israel, that by this time tomorrow, or the next day at the latest, I will talk to my father and let you know at once how he feels about you. If he speaks favorably about you, I will let you know. But if he is angry and wants you killed, may the LORD strike me and even kill me if I don't warn you so you can escape and live. May the LORD be with you as he used to be with my father. And may you treat me with the faithful love of the LORD as long as I live. But if I die, treat my family with this faithful love." . . .

So Jonathan made a solemn pact with David, saying, "May the LORD destroy all your enemies!" . . .

Then Jonathan said, . . . "The day after tomorrow, toward evening, go to the place where you hid before, and wait there by the stone pile. I will come out and shoot three arrows to the side of the stone pile as though I were shooting at a target. Then I will send a boy to bring the arrows back. If you hear me tell him, 'They're on this side,' then you will know, as surely as the LORD lives, that all is well, and there is no trouble. But if I tell him, 'Go farther—the arrows are still ahead of you,' then it will mean that you must leave immediately, for the LORD is sending you away. And may the LORD make us keep our promises to each other, for he has witnessed them."

REFLECT

After climbing out a window and running for his life, David must have begun to wonder whether he'd somehow gotten his wires crossed and was never intended to be Israel's next king after all. In fact, Jonathan was likely the only person he could trust. But what a gift Jonathan was. Through him, God reminded David that he was loved, that he wasn't alone, and that he indeed would be king. Sometimes we forget to open our eyes and see those around us as God's gifts.

• Imagine being in David's position. What might have been going on in his mind and heart? What might his prayers have been like?

Grounded

•

151

- Who is your most trusted friend? What is the biggest sacrifice that friend has made for you? What is the biggest sacrifice you have made for that friend?

- Identify three or four seasons in your life that were painful or difficult. Who were the people God blessed you with during those seasons?

RESPOND

Father, thank you for the way you remind me of your presence and love through other people. Thank you especially for the friends and acquaintances you have placed in my life during seasons of loneliness and pain. Use me to console others and extend your love during their times of difficulty. Give me eyes to see the lonely and the hurting, and courage to bring them comfort. Amen.

DAY 11

12-28

GO IN PEACE

a prayer to open   My Lord, my God, show me your heart. Ground me in your presence. Draw me near and hold me close.

READ 1 SAMUEL 20:24-42

When the new moon festival began . . . David's place was empty. Saul didn't say anything about it that day, for he said to himself, "Something must have made David ceremonially unclean." But when David's place was empty again the next day, Saul asked Jonathan, "Why hasn't the son of Jesse been here for the meal either yesterday or today?"

Jonathan replied, "David earnestly asked me if he could go to Bethlehem. He said, 'Please let me go, for we are having a family sacrifice. My brother demanded that I be there. So please let me get away to see my brothers.' That's why he isn't here at the king's table."

Saul boiled with rage at Jonathan. "You stupid son of a whore!" he swore at him. "Do you think I don't know that you want him to be king in your place? . . . As long as that son of Jesse is alive, you'll never be king. Now go and get him so I can kill him!"

"But why should he be put to death?" Jonathan asked his father. "What has he done?" Then Saul hurled his spear at Jonathan, intending to kill him. So at last Jonathan realized that his father was really determined to kill David.

Jonathan left the table in fierce anger and refused to eat on that second day of the festival, for he was crushed by his father's shameful behavior toward David.

The next morning . . . Jonathan went out into the field and took a young boy with him to gather his arrows. "Start running," he told the boy, "so you can find the arrows as I shoot them." So the boy ran, and Jonathan shot an arrow beyond him. When the boy had almost reached the arrow, Jonathan shouted, "The arrow is still ahead of you. Hurry, hurry, don't wait." So the boy quickly gathered up the arrows and ran back to his master. . . . Only Jonathan and David understood the signal. Then Jonathan gave his bow and arrows to the boy and told him to take them back to town.

As soon as the boy was gone, David came out from where he had been hiding near the stone pile. . . . Both of them were in tears as they embraced each other and said good-bye. . . .

At last Jonathan said to David, "Go in peace, for we have sworn loyalty to each other in the LORD's name. The LORD is the witness of a bond between us and our children forever."

Saul finally showed his true intentions at the feast table before all his guests. His extreme outburst against his own son must have created quite a scene. For David, Saul's anger meant exile and heartbreak. Not only would David have to live on the run, with no hope of reconciliation with his king, but he would also lose his best friend and confidant, Jonathan, who would have to remain with Saul and cut off contact with David. Yet Jonathan and David parted in peace and somehow, through their mutual love of God, remained connected to one another.

- What emotions must Jonathan have experienced as he sat with his father at the table, knowing the man would likely ask about David's whereabouts? What would the experience have been like for the others sitting at the table?

- What dinner parties or family gatherings have you attended where someone burst into a fit of anger or instigated a verbal or physical fight? How was it resolved? What has been the lasting impact?

- Have you had a relationship that ended based on circumstances beyond your control? How did you manage the pain? Where did you see God in the midst of that experience?

RESPOND

Father, thank you for friendships like that between David and Jonathan. Thank you for relationships that have touched my soul and brought me closer to you. Help me cherish the friends in my life and have the courage to tell them how much they mean to me. Show me how to be a better friend, one who seeks to honor you through my words and actions. Amen.

DAY 12

1 -6 - 2020

A HEART AFTER GOD'S WISDOM

a prayer to open   My Lord, my God, show me your heart. Ground me in your presence.
Draw me near and hold me close.

READ 1 SAMUEL 23:7-28

Saul soon learned that David was at Keilah. "Good!" he exclaimed. . . . "God has handed him over to me, for he has trapped himself in a walled town!" So Saul mobilized his entire army to . . . besiege David and his men.

But David learned of Saul's plan and told Abiathar the priest to bring the ephod and ask the LORD what he should do. Then David prayed, "O LORD, God of

Israel, I have heard that Saul is planning to come and destroy Keilah because I am here. Will the leaders of Keilah betray me to him? And will Saul actually come as I have heard? O LORD, God of Israel, please tell me."

And the LORD said, "He will come."

Again David asked, "Will the leaders of Keilah betray me and my men to Saul?"

And the LORD replied, "Yes, they will betray you."

So David and his men . . . left Keilah and began roaming the countryside. Word soon reached Saul that David had escaped. . . . David now stayed in the strongholds of the wilderness and in the hill country of Ziph. Saul hunted him day after day, but God didn't let Saul find him.

One day . . . David received the news that Saul was on the way to Ziph to search for him and kill him. Jonathan went to find David and encouraged him to stay strong in his faith in God. "Don't be afraid," Jonathan reassured him. "My father will never find you! You are going to be the king of Israel, and I will be next to you, as my father, Saul, is well aware." So the two of them renewed their solemn pact before the LORD. . . .

But now the men of Ziph went to Saul in Gibeah and betrayed David to him. "We know where David is hiding," they said. . . . "Come down whenever you're ready, O king, and we will catch him and hand him over to you!"

"The LORD bless you," Saul said. . . . "Go and check again to be sure of where he is staying and who has seen him there. . . . Then I'll go with you. And if he is in the area at all, I'll track him down, even if I have to search every hiding place in Judah!" So the men of Ziph returned home ahead of Saul.

Meanwhile, David and his men had moved into the wilderness. . . . When David heard that Saul and his men were searching for him, he went even farther into the wilderness to the great rock, and he remained there. . . . But Saul kept after him in the wilderness.

Saul and David were now on opposite sides of a mountain. Just as Saul and his men began to close in on David and his men, an urgent message reached Saul that the Philistines were raiding Israel again. So Saul quit chasing David and returned to fight the Philistines. Ever since that time, the place where David was camped has been called the Rock of Escape.

REFLECT

In this passage, Saul stopped seeking God's guidance entirely and was overtaken by his desire to murder David. Saul had relied on his own wisdom and failed to defend his people and defeat the Philistines. David, on the other hand, specifically sought God's will before acting, and God protected him. We have the same choice as Saul and David—God still speaks to his people today, communicating his will primarily through Scripture. Will we listen, or will we follow our own wisdom?

- Where do you see God's presence and intervention in this passage?

- How can you tell the difference between God's wisdom and your own? What most often motivates your wisdom in a situation?

- In what area of your life are you currently wanting to know God's will and wisdom? What are some steps you can take to seek clarity?

RESPOND

Father, I need your wisdom and guidance. So often I have relied on my own wisdom, motivated by my desires instead of yours. Please lead me in your ways and keep me attuned to your Spirit. Guide me as I make decisions and engage with my family and friends. Transform my heart and mind so I reflect Christ's love to the world. May your will be done in and through me. Amen.

YOU WILL SURELY BE KING

a prayer to open   My Lord, my God, show me your heart. Ground me in your presence. Draw me near and hold me close.

READ 1 SAMUEL 24:1-22

After Saul returned from fighting the Philistines, he was told that David had gone into the wilderness of En-gedi. So Saul chose 3,000 elite troops from all Israel and went to search for David and his men. . . .

Saul went into a cave to relieve himself. But as it happened, David and his men were hiding farther back in that very cave!

"Now's your opportunity!" David's men whispered to him. "Today the LORD is telling you, 'I will certainly put your enemy into your power, to do with as you wish.'" So David crept forward and cut off a piece of the hem of Saul's robe.

But then David's conscience began bothering him because he had cut Saul's robe. He said to his men, "The LORD forbid that I should do this to my lord the king. I shouldn't attack the LORD's anointed one, for the LORD himself has chosen him." So David restrained his men and did not let them kill Saul.

After Saul had left the cave and gone on his way, David came out and shouted after him, "My lord the king!" And when Saul looked around, David bowed low before him.

Then he shouted to Saul, "Why do you listen to the people who say I am trying to harm you? This very day you can see with your own eyes it isn't true. For the LORD placed you at my mercy back there in the cave. Some of my men told me to kill you, but I spared you. For I said, 'I will never harm the king—he

is the LORD's anointed one.' Look, my father, at what I have in my hand. It is a piece of the hem of your robe! I cut it off, but I didn't kill you. This proves that I am not trying to harm you and that I have not sinned against you, even though you have been hunting for me to kill me.

"May the LORD judge between us. Perhaps the LORD will punish you for what you are trying to do to me, but I will never harm you. As that old proverb says, 'From evil people come evil deeds.' So you can be sure I will never harm you. . . . May the LORD therefore judge which of us is right and punish the guilty one. He is my advocate, and he will rescue me!" . . .

When David had finished speaking, Saul called back, "Is that really you, my son David?" . . . And he said to David, "You are a better man than I am, for you have repaid me good for evil. Yes, you have been amazingly kind to me today, for when the LORD put me in a place where you could have killed me, you didn't do it. . . . May the LORD reward you well for the kindness you have shown me today. And now I realize that you are surely going to be king, and that the kingdom of Israel will flourish under your rule. Now swear to me by the LORD that when that happens you will not kill my family." . . .

So David promised this to Saul with an oath.

REFLECT

David could have stopped his life of running and hiding. He could have put to rest his constant fear of being killed. He could have taken the throne that rightfully belonged to him. The circumstances even suggested that God had delivered Saul into David's hands. But David chose to let Saul go. Such restraint is hard to imagine, given that David had been fleeing Saul's sword since the day he killed Goliath. But David's devotion to and trust in God compelled him not to take Saul's life or his throne. Those were matters to be left to God alone. How often we seek to fill his job description instead of our own. God invites us to release to him what is his and focus solely on what he's given us to do.

- Imagine being in David's position: in the cave with Saul, knowing you could finally stop living in fear and hiding in the forest, and being goaded to take action by the men who follow you. What thoughts would you have? How would you respond?

- When have you had an opportunity to grab your life by the reins but decided not to? What motivated you to not do so? Was it a desire not to be caught or break the rules? Was it a desire not to grieve your relationship with God but to choose to trust him instead? Is there a difference?

- What spiritual practices—prayer, reading and reflecting on Bible passages, worship, or others—help you grow in your devotion to and trust in God? Do you regularly incorporate these into your daily life? Why or why not?

RESPOND

Father, thank you for providing an example of what a devoted heart looks like. I long for my devotion to increase and for my trust in you to grow. You have only given me reasons to trust you, yet my heart can be overtaken so easily by fear and doubt. Remind me of your presence, and, by your grace and love, give me opportunities to know you more. Amen.

HOW THE MIGHTY HAVE FALLEN!

a prayer to open   My Lord, my God, show me your heart. Ground me in your presence. Draw me near and hold me close.

READ 2 SAMUEL 1:19-27

Your pride and joy, O Israel, lies dead on the hills!
  Oh, how the mighty heroes have fallen! . . .
O mountains of Gilboa,
  let there be no dew or rain upon you,
  nor fruitful fields producing offerings of grain.
For there the shield of the mighty heroes was defiled;
  the shield of Saul will no longer be anointed with oil.
The bow of Jonathan was powerful,
  and the sword of Saul did its mighty work.
They shed the blood of their enemies
  and pierced the bodies of mighty heroes.
How beloved and gracious were Saul and Jonathan!

They were together in life and in death.
They were swifter than eagles,
  stronger than lions.
O women of Israel, weep for Saul,
for he dressed you in luxurious scarlet clothing,
  in garments decorated with gold.
Oh, how the mighty heroes have fallen in battle!
Jonathan lies dead on the hills.
How I weep for you, my brother Jonathan!
  Oh, how much I loved you!
And your love for me was deep,
  deeper than the love of women!
Oh, how the mighty heroes have fallen!
  Stripped of their weapons, they lie dead.

After David spared Saul's life in the cave, he spent several more years on the run, sparing the king's life a second time and taking up residence among the Philistines. During this time, David continued to fight battles on behalf of God's people, even defeating the Amalekites along the way. However, the Philistines waged war against the Israelites and eventually caught up with Saul and his sons. They killed three of Saul's sons, including Jonathan. Saul was wounded critically and fell on his own sword to kill himself.

David's time to be king had finally arrived, yet he did not rejoice at Saul's death. Instead, David penned a beautiful, heart-wrenching lament for Saul, the LORD's anointed; for his beloved friend, Jonathan; and for the nation of Israel. May our love for God, like David's, translate to love even for our most persistent enemies.

- Think over Saul's life as we have traced it through this study. What was his biggest tragedy?

- What has been the greatest loss of your life? What was your grieving process like? Where did you see God in the midst of your pain?

- Where have you experienced God's faithfulness to his promises? How can you help yourself remember those seasons of faithfulness in the midst of doubt, suffering, and fear?

RESPOND

Father, thank you for your faithfulness. Thank you that your promises are true and that you are reliable and trustworthy. Help me remember the ways you have been faithful in my life and throughout history, especially when I suffer loss or when I doubt your goodness and presence. Give me the courage and strength to follow Jesus all of my days, and by your grace, set me on the right path when I stray. Amen.

DAY 15

A PROMISE FULFILLED

a prayer to open   My Lord, my God, show me your heart. Ground me in your presence. Draw me near and hold me close.

READ 2 SAMUEL 2:1-7; 5:1-13

After this, David asked the LORD, "Should I move back to one of the towns of Judah?"

"Yes," the LORD replied.

Then David asked, "Which town should I go to?"

"To Hebron," the LORD answered. . . .

So David and his wives and his men and their

Grounded

•

families all moved to Judah, and they settled in the villages near Hebron. Then the men of Judah came to David and anointed him king over the people of Judah.

When David heard that the men of Jabesh-gilead had buried Saul, he sent them this message: "May the LORD bless you for being so loyal to your master Saul and giving him a decent burial. May the LORD be loyal to you in return and reward you with his unfailing love! And I, too, will reward you for what you have done. Now that Saul is dead, I ask you to be my strong and loyal subjects like the people of Judah, who have anointed me as their new king." . . .

Then all the tribes of Israel went to David at Hebron and told him, "We are your own flesh and blood. In the past, when Saul was our king, you were the one who really led the forces of Israel. And the LORD told you, 'You will be the shepherd of my people Israel.'" . . .

King David made a covenant before the LORD with all the elders of Israel. And they anointed him king of Israel.

David was thirty years old when he began to reign, and he reigned forty years in all. He had reigned over Judah from Hebron for seven years and six months, and from Jerusalem he reigned over all Israel and Judah for thirty-three years.

David then led his men to Jerusalem to fight against the Jebusites. . . . The Jebusites taunted David, saying, "You'll never get in here! Even the blind and lame could keep you out!" . . . But David captured the fortress of Zion. . . .

David made the fortress his home, and he called it the City of David. . . . And David became more and more powerful, because the LORD God of Heaven's Armies was with him.

Then King Hiram of Tyre sent messengers to David, along with cedar timber and carpenters and stonemasons, and they built David a palace. And David realized that the LORD had confirmed him as king over Israel and had blessed his kingdom for the sake of his people Israel. . . .

David married more concubines and wives, and they had more sons and daughters.

REFLECT

When Abraham, the founding father of the nation of Israel, and his wife, Sarah, were in their nineties and childless, God promised them, "I will make you very fruitful; I will make nations of you, and kings will come from you" (Genesis 17:6, NIV). When Abraham's descendant David became king centuries later, God's promise began to be fulfilled.

- What kind of emotion is stirred in you as you reflect on the fulfillment of God's promise to Abraham?

- Up to this point in the story of David, we see David as a man who seeks God's will and then obeys his instructions. When have you known God's will but decided to disobey his direction? What caused you to act as you did? How did your actions affect your relationships with God and with others?

- How do you seek to determine God's will and guidance for your life?

RESPOND

Father, thank you for keeping your promises. Thank you that you remain faithful even when I am unfaithful to you. I stand in awe of your goodness and love. Create in me a heart that seeks your will, asks for your guidance, and then has the fortitude and courage to obey even in the face of obstacles and fear. Help me stay attuned to your voice and keep my eyes fixed on you. Amen.

A FOREVER KINGDOM

a prayer to open   My Lord, my God, show me your heart.   Ground me in your presence.
Draw me near and hold me close.

READ 2 SAMUEL 7:1-16

When King David was settled in his palace and the LORD had given him rest from all the surrounding enemies, the king summoned Nathan the prophet. "Look," David said, "I am living in a beautiful cedar palace, but the Ark of God is out there in a tent!"

Nathan replied to the king, "Go ahead and do whatever you have in mind, for the LORD is with you."

But that same night the LORD said to Nathan,

"Go and tell my servant David, 'This is what the LORD has declared: Are you the one to build a house for me to live in? I have never lived in a house, from the day I brought the Israelites out of Egypt until this very day. . . . Yet no matter where I have gone with the Israelites, I have never once complained to . . . the shepherds of my people Israel.'" . . .

"Now go and say to my servant David, 'This is what the LORD of Heaven's Armies has declared: I took you from tending sheep in the pasture and selected you to be the leader of my people Israel. I have been with you wherever you have gone, and I

have destroyed all your enemies before your eyes. Now I will make your name as famous as anyone who has ever lived on the earth! And I will provide a homeland for my people Israel, planting them in a secure place where they will never be disturbed. Evil nations won't oppress them as they've done in the past, starting from the time I appointed judges to rule my people Israel. And I will give you rest from all your enemies.

"'Furthermore, the LORD declares that he will make a house for you—a dynasty of kings! . . . I will raise up one of your descendants, your own offspring, and I will make his kingdom strong. . . . I will secure his royal throne forever. I will be his father, and he will be my son. If he sins, I will correct and discipline him with the rod, like any father would do. But my favor will not be taken from him as I took it from Saul, whom I removed from your sight. Your house and your kingdom will continue before me for all time, and your throne will be secure forever.'"

REFLECT

In this passage, we see God's sweeping promises to David and the Israelite people—promises that went far beyond what David could have imagined. God promised not only that a son of David would build him a house but that David's kingdom would endure forever. In this way, God foreshadowed the coming King, Jesus—the son of David and son of Abraham (see Matthew 1:1), who will reign forever.

- How might David have felt when God rejected his plan to build him a temple?

- Do you ever find yourself believing that someone else's calling is worthier or grander than yours? How does comparing yourself to that person make you feel?

- What has God uniquely called you to be and do? When you are feeling disappointed about your contributions in this world, who in your life can help affirm your talents and gifts?

Grounded

•

Father, thank you for your promises to David and your promise that Jesus Christ will reign as King forever. Thank you for the ways you have gifted me uniquely to serve you. When I compare myself to others, remind me who you made me to be and what you've called me to do. Please give me the presence of mind to affirm others for the ways you have made and gifted them. Amen.

DAY 17

THE LORD'S GREAT LOVE

a prayer to open   My Lord, my God, show me your heart.   Ground me in your presence.
Draw me near and hold me close.

READ PSALM 89:1-18, 28-37

I will sing of the LORD's unfailing love forever!
Young and old will hear of your faithfulness.
Your unfailing love will last forever.
Your faithfulness is as enduring as the heavens.
The LORD said, "I have made a covenant with David, my chosen servant.
I have sworn this oath to him:
'I will establish your descendants as kings forever;
they will sit on your throne from now until eternity.'"
All heaven will praise your great wonders, LORD;
myriads of angels will praise you for your faithfulness.
For who in all of heaven can compare with the LORD?
What mightiest angel is anything like the LORD? . . .
O LORD God of Heaven's Armies!
Where is there anyone as mighty as you, O LORD?
You are entirely faithful.
You rule the oceans.
You subdue their storm-tossed waves.
You crushed the great sea monster.
You scattered your enemies with your mighty arm.
The heavens are yours, and the earth is yours;
everything in the world is yours—you created it all. . . .
Powerful is your arm!
Strong is your hand!
Your right hand is lifted high in glorious strength.

Righteousness and justice are the foundation of your throne.
Unfailing love and truth walk before you as attendants.
Happy are those who hear the joyful call to worship,
for they will walk in the light of your presence, LORD.
They rejoice all day long in your wonderful reputation.
They exult in your righteousness.
You are their glorious strength.
It pleases you to make us strong.
Yes, our protection comes from the LORD,
and he, the Holy One of Israel, has given us our king. . . .
"I will love him and be kind to him forever;
my covenant with him will never end.
I will preserve an heir for him;
his throne will be as endless as the days of heaven.
But if his descendants forsake my instructions and fail to obey my regulations, . . .
then I will punish their sin with the rod,
and their disobedience with beating.
But I will never stop loving him
nor fail to keep my promise to him. . . .
I have sworn an oath to David,
and in my holiness I cannot lie:
His dynasty will go on forever;
his kingdom will endure as the sun.
It will be as eternal as the moon,
my faithful witness in the sky!"

Scholars believe that this psalm was written by a musician who lived during David's reign. It confirms what has come to be known as the Davidic covenant, or God's promise to David (see 2 Samuel 7:11-16), which states that the Messiah would come from David's line and the tribe of Judah and establish a Kingdom that would last forever. In the midst of uncertainty and despair, the psalmist holds on to what he knows is true: God keeps his promises. Even when we don't see a clear path to what he has promised, we can trust in his faithfulness.

- What does it mean to you that God is faithful to his promises? How have you experienced his faithfulness? How might you share with others the story of God's faithfulness in your life?

- In verse 15, we read that those who "walk in the light of" God's presence are blessed. What does it mean to walk in the light of God's presence?

- Reflect on a time that you have felt uncertain or confused about your future. What promises of God were you (or are you) relying on?

RESPOND

Use Psalm 89:1-18 as a prayer for today.

DAY 18

TEMPTATION STRIKES

a prayer to open   My Lord, my God, show me your heart. Ground me in your presence. Draw me near and hold me close.

READ 2 SAMUEL 11:1-17

In the spring . . . when kings normally go out to war, David sent Joab and the Israelite army to fight the Ammonites. . . . However, David stayed behind in Jerusalem.

Late one afternoon . . . David got out of bed and was walking on the roof of the palace. As he looked out over the city, he noticed a woman of unusual beauty taking a bath. He sent someone to find out who she was, and he was told, "She is Bathsheba, the daughter of Eliam and the wife of Uriah the Hittite." Then David sent messengers to get her; and when she came to the palace, he slept with her. . . . Then she returned home. Later, when Bathsheba discovered that she was pregnant, she sent David a message, saying, "I'm pregnant."

Then David sent word to Joab: "Send me Uriah the Hittite." So Joab sent him to David. When Uriah arrived, David asked him how Joab and the army were getting along and how the war was progressing. Then he told Uriah, "Go on home and relax." David even sent a gift to Uriah after he had left the palace. But Uriah didn't go home. He slept that night at the palace entrance with the king's palace guard.

When David heard that Uriah had not gone home, he summoned him and asked, "What's the matter?

Grounded

•

161

Why didn't you go home last night after being away for so long?"

Uriah replied, "The Ark and the armies of Israel and Judah are living in tents, and Joab and my master's men are camping in the open fields. How could I go home to wine and dine and sleep with my wife? I swear that I would never do such a thing."

"Well, stay here today," David told him, "and tomorrow you may return to the army." So Uriah stayed in Jerusalem that day and the next. But . . .

again he slept at the palace entrance with the king's palace guard.

So the next morning David wrote a letter to Joab and gave it to Uriah to deliver. The letter instructed Joab, "Station Uriah on the front lines where the battle is fiercest. Then pull back so that he will be killed." So . . . when the enemy soldiers came out of the city to fight, Uriah the Hittite was killed along with several other Israelite soldiers.

REFLECT

Up to this point in David's life, he seemed perfect and invincible. But now we see that he was a flawed man, prone—just like the rest of us—to wander away from God's path and toward lust, abuse of power, deception, and self-preservation. However, as this story unfolds, we'll notice that David's relationship with God and his deep understanding of God's love and mercy always drew him back to God in repentance.

- Before sleeping with Bathsheba, David made a series of decisions that enabled his sin. What were they?

- What is the greatest temptation you face? What kinds of decisions make you more likely to give in to your temptations?

- When was the last time you gave in to a temptation? How did you experience God in the midst of that temptation?

RESPOND

Father, thank you for the mercy and grace you offer through Jesus Christ. I need strength in the midst of temptation. My desire is to honor you with my mind, my body, and my words, yet so often I turn to relationships, substances, or other things out of fear, lack of trust, or loneliness. Help me identify the things that set me up for giving in to temptation and turn me away from you. May I see you in the midst of my temptation and sin and, in your mercy and grace, turn my heart back to you. Amen.

DAY 19

I HAVE SINNED AGAINST THE LORD

a prayer to open   My Lord, my God, show me your heart. Ground me in your presence.
Draw me near and hold me close.

The LORD sent Nathan the prophet to tell David this story: "There were two men in a certain town. One was rich, and one was poor. The rich man owned a great many sheep and cattle. The poor man owned nothing but one little lamb he had bought. He raised that little lamb, and it grew up with his children. It ate from the man's own plate and drank from his cup. . . . One day a guest arrived at the home of the rich man. But instead of killing an animal from his own flock or herd, he took the poor man's lamb and killed it and prepared it for his guest."

David was furious. "As surely as the LORD lives," he vowed, "any man who would do such a thing deserves to die! He must repay four lambs to the poor man for the one he stole and for having no pity."

Then Nathan said to David, "You are that man! The LORD, the God of Israel, says: I anointed you king of Israel and saved you from the power of Saul. . . . I would have given you much, much more. Why, then, have you despised the word of the LORD and done this horrible deed? For you have murdered Uriah the Hittite . . . and stolen his wife. From this time on, your family will live by the sword because you have despised me. . . .

"This is what the LORD says: Because of what you have done, I will cause your own household to rebel against you. I will give your wives to another man before your very eyes, and he will go to bed with them in public view. You did it secretly, but I will make this happen to you openly in the sight of all Israel."

Then David confessed to Nathan, "I have sinned against the LORD."

Nathan replied, "Yes, but the LORD has forgiven you, and you won't die for this sin. Nevertheless, because you have shown utter contempt for the word of the LORD . . . your child will die."

After Nathan returned to his home, the LORD sent a deadly illness to the child of David and Uriah's wife. David begged God to spare the child. He went without food and lay all night on the bare ground. . . .

Then on the seventh day the child died. David's advisers were afraid to tell him. . . . "What drastic thing will he do when we tell him the child is dead?"

When David saw them whispering, he realized what had happened. "Is the child dead?" he asked.

"Yes," they replied, "he is dead."

Then David got up from the ground, washed himself, put on lotions, and changed his clothes. He went to the Tabernacle and worshiped the LORD. After that, he returned to the palace and was served food and ate.

His advisers were amazed. "We don't understand you," they told him. "While the child was still living, you wept and refused to eat. But now that the child is dead, you have stopped your mourning and are eating again."

David replied, "I fasted and wept while the child was alive, for I said, 'Perhaps the LORD will be gracious to me and let the child live.' But why should I fast when he is dead? Can I bring him back again? I will go to him one day, but he cannot return to me."

Then David comforted Bathsheba, his wife. . . . She became pregnant and gave birth to a son, and David named him Solomon. The LORD loved the child and sent word through Nathan the prophet that they should name him Jedidiah (which means "beloved of the LORD"), as the LORD had commanded.

REFLECT

We never learn much about Nathan, but we see by his words and authority that he was a prophet who spoke on God's behalf. Nathan's use of a parable—especially one that would have struck a chord with a former shepherd and helped him see his own sinfulness—was obviously God-directed. It would have been dangerous for Nathan to call the king out on his extreme and violent conduct directly, so leading David to condemn himself was the only way. We can be so defensive and self-justifying that sometimes we simply cannot hear truth that comes head on. We need someone to tell us that truth in an indirect way that gets around our defenses.

• How did David respond when he realized he was the man in Nathan's parable? What did Nathan say on God's behalf in response?

- When has someone told you a truth that was hard to hear? How did you receive that truth? What was your response?
- When have you suffered the consequences of your own wrongdoing? What were those consequences? How did you handle them?

RESPOND

Father, thank you for truth tellers. Please bring them into my life and give me ears to hear what they have to say. When someone points out my wrongdoing, help me respond as David did: with a truly repentant heart that desires to be restored and transformed. Help me see your love and correction in the midst of the consequences of my sin, and give me the ability to continue to grow in my devotion to you. Amen.

DAY 20

HAVE MERCY ON ME!

a prayer to open My Lord, my God, show me your heart. Ground me in your presence. Draw me near and hold me close.

READ PSALM 51:1-17

Have mercy on me, O God,
  because of your unfailing love.
Because of your great compassion,
  blot out the stain of my sins.
Wash me clean from my guilt.
  Purify me from my sin.
For I recognize my rebellion;
  it haunts me day and night.
Against you, and you alone, have I sinned;
  I have done what is evil in your sight.
You will be proved right in what you say,
  and your judgment against me is just.
For I was born a sinner—
  yes, from the moment my mother
    conceived me.
But you desire honesty from the womb,
  teaching me wisdom even there.
Purify me from my sins, and I will be clean;
  wash me, and I will be whiter than snow.
Oh, give me back my joy again;
  you have broken me—
  now let me rejoice.

Don't keep looking at my sins.
  Remove the stain of my guilt.
Create in me a clean heart, O God.
  Renew a loyal spirit within me.
Do not banish me from your presence,
  and don't take your Holy Spirit from me.
Restore to me the joy of your salvation,
  and make me willing to obey you.
Then I will teach your ways to rebels,
  and they will return to you.
Forgive me for shedding blood, O God who
    saves;
  then I will joyfully sing of your forgiveness.
Unseal my lips, O Lord,
  that my mouth may praise you.
You do not desire a sacrifice, or I would
    offer one.
  You do not want a burnt offering.
The sacrifice you desire is a broken spirit.
  You will not reject a broken and repentant
    heart, O God.

David's song of repentance in Psalm 51 is beautiful not only in the way it displays David's heart toward God but also in the way it can deepen and expand our understanding of who God is. David is confident that based on his contrite heart, God will cleanse him, purify his heart, and renew his desire to follow God's ways. Oh that we could have this same confidence—that whenever we stray or rebel, we would return to God, knowing that he is good and will cleanse us and give us new strength to follow him.

- What phrase in this psalm most stands out to you? Why?

- Based on this passage, what must you do to receive God's forgiveness?

- Is there a wrongdoing you have committed that you feel God won't forgive? What parts of this psalm give you confidence that he will forgive you when you repent?

RESPOND

Father, thank you for the truth of the words in David's song of repentance. Bring to mind any wrongdoing for which I have not truly repented, and help me seek your forgiveness wholeheartedly. Purify my heart and renew my desire to follow you with my whole self: my heart, mind, soul, and strength. Remind me of your unending love and compassion when I fail. May my lips always praise you. Amen.

DAY 21

BETRAYAL!

a prayer to open   My Lord, my God, show me your heart. Ground me in your presence.
Draw me near and hold me close.

READ 2 SAMUEL 15:1-16

Absalom bought a chariot and horses, and he hired fifty bodyguards to run ahead of him. He got up early every morning and went out to the gate of the city. When people brought a case to the king for judgment, . . . Absalom would say, "You've really got a strong case here! It's too bad the king doesn't have anyone to hear it. I wish I were the judge. Then everyone could bring their cases to me for judgment, and I would give them justice!"

When people tried to bow before him, Absalom wouldn't let them. Instead, he took them by the hand and kissed them, . . . and so he stole the hearts of all the people of Israel.

After four years, Absalom said to the king, "Let me go to Hebron to offer a sacrifice to the LORD and fulfill a vow I made to him. . . . I promised to sacrifice to the LORD in Hebron if he would bring me back to Jerusalem."

"All right," the king told him. "Go and fulfill your vow."

While he was [in Hebron], he sent secret messengers to all the tribes of Israel to stir up a rebellion against the king. "As soon as you hear the ram's horn," his message read, "you are to say, 'Absalom has been crowned king in Hebron.'" He took 200 men from Jerusalem with him as guests, but

Grounded

•

165

they knew nothing of his intentions. While Absalom was offering the sacrifices, he sent for Ahithophel, one of David's counselors. . . . Soon many others also joined Absalom. . . .

A messenger soon arrived in Jerusalem to tell David, "All Israel has joined Absalom in a conspiracy against you!"

"Then we must flee at once, or it will be too late!" David urged his men. "Hurry! If we get out of the city before Absalom arrives, both we and the city of Jerusalem will be spared from disaster."

"We are with you," his advisers replied. "Do what you think is best."

So the king and all his household set out at once. He left no one behind except ten of his concubines to look after the palace.

REFLECT

Not long after David slept with Bathsheba and had her husband, Uriah, killed, David and his family began to suffer for his sin, just as Nathan had prophesied in 2 Samuel 12:10-12. David's son Amnon raped David's daughter, Tamar. When David failed to take any action, David's son Absalom killed Amnon and was forced into exile. When Absalom finally returned three years later, David welcomed him back and Absalom began conspiring to take his father's throne. So often we think our sin is merely personal and that no one will get hurt by the things we do in private, but as we see in David's life, sin has a way of wreaking havoc in ways we never intended. Although God is faithful to forgive—and in Christ we are forgiven and freed from the ultimate consequences of sin—the earthly consequences can still be devastating.

- What did Absalom do to slowly gain followers and turn people against David?

- Have you ever had someone betray you? How did it make you feel? How did you respond to that person?

- Have you ever betrayed someone? What led you to do what you did? What consequences of that betrayal did you experience?

RESPOND

Father, thank you that you are trustworthy and that your promises are true. Help me reflect your faithfulness in the world and fulfill the promises I have made to the people in my life. For those I have betrayed in some way, please forgive me and give me the courage to seek their forgiveness. When I am betrayed, allow my heart to be filled with grace and the willingness to reconcile. Amen.

DAVID WEPT

a prayer to open   My Lord, my God, show me your heart.   Ground me in your presence.
Draw me near and hold me close.

READ 2 SAMUEL 15:23-36

Everyone cried loudly as the king and his followers passed by. . . . Zadok and all the Levites also came along, carrying the Ark of the Covenant of God. . . .

Then the king instructed Zadok to take the Ark of God back into the city. "If the LORD sees fit," David said, "he will bring me back to see the Ark and the Tabernacle again. But if he is through with me, then let him do what seems best to him."

The king also told Zadok the priest, "Look, here is my plan. You and Abiathar should return quietly to the city with your son Ahimaaz and Abiathar's son Jonathan. I will stop at the shallows of the Jordan River and wait there for a report from you." . . .

David walked up the road to the Mount of Olives, weeping as he went. His head was covered and his feet were bare as a sign of mourning. And the people who were with him covered their heads and wept as they climbed the hill. When someone told David that his adviser Ahithophel was now backing Absalom, David prayed, "O LORD, let Ahithophel give Absalom foolish advice!"

When David reached the summit of the Mount of Olives where people worshiped God, Hushai the Arkite was waiting there for him. Hushai had torn his clothing and put dirt on his head as a sign of mourning. But David told him, "If you go with me, you will only be a burden. Return to Jerusalem and tell Absalom, 'I will now be your adviser, O king, just as I was your father's adviser in the past.' Then you can frustrate and counter Ahithophel's advice. Zadok and Abiathar, the priests, will be there. Tell them about the plans being made in the king's palace, and they will send their sons Ahimaaz and Jonathan to tell me what is going on."

REFLECT

David was betrayed not only by his son Absalom but also by his trusted adviser Ahithophel. As he fled Jerusalem to escape these coconspirators, David must have been grieving about returning to a life on the run, wondering what would become of his kingdom and God's promise that it would endure forever. Indeed, there is nothing quite like betrayal to cause us to doubt ourselves and God's presence and provision in our lives.

• Why did David weep as he walked up the Mount of Olives?

• What situation in your life do you need to release to God's care and ask him, as David did, to do whatever seems good to him?

• Is there anyone in your life who has been betrayed by a spouse, friend, or colleague? How might you reach out to listen to that person's story and empathize with the pain he or she has experienced?

RESPOND

Father, there is so much betrayal and heartbreak in the world. Help me be a person who can be trusted, keeps promises, and remains faithful. I surrender, as best I can, every part of my life to you. Do with my life whatever seems good in your eyes. Help me be an empathetic listening ear to the hurting and betrayed. Amen.

A LORD WHO INTERVENES

a prayer to open   My Lord, my God, show me your heart. Ground me in your presence.
Draw me near and hold me close.

READ 2 SAMUEL 16:15-23

Meanwhile, Absalom and all the army of Israel arrived at Jerusalem. . . . When David's friend Hushai the Arkite arrived, he went immediately to see Absalom. "Long live the king!" he exclaimed. . . .

"Is this the way you treat your friend David?" Absalom asked him. "Why aren't you with him?"

"I'm here because I belong to the man who is chosen by the LORD and by all the men of Israel," Hushai replied. "And anyway, why shouldn't I serve you?" . . .

Then Absalom turned to Ahithophel and asked him, "What should I do next?"

Ahithophel told him, "Go and sleep with your father's concubines. . . . Then all Israel will know that you have insulted your father beyond hope of reconciliation, and they will throw their support to you." So they set up a tent on the palace roof where everyone could see it, and Absalom went in and had sex with his father's concubines.

Absalom followed Ahithophel's advice, just as David had done.

REFLECT

In this scene, we see God intervene to save David's life by answering his prayer that Ahithophel's advice be turned to foolishness (see 2 Samuel 15:31). Such a contrast between David and Saul! Both were leaders who committed wrongdoings, but Saul defended, justified, and blamed; David repented. As a result, God did not abandon him as king and protected him from his enemies, ensuring that David's reign would continue as promised. God is quick to forgive when we turn to him, but so often we act like Saul instead of like David.

- Why did Absalom respond to Hushai's pledge of loyalty as he did?

- What must it have been like to be in Hushai's position—falsely pledging his loyalty to Absalom, giving advice that was contrary to the trusted Ahithophel, and sneaking around to make sure David got the news about what Absalom was planning?

- When has God intervened to protect you? What happened?

RESPOND

Father, thank you for all the times you have protected me. I am so grateful that you are a God who intervenes when I am in trouble and walks with me in the midst of my pain. Thank you for your presence in the midst of betrayal, heartache, and sorrow. Use me to advance your plans in this world and to be a help to those praying for relief and solace for their suffering. Amen.

I CALL OUT TO THE LORD

a prayer to open   My Lord, my God, show me your heart. Ground me in your presence.
Draw me near and hold me close.

READ PSALM 3

O LORD, I have so many enemies;
  so many are against me.
So many are saying,
  "God will never rescue him!"
But you, O LORD, are a shield around me;
  you are my glory, the one who holds my head
    high.
I cried out to the LORD,
  and he answered me from his holy mountain.
I lay down and slept,

yet I woke up in safety,
  for the LORD was watching over me.
I am not afraid of ten thousand enemies
  who surround me on every side.
Arise, O LORD!
  Rescue me, my God!
Slap all my enemies in the face!
  Shatter the teeth of the wicked!
Victory comes from you, O LORD.
  May you bless your people.

REFLECT

David wrote this psalm when he was running for his life and surrounded by men loyal to his son Absalom. David's men were outnumbered and being chased, and things looked hopeless. Yet David's faith sustained him and he remained confident that God would deliver him from his enemies. Oh that we could remain confident in God's promises when everything seems to be falling apart and we can't see any light in the darkness.

• Consider a time when you felt surrounded on all sides by enemies (whether people or circumstances). How did you respond? How did you experience God during that time?

• What spiritual practices can help you build your faith during seasons of calm in order to prepare you for times of unrest? Which of these practices can you incorporate into your daily routine?

• Who do you know to be struggling or feeling overwhelmed in some way? How might you be able to encourage that individual in their faith this week?

RESPOND

Father, thank you for David and his example of faith in the midst of chaos and unrest. Strengthen my faith and grow my desire to meet with you each day so I can know you more and experience your power and presence. Protect me from enemies who try to pull me away from you and deter me from your plans for my life. Give me the words and presence of mind to encourage others in their faith this week. Amen.

MY SON, MY SON!

a prayer to open   My Lord, my God, show me your heart. Ground me in your presence.
Draw me near and hold me close.

READ 2 SAMUEL 18:14-33

"Enough of this nonsense," Joab said. Then he took three daggers and plunged them into Absalom's heart as he dangled, still alive, in the great tree. Ten of Joab's young armor bearers then surrounded Absalom and killed him.

Then Joab blew the ram's horn, and his men returned from chasing the army of Israel. They threw Absalom's body into a deep pit . . . and piled a great heap of stones over it. And all Israel fled to their homes.

During his lifetime, Absalom had built a monument to himself in the King's Valley, for he said, "I have no son to carry on my name." He named the monument after himself, and it is known as Absalom's Monument to this day.

Then Zadok's son Ahimaaz said, "Let me run to the king with the good news that the LORD has rescued him from his enemies."

"No," Joab told him, "it wouldn't be good news to the king that his son is dead. You can be my messenger another time, but not today."

Then Joab said to a man from Ethiopia, "Go tell the king what you have seen." The man bowed and ran off.

But Ahimaaz continued to plead with Joab, "Whatever happens, please let me go, too."

"Why should you go, my son?" Joab replied. "There will be no reward for your news."

"Yes, but let me go anyway," he begged.

Joab finally said, "All right, go ahead." . . .

While David was sitting between the inner and outer gates of the town, the watchman climbed to the roof of the gateway by the wall. As he looked, he saw a lone man running toward them. He shouted the news down to David, and the king replied, "If he is alone, he has news."

As the messenger came closer, the watchman saw another man running toward them. He shouted down, "Here comes another one!"

The king replied, "He also will have news."

"The first man runs like Ahimaaz son of Zadok," the watchman said.

"He is a good man and comes with good news," the king replied.

Then Ahimaaz cried out to the king, "Everything is all right!" He bowed before the king with his face to the ground and said, "Praise to the LORD your God, who has handed over the rebels who dared to stand against my lord the king."

"What about young Absalom?" the king demanded. "Is he all right?"

Ahimaaz replied, "When Joab told me to come, there was a lot of commotion. But I didn't know what was happening."

"Wait here," the king told him. So Ahimaaz stepped aside.

Then the man from Ethiopia arrived and said, "I have good news for my lord the king. Today the LORD has rescued you from all those who rebelled against you."

"What about young Absalom?" the king demanded. "Is he all right?"

And the Ethiopian replied, "May all of your enemies, my lord the king, both now and in the future, share the fate of that young man!"

The king was overcome with emotion. . . . He cried, "O my son Absalom! My son, my son Absalom! If only I had died instead of you! O Absalom, my son, my son."

REFLECT

Just before the scene in this passage, David had sent his troops to battle the army of Israel and ordered his men to be gentle with Absalom, the army's commander. David's troops were successful. They defeated the army—but they also killed Absalom. So from a king's perspective, David got everything he could have wanted: The coup had been defeated and his kingdom would be restored to him. But he'd lost his beloved son, and here we see a father with a broken heart. Despite the ways Absalom had betrayed him and sought to destroy him and his kingdom, David never disowned or turned his back on his son. He was a man with a heart for God's heart.

- Why was the monument Absalom built of himself mentioned in this particular part of the story?

- At the heart of Absalom's rebellion was a misuse of his power as the heir to the throne. When have you used, or been tempted to use, the power you had over someone else to get what you wanted? What were the consequences of your actions?

- Consider whatever power God has given you over others at your job, in your family, or among your friends. Is that power spiritual, financial, or relational? For what purpose do you believe God has given you such power? How do you guard against its misuse?

RESPOND

Father, forgive me for the times I have misused power you have entrusted to me. Help me use whatever power I have to honor you and build up others. Help me grow in humility and be on guard against allowing my pride to override what you seek to accomplish through me. Give me eyes to see the powerless and ears to hear how you are calling me to respond to them. Amen.

DAY 26

CRITICIZED AND INSULTED

a prayer to open   My Lord, my God, show me your heart. Ground me in your presence.
Draw me near and hold me close.

READ 2 SAMUEL 16:5-13

As King David came to Bahurim, a man came out of the village cursing them. It was Shimei son of Gera, from the same clan as Saul's family. . . . "Get out of here, you murderer, you scoundrel!" he shouted at David. "The LORD is paying you back for all the bloodshed in Saul's clan. You stole his throne, and now the LORD has given it to your son Absalom." . . .

"Why should this dead dog curse my lord the king?" Abishai son of Zeruiah demanded. "Let me go over and cut off his head!"

"No!" the king said. "Who asked your opinion! . . . If the LORD has told him to curse me, who are you to stop him?"

Then David said to Abishai and to all his servants, "My own son is trying to kill me. Doesn't this relative of Saul have even more reason to do so? Leave him alone and let him curse, for the LORD has told him to do it. And perhaps the LORD will see that I am being wronged and will bless me because of these curses today." So David and his men continued down the road, and Shimei kept pace with them on a nearby hillside, cursing and throwing stones and dirt at David.

We have gone back in time a bit with this passage in order to meet a man who will appear repeatedly in David's life. While David was still on the run from Absalom, he encountered Shimei, a blood relative of Saul who believed that David had wrongly usurped Saul's throne. David's remarkable restraint in sparing Shimei's life despite his insults and rock throwing suggests that David was back in step with God's will. After all, he would have had every right to kill Shimei. He laid down his rights to preserve Shimei's life.

- Why do you think David spared Shimei's life?

- When have you been insulted or criticized recently? How did it make you feel? How did you respond?

- In an average week, how often do you criticize other people (including people you don't know)? What feelings or events typically lead you to criticize others?

RESPOND

Father, forgive me for criticizing the people in my life, both those I know and those I don't. I want to be an encourager, someone who builds up others with my words and actions. Give me a spirit of gentleness and patience so I see the best in others and can bring blessings instead of insults or judgment. Help me turn to you when criticism comes my way and remember that my identity and worth are found in you alone. Amen.

DAY 27

DO NOT HOLD ME GUILTY

a prayer to open   My Lord, my God, show me your heart. Ground me in your presence. Draw me near and hold me close.

READ 2 SAMUEL 19:9-23

And throughout all the tribes of Israel there was much discussion and argument going on. The people were saying, "The king rescued us from our enemies and saved us from the Philistines, but Absalom chased him out of the country. Now Absalom, whom we anointed to rule over us, is dead. Why not ask David to come back and be our king again?"

Then King David sent Zadok and Abiathar, the priests, to say to the elders of Judah, "Why are you the last ones to welcome back the king into his palace? For I have heard that all Israel is ready. You are my relatives, my own tribe, my own flesh and blood! So why are you the last ones to welcome back the king?" And David told them to tell Amasa, "Since you are my own flesh and blood, like Joab, may God strike me and even kill me if I do not appoint you as commander of my army in his place."

Then Amasa convinced all the men of Judah, and they responded unanimously . . . , "Return to us, and bring back all who are with you."

So the king started back to Jerusalem. And when

he arrived at the Jordan River, the people of Judah came . . . to meet him and escort him across the river. Shimei son of Gera . . . hurried across with the men of Judah to welcome King David. A thousand other men from the tribe of Benjamin were with him. . . . They rushed down to the Jordan to meet the king. They crossed the shallows of the Jordan to bring the king's household across the river, helping him in every way they could.

As the king was about to cross the river, Shimei fell down before him. "My lord the king, please forgive me," he pleaded. "Forget the terrible thing your servant did when you left Jerusalem. May the king put it out of his mind. I know how much I sinned. That is why I have come here today, the very first person in all Israel to greet my lord the king."

Then Abishai son of Zeruiah said, "Shimei should die, for he cursed the LORD's anointed king!"

"Who asked your opinion, you sons of Zeruiah!" David exclaimed. "Why have you become my adversary today? This is not a day for execution, for today I am once again the king of Israel!" Then, turning to Shimei, David vowed, "Your life will be spared."

REFLECT

Although Absalom had been killed and his coup defeated, the battle between his and David's supporters continued. Once David was welcomed back to Jerusalem as king, Shimei was the first to greet him and beg David's forgiveness for his extreme disloyalty during the coup. David spared Shimei's life again, despite cries from David's supporters to have him executed. Notably, however, David did not forgive Shimei. In fact, years later, on his deathbed, David ordered that Shimei be killed. As we see in David, even when we seek after God, vengeance and bitterness can bury themselves deeply in our hearts.

- Why did David spare Shimei's life a second time?

- What's the difference between withholding vengeance in the face of wrongdoing and forgiving a person for his or her wrongdoing?

- When have you withheld vengeance but not actually forgiven someone for a wrongdoing? What would forgiveness in that situation have looked like? How might you take a step toward forgiveness even now?

RESPOND

Father, thank you that you not only withhold your vengeance from me but also forgive me through the sacrifice of Jesus Christ. Help me remember this fact as I move through my life and experience hurt, betrayal, and criticism. Grow in me a desire and ability to forgive when I have been wronged and to turn from any thoughts of vengeance. Amen.

I CALLED TO THE LORD

a prayer to open   My Lord, my God, show me your heart. Ground me in your presence. Draw me near and hold me close.

Grounded

David sang this song to the LORD on the day the LORD rescued him from all his enemies and from Saul. He sang:

"The LORD is my rock, my fortress, and my savior;
my God is my rock, in whom I find protection.
He is my shield, the power that saves me, and my place of safety.
He is my refuge, my savior,
the one who saves me from violence.
I called on the LORD, who is worthy of praise,
and he saved me from my enemies.
The waves of death overwhelmed me;
floods of destruction swept over me.
The grave wrapped its ropes around me;
death laid a trap in my path.
But in my distress I cried out to the LORD;
yes, I cried to my God for help.
He heard me from his sanctuary;
my cry reached his ears.
Then the earth quaked and trembled.
The foundations of the heavens shook;
they quaked because of his anger. . . .
He opened the heavens and came down;
dark storm clouds were beneath his feet.
Mounted on a mighty angelic being, he flew,
soaring on the wings of the wind.
He shrouded himself in darkness,
veiling his approach with dense rain clouds.
A great brightness shone around him,
and burning coals blazed forth.
The LORD thundered from heaven;
the voice of the Most High resounded.
He shot arrows and scattered his enemies;
his lightning flashed, and they were confused.
Then at the command of the LORD,
at the blast of his breath,
the bottom of the sea could be seen,
and the foundations of the earth were laid bare.
He reached down from heaven and rescued me;
he drew me out of deep waters.
He rescued me from my powerful enemies,
from those who hated me and were too strong for me.
They attacked me at a moment when I was in distress,
but the LORD supported me.
He led me to a place of safety;
he rescued me because he delights in me.
The LORD rewarded me for doing right;
he restored me because of my innocence.
For I have kept the ways of the LORD;
I have not turned from my God to follow evil.
I have followed all his regulations;
I have never abandoned his decrees.
I am blameless before God;
I have kept myself from sin.
The LORD rewarded me for doing right.
He has seen my innocence.
To the faithful you show yourself faithful;
to those with integrity you show integrity.
To the pure you show yourself pure,
but to the crooked you show yourself shrewd.
You rescue the humble,
but your eyes watch the proud and humiliate them.
O LORD, you are my lamp.
The LORD lights up my darkness.
In your strength I can crush an army;
with my God I can scale any wall.
God's way is perfect.
All the LORD's promises prove true.
He is a shield for all who look to him for protection.
For who is God except the LORD?
Who but our God is a solid rock?
God is my strong fortress,
and he makes my way perfect.
He makes me as surefooted as a deer,
enabling me to stand on mountain heights.
He trains my hands for battle;
he strengthens my arm to draw a bronze bow.
You have given me your shield of victory;
your help has made me great.
You have made a wide path for my feet
to keep them from slipping."

REFLECT

These words come near the end of David's life and represent his song of thanksgiving to the Lord. Nothing quite captures David's approach to life as much as this statement: "I called on the LORD" (verse 4). Through his harrowing experiences as a shepherd, years on the run from Saul, betrayal, his own sinfulness and its consequences, and persecution and insult, David continually called on the Lord. And the Lord was David's great deliverer, forgiver, and refuge—as he is ours.

- What promise in David's song of thanksgiving do you need to remember and hold on to?

- In what area of life do you need to "call to the Lord" for deliverance, guidance, protection, provision, or repentance?

- If you wrote a song of thanksgiving to the Lord based on your life so far, what words would you use to describe God? What acts of deliverance would you include?

RESPOND

Father, you are the Great Deliverer. As I reflect on the events of my life—including times of joy and pain, confusion and clarity, the mountaintops and the valleys—I see that you have been present all along. You are my rock and refuge, my constant companion. As you did with David, you arm me with strength and keep my way secure. You make my feet like the feet of a deer and cause me to stand on the heights. You train my hands for battle and make your saving help my shield. You provide a broad path for my feet so my ankles do not give way. May I forever praise you. Amen.

DAY 29

FINAL INSTRUCTIONS

a prayer to open My Lord, my God, show me your heart. Ground me in your presence.
Draw me near and hold me close.

READ 1 KINGS 2:1-12

As the time of King David's death approached, he gave this charge to his son Solomon:

"I am going where everyone on earth must someday go. Take courage and be a man. Observe the requirements of the LORD your God, and follow all his ways. . . . If you do this, then the LORD will keep the promise he made to me. He told me, 'If your descendants live as they should and follow me faithfully with all their heart and soul, one of them will always sit on the throne of Israel.'

"And there is something else. You know what Joab son of Zeruiah did to me when he murdered my two army commanders, Abner son of Ner and Amasa son of Jether. He pretended that it was an act of war, but it was done in a time of peace, staining his belt and sandals with innocent blood. Do with him what

you think best, but don't let him grow old and go to his grave in peace.

"Be kind to the sons of Barzillai of Gilead. Make them permanent guests at your table, for they took care of me when I fled from your brother Absalom.

"And remember Shimei son of Gera, the man from Bahurim in Benjamin. He cursed me with a terrible curse as I was fleeing to Mahanaim. When he came down to meet me at the Jordan River, I swore by the LORD that I would not kill him. But that oath does not make him innocent. You are a wise man, and you will know how to arrange a bloody death for him."

Then David died and was buried with his ancestors. . . . Solomon became king . . . and his kingdom was firmly established.

David's final words to his son and heir to the throne, Solomon, are surprising for a man after God's own heart. David revealed long-held grudges against Joab and Shimei, essentially instructing Solomon to have both killed for their actions years earlier. In fact, although David spared Shimei's life twice, his inability or refusal to actually forgive Shimei when asked ultimately allowed vengeance to win out. Despite this disappointing evidence of David's flaws, God still did what he promised he would: He established Solomon's rule. In this, we see that God is faithful and will accomplish his purposes regardless of our unfaithfulness.

- What was your reaction to reading David's final words and instructions to Solomon?

- When in your life have you strayed from God's ways? How did you experience his faithfulness during that time?

- When have you been disappointed by the flaws or failures of someone you respect? What impact did your disappointment in that person have on you? How has that disappointment been resolved?

RESPOND

Father, thank you for your faithfulness even in the midst of my waywardness. Thank you for the reminder that David was human and flawed and that you loved him and kept your promises to him even so. Thank you that because of my faith in Jesus, you see me as righteous and pure. Help me empathize with the flaws and failures of others and see them as you do instead of with eyes of condemnation. Amen.

DAY 30

PRAISE THE LORD, MY SOUL

a prayer to open   My Lord, my God, show me your heart. Ground me in your presence. Draw me near and hold me close.

READ PSALM 103

Let all that I am praise the LORD;
  with my whole heart, I will praise his holy name.
Let all that I am praise the LORD;
  may I never forget the good things he does for me.
He forgives all my sins
  and heals all my diseases.
He redeems me from death

and crowns me with love and tender mercies.
He fills my life with good things.
  My youth is renewed like the eagle's!
The LORD gives righteousness
  and justice to all who are treated unfairly. . . .
The LORD is compassionate and merciful,
  slow to get angry and filled with unfailing love. . . .
He does not punish us for all our sins;

he does not deal harshly with us, as we
deserve.
For his unfailing love toward those who fear him
is as great as the height of the heavens above
the earth.
He has removed our sins as far from us
as the east is from the west.
The LORD is like a father to his children,
tender and compassionate to those who fear
him.
For he knows how weak we are;
he remembers we are only dust. . . .
The wind blows, and we are gone—
as though we had never been here.

But the love of the LORD remains forever
with those who fear him.
His salvation extends to the children's children
of those who are faithful to his covenant,
of those who obey his commandments!
The LORD has made the heavens his throne;
from there he rules over everything.
Praise the LORD, you angels,
you mighty ones who carry out his plans,
listening for each of his commands. . . .
Praise the LORD, everything he has created,
everything in all his kingdom.
Let all that I am praise the LORD.

REFLECT

In this stirring, expansive psalm, we see David's heart for God on full display, and his overwhelming desire to praise and serve God with his whole heart, mind, and soul inspires us to do the same.

- Having studied the life of David, how would you describe him? What have you learned from him?

- What does a heart for God look like in your particular circumstances?

- In what ways have your faith and understanding of God grown over the past several weeks as you have studied the life of David and his heart for God?

RESPOND

Use Psalm 103 as a prayer for today.

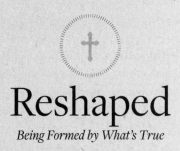

Reshaped

Being Formed by What's True

WHEN I WAS little, my sister Tracey and I went to a babysitter's house every day after school, and our mom picked us up on her way home from work. At home, Tracey and I would climb into our parents' bed while Mom changed out of her work clothes and talked to us about our days. One day as we were sitting on the bed while Mom was in the bathroom, I noticed something odd. My parents had a closet that held my mom's clothes on the left and my dad's on the right. On this day, the doors on my dad's side were open and a belt hung over the knob on the door. All his clothes were gone.

I don't remember what I felt in that moment, but I recall asking my mom, "Where's Dad's stuff?" At this, she came over to the bed, wedged herself between Tracey and me, and told us she and Dad were separating. I hadn't known this was coming; they didn't fight or show any outward signs that ending their relationship was a possibility. Yet they separated and at some later date divorced.

Even today I don't know fully what happened. I know only that if someone were to ask me what one experience has most shaped my life, the answer is obvious: my parents' divorce. That one event, and really all that accompanied it, still affects me. The divorce undoubtedly shaped my sister, too, and each of my parents in their own way. I don't hold any bad feelings toward my parents or blame them for anything, but this was the formative event of my life.

Recently, I wrote a letter to my seven-year-old self. I wanted to enter into this profound reshaping phase of my life with the perspective I have now, choosing to be open to how God has molded me through what's true about him, me, and the story he's been writing since the beginning of time.

Dear Kellye,
You're seven years old, and I see it in you already: the broken heart, the fear,
and the confusion. Darling girl, my heart hurts for you because thirty-five
years later, your heart still hurts. You still withdraw to the quiet places—
where the trees tower above, the clouds blow by, and the worms hide in
the grass—and beg to be put back together. Was there a time when you
smiled freely and laughed without constraint? When you woke up without

the sadness and fear of being left and unseen? Was there a time when you trusted, or have always carried the absolute certainty that you were and would always be alone?

I wish I could tell you it gets better, but years lie ahead when what you've just been through will haunt you. You'll wonder if anyone could love you and if everyone will leave. You're going to make decisions to cope with your pain that will break you apart even more. People will do things to you that will open and deepen your wounds. There will be a time when you don't know who you are and you will conclude you cannot love and cannot be loved. You will survive that time only because someone is saving you in order to heal you.

So this is a good time to tell you that there is a healer. You'll have to say yes, and he won't heal you overnight. In fact, your own healing is going to feel more painful at times than the original hurt ever did. But this healer desires your wholeness. He will collect all your broken pieces and put you back together. While that's happening, though, you'll lament and cry over just how much of you has fallen apart over the years. You will want to close your eyes, run away, and hide. Despair will threaten to overtake you.

The healer will send some people along. Pay attention. These are the ones he will use to restore you and redeem all you've been through and suffered. They won't be people you expect, but listen, my darling, listen. Each one has something to say, a wound to heal. I know it will be difficult, but you're going to have to show these people where it hurts. The fear and mistrust that sticks to you won't go anywhere until you let these friends in and trust them. They will tell you about the healer and all he's done and continues to do for you. They will actually show you who he is and what he desires for you. They will love you and be faithful to you. They will stay. Do you hear me? They will stay. They will give you reason to laugh and cast off the sadness. You can trust them. You can love them.

You're going to be okay, in the end, and along the way you will believe that all is well in the deepest parts of your soul. You will know you're loved and you will see what the healer has done and is doing. You'll laugh more and more. Your sadness will dissipate. Just keep walking forward, keep going to the quiet places. Keep being who you are.

Always,
Kellye

We all have been shaped by traumatic and painful experiences in our lives. And there is no question we are also shaped by good, positive experiences. What one event or experience has most shaped your life? Are you willing to be reshaped (or perhaps even further shaped) by what's true? Are you willing to enter into

God's powerful, gracious, and loving hands and allow him to show you who he is and who you are and to form you into wholeness as he always intended? The next fifty-four days will help you do just that. We will soak in the truth of the Psalms and allow their eternal truths to shape and reshape our hearts, minds, and actions.

SHAPED BY GOD'S WORD

a prayer to open

Here's my heart, Lord. Speak what is true.
Here's my life, Lord. Speak what is true.

READ PSALM 1

Oh, the joys of those who do not
    follow the advice of the wicked,
    or stand around with sinners,
    or join in with mockers.
But they delight in the law of the LORD,
    meditating on it day and night.
They are like trees planted along the riverbank,
    bearing fruit each season.
Their leaves never wither,
    and they prosper in all they do.

But not the wicked!
    They are like worthless chaff, scattered by the
    wind.
They will be condemned at the time of
    judgment.
    Sinners will have no place among the godly.
For the LORD watches over the path of the
    godly,
    but the path of the wicked leads to
    destruction.

REFLECT

The things we do on a regular basis are the things that shape us. When we exercise and eat vegetables regularly, we become people who are more likely to be physically healthy. When we sleep eight hours a night, we become people who are more likely to be well rested. Psalm 1 reminds us that when we meditate on Scripture daily, we become people who are more likely to follow God's ways and turn away from things that lead to disappointment and heartache. How might our lives be shaped if our days began and ended with Scripture?

- Read this passage again slowly. What word or phrase stands out to you? Why do you think that particular word or phrase speaks to you? What does it say?

- What regular practices do you have built into each day, each week, and each month? Which of these routines shape your mind, heart, and body for the positive? Which for the negative?

- What emotions and thoughts occupy your mind and heart the most during a typical day? In what ways do the things you read, listen to, and watch contribute to those emotions and thoughts?

Reshaped

•

Watch over me, Lord, and help me walk in step with you. Plant in me a deep hunger for your Word, and focus my mind on the things that matter to you. Give me the resolve and courage to run from the things that distract me from you, that pull me away from your plans for me, and that lead me down a path of destruction. Mold my heart and character to reflect yours. Amen.

DAY 2

SUBMIT TO GOD'S SON

a prayer to open

Here's my heart, Lord. Speak what is true.
Here's my life, Lord. Speak what is true.

READ PSALM 2

Why are the nations so angry?
  Why do they waste their time with futile
    plans?
The kings of the earth prepare for battle;
  the rulers plot together
against the LORD
  and against his anointed one.
"Let us break their chains," they cry,
  "and free ourselves from slavery to God."
But the one who rules in heaven laughs.
  The Lord scoffs at them.
Then in anger he rebukes them,
  terrifying them with his fierce fury.
For the Lord declares, "I have placed my chosen
    king on the throne
  in Jerusalem, on my holy mountain."

The king proclaims the LORD's decree:
  "The LORD said to me, 'You are my son.
    Today I have become your Father.
Only ask, and I will give you the nations as your
    inheritance,
  the whole earth as your possession.'" . . .
Now then, you kings, act wisely!
  Be warned, you rulers of the earth!
Serve the LORD with reverent fear,
  and rejoice with trembling.
Submit to God's royal son, or he will become
    angry,
  and you will be destroyed in the midst of all
    your activities—
for his anger flares up in an instant.
  But what joy for all who take refuge in him!

REFLECT

In Psalm 1, we read about the choice we each have to walk in step with the wicked or follow the ways of God. Psalm 2 sets up a similar choice for the nations of the earth: They can either serve and submit to God or go their own way. When we read this psalm, we may wonder what it has to do with us today. It is a stark reminder of who is in charge and who is at the center. Often it seems that our fate and ability to live in the ways we desire are tied to the person or people in power. And to a certain extent, this is true—though temporary. Ultimately, as this psalm makes clear, God is at the center of all things and is ruling over all things. Nations and rulers come and go; God remains constant and never-changing. How might our thoughts and responses to injustice or harm be shaped if we remembered his constancy and sovereignty over all things?

- Read today's psalm again slowly. What word or phrase stands out to you? Why do you think that particular word or phrase speaks to you? What does it say?

- What is your typical reaction when you learn of an injustice carried out by the government of the country you live in? What hope do you see in the midst of injustice?

- As you reflect, what do you sense God seeking to shape in you as you remember that the end of the story of human history is not injustice, despair, and evil kings but rather hope, justice, and goodness under the reign of Jesus Christ?

RESPOND

Lord, injustice seems to rule the world. There are bright spots here and there, but from what we can see, governmental corruption rules more than compassion, peace, and justice. When my heart falls into despair over the state of things—and especially the ruling authorities—remind me of the truth that no matter who is governing the nations, you remain at the center of all things, rule over all things, and are working to make all things new. Allow this truth to shape my every thought and response to the good and the evil I see in the world. May I applaud and encourage the peacemakers and find my joy in you alone. Amen.

DAY 3

HEAR MY PRAYER

a prayer to open

Here's my heart, Lord. Speak what is true.
Here's my life, Lord. Speak what is true.

READ PSALM 4

Answer me when I call to you,
  O God who declares me innocent.
Free me from my troubles.
  Have mercy on me and hear my prayer.
How long will you people ruin my reputation?
  How long will you make groundless accusations?
  How long will you continue your lies?
You can be sure of this:
  The LORD set apart the godly for himself.
  The LORD will answer when I call to him.
Don't sin by letting anger control you.

Think about it overnight and remain silent.
Offer sacrifices in the right spirit,
  and trust the LORD.
Many people say, "Who will show us better times?"
  Let your face smile on us, LORD.
You have given me greater joy
  than those who have abundant harvests of grain and new wine.
In peace I will lie down and sleep,
  for you alone, O LORD, will keep me safe.

Between fifty and seventy million Americans suffer from sleep disorders or deprivation,[5] which means that many of us don't lie down and sleep in peace. Fear, anxiety, stress, and the 24/7 nature of our culture keep us awake. This psalm promises that when we place our trust in God, releasing to him our families, our jobs, our desires, and our dreams, he will fill us with joy and peace. How might our lives be shaped if we were to turn over every aspect of ourselves to God?

- Read this passage again slowly. What word or phrase stands out to you? Why do you think that particular word or phrase speaks to you? What does it say?

- What worries or fears keep you up or wake you up at night (whether it's every night or just once in a while)?

- Think about the area of your life that you worry about most. What one step could you take to begin to release that area to God's care and provision?

RESPOND

I long for your joy and peace to fill my soul and ease my mind, Lord. Illuminate for me the things I'm holding on to too tightly—things I need to release to your care. I want to trust every aspect of my life to you, but at times I am not even sure how to do that. Show me, and help me release my life into your care. Amen.

DAY 4

WRONGLY ACCUSED

a prayer to open

Here's my heart, Lord. Speak what is true.
Here's my life, Lord. Speak what is true.

READ PSALM 7:1-9

I come to you for protection, O Lord my God.
    Save me from my persecutors—rescue me! . . .
O Lord my God, if I have done wrong
    or am guilty of injustice,
if I have betrayed a friend
    or plundered my enemy without cause,
then let my enemies capture me.
    Let them trample me into the ground
    and drag my honor in the dust.
Arise, O Lord, in anger!

Stand up against the fury of my enemies!
    Wake up, my God, and bring justice!
Gather the nations before you.
    Rule over them from on high. . . .
Declare me righteous, O Lord,
    for I am innocent, O Most High!
End the evil of those who are wicked,
    and defend the righteous.
For you look deep within the mind and heart,
    O righteous God.

We've read about it in the news—someone in the wrong place at the wrong time, accused of a crime he or she didn't commit. These stories pull at our hearts because we know deep within us what it means to be wrongly accused. Not of a crime, necessarily—accusation can be an internal, spiritual battle as well.

Psalm 7 plays on two levels. The first is that we actually can be accused of something we didn't do: sharing a secret we were sworn to keep, gossiping about another person, acting in a way that was detrimental to a friend, or even committing a crime. When this happens, we can be driven to prove our innocence and can drown in our desire to bring the real wrongdoers to justice. The second—and perhaps more relevant—level on which this psalm operates is the spiritual level. Jesus called Satan "the father of lies" (see John 8:44), and in Revelation, Satan is called "the accuser" (see 12:10). Satan's specialty is to get us to believe lies about ourselves. Some of us believe the lie that we are worthless and unredeemable. Others believe that we can't be forgiven and that our past will always have a hold on us. Still others believe that we should forever be ashamed of what we've done or what's been done to us. When we hear these lies, we can run to God for refuge and ask him to remind us who we are in him. Our identity is in Christ; we are loved and forgiven; we are freed. And we can call on God to stand against Satan on our behalf. How might our lives be shaped if, when the accusations came, we turned our hearts immediately to God for refuge?

- Read this passage again slowly. What word or phrase stands out to you? Why do you think that particular word or phrase speaks to you? What does it say?

- What are the false accusations that most often plague your thoughts? Under what circumstances are you tempted to believe that these accusations are true?

- Take a moment in silence, remembering that you are in God's loving presence, and ask him to remind you of what's true of you. Write down whatever comes to mind.

Lord, thank you for my identity in Christ and all that I am because of him. When my mind slips into old ways of thinking or when Satan whispers lies into my mind and heart, rescue me! Remind me of what you say is true of me, what has become my true identity in Christ. Turn my attention to you and the work you've given me to do. Run Satan off and grant me the freedom to know I am secure in your love. Amen.

THE LORD STILL RULES

a prayer to open

Here's my heart, Lord. Speak what is true.
Here's my life, Lord. Speak what is true.

READ PSALM 11

I trust in the LORD for protection.
So why do you say to me,
 "Fly like a bird to the mountains for safety!
The wicked are stringing their bows
 and fitting their arrows on the bowstrings.
They shoot from the shadows
 at those whose hearts are right.
The foundations of law and order have
 collapsed.
 What can the righteous do?"
But the LORD is in his holy Temple;

the LORD still rules from heaven.
He watches everyone closely,
 examining every person on earth.
The LORD examines both the righteous and the
 wicked.
He hates those who love violence.
He will rain down blazing coals and burning
 sulfur on the wicked,
 punishing them with scorching winds.
For the righteous LORD loves justice.
 The virtuous will see his face.

REFLECT

There are times we feel under attack, as though threats to our safety and our fundamental beliefs are being lobbed at us from all directions. In this psalm, the attack comes from the taut bows of the wicked and the collapse of law and order. In our lives, it's sickness, job loss, family disputes, systemic injustice, economic downturn, governmental uncertainty. Whatever the threat, though, it's clear the psalmist would have the same response: "The LORD still rules from heaven" (verse 4). No matter the chaos or uncertainty, no matter what bows are aimed at us or what foundations of the world collapse, the Lord still rules. And God examines our hearts in the midst of this chaos, searching for those who remain faithful, stay open to his soft whispers, and continue to love in the face of hardship and hatred. How might our lives be shaped if we could say with confidence, no matter the circumstances, "The LORD still rules from heaven"?

- Read this passage again slowly. What word or phrase stands out to you? Why do you think that particular word or phrase speaks to you? What does it say?

- What is currently threatening your sense of security, peace, or overall well-being? What thoughts or fears keep you up at night? What comfort does the truth that "the Lord still rules" bring?

- What do you sense God is seeking to show you about who he is in the midst of the threats you are currently facing?

RESPOND

Lord, give me strength to stand firm against anything and everything that threatens my deep sense of well-being. I know that in you I have life and peace and that nothing can separate me from your love—nothing. When outside circumstances or internal struggles pull at me and seduce me into thinking my foundation is shaky, remind me again and again that you rule. You still rule. You still rule from heaven. You are my stronghold and my safety. No matter how chaotic the world seems, you still rule. May I have a heart that stays true, hears your voice, and reaches out in love. Amen.

CONSTANT AWARENESS

a prayer to open
Here's my heart, Lord. Speak what is true.
Here's my life, Lord. Speak what is true.

READ PSALM 14

Only fools say in their hearts,
  "There is no God."
They are corrupt, and their actions are evil;
  not one of them does good!
The LORD looks down from heaven
  on the entire human race;
he looks to see if anyone is truly wise,
  if anyone seeks God.
But no, all have turned away;
  all have become corrupt.

No one does good,
  not a single one!
Will those who do evil never learn? . . .
Terror will grip them,
  for God is with those who obey him.
The wicked frustrate the plans of the oppressed,
  but the LORD will protect his people. . . .
When the LORD restores his people,
  Jacob will shout with joy, and Israel will
    rejoice.

REFLECT

Most of us would never say, "There is no God." In fact, we are reading God's Word and seeking to hear from him because we believe there is a God. We would describe him as loving, faithful, and powerful. We call ourselves followers of Jesus, who we believe is God incarnate, God in the flesh. The question for us is not whether we would say there is a God but this: Do we *live* as though there is a God? If an outside observer examined our decisions, relationships, actions, words, thoughts, and attitudes, would they come to the conclusion that we are seeking after God, believing he exists and is present here and now, working good, and available and willing to help us? This psalm suggests that when we deny God's active presence in the world by the way we live, we might as well scream out, "There is no God!" How might our lives be shaped if we lived in the constant awareness of God's presence?

• Read this passage again slowly. What word or phrase stands out to you? Why do you think that particular word or phrase speaks to you? What does it say?

• In what area of your life have you all but said, "There is no God," with your actions and attitudes? Take a moment, remembering you are in God's loving

Reshaped

•

187

presence, to confess that reality to him. Listen for his word of assurance that you are forgiven.

- What barriers seem to keep you from being aware of God's presence and work in the world? What practices or habits might you adopt so that you can seek after him in every aspect of your life?

RESPOND

Remind me of your presence, Lord. Open my eyes to where you are working in the world and inviting me to participate. I want to be among the wise—among those who seek after you in every aspect of their lives. Show me where I'm holding you at bay, keeping my distance, and asserting my independence. Make me more dependent, increasingly surrendered, and ever mindful of the restoration you are bringing forth. Amen.

DAY 7

A REFUGE IN THE STORM

a prayer to open

Here's my heart, Lord. Speak what is true.
Here's my life, Lord. Speak what is true.

READ PSALM 16

Keep me safe, O God,
  for I have come to you for refuge.
I said to the LORD, "You are my Master!
  Every good thing I have comes from you."
The godly people in the land
  are my true heroes!
  I take pleasure in them!
Troubles multiply for those who chase after
  other gods. . . .
LORD, you alone are my inheritance, my cup of
  blessing.
  You guard all that is mine.
The land you have given me is a pleasant land.

What a wonderful inheritance!
I will bless the LORD who guides me;
  even at night my heart instructs me.
I know the LORD is always with me.
  I will not be shaken, for he is right beside me.
No wonder my heart is glad, and I rejoice.
  My body rests in safety.
For you will not leave my soul among
    the dead
  or allow your holy one to rot in the grave.
You will show me the way of life,
  granting me the joy of your presence
  and the pleasures of living with you forever.

REFLECT

When children get scared, they run and hide under their bedcovers, in the closet, or in the arms of their mothers or fathers. We adults usually don't run to those same places when we're afraid, but most of us still seek refuge somewhere. How might our lives be shaped if we saw God as our refuge, the place where we could find not only security and safety but also joy and life?

- Read this passage again slowly. What word or phrase stands out to you? Why do you think that particular word or phrase speaks to you? What does it say?

- When you were a child, where did you run for security and safety? What was it about that place that brought comfort?

- In what ways do you cope with fear and anxiety today? What (or who) are you likely to seek out when you are most afraid or anxious?

RESPOND

Lord, you alone are my true and lasting refuge, yet I seek safety and comfort in many temporary things—things that fade and can be shaken. When I am afraid, remind me of your presence and your eternity. Give me eyes that see beyond my immediate circumstances, and a heart that praises you even in the midst of fear and the unknown. Be my refuge, my joy, my life. Amen.

CALL TO THE LORD

a prayer to open

Here's my heart, Lord. Speak what is true.
Here's my life, Lord. Speak what is true.

READ PSALM 18:1-24

I love you, LORD;
  you are my strength.
The LORD is my rock, my fortress, and my savior;
  my God is my rock, in whom I find protection.
He is my shield, the power that saves me,
  and my place of safety.
I called on the LORD, who is worthy of praise,
  and he saved me from my enemies.
The ropes of death entangled me;
  floods of destruction swept over me.
The grave wrapped its ropes around me;
  death laid a trap in my path.
But in my distress I cried out to the LORD;
  yes, I prayed to my God for help.
He heard me from his sanctuary;
  my cry to him reached his ears.
Then the earth quaked and trembled.
  The foundations of the mountains shook;
  they quaked because of his anger.
Smoke poured from his nostrils;
  fierce flames leaped from his mouth.
  Glowing coals blazed forth from him.
He opened the heavens and came down;
  dark storm clouds were beneath his feet.

Mounted on a mighty angelic being, he flew,
  soaring on the wings of the wind.
He shrouded himself in darkness,
  veiling his approach with dark rain clouds.
Thick clouds shielded the brightness
  around him
  and rained down hail and burning coals.
The LORD thundered from heaven;
  the voice of the Most High resounded
  amid the hail and burning coals.
He shot his arrows and scattered his enemies;
  great bolts of lightning flashed, and they were
  confused.
Then at your command, O LORD,
  at the blast of your breath,
the bottom of the sea could be seen,
  and the foundations of the earth were laid
  bare.
He reached down from heaven
  and rescued me;
  he drew me out of deep waters.
He rescued me from my powerful enemies,
  from those who hated me and were too
  strong for me.

They attacked me at a moment when I was in
distress,
    but the LORD supported me.
He led me to a place of safety;
    he rescued me because he delights in me.
The LORD rewarded me for doing right;
    he restored me because of my innocence.
For I have kept the ways of the LORD;

I have not turned from my God to follow evil.
I have followed all his regulations;
    I have never abandoned his decrees.
I am blameless before God;
    I have kept myself from sin.
The LORD rewarded me for doing right.
    He has seen my innocence.

REFLECT

Calling out to God when hardship comes is often something we resort to after all other options have run out. What if calling out to God was our first response to distress? What if we called out to him at the first sign of difficulty? What might we see him do to rescue us? How might our lives be shaped if prayer were our leading thought instead of an afterthought?

- Read this passage again slowly. What word or phrase stands out to you? Why do you think that word or phrase speaks to you?

- Reflect on the last time God clearly answered one of your prayers. What was your prayer? How did he respond? What was your reaction?

- Is there something going on in your life that seems too big or too hard for you to handle but about which you haven't yet prayed? How might you bring that issue before God and call out for his help?

RESPOND

Lord, thank you that you hear me when I call out to you. I want to be a person who truly believes that you are a rescuer, a God who reaches into my life when I seek you. When pain and struggle enter my life, remind me of your presence and goodness. Prompt my preoccupied, worried mind to share with you the burdens I carry and the ways I need you. Amen.

DAY 9

MAY GOD BLESS YOU

a prayer to open

Here's my heart, Lord. Speak what is true.
Here's my life, Lord. Speak what is true.

READ PSALM 20:1-5

In times of trouble, may the LORD answer
your cry.
    May the name of the God of Jacob keep you
safe from all harm.

May he send you help from his sanctuary
    and strengthen you from Jerusalem.
May he remember all your gifts
    and look favorably on your burnt offerings.

May he grant your heart's desires
and make all your plans succeed.
May we shout for joy when we hear of
your victory

and raise a victory banner in the name of
our God.
May the LORD answer all your prayers.

REFLECT

Blessing others is a spiritual discipline that we rarely practice in our culture. Perhaps it feels too formal, or perhaps we lack the confidence to speak so boldly about what God will do or the promises he has made. Every person we lock eyes with is facing a battle of some kind, and we have an opportunity to encourage and build others up by reminding them of God's presence, power, and promises. The apostle Paul did this in every letter he wrote (for example, 2 Corinthians 13:14; Ephesians 3:14-21; 1 Thessalonians 5:23-24). How might our lives be shaped if we were to take up the spiritual practice of blessing the people in our lives who are facing difficulty and have lost confidence in God's willingness or ability to grant them victory?

- Read this passage again slowly. What word or phrase stands out to you? Why do you think that particular word or phrase speaks to you? What does it say?

- Who came to mind when you read today's psalm? How might you adapt the words of this psalm to be a blessing over that person?

- What would prevent you from speaking a blessing based on Psalm 20 over a friend or family member you know is struggling? In what area do you need God to strengthen your confidence in him?

RESPOND

Lord, I want to be a blessing to those around me. Fill me with your presence and power, and remind me of your long-standing, time-tested promises to rescue and be with those who love you. Let my faith be something others can lean on when they can't muster the memory of your goodness and faithfulness. Untangle my tongue and grant me confidence and boldness to speak words of life and hope to the battle weary. Amen.

CELEBRATING GOD'S GOODNESS

a prayer to open

Here's my heart, Lord. Speak what is true.
Here's my life, Lord. Speak what is true.

Reshaped

•

How the king rejoices in your strength, O Lord!
 He shouts with joy because you give him
 victory.
For you have given him his heart's desire;
 you have withheld nothing he requested.
You welcomed him back with success and
 prosperity.
 You placed a crown of finest gold on his head.
He asked you to preserve his life,
 and you granted his request.

The days of his life stretch on forever.
Your victory brings him great honor,
 and you have clothed him with splendor and
 majesty.
You have endowed him with eternal blessings
 and given him the joy of your presence.
For the king trusts in the Lord.
 The unfailing love of the Most High will keep
 him from stumbling.

REFLECT

How often do we pray for something or ask God to carry us through a hard time but then forget to celebrate and praise him for answering our prayers? Or how often do we fail to express our hearts' desires to God for fear he won't hear us or answer our pleas? This psalm reminds us that God wants to fulfill our deepest desires—the longings in us to be loved and known, to be seen and forgiven, to have purpose and meaning. And when he does, when we find ourselves in those moments of deep contentment, may we celebrate and thank him for his faithfulness and graciousness. How might our lives be shaped if we celebrated God's goodness to us, thanking and praising him for hearing and blessing us?

- Read this passage again slowly. What word or phrase stands out to you? Why do you think that particular word or phrase speaks to you? What does it say?

- Where do you see God's goodness to you over the past six months? What do you want to say to him about whatever you identified?

- Sit quietly for a couple of minutes and ask God to help you identify the desires in your heart that persist and long to be filled. Where do you sense discontentment? Where do you feel a longing for things to be different? What is your prayer?

RESPOND

Lord, you know my deepest desires, as well as those that sit right on the surface. Awaken me to what underlies the sense of longing I have in the places I feel discontent or anxious. Remind me that you're making me whole, making me new, shoring up the holes in my heart and soul. Grant me the desires of my heart. Fill me with your presence. Amen.

OPEN HANDS

a prayer to open

Here's my heart, Lord.   Speak what is true.
Here's my life, Lord.   Speak what is true.

READ PSALM 23

The LORD is my shepherd;
  I have all that I need.
He lets me rest in green meadows;
  he leads me beside peaceful streams.
He renews my strength.
He guides me along right paths,
  bringing honor to his name.
Even when I walk
  through the darkest valley,
I will not be afraid,
  for you are close beside me.

Your rod and your staff
  protect and comfort me.
You prepare a feast for me
  in the presence of my enemies.
You honor me by anointing my head with oil.
  My cup overflows with blessings.
Surely your goodness and unfailing love will
  pursue me
all the days of my life,
and I will live in the house of the LORD
  forever.

REFLECT

To say that God is like something else—something we can more easily understand—is a technique we see throughout the Bible. Jesus often used parables and stories to illustrate what God is like. Psalm 23 has much more to say about what God is like than almost any other description in the Scriptures. It depicts God as both a shepherd and a host of a great feast. The shepherd is not some far-off presence in the life of a sheep. The shepherd stays close, keeping his sheep from wandering away, being attacked by predators, or falling into danger. He gathers his sheep together to rest and be restored and nourished. The host welcomes and seeks to please his guest, honoring her presence and offering abundant food and drink. The shepherd can do his job only if the sheep is willing to be led. And a host can provide for and honor his guest only if the guest is willing to receive what the host offers. How might our lives be shaped if we opened our hands and hearts every day to receive the shepherd's guidance and rest and the host's abundant provision?

- Read this passage again slowly. What word or phrase stands out to you? Why do you think that particular word or phrase speaks to you? What does it say?

- In what area of your life have you wandered away from the shepherd, refusing his guidance and rest? What do you hear God whispering to you?

- In what area of your life are you rejecting or resisting God's abundant provision? (This might be reflected in an inability to be content with what he has provided or an inability to receive blessings out of guilt or pride.)

Lord, my shepherd and host, draw me close. I don't want to wander away, yet I'm so prone to doing that, so tempted at times, as if I'll stumble upon something better. You are my guide and protector, my provider and place of rest. Whatever is in me—pride, guilt, shame, fear—that prevents me from receiving you and saying yes, remove it, cast it away. Open me to receive. Amen.

DAY 12

A LOVING TEACHER

a prayer to open

Here's my heart, Lord. Speak what is true.
Here's my life, Lord. Speak what is true.

READ PSALM 25:1-21

O LORD, I give my life to you.
　I trust in you, my God!
Do not let me be disgraced,
　or let my enemies rejoice in my defeat.
No one who trusts in you will ever be disgraced,
　but disgrace comes to those who try to
　　deceive others.
Show me the right path, O LORD;
　point out the road for me to follow.
Lead me by your truth and teach me,
　for you are the God who saves me.
All day long I put my hope in you.
Remember, O LORD, your compassion and
　unfailing love,
　which you have shown from long ages past.
Do not remember the rebellious sins of my
　youth.
　Remember me in the light of your unfailing
　　love,
　for you are merciful, O LORD.
The LORD is good and does what is right;
　he shows the proper path to those who go
　　astray.
He leads the humble in doing right,
　teaching them his way.
The LORD leads with unfailing love and
　faithfulness

all who keep his covenant and obey his
　demands.
For the honor of your name, O LORD,
　forgive my many, many sins.
Who are those who fear the LORD?
　He will show them the path they should
　　choose.
They will live in prosperity,
　and their children will inherit the land.
The LORD is a friend to those who fear him.
　He teaches them his covenant.
My eyes are always on the LORD,
　for he rescues me from the traps of my
　　enemies.
Turn to me and have mercy,
　for I am alone and in deep distress.
My problems go from bad to worse.
　Oh, save me from them all!
Feel my pain and see my trouble.
　Forgive all my sins.
See how many enemies I have
　and how viciously they hate me!
Protect me! Rescue my life from them!
　Do not let me be disgraced, for in you I take
　　refuge.
May integrity and honesty protect me,
　for I put my hope in you.

REFLECT

Sometimes, in the back of our minds, we tend to think that God has a scoreboard in his heavenly office and marks us down a point each time we fail. But this psalm reminds us that we are not victims of God's scorekeeping; we are students of his ways, and he will teach and guide us to follow in his path. We need only be willing to learn and when we make mistakes seek his forgiveness and correction and get back up to try again. How might our lives be shaped if we saw ourselves as students of a loving, wise, and faithful teacher?

- Read this passage again slowly. What word or phrase stands out to you? Why do you think that particular word or phrase speaks to you? What does it say?

- Who is the best teacher or mentor you have ever had? What characteristics made that person helpful in your learning?

- In the past, how have you imagined God responding to you in the midst of your failures to follow in his ways? Does your imaginative portrait of him differ from how you have actually experienced him or from what Scripture describes? How so?

RESPOND

Lord, I want to be a student of your ways and your will. Forgive me for the times I have seen you as a scorekeeper, tyrant, or taskmaster instead of the loving, grace-giving teacher you are. Fill my mind with your words of love and mercy. Convict my heart when I go astray, correct my thoughts when they misrepresent you, and put me back on the right path so that all I am and all I do honors you. Amen.

DAY 13

MINDFUL OF YOUR UNFAILING LOVE

a prayer to open

Here's my heart, Lord. Speak what is true.
Here's my life, Lord. Speak what is true.

READ PSALM 26

Declare me innocent, O Lord,
  for I have acted with integrity;
  I have trusted in the Lord without wavering.
Put me on trial, Lord, and cross-examine me.
  Test my motives and my heart.
For I am always aware of your unfailing love,
  and I have lived according to your truth.
I do not spend time with liars
  or go along with hypocrites.
I hate the gatherings of those who do evil,
  and I refuse to join in with the wicked.
I wash my hands to declare my innocence.
  I come to your altar, O Lord,

singing a song of thanksgiving
  and telling of all your wonders.
I love your sanctuary, Lord,
  the place where your glorious presence dwells.
Don't let me suffer the fate of sinners.
  Don't condemn me along with murderers.
Their hands are dirty with evil schemes,
  and they constantly take bribes.
But I am not like that; I live with integrity.
  So redeem me and show me mercy.
Now I stand on solid ground,
  and I will publicly praise the Lord.

Reshaped

•

195

What if the beginning of a blameless life is not sin management but rather mindfulness of God's unfailing love and reliance on his faithfulness? So often when we reflect on our lives, our starting point is our own frailties, weaknesses, and sin. But what if before we considered how to follow in God's ways or determined how to turn from our own selfish desires or destructive behaviors (which are also worthy tasks) we first remembered his unfailing love for us and enduring faithfulness toward us? Indeed, what if God's unfailing love and enduring faithfulness were the starting points of all our thoughts? If we start there each morning, we will more easily be able to say no to deceitful ways and stand strong in the face of those who seek to pull us away from God's path. How might our lives be shaped if we kept his unfailing love and enduring faithfulness at the top of our minds?

- Read this passage again slowly. What word or phrase stands out to you? Why do you think that particular word or phrase speaks to you? What does it say?

- What does it mean that God loves you unfailingly? What does it mean that he is faithful? (Make these personal. For example, "The fact that God loves me unfailingly means that even when I do [or am] _____, he loves me.")

- Reflect on your greatest temptation—the thing that most often pulls you toward selfishness or behavior that is destructive to you or others. How might becoming mindful of God's unfailing love for you in those moments affect your ability to resist?

RESPOND

Lord, you love me, unfailingly, without hesitation, all the time. I don't understand this kind of love. Allow me to know it from you. Let this truth be the thing that I wake up knowing. Let it inform how I think, what I say, and all I do. When fear overtakes me or when shame comes knocking on my door, remind me that I am loved. I have nothing to fear. I cannot get away from your love—your love is unfailing. Help me remember. Amen.

UNMATCHED POWER

a prayer to open

Here's my heart, Lord. Speak what is true.
Here's my life, Lord. Speak what is true.

READ PSALM 29

Honor the LORD, you heavenly beings;
  honor the LORD for his glory and strength.
Honor the LORD for the glory of his name.

Worship the LORD in the splendor of his
  holiness.
The voice of the LORD echoes above the sea.

The God of glory thunders.
The LORD thunders over the mighty sea.
The voice of the LORD is powerful;
the voice of the LORD is majestic. . . .
The voice of the LORD strikes
with bolts of lightning.
The voice of the LORD makes the barren
wilderness quake;

the LORD shakes the wilderness of Kadesh.
The voice of the LORD twists mighty oaks
and strips the forests bare.
In his Temple everyone shouts, "Glory!"
The LORD rules over the floodwaters.
The LORD reigns as king forever.
The LORD gives his people strength.
The LORD blesses them with peace.

REFLECT

There's nothing like a thunderstorm—or flood, hurricane, or earthquake—to remind us just how small we are. Technology gives us the ability to better predict each of these weather phenomena, and preparedness training and strategies help us when storms or natural disasters strike. But no matter how strong our desire to do so, we have no ability to stop, change, or control any aspect of the weather. That power resides in God alone. Indeed, in this psalm, his strength is compared to the power we experience in storms.

God is not just as powerful as the most powerful storm, though. His power extends beyond the physical world. He reigns over every storm. Yes, with a single command, Jesus stilled the storm raging on the Sea of Galilee. But he also made the paralyzed walk, the blind see, and the deaf hear. He set people free from demons. He raised the dead to life. God gives his people strength and blesses them with peace. In other words, he also reigns over the storms we carry inside us and is able to bring strength and peace to our souls—in the midst of the storms we face. How might our lives be shaped if we were to acknowledge God's unmatched power over the physical world as well as over our minds, hearts, and souls?

- Read this passage again slowly. What word or phrase stands out to you? Why do you think that particular word or phrase speaks to you? What does it say?

- Under what circumstances do you most often face your powerlessness? What feelings arise in the midst of those circumstances?

- In what area of your life do you need to acknowledge God's power and ability to bring strength and peace? How might you write today's psalm to reflect that acknowledgment?

RESPOND

Lord, awaken me to your unmatched power and strength. When storms hit—whether physical, relational, emotional, or spiritual—remind me that you rule over every storm. Nothing I face is outside your control or beyond your reach. Release my heart from the grip of fear and worry and fill me with the faith—even in the worst of storms—that you are with me. You are my refuge. You are my strength. You are my peace. Amen.

AND YOU FORGAVE ME

a prayer to open

Here's my heart, Lord. Speak what is true.
Here's my life, Lord. Speak what is true.

READ PSALM 32

Oh, what joy for those
  whose disobedience is forgiven,
  whose sin is put out of sight!
Yes, what joy for those
  whose record the LORD has cleared
    of guilt,
  whose lives are lived in complete honesty!
When I refused to confess my sin,
  my body wasted away,
  and I groaned all day long.
Day and night your hand of discipline was
    heavy on me.
  My strength evaporated like water in the
    summer heat.
Finally, I confessed all my sins to you
  and stopped trying to hide my guilt.
I said to myself, "I will confess my rebellion to
    the LORD."
  And you forgave me! All my guilt is gone.

Therefore, let all the godly pray to you while
    there is still time,
  that they may not drown in the floodwaters of
    judgment.
For you are my hiding place;
  you protect me from trouble.
  You surround me with songs of victory.
The LORD says, "I will guide you along the best
    pathway for your life.
  I will advise you and watch over you.
Do not be like a senseless horse or mule
  that needs a bit and bridle to keep it under
    control."
Many sorrows come to the wicked,
  but unfailing love surrounds those who trust
    the LORD.
So rejoice in the LORD and be glad, all you who
    obey him!
  Shout for joy, all you whose hearts are pure!

REFLECT

Confessing our wrongdoing to another person can be really scary. We can feel ashamed of ourselves. It can seem too vulnerable to expose ourselves. We can feel disappointed to have hurt another person or worried about ruining a relationship. We can be afraid to tarnish our image or reputation. We might be concerned that the other person will not forgive us. These are all legitimate fears. We have no way of knowing how others will respond when we confess. But we *do* know how God will respond: He will forgive us. Period. It's in his character to forgive us. It's who he is, always and forever. How might our lives be shaped if we really believed to our core that God forgives us when we confess?

- Read this passage again slowly. What word or phrase stands out to you? Why do you think that particular word or phrase speaks to you? What does it say?

- Have you ever confessed a wrongdoing to another person? How did it feel? What was hard about it? How did you feel afterward?

- What keeps you from confessing your wrongdoing to God? As you look back on the past week, what things do you need to confess? God is trustworthy. Give confession a try.

You see every part of me, Lord—the good and the bad. You see the darkest thoughts and the secret actions, and you love me fully and faithfully. I confess that I have not loved you with my whole heart and have not loved others as you have loved me. In your mercy, forgive me. Give me the strength to love others well today, just as you love me. Amen.

DAY 16

THE PLANS OF THE LORD

a prayer to open

Here's my heart, Lord. Speak what is true.
Here's my life, Lord. Speak what is true.

READ PSALM 33:4-11

For the word of the LORD holds true,
  and we can trust everything he does.
He loves whatever is just and good;
  the unfailing love of the LORD fills the earth.
The LORD merely spoke,
  and the heavens were created.
He breathed the word,
  and all the stars were born.
He assigned the sea its boundaries

and locked the oceans in vast reservoirs.
Let the whole world fear the LORD,
  and let everyone stand in awe of him.
For when he spoke, the world began!
  It appeared at his command.
The LORD frustrates the plans of the nations
  and thwarts all their schemes.
But the LORD's plans stand firm forever;
  his intentions can never be shaken.

REFLECT

In a complicated book or movie, it can be hard not to lose the plot and get lost in the details. An interesting character might distract from the central story line. Or a particular scene might hold our attention too long or for the wrong reasons. And sometimes we just don't have the patience to see how the story will unfold. We do this in our lives, too. We lose the plot of the story we're in. We get distracted. We can begin to think the story is all about us and our circle of family and friends. We focus on the pain we're experiencing. And although those things matter, we lose sight of the grander story that is getting written over the course of our lives and history. From the moment sin entered the world, God has been making all things new—working to restore and redeem everything through Christ. That's the story. Plans or plots or schemes or scenarios that fall outside God's plans, which stand firm forever, either are distractions and diversions or will be used by God to restore and redeem. How might our lives be shaped if we stayed clear on the plot and looked at all things through the lens of his plans to restore and redeem?

• Read this passage again slowly. What word or phrase stands out to you? Why do you think that particular word or phrase speaks to you? What does it say?

Reshaped

•

199

- Reflect on the most significant relational upheaval you've experienced in your life. How does that experience fit into God's plans to restore and redeem all things?

- Who in your life needs a reminder of the story they're in because of having gotten distracted or diverted from the plot? Ask God to bring someone to mind and give you the words and grace to encourage them.

RESPOND

Lord, I get so distracted! I get pulled into mini-dramas and side stories. I get overwhelmed by the sins and failures of my past and worries about my future. Don't let me forget the plot! You're making all things new, even in this moment, working to restore and redeem. As I look at those around me, give me eyes of love and restoration. Show me what grace I need to extend and truth I need to speak. Give me words that will build up and encourage. Let me be part of your plans. Let me be an instrument in your hands. Amen.

SEEK PEACE AND PURSUE IT

a prayer to open

Here's my heart, Lord. Speak what is true.
Here's my life, Lord. Speak what is true.

READ PSALM 34

I will praise the LORD at all times.
  I will constantly speak his praises.
I will boast only in the LORD;
  let all who are helpless take heart.
Come, let us tell of the LORD's greatness;
  let us exalt his name together.
I prayed to the LORD, and he answered me.
  He freed me from all my fears.
Those who look to him for help will be radiant
    with joy;
  no shadow of shame will darken their faces.
In my desperation I prayed, and the LORD
    listened;
  he saved me from all my troubles.
For the angel of the LORD is a guard;
  he surrounds and defends all who fear him.
Taste and see that the LORD is good.
  Oh, the joys of those who take refuge in him!
Fear the LORD, you his godly people,
  for those who fear him will have all they need.
Even strong young lions sometimes go hungry,
  but those who trust in the LORD will lack no
    good thing.

Come, my children, and listen to me,
  and I will teach you to fear the LORD.
Does anyone want to live a life
  that is long and prosperous?
Then keep your tongue from speaking evil
  and your lips from telling lies!
Turn away from evil and do good.
  Search for peace, and work to maintain it.
The eyes of the LORD watch over those who do
    right;
  his ears are open to their cries for help.
But the LORD turns his face against those who
    do evil;
  he will erase their memory from the earth.
The LORD hears his people when they call to him
    for help.
  He rescues them from all their troubles.
The LORD is close to the brokenhearted;
  he rescues those whose spirits are crushed.
The righteous person faces many troubles,
  but the LORD comes to the rescue each time.
For the LORD protects the bones of the
    righteous;

not one of them is broken!
Calamity will surely destroy the wicked,
and those who hate the righteous will be
punished.

But the Lord will redeem those who serve him.
No one who takes refuge in him will be
condemned.

REFLECT

Words are powerful. What we say can affirm, empower, and bring peace. But our words can also tear down, silence the voices of others, and start war. We praise God with the same mouth that gossips, complains, and curses. How might our lives be shaped if we kept our lips from lies and gossip and used our words to build up others, seek peace, and speak good?

- Read this passage again slowly. What word or phrase stands out to you? Why do you think that word or phrase speaks to you? What does it say?

- Reflect on the last time you used your words to gossip or speak ill of another person. What motivated you to say what you did (for example, envy, anger, resentment, hard-heartedness, hurt)?

- Are there certain people with whom you tend to gossip or speak ill of others more than you otherwise would? Who are those people? What about your relationships with them—or your sense of self when you're around them—causes you to slip into gossip?

RESPOND

Lord, I know the power that words have on me—the joy of being lifted up by good words and the pain and shame of harsh, hurtful words. I have been gossiped about, spoken ill of, and teased. And I have done the same to friends and enemies alike. Forgive me. Let my words be only tools to build up others and speak good into the world. Transform the parts of my heart that lead me to use words as weapons instead of balm. Amen.

DAY 18

TRUST IN THE LORD AND DO GOOD

a prayer to open

Here's my heart, Lord.   Speak what is true.
Here's my life, Lord.   Speak what is true.

READ PSALM 37:1-24

Don't worry about the wicked
or envy those who do wrong.
For like grass, they soon fade away.
Like spring flowers, they soon wither.

Trust in the Lord and do good.
Then you will live safely in the land and
prosper.
Take delight in the Lord,

Reshaped

•

and he will give you your heart's desires.
Commit everything you do to the LORD.
Trust him, and he will help you.
He will make your innocence radiate like the
dawn,
and the justice of your cause will shine like the
noonday sun.
Be still in the presence of the LORD,
and wait patiently for him to act.
Don't worry about evil people who prosper
or fret about their wicked schemes.
Stop being angry!
Turn from your rage!
Do not lose your temper—
it only leads to harm.
For the wicked will be destroyed,
but those who trust in the LORD will possess
the land.
Soon the wicked will disappear.
Though you look for them, they will be gone.
The lowly will possess the land
and will live in peace and prosperity.
The wicked plot against the godly;
they snarl at them in defiance.
But the Lord just laughs,
for he sees their day of judgment coming.
The wicked draw their swords

and string their bows
to kill the poor and the oppressed,
to slaughter those who do right.
But their swords will stab their own hearts,
and their bows will be broken.
It is better to be godly and have little
than to be evil and rich.
For the strength of the wicked will be shattered,
but the LORD takes care of the godly.
Day by day the LORD takes care of the innocent,
and they will receive an inheritance that lasts
forever.
They will not be disgraced in hard times;
even in famine they will have more than
enough.
But the wicked will die.
The LORD's enemies are like flowers in a field—
they will disappear like smoke.
The wicked borrow and never repay,
but the godly are generous givers.
Those the LORD blesses will possess the land,
but those he curses will die.
The LORD directs the steps of the godly.
He delights in every detail of their lives.
Though they stumble, they will never fall,
for the LORD holds them by the hand.

REFLECT

It is easy to get discouraged about the overwhelming amount of injustice and pain
in our world, which is so often characterized by broken governments, oppressive
systems, and discriminatory cultural practices. We may wonder, *Does God really
see what's happening? Does he really care? When is he going to make things right?* This
psalm reminds us that the essence of our faith in God is our belief that he will right
the wrongs of the world. Our job is to continue doing good, aligning ourselves
with his ways in the world and trusting that he will ultimately bring justice. How
might our lives be shaped if we were to see injustice, do our parts, and stand firm
in the belief that all wrongs will be righted in the end?

- Read this passage again slowly. What word or phrase stands out to you? Why
  do you think that word or phrase speaks to you? What does it say?

- When you see injustice in the world, what is your typical reaction (sorrow,
  anger, compassion, apathy, a desire to act, defensiveness)? Why do you think
  you respond that way? How do the words of this psalm influence how you
  might respond in the future?

- What do you do when you are treated unfairly? What determines whether
  you speak up or not? How do the words of this psalm affect how you might
  respond in the future?

Lord, I need to be reminded of your presence in this world filled with injustice. I want to join in the good you're doing and be part of your restoration. Fill me with passion for those who are mistreated or oppressed, and give me the humility to forgive anyone who does me wrong. Allow my heart to delight in you and reflect your coming Kingdom each and every day. Amen.

DAY 19

ON THE LOOKOUT

a prayer to open

Here's my heart, Lord.   Speak what is true.
Here's my life, Lord.   Speak what is true.

READ PSALM 40:1-10

I waited patiently for the LORD to help me,
and he turned to me and heard my cry.
He lifted me out of the pit of despair,
out of the mud and the mire.
He set my feet on solid ground
and steadied me as I walked along.
He has given me a new song to sing,
a hymn of praise to our God.
Many will see what he has done and be
amazed.
They will put their trust in the LORD.
Oh, the joys of those who trust the LORD,
who have no confidence in the proud
or in those who worship idols.
O LORD my God, you have performed many
wonders for us.
Your plans for us are too numerous to list.
You have no equal.
If I tried to recite all your wonderful deeds,

I would never come to the end of them.
You take no delight in sacrifices or offerings.
Now that you have made me listen, I finally
understand—
you don't require burnt offerings or sin
offerings.
Then I said, "Look, I have come.
As is written about me in the Scriptures:
I take joy in doing your will, my God,
for your instructions are written on my heart."
I have told all your people about your justice.
I have not been afraid to speak out,
as you, O LORD, well know.
I have not kept the good news of your justice
hidden in my heart;
I have talked about your faithfulness and
saving power.
I have told everyone in the great assembly
of your unfailing love and faithfulness.

REFLECT

This psalm could be summarized in four short sentences:

I cried out to God.
He heard my cry and saved me.
My eyes were opened to his goodness and
power.

Now I can't help but tell everyone about who
God is and what he's done!

This experience is universal for followers of Jesus. Each of us has a story to tell that follows this pattern. After all, this is the way God works. He doesn't force himself on us, but when we cry out to him, not only does he listen, but he acts.

And he acts to save—whether in the macro sense of saving us through Jesus' death and resurrection or in the micro sense, such as saving us from anxiety and worry when we pray for peace. The only question is whether we have eyes to see God's saving acts for what they are and praise him for those acts. In the New Testament story about the ten lepers Jesus healed, the ten lepers called out, "Jesus, Master, have pity on us!" (Luke 17:12-13, NIV). Jesus healed all of them, but only one praised God and thanked Jesus for saving him from a continued life of physical deformity and social alienation. Only one had eyes to see God's goodness and power in the healing and responded with gratitude and worship. How might our lives be shaped if we constantly looked for God's saving acts, expressed our thanks to him for these acts, and then shared about them with others?

- Read this passage again slowly. What word or phrase stands out to you? Why do you think that word or phrase speaks to you? What does it say?

- Reflect on the pattern set out in today's psalm, expressed in the four statements above. To which of the four statements do you feel resistance? Why do you think that is?

- How have you seen God act in your life over the past month? What was your response? Who do you think could benefit from hearing about your experience?

RESPOND

Thank you for hearing me, Lord. Thank you that at the softest whisper in my soul for help, you are listening. Thank you that I don't even have to have the words fully formed before you hear and act. Keep saving me; keep refining me and transforming me. May I never take for granted the ways you act in my life out of your goodness and mercy. And may I be an extension of these very traits to others so that to come to know me is to be introduced to you. Amen.

DAY 20

SEEKING TO UNDERSTAND

SACRED QUESTIONS

a prayer to open

Here's my heart, Lord. Speak what is true.
Here's my life, Lord. Speak what is true.

READ PSALM 41:1-12

Oh, the joys of those who are kind to the poor!
   The LORD rescues them when they are in
      trouble.
   The LORD protects them

and keeps them alive.
He gives them prosperity in the land
   and rescues them from their enemies.
The LORD nurses them when they are sick

and restores them to health.
"O LORD," I prayed, "have mercy on me.
  Heal me, for I have sinned against you."
But my enemies say nothing but evil about me.
  "How soon will he die and be forgotten?"
    they ask.
They visit me as if they were my friends,
  but all the while they gather gossip,
  and when they leave, they spread it
    everywhere.
All who hate me whisper about me,
  imagining the worst. . . .

Even my best friend, the one I trusted
    completely,
  the one who shared my food, has turned
    against me.
LORD, have mercy on me.
  Make me well again, so I can pay them back!
I know you are pleased with me,
  for you have not let my enemies triumph over
    me.
You have preserved my life because I am
    innocent;
  you have brought me into your presence
    forever.

REFLECT _____

Can we see ourselves in the faces of those we consider poor? That's the question this psalm seems to ask. Indeed, in large part, our relative wealth or poverty depends upon where we were born, the parents we had, and the opportunities presented to us. For many of us, a sudden illness, job loss, bad decision, or natural disaster could mean we're suddenly unable to care for ourselves and our families. Yet so often we distance ourselves from those who have less, concluding that we have nothing in common with them and certainly nothing to learn from them. In fact, we are subtly told that we've "made it" the more isolated we are from those who have less. How might our lives be shaped if we identified more closely with those who have less than we do, seeking to learn and understand instead of looking down our noses, passing judgment, and creating distance?

- Read this passage again slowly. What word or phrase stands out to you? Why do you think that word or phrase speaks to you? What does it say?

- What barriers exist between you and those who have substantially less? As you reflect on today's psalm, what invitation do you sense God extending to you related to those who have less than you?

- How might you learn from and seek to understand those who have substantially less? What value do you think that would hold for you as a follower of Jesus?

RESPOND _____

Lord, thank you for the ways you have blessed and provided for me. I know there are many people in the world who have substantially less than I do. Expand my heart and open my eyes to those around me who you would call me to learn from and seek to understand. I want to love like you do and honor everyone regardless of status or income. Correct me when I attribute more value to the rich and powerful, and remind me that it is only by your grace that I have what I have. Amen.

Reshaped

•

205

I WILL YET PRAISE HIM

a prayer to open

Here's my heart, Lord.   Speak what is true.
Here's my life, Lord.   Speak what is true.

READ PSALM 42

As the deer longs for streams of water,
   so I long for you, O God.
I thirst for God, the living God.
   When can I go and stand before him?
Day and night I have only tears for food,
   while my enemies continually taunt me,
      saying,
   "Where is this God of yours?"
My heart is breaking
   as I remember how it used to be:
I walked among the crowds of worshipers,
   leading a great procession to the house of
      God,
singing for joy and giving thanks
   amid the sound of a great celebration!
Why am I discouraged?
   Why is my heart so sad?
I will put my hope in God!
   I will praise him again—
      my Savior and my God!

Now I am deeply discouraged,
   but I will remember you. . . .
I hear the tumult of the raging seas
   as your waves and surging tides sweep over
      me.
But each day the LORD pours his unfailing love
      upon me,
   and through each night I sing his songs,
      praying to God who gives me life.
"O God my rock," I cry,
   "why have you forgotten me?
Why must I wander around in grief,
   oppressed by my enemies?"
Their taunts break my bones.
   They scoff, "Where is this God of yours?"
Why am I discouraged?
   Why is my heart so sad?
I will put my hope in God!
   I will praise him again—
      my Savior and my God!

REFLECT

If we believe in Jesus Christ—the one who rescued and forgave us—shouldn't we always be filled with joy and hope? This psalm reflects what many of us feel from time to time. Our circumstances hijack our emotions and lead us into despair, confusion, or doubt. How might our lives be shaped if, when we are overwhelmed by our circumstances, we praise God and remember who he is and what he has done, even when we don't see or feel him?

- Read this passage again slowly. What word or phrase stands out to you? Why do you think that word or phrase speaks to you? What does it say?

- What kinds of experiences or circumstances tend to hijack your emotions? What do you tell yourself in those moments?

- Write down what you know to be true about God. How might you recall these truths during times you are questioning his goodness, his presence, or your own security in him?

Thank you, Lord, that you are bigger than any circumstance I might face. Even when my emotions blur my perspective and muddle the truth, you direct your love toward me. Even when things seem to be spinning out of control, I am completely secure in you. Even when I feel alone and abandoned, you are with me. Bring these truths to my mind when I am tempted toward despair or doubt. My hope is in you. Amen.

 DAY 22

BE STILL

a prayer to open

Here's my heart, Lord.   Speak what is true.
Here's my life, Lord.   Speak what is true.

READ PSALM 46

God is our refuge and strength,
   always ready to help in times of trouble.
So we will not fear when earthquakes come
   and the mountains crumble into the sea.
Let the oceans roar and foam.
   Let the mountains tremble as the waters
   surge!
A river brings joy to the city of our God,
   the sacred home of the Most High.
God dwells in that city; it cannot be destroyed.
   From the very break of day, God will protect it.
The nations are in chaos,
   and their kingdoms crumble!
God's voice thunders,

and the earth melts!
The LORD of Heaven's Armies is here among us;
   the God of Israel is our fortress.
Come, see the glorious works of the LORD:
   See how he brings destruction upon the
   world.
He causes wars to end throughout the earth.
   He breaks the bow and snaps the spear;
   he burns the shields with fire.
"Be still, and know that I am God!
   I will be honored by every nation.
   I will be honored throughout the world."
The LORD of Heaven's Armies is here among us;
   the God of Israel is our fortress.

REFLECT

Sometimes watching the evening news feels like having a front-row seat to the end of the world. Civil wars rage; hundreds of millions of people are hungry, lack clean water, and have been driven from their homes; and natural disasters such as typhoons, earthquakes, hurricanes, wildfires, and volcanic eruptions relentlessly destroy entire communities. How do we respond? Do we fall into despair? Do we let fear paralyze us and cause us to withdraw? In this psalm, God tells us to be still and release our fear because he is with us, he is in control, and his goodness will prevail. How might our lives be shaped if we were to release our fears and remember God's reign, presence, and goodness?

- Read this passage again slowly. What word or phrase stands out to you? Why do you think that word or phrase speaks to you? What does it say?

Reshaped

•

- What events, tragedies, and disasters in the world make you afraid for your family, the world, or the future? What are you afraid of? Why are you afraid?

- Is there something currently causing fear in your family, workplace, community, or church? What is it? How can you, as a follower of Jesus, help combat the escalation of fear around that particular issue?

RESPOND

Lord, I want to make decisions based on love, not fear. I want to say words brought about by love, not fear. I want my life to point people to love, not fear. Help me see where fear has a hold on me so I can release that fear to you. Help me become someone who de-escalates fear when it flares and brings encouragement when hope fades. May your love cast out every fear, and may your peace cover every worry. Amen.

ACQUIRING WISDOM, NOT MONEY

a prayer to open

Here's my heart, Lord. Speak what is true.
Here's my life, Lord. Speak what is true.

READ PSALM 49:12-20

Their fame will not last.
  They will die, just like animals.
This is the fate of fools,
  though they are remembered as
    being wise.
Like sheep, they are led to the grave,
  where death will be their shepherd.
In the morning the godly will rule over them.
  Their bodies will rot in the grave,
  far from their grand estates.
But as for me, God will redeem my life.
  He will snatch me from the power of the
    grave.

So don't be dismayed when the wicked grow
    rich
  and their homes become ever more splendid.
For when they die, they take nothing with them.
  Their wealth will not follow them into the
    grave.
In this life they consider themselves fortunate
  and are applauded for their success.
But they will die like all before them
  and never again see the light of day.
People who boast of their wealth don't
    understand;
  they will die, just like animals.

REFLECT

We get so caught up with admiring the wealthy and acquiring wealth in our culture. Money tricks us into thinking that those who have it are indestructible. Indeed, if we could be objective, we would be shocked at the lengths we go to in order to find security in money. We strive to get to whatever the next level is in our context, often putting our families and health at risk. Trying to "keep up" with our neighbors or coworkers drives us to live beyond our means and chain ourselves to unthinkable amounts of debt. We end up serving money instead of making money serve us. Money and stuff can neither save us from death nor grant us life, and it's those who know and live out this truth whom we can call wise. They understand. How might our lives be shaped if we shifted our focus from admiring the wealthy and acquiring wealth to admiring the wise and acquiring wisdom?

- Read this passage again slowly. What word or phrase stands out to you? Why do you think that word or phrase speaks to you? What does it say?

- Take a few moments, remembering you are in God's loving presence, to reflect on the extent to which you seek security in money or possessions. Examine how you spend your time and energy. Consider what worries you or keeps you up at night. What did God bring to mind?

- What practices tend to build your trust in God and your ability to find your security in him instead of in things such as money and possessions?

RESPOND

Lord, keep me centered on you. Oh how my heart can wander. Forgive me. When my loyalty shifts to other things, such as money and possessions, bring me back to you. Give me strength and courage to live differently than this culture dictates. In the moments or seasons when money seems more palpable and real than you do, keep me faithful to you. Help me grow in wisdom and understanding so my life reflects devotion to you and nothing else. Amen.

DAY 24

THEN I WILL TEACH

a prayer to open

Here's my heart, Lord.   Speak what is true.
Here's my life, Lord.   Speak what is true.

READ PSALM 51:1-17

Have mercy on me, O God,
  because of your unfailing love.
Because of your great compassion,
  blot out the stain of my sins.
Wash me clean from my guilt.
  Purify me from my sin.
For I recognize my rebellion;
  it haunts me day and night.
Against you, and you alone, have I sinned;
  I have done what is evil in your sight.
You will be proved right in what you say,
  and your judgment against me is just.

For I was born a sinner—
  yes, from the moment my mother conceived
  me.
But you desire honesty from the womb,
  teaching me wisdom even there.
Purify me from my sins, and I will be clean;
  wash me, and I will be whiter than snow.
Oh, give me back my joy again;
  you have broken me—
  now let me rejoice.
Don't keep looking at my sins.
  Remove the stain of my guilt.

Reshaped •

Create in me a clean heart, O God.
  Renew a loyal spirit within me.
Do not banish me from your presence,
  and don't take your Holy Spirit from me.
Restore to me the joy of your salvation,
  and make me willing to obey you.
Then I will teach your ways to rebels,
  and they will return to you.
Forgive me for shedding blood, O God who
  saves;

then I will joyfully sing of your forgiveness.
Unseal my lips, O Lord,
  that my mouth may praise you.
You do not desire a sacrifice, or I would offer
  one.
You do not want a burnt offering.
The sacrifice you desire is a broken spirit.
  You will not reject a broken and repentant
  heart, O God.

REFLECT_____

This psalm contains a heartfelt confession and reveals utter trust in God's forgiveness and compassion. It also teaches something many of us have never considered: What if our being cleansed from sin is not for our sake alone? The writer of this psalm asks God for a pure heart, a steadfast spirit, and restoration *so that* he can teach other transgressors about God's compassion, mercy, and forgiveness. What could our families, friends, and neighbors learn from the way God has poured out his grace on us? How might our lives be shaped if we were to confess and repent—not only to receive forgiveness, but also to share our story of God's loving forgiveness with others?

• Read this passage again slowly. What word or phrase stands out to you? Why do you think that word or phrase speaks to you? What does it say?

• Identify two or three specific wrongdoings you have confessed to God in the recent past. What would you say if a friend asked you, "What difference did it make when you confessed?"

• According to this psalm, what are the things God gives us when we come to him with a contrite heart? How might you describe these things to a friend who asks you how you know that God has forgiven you?

RESPOND_____

Lord, thank you for your forgiveness and willingness to cleanse me of all sin, create in me a pure heart, and restore me to joy. Give me the courage to share the story of your forgiveness in my life with others so they too can know the peace and freedom that comes when we turn to you. May my life display the truth of your forgiveness. Amen.

WHEN I AM AFRAID

a prayer to open

Here's my heart, Lord. Speak what is true.
Here's my life, Lord. Speak what is true.

READ PSALM 56

O God, have mercy on me,
for people are hounding me.
My foes attack me all day long.
I am constantly hounded by those who
slander me,
and many are boldly attacking me.
But when I am afraid,
I will put my trust in you.
I praise God for what he has promised.
I trust in God, so why should I be afraid?
What can mere mortals do to me?
They are always twisting what I say;
they spend their days plotting to harm me.
They come together to spy on me—
watching my every step, eager to kill me.
Don't let them get away with their
wickedness;
in your anger, O God, bring them down.

You keep track of all my sorrows.
You have collected all my tears in your bottle.
You have recorded each one in your book.
My enemies will retreat when I call to you for
help.
This I know: God is on my side!
I praise God for what he has promised;
yes, I praise the LORD for what he has
promised.
I trust in God, so why should I be afraid?
What can mere mortals do to me?
I will fulfill my vows to you, O God,
and will offer a sacrifice of thanks for your
help.
For you have rescued me from death;
you have kept my feet from slipping.
So now I can walk in your presence, O God,
in your life-giving light.

REFLECT

None of us is immune to fear. The question is, what will we do when we're afraid? After all, fear can be debilitating and prevent us from acting as God calls. If we are afraid to travel somewhere he has called us and we bail on the trip as a result, we will miss what he has in store for us there. If we are afraid to have a hard conversation with someone even though we know it's what the relationship needs, we may miss a healing opportunity. If we are afraid of a grand tragedy that might strike, and that fear keeps us from living fully in the present moment, we will be too focused on what could be and fail to see what is. God acts in the here and now, and fear is our biggest barrier to experiencing his presence and following in his ways. How might our lives be shaped if when we are afraid we turn our trust to God?

- Read this passage again slowly. What word or phrase stands out to you? Why do you think that word or phrase speaks to you? What does it say?

- What are some fears that keep you from fully experiencing God's presence? What underlies those fears?

- Reflect on whether there is something God is calling you to do that you've been avoiding out of fear. What comes to mind? What step do you sense him inviting you to take?

Reshaped

Free me from fear, Lord. Increase my ability to trust you, and show me how to actually do it. When fear strikes, I can feel paralyzed and uncertain about how exactly to return to you. You know my deepest fears and how I cope with them. Bring healing to what underlies those fears, and when they arise, give me the presence of mind to say, *Why should I be afraid? I trust in God.* As best I know how, I trust you and long to trust you more. Help me. Amen.

DAY 26

A W A K E , M Y S O U L !

a prayer to open

Here's my heart, Lord. Speak what is true.
Here's my life, Lord. Speak what is true.

READ PSALM 57

Have mercy on me, O God, have mercy!
　I look to you for protection.
I will hide beneath the shadow of your wings
　until the danger passes by.
I cry out to God Most High,
　to God who will fulfill his purpose for me.
He will send help from heaven to rescue me,
　disgracing those who hound me.
My God will send forth his unfailing love and
　faithfulness. . . .
Be exalted, O God, above the highest heavens!
　May your glory shine over all the earth.
My enemies have set a trap for me.
　I am weary from distress.

They have dug a deep pit in my path,
　but they themselves have fallen into it.
My heart is confident in you, O God;
　my heart is confident.
　No wonder I can sing your praises!
Wake up, my heart!
　Wake up, O lyre and harp!
　I will wake the dawn with my song.
I will thank you, Lord, among all the people.
　I will sing your praises among the nations.
For your unfailing love is as high as the heavens.
　Your faithfulness reaches to the clouds.
Be exalted, O God, above the highest heavens.
　May your glory shine over all the earth.

REFLECT

Have you ever been reading a book and realized halfway down the page that you actually weren't taking in anything? Your eyes were scanning the page, but your brain was not computing the words. We live our lives like this sometimes: We wake up, go through our daily routines and tasks, go to bed, and then wake up the next morning to do it all again. Every day can start to feel the same, and our duties and responsibilities seem never-ending. Our souls glaze over the beauty and uniqueness and wonder of life; they are asleep. How might our lives be shaped if we were to awaken our souls to noticing God's love and light as it breaks into our world each day?

- Read this passage again slowly. What word or phrase stands out to you? Why do you think that word or phrase speaks to you? What does it say?

- Where do you most often experience God's presence? Reflect on the last time you sensed his nearness. What did you feel? How did that experience affect you?

- What helps you notice God's presence and fingerprints throughout your day (being in creation, slowing down, praying, being quiet, serving others, worshiping)? How can you incorporate these elements into your day more often?

RESPOND

Awaken my soul, Lord! Open my eyes to seeing all the beauty you put on display each day. Help me notice the sparks of your Kingdom, both in the midst of joy and in the midst of pain. Allow my soul to be awake to your presence and your whispers. Light in me a desire to participate with you as you bring your Kingdom to "earth, as it is in heaven" (Matthew 6:10). Fill my heart with worship for you, and my mouth with thanksgiving for all you do and in all circumstances. Amen.

REMEMBERING GOD'S CHARACTER

a prayer to open

Here's my heart, Lord. Speak what is true.
Here's my life, Lord. Speak what is true.

READ PSALM 62

I wait quietly before God,
  for my victory comes from him.
He alone is my rock and my salvation,
  my fortress where I will never be shaken.
So many enemies against one man—
  all of them trying to kill me. . . .
They plan to topple me from my high position.
  They delight in telling lies about me.
They praise me to my face
  but curse me in their hearts.
Let all that I am wait quietly before God,
  for my hope is in him.
He alone is my rock and my salvation,
  my fortress where I will not be shaken.
My victory and honor come from God alone.
  He is my refuge, a rock where no enemy can
    reach me.
O my people, trust in him at all times.

Pour out your heart to him,
  for God is our refuge.
Common people are as worthless as a puff of
  wind,
  and the powerful are not what they appear
    to be.
If you weigh them on the scales,
  together they are lighter than a breath of air.
Don't make your living by extortion
  or put your hope in stealing.
And if your wealth increases,
  don't make it the center of your life.
God has spoken plainly,
  and I have heard it many times:
Power, O God, belongs to you;
  unfailing love, O Lord, is yours.
Surely you repay all people
  according to what they have done.

The wisdom of waiting for someone—particularly in the midst of a storm—depends upon the character of that person. Are they trustworthy? Reliable? Strong enough to get us through what we're facing? These are the questions we ask—probably subconsciously—about God. Is he really trustworthy? Reliable? Strong enough to get us through what we're facing? We wonder, and often we place our trust in other things that seem secure. But the psalmist counsels us to wait and to trust. God is trustworthy and reliable. He has the strength and power to get us through whatever we face. Even when we feel certain that we cannot make it through or that God is absent, we can trust him. He's not only powerful but also loving—unfailingly so. How might our lives be shaped if, in the midst of storms, we remembered God's character and let the truth of who he is lead us to trust?

- Read this passage again slowly. What word or phrase stands out to you? Why do you think that word or phrase speaks to you? What does it say?

- Where have you been withholding your trust of God for fear that he might not come through? What would increase your willingness to trust?

- What aspect of God's character do you need to be reminded of consistently? What will help you remember that truth?

RESPOND

Lord, I know your character based on my own experience and what I read in the Scriptures, and still I don't fully trust you with every area of my life. Remind me of your unfailing love, unmatched power, and ability to bring peace in the midst of storms. Remind me of your willingness to rescue me and be my refuge. Be the center of my life, my stronghold, and my light. Amen.

DAY 28

I REMEMBER YOU

a prayer to open

Here's my heart, Lord. Speak what is true.
Here's my life, Lord. Speak what is true.

READ PSALM 63

O God, you are my God;
  I earnestly search for you.
My soul thirsts for you;
  my whole body longs for you
in this parched and weary land
  where there is no water.
I have seen you in your sanctuary

and gazed upon your power and glory.
Your unfailing love is better than life itself;
  how I praise you!
I will praise you as long as I live,
  lifting up my hands to you in prayer.
You satisfy me more than the richest feast.
I will praise you with songs of joy.

I lie awake thinking of you,
   meditating on you through the night.
Because you are my helper,
   I sing for joy in the shadow of your wings.
I cling to you;
   your strong right hand holds me
      securely.

But those plotting to destroy me will come to
   ruin.
They will go down into the depths of the
   earth. . . .
But the king will rejoice in God.
   All who swear to tell the truth will praise him,
   while liars will be silenced.

REFLECT

There are times when it feels as though God is far away. We don't sense his presence, we feel alone, and we wonder if he was ever there at all. We long for a fresh touch of his love and grace, but it doesn't come. This psalm reminds us to keep holding on to what we know to be true—we have experienced his presence and we have seen his power in our lives—and praise him for who we know him to be. How might our lives be shaped if in moments of God's seeming absence we remember his faithfulness and worship him?

- Read this passage again slowly. What word or phrase stands out to you? Why do you think that word or phrase speaks to you? What does it say?

- Reflect on a time during which you longed for God but couldn't sense his presence. How did you navigate that time? What thoughts and feelings went through your mind? How did that time come to an end, or how do you hope it will come to an end?

- List two or three times in your life when God's presence was noticeably evident. Who would be a good person to share your list with so that when you have doubts or don't sense God's presence, your friend can remind you and encourage you to sing his praise even then? Make plans to share your list with this person.

RESPOND

You, Lord, are my Lord. I seek you and thirst for your presence. I have seen you work in my life in small and big ways. You delight in me and have walked with me in valleys. You have appeared to me in the kindness and grace of friends, family, and strangers. You will never leave me. When I cannot feel your presence, remind me of the times I unmistakably sensed your love and goodness, and open my eyes to your presence. Amen.

COME AND SEE

a prayer to open

Here's my heart, Lord. Speak what is true.
Here's my life, Lord. Speak what is true.

READ PSALM 66

Shout joyful praises to God, all the earth!
  Sing about the glory of his name!
  Tell the world how glorious he is.
Say to God, "How awesome are your deeds!
  Your enemies cringe before your mighty
    power.
Everything on earth will worship you;
  they will sing your praises,
  shouting your name in glorious songs."
Come and see what our God has done,
  what awesome miracles he performs for
    people!
He made a dry path through the Red Sea,
  and his people went across on foot.
  There we rejoiced in him.
For by his great power he rules forever.
  He watches every movement of the nations;
  let no rebel rise in defiance.
Let the whole world bless our God
  and loudly sing his praises.
Our lives are in his hands,
  and he keeps our feet from stumbling.
You have tested us, O God;
  you have purified us like silver.

You captured us in your net
  and laid the burden of slavery on our backs.
Then you put a leader over us.
  We went through fire and flood,
  but you brought us to a place of great
    abundance.
Now I come to your Temple with burnt offerings
  to fulfill the vows I made to you—
yes, the sacred vows that I made
  when I was in deep trouble.
That is why I am sacrificing burnt offerings to
    you—
  the best of my rams as a pleasing aroma,
  and a sacrifice of bulls and male goats.
Come and listen, all you who fear God,
  and I will tell you what he did for me.
For I cried out to him for help,
  praising him as I spoke.
If I had not confessed the sin in my heart,
  the Lord would not have listened.
But God did listen!
  He paid attention to my prayer.
Praise God, who did not ignore my prayer
  or withdraw his unfailing love from me.

REFLECT

In many of our churches, worship is a pretty tame affair. Our hearts are in it, but we sway only slightly, not wanting to invade the space of the person next to us. This psalmist seems far from tame; it's no stretch to imagine him shouting and jumping, raising his hands and clapping with vigor! God had acted, and the psalmist just couldn't contain his praise. He wanted everyone to know what God had done on this particular occasion and all throughout history. "Come and see" (verse 5), he said, inviting anyone who would listen. Implied in his invitation was the assurance that God is not far off or aloof but present and active. How might our lives be shaped if, in response to God's acts, we allowed praise and thanksgiving to overtake us and invited others into our experience?

- Read this passage again slowly. What word or phrase stands out to you? Why do you think that word or phrase speaks to you? What does it say?

- What "come and see" experience have you had recently that makes you shake your head in awe at God's greatness and love for you? If no one were watching, how would you want to express your praise and thanksgiving to God?

- Spend a few minutes in prayer, asking God to bring someone to mind who needs to hear your "come and see" story. What about your story do you think will connect with that person?

RESPOND

Lord, there are so many ways you have acted in my life and in history that spark awe in me when I consider them. Just thinking of the saving love and grace of Jesus is enough, but you have done even more. You have acted in my life in ways that make me know you are real, you are loving, and you are powerful. Thank you, thank you, thank you! May I never fail to praise and thank you. Remind me to invite others into my thanksgiving so those who know you can be encouraged and reminded and those who don't yet know you might come to believe. Use me to tell your story. Amen.

DAY 30

BLESSINGS TO SHARE

a prayer to open

Here's my heart, Lord. Speak what is true.
Here's my life, Lord. Speak what is true.

READ PSALM 67

May God be merciful and bless us.
 May his face smile with favor on us.
May your ways be known throughout the earth,
 your saving power among people everywhere.
May the nations praise you, O God.
 Yes, may all the nations praise you.
Let the whole world sing for joy,
 because you govern the nations with justice

and guide the people of the whole world.
May the nations praise you, O God.
 Yes, may all the nations praise you.
Then the earth will yield its harvests,
 and God, our God, will richly bless us.
Yes, God will bless us,
 and people all over the world will fear him.

REFLECT

This psalm was written well before Jesus walked the earth, but it's hard not to hear in it echoes of Jesus' words to us: "You are the light of the world" (Matthew 5:14). Indeed, the psalmist prays that God's mercy and blessing would be upon his people, but not for the sake of his people alone. He prays that God's blessing on his people will bring blessing to the whole world. The fact that Jesus has saved us and given us life in him is a gift to us, of course, but it is not for our sake alone. We are called to share the blessing we have received in Christ with everyone God puts on our path. How might our lives be shaped if we saw the blessings we receive from God as not just for ourselves but also for others?

Reshaped

- Read this passage again slowly. What word or phrase stands out to you? Why do you think that word or phrase speaks to you? What does it say?

- What blessings has God given you that you have shared with others? What blessings have you been a bit stingier about sharing? Why do you think that is?

- Consider all the places you frequent: work, stores, community centers, local businesses. How is God calling you uniquely to be a light in those places?

RESPOND

Lord, thank you for every good and perfect gift you have given me. Let me never take your blessings for granted or keep them to myself. Show me how to be a light wherever you have placed me, and give me the right words and spirit to point those I encounter to you. May your ways, love, and saving power be known throughout the whole earth. Amen.

DAY 31

OPEN TO TRUTH

a prayer to open

Here's my heart, Lord. Speak what is true.
Here's my life, Lord. Speak what is true.

READ PSALM 73:21-26

Then I realized that my heart was bitter,
and I was all torn up inside.
I was so foolish and ignorant—
I must have seemed like a senseless animal
to you.
Yet I still belong to you;
you hold my right hand.
You guide me with your counsel,

leading me to a glorious destiny.
Whom have I in heaven but you?
I desire you more than anything on earth.
My health may fail, and my spirit may grow
weak,
but God remains the strength of my heart;
he is mine forever.

REFLECT

Bitterness can have such a deep hold on us that we don't even know it's there. Others see it. They hear it in our words and our silent judgment. They know it by our criticism, cynicism, and complaints. What will make us realize that our hearts have turned to bitterness and we've lost hope? Often we can't come to awareness on our own. We need the Holy Spirit to convict us and remind us of God's presence and active redemption. We need friends to call us out. We need practices that will cultivate hope, patience, and compassion. How might our lives be shaped if we were open to the Spirit's truth and our friends' correction in order to rid ourselves of bitterness?

- Read this passage again slowly. What word or phrase stands out to you? Why do you think that word or phrase speaks to you? What does it say?

- Take a few minutes, remembering you are in God's loving presence, to reflect on your heart. Where has bitterness taken root? Why do you think bitterness has taken root? Where do you sense bitterness getting a foothold? What practices might help you rid yourself of this growing bitterness?

- What circumstances, relationships, and activities tend to turn your heart toward bitterness? What changes do you need to make to rid yourself of the bitterness these things create?

RESPOND

Lord, may all bitterness toward others be rooted out of my heart. I want none of that choking out the hope I have in you or the love I long to share with the people in my life. Give me eyes to see when bitterness is taking over and judgment is my first instinct. Grow my capacity for patience and compassion. Where I am prone to bitterness because of circumstance or the people I am with, show me a way out. Show me the way of hope. Amen.

DAY 32

REMEMBER ME

a prayer to open

Here's my heart, Lord. Speak what is true.
Here's my life, Lord. Speak what is true.

READ PSALM 77

I cry out to God; yes, I shout.
  Oh, that God would listen to me!
When I was in deep trouble,
  I searched for the Lord.
All night long I prayed, with hands lifted toward heaven,
  but my soul was not comforted.
I think of God, and I moan,
  overwhelmed with longing for his help.
You don't let me sleep.
  I am too distressed even to pray!
I think of the good old days,
  long since ended,
when my nights were filled with joyful songs.
  I search my soul and ponder the difference now.
Has the Lord rejected me forever?
  Will he never again be kind to me?
Is his unfailing love gone forever?

Have his promises permanently failed?
Has God forgotten to be gracious?
  Has he slammed the door on his compassion?
And I said, "This is my fate;
  the Most High has turned his hand against me."
But then I recall all you have done, O LORD;
  I remember your wonderful deeds of long ago.
They are constantly in my thoughts.
  I cannot stop thinking about your mighty works.
O God, your ways are holy.
  Is there any god as mighty as you?
You are the God of great wonders!
  You demonstrate your awesome power among the nations.
By your strong arm, you redeemed your people,
  the descendants of Jacob and Joseph.

Reshaped

When the Red Sea saw you, O God,
　its waters looked and trembled!
　The sea quaked to its very depths.
The clouds poured down rain;
　the thunder rumbled in the sky.
　Your arrows of lightning flashed.
Your thunder roared from the whirlwind;
　the lightning lit up the world!

The earth trembled and shook.
Your road led through the sea,
　your pathway through the mighty waters—
　a pathway no one knew was there!
You led your people along that road like a flock
　of sheep,
　with Moses and Aaron as their shepherds.

REFLECT

When we are in the depths of despair and have experienced an unthinkable heartbreak, our minds can become scattered and overwhelmed with a desire to immediately fix the pain. We can feel unanchored and desperate. How do we find our way back to hope? How do we stay connected to God? The author of this psalm tells us the key: remember. How might our lives be shaped if in the midst of our lowest points we recall how God's presence, provision, and power have showed up for us in the past?

• Read this passage again slowly. What word or phrase stands out to you? Why do you think that word or phrase speaks to you? What does it say?

• Reflect on the last time you went through a valley and found yourself unanchored, desperate, or groaning. In what ways did God show himself to you?

• Who do you know who is in a valley right now? How can you bring God's love and peace to them? How can you help that person remember the ways God walked with them through the last valley and know that he is faithful to do the same this time?

RESPOND

Lord, I have known despair and deep pain. I know what it is to groan in desperation for the hurt to be removed and to long for immediate healing. Yet I know your presence in the midst of these valleys. I remember the ways you have walked with me before. Use me to bring hope to someone today—someone who is in a valley and feels unanchored. Allow me to be your presence to a desperate, longing soul. Amen.

DAY 33

AN EXPECTANT SPIRIT

a prayer to open

Here's my heart, Lord.　Speak what is true.
Here's my life, Lord.　Speak what is true.

How lovely is your dwelling place,
  O Lord of Heaven's Armies.
I long, yes, I faint with longing
  to enter the courts of the Lord.
With my whole being, body and soul,
  I will shout joyfully to the living God.
Even the sparrow finds a home,
  and the swallow builds her nest and raises
    her young
at a place near your altar,
  O Lord of Heaven's Armies, my King and my
    God!
What joy for those who can live in your house,
  always singing your praises.
What joy for those whose strength comes from
    the Lord,
  who have set their minds on a pilgrimage to
    Jerusalem.
When they walk through the Valley of Weeping,
  it will become a place of refreshing springs.
  The autumn rains will clothe it with blessings.

They will continue to grow stronger,
  and each of them will appear before God in
    Jerusalem.
O Lord God of Heaven's Armies, hear my
    prayer.
  Listen, O God of Jacob.
O God, look with favor upon the king, our
    shield!
  Show favor to the one you have anointed.
A single day in your courts
  is better than a thousand anywhere else!
I would rather be a gatekeeper in the house of
    my God
  than live the good life in the homes of the
    wicked.
For the Lord God is our sun and our shield.
  He gives us grace and glory.
The Lord will withhold no good thing
  from those who do what is right.
O Lord of Heaven's Armies,
  what joy for those who trust in you.

REFLECT

Before Christ, God's people experienced his presence in the physical Temple in Jerusalem. They traveled from far away throughout the year to visit the Temple, where they found refreshment and renewal. Experiencing God's presence there enabled them to return to their towns and continue to follow in his ways. Since Christ, we no longer need to visit a physical temple in order to experience God's presence. God lives in and among his people. As Paul described to the church in Corinth, "Don't you know that you yourselves are God's temple and that God's Spirit dwells in your midst? If anyone destroys God's temple, God will destroy that person; for God's temple is sacred, and you together are that temple" (1 Corinthians 3:16-17, NIV). When we are among other believers, we experience God's presence in a unique way. We know the love and strength and refreshment of Christ in and through the people with whom we are gathered. And when we have had a taste of Christ's presence, our bodies and souls long for more. How might our lives be shaped if each time we gathered with other believers, we expected to experience and help others experience God's presence in a unique way that would bring refreshment and renewal?

- Read this passage again slowly. What word or phrase stands out to you? Why do you think that word or phrase speaks to you? What does it say?

- When do you feel a sense of longing for God's presence?

- Reflect on a time recently when you were refreshed and renewed while gathered with other believers. How did you experience God's presence in and through the people you were with?

I long to know your presence, Lord—to experience your healing and refreshment and to be reminded of your goodness. With you I find healing and wholeness, light and hope. Don't let me forget the power of gathering with your people and the restoration that brings to my mind, heart, and soul. Allow me to be a refreshment to others whose souls are depleted or hearts are hurting. Amen.

DAY 34

AN UNDIVIDED HEART

a prayer to open

Here's my heart, Lord. Speak what is true.
Here's my life, Lord. Speak what is true.

READ PSALM 86

Bend down, O LORD, and hear my prayer;
  answer me, for I need your help.
Protect me, for I am devoted to you.
  Save me, for I serve you and trust you.
  You are my God.
Be merciful to me, O Lord,
  for I am calling on you constantly.
Give me happiness, O Lord,
  for I give myself to you.
O Lord, you are so good, so ready to forgive,
  so full of unfailing love for all who ask for your
    help.
Listen closely to my prayer, O LORD;
  hear my urgent cry.
I will call to you whenever I'm in trouble,
  and you will answer me.
No pagan god is like you, O Lord.
  None can do what you do!
All the nations you made
  will come and bow before you, Lord;
  they will praise your holy name.
For you are great and perform wonderful deeds.
  You alone are God.

Teach me your ways, O LORD,
  that I may live according to your truth!
Grant me purity of heart,
  so that I may honor you.
With all my heart I will praise you, O Lord my
    God.
  I will give glory to your name forever,
for your love for me is very great.
  You have rescued me from the depths of
    death.
O God, insolent people rise up against me;
  a violent gang is trying to kill me.
  You mean nothing to them.
But you, O Lord,
  are a God of compassion and mercy,
slow to get angry
  and filled with unfailing love and faithfulness.
Look down and have mercy on me.
  Give your strength to your servant;
  save me, the son of your servant.
Send me a sign of your favor.
  Then those who hate me will be put to shame,
  for you, O LORD, help and comfort me.

REFLECT

In this psalm, the author asks God for purity of heart, or put another way, an "undivided heart" (verse 11, NIV). Most of us have a hard time even imagining what an undivided heart would be like. So many things vie for our attention and devotion. We are constantly pulled in different directions. What would it feel like to be undivided? How might our lives be shaped by a prayer each day that we would have undivided hearts, singularly devoted to God and centered on his presence and purposes?

- Read this passage again slowly. What word or phrase stands out to you? Why do you think that word or phrase speaks to you? What does it say?

- How would you complete this sentence? _____ *keeps me from having an undivided heart, centered on God and his purposes.* (For example, a particular relationship, a busy schedule, lack of clarity about how to have an undivided heart, responsibilities with young kids, work schedule.) Is there any element of fear underneath what you identified?

- What changes would you need to make to allow yourself to fully partner with God's attempts to give you an undivided heart, centered in his purposes and equipped to be a light in the world?

RESPOND

I need your help, Lord. My heart is divided among so many things. Please give me an undivided heart. Show me what I need to let go of so I can be less scattered. Make clear what you are calling me to in this season, and give me the courage to listen and follow. Open my eyes to the parts of me you seek to redeem and restore. Give me an undivided heart that yields to your work in me and in the world. Amen.

IN THE DARKNESS

a prayer to open

Here's my heart, Lord. Speak what is true.
Here's my life, Lord. Speak what is true.

READ PSALM 88

O LORD, God of my salvation,
  I cry out to you by day.
  I come to you at night.
Now hear my prayer;
  listen to my cry.
For my life is full of troubles,
  and death draws near.
I am as good as dead,
  like a strong man with no strength left.
They have left me among the dead,
  and I lie like a corpse in a grave.
I am forgotten,
  cut off from your care.
You have thrown me into the lowest pit,
  into the darkest depths.
Your anger weighs me down;
  with wave after wave you have engulfed me.

You have driven my friends away
  by making me repulsive to them.
I am in a trap with no way of escape.
  My eyes are blinded by my tears.
Each day I beg for your help, O LORD;
  I lift my hands to you for mercy.
Are your wonderful deeds of any use to the
    dead?
  Do the dead rise up and praise you?
Can those in the grave declare your unfailing
    love?
  Can they proclaim your faithfulness in the
    place of destruction?
Can the darkness speak of your wonderful
    deeds?
  Can anyone in the land of forgetfulness talk
    about your righteousness?

O LORD, I cry out to you.
  I will keep on pleading day by day.
O LORD, why do you reject me?
  Why do you turn your face from me?
I have been sick and close to death since my
    youth.
  I stand helpless and desperate before your
    terrors.

Your fierce anger has overwhelmed me.
  Your terrors have paralyzed me.
They swirl around me like floodwaters all day
    long.
  They have engulfed me completely.
You have taken away my companions and loved
    ones.
  Darkness is my closest friend.

REFLECT

In this psalm, the author asks a question nearly all of us have asked at one point or another: Is God present in the darkness? When we have our lowest lows, when we are suffering or dying—or someone we love is dying—is God there? Does he see our pain? Does he know our despair? And if the answer is yes, why are we so often unable to sense his presence? In Old Testament days—before Jesus—God's people did not have the assurance of life after death with God. Darkness seemed to prevail. Indeed sometimes even today we feel and live this way, forgetting that in Christ and through Christ, death is not the end. Just as he resurrected from the dead, so too will we (John 11:25-26). Although this truth may not always find its way into our hearts and minds as we experience darkness, it is our lifeline. If today's psalm were our lament, we might end it this way: "I hold on to the hope I have in Jesus Christ. I will be raised to life. Death and darkness will not prevail." How might our lives be shaped if, in the midst of despair and darkness, our lament was always paired with the hope we have in Christ?

- Read this passage again slowly. What word or phrase stands out to you? Why do you think that word or phrase speaks to you? What does it say?

- What pointed questions do you want to pose to God about your own suffering, the suffering of friends or family members, or the suffering in the world? Remembering that you are in his loving presence, ask God the questions you are longing to voice. Listen for how he responds.

- Reflect on seasons of darkness you have walked through. How did you hold on to hope? Or if you were unable to, how did you make it through those times? If you're in a season of darkness now, who could you invite into your life to be hopeful on your behalf?

RESPOND

Lord, thank you for light, life, and resurrection through Jesus! How my heart would despair if I couldn't hold on to the hope I have in him. In those moments or seasons when darkness falls upon me, help me remember the life that awaits me in your presence forever. Do not let me forget the hope I have, and surround me with friends who can remind me that death does not prevail. And may I bring hope to those who suffer and be a light to those who despair. When I suffer, grant me mercy and allow me to know the gift and joy of your presence. Amen.

FULLY DEVOTED

a prayer to open

Here's my heart, Lord. Speak what is true.
Here's my life, Lord. Speak what is true.

READ PSALM 96

Sing a new song to the LORD!
Let the whole earth sing to the LORD!
Sing to the LORD; praise his name.
Each day proclaim the good news that he
saves.
Publish his glorious deeds among the nations.
Tell everyone about the amazing things he
does.
Great is the LORD! He is most worthy of praise!
He is to be feared above all gods.
The gods of other nations are mere idols,
but the LORD made the heavens!
Honor and majesty surround him;
strength and beauty fill his sanctuary.
O nations of the world, recognize the LORD;
recognize that the LORD is glorious and
strong.

Give to the LORD the glory he deserves!
Bring your offering and come into his courts.
Worship the LORD in all his holy splendor.
Let all the earth tremble before him.
Tell all the nations, "The LORD reigns!"
The world stands firm and cannot be shaken.
He will judge all peoples fairly.
Let the heavens be glad, and the earth rejoice!
Let the sea and everything in it shout his
praise!
Let the fields and their crops burst out with joy!
Let the trees of the forest sing for joy
before the LORD, for he is coming!
He is coming to judge the earth.
He will judge the world with justice,
and the nations with his truth.

REFLECT

Even though many of us have a deep sense that it isn't good or healthy to idolize things or people, idols have a grip on most of us in one way or another, in ways we don't even realize. We tend to turn things that are otherwise good—such as a desire for relationship, adequate income, a fulfilling job, or God-given talents—into idols as a way to cope with difficulty or unresolved wounds. Idols take over our minds and hearts. They tempt us to pursue them instead of God. This psalm reminds us of what we already instinctively know but easily forget: All gods but God are idols, unable to provide satisfaction, help, or hope. How might our lives be shaped if we were to get honest about the things that have a hold on us?

- Read this passage again slowly. What word or phrase stands out to you? Why do you think that word or phrase speaks to you? What does it say?

- What things and people absorb your thoughts and heart more than God (your job, money, image, family, singleness, pain)? What do you pursue more than you pursue God (sex, intimacy, alcohol, drugs, recognition, success, freedom, approval)?

- Who in your life can call you out when you begin to allow those things to take your heart away from God? What's a step you can take this week to get honest with that person about what idol has a hold on you?

Reshaped

•

225

I deeply desire, Lord, that my heart would be fully yours. Why do I get pulled away so easily? Why do temporary pleasures or fixes that bring short-term satisfaction have such a hold on me at times? Help me see clearly what I'm placing ahead of you as idols, and help me be honest with someone in my life about those things so they can help me be free. May my full devotion be to you. Amen.

DAY 37

WE ARE HIS

a prayer to open

Here's my heart, Lord. Speak what is true.
Here's my life, Lord. Speak what is true.

READ PSALM 100

Shout with joy to the LORD, all the earth!
    Worship the LORD with gladness.
    Come before him, singing with joy.
Acknowledge that the LORD is God!
    He made us, and we are his.
    We are his people, the sheep of his
        pasture.

Enter his gates with thanksgiving;
    go into his courts with praise.
    Give thanks to him and praise his name.
For the LORD is good.
    His unfailing love continues forever,
    and his faithfulness continues to each
        generation.

REFLECT

How do you introduce yourself when you first meet someone? Is it often based on your relationship to someone else—being so-and-so's spouse or so-and-so's friend? Relationship to others defines us in so many ways. But in this psalm, our most fundamental identity is established: "He made us, and we are his" (verse 3). However else we may define, introduce, or perceive ourselves, we are first and foremost God's. How might our lives be shaped if we were to wake up each morning and go to bed each night reminding ourselves of this truth?

- Read this passage again slowly. What word or phrase stands out to you? Why do you think that word or phrase speaks to you? What does it say?

- What emotions do you feel when you read and receive the truth that you are God's?

- What does it mean that you are his? How does this truth influence your view of yourself? How does it influence your interactions with others? What might your relationships look like if you felt secure as God's beloved?

I am yours, Lord. Above all else, I am yours. Remind me of this truth throughout each day. I forget so quickly, sometimes at the slightest criticism or difficulty. Help me remember when I open my eyes in the morning and as I drift off to sleep at night that I am yours. Allow this truth to sink deeply into my soul. Let it mark my actions and reactions and drive my thoughts and words. I am yours. Above all else, I am yours. Amen.

ALL OF CREATION

a prayer to open

Here's my heart, Lord. Speak what is true.
Here's my life, Lord. Speak what is true.

READ PSALM 104:1-34

Let all that I am praise the LORD.
O LORD my God, how great you are!
  You are robed with honor and majesty.
  You are dressed in a robe of light.
You stretch out the starry curtain of the
    heavens;
  you lay out the rafters of your home in the rain
    clouds.
You make the clouds your chariot;
  you ride upon the wings of the wind.
The winds are your messengers;
  flames of fire are your servants.
You placed the world on its foundation
  so it would never be moved.
You clothed the earth with floods of water,
  water that covered even the mountains.
At your command, the water fled;
  at the sound of your thunder, it hurried away.
Mountains rose and valleys sank
  to the levels you decreed.
Then you set a firm boundary for the seas,
  so they would never again cover the earth.
You make springs pour water into the ravines,
  so streams gush down from the mountains.
They provide water for all the animals,
  and the wild donkeys quench their thirst.
The birds nest beside the streams
  and sing among the branches of the trees.
You send rain on the mountains from your
    heavenly home,
  and you fill the earth with the fruit of your
    labor.
You cause grass to grow for the livestock

and plants for people to use.
You allow them to produce food from the
    earth—
  wine to make them glad,
olive oil to soothe their skin,
  and bread to give them strength. . . .
High in the mountains live the wild goats,
  and the rocks form a refuge for the hyraxes.
You made the moon to mark the seasons,
  and the sun knows when to set.
You send the darkness, and it becomes night,
  when all the forest animals prowl about.
Then the young lions roar for their prey,
  stalking the food provided by God. . . .
People go off to their work,
  where they labor until evening.
O LORD, what a variety of things you have
    made!
  In wisdom you have made them all.
  The earth is full of your creatures.
Here is the ocean, vast and wide,
  teeming with life of every kind,
  both large and small.
See the ships sailing along,
  and Leviathan, which you made to play in
    the sea.
They all depend on you
  to give them food as they need it.
When you supply it, they gather it.
  You open your hand to feed them,
  and they are richly satisfied. . . .
When you give them your breath, life is created,
  and you renew the face of the earth.

Reshaped

•

> May the glory of the LORD continue forever!
>   The LORD takes pleasure in all he has made!
> The earth trembles at his glance;
>   the mountains smoke at his touch.

> I will sing to the LORD as long as I live.
>   I will praise my God to my last breath!
> May all my thoughts be pleasing to him,
>   for I rejoice in the LORD.

REFLECT _____

The poet Elizabeth Barrett Browning wrote,

> *Earth's crammed with heaven,*
> *And every common bush afire with God;*
> *But only he who sees, takes off his shoes;*
> *The rest sit round it and pluck blackberries.*[6]

She captured the psalmist's sentiments exactly. The author begs us to take notice of all God has made, all he sustains, and all he provides. How might our lives be shaped if we were to pay attention to the stunning details of creation—big and small—more often?

- Read the Bible passage again slowly. What word or phrase stands out to you? Why do you think that word or phrase speaks to you? What does it say?

- Which season of the year is your favorite? What parts of creation do you notice most in that season?

- What part of creation most represents God's power and majesty for you? What part of creation most represents his care and provision for you?

RESPOND _____

Thank you for every single detail of creation, Lord. I am in awe of your care and your majesty. You made and sustain all that I see, and still you speak into my individual heart and seek to guide my every step. Thank you. Open my eyes to the beauty and intricacy of this world, and fill my heart with childlike wonder. Amen.

DAY 39

LOVE THE LORD YOUR GOD

a prayer to open

Here's my heart, Lord. Speak what is true.
Here's my life, Lord. Speak what is true.

Give thanks to the LORD and proclaim his
greatness.
Let the whole world know what he has done.
Sing to him; yes, sing his praises.
Tell everyone about his wonderful deeds.
Exult in his holy name;
rejoice, you who worship the LORD.
Search for the LORD and for his strength;

continually seek him.
Remember the wonders he has performed,
his miracles, and the rulings he has given. . . .
He is the LORD our God.
His justice is seen throughout the land.
He always stands by his covenant—
the commitment he made to a thousand
generations.

REFLECT _____

These first eight verses of today's psalm give us a road map for loving God: Give thanks. Proclaim God's greatness. Sing his praises. Tell everyone what God does. Exult in his name. Rejoice! Search for and seek the Lord. Remember what God has done. Remember who he is.

Note in this psalm the absence of offering sacrifices and following a set of rules. These are absent not because of their lack of importance (we learn in the New Testament that God wants our whole lives as a living sacrifice and calls us to holiness) but because if we love God in the way the psalmist instructs here, all else will follow. As we grow in our ability to believe God, to trust in who he is, to see and remember all he has done in our lives and in the world, obedience to his path, thankfulness for his faithfulness, and a surrender of our lives to him will flow naturally. How might our lives be shaped if we regularly practiced the instructions of this psalm?

- Read this passage again slowly. What word or phrase stands out to you? Why do you think that word or phrase speaks to you? What does it say?

- As you read through the list of ways we show our love for God, what comes naturally for you? Which is more difficult? What would help you grow in the area you feel least capable?

- If a friend were to ask you how to love God, what practical counsel would you give?

RESPOND _____

Thank you, Lord, for the ability to worship you and know you. What a miracle it is that you have acted in my life and in the world in ways that inspire awe and wonder in my heart and mind! Let my mouth always praise you and tell about what you've done. Let my life show the world your goodness and grace. Forgive me when I forget to be grateful for or content with what you've given me. Center my heart on you, and allow me to love my neighbor as myself. Amen.

Reshaped

THE BEGINNING OF WISDOM

a prayer to open

Here's my heart, Lord. Speak what is true.
Here's my life, Lord. Speak what is true.

READ PSALM 111

Praise the LORD!
I will thank the LORD with all my heart
as I meet with his godly people.
How amazing are the deeds of the LORD!
All who delight in him should ponder them.
Everything he does reveals his glory and
majesty.
His righteousness never fails.
He causes us to remember his wonderful
works.
How gracious and merciful is our LORD!
He gives food to those who fear him;
he always remembers his covenant.
He has shown his great power to his people
by giving them the lands of other nations.
All he does is just and good,
and all his commandments are trustworthy.
They are forever true,
to be obeyed faithfully and with integrity.
He has paid a full ransom for his people.
He has guaranteed his covenant with them
forever.
What a holy, awe-inspiring name he has!
Fear of the LORD is the foundation of true
wisdom.
All who obey his commandments will grow in
wisdom.
Praise him forever!

REFLECT

Almost all of us know people we would describe as wise. They seem to have access to deeper wells of knowledge and often have experience beyond what their years would suggest. How do we grow in wisdom? The psalmist tells us that wisdom begins when we trust God and commit to following him ("fear of the LORD" [verse 10]). In James 1:5, we are told that if we lack wisdom, we should ask God and it will be given to us. How might our lives be shaped if we were to ask God to give us the wisdom we need when we face difficult decisions or hard circumstances?

- Read this passage again slowly. What word or phrase stands out to you? Why do you think that word or phrase speaks to you? What does it say?

- Who comes to mind when you think of wisdom? What characteristics does that person have?

- In what area of your life do you need wisdom right now? How does Scripture advise you to handle that situation? Ask God for his wisdom in the area you need.

RESPOND

Thank you, Lord, for your promise of wisdom. Thank you for the guidance and counsel you provide in Scripture. Please give me your wisdom to face the decisions I need to make today, whether big or small. Direct my mind to Scripture passages that should guide and inform me. Give me the awareness and the resolve to walk in your ways, committed fully to your desires for my life. Amen.

TO FREELY GIVE

a prayer to open
Here's my heart, Lord. Speak what is true.
Here's my life, Lord. Speak what is true.

READ PSALM 112

Praise the LORD!
How joyful are those who fear the LORD
and delight in obeying his commands.
Their children will be successful everywhere;
an entire generation of godly people will be
blessed.
They themselves will be wealthy,
and their good deeds will last forever.
Light shines in the darkness for the godly.
They are generous, compassionate, and
righteous.
Good comes to those who lend money
generously
and conduct their business fairly.
Such people will not be overcome by evil.

Those who are righteous will be long
remembered.
They do not fear bad news;
they confidently trust the LORD to care for
them.
They are confident and fearless
and can face their foes triumphantly.
They share freely and give generously to those
in need.
Their good deeds will be remembered
forever.
They will have influence and honor.
The wicked will see this and be infuriated.
They will grind their teeth in anger;
they will slink away, their hopes thwarted.

REFLECT

Flip on your television or radio any time of day, and within minutes you are likely to hear about two things: spending and saving. Both are a necessary part of life, of course, but how often are we encouraged in our culture to give generously and freely? God's Word says far more about giving than about spending or saving. In this psalm, we are reminded not only of God's heart for the poor but also of how giving affects the human heart. Those who are generous and lend freely will have no fear of bad news, their hearts will remain steadfast and secure, and they will trust the Lord. In other words, although we associate giving with a loss of something (money, time, energy), it actually results in gains (security, trust, peace). How might our lives be shaped if we realized that giving freely and generously will result in great gains for our hearts and souls?

- Read this passage again slowly. What word or phrase stands out to you? Why do you think that word or phrase speaks to you? What does it say?

- When you give of your money, time, or energy, what do you feel you are sacrificing? What most often keeps you from giving to those who are poor?

- Reflect on a time you gave freely and generously. How did you feel? How did you experience God in the midst of your giving?

Reshaped

231

Lord, expand my heart to love and give freely to those beyond my friends and family. Give me eyes to see need and a heart that longs to respond generously even if it means sacrifice or discomfort. Grow my trust in you, banish all fear that causes me to cling to that which is "mine," and fill me with a desire to give. Use my money, my gifts, and my time—all of which are yours—to build your Kingdom and extend your love to those who need it most. Amen.

DAY 42

JUST LIKE HIM

a prayer to open

Here's my heart, Lord. Speak what is true.
Here's my life, Lord. Speak what is true.

READ PSALM 115

Not to us, O LORD, not to us,
   but to your name goes all the glory
   for your unfailing love and faithfulness.
Why let the nations say,
   "Where is their God?"
Our God is in the heavens,
   and he does as he wishes.
Their idols are merely things of silver and gold,
   shaped by human hands.
They have mouths but cannot speak,
   and eyes but cannot see.
They have ears but cannot hear,
   and noses but cannot smell.
They have hands but cannot feel,
   and feet but cannot walk,
   and throats but cannot make a sound.
And those who make idols are just like them,
   as are all who trust in them.
O Israel, trust the LORD!

He is your helper and your shield. . . .
All you who fear the LORD, trust the LORD!
   He is your helper and your shield.
The LORD remembers us and will bless us.
   He will bless the people of Israel. . . .
He will bless those who fear the LORD,
   both great and lowly.
May the LORD richly bless
   both you and your children.
May you be blessed by the LORD,
   who made heaven and earth.
The heavens belong to the LORD,
   but he has given the earth to all humanity.
The dead cannot sing praises to the LORD,
   for they have gone into the silence of the
   grave.
But we can praise the LORD
   both now and forever!
Praise the LORD!

REFLECT

It's so easy to look back on ancient times and think how ridiculous it was for people to have put their trust in wooden figures or pieces of gold and silver. Who would ever think handmade objects were gods? But our hearts are no less deceived. All of us attach to temporary, powerless objects, ideas, and people. Although we long to be like Jesus, our hearts lead us to treat other people and things like gods. We chase fame, money, status, power, and perfection, and before we know what's happening, we become just like our idols. If we put our trust in status, believing that the way others see us is what determines our value, we will see others through this same lens, where only those who have reached a certain level are worthy of our attention. John the apostle said that God is love and that as we live in him, our love grows more perfect (see 1 John 4:16-17). In other words, only when God is at the center of our lives will we become more like him. If money or fame or power or perfection is at the center of our lives (and hearts), we will not become more like Christ; any effort will be fruitless. How might our lives be shaped if, with gut-wrenching honesty, we named the things and people and ideas that regularly find their way into the number one position in our hearts?

- Read this passage again slowly. What word or phrase stands out to you? Why do you think that word or phrase speaks to you? What does it say?

- What are your idols? Why do you think your heart tends to attach to whatever you identified?

- In what areas of your life do you feel stuck in your growth toward Christlikeness? Reflect on whether there is an idol at the heart of that "stuck-ness." Ask God to give you eyes to see what you're pursuing more than love.

RESPOND

Oh, Lord, it's embarrassing to see the kinds of things my heart attaches to for safety or control or temporary satisfaction. I need you at the center of my heart. I can be so easily fooled by the temptations of this world and the things this culture puts on a pedestal. What I desire most is to love like Jesus in every sense. Help me live in you, put my trust in you, rely on you, and attach to only you. In the places I am stuck, free me and give me the strength and opportunity to grow. Amen.

DAY 43

RETURN TO YOUR REST

a prayer to open

Here's my heart, Lord. Speak what is true.
Here's my life, Lord. Speak what is true.

READ PSALM 116

I love the LORD because he hears my voice
  and my prayer for mercy.
Because he bends down to listen,
  I will pray as long as I have breath!
Death wrapped its ropes around me;
  the terrors of the grave overtook me.
I saw only trouble and sorrow.
Then I called on the name of the LORD:
  "Please, LORD, save me!"
How kind the LORD is! How good he is!

So merciful, this God of ours!
The LORD protects those of childlike faith;
  I was facing death, and he saved me.
Let my soul be at rest again,
  for the LORD has been good to me.
He has saved me from death,
  my eyes from tears,
  my feet from stumbling.
And so I walk in the LORD's presence
  as I live here on earth!

Reshaped

•

I believed in you, so I said,
  "I am deeply troubled, LORD."
In my anxiety I cried out to you,
  "These people are all liars!"
What can I offer the LORD
  for all he has done for me?
I will lift up the cup of salvation
  and praise the LORD's name for saving me.
I will keep my promises to the LORD
  in the presence of all his people.
The LORD cares deeply
  when his loved ones die.

O LORD, I am your servant;
  yes, I am your servant, born into your
    household;
  you have freed me from my chains.
I will offer you a sacrifice of thanksgiving
  and call on the name of the LORD.
I will fulfill my vows to the LORD
  in the presence of all his people—
in the house of the LORD
  in the heart of Jerusalem.
Praise the LORD!

REFLECT _____

Rest is evasive in our culture. We value productivity, achievement, and success above almost everything else. And so we push our bodies, minds, and souls beyond what they can bear and end up weary, sick, and scattered. In this psalm, we hear how we can counsel our own souls: "Let my soul be at rest again, for the LORD has been good to me." How might our lives be shaped if we sought out rest for our souls on a regular basis?

- Read this passage again slowly. What word or phrase stands out to you? Why do you think that word or phrase speaks to you? What does it say?

- If you had two days to yourself, what would be restorative to your body, mind, and soul? If you had only one day, how might you rest?

- What is one thing you could do to create a little more rest in your life? Is there something you need to say no to? Is there a conversation you need to have? Is there a routine you need to establish—or discontinue?

RESPOND _____

Thank you, Lord, for your goodness to me. Help me remember that you are in control and that I can experience rest without fear or anxiety. I know I am at my best when I am filled with your Spirit and living with open hands and an open heart. Guide me as I seek to build rest into my life. Remind me of your goodness and your desire for me to trust you fully. Amen.

DAY 44

HERE'S MY HEART

a prayer to open

Here's my heart, Lord. Speak what is true.
Here's my life, Lord. Speak what is true.

You have done many good things for me, LORD,
just as you promised.
I believe in your commands;
now teach me good judgment and
knowledge.
I used to wander off until you disciplined me;
but now I closely follow your word.
You are good and do only good;
teach me your decrees.
Arrogant people smear me with lies,
but in truth I obey your commandments with
all my heart.
Their hearts are dull and stupid,
but I delight in your instructions.
My suffering was good for me,
for it taught me to pay attention to your
decrees.
Your instructions are more valuable to me
than millions in gold and silver.
You made me; you created me.

Now give me the sense to follow your
commands.
May all who fear you find in me a cause for joy,
for I have put my hope in your word.
I know, O LORD, that your regulations are fair;
you disciplined me because I needed it.
Now let your unfailing love comfort me,
just as you promised me, your servant.
Surround me with your tender mercies so I may
live,
for your instructions are my delight.
Bring disgrace upon the arrogant people who
lied about me;
meanwhile, I will concentrate on your
commandments.
Let me be united with all who fear you,
with those who know your laws.
May I be blameless in keeping your decrees;
then I will never be ashamed.

REFLECT

The words of this psalm may seem more like aspiration than reality. Is it possible for our wayward hearts to obey God's commands fully? Do we need to try harder? Yes and no. Just trying harder isn't the answer. Rather, God asks us to surrender our hearts to him and partner with his Spirit as he transforms us over time into people who naturally obey his commands. This is a lifelong process, but by God's guidance and grace, our desires eventually become his desires, and our ways his ways. How might our lives be shaped if we began each day by surrendering our hearts anew to his transformative work?

- Read this passage again slowly. What word or phrase stands out to you? Why do you think that word or phrase speaks to you? What does it say?

- Which of God's commands are hardest for you to follow? Why? Describe to God the difficulty you are having. Is there a friend or family member you could also share that with this week?

- Reflect on the areas of your life that seem out of step with God's desires for you. What needs to be transformed or healed in you in order for you to be more aligned with God? What do you sense him asking of you to partner with him in that transformation?

RESPOND

Lord, I pray that this psalm would be true of me. Help me surrender my heart to you and your work more fully. Be merciful and gentle with me as you guide me. Transform my desires to align with yours. Heal the hurts and wounds that can misguide my steps and reactions. I give you my heart. Amen.

MY HELP COMES FROM THE LORD

a prayer to open

Here's my heart, Lord. Speak what is true.
Here's my life, Lord. Speak what is true.

READ PSALM 121

I look up to the mountains—
  does my help come from there?
My help comes from the LORD,
  who made heaven and earth!
He will not let you stumble;
  the one who watches over you will not
  slumber.
Indeed, he who watches over Israel
  never slumbers or sleeps.
The LORD himself watches over you!

The LORD stands beside you as your protective
  shade.
The sun will not harm you by day,
  nor the moon at night.
The LORD keeps you from all harm
  and watches over your life.
The LORD keeps watch over you as you come
  and go,
  both now and forever.

REFLECT

Help doesn't always come in the way we anticipate. Sometimes it appears out of nowhere, without us even asking. Sometimes it seems delayed. Sometimes it comes by way of a person we never expected. Sometimes we even turn down help because it comes in a manner we didn't plan on or foresee. How might our lives be shaped if we truly embraced the promises in this psalm and always had our hearts open to receiving help in whatever way God chose to send it?

- Read this passage again slowly. What word or phrase stands out to you? Why do you think that word or phrase speaks to you? What does it say?

- What are you currently facing that seems overwhelming? What help do you need? Ask God to provide it.

- Who has God used in your life to bring help in difficult circumstances? Who do you sense him prompting you to help, and how?

RESPOND

Lord, my help comes from you. You will not let my foot slip. You watch over me and do not slumber. I am hidden in your shadow, protected and kept from harm. I know that my perspective is smaller than yours, so open my eyes to the aid you send, and give me the wisdom to receive it—in whatever way you choose to send it. Use me to bring help to those who need it. Thank you for your ever-present help. Amen.

IN THE WAITING

a prayer to open

Here's my heart, Lord. Speak what is true.
Here's my life, Lord. Speak what is true.

READ PSALM 130

From the depths of despair, O LORD,
  I call for your help.
Hear my cry, O Lord.
  Pay attention to my prayer.
LORD, if you kept a record of our sins,
  who, O Lord, could ever survive?
But you offer forgiveness,
  that we might learn to fear you.
I am counting on the LORD;
  yes, I am counting on him.

I have put my hope in his word.
I long for the Lord
  more than sentries long for the dawn,
  yes, more than sentries long for the dawn.
O Israel, hope in the LORD;
  for with the LORD there is unfailing love.
  His redemption overflows.
He himself will redeem Israel
  from every kind of sin.

REFLECT

Have you ever watched kids wait in line to ride a roller coaster? They can hardly stand still. They jump and yell. They swing on the ropes and bars that mark off the waiting area. They bump into the people ahead of them. They have great expectations for what the ride will be like: thrilling and a little scary. How might our lives be shaped if we were to wait with this kind of great expectation for God's actions in and restoration of the world?

- Read this passage again slowly. What word or phrase stands out to you? Why do you think that word or phrase speaks to you? What does it say?

- Reflect on a time you have waited on an action or answer from God. How did you experience the waiting? How did he ultimately respond?

- What are you currently waiting on God for? How does it feel to be waiting? What emotions are you experiencing?

RESPOND

Lord, thank you for times of waiting and for the transformation you do in me during those times. Please mold my character so it reflects your will and so I may serve in your Kingdom. Give me patience and allow me to trust your timing and provision. May I wait with great expectation for how you will reveal your ways and guide me. May I experience your presence in the midst of my waiting. Amen.

THE GOODNESS OF UNITY

a prayer to open

Here's my heart, Lord. Speak what is true.
Here's my life, Lord. Speak what is true.

READ PSALM 133

How wonderful and pleasant it is
    when brothers live together in harmony!
For harmony is as precious as the anointing oil
    that was poured over Aaron's head. . . .
Harmony is as refreshing as the dew from
    Mount Hermon

that falls on the mountains of Zion.
And there the LORD has pronounced his
    blessing,
even life everlasting.

REFLECT

Division characterizes our culture today, no matter where we might find ourselves. Fracture and party lines are the pervasive norms under which we live. Unity is so rare that it is newsworthy and surprising when it happens.

Unity in the church is just as uncommon. We are divided over doctrinal, social, and stylistic issues. We leave little room for other people, and instead of bearing with one another, we leave one another. When unity does arise, there is hardly anything more beautiful. Think of the way people rally together when natural disasters strike. Lines of distinction that we normally draw disappear. Arguments over who holds the right beliefs fade. Goodness emerges. We remember our similarities instead of our differences. We remember that none of us really has control or is secure in this world. How might our lives be shaped if we sought unity—looked for our similarities and bore with one another—in our everyday circumstances?

- Read this passage again slowly. What word or phrase stands out to you? Why do you think that word or phrase speaks to you? What does it say?

- Reflect on what creates division and fracture among God's people. How have you contributed to this division? How have you sought to build up unity? What do you sense God calling you to contribute in the current climate of disunity?

- Where is there division in your own life? What step do you need to take to foster unity? What holds you back? What do you need from God to help you overcome whatever is standing in your way?

Lord, thank you for the moments of unity among people—and among your people—that I have experienced. I have the choice to be a bridge builder or bridge burner. In moments of strife or when my emotions are negatively triggered, fill me with your Spirit and give me the courage to bring peace instead of division. Allow me to experience the goodness of unity that reigns in your Kingdom. May your love in and through me be evident in the words I say and the actions I take. Amen.

DAY 48

PRACTICING HUMILITY

a prayer to open

Here's my heart, Lord. Speak what is true.
Here's my life, Lord. Speak what is true.

READ PSALM 138

I give you thanks, O LORD, with all my heart;
  I will sing your praises before the gods.
I bow before your holy Temple as I worship.
  I praise your name for your unfailing love and
    faithfulness;
for your promises are backed
  by all the honor of your name.
As soon as I pray, you answer me;
  you encourage me by giving me strength.
Every king in all the earth will thank you, LORD,
  for all of them will hear your words.
Yes, they will sing about the LORD's ways,

  for the glory of the LORD is very great.
Though the LORD is great, he cares for the
    humble,
  but he keeps his distance from the proud.
Though I am surrounded by troubles,
  you will protect me from the anger of my
    enemies.
You reach out your hand,
  and the power of your right hand saves me.
The LORD will work out his plans for my life—
  for your faithful love, O LORD, endures forever.
Don't abandon me, for you made me.

REFLECT

Only the humble can give wholehearted thanks to God for whatever provision comes. Only the humble can reserve their worship for him alone when other gods call out to them. Only the humble can bow fully before God in acknowledgment of their need for mercy. Only the humble see their need for his strength and encouragement. Growing in humility begins with giving him thanks for what we have, worshiping him even when we aren't in the mood, surrendering our hearts piece by piece in acknowledgment of our need for his healing and power, and seeking his direction when we think we know exactly what to do. How might our lives be shaped if we practiced humility moment by moment, day by day?

- Read this passage again slowly. What word or phrase stands out to you? Why do you think that word or phrase speaks to you? What does it say?

Reshaped

- What experience or practice has helped form a spirit of humility in you? What continues to keep you humble?

- Take a few minutes in prayer, remembering that you are in God's loving presence, and ask him to show you the ways pride persists in your heart. How is he inviting you to respond to whatever he revealed?

RESPOND

Lord, give me a spirit of humility—one that's quick to give you thanks and praise, acknowledge my dependence upon you, and seek after you in every aspect of my life. Give me eyes that see others as you do and see myself clearly so I don't elevate myself and my needs above those of others. Thank you for your love and faithfulness. Let me never take your saving grace for granted. Amen.

EVERY PART OF YOU

a prayer to open

Here's my heart, Lord. Speak what is true.
Here's my life, Lord. Speak what is true.

READ PSALM 139

O LORD, you have examined my heart
  and know everything about me.
You know when I sit down or stand up.
  You know my thoughts even when I'm far
    away.
You see me when I travel
  and when I rest at home.
  You know everything I do.
You know what I am going to say
  even before I say it, LORD.
You go before me and follow me.
  You place your hand of blessing on my head.
Such knowledge is too wonderful for me,
  too great for me to understand!
I can never escape from your Spirit!
  I can never get away from your presence!
If I go up to heaven, you are there;
  if I go down to the grave, you are there.
If I ride the wings of the morning,
  if I dwell by the farthest oceans,
even there your hand will guide me,
  and your strength will support me.
I could ask the darkness to hide me
  and the light around me to become night—
  but even in darkness I cannot hide from you.
To you the night shines as bright as day.
  Darkness and light are the same to you.

You made all the delicate, inner parts of my
  body
  and knit me together in my mother's womb.
Thank you for making me so wonderfully
  complex!
  Your workmanship is marvelous—how well I
    know it.
You watched me as I was being formed in utter
  seclusion,
  as I was woven together in the dark of the
    womb.
You saw me before I was born.
  Every day of my life was recorded in your
    book.
Every moment was laid out
  before a single day had passed.
How precious are your thoughts about me,
  O God.
  They cannot be numbered!
I can't even count them;
  they outnumber the grains of sand!
And when I wake up,
  you are still with me! . . .
Search me, O God, and know my heart;
  test me and know my anxious thoughts.
Point out anything in me that offends you,
  and lead me along the path of everlasting life.

It is hard to imagine that anyone knows us completely—our desires, pain, fears, failures, and deepest thoughts. But God knows every part of us because he carefully crafted us and we are ever in his presence and care. This psalm reminds us that the one who made and sustains us knows and loves every part of who we are. How might our lives be shaped if we remembered the care with which we were made and the love with which we are sustained?

- Read this passage again slowly. What word or phrase stands out to you? Why do you think that word or phrase speaks to you? What does it say?

- What parts of you seem unlovable? How do you think God views those parts of you?

- Do you know someone who feels unlovable in some way or has a low view of their worth? How can you communicate what is in Psalm 139 to that person this week?

RESPOND

Search me, Lord, and know my heart to the very bottom. Test me and know my fears, anxious thoughts, and worry. See if there is any offensive way in me—my words, my actions, or my character—and lead me in your way, the way that lasts forever. Amen.

DAY 50

THE KINDNESS OF TRUTH

a prayer to open

Here's my heart, Lord. Speak what is true.
Here's my life, Lord. Speak what is true.

READ PSALM 141

O LORD, I am calling to you. Please hurry!
  Listen when I cry to you for help!
Accept my prayer as incense offered to you,
  and my upraised hands as an evening
    offering.
Take control of what I say, O LORD,
  and guard my lips.
Don't let me drift toward evil
  or take part in acts of wickedness.
Don't let me share in the delicacies
  of those who do wrong.
Let the godly strike me!
  It will be a kindness!
If they correct me, it is soothing medicine.
  Don't let me refuse it.

But I pray constantly
  against the wicked and their deeds.
When their leaders are thrown down from a
    cliff,
  the wicked will listen to my words and find
    them true.
Like rocks brought up by a plow,
  the bones of the wicked will lie scattered
    without burial.
I look to you for help, O Sovereign LORD.
  You are my refuge; don't let them kill me.
Keep me from the traps they have set for me,
  from the snares of those who do wrong.
Let the wicked fall into their own nets,
  but let me escape.

Reshaped

•

The conditions of our hearts are revealed by our reactions to stressful or difficult situations. The words that come out of our mouths say something about the anger, resentment, unrest, and fear deep within us. This psalm reminds us that sometimes the greatest kindness a person can offer (although it may not feel like kindness at the time) is the truth about how he or she experiences us in stressful conditions. That truth helps us see what's in our hearts. How might our lives be shaped if we were able to hear truth from others as a kindness from God aimed at transforming us into Christlikeness?

- Read this passage again slowly. What word or phrase stands out to you? Why do you think that word or phrase speaks to you? What does it say?

- Reflect on the last time you were under very stressful circumstances. How would an objective person have experienced your words and actions during that time? What do you think your words and actions revealed about your heart?

- Who speaks truth to you? What are the ways you encourage that person to share truth with you? What are the ways you (perhaps even subconsciously) discourage them from being fully truthful?

RESPOND

Lord, thank you for placing people in my life who will be truthful with me, not as a criticism but as an extension of your kindness. Help me lower my defenses and be open to the transforming work you seek to do in me through other people. Show me the places in my heart that still don't reflect your heart and character. Allow me to receive your correction wholeheartedly so I can better reflect to the world who you are. Amen.

FOR WHO HE IS

a prayer to open

Here's my heart, Lord. Speak what is true.
Here's my life, Lord. Speak what is true.

READ PSALM 145

I will exalt you, my God and King,
　and praise your name forever and ever.
I will praise you every day;
　yes, I will praise you forever.
Great is the LORD! He is most worthy of praise!
　No one can measure his greatness.

Let each generation tell its children of your
　mighty acts;
　let them proclaim your power.
I will meditate on your majestic, glorious
　splendor
　and your wonderful miracles.

Your awe-inspiring deeds will be on every
tongue;
I will proclaim your greatness.
Everyone will share the story of your wonderful
goodness;
they will sing with joy about your
righteousness.
The LORD is merciful and compassionate,
slow to get angry and filled with unfailing
love.
The LORD is good to everyone.
He showers compassion on all his creation.
All of your works will thank you, LORD,
and your faithful followers will praise you.
They will speak of the glory of your kingdom;
they will give examples of your power.
They will tell about your mighty deeds
and about the majesty and glory of your
reign.
For your kingdom is an everlasting kingdom.
You rule throughout all generations.

The LORD always keeps his promises;
he is gracious in all he does.
The LORD helps the fallen
and lifts those bent beneath their loads.
The eyes of all look to you in hope;
you give them their food as they need it.
When you open your hand,
you satisfy the hunger and thirst of every living
thing.
The LORD is righteous in everything he does;
he is filled with kindness.
The LORD is close to all who call on him,
yes, to all who call on him in truth.
He grants the desires of those who fear him;
he hears their cries for help and rescues them.
The LORD protects all those who love him,
but he destroys the wicked.
I will praise the LORD,
and may everyone on earth bless his holy
name
forever and ever.

REFLECT

We have a tendency in our prayers and praise to celebrate God for the things we see him do. And this is a good thing; we see examples throughout Scripture of this kind of praise. But this psalm reminds us that God's actions in the world flow out of his character. How might our lives and prayers be shaped if we praised him not only for his actions in the world but also for who he is?

- Read this passage again slowly. What word or phrase stands out to you? Why do you think that word or phrase speaks to you? What does it say?

- Look back at every phrase in this psalm that begins with the words "The LORD . . ." and list God's characteristics. For which one of these characteristics are you most grateful today? Why?

- Consider the last time you experienced God acting in your life. What did his actions reveal to you about his character?

RESPOND

Thank you, Lord, for who you are. So often I look for what you are doing and how you are acting. I lose sight of who you are and what your actions reveal about you—your grace, compassion, goodness, trustworthiness, faithfulness, righteousness, and nearness. Remind me of who you are, Lord, in my moments of joy and my moments of sadness. And regardless of my circumstances, may I see your character shining through. Amen.

TRUST IN GOD ALONE

a prayer to open

Here's my heart, Lord. Speak what is true.
Here's my life, Lord. Speak what is true.

READ PSALM 146

Praise the LORD!
Let all that I am praise the LORD.
  I will praise the LORD as long as I live.
  I will sing praises to my God with my dying
    breath.
Don't put your confidence in powerful people;
  there is no help for you there.
When they breathe their last, they return to the
    earth,
  and all their plans die with them.
But joyful are those who have the God of Israel
    as their helper,
  whose hope is in the LORD their God.
He made heaven and earth,
  the sea, and everything in them.

He keeps every promise forever.
He gives justice to the oppressed
  and food to the hungry.
The LORD frees the prisoners.
  The LORD opens the eyes of the blind.
The LORD lifts up those who are weighed down.
  The LORD loves the godly.
The LORD protects the foreigners among us.
  He cares for the orphans and widows,
  but he frustrates the plans of the wicked.
The LORD will reign forever.
  He will be your God, O Jerusalem, throughout
    the generations.
Praise the LORD!

REFLECT

We put great hope in our politicians, teachers, pastors, and others with authority. And we can be greatly disappointed when they do not live up to our expectations. Often the pain we feel when they let us down reveals more about us than about them, revealing where we may have misplaced our hope. The author of this psalm instructs us not to put our trust in human beings but to place our trust in God alone. How might our lives be shaped if we remembered our authority figures' humanity and frailty and placed our hope in God alone?

- Read this passage again slowly. What word or phrase stands out to you? Why do you think that word or phrase speaks to you? What does it say?

- Identify someone in authority who has let you down and caused you pain as a result. Were your expectations too high? Were they misplaced? If so, how? If not, how can you pray for that person in their humanity and frailty?

- What does it look like to place your trust and hope in God alone? Where have your expectations in people been misplaced most frequently? What might this reveal about your own heart?

RESPOND

I need your help, Lord. I can be tempted to place the full weight of my hope and expectations on human beings. Of course, they cannot bear such a burden and I am setting myself up for disappointment. Help me know how to respect and honor those in authority while acknowledging and being gracious about their humanity. Show me how to place my hope and trust in you and you alone. Amen.

HE HEALS THE BROKENHEARTED

a prayer to open

Here's my heart, Lord. Speak what is true.
Here's my life, Lord. Speak what is true.

READ PSALM 147

Praise the LORD!
How good to sing praises to our God!
  How delightful and how fitting!
The LORD is rebuilding Jerusalem
  and bringing the exiles back to Israel.
He heals the brokenhearted
  and bandages their wounds.
He counts the stars
  and calls them all by name.
How great is our Lord! His power is absolute!
  His understanding is beyond comprehension!
The LORD supports the humble,
  but he brings the wicked down into the dust.
Sing out your thanks to the LORD;
  sing praises to our God with a harp.
He covers the heavens with clouds,
  provides rain for the earth,
  and makes the grass grow in mountain
    pastures.
He gives food to the wild animals
  and feeds the young ravens when they cry.
He takes no pleasure in the strength of a horse
  or in human might.

No, the LORD's delight is in those who fear him,
  those who put their hope in his unfailing love.
Glorify the LORD, O Jerusalem!
  Praise your God, O Zion!
For he has strengthened the bars of your gates
  and blessed your children within your walls.
He sends peace across your nation
  and satisfies your hunger with the finest
    wheat.
He sends his orders to the world—
  how swiftly his word flies!
He sends the snow like white wool;
  he scatters frost upon the ground like ashes.
He hurls the hail like stones.
  Who can stand against his freezing cold?
Then, at his command, it all melts.
  He sends his winds, and the ice thaws.
He has revealed his words to Jacob,
  his decrees and regulations to Israel.
He has not done this for any other nation;
  they do not know his regulations.
Praise the LORD!

REFLECT

As a whole, the Psalms reveal God's love and concern for the hurting: the oppressed, the lonely, the disconnected, the imprisoned. God draws close to, heals, and seeks to restore and connect brokenhearted people to himself and to community. We all have experienced a broken heart in one way or another, and we all likely know someone whose heart has been broken recently. In this psalm, we are assured that it is to these very people—those with broken hearts and wounded souls—that God directs his healing and care. How might our lives be shaped by the assurance of his healing and nearness when we are hurting?

• Read this passage again slowly. What word or phrase stands out to you? Why do you think that word or phrase speaks to you? What does it say?

• How do you sense God inviting you to participate in the healing of someone who is brokenhearted?

• What would it look like to turn over the hurting parts of your heart to God for healing? What is one step you could take?

Reshaped

•

245

Lord, my heart—including the whole parts, broken parts, hurting parts, healed parts—is yours. I give it to you and ask you to piece it together so it aligns with who you are and who you made me to be. Come close to me and allow me to know your healing. Use me in this world—so full of brokenness, goodness, pain, and beauty—to help heal, build up, and lavish grace so that everyone I encounter will come to know you. Amen.

PRAISE THE LORD

a prayer to open

Here's my heart, Lord. Speak what is true.
Here's my life, Lord. Speak what is true.

READ PSALM 150

Praise the LORD!
Praise God in his sanctuary;
  praise him in his mighty heaven!
Praise him for his mighty works;
  praise his unequaled greatness!
Praise him with a blast of the ram's horn;
  praise him with the lyre and harp!

Praise him with the tambourine and dancing;
  praise him with strings and flutes!
Praise him with a clash of cymbals;
  praise him with loud clanging cymbals.
Let everything that breathes sing praises to the
  LORD!
Praise the LORD!

REFLECT

After drinking deeply from the Psalms and opening ourselves to their shaping force, what can we do but praise the Lord with every tool we have at our disposal? Today it may not be a harp or lyre or timbrel or cymbal, but there is no doubt after fifty-four days of soaking in the spectrum of emotion presented in the Psalms that God has acted in our hearts, changed something that was headed in the wrong direction, transformed a bad decision, or healed a wound.

- What has God changed, transformed, or healed in your heart as you've read through the Psalms?

- What truths from the Psalms do you want to regularly shape your life over the next year?

- What words from the Psalms resonated most deeply with you as you read?

RESPOND

Lord, thank you for the compelling, life-changing words of the Psalms and for your presence in the midst of those words. Thank you for what you've done in my life as I've read and reflected on them. Continue to transform me into the likeness of Christ through the truths you implanted in me. May my life reflect my praise and worship of your name, my devotion to you, and my heart's desire to live in your presence forever. Amen.

Centered

Loving Like Jesus

I'M REALLY NOT very good at love. Several years ago, a friend told me that her father-in-law would likely die in a matter of days. My first thought—the first one—was not one of sadness, compassion, or empathy but of regret over how his death would affect a gathering I had planned. Then came guilt and shame.

At my core, I am selfish, protective, and stingy. I'd love to say I was having an off day when this friend shared her sorrow. But I could tell a hundred other stories just like this one, varying only in degree of self-centeredness. So I can't help but think I've been set up to fail when I read these words from Jesus: "The most important commandment is this: 'Listen, O Israel! The LORD our God is the one and only LORD. And you must love the LORD your God with all your heart, all your soul, all your mind, and all your strength.' The second is equally important: 'Love your neighbor as yourself.' No other commandment is greater than these" (Mark 12:29-31). I long to be able to love well consistently and authentically, but the gap between this desire and what I'm actually capable of seems impassable.

I know I'm not alone; this is the story of human history, from Adam and Eve to Moses to the Israelites to David to Jesus' disciples to us today. None of us naturally is very good at love—on our own. In partnership with the Holy Spirit, though, we can begin to love as Jesus does.

To live lives centered on love and carry love into every relationship, we must first know what love is and what it isn't. We must see what love does and what it doesn't do. Under the inspiration of the Holy Spirit, the apostle Paul made these things very clear in Romans 12 and 1 Corinthians 13:

What love is:	What love does:
Patient	Leaves room for God
Kind	Knows the lowly
Generous	Shows empathy
Humble	Seeks second place
Others-focused	Shares resources
Honoring	Lifts others up
Even-tempered	Pursues peace

Forgiving	Rejects revenge and blesses
Energized by truth	Hates evil and clings to good
Protective	Stands firm in hardship
Trusting	Joyfully hopes
Persistent	Prays

For the next twenty-five days, we will spend time in just these sections of Scripture. Perhaps more than any other passage in Scripture, 1 Corinthians 13:1-8 shows us the centrality of love—and not doctrine, belief, faith, or even hope—in the life of a Christian. Romans 12:9-21 is Paul's description of what love does and does not do in relationships with others. There is a close tie between how Paul describes what love is in 1 Corinthians 13 and what it does in Romans 12. And that is why we'll alternate between these passages each day, beginning first with a definition of what love is and then moving to what love does.

We know we are called to love. Yet time and again, we run into the reality that we are not good at it. The invitation of this section is to practice love. Some days we will fail, and other days we will succeed. But the more we practice, the better we will get.

I've been practicing love through forgiveness. Although Jesus says over and over to forgive, I still find it difficult. A while back, someone hurt me emotionally. I desired to forgive her fully, but I noticed that unforgiveness lingered. I began to practice—to pray each morning that God would bless her, fill her with joy, and pour out his favor upon her so she would know how loved and valued she was. After a few weeks of earnestly praying, I noticed a warmth toward her. The unforgiveness that had a hold on me had faded. As I blessed her, I forgave her. What once seemed impossible became more natural with practice. Love is this way: As we practice love, we become more naturally loving.

LOVE IS PATIENT

Begin by quieting your body and mind, remembering you are in God's loving presence. Open your hands to reflect with your body your desire for a heart that's open to whatever he has for you today. Spend a minute in silence.

READ 1 CORINTHIANS 13:1-8

If I could speak all the languages of earth and of angels, but didn't love others, I would only be a noisy gong or a clanging cymbal. If I had the gift of prophecy, and if I understood all of God's secret plans and possessed all knowledge, and if I had such faith that I could move mountains, but didn't love others, I would be nothing. If I gave everything I have to the poor and even sacrificed my body, I could boast about it; but if I didn't love others, I would have gained nothing.

Love is patient and kind. Love is not jealous or boastful or proud or rude. It does not demand its own way. It is not irritable, and it keeps no record of being wronged. It does not rejoice about injustice but rejoices whenever the truth wins out. Love never gives up, never loses faith, is always hopeful, and endures through every circumstance.

Prophecy and speaking in unknown languages and special knowledge will become useless. But love will last forever!

REFLECT

Love bears with flaws, shortcomings, and weaknesses.
   Love abides amidst annoyance and provocation.
   Love is not irritable and short tempered.
   Love is long-suffering, forgiving, and forbearing.

- Spend a few moments in silence, reflecting on the truth that love bears with flaws, shortcomings, and weaknesses. In whom have you seen this kind of love? Where do you see it in your own life?

- Where do you see the patience of love reflected in Jesus' life?

- Sit quietly and ask God to speak what's true of your heart when it comes to patience in your relationships. What did he show you? How is he inviting you to extend that patience?

RESPOND

Father, you are love. Jesus, you are love. Holy Spirit, you are love.
Shape me into the image of love, and lead me in the way of love. Amen.

LOVE LEAVES ROOM FOR GOD

Begin by quieting your body and mind, remembering you are in God's loving presence. Open your hands to reflect with your body your desire for a heart that's open to whatever he has for you today. Spend a minute in silence.

READ ROMANS 12:9-21

Don't just pretend to love others. Really love them. Hate what is wrong. Hold tightly to what is good. Love each other with genuine affection, and take delight in honoring each other. Never be lazy, but work hard and serve the Lord enthusiastically. Rejoice in our confident hope. Be patient in trouble, and keep on praying. When God's people are in need, be ready to help them. Always be eager to practice hospitality.

Bless those who persecute you. Don't curse them; pray that God will bless them. Be happy with those who are happy, and weep with those who weep. Live in harmony with each other. Don't be too proud to enjoy the company of ordinary people. And don't think you know it all!

Never pay back evil with more evil. Do things in such a way that everyone can see you are honorable. Do all that you can to live in peace with everyone.

Dear friends, never take revenge. Leave that to the righteous anger of God. For the Scriptures say,

"I will take revenge;
  I will pay them back,"
  says the LORD.

Instead,

"If your enemies are hungry, feed them.
  If they are thirsty, give them something to drink.
In doing this, you will heap
  burning coals of shame on their heads."

Don't let evil conquer you, but conquer evil by doing good.

REFLECT

Love calls us to allow space for God to work, transform, and correct. Where we want to stick our noses in, love says, "Leave room for God. Know that he sees. Know that he's working."

- What relationships come to mind when you reflect on the refrain "Leave room for God. Know that he sees. Know that he's working"? Why? Ask God to help you understand what he might be inviting you to see or do.

- How might leaving room for God to work, transform, and correct cultivate patience in your relationships?

- What most frequently keeps you from leaving room for God?

RESPOND

Father, you are love. Jesus, you are love. Holy Spirit, you are love. Shape me into the image of love, and lead me in the way of love. Amen.

LOVE IS KIND

Begin by quieting your body and mind, remembering you are in God's loving presence. Open your hands to reflect with your body your desire for a heart that's open to whatever he has for you today. Spend a minute in silence.

READ 1 CORINTHIANS 13:1-8 (see page 249)

REFLECT

Love shows forth goodness in action.
>Love goes out of its way to be compassionate and courteous.
>Love is not cruel or insensitive.
>Love is thoughtful, gracious, and gentle.

- Spend a few moments in silence, reflecting on the truth that love goes out of its way to be not only courteous but also compassionate. In whom have you seen this kind of love? Where do you see it in your own life?

- Where do you see the kindness of love reflected in Jesus' life?

- Sit quietly and ask God to speak what's true of your heart when it comes to kindness in your relationships. What did he show you? How is he inviting you to extend that kindness?

RESPOND

Father, you are love. Jesus, you are love. Holy Spirit, you are love.
Shape me into the image of love, and lead me in the way of love. Amen.

LOVE KNOWS THE LOWLY

Begin by quieting your body and mind, remembering you are in God's loving presence. Open your hands to reflect with your body your desire for a heart that's open to whatever he has for you today. Spend a minute in silence.

READ ROMANS 12:9-21 (see page 250)

Centered

•

Love calls us to reach out to people who are marginalized, those deemed outsiders or outliers. When we want to protect our reputations and escape into comfort, love says, "Know the lowly. Get close. Stand near."

- What relationships come to mind when you reflect on the refrain "Know the lowly. Get close. Stand near"? Why? Ask God to help you understand what he might be inviting you to see or do.

- How might reaching out to people who are marginalized or spending time with people of low position cultivate kindness in you?

- What most frequently keeps you from getting to know people outside your normal circles?

RESPOND

Father, you are love. Jesus, you are love. Holy Spirit, you are love.
Shape me into the image of love, and lead me in the way of love. Amen.

DAY 5

LOVE IS GENEROUS

Begin by quieting your body and mind, remembering you are in God's loving presence. Open your hands to reflect with your body your desire for a heart that's open to whatever he has for you today. Spend a minute in silence.

READ 1 CORINTHIANS 13:1-8 (see page 249)

REFLECT

Love lavishes itself freely and unreservedly.
  Love wants the best for others.
  Love is not stingy or jealous.
  Love is openhanded, willing, and abundant.

- Spend a few moments in silence, reflecting on the truth that love is openhanded, willing, and abundant. In whom have you seen this kind of love? Where do you see it in your own life?

- Where do you see the generosity of love reflected in Jesus' life?

- Sit quietly and ask God to speak what's true of your heart when it comes to generosity in your relationships. What did he show you? How is he inviting you to extend that generosity?

Father, you are love. Jesus, you are love. Holy Spirit, you are love.
Shape me into the image of love, and lead me in the way of love. Amen.

LOVE SHOWS EMPATHY

Begin by quieting your body and mind, remembering you are in God's loving presence. Open your hands to reflect with your body your desire for a heart that's open to whatever he has for you today. Spend a minute in silence.

READ ROMANS 12:9-21 (see page 250)

REFLECT

Love calls us to show empathy and seek to understand. When we want to jump to judgment or slide into indifference, love says, "Be present. Stand in their shoes. See through their eyes."

• What relationships come to mind when you reflect on the refrain "Be present. Stand in their shoes. See through their eyes"? Why? Ask God to help you understand what he might be inviting you to see or do.

• How might putting yourself in another person's shoes cultivate generosity in you?

• What most frequently keeps you from showing empathy or seeking to understand others?

RESPOND

Father, you are love. Jesus, you are love. Holy Spirit, you are love.
Shape me into the image of love, and lead me in the way of love. Amen.

LOVE IS HUMBLE

Begin by quieting your body and mind, remembering you are in God's loving presence. Open your hands to reflect with your body your desire for a heart that's open to whatever he has for you today. Spend a minute in silence.

READ 1 CORINTHIANS 13:1-8 (see page 249)

REFLECT _____

Love seeks the low position, the least desirable seat.
> Love lets others go first.
> Love is not prideful or pretentious.
> Love is unassuming, meek, and simple.

- Spend a few moments in silence, reflecting on the truth that love seeks the low position and lets others go first. In whom have you seen this kind of love? Where do you see it in your own life?

- Where do you see the humility of love reflected in Jesus?

- Sit quietly and ask God to speak what's true of your heart when it comes to humility in your relationships. What did he show you? How is he inviting you to exercise that humility?

RESPOND _____

Father, you are love. Jesus, you are love. Holy Spirit, you are love.
Shape me into the image of love, and lead me in the way of love. Amen.

DAY 8

LOVE SEEKS SECOND PLACE

Begin by quieting your body and mind, remembering you are in God's loving presence. Open your hands to reflect with your body your desire for a heart that's open to whatever he has for you today. Spend a minute in silence.

READ ROMANS 12:9-21 (see page 250)

REFLECT _____

Love calls us to submit to one another and hand over the spotlight. When we long for recognition and our desire to be first overwhelms us, love says, "Seek second place. Stand back. Let others go first."

- What relationships come to mind when you reflect on the refrain "Seek second place. Stand back. Let others go first"? Why? Ask God to help you understand what he might be inviting you to see or do.

- How might handing over the spotlight or submitting to someone else cultivate humility in you?

- What most frequently keeps you from seeking second place and rejoicing in the success of others?

Father, you are love. Jesus, you are love. Holy Spirit, you are love.
Shape me into the image of love, and lead me in the way of love. Amen.

LOVE IS OTHERS-FOCUSED

Begin by quieting your body and mind, remembering you are in God's loving presence. Open your hands to reflect with your body your desire for a heart that's open to whatever he has for you today. Spend a minute in silence.

READ 1 CORINTHIANS 13:1-8 (see page 249)

REFLECT

Love looks for ways to serve, help, and lift up others.
> Love shares.
> Love is not self-seeking or self-centered.
> Love is considerate, genuine, and caring.

- Spend a few moments in silence, reflecting on the truth that love shares with others and cares for others. In whom have you seen this kind of love? Where do you see it in your own life?

- Where do you see the others-focused nature of love reflected in Jesus' life?

- Sit quietly and ask God to speak what's true of your heart when it comes to being others-focused in your relationships. What did he show you? How is he inviting you to focus less on yourself?

RESPOND

Father, you are love. Jesus, you are love. Holy Spirit, you are love.
Shape me into the image of love, and lead me in the way of love. Amen.

LOVE SHARES RESOURCES

Begin by quieting your body and mind, remembering you are in God's loving presence. Open your hands to reflect with your body your desire for a heart that's open to whatever he has for you today. Spend a minute in silence.

READ ROMANS 12:9-21 (see page 250)

REFLECT _____

Love calls us to share our resources—our money, time, energy, and gifts. When we close our fists tightly or give only to those we consider deserving, love says, "Share what you have. Open your hands. Don't be afraid."

- What relationships come to mind when you reflect on the refrain "Share what you have. Open your hands. Don't be afraid"? Why? Ask God to help you understand what he might be inviting you to see or do.

- How might freely sharing your money, time, energy, and gifts cultivate your desire and ability to focus on others more than on yourself?

- What most frequently keeps you from unreservedly sharing what you have?

RESPOND _____

Father, you are love. Jesus, you are love. Holy Spirit, you are love.
Shape me into the image of love, and lead me in the way of love. Amen.

LOVE IS HONORING

Begin by quieting your body and mind, remembering you are in God's loving presence. Open your hands to reflect with your body your desire for a heart that's open to whatever he has for you today. Spend a minute in silence.

READ 1 CORINTHIANS 13:1-8 (see page 249)

REFLECT _____

Love sees beyond flaws and failures.
Love picks up the fallen and lifts up the downtrodden.
Love is not demeaning or diminishing.
Love is encouraging, edifying, and dignifying.

- Spend a few moments in silence, reflecting on the truth that love sees beyond flaws and failures. In whom have you seen this kind of love? Where do you see it in your own life?

- Where do you see the honoring nature of love reflected in Jesus' life?

- Sit quietly and ask God to speak what's true of your heart when it comes to honoring others in your relationships. What did he show you? How is he inviting you to extend honor?

RESPOND_____

Father, you are love. Jesus, you are love. Holy Spirit, you are love.
Shape me into the image of love, and lead me in the way of love. Amen.

LOVE HONORS OTHERS

Begin by quieting your body and mind, remembering you are in God's loving presence. Open your hands to reflect with your body your desire for a heart that's open to whatever he has for you today. Spend a minute in silence.

READ ROMANS 12:9-21 (see page 250)

REFLECT_____

Love calls us to see God's image in every person. When we look down on others or see them as less, love says, "Honor others. Hold them in high regard, as men and women made in God's very image and loved so much that Christ died to save them."

- What relationships come to mind when you reflect on the refrain "Honor others. Hold them in high regard, as men and women made in God's image and loved so much that Christ died to save them"? Why? Ask God to help you understand what he might be inviting you to see or do.

- How might remembering that each person you see was made in God's image cultivate your desire and ability to honor others above yourself?

- What most frequently keeps you from seeing God's image in others?

RESPOND_____

Father, you are love. Jesus, you are love. Holy Spirit, you are love.
Shape me into the image of love, and lead me in the way of love. Amen.

LOVE IS EVEN-TEMPERED

Begin by quieting your body and mind, remembering you are in God's loving presence. Open your hands to reflect with your body your desire for a heart that's open to whatever he has for you today. Spend a minute in silence.

READ 1 CORINTHIANS 13:1-8 (see page 249)

REFLECT

Love remains calm in the chaos.
  Love looks for ways to mend what's broken.
  Love doesn't fly off the handle.
  Love is levelheaded, steady, and constant.

- Spend a few moments in silence, reflecting on the truth that love is calm and looks for ways to mend what's broken. In whom have you seen this kind of love? Where do you see it in your own life?

- Where do you see even-tempered love reflected in Jesus' life?

- Sit quietly and ask God to speak what's true of your heart when it comes to being even-tempered in your relationships. What did he show you? How is he inviting you to be even-tempered?

RESPOND

Father, you are love. Jesus, you are love. Holy Spirit, you are love.
Shape me into the image of love, and lead me in the way of love. Amen.

LOVE PURSUES PEACE

Begin by quieting your body and mind, remembering you are in God's loving presence. Open your hands to reflect with your body your desire for a heart that's open to whatever he has for you today. Spend a minute in silence.

READ ROMANS 12:9-21 (see page 250)

Love calls us to build bridges when conflict seems inevitable, to be peacemakers when war would be easier. When we'd rather turn our backs and slam the door or seek revenge or silently stew, love says, "Pursue peace. Reach out. Swallow your pride. Forgive. Extend your hands."

- What relationships come to mind when you reflect on the refrain "Pursue peace. Reach out. Swallow your pride. Forgive. Extend your hands"? Why? Ask God to help you understand what he might be inviting you to see or do.

- How might purposefully building bridges in areas of conflict cultivate your desire and ability to pursue peace in all situations?

- What most frequently keeps you from pursuing peace and reaching out in the midst of conflict?

RESPOND

Father, you are love. Jesus, you are love. Holy Spirit, you are love.
Shape me into the image of love, and lead me in the way of love. Amen.

DAY 15

LOVE IS FORGIVING

Begin by quieting your body and mind, remembering you are in God's loving presence. Open your hands to reflect with your body your desire for a heart that's open to whatever he has for you today. Spend a minute in silence.

READ 1 CORINTHIANS 13:1-8 (see page 249)

REFLECT

Love absorbs the blows and releases the offender.
  Love extends its hands and blesses.
  Love is not bloodthirsty or vengeful.
  Love is healing, liberating, and sparing.

- Spend a few moments in silence, reflecting on the truth that love forgives and blesses. In whom have you seen this kind of love? Where do you see it in your own life?

- Where do you see the forgiving nature of love reflected in Jesus' life?

- Sit quietly and ask God to speak what's true of your heart when it comes to forgiveness in your relationships. What did he show you? How is he inviting you to extend that forgiveness?

RESPOND

Father, you are love. Jesus, you are love. Holy Spirit, you are love.
Shape me into the image of love, and lead me in the way of love. Amen.

DAY 16

LOVE REJECTS REVENGE AND BLESSES

Begin by quieting your body and mind, remembering you are in God's loving presence. Open your hands to reflect with your body your desire for a heart that's open to whatever he has for you today. Spend a minute in silence.

READ ROMANS 12:9-21 (see page 250)

REFLECT

Love calls us to reject revenge and extend blessing to our enemies and betrayers. When everything in us wants to punish, punch back, and pay back, love says, "No revenge, only blessing. Extend your hands and seek only good. Bless and seek the good of your enemies."

- What relationships come to mind when you reflect on the refrain "No revenge, only blessing. Extend your hands and seek only good. Bless and seek the good of your enemies"? Why? Ask God to help you understand what he might be inviting you to see or do.

- How might blessing your enemies and seeking their good cultivate your desire and ability to forgive not only those enemies but others?

- What most frequently keeps you from praying for your enemies or releasing your desire for revenge?

RESPOND

Father, you are love. Jesus, you are love. Holy Spirit, you are love.
Shape me into the image of love, and lead me in the way of love. Amen.

LOVE IS ENERGIZED BY TRUTH

Begin by quieting your body and mind, remembering you are in God's loving presence. Open your hands to reflect with your body your desire for a heart that's open to whatever he has for you today. Spend a minute in silence.

READ 1 CORINTHIANS 13:1-8 (see page 249)

REFLECT _____

Love flourishes where truth prevails.
> Love focuses on what is good and pure.
> Love doesn't give in or get drowned out by evil.
> Love is true, right, and noble.

- Spend a few moments in silence, reflecting on the truth that love flourishes where truth prevails. In whom have you seen this kind of love? Where have you seen someone show love through telling the truth? How has someone shown you love by speaking truth to you?

- Where do you see the truth of love reflected in Jesus' life?

- Sit quietly and ask God to speak what's true of your heart when it comes to truth in your relationships. What did he show you? How is he inviting you to exercise truth?

RESPOND _____

Father, you are love. Jesus, you are love. Holy Spirit, you are love.
Shape me into the image of love, and lead me in the way of love. Amen.

LOVE HATES EVIL
AND CLINGS TO GOOD

Begin by quieting your body and mind, remembering you are in God's loving presence. Open your hands to reflect with your body your desire for a heart that's open to whatever he has for you today. Spend a minute in silence.

READ ROMANS 12:9-21 (see page 250)

REFLECT

Love calls us to turn from evil—to run to what is noble, lovely, true, right, and pure. When the broken parts of us seek out solace in deception, lust, greed, or fear, love says, "Cling to the good. Lift up your eyes. Don't get dragged down. You know what's true. You know what's right. Run to the good."

- What relationships come to mind when you reflect on the refrain "Cling to the good. Lift up your eyes. Don't get dragged down. You know what's true. You know what's right. Run to the good"? Why? Ask God to help you understand what he might be inviting you to see or do.

- How might purposefully seeking out good and focusing your mind on what is noble, lovely, true, right, and pure cultivate your desire and ability to overcome temptation?

- What most frequently keeps you from being able to cling to what is good and turn away from less noble and pure desires?

RESPOND

Father, you are love. Jesus, you are love. Holy Spirit, you are love.
Shape me into the image of love, and lead me in the way of love. Amen.

DAY 19

LOVE IS PROTECTIVE

Begin by quieting your body and mind, remembering you are in God's loving presence. Open your hands to reflect with your body your desire for a heart that's open to whatever he has for you today. Spend a minute in silence.

READ 1 CORINTHIANS 13:1-8 (see page 249)

REFLECT

Love offers refuge and support.
    Love fends off attackers.
    Love does not abandon or endanger.
    Love is watchful, devoted, and nurturing.

SACRED QUESTIONS

- Spend a few moments in silence, reflecting on the truth that love offers refuge and support. In whom have you seen this kind of love? Where do you see it in your own life?

- Where do you see the protectiveness of love reflected in Jesus' life?

- Sit quietly and ask God to speak what's true of your heart when it comes to protectiveness in your relationships. What did he show you? How is he inviting you to extend that protectiveness?

RESPOND_____

Father, you are love. Jesus, you are love. Holy Spirit, you are love.
Shape me into the image of love, and lead me in the way of love. Amen.

DAY 20

LOVE STANDS FIRM IN HARDSHIP

Begin by quieting your body and mind, remembering you are in God's loving presence. Open your hands to reflect with your body your desire for a heart that's open to whatever he has for you today. Spend a minute in silence.

READ ROMANS 12:9-21 (see page 250)

REFLECT_____

Love does not jump ship at the slightest sign of a storm. Love stands firm in hardship despite the fear, uncertainty, or momentary suffering. When we are beating back fear and pain, expecting the worst, and losing hope, love says, "Stand firm. Stay in it. You are not alone."

- What relationships come to mind when you reflect on the refrain "Stand firm. Stay in it. You are not alone"? Why? Ask God to help you understand what he might be inviting you to see or do.

- How might standing firm in the midst of fear, uncertainty, or suffering cultivate your ability and desire to protect those you love?

- What most frequently keeps you from remaining steady and present in the stormy seasons of relationships?

RESPOND_____

Father, you are love. Jesus, you are love. Holy Spirit, you are love.
Shape me into the image of love, and lead me in the way of love. Amen.

Centered

•

LOVE IS TRUSTING

Begin by quieting your body and mind, remembering you are in God's loving presence. Open your hands to reflect with your body your desire for a heart that's open to whatever he has for you today. Spend a minute in silence.

READ 1 CORINTHIANS 13:1-8 (see page 249)

REFLECT_____

Love reaches out in faith and hope.
>Love remembers what's true.
>Love doesn't despair or shut down.
>Love is confident, brave, and expectant.

- Spend a few moments in silence, reflecting on the truth that love reaches out in faith and hope. In whom have you seen the kind of love that doesn't shut down or despair but remains expectant and confident? Where do you see it in your own life?

- Where do you see the trusting nature of love reflected in Jesus' life?

- Sit quietly and ask God to speak what's true of your heart when it comes to trust in your relationships. What did he show you? How is he inviting you to exercise trust?

RESPOND_____

Father, you are love. Jesus, you are love. Holy Spirit, you are love.
Shape me into the image of love, and lead me in the way of love. Amen.

LOVE JOYFULLY HOPES

Begin by quieting your body and mind, remembering you are in God's loving presence. Open your hands to reflect with your body your desire for a heart that's open to whatever he has for you today. Spend a minute in silence.

READ ROMANS 12:9-21 (see page 250)

Love calls us to be joyful in hope, not skittish and worried or letting the ups and downs of our lives and the world dictate the states of our souls and hearts. When the world tells us that we should despair, that hate is winning, and that self-protection is our only remedy, love says, "The Kingdom of God has come. Love has prevailed. All things are being redeemed and restored. Be joyful in hope!"

- What relationships come to mind when you reflect on the refrain "The Kingdom of God has come. Love has prevailed. All things are being redeemed and restored. Be joyful in hope!"? Why? Ask God to help you understand what he might be inviting you to see or do.

- How might remembering God's redemption and restoration through Jesus Christ cultivate trust in your relationships?

- What most frequently keeps you from resting in joyful hope?

RESPOND _____

Father, you are love. Jesus, you are love. Holy Spirit, you are love.
Shape me into the image of love, and lead me in the way of love. Amen.

DAY 23

LOVE IS PERSISTENT

Begin by quieting your body and mind, remembering you are in God's loving presence. Open your hands to reflect with your body your desire for a heart that's open to whatever he has for you today. Spend a minute in silence.

READ 1 CORINTHIANS 13:1-8 (see page 249)

REFLECT _____

Love perseveres to the end.
    Love sees things through.
    Love isn't temporary and temperamental.
    Love is unwavering, tenacious, and enduring.

- Spend a few moments in silence, reflecting on the truth that love sees things through. In whom have you seen this kind of love? Where do you see it in your own life?

- Where do you see the persistence of love reflected in Jesus' life?

- Sit quietly and ask God to speak what's true of your heart when it comes to persistence in your relationships. What did he show you? How is he inviting you to exercise that persistence?

RESPOND_____

Father, you are love. Jesus, you are love. Holy Spirit, you are love.
Shape me into the image of love, and lead me in the way of love. Amen.

DAY 24

LOVE PRAYS

Begin by quieting your body and mind, remembering you are in God's loving presence. Open your hands to reflect with your body your desire for a heart that's open to whatever he has for you today. Spend a minute in silence.

READ ROMANS 12:9-21 (see page 250)

REFLECT_____

Love calls us to pray—fervently, faithfully—for transformation, for family, for friends, for enemies, for the world, for God's Kingdom to come on earth as it is in heaven. When we are tempted by self-pity, self-protection, or self-focus, love says, "Pray. Ask God. Tell your Creator and Sustainer. Turn to your great comforter, the one who intercedes. Pray."

- What relationships come to mind when you reflect on the refrain "Pray. Ask God. Tell your Creator and Sustainer. Turn to your great comforter, the one who intercedes. Pray"? Why? Ask God to help you understand what he might be inviting you to see or do.

- How might praying honestly and openly for yourself and others cultivate your ability to be persistent in the way you love others?

- What most frequently keeps you from praying or being open with God in prayer?

RESPOND_____

Father, you are love. Jesus, you are love. Holy Spirit, you are love.
Shape me into the image of love, and lead me in the way of love. Amen.

SACRED QUESTIONS

LOVE NEVER FAILS

Begin by quieting your body and mind, remembering you are in God's loving presence. Open your hands to reflect with your body your desire for a heart that's open to whatever he has for you today. Spend a minute in silence.

READ 1 CORINTHIANS 13:1-8 (see page 249)

REFLECT

Love never fails.
    Love knows no end.
    Love goes on forever.

- What impact does the truth that God's love never fails, knows no end, and goes on forever have on your relationships?
- What does it mean to love like Jesus?
- Sit quietly and ask God to speak what's true of your heart when it comes to loving like Jesus those you are in relationship with. What did God show you?

RESPOND

Father, you are love. Jesus, you are love. Holy Spirit, you are love.
Shape me into the image of love, and lead me in the way of love. Amen.

Blessed

Opening Your Eyes to the Kingdom of God

IN 2013 I resigned my partnership in my law firm and ventured into the world of "poverty law." I had led a legal-aid ministry at the Willow Creek Care Center five years earlier, and now I was formally joining the church's staff team. I moved from spending nearly every day with those who are inordinately blessed by the world's standards to spending my days among those whom our culture casts aside, ignores, oppresses, and criticizes. Before, my typical month involved first-class flights to four-star hotels; dinners at expensive restaurants; discussions about second homes in Vail, Marco Island, or St. Barts; and conflicts over millions of dollars in profits. Spend fifteen years in that kind of world, and nothing seems abnormal or excessive.

Now, the reality of those who are poor and hungry was not a blind spot for me. But what I experienced as I made the move to full-time ministry was nothing short of a revelation. The most concise way to describe it is that I ran headlong into the Beatitudes:

- A Mexican dad who was being deported and mourned that he would be separated from his wife and their young son. He prayed fervently for me after I met with him and shared his limited legal options.

- An Indian woman who tearfully shared about being discriminated against at a local grocery chain. She wondered if there was any way for me to get her harasser to stop.

- A man who asked what to do after the State of Illinois demolished his house without notice or payment. His family treasures and memories had been stored in that house.

- A young mother of three who sought to have an order of protection lifted so her children could have a relationship with their father. She'd obtained the order to protect herself, and she worried about whether lifting it was the right thing to do.

- A small-business owner who asked about mediation options to resolve a dispute with his business partner. He didn't want to go to court when they were both Christians.

- A Mexican woman who sought help in getting paid for her weekly overtime hours. Her employer was withholding payment, assuming wrongly that she was an undocumented immigrant.

I can still see every face, feel every hand in mine as we prayed together. Of course, no one I met with was perfect or wholly righteous. But I believe that these people were precisely who Jesus had in mind as he spoke about the blessed.

I have long thought about the soul impact of my legal-aid ministry experience. Yes, the interactions themselves formed compassion and love in me, but God also used each person to give me a glimpse of his Kingdom. I saw true humility and meekness; full hearts, faithful workers, devoted moms and dads; reconcilers and people who hungered for righteousness—all in the midst of trying, unfair, often oppressive circumstances. The depth of character and perseverance of those people still inspires me and far outweighs any legal advice I ever dispensed.

My prayer is that I don't ever forget their faces and hands and stories. I don't want to be confused about what Jesus meant when he used the term *blessed*. May I never be tempted to believe that what the world holds in high regard—self-dependence, money, power, physical beauty, status—bears any resemblance to what God holds in high regard—poverty of spirit, mourning, meekness, a hunger and thirst for righteousness, mercy, purity of heart, and peace. In this ten-day section, we will see how Jesus reversed traditional notions of blessedness and revealed the stark contrast between our world and the Kingdom of God. Let's reflect on each of Jesus' "blessed" statements and pray that God will open our eyes to his Kingdom.

DAY 1

BLESSED

a prayer to open

Give me eyes to see, Lord—
to see your Kingdom, your heart, your love. Give me eyes to see.

READ MATTHEW 5:1-12 _____

One day as he saw the crowds gathering, Jesus went up on the mountainside and sat down. His disciples gathered around him, and he began to teach them.

"God blesses those who are poor and realize their need for him,
for the Kingdom of Heaven is theirs.
God blesses those who mourn,
for they will be comforted.

God blesses those who are humble,
for they will inherit the whole earth.
God blesses those who hunger and thirst for justice,
for they will be satisfied.
God blesses those who are merciful,
for they will be shown mercy.
God blesses those whose hearts are pure,
for they will see God.

God blesses those who work for peace,
for they will be called the children
of God.
God blesses those who are persecuted for
doing right,
for the Kingdom of Heaven is theirs.

"God blesses you when people mock you and persecute you and lie about you and say all sorts of evil things against you because you are my followers. Be happy about it! Be very glad! For a great reward awaits you in heaven. And remember, the ancient prophets were persecuted in the same way."

REFLECT

In the Sermon on the Mount, Jesus spoke to his followers about living in light of his inauguration of the Kingdom of God. With his arrival, something significant had changed—a new era had begun. Yet the old era remained as well. So Jesus taught his disciples how to live in the new while still facing a world that was part of the old. Jesus began his Sermon with what have come to be known as the Beatitudes, nine statements identifying those who are considered "blessed" in God's eyes. Are the blessed the rich and powerful? Those the world elevates and honors? Jesus said no. He reversed traditional notions of blessedness and revealed the stark contrast between our world and the Kingdom of God. In the Kingdom of God, the blessed are those the world looks down upon and casts aside.

- What status symbols or worldly attributes do you tend to revere and honor? (To get at this, reflect on what elicits envy in you.)

- Sit silently for a few seconds and notice who comes to mind as you read the Beatitudes—a person you know or have seen, or a category or group of people. Why do you think that person or people group came to mind? Which of the Beatitudes do you believe brought that person or people group to mind?

- Read today's passage again slowly. Where did you have a sense of longing? Where did you feel resistance? Why?

RESPOND

Father, open my eyes to your Kingdom today. As my day unfolds, allow me to really see those I normally overlook. Remove the barriers, the assumptions, and the biases that cause me to dismiss or turn away from the people who don't fit my vision of the honorable and distinguished. Show me how I am conforming to the ways of this world instead of living according to the values of your Kingdom. As best as I know how, I open my hands and heart before you and ask that your will would be done and that your Kingdom would come in and through me. Amen.

BLESSED ARE THE POOR IN SPIRIT

a prayer to open   Give me eyes to see, Lord—
to see your Kingdom, your heart, your love. Give me eyes to see.

READ MATTHEW 5:1-12 (see pages 270–271)

REFLECT

Most of us have an inherent sense of what it means to be poor in spirit. Certain people come to mind—those who are humble, open, and at peace in an unusual way. They are gentle in spirit, and something makes us want to be near them when our souls are in states of unrest. Their total dependence on God draws us in and makes us pay attention. They bring us closer to the heart of Jesus. This should come as no surprise. After all, Jesus exemplified poverty of spirit. Paul described Jesus this way:

> Who, being in very nature God,
>   did not consider equality with God something
>   to be used to his own advantage;
>   rather, he made himself nothing
>   by taking the very nature of a servant,
> being made in human likeness.
> And being found in appearance as a man,
>   he humbled himself
>   by becoming obedient to death—
>   even death on a cross!

PHILIPPIANS 2:6-8, NIV

The Kingdom of God belongs to the poor in spirit.

- Reflect on a time in your life when you felt totally dependent on God. What did you learn about him during that time? What did you learn about yourself?

- How would you describe the opposite of "poor in spirit"? What does that look like in your own life?

- What practices, relationships, and circumstances tend to keep you dependent on God? What habits, situations, and people cause you to exert control and act independently?

RESPOND

Father, I long for your blessing. I long to have a heart that looks like yours, that seeks to bless and love and forgive rather than judge and condemn and withhold grace. I long for a surrendered, dependent soul—one that mourns over the heartbroken, the lost, the oppressed, and the sick. Help me, Lord, to release my grip on the things of the world today, and empower me by your Spirit to seek your Kingdom and your values. My life and all that I am is yours. Amen.

BLESSED ARE THOSE WHO MOURN

a prayer to open   Give me eyes to see, Lord—
                                        to see your Kingdom, your heart, your love. Give me eyes to see.

READ MATTHEW 5:1-12 (see pages 270–271)

REFLECT_____

When we mourn, sadness and emptiness overtake us, and those around us can feel the depth of our sorrow. But when Jesus spoke of those who mourn—and called them blessed—he wasn't referring to those who have experienced a personal loss. Jesus spoke instead of those who carry sorrow over a world in rebellion against God—those who look around them and mourn as they see people chasing after money, power, and status. These people mourn unforgiveness, deception, and injustice. They mourn the friend, coworker, or neighbor who gets so caught up in this world and all it claims to offer that they miss the Kingdom of God.

Blessed are those who mourn. Those whose eyes are fixed on the Kingdom of God—who, though they may suffer persecution or be treated as outcasts, don't go astray and fall for short-term worldly promises—will be comforted.

- What practices, behaviors, attitudes, and ideas in our world today should disciples of Jesus Christ be mourning? (Start with a wide lens—looking at the world—and then focus on your country, your community, and your home.)

- Reflect on something in our world that you mourn over. What causes you to mourn? How might you bring that mourning before God?

- As you reflect on your own life, in what areas—big or small—do you see rebellion against God's ways or desires for you? Sit quietly, remembering you are in his loving presence, and ask him to illuminate how you are still seeking after what the world values.

RESPOND_____

Father, this is your world. You created every part of it. You sustain it. Yet we turn our backs on you and run away from your loving call to us. Show me the ways that, though I profess to love and follow you, my heart still chases after the things of this world. Root out the desires within me that look to be satisfied by anything other than you. Help me see and then mourn over the ways I am in rebellion against you and in league with the culture around me. Give me a heart that mourns the unforgiveness, lack of peace, deception, and injustice in my own home, my community, my country, and the wider world. And remind me that you are the comfort of those who mourn. May your Kingdom come. Amen.

BLESSED ARE THE MEEK

a prayer to open   Give me eyes to see, Lord—
                        to see your Kingdom, your heart, your love. Give me eyes to see.

READ MATTHEW 5:1-12 (see pages 270–271)

REFLECT

We don't use the word *meek* in our culture much; in fact, it holds a negative connotation. We associate *meek* with *weak*. But the meek are not the weak; they are those who have suffered but, instead of seeking revenge, seek God's glory and the blessing of their enemies. There is no better image of the meek than Jesus at his death. After soldiers nailed his hands and feet to the cross, Jesus did not seek revenge. He did not seek justice for himself. He did not cry out curses over his fellow Jews, the soldiers, or the governing authorities. Rather, Jesus said, "Father, forgive them, for they do not know what they are doing" (Luke 23:34, NIV). When we are wronged or caused to suffer, we so often want revenge or to curse the wrongdoer. Yet blessed are the meek. The harder path—the path of Jesus—is to bless and seek the good of those who have hurt us. The meek will inherit the earth.

• Reflect on a time you were wronged and responded by punishing your wrongdoer either with words or actions. What comes to mind? How do you wish you had responded?

• What are the practices or routines that keep your soul at peace and generate a gentle, forgiving spirit in you? In contrast, when do you tend to find yourself less willing to forgive or extend the benefit of the doubt?

• Consider whether there is someone in your life you are punishing, whether by withholding your love or forgiveness, because of something they did to you. What would God need to change in you for you to bless that person instead?

RESPOND

Father, forgive my selfishness, my self-focused soul. Small offenses trigger in me not a desire to forgive and reconcile but a desire to punish by withdrawing or to harm by lashing out. I seek my own welfare, my own righteousness. I turn inward. But something deep in me wants to be free—free to love and free to forgive. Help me embrace the freedom you have given and modeled. When I am hurt or feel betrayed, let me seek your glory instead of idolizing my pain. Guide me today to love and desire what is best for those who have caused me pain, big or small. Amen.

BLESSED ARE THOSE WHO HUNGER AND THIRST FOR RIGHTEOUSNESS

a prayer to open   Give me eyes to see, Lord—
to see your Kingdom, your heart, your love. Give me eyes to see.

READ MATTHEW 5:1-12 (see pages 270–271)

REFLECT

When we think of righteousness, most of us conjure up self-righteousness. Or maybe we think of people who always want to demonstrate the rightness of their thinking. But righteousness is something else entirely. Righteousness is all things as they were meant to be, in right relationship with one another. We have never seen the world in this way God intended, except perhaps in a glimpse here and there. Yet within our hearts we seem to long to remember another way. In Ecclesiastes 3:11, we read that God has "set eternity in the human heart; yet no one can fathom what God has done from beginning to end" (NIV). Though our bodies desire food and water, our hearts long for connection, and our minds seek knowledge and information, we have a deeper longing. And the more we follow Jesus—the closer we hold ourselves to his presence—the stronger this longing grows. We begin to ache for the forgiveness of all sin; the restoration of all that has withered and died; and the full and final reign of God's love, peace, and justice on earth. Those who hunger and thirst for righteousness will not be left unsatisfied. They will be filled.

• Reflect on a time you caught a glimpse of things as they were meant to be. Perhaps it was an act of forgiveness, mercy, or compassion; a moment of purehearted joy; a time of unity within your family, community, or church; or an example of an injustice being made right. How did your soul respond in that moment?

• Imagine for a moment what righteousness would look like in your community. Begin with the relationships in your family, and then consider your neighbors and the schools, businesses, and restaurants in your town or city. What would forgiveness, restoration, and renewal look like in those places?

• Identify one thing you are longing for most in your life right now. What deeper desire underlies the longing?

Father, I long for things the way you created and intended them to be. I can see the brokenness in the world easily—it's all around. Open my eyes to the places and spaces where your Kingdom is breaking through and things are as they should be. Hold me close to you so my desire for what is right and good and pure grows and drives what I do and how I am in this world. May my longings and desires always lead me to you, and may I find satisfaction in you alone. May your Kingdom come on earth as it is in heaven. Amen.

DAY 6

BLESSED ARE THE MERCIFUL

a prayer to open   Give me eyes to see, Lord—
to see your Kingdom, your heart, your love. Give me eyes to see.

READ MATTHEW 5:1-12 (see pages 270–271)

REFLECT

Our world prefers judgment to mercy. It's easier and more natural for most of us. This is especially true in our day of anonymous (or not-so-anonymous) comments online. Consider how often social media posts are dominated by words of judgment and cries for punishment as opposed to calls for mercy and compassion. In fact, those who grant mercy are often condemned as weak, naive, or somehow opposed to justice. But the merciful—those who respond with compassionate action—will be the ones to whom God will show mercy. Think of the way Jesus called out to Zacchaeus, the hated tax collector who climbed a sycamore-fig tree to catch a glimpse of Jesus teaching (see Luke 19:1-10). Jesus knew about all the ways Zacchaeus had cheated and stolen from his own people, yet Jesus didn't try to keep his distance; he moved toward Zacchaeus with compassion, seeing beyond his sin. The Gospels are filled with similar accounts of Jesus extending mercy toward sinners instead of judgment. The merciful will be shown mercy.

- In Jesus' day, tax collectors were universally recognized as sinners. Who are the universally recognized sinners of our day? Reflect on what's in your heart about this group of people. How do you speak of them, think about them, treat them? With judgment or mercy? Some combination? What would compassionate action toward those people look like?

- Read Matthew 18:21-35, the parable of the unmerciful servant. Prayerfully consider where you see yourself in the story: as the king, as the servant who owed the debt to the king, as the fellow servant, or as an observer. What next step might the Holy Spirit be inviting you to take?

- Reflect on whether there is someone from whom you are withholding mercy, seeing only their sin or offense. What good do you see or have you seen in that person? What would a generous extension of mercy toward them look like?

RESPOND

Father, thank you for your mercy. Thank you that you look at me not through a lens of judgment but through one of mercy. I am so quick to judge and identify the faults and shortcomings of others. Thank you that your eyes see what I can become by your grace and guidance. Examine my heart, Lord, and show me where I am stingy with mercy, lacking in grace, and refusing to love. Break through whatever it is that allows me to receive your mercy and love so greedily yet refuse to give it as generously. Please provide me an opportunity today to be merciful, and help me know your will and follow it. Amen.

DAY 7

BLESSED ARE THE PURE IN HEART

a prayer to open

Give me eyes to see, Lord—
to see your Kingdom, your heart, your love. Give me eyes to see.

READ MATTHEW 5:1-12 (see pages 270–271)

REFLECT

On several occasions, Jesus confronted the Pharisees and teachers of the law about the true states of their hearts. He once said to them, "On the outside you appear to people as righteous but on the inside you are full of hypocrisy and wickedness" (Matthew 23:28, NIV; see also verses 25-27). Don't we know this phenomenon all too well? We present ourselves one way to the world, but something else entirely is going on within us. We are proud to take the moral high ground, but all the while our hearts are filled with anger, greed, self-indulgence, envy, or lust. A pure heart is fully surrendered for God to carry out his transformation. The secret sins of the heart are not hidden and covered over but confessed and presented to God for healing and restoration. A purehearted person knows they have no reason to be self-righteous and to consider themselves morally superior, to be impressed by their own goodness. The pure in heart will see God.

- Where do you see inconsistencies between what you present to the world and what is actually going on in your heart?

- Spend a minute in silent reflection, asking God to examine your heart and illuminate any impurities deep within. As words and ideas come to mind, remember that you are in God's loving presence, and confess and present those things to him. Ask him for healing and restoration in the areas he showed you.

- Read James 3:13-18. Write two columns that compare earthly wisdom with the wisdom that comes from heaven. Prayerfully consider why Jesus would say that the pure in heart will see God. What next step might the Holy Spirit be inviting you to take?

RESPOND

Father, make my heart pure. Help me surrender fully and completely to you. Relieve me of any notion that I am morally superior or better than anyone else. Instead, give me a heart that can learn from others, loves with humility and compassion, and sees people through your eyes. When I think too highly of myself, bring me back to reality. Be merciful and gentle. Transform me so that my heart reflects the heart of Jesus. May your Kingdom come in and through me. Amen.

DAY 8

BLESSED ARE THE PEACEMAKERS

a prayer to open Give me eyes to see, Lord—
to see your Kingdom, your heart, your love. Give me eyes to see.

READ MATTHEW 5:1-12 (see pages 270–271)

REFLECT

Jesus' audience would have understood *peace* to mean much more than what we understand it to mean today. He was calling to mind the rich Jewish concept of *shalom*. *Shalom* is a Hebrew word that means wholeness and describes the status of people living in harmony with one another. Of course, Jesus was the ultimate peacemaker, who, through great sacrifice, reconciled us with the Father and moves us toward wholeness and healing. The peacemakers of our world are those who help us move toward shalom—toward harmony and unity. But peacemaking is not for the faint of heart. It involves bridging gaps caused by acts of war and violence, betrayal and abandonment, and a lack of understanding and compassion. Making peace in our own relationships often means giving up our desire for vengeance or our need to be vindicated. But as we become peacemakers, Jesus says, we will be called children of God.

- When you think of a lack of peace in the world today, what comes to mind? What role might you play in being a peacemaker in that area?

- Consider Jesus' words as they apply in your life. Where is peace reigning, and where is it lacking? In the relationships in which shalom is lacking, what part have you played to foster or cause the absence of peace?

- Take a moment in silence, remembering you are in God's loving presence, and ask him to bring to mind any relationships in your life in which brokenness instead of wholeness prevails. As you consider what it would take for you to move toward shalom, what resistance do you feel? What sacrifice would be required?

RESPOND

Father, thank you for Jesus, the Prince of Peace. Thank you that at such high cost, he reconciled me to you so that I can partake of your peace and receive healing. Often it is the absence of peace that reigns, in both my soul and my relationships. The sacrifice of my ego or position or plans seems too great much of the time. But it is because my grip on the things of this world is tight, and my eyes have been seduced by a competing kingdom. To pursue your peace, I need your heart, your eyes, and your desires. Transform me and show me the path to peace. Amen.

BLESSED ARE THOSE WHO ARE PERSECUTED BECAUSE OF RIGHTEOUSNESS

a prayer to open   Give me eyes to see, Lord—
                           to see your Kingdom, your heart, your love.   Give me eyes to see.

READ MATTHEW 5:1-12 (see pages 270–271)

REFLECT

Persecution—at least as the early followers of Jesus experienced it—isn't common in most places today. Although there are certain areas where Christians can be and are killed for following Jesus, for most of us, persecution comes in less obvious ways, such as insults or social rejection. Sometimes this kind of persecution is linked to beliefs, and sometimes it's linked to action. Jesus seems to be addressing the persecution his followers receive not necessarily when they profess faith in him but rather when they act rightly or for a just cause. Consider an office environment in which all the employees regularly disparage their boss. It has become a sport, and each week the comments get more demeaning. A new employee starts at the company and after a couple of days of experiencing this office sport decides she can't participate in it. It isn't right. What will the response be from her coworkers? Most likely she'll be cast out, considered strange and not part of the team. And her boss will probably never know that she took a stand in this way and refused to take part. The Kingdom of heaven belongs to those who are persecuted because of righteousness.

- Who comes to mind when you think of people consistently doing the right thing even when it's difficult?

- Consider a time you had a choice between acting rightly and taking the easier road of going along with the crowd, and you decided to just go along with the crowd. What got in the way of your doing the right thing?

- Reflect on the realms in your life in which you are most likely to avoid doing the right thing in order to not be rejected socially or insulted. What action (or nonaction) do you sense God inviting you to take? What would you need from him to be able to take that action?

RESPOND_____

Father, I want to seek after your Kingdom and your righteousness above all else. I want to act rightly in every situation. And yet I know I fall short time and time again. Help me see the areas in my life where I'm more apt to try to avoid social rejection and insults. Allow me to discern how to do the right thing in your strength. Let me be an example of someone who is unafraid to stand up for a just cause and against those things that demean and devalue. I need your wisdom to know the right thing, and your strength to do it. May your Kingdom come on earth as it is in heaven. Amen.

BLESSED ARE YOU WHEN PEOPLE INSULT YOU BECAUSE OF ME

a prayer to open

Give me eyes to see, Lord— to see your Kingdom, your heart, your love. Give me eyes to see.

READ MATTHEW 5:1-12 (see pages 270–271)

Jesus knew what would happen to those who chose to follow him. He initiated a new order—a revolution that would upset worldly power structures, authority figures, and typical ways of thinking and acting. Thus, those who follow him—advocating peace, extending love to the hated, and serving the outcasts—are bound to be disliked as he was. In this last beatitude, he gave a preview of not only what will happen on earth (insults, persecution, and lies) but also what will happen in heaven: a great reward. If we never experience any discomfort, never hear an insult, never elicit a confused look, and never draw criticism for the way we live, we have to ask ourselves if we're really practicing Jesus' teachings.

- Jesus taught that there would be a cost in this life to anyone who followed him (see Luke 14:25-27). What has been the cost of following Jesus in your life? Why do you think that might be important to reflect upon from time to time?

- In what ways have you insulated yourself or compartmentalized your faith in Jesus in order to avoid persecution or ridicule? What do you fear would happen if you were more open?

- How do you sense God calling you into deeper levels of commitment and obedience to the way of Jesus? What fears, anxiety, and hesitations do you have? What would you need from God to be able to do what he's calling you to do?

RESPOND

Father, thank you for the challenge of what it means to follow Jesus and the reminder that there is a cost. I want to love and serve radically—differently than the world does. I want to be brave and unconcerned for my own reputation and self-preservation. Show me where I'm acting in fear by retreating to what's safe or what's comfortable. Awaken me to where I've fallen asleep, and incite a new boldness of spirit in me so I can follow you wholeheartedly and unafraid. Open my heart and hands so I can love as Jesus modeled, no matter the cost. Amen.

Empowered

Aligning with the Holy Spirit

ON A JANUARY morning in 2009, just weeks after I had given my life over to Christ on December 20, I was riding the train downtown to my office. I settled into my seat and cracked open a book, but after only a couple of pages, five words came into my mind: *Take the marine to lunch.*

I had not been thinking about lunch. I had not been thinking about the homeless marine who sat on the Jackson Street Bridge by my office, though I'd passed him dozens of times in the past several months. And I had never heard words from God, but I was sure these were from him. So what else could I do? I was going to follow.

I got off the train and walked toward my office, knowing I would pass the marine. I was so excited because I had been longing for God to give me a specific and tangible way to follow him. My plan was to get a peek at the marine and approach him later in the day to ask him to join me for lunch. As I walked by, he looked as he always did, with his green military-issued bag and cardboard-box pieces that read, "Please help. Former marine. God bless you."

I had several tasks to do that morning, but I was distracted, knowing that at noon I would be asking the marine to lunch. What would I say? How would I broach the subject? Would I tell him the reason I was inviting him? My office window just happened to face the spot on the bridge where the marine sat, so for the next several hours, I glanced down, trying to get a better feel for how the conversation might go. A few minutes before noon, I looked out the window one last time before heading out on my mission. He was gone.

I was crushed. I knew I had missed something, but I didn't understand how or why. I was so disappointed, but I prayed, "I'm here. I will do what you ask."

For the next four months, I passed by the marine's spot on the bridge. He had not returned, not even once. I began to wonder if he had been a figment of my imagination. I doubted that God had asked me to take him to lunch. I doubted he whispered anymore at all.

Then, on May 7, 2009, the marine was back—scraggly beard and baseball cap, cardboard sign attached to his bag, yellow and black cup for money out in front of him. I felt nervous and unsure about what to do. After saying a prayer,

I approached him and said hello. He looked up at me. I asked if I could get him something to eat. He'd just eaten, so he asked for a mere five dollars to cover his shortfall for a room that night at a men's hotel down the street. He was younger than I'd thought, just a couple of years older than I was, and the way he talked reminded me of friends I had. He wore black jeans and black boots and sat with his legs crossed. I gave him a five-dollar bill. We exchanged names—his is Joe— and then I went on to work.

The following Monday I stopped to chat again. This time Joe was hungry, so I got him a muffin and some coffee. He asked why I was being so nice to him when I didn't even know him, and I could only say, "Well, God told me to." This started a longer conversation. I'd noticed that he had a Bible on his lap. I asked if he was a Christ follower. He said yes and began to tell me his story:

"I started going to a church on the south side in November. I really liked it. It was different from other churches I'd been to."

My mind started running, thinking of my own story: my first time to my church in November, how different it was from my prior experience.

He continued, "I kept going, each week. And then one weekend in December . . ." He talked about an altar call the pastor at the church made. I stopped listening and started praying: *God, please let him say he came to know you on December twentieth. Please, God, just let him say December twentieth.* My insides started jumping. My heart was pounding. "I'll never forget the day it happened," he said. "It was December twentieth. The pastor asked if I wanted to accept Jesus Christ as my Savior. And I did."

December twentieth. December 20, 2008. I wanted to laugh, to cry. Of all the people in the world, of all the days, of all the months, of all the years. This man, homeless, jobless, hungry—and me, on my way to work as a lawyer, with a home, full from breakfast. Two strangers on a bridge. God found us, picked us out, on the *very same day*. And not only that, but then he brought us together in a most unlikely way.

The Holy Spirit came to me in a gentle whisper, saying, *Take the marine to lunch.* And that day on the bridge began a whole new story for Joe and for me—a story God had planned all along. We went through years of life just as brothers and sisters in Christ do: birthdays, Thanksgivings, Christmases, cancer, job offers, spiritual hunger and mentoring, difficult conversations, celebrations, miracles, anniversaries, and stories of war, grace, forgiveness, and pain.

God used my friendship with Joe to teach me about who my Father is and demonstrate powerfully that he is present and active in this world. As I abide in Christ and allow God to reshape my heart, my ability to discern what God is doing in the world increases. I can align with the Holy Spirit, say yes to his promptings, and be part of the greatest story being told. If I ever doubt, I need only look back on that day in May 2009 when God showed me in an unmistakable way, *I am here. I am real. I love you.*

In this section, we will spend fifty-six days in the book of Acts, studying the supernatural activity and human participation that launched the church. We'll practice aligning with God's movement in our day. So many of us live as though the Holy Spirit is no longer active in our world. We marvel at the miracles performed in the early church and at the courage those first believers displayed, but we doubt that anything like what happened then could happen today. As a result, we either exhaust ourselves attempting to do good works without God or sit back and wait for his Kingdom to come without our involvement. What we so often forget is that the Holy Spirit is active and even now redeeming and restoring all things. God invites us to align with this work based on how he made us, where he has placed us, and how he has gifted us.

THE GIFT MY FATHER PROMISED

a prayer to open

Holy Spirit, come. Center my heart.
Fill my mind. Guide my steps.

READ ACTS 1:3-11

During the forty days after [Jesus] suffered and died, he appeared to the apostles . . . and he proved to them in many ways that he was actually alive. And he talked to them about the Kingdom of God. . . .

He commanded them, "Do not leave Jerusalem until the Father sends you the gift he promised, as I told you before. John baptized with water, but in just a few days you will be baptized with the Holy Spirit."

So when the apostles were with Jesus, they kept asking him, "Lord, has the time come for you to free Israel and restore our kingdom?"

He replied, "The Father alone has the authority to set those dates and times, and they are not for you to know. But you will receive power when the Holy Spirit comes upon you. And you will be my witnesses, telling people about me everywhere—in Jerusalem, throughout Judea, in Samaria, and to the ends of the earth."

REFLECT

Jesus' resurrection and ascension were not the end of the story. As we dive into this sequel to Luke's Gospel account, we discover that as followers of Jesus, we are not merely in a holding pattern until Christ returns. Each of us has a role to play in the redemption and restoration of the world. But we are not left to our own strength—Jesus promised to (and did) send the Holy Spirit to supernaturally empower his followers to bring healing, reconciliation, and love to a broken world.

Empowered

•

- Read this passage again. What word or phrase stands out to you? Sit quietly, reminding yourself that you are in God's loving presence, and ask him to show you how that word or phrase connects to your life.

- Reflect on a broken relationship in your life that you have seen restored or reconciled. What was required for that to happen? What role did you play?

- Where do you currently see broken relationships and systems in your work, community, or family? As a follower of Jesus, what role can you play in bringing healing?

RESPOND

Father, thank you for Jesus' last words to his disciples and the incredible truth that I have a role to play in your redemption and restoration of all things. Thank you for the gift of your Holy Spirit and the power to share the gospel and bring reconciliation and healing to people who are hurting and systems that are broken. Help me access that power and allow it to inform my words and drive my actions. Give me supernatural strength and wisdom to fulfill my role in your plan for this world. Amen.

DAY 2

CHOSEN

a prayer to open

Holy Spirit, come. Center my heart.
Fill my mind. Guide my steps.

READ ACTS 1:13-26

Peter, John, James, Andrew, Philip, Thomas, Bartholomew, Matthew, James (son of Alphaeus), Simon (the zealot), and Judas (son of James) . . . all met together and were constantly united in prayer, along with Mary the mother of Jesus, several other women, and the brothers of Jesus.

During this time, when about 120 believers were together in one place, Peter stood up and addressed them. "Brothers," he said, "the Scriptures had to be fulfilled concerning Judas, who guided those who arrested Jesus. This was predicted long ago by the Holy Spirit, speaking through King David. Judas was one of us and shared in the ministry with us. . . . We must choose a replacement for Judas from among

the men who were with us the entire time we were traveling with the Lord Jesus—from the time he was baptized by John until the day he was taken from us. Whoever is chosen will join us as a witness of Jesus' resurrection."

So they nominated two men: Joseph called Barsabbas (also known as Justus) and Matthias. Then they all prayed, "O Lord, you know every heart. Show us which of these men you have chosen as an apostle to replace Judas in this ministry, for he has deserted us and gone where he belongs." Then they cast lots, and Matthias was selected to become an apostle with the other eleven.

REFLECT

Upon returning to Jerusalem, where they would wait for the Holy Spirit, the eleven apostles gathered with Jesus' other disciples to wrestle with how to carry out their mission now that they were one apostle short of what Jesus had ordained (twelve, symbolizing the twelve tribes of Israel). They turned to the Scriptures for guidance, and after reflecting on Psalms 69 and 109, they concluded that they should identify someone to take Judas's place. Barsabbas and Matthias were nominated, and through the casting of lots, God made it known that Matthias was his choice.

- Read this passage again. What word or phrase stands out to you? Sit quietly, reminding yourself that you are in God's loving presence, and ask him to show you how that word or phrase connects to your life.

- Has there been a time in your life in which someone else was chosen ahead of you to do a job or fulfill a particular role or purpose? What did it feel like not to be chosen? What have you learned about yourself based on that experience?

- Reflect on the various roles you currently hold: spouse, parent, sibling, child, employee, friend, neighbor. How would you approach each of those roles differently if you considered yourself chosen for them, as opposed to just having fallen into them?

RESPOND

Father, thank you that you have placed me in the world you created and called good. Open the eyes of my heart to see that you have chosen me, by your grace and goodness, to fill the roles in which I find myself in my family, work, church, and community. Help me carry out your will and purpose in each role, whether I find it personally satisfying or not. Empower me by your Holy Spirit to reflect the good you created and are seeking to restore. Amen.

DAY 3

HIS SPIRIT POURED OUT

a prayer to open   Holy Spirit, come. Center my heart.
                                                Fill my mind. Guide my steps.

READ ACTS 2:1-21

On the day of Pentecost all the believers were meeting together in one place. Suddenly, there was a sound from heaven like the roaring of a mighty windstorm, and it filled the house where they were sitting. Then, what looked like flames or tongues of fire appeared and settled on each of them. And everyone present was filled with the Holy Spirit and began speaking in other languages, as the Holy Spirit gave them this ability.

At that time there were devout Jews from every nation living in Jerusalem. When they heard the loud noise, everyone came running, and they were bewildered to hear their own languages being spoken by the believers.

They were completely amazed. "How can this be?" they exclaimed. "These people are all from Galilee, and yet we hear them speaking in our own native languages . . . about the wonderful things God has done!" They stood there amazed and perplexed. "What can this mean?" they asked each other.

But others in the crowd ridiculed them, saying, "They're just drunk, that's all!"

Then Peter stepped forward with the eleven other apostles and shouted to the crowd, "Listen carefully, all of you, fellow Jews and residents of Jerusalem! Make no mistake about this. These people are not drunk, as some of you are assuming. . . . No, what you see was predicted long ago by the prophet Joel:

'In the last days,' God says,
     'I will pour out my Spirit upon all people.
Your sons and daughters will prophesy.
     Your young men will see visions,
     and your old men will dream dreams. . . .
But everyone who calls on the name of the Lord
     will be saved.'"

REFLECT

In Old Testament times, God granted his Holy Spirit to only a select few for specific purposes and for a limited time. But upon the resurrection and ascension of Jesus, something brand new happened. The Holy Spirit became available to all who believe in Jesus, and for the first time in history, God's people could access the power of God to share the gospel, participate in his restoration, and live a Spirit-led life.

- Read this passage again. What word or phrase stands out to you? Sit quietly, reminding yourself that you are in God's loving presence, and ask him to show you how that word or phrase connects to your life.

- Have you experienced the supernatural power of the Holy Spirit? When? How would you describe it to a friend?

- What areas of your life have you tended to see as disconnected from God's purposes and plans in the world (for example, your work, sexuality, pain, success, or failure)? What would those things look like under the Holy Spirit's power and guidance?

RESPOND

Father, thank you for the gift of your Holy Spirit. I pray for the ability to remember your presence with me and your promise and willingness to guide and empower my thoughts, words, and actions to carry out your purposes in the world. As best as I know how, I present to you those parts of my life I have considered secular and nonspiritual, and I pray that I would see your power and presence even there. I am open to you. Amen.

DAY 4

GOD OF THE SECOND CHANCE

a prayer to open

Holy Spirit, come. Center my heart.
Fill my mind. Guide my steps.

"God publicly endorsed Jesus the Nazarene by doing powerful miracles, wonders, and signs through him, as you well know. But God knew what would happen, and his prearranged plan was carried out when Jesus was betrayed. With the help of lawless Gentiles, you nailed him to a cross and killed him. But God released him from the horrors of death and raised him back to life, for death could not keep him in its grip. King David said this about him:

'I see that the LORD is always with me.
I will not be shaken, for he is right beside me.
No wonder my heart is glad,
and my tongue shouts his praises!
My body rests in hope.
For you will not leave my soul among the dead
or allow your Holy One to rot in the grave.
You have shown me the way of life,
and you will fill me with the joy of your presence.'

"Dear brothers, think about this! You can be sure that the patriarch David wasn't referring to himself, for he died and was buried, and his tomb is still here among us. But he was a prophet, and he knew God had promised with an oath that one of David's own descendants would sit on his throne. David was looking into the future and speaking of the Messiah's resurrection. . . .

"God raised Jesus from the dead, and we are all witnesses of this. Now he is exalted to the place of highest honor in heaven, at God's right hand. And the Father, as he had promised, gave him the Holy Spirit to pour out upon us. . . . For David himself never ascended into heaven, yet he said,

'The LORD said to my Lord,
"Sit in the place of honor at my right hand
until I humble your enemies,
making them a footstool under your feet."'

"So let everyone in Israel know for certain that God has made this Jesus, whom you crucified, to be both Lord and Messiah!"

Peter's words pierced their hearts, and they said to him and to the other apostles, "Brothers, what should we do?"

Peter replied, "Each of you must repent of your sins and turn to God, and be baptized in the name of Jesus Christ for the forgiveness of your sins. Then you will receive the gift of the Holy Spirit. This promise is to you, to your children, and to those far away—all who have been called by the Lord our God." . . .

Those who believed what Peter said were baptized and added to the church that day—about 3,000 in all.

All the believers devoted themselves to the apostles' teaching, and to fellowship, and to sharing in meals (including the Lord's Supper), and to prayer.

A deep sense of awe came over them all, and the apostles performed many miraculous signs and wonders. And all the believers met together in one place and shared everything they had. They sold their property and possessions and shared the money with those in need. They worshiped together at the Temple each day, met in homes for the Lord's Supper, and shared their meals with great joy and generosity—all the while praising God and enjoying the goodwill of all the people. And each day the Lord added to their fellowship those who were being saved.

REFLECT

Our God grants second chances. And there is no better example of that truth than what we see in this passage. Peter explained to those gathered that the coming of the Holy Spirit was brought about by the resurrection and ascension of Jesus. And God had promised that very event long ago through the prophets. Despite Peter's listeners' involvement in Jesus' death, they still could receive forgiveness and the Holy Spirit by repenting. The same is true for us. Regardless of anything we have ever done—no matter how destructive, immoral, or dark—we can receive forgiveness by turning to God with repentant hearts.

- Read this passage again. What word or phrase stands out to you? Sit quietly, reminding yourself that you are in God's loving presence, and ask him to show you how that word or phrase connects to your life.

- Reflect on a time you asked someone for a second chance. How did it feel to ask? What was the response?

- When have you failed to model God by refusing someone a second chance? What motivated you to withhold a second chance?

RESPOND

Father, thank you for the many second chances you have extended to me. Thank you for the way you continue to transform me and mold me into your likeness. I want to be someone who freely grants second chances and extends your generous grace in this world full of judgment, condemnation, and hate. Remind me of your Holy Spirit's presence and your power within me to be a giver of second chances. Amen.

DAY 5

FILLED WITH WONDER AND AMAZEMENT

a prayer to open

Holy Spirit, come. Center my heart.
Fill my mind. Guide my steps.

READ ACTS 3:1-8

As [Peter and John] approached the Temple, a man lame from birth was being carried in. Each day he was put beside the Temple gate, the one called the Beautiful Gate, so he could beg from the people going into the Temple. When he saw Peter and John about to enter, he asked them for some money.

Peter and John looked at him intently, and Peter said, "Look at us! . . . I don't have any silver or gold for you. But I'll give you what I have. In the name of Jesus Christ the Nazarene, get up and walk!"

Then Peter took the lame man by the right hand and helped him up. And as he did, the man's feet and ankles were instantly healed and strengthened. He jumped up, stood on his feet, and began to walk! Then, walking, leaping, and praising God, he went into the Temple with them.

REFLECT

We see in this passage the first healing Jesus accomplished through his disciples after his ascension and the wonder and amazement that followed. Imagine being present to see a man walk who had been paralyzed since birth. Before Peter healed the lame man, something critical happened: Peter looked at the man and instructed the man to look at him. We don't know exactly why Peter did this, but it is a powerful moment in which a man who was likely constantly overlooked was given permission to be seen just as he was. A kind of leveling seems to have happened between the men: one an apostle, one a beggar, but both equal in the eyes of Jesus.

- Read this passage again. What word or phrase stands out to you? Sit quietly, reminding yourself that you are in God's loving presence, and ask him to show you how that word or phrase connects to your life.

- Reflect on your daily routine, from the moment you first leave your home to the moment you return. Who are the people you tend to overlook or fail to see? Why do you think that is?

- Who do you allow to really see you—your weaknesses, vulnerabilities, sin, and failures? What makes you feel safe with those people? Are you someone before whom your friends and family members allow themselves to be seen? What do you think makes you safe or unsafe? (Are you judgmental, critical, hope-filled, encouraging?)

RESPOND

Father, thank you for the restoration and healing that is available through Christ. May I always be open to your desire to restore and heal those parts of my heart, mind, and body that are broken. And give me eyes to see those I have overlooked in my busyness, brokenness, or apathy. Help me be a person in whose presence it is safe to be seen—free of judgment, condemnation, and criticism. Transform all that is in me that diminishes or dismisses the unique beauty and chosenness of others. Amen.

TIMES OF REFRESHING

a prayer to open   Holy Spirit, come. Center my heart.
                                               Fill my mind. Guide my steps.

READ ACTS 3:9-21

All the people saw him walking and heard him praising God. When they realized he was the lame beggar they had seen so often at the Beautiful Gate, they were absolutely astounded! . . .

Peter . . . addressed the crowd. . . . "What is so surprising about this? And why stare at us as though we had made this man walk by our own power or godliness? . . . [God] has brought glory to his servant Jesus by doing this. This is the same Jesus whom you handed over and rejected before Pilate. . . . You killed the author of life, but God raised him from the dead. And we are witnesses of this fact!

"Through faith in the name of Jesus, this man was healed. . . . Faith in Jesus' name has healed him before your very eyes.

"Friends, I realize that what you and your leaders did to Jesus was done in ignorance. But God was fulfilling what all the prophets had foretold about the Messiah—that he must suffer these things. Now repent of your sins and turn to God, so that your sins may be wiped away. Then times of refreshment will come from the presence of the Lord, and he will again send you Jesus, your appointed Messiah. For he must remain in heaven until the time for the final restoration of all things, as God promised long ago through his holy prophets."

It's easy to read the story of the healed beggar and consider it irrelevant other than as something amazing that happened long ago. We may even wonder if such healings still occur in our day. Moments after the lame man began to walk, though, Peter immediately shifted the onlookers' attention away from the man and toward Jesus, wanting them to realize that the man's physical healing was just a glimpse of what is to come for all who believe. Because of Jesus' resurrection, anyone who turns to God will be restored to wholeness in body, mind, and soul when Jesus returns and God's Kingdom is fully realized.

- Read this passage again. What word or phrase stands out to you? Sit quietly, reminding yourself that you are in God's loving presence, and ask him to show you how that word or phrase connects to your life.

- Reflect on the word *broken*. What comes to mind? What in your life is broken? What would healing and wholeness look like? What would healing enable for you?

- How has God used what's broken in you for good, whether in your life or someone else's?

RESPOND

Father, thank you for the promise that through Jesus and because of your goodness and mercy, there will be a day when every broken part of me will be made whole again. I pray for patience and grace in the meantime. Use my weaknesses for your purposes. Allow my life to reflect the hope I have in you and point people to the only source for redemption, restoration, and refreshment. Amen.

DAY 7

THE ONLY WAY

a prayer to open

Holy Spirit, come. Center my heart.
Fill my mind. Guide my steps.

READ ACTS 4:1-20

While Peter and John were speaking to the people, they were confronted by the priests, the captain of the Temple guard, and some of the Sadducees. These leaders were very disturbed that Peter and John were teaching the people that through Jesus there is a resurrection of the dead. They arrested them and, since it was already evening, put them in jail until morning. But many of the people who heard their message believed it. . . .

The next day the council of all the rulers and elders and teachers of religious law met in Jerusalem. . . . They brought in the two disciples and demanded, "By what power, or in whose name, have you done this?"

Then Peter, filled with the Holy Spirit, said to

them, "Rulers and elders of our people, are we being questioned today because we've done a good deed for a crippled man? Do you want to know how he was healed? Let me clearly state to all of you and to all the people of Israel that he was healed by the powerful name of Jesus Christ the Nazarene, the man you crucified but whom God raised from the dead. . . . There is salvation in no one else! " . . .

The members of the council were amazed when they saw the boldness of Peter and John, for they could see that they were ordinary men with no special training in the Scriptures. They also recognized them as men who had been with Jesus. . . .

"What should we do with these men?" they asked each other. "We can't deny that they have performed a miraculous sign, and everybody in Jerusalem knows about it. But to keep them from spreading their propaganda any further, we must warn them not to speak to anyone in Jesus' name again." So they called the apostles back in and commanded them never again to speak or teach in the name of Jesus.

But Peter and John replied, "Do you think God wants us to obey you rather than him? We cannot stop telling about everything we have seen and heard."

REFLECT

Peter's and John's belief in the Resurrection and in salvation in Jesus alone put them at odds with the religious leaders. Such beliefs threatened the leaders' authority and the structures upon which their authority was based. The disciples were such a threat that the authorities commanded them on multiple occasions not to speak the name of Jesus. We face similar problems today: Many people in positions of power find the notion that Jesus is the only means to salvation too exclusive, too narrow, and an affront to modern ways of thinking. The name of Jesus continues to threaten power structures and authorities that seek to advance anything other than God's Kingdom. Will we shut our mouths or follow the example of Peter and John?

- Read this passage again. What word or phrase stands out to you? Sit quietly, reminding yourself that you are in God's loving presence, and ask him to show you how that word or phrase connects to your life.

- Why is it good news that Jesus is the only way of salvation? How would you answer this question when speaking with a friend or colleague who doesn't believe in him?

- What are the power structures and authorities that the name of Jesus threatens in our country? How could you reflect God's love and light to those structures and authorities? (Consider your social-media posts, words about political figures and structures, the way you pray, how you debate important issues, and so on.)

RESPOND

Father, thank you for salvation through Jesus. Help me to be a light in this world. I want to represent a different way—the way of Jesus, the way of love and grace. By your Holy Spirit, grant me the power to walk in the ways of Jesus even when it is unpopular and I am criticized. Give me the words to share your invitation to life that is truly life through Christ. And more than anything else, let my life speak the hope I hold and the forgiveness I know. Amen.

ENABLE US
BY YOUR POWER, LORD

a prayer to open

Holy Spirit, come. Center my heart.
Fill my mind. Guide my steps.

READ ACTS 4:23-31

Peter and John returned to the other believers and told them what the leading priests and elders had said.... All the believers lifted their voices together in prayer to God: "O Sovereign Lord, Creator of heaven and earth, the sea, and everything in them—you spoke long ago by the Holy Spirit through our ancestor David, your servant, saying,

'Why were the nations so angry?
  Why did they waste their time with futile plans?
The kings of the earth prepared for battle;
  the rulers gathered together
against the LORD
  and against his Messiah.'

"In fact, this has happened here in this very city! For Herod Antipas, Pontius Pilate the governor, the Gentiles, and the people of Israel were all united against Jesus, your holy servant, whom you anointed. But everything they did was determined beforehand according to your will. And now, O Lord, hear their threats, and give us, your servants, great boldness in preaching your word. Stretch out your hand with healing power; may miraculous signs and wonders be done through the name of your holy servant Jesus."

After this prayer, the meeting place shook, and they were all filled with the Holy Spirit. Then they preached the word of God with boldness.

REFLECT

This passage gives us a powerful example of how we might pray when our circumstances overwhelm us. Jesus had told the disciples that they would spread the gospel to the ends of the earth, but then they were arrested before even getting out of Jerusalem. How discouraged and disappointed they must have felt. But instead of giving up, they prayed, acknowledging to God and to each other God's sovereignty and power, reminding themselves with the words of Psalm 2 that opposition was to be expected, and asking God to enable them to do what Jesus had called them to do. Their prayer caused the building in which they met to shake, and God responded with a special outpouring of the Holy Spirit and grace.

- Read this passage again. What word or phrase stands out to you? Sit quietly, reminding yourself that you are in God's loving presence, and ask him to show you how that word or phrase connects to your life.

- Reflect on the last time you felt disappointed by something. What caused your disappointment? How did you respond?

- What circumstances do you find yourself in now that are discouraging or disappointing? Write out a prayer like the one the disciples used—not because the words are magic, but as a way to remember who God is, to remind yourself of the reality of life in a broken world, and to ask for the provision to carry out all that God has asked you to be and do.

Use the prayer you wrote out as your way of responding today.

DECEIT AND DEATH

a prayer to open

Holy Spirit, come. Center my heart.
Fill my mind. Guide my steps.

READ ACTS 5:1-16

There was a certain man named Ananias who, with his wife, Sapphira, sold some property. He brought part of the money to the apostles, claiming it was the full amount. With his wife's consent, he kept the rest.

Then Peter said, "Ananias, why have you let Satan fill your heart? You lied to the Holy Spirit, and you kept some of the money for yourself. The property was yours to sell or not sell, as you wished. And after selling it, the money was also yours to give away. How could you do a thing like this? You weren't lying to us but to God!"

As soon as Ananias heard these words, he fell to the floor and died. Everyone who heard about it was terrified. Then some young men got up, wrapped him in a sheet, and took him out and buried him.

About three hours later his wife came in, not knowing what had happened. Peter asked her, "Was this the price you and your husband received for your land?"

"Yes," she replied, "that was the price."

And Peter said, "How could the two of you even think of conspiring to test the Spirit of the Lord like this? The young men who buried your husband are just outside the door, and they will carry you out, too."

Instantly, she fell to the floor and died. When the young men came in and saw that she was dead, they carried her out and buried her beside her husband. Great fear gripped the entire church and everyone else who heard what had happened.

The apostles were performing many miraculous signs and wonders among the people. And all the believers were meeting regularly at the Temple in the area known as Solomon's Colonnade. But no one else dared to join them, even though all the people had high regard for them. Yet more and more people believed and were brought to the Lord—crowds of both men and women. As a result of the apostles' work, sick people were brought out into the streets on beds and mats so that Peter's shadow might fall across some of them as he went by. Crowds came from the villages around Jerusalem, bringing their sick and those possessed by evil spirits, and they were all healed.

REFLECT

In this story of Ananias and Sapphira, we discover an amazing (and heartbreaking) parallel to the story of Adam and Eve. Satan and human sin were alive and well at the beginning of the church, just as they were in the Garden of Eden, yet this story is sandwiched between a report of the supernatural generosity of early believers and the telling of Peter healing the sick simply by virtue of his shadow falling upon them. The lesson is not that Ananias and Sapphira should have given 100 percent of their property over; Peter makes that clear. The sin that so undermined the church was deceit and a desire to seem more generous than what was

Empowered

•

true. Although such harsh and immediate judgment from God is rare, we see how destructive he views deceit and how protective he is of the church.

- Read this passage again. What word or phrase stands out to you? Sit quietly, reminding yourself that you are in God's loving presence, and ask him to show you how that word or phrase connects to your life.

- Why do you think deceit is so destructive to a community? In what circumstances have you seen its detrimental effects?

- Reflect on your own words and actions, and consider in what areas of your life you may be acting in a less-than-honest way: saying untrue things, exaggerating the truth, or failing to disclose the whole truth. What underlies the way you are behaving? Fear, insecurity, greed, lust, or something else? What is one step toward living truthfully that you can take this week?

RESPOND

Father, thank you for the reminder about how destructive lying and deceit are to your church and how offensive they are to you. How easy it is to allow half-truths or exaggerations to escape my lips in order to build myself up and be seen as important or right or better than I am. And how easy it is to withhold the truth if it will make me look good. Forgive me. Transform me. I want to be honest and authentic and to stand firmly in the truth. Give me the strength to live with full authenticity. May it be so.

DAY 10

I WILL BUILD MY CHURCH

a prayer to open

Holy Spirit, come. Center my heart.
Fill my mind. Guide my steps.

READ ACTS 5:17-42

The high priest and his officials . . . were filled with jealousy. They arrested the apostles and put them in the public jail. But an angel of the Lord came at night, opened the gates of the jail, and brought them out. Then he told them, "Go to the Temple and give the people this message of life!"

So at daybreak the apostles entered the Temple . . . and immediately began teaching.

When the high priest and his officials arrived, they convened . . . the full assembly of the elders of Israel. Then they sent for the apostles to be brought from the jail for trial. But when the Temple guards went to the jail, the men were gone. So they returned to the council and reported, "The jail was securely locked, with the guards standing outside, but when we opened the gates, no one was there!"

When the captain of the Temple guard and the leading priests heard this, they were perplexed, wondering where it would all end. Then someone arrived with startling news: "The men you put in jail are standing in the Temple, teaching the people!"

The captain went with his Temple guards and arrested the apostles, but without violence, for they were afraid the people would stone them. Then they brought the apostles before the high council. . . . "We gave you strict orders never again to teach in this man's name!" [the high priest] said. "Instead, you have filled all Jerusalem with your teaching about him, and you want to make us responsible for his death!"

But Peter and the apostles replied, "We must obey God rather than any human authority. The God of our ancestors raised Jesus from the dead after you killed him. . . . Then God put him in the place of honor at his right hand as Prince and Savior. He did this so the people of Israel would repent of their sins and be forgiven. We are witnesses of these things and so is the Holy Spirit, who is given by God to those who obey him."

When they heard this, the high council was furious and decided to kill them. But one member, a Pharisee named Gamaliel, who was an expert in religious law and respected by all the people, stood up and ordered that the men be sent outside. . . . Then he said to his colleagues, "Men of Israel, take care what you are planning to do to these men! Some time ago there was that fellow Theudas, who pretended to be someone great. About 400 others joined him, but he was killed, and all his followers went their various ways. The whole movement came to nothing. After him, at the time of the census, there was Judas of Galilee. He got people to follow him, but he was killed, too, and all his followers were scattered.

"So my advice is, leave these men alone. Let them go. If they are planning and doing these things merely on their own, it will soon be overthrown. But if it is from God, you will not be able to overthrow them. You may even find yourselves fighting against God!"

The others accepted his advice. They called in the apostles and had them flogged. Then they ordered them never again to speak in the name of Jesus, and they let them go.

The apostles left the high council rejoicing that God had counted them worthy to suffer disgrace for the name of Jesus. And every day . . . they continued to teach and preach this message: "Jesus is the Messiah."

REFLECT _____

"I tell you that you are Peter, and on this rock I will build my church, and the gates of Hades will not overcome it" (Matthew 16:18, NIV). These words of Jesus to Peter come to life in the book of Acts as we read about Peter's persecution, imprisonment, and flogging. God intervened in two significant ways to free Peter and the other apostles so they could continue their Jesus-ordained mission. First, God opened the prison doors in the middle of the night. Second, he used a member of the Sanhedrin (the highest Jewish authoritative body) to free the apostles. These supernatural acts show Jesus' faithfulness to his promise to build his church. They should fill us with hope that nothing then or now will prevent or inhibit him from making good on that promise.

- Read this passage again. What word or phrase stands out to you? Sit quietly, reminding yourself that you are in God's loving presence, and ask him to show you how that word or phrase connects to your life.

- Reflect on whether your life—your decisions, relationships, calendar, words—demonstrates your belief that Jesus' promises are true. Where do you see gaps? What do the gaps reveal to you?

- What experiences and truths remind you of Christ's faithfulness? How might you keep those experiences and truths close at hand when doubt creeps into your mind and heart?

Father, thank you for your faithfulness. Whether I am filled with faith or overcome by doubt, you remain trustworthy. Help me live a life that reflects my belief in your promises. Remind me of how you have been faithful. When my circumstances or the circumstances of the world overwhelm me, bring to mind the promises you have made in your Scriptures. May my words and actions evidence the hope I have in you. Amen.

SO THE WORD OF GOD SPREAD

a prayer to open

Holy Spirit, come. Center my heart.
Fill my mind. Guide my steps.

READ ACTS 6:1-7

But as the believers rapidly multiplied, there were rumblings of discontent. The Greek-speaking believers complained about the Hebrew-speaking believers, saying that their widows were being discriminated against in the daily distribution of food.

So the Twelve called a meeting of all the believers. They said, "We apostles should spend our time teaching the word of God, not running a food program. And so, brothers, select seven men who are well respected and are full of the Spirit and wisdom. We will give them this responsibility.

Then we apostles can spend our time in prayer and teaching the word."

Everyone liked this idea, and they chose the following: Stephen (a man full of faith and the Holy Spirit), Philip, Procorus, Nicanor, Timon, Parmenas, and Nicolas of Antioch (an earlier convert to the Jewish faith). These seven were presented to the apostles, who prayed for them as they laid their hands on them.

So God's message continued to spread. The number of believers greatly increased in Jerusalem, and many of the Jewish priests were converted, too.

REFLECT

Conflict and confusion within the church can prevent the effective presentation of the gospel and inhibit the church's ability to demonstrate the love and union it professes. As we see in this passage, one of the ways to begin to resolve conflict and clear up confusion is to encourage and enable every believer to use his or her spiritual gifts to serve. This is precisely what the apostles did in asking the community of believers to identify seven people gifted in caring for the widows among them and allow the apostles to do what God had called and gifted them to do. Because the apostles served in their areas of gifting, "the word of God spread" (verse 7, NIV).

- Read this passage again. What word or phrase stands out to you? Then sit quietly, reminding yourself that you are in God's loving presence, and ask him to show you how that word or phrase connects to your life.

- Reflect on a season in your life (maybe it's now) in which you served in a way that was outside your gifts. How did that feel? How fruitful or fulfilling was your time serving in this area? (For a list of spiritual gifts, take a look at 1 Corinthians 12:1-11 and Romans 12:4-8.) Compare that feeling to times you've served according to how God has gifted you. What is the difference?

• When you serve in the ways God has gifted you—whether in your church, family, or community—what do onlookers come to know about Jesus through you?

RESPOND

Father, thank you for the diverse ways you have dispersed gifts among your followers. Give me eyes to see not only how I contribute to your purposes through my gifts but also how those around me contribute. Remind me that this is what allows your Word to spread. Forgive me for times I may have elevated certain gifts above others and thereby elevated certain people above others. Use me to encourage every person I encounter to be who you've made them to be. And may all of my life—every thought, word, and action—honor you and advance your Kingdom here on earth. Amen.

DAY 12

OPEN MY EYES!

a prayer to open

Holy Spirit, come. Center my heart.
Fill my mind. Guide my steps.

READ ACTS 6:8-13; 7:1-29

Stephen, a man full of God's grace and power, performed amazing miracles and signs among the people. But one day some men . . . started to debate with him. . . . None of them could stand against the wisdom and the Spirit with which Stephen spoke.

So they persuaded some men to lie about Stephen, saying, "We heard him blaspheme Moses, and even God." This roused the people, the elders, and the teachers of religious law. So they arrested Stephen and brought him before the high council.

The lying witnesses said, "This man is always speaking against the holy Temple and against the law of Moses." . . .

Then the high priest asked Stephen, "Are these accusations true?"

This was Stephen's reply: . . . "Listen to me. Our glorious God appeared to our ancestor Abraham. . . . God told him, 'Leave your native land and your relatives, and come into the land that I will show you.' So Abraham left the land [and] God brought him here to the land where you now live.

"But God gave him no inheritance here. . . . God did promise, however, that eventually the whole land would belong to Abraham and his descendants— even though he had no children yet. God also told him that his descendants would live in a foreign land, where they would be oppressed as slaves for 400 years. 'But I will punish the nation that enslaves them,' God said, 'and in the end they will come out and worship me here in this place.'

"God also gave Abraham the covenant of circumcision at that time. So when Abraham became the father of Isaac, he circumcised him on the eighth day. And the practice was continued when Isaac became the father of Jacob, and when Jacob became the father of the twelve patriarchs of the Israelite nation.

"These patriarchs were jealous of their brother Joseph, and they sold him to be a slave in Egypt. But God was with him and rescued him from all his troubles. And God gave him favor before Pharaoh, king of Egypt. God also gave Joseph unusual

Empowered

•

wisdom, so that Pharaoh appointed him governor over all of Egypt. . . .

"But a famine came upon Egypt and Canaan . . . and our ancestors ran out of food. Jacob heard that there was still grain in Egypt, so he sent his sons—our ancestors—to buy some. The second time they went, Joseph revealed his identity to his brothers, and they were introduced to Pharaoh. Then Joseph sent for his father, Jacob, and all his relatives to come to Egypt. . . . So Jacob went to Egypt. He died there, as did our ancestors. . . .

"As the time drew near when God would fulfill his promise to Abraham, the number of our people in Egypt greatly increased. But then a new king came to the throne of Egypt. . . . This king exploited our people and oppressed them, forcing parents to abandon their newborn babies so they would die.

"At that time Moses was born. . . . His parents cared for him at home for three months. When they had to abandon him, Pharaoh's daughter adopted him and raised him as her own son. Moses was taught all the wisdom of the Egyptians, and he was powerful in both speech and action.

"One day when Moses was forty years old, he decided to visit his relatives, the people of Israel. He saw an Egyptian mistreating an Israelite. So Moses came to the man's defense and avenged him, killing the Egyptian. Moses assumed his fellow Israelites would realize that God had sent him to rescue them, but they didn't.

"The next day he visited them again and saw two men of Israel fighting. He tried to be a peacemaker. 'Men,' he said, 'you are brothers. Why are you fighting each other?'

"But the man in the wrong pushed Moses aside. 'Who made you a ruler and judge over us?' he asked. 'Are you going to kill me as you killed that Egyptian yesterday?' When Moses heard that, he fled the country and lived as a foreigner in the land of Midian. There his two sons were born."

REFLECT

Stephen was chosen as one of seven men to oversee the daily distribution of food to the Christian widows living in Jerusalem. He also performed miracles and received great opposition and criticism. His words, wisdom, and wonders—all gifts from the Holy Spirit—represented new movement by God in the world, one that looked different from what people expected. So those who were entrenched in the old ways didn't recognize that Stephen's words and actions represented the fulfillment of the very promises God had made to the Jewish people through Abraham and Moses. Instead of defending himself against their accusations point by point, Stephen responded to his accusers by reminding them of the bigger story in which they found themselves. We all need this reminder from time to time. We get stuck in our small stories and lose track of God's story and all he might be inviting us to be a part of for his Kingdom and the sake of others.

- Read this passage again. What word or phrase stands out to you? Sit quietly, reminding yourself that you are in God's loving presence, and ask him to show you how that word or phrase connects to your life.

- What are the ways you generally expect God to be present, speak to you, or respond to you? What are those expectations based on? Do they in some way limit your ability to hear from him in new ways?

- In what area of your life right now are you longing to see God intervene or act but sensing only silence and inaction? How might this area of your life be a bigger part of his story?

Father, open my eyes! I want to see where you're at work and align with what you're doing in my life. Remove any barriers in me that blind me from noticing your presence. Remind me of the grander story you're weaving together so I can share that story with others. Empower me by your Holy Spirit to be patient and notice you in unexpected places. Amen.

DAY 13

THE HARSH TRUTH

a prayer to open

Holy Spirit, come. Center my heart.
Fill my mind. Guide my steps.

READ ACTS 7:30-53

"Forty years later, in the desert near Mount Sinai, an angel appeared to Moses in the flame of a burning bush. When Moses saw it, he was amazed at the sight. As he went to take a closer look, the voice of the LORD called out to him, 'I am the God of your ancestors—the God of Abraham, Isaac, and Jacob.' Moses shook with terror and did not dare to look.

"Then the LORD said to him, 'Take off your sandals, for you are standing on holy ground. I have certainly seen the oppression of my people in Egypt. I have heard their groans and have come down to rescue them. Now go, for I am sending you back to Egypt.'

"So God sent back the same man his people had previously rejected. . . . Through the angel who appeared to him in the burning bush, God sent Moses to be their ruler and savior. And by means of many wonders and miraculous signs, he led them out of Egypt, through the Red Sea, and through the wilderness for forty years.

"Moses himself told the people of Israel, 'God will raise up for you a Prophet like me from among your own people.' Moses was with our ancestors . . . when the angel spoke to him at Mount Sinai. And there Moses received life-giving words to pass on to us.

"But our ancestors refused to listen to Moses. They rejected him and wanted to return to Egypt. They told Aaron, 'Make us some gods who can lead us, for we don't know what has become of this Moses, who brought us out of Egypt.' So they made an idol shaped like a calf, and they sacrificed to it and celebrated over this thing they had made. Then God turned away from them and abandoned them to serve the stars of heaven as their gods! In the book of the prophets it is written,

'Was it to me you were bringing sacrifices and offerings
    during those forty years in the wilderness, Israel?
No, you carried your pagan gods . . .
    and the images you made to worship them.
So I will send you into exile
    as far away as Babylon.'

"Our ancestors carried the Tabernacle with them through the wilderness. It was constructed according to the plan God had shown to Moses. Years later, when Joshua led our ancestors in battle against the nations that God drove out of this land, the Tabernacle was taken with them into their new territory. And it stayed there until the time of King David.

"David found favor with God and asked for the privilege of building a permanent Temple for the God of Jacob. But it was Solomon who actually built it. However, the Most High doesn't live in temples made by human hands. As the prophet says,

'Heaven is my throne,
    and the earth is my footstool.
Could you build me a temple as good as that?'
    asks the LORD.
'Could you build me such a resting place?
    Didn't my hands make both heaven and earth?'

"You stubborn people! You are heathen at heart and deaf to the truth. Must you forever resist the Holy Spirit? That's what your ancestors did, and so do you! Name one prophet your ancestors didn't persecute! They even killed the ones who predicted the coming of the Righteous One—the Messiah whom you betrayed and murdered. You deliberately disobeyed God's law, even though you received it from the hands of angels."

REFLECT

Imagine if someone were to lay before you all the ways you have rebelled against God—which is what Stephen did for the Jewish leaders. How would it feel to come face to face with all the times you idolized relationships, tangible things, or your own feelings; all the times you turned your back on God because something "better" came along that fulfilled an immediate need; or all the ways that, through selfish or reckless decisions, you undermined who he made you to be? This kind of truth is hard to hear and yet so necessary to hear in order to experience God's transformation and fulfill our callings.

- Read this passage again. What word or phrase stands out to you? Sit quietly, reminding yourself that you are in God's loving presence, and ask him to show you how that word or phrase connects to your life.

- Reflect on a time when someone pointed out a destructive or sinful behavior in you. How was the message delivered? How did you respond? Were you able to receive that truth in the moment? If not, why not? What would have made you more able to receive the truth about yourself?

- Is there anyone in your life right now who could benefit from hearing the truth about a destructive pattern, sinful behavior, or ungodly character lapse? What is your role to play? If you sense God's gentle nudge to "be Stephen" for this person, how might you balance truth and grace in that conversation so their eyes might be opened?

RESPOND

Father, thank you that in a world in which everything seems relative, there is truth—an actual path that is good and right. When I look back and see the trail of rebellion in my life—and all the consequences that have resulted—I also can see how you have continued to pursue me, forgive me, and guide me back to you. Thank you for truth tellers in my life. Give me the humility to hear from them even if their words or attitudes are harsh. May the truth I share always be accompanied by grace. Amen.

TO SUFFER WITH CHRIST

a prayer to open

Holy Spirit, come. Center my heart.
Fill my mind. Guide my steps.

READ ACTS 7:54–8:3

The Jewish leaders were infuriated by Stephen's accusation, and they shook their fists at him in rage. But Stephen, full of the Holy Spirit, gazed steadily into heaven and saw the glory of God, and he saw Jesus standing in the place of honor at God's right hand. And he told them, "Look, I see the heavens opened and the Son of Man standing in the place of honor at God's right hand!"

Then they put their hands over their ears and began shouting. They rushed at him and dragged him out of the city and began to stone him. His accusers took off their coats and laid them at the feet of a young man named Saul.

As they stoned him, Stephen prayed, "Lord Jesus, receive my spirit." He fell to his knees, shouting, "Lord, don't charge them with this sin!" And with that, he died.

Saul was one of the witnesses, and he agreed completely with the killing of Stephen.

A great wave of persecution began that day . . . and all the believers except the apostles were scattered through the regions of Judea and Samaria. . . . But Saul was going everywhere to destroy the church. He went from house to house, dragging out both men and women to throw them into prison.

REFLECT

Stephen's truth was too much for his audience to bear, and he became the first martyr of the early church. The suffering Stephen endured is hard to imagine— particularly in our day, when, in most places in the West, we can gather and share our faith freely. Also, we find suffering unacceptable and seek to avoid it at all costs. We censor ourselves and are tempted to back off if we sense that our beliefs will cause us or someone else the slightest discomfort. Stephen's example shows us how our human suffering is a way of identifying with Christ's suffering and thereby helps us know Jesus more deeply. Could our small versions of suffering—which may happen because we forgive over and over, stand up for the vulnerable and oppressed, pray for our enemies, and give generously—actually be gifts?

- Read this passage again. What word or phrase stands out to you? Sit quietly, reminding yourself that you are in God's loving presence, and ask him to show you how that word or phrase connects to your life.

- What are some ways you avoid suffering and pain in relationships? Recall a time when you experienced growth, beauty, or goodness that came as a result of your suffering and pain.

- Reflect on a time you experienced suffering—humiliation, reputational damage, disappointment, sadness, or even physical pain—as a result of living out your faith in Jesus. How did you navigate that suffering? How did it affect your conduct or your faith? If you have not suffered in any of these ways, why do you think that is?

Empowered

•

Father, thank you for the example of Stephen and how he responded to suffering: forgiving his attackers and turning his attention to you. Too often I seek to avoid pain. I can be leery about forgiving others unless I sense their repentance; I can be cautious about offering someone grace lest they take advantage of me; I sometimes lash out at enemies, either with my words or my thoughts, instead of loving them. Give me courage to suffer with Christ—not to step into suffering for its own sake, but to see it as a gift that helps me better identify with you. Amen.

DAY 15

A RIGHT HEART

a prayer to open

Holy Spirit, come. Center my heart.
Fill my mind. Guide my steps.

READ ACTS 8:4-25

The believers who were scattered preached the Good News about Jesus wherever they went. Philip . . . went to the city of Samaria and told the people there about the Messiah. Crowds listened intently to Philip because they were eager to hear his message and see the miraculous signs he did. Many evil spirits were cast out, screaming as they left their victims. And many who had been paralyzed or lame were healed. So there was great joy in that city.

A man named Simon had been a sorcerer there for many years, amazing the people of Samaria and claiming to be someone great. Everyone, from the least to the greatest, often spoke of him as "the Great One—the Power of God." They listened closely to him because for a long time he had astounded them with his magic.

But now the people believed Philip's message of Good News concerning the Kingdom of God and the name of Jesus Christ. As a result, many men and women were baptized. Then Simon himself believed and was baptized. He began following Philip wherever he went, and he was amazed by the signs and great miracles Philip performed.

When the apostles in Jerusalem heard that the people of Samaria had accepted God's message, they sent Peter and John there. As soon as they arrived, they prayed for these new believers to receive the Holy Spirit. The Holy Spirit had not yet come upon any of them, for they had only been baptized in the name of the Lord Jesus. Then Peter and John laid their hands upon these believers, and they received the Holy Spirit.

When Simon saw that the Spirit was given when the apostles laid their hands on people, he offered them money to buy this power. "Let me have this power, too," he exclaimed, "so that when I lay my hands on people, they will receive the Holy Spirit!"

But Peter replied, "May your money be destroyed with you for thinking God's gift can be bought! You can have no part in this, for your heart is not right with God. Repent of your wickedness and pray to the Lord. Perhaps he will forgive your evil thoughts, for I can see that you are full of bitter jealousy and are held captive by sin."

"Pray to the Lord for me," Simon exclaimed, "that these terrible things you've said won't happen to me!"

After testifying and preaching the word of the Lord in Samaria, Peter and John returned to Jerusalem. And they stopped in many Samaritan villages along the way to preach the Good News.

REFLECT

Stephen's death caused many disciples to scatter away from Jerusalem for fear of persecution. And for some, their first stop was Samaria, just as Jesus had predicted (see Acts 1:8). There the disciples confronted a new problem: people's desire to use the Holy Spirit for their own power or fame, which Simon the Sorcerer seemed to desire above all else. Although he claimed to believe in Jesus and was even baptized, something in his heart was not right. He did not want the gift of God's Holy Spirit, a relationship with Jesus, or the ability to invite others into that relationship; what Simon wanted was God's power so he could amass fame. He sought not to follow God but to be God. How often do we seek God's power to overcome difficulty but resist his presence to guide us into love or service or generosity?

- Read this passage again. What word or phrase stands out to you? Sit quietly, reminding yourself that you are in God's loving presence, and ask him to show you how that word or phrase connects to your life.

- Have you ever sought a relationship with someone just to gain power or fame, or perhaps to fulfill an unmet need? Why did you really want that thing?

- Examine your relationship with God. What evidence do you see of an actual relationship? Do you spend time with him? Does your conduct and attitude reflect time spent with him? Are there times you want the power of God but resist guidance and correction? Is there any area in which you are held captive by sin or bitterness and you push him away?

RESPOND_____

Father, I want a heart that is right with you. There are times I seek your power and ability to resolve my problems but resist your presence and love. When I slow down and quiet my heart before you, I recognize that what my soul really desires is to walk with you, hear your voice, and allow you to correct and guide my steps. I want to turn my heart over to you to be transformed. Help me surrender my hands to you for your purposes. Help me submit my mind and thoughts to you so you can align them with your love and holiness. I pray that your Holy Spirit would make your will known and done in and through me. Amen.

DAY 16

EARS TO HEAR

a prayer to open

Holy Spirit, come. Center my heart.
Fill my mind. Guide my steps.

READ ACTS 8:26-40 _____

As for Philip, an angel of the Lord said to him, "Go south down the desert road that runs from Jerusalem to Gaza." So he started out, and he met the treasurer of Ethiopia, a eunuch of great authority under the Kandake, the queen of Ethiopia. The eunuch had gone to Jerusalem to worship, and he was now returning. Seated in his carriage, he was reading aloud from the book of the prophet Isaiah.

The Holy Spirit said to Philip, "Go over and walk along beside the carriage."

Philip ran over and heard the man reading from the prophet Isaiah. Philip asked, "Do you understand what you are reading?"

The man replied, "How can I, unless someone instructs me?" And he urged Philip to come up into the carriage and sit with him.

The passage of Scripture he had been reading was this:

"He was led like a sheep to the slaughter.
And as a lamb is silent before the shearers,
he did not open his mouth.

He was humiliated and received no justice.
Who can speak of his descendants?
For his life was taken from the earth."

The eunuch asked Philip, "Tell me, was the prophet talking about himself or someone else?" So beginning with this same Scripture, Philip told him the Good News about Jesus.

As they rode along, they came to some water, and the eunuch said, "Look! There's some water! Why can't I be baptized?" He ordered the carriage to stop, and they went down into the water, and Philip baptized him.

When they came up out of the water, the Spirit of the Lord snatched Philip away. The eunuch never saw him again but went on his way rejoicing. Meanwhile, Philip found himself farther north. . . . He preached the Good News there and in every town along the way until he came to Caesarea.

REFLECT _____

Philip was one of the seven men, along with Stephen, appointed to care for the widows in the early-church community (see Acts 6:1-7), yet in this passage, we see Philip sent out with a task that God would reveal only as it presented itself. We don't know whether approaching a chariot with a foreign finance official inside would have been within Philip's comfort zone. Given what we do know, it seems unlikely. But the Holy Spirit empowered him and gave him the words and boldness he needed to share the gospel about Jesus with the Ethiopian eunuch, who became the first foreign Christ follower recorded in Scripture. With Holy Spirit–prompted words and Holy Spirit–empowered boldness, we too can overcome any fears we might have to share the good news about Jesus with anyone on our paths.

- Read this passage again. What word or phrase stands out to you? Sit quietly, reminding yourself that you are in God's loving presence, and ask him to show you how that word or phrase connects to your life.

- What fears or concerns do you feel when God prompts you to have a spiritual conversation with a stranger? What underlies those fears or concerns? How might you overcome them in order to allow the Holy Spirit to use you?

- When you believe you have heard God "whisper" to you—whether through Scripture, in your heart, through other people, or in some other way—how do you typically respond? With whom do you share what you've heard to help you discern whether it is from God and what your next steps should be?

Father, thank you that by your Holy Spirit, you speak to me. Thank you that you are still sending your followers out to share the good news about Jesus. I want to be someone who is open to hearing and responding to your callings and divine assignments. Give me ears to hear you and courage to obey as Philip did. Help me discern your voice and seek guidance from wise friends or mentors when I'm unsure of your direction. May I always act in love and point those I encounter to you. Amen.

THE COURAGE TO ACT

a prayer to open   Holy Spirit, come. Center my heart.
                                       Fill my mind. Guide my steps.

READ ACTS 9:1-25

Saul was uttering threats with every breath and was eager to kill the Lord's followers. So he went to the high priest. He requested letters addressed to the synagogues in Damascus, asking for their cooperation in the arrest of any followers of the Way he found there. He wanted to bring them . . . back to Jerusalem in chains.

As he was approaching Damascus on this mission, a light from heaven suddenly shone down around him. He fell to the ground and heard a voice saying to him, "Saul! Saul! Why are you persecuting me?"

"Who are you, lord?" Saul asked.

And the voice replied, "I am Jesus, the one you are persecuting! Now get up and go into the city, and you will be told what you must do."

The men with Saul stood speechless, for they heard the sound of someone's voice but saw no one! Saul picked himself up off the ground, but when he opened his eyes he was blind. So his companions led him by the hand to Damascus. He remained there blind for three days and did not eat or drink.

Now there was a believer in Damascus named Ananias. The Lord spoke to him in a vision, calling, "Ananias!"

"Yes, Lord!" he replied.

The Lord said, "Go over to Straight Street, to the house of Judas. When you get there, ask for a man from Tarsus named Saul. He is praying to me right now. I have shown him a vision of a man named Ananias coming in and laying hands on him so he can see again."

"But Lord," exclaimed Ananias, "I've heard many people talk about the terrible things this man has done to the believers in Jerusalem! And he is authorized by the leading priests to arrest everyone who calls upon your name."

But the Lord said, "Go, for Saul is my chosen instrument to take my message to the Gentiles and to kings, as well as to the people of Israel. And I will show him how much he must suffer for my name's sake."

So Ananias went and found Saul. He laid his hands on him and said, "Brother Saul, the Lord Jesus, who appeared to you on the road, has sent me so that you might regain your sight and be filled with the Holy Spirit." Instantly something like scales fell from Saul's eyes, and he regained his sight. Then he got up and was baptized. Afterward he ate some food and regained his strength.

Saul stayed with the believers in Damascus for a few days. And immediately he began preaching about Jesus in the synagogues, saying, "He is indeed the Son of God!"

All who heard him were amazed. "Isn't this the same man who caused such devastation among Jesus' followers in Jerusalem?" they asked. "And didn't he come here to arrest them and take them in chains to the leading priests?"

Saul's preaching became more and more powerful, and the Jews in Damascus couldn't refute his proofs that Jesus was indeed the Messiah. After a while some of the Jews plotted together to kill him. They were watching for him day and night at the city gate so they could murder him, but Saul was told about their plot. So during the night, some of the other believers lowered him in a large basket through an opening in the city wall.

Empowered

●

The story of Saul's encounter with Jesus on the road to Damascus is a compelling example of God's intervention in an individual's life. The fact that Saul was the leading persecutor of those who followed Jesus and then became the loudest voice for Christ the world has known is in itself miraculous. Equally miraculous, though, are Ananias's actions and his courage to follow God's seemingly outrageous and dangerous instruction to lay hands on this man who had set out to put people like Ananias in prison. This might not be the kind of task God will assign all of us, but perhaps we would see the miraculous more often if we trusted the Holy Spirit as Ananias did.

- Read this passage again. What word or phrase stands out to you? Sit quietly, reminding yourself that you are in God's loving presence, and ask him to show you how that word or phrase connects to your life.

- Reflect on a time you experienced something you would describe as miraculous. What were the circumstances? What was your relationship with God like during that time?

- When was the last time you took what felt like a great step of faith? What happened? How did you experience God then?

RESPOND

Father, thank you that you still intervene in individual lives and transform hearts. Thank you for drawing me to you and allowing me to understand your goodness and grace in Jesus. Thank you for your willingness to pull me into the light and relieve my spiritual blindness. Help me notice where you're at work so I can participate in what you're doing. Enable me by your Spirit to act in faith and experience the miraculous. Fill me with courage and a desire to respond without hesitation when you call me to act. Amen.

DAY 18

RAISED TO LIFE

a prayer to open

Holy Spirit, come. Center my heart.
Fill my mind. Guide my steps.

READ ACTS 9:26-42

When Saul arrived in Jerusalem, he tried to meet with the believers, but they were all afraid of him. They did not believe he had truly become a believer! Then Barnabas brought him to the apostles and told them how Saul had seen the Lord on the way to Damascus and how the Lord had spoken to Saul. He also told them that Saul had preached boldly in the name of Jesus in Damascus.

So Saul stayed with the apostles and went all around Jerusalem with them, preaching boldly in the name of the Lord. He debated with some Greek-speaking Jews, but they tried to murder him. When the believers heard about this, they took him down to Caesarea and sent him away to Tarsus, his hometown.

The church then had peace throughout Judea, Galilee, and Samaria, and it became stronger as the believers lived in the fear of the Lord. And with the encouragement of the Holy Spirit, it also grew in numbers.

Meanwhile, Peter traveled from place to place, and he came down to visit the believers in the town of Lydda. There he met a man named Aeneas, who had been paralyzed and bedridden for eight years. Peter said to him, "Aeneas, Jesus Christ heals you! Get up, and roll up your sleeping mat!" And he was healed instantly. Then the whole population of Lydda and Sharon saw Aeneas walking around, and they turned to the Lord.

There was a believer in Joppa named Tabitha (which in Greek is Dorcas). She was always doing kind things for others and helping the poor. About this time she became ill and died. Her body was washed for burial and laid in an upstairs room. But the believers had heard that Peter was nearby at Lydda, so they sent two men to beg him, "Please come as soon as possible!"

So Peter returned with them; and as soon as he arrived, they took him to the upstairs room. The room was filled with widows who were weeping and showing him the coats and other clothes Dorcas had made for them. But Peter asked them all to leave the room; then he knelt and prayed. Turning to the body he said, "Get up, Tabitha." And she opened her eyes! When she saw Peter, she sat up! He gave her his hand and helped her up. Then he called in the widows and all the believers, and he presented her to them alive.

The news spread through the whole town, and many believed in the Lord.

REFLECT

Luke wrote the stories of Aeneas's healing and Tabitha's resurrection in such an understated way that it almost requires a double take. A man paralyzed for eight years could now walk, and a woman who was dead was raised to life! We know little about Tabitha—only that she was dedicated to the poor—and even less about Aeneas. They seem to have been people going about their lives in quietude—perhaps just like us—until the supernatural happened.

- Read this passage again. What word or phrase stands out to you? Sit quietly, reminding yourself that you are in God's loving presence, and ask him to show you how that word or phrase connects to your life.

- Reflect on whether there is a part of your work, service, or identity that seems to be constantly overlooked by those around you or whose opinion and encouragement matters to you. How does it feel to be unseen or overlooked?

- Who came to mind when you read the stories of Aeneas and Tabitha? Someone with a chronic illness or disability? Someone who serves faithfully and without fanfare? How could you affirm or notice that person?

RESPOND

Father, thank you that you see me and that nothing I do goes unnoticed in your eyes. Fill me with a desire to serve the poor and extend kindness. Help me to remain faithful whether or not what I do or who I am is celebrated, affirmed, or noticed. Open my eyes to those around me, and use me to affirm the good works and faithfulness of others. May the faithful feel your favor and blessing. Amen.

ONE IN CHRIST

a prayer to open

Holy Spirit, come. Center my heart.
Fill my mind. Guide my steps.

READ ACTS 10:1-33

In Caesarea there lived a Roman army officer named Cornelius, who was a captain of the Italian Regiment. He was a devout, God-fearing man, as was everyone in his household. He gave generously to the poor and prayed regularly to God. One afternoon . . . he had a vision in which he saw an angel of God coming toward him. "Cornelius!" the angel said.

Cornelius stared at him in terror. "What is it, sir?" he asked the angel.

And the angel replied, "Your prayers and gifts to the poor have been received by God as an offering! Now send some men to Joppa, and summon a man named Simon Peter." . . .

As soon as the angel was gone, Cornelius called two of his household servants and a devout soldier, one of his personal attendants. He told them what had happened and sent them off to Joppa.

The next day as Cornelius's messengers were nearing the town, Peter went up on the flat roof to pray. It was about noon, and he was hungry. But while a meal was being prepared, he fell into a trance. He saw the sky open, and something like a large sheet was let down by its four corners. In the sheet were all sorts of animals, reptiles, and birds. Then a voice said to him, "Get up, Peter; kill and eat them."

"No, Lord," Peter declared. "I have never eaten anything that our Jewish laws have declared impure and unclean."

But the voice spoke again: "Do not call something unclean if God has made it clean." The same vision was repeated three times. Then the sheet was suddenly pulled up to heaven.

Peter was very perplexed. What could the vision mean? Just then the men sent by Cornelius [arrived]. . . .

As Peter was puzzling over the vision, the Holy

Spirit said to him, "Three men have come looking for you. Get up, go downstairs, and go with them without hesitation. Don't worry, for I have sent them."

So Peter went down and said, "I'm the man you are looking for. Why have you come?"

They said, "We were sent by Cornelius, a Roman officer. He is a devout and God-fearing man, well respected by all the Jews. A holy angel instructed him to summon you to his house so that he can hear your message." So Peter invited the men to stay for the night. The next day he went with them, accompanied by some of the brothers from Joppa.

They arrived in Caesarea the following day. Cornelius was waiting for them and had called together his relatives and close friends. As Peter entered his home, Cornelius fell at his feet and worshiped him. But Peter pulled him up and said, "Stand up! I'm a human being just like you!" So they talked together and went inside, where many others were assembled.

Peter told them, "You know it is against our laws for a Jewish man to enter a Gentile home like this or to associate with you. But God has shown me that I should no longer think of anyone as impure or unclean. So I came without objection as soon as I was sent for. Now tell me why you sent for me."

Cornelius replied, "Four days ago I was praying in my house. . . . Suddenly, a man in dazzling clothes was standing in front of me. He told me, 'Cornelius, your prayer has been heard, and your gifts to the poor have been noticed by God! Now send messengers to Joppa, and summon a man named Simon Peter. . . .' So I sent for you at once, and it was good of you to come. Now we are all here, waiting before God to hear the message the Lord has given you."

REFLECT

In Galatians 3:28, the apostle Paul wrote, "There is neither Jew nor Gentile, neither slave nor free, nor is there male and female, for you are all one in Christ Jesus" (NIV). We see this theology worked out in practical, real-life terms in this passage about Peter and Cornelius. It is such an important moment in the church that it's the longest story in Acts, and Luke repeated it multiple times. Indeed, prior to Peter and Cornelius's encounter, the barrier between Jews and Gentiles was impenetrable. But here, by the power of the Holy Spirit, that barrier fell. Barriers between and among Christians persist to this day. Though Paul tells us that we are all one in Christ Jesus, we can't quite seem to embrace this reality. We want to label and categorize based on any number of reasons. Only as we are surrendered to the Spirit can we live into the truth that our first and fundamental identity is in Christ.

- Read this passage again. What word or phrase stands out to you? Sit quietly, reminding yourself that you are in God's loving presence, and ask him to show you how that word or phrase connects to your life.

- What are the most prominent barriers you see between Christians? Which of those barriers do you contribute to? Which do you seek to tear down by practicing love, forgiveness, and openness to the Holy Spirit's leadership and direction?

- What practices tend to open your heart to people who are different from you? What tends to make you less open and more judgmental?

RESPOND_____

Father, thank you for the Holy Spirit and how you guide and direct your followers in such personal and powerful ways. I pray that you would continue to break down barriers in this day to increase the unity in your church. Lead me, by your Spirit, to see the ways I erect or maintain walls, and help me instead to be a bridge builder, reconciler, and peacemaker. Amen.

DAY 20

THE GOOD NEWS OF PEACE

a prayer to open

Holy Spirit, come. Center my heart.
Fill my mind. Guide my steps.

READ ACTS 10:34-48_____

Peter replied, "I see very clearly that God shows no favoritism. In every nation he accepts those who fear him and do what is right. This is the message of Good News for the people of Israel—that there is peace with God through Jesus Christ, who is Lord of all. You know what happened throughout Judea, beginning in Galilee, after John began preaching his message of baptism. And you know that God anointed Jesus of Nazareth with the Holy Spirit and with power. Then Jesus went around doing good and healing all who were oppressed by the devil, for God was with him.

"And we apostles are witnesses of all he did throughout Judea and in Jerusalem. They put him to death by hanging him on a cross, but God raised him to life on the third day. Then God allowed him to appear . . . to us whom God had chosen in advance to be his witnesses. We were those who ate and drank with him after he rose from the dead. And he ordered us to preach everywhere and to testify that Jesus is the one appointed by God to be the judge of all—the living and the dead. He is the one all the prophets testified about, saying that everyone who believes in him will have their sins forgiven through his name."

Even as Peter was saying these things, the Holy Spirit fell upon all who were listening to the message.

The Jewish believers who came with Peter were amazed that the gift of the Holy Spirit had been poured out on the Gentiles, too. For they heard them speaking in other tongues and praising God.

Then Peter asked, "Can anyone object to their being baptized, now that they have received the Holy Spirit just as we did?" So he gave orders for them to be baptized in the name of Jesus Christ.

REFLECT_____

Jesus' promise that his disciples would be his witnesses to the ends of the earth implied that the salvation and life he offered would be opened to everyone, not just the Jewish people who, up to that point in history, had a privileged position as God's chosen. Here, with Peter's witnessing words to Cornelius and his family, the Holy Spirit came, as promised, to the Gentiles. And because of the parallels to Pentecost in Jerusalem (see Acts 2), there was no mistaking what happened. Peter called Jesus' message the "good news of peace" (10:36, NIV) to stress that Christ enabled not only reconciliation of people to God but also reconciliation between people.

- Read this passage again. What word or phrase stands out to you? Sit quietly, reminding yourself that you are in God's loving presence, and ask him to show you how that word or phrase connects to your life.

- How has Christ brought peace into your relationships? Where is peace still lacking?

- What are some concrete ways you are extending the peace Jesus made possible? How might you be inhibiting this peace?

RESPOND_____

Father, thank you for the peace of Christ—the reconciliation he brought to all people. I want to be an instrument of that peace. Empower me by your Holy Spirit to seek reconciliation and restoration, build bridges and common ground, welcome the stranger, and reach out to the isolated. Use me to share the good news of peace, and show me the ways I inhibit the restoration you seek to accomplish in my life and in my relationships. Amen.

DAY 21

REPENTANCE THAT LEADS TO LIFE

a prayer to open

Holy Spirit, come. Center my heart.
Fill my mind. Guide my steps.

Soon the news reached the apostles and other believers in Judea that the Gentiles had received the word of God. But when Peter arrived back in Jerusalem, the Jewish believers criticized him. "You entered the home of Gentiles and even ate with them!" they said.

Then Peter told them exactly what had happened. "I was in the town of Joppa," he said, "and while I was praying, I went into a trance and saw a vision. Something like a large sheet was let down by its four corners from the sky. And it came right down to me. When I looked inside the sheet, I saw all sorts of tame and wild animals, reptiles, and birds. And I heard a voice say, 'Get up, Peter; kill and eat them.'

"'No, Lord,' I replied. 'I have never eaten anything that our Jewish laws have declared impure or unclean.'

"But the voice from heaven spoke again: 'Do not call something unclean if God has made it clean.' This happened three times before the sheet and all it contained was pulled back up to heaven.

"Just then three men who had been sent from Caesarea arrived at the house where we were staying. The Holy Spirit told me to go with them and not to worry that they were Gentiles. These six brothers here accompanied me, and we soon entered the home of the man who had sent for us. He told us how an angel had appeared to him in his home and had told him, 'Send messengers to Joppa, and summon a man named Simon Peter. He will tell you how you and everyone in your household can be saved!'

"As I began to speak," Peter continued, "the Holy Spirit fell on them, just as he fell on us at the beginning. Then I thought of the Lord's words when he said, 'John baptized with water, but you will be baptized with the Holy Spirit.' And since God gave these Gentiles the same gift he gave us when we believed in the Lord Jesus Christ, who was I to stand in God's way?"

When the others heard this, they stopped objecting and began praising God. They said, "We can see that God has also given the Gentiles the privilege of repenting of their sins and receiving eternal life."

REFLECT

Every time God does something new or extends an invitation to more people, controversy results. Peter's involvement with Cornelius and his family did not sit well with a small group of Jewish Christians (the "circumcised believers" [verse 2, NIV]) who wanted to remain among the privileged and make newcomers abide by their rules and traditions. Once Peter explained how his experience had been predicted by Jesus, the objectors relented and realized that God's invitation to life through repentance was much bigger than they had previously believed. This is undoubtedly true in our day too: We shrink God's invitation to fit our standards about who should be in and who should be out. But God is always calling to those on the fringes, those who are ignored. His invitation is for all.

- Read this passage again. What word or phrase stands out to you? Sit quietly, reminding yourself that you are in God's loving presence, and ask him to show you how that word or phrase connects to your life.

- What comes to mind when you hear the word *repentance*? How does repentance lead to life?

- In what ways do you find yourself seeking to limit God's invitation? Who have you thought is beyond God's reach?

Empowered

•

313

Father, thank you for the gift of repentance that leads to life—an eternal life and a life in Christ now. Remind me of your compassion and mercy so I can turn to you with openness and without fear of punishment or condemnation. Forgive me for attempting to limit your invitation to those I deem acceptable or worthy. Show me how to reach out, share your love, and live in a way that leads others to you. Lead me by your Spirit. Amen.

DAY 22

GOD'S GRACE AT WORK

a prayer to open

Holy Spirit, come. Center my heart.
Fill my mind. Guide my steps.

READ ACTS 11:19-30

The believers who had been scattered during the persecution after Stephen's death traveled as far as Phoenicia, Cyprus, and Antioch of Syria. They preached the word of God, but only to Jews. However, some of the believers who went to Antioch from Cyprus and Cyrene began preaching to the Gentiles about the Lord Jesus. The power of the Lord was with them, and a large number of these Gentiles believed and turned to the Lord.

When the church at Jerusalem heard what had happened, they sent Barnabas to Antioch. When he arrived and saw this evidence of God's blessing, he was filled with joy, and he encouraged the believers to stay true to the Lord. Barnabas was a good man, full of the Holy Spirit and strong in faith. And many people were brought to the Lord.

Then Barnabas went on to Tarsus to look for Saul. When he found him, he brought him back to Antioch. Both of them stayed there with the church for a full year, teaching large crowds of people. . . .

During this time some prophets traveled from Jerusalem to Antioch. One of them named Agabus stood up in one of the meetings and predicted by the Spirit that a great famine was coming upon the entire Roman world. (This was fulfilled during the reign of Claudius.) So the believers in Antioch decided to send relief to the brothers and sisters in Judea, everyone giving as much as they could. This they did, entrusting their gifts to Barnabas and Saul to take to the elders of the church in Jerusalem.

REFLECT

Barnabas means "Son of Encouragement" (see Acts 4:36), and in the city of Antioch, we see Barnabas live up to his name. Often we fail to encourage others because we are jealous of their success, how we see God working in them, or the gifts and skills they have been given. Sometimes we fail to encourage others just because we are self-focused and forget how helpful it can be to affirm someone during good times or to lift them up during difficult times. Barnabas had certain character traits that allowed him to be an encourager: He was able to see God's grace at work, seeing God's grace made him glad, and he was full of faith.

- Read this passage again. What word or phrase stands out to you? Sit quietly, reminding yourself that you are in God's loving presence, and ask him to show you how that word or phrase connects to your life.

- How would you grade yourself as an encourager? What do you think stops you from encouraging others more often?

- Who is your biggest encourager, bringing you affirmation when God is at work in you or reassurance during difficulty? Call that person to say thanks and share why his or her encouragement has mattered to you.

RESPOND

Father, thank you for all the ways your grace is at work in this world. So often my eyes see only despair and brokenness. Allow me to catch glimpses of your Kingdom in my family interactions, my workplace relationships, and everyday kindnesses. Remind me of your abundance, and banish the envy that stops me from encouraging others. May your grace always fill me with joy, and may your Spirit be evident in me as I seek to point those I encounter to you. Amen.

HOPE IN THE MIDST OF SORROW

a prayer to open

Holy Spirit, come. Center my heart.
Fill my mind. Guide my steps.

READ ACTS 12:1-25

About that time King Herod Agrippa began to persecute some believers in the church. He had the apostle James (John's brother) killed with a sword. When Herod saw how much this pleased the Jewish people, he also arrested Peter. (This took place during the Passover celebration.) Then he imprisoned him, placing him under the guard of four squads of four soldiers each. Herod intended to bring Peter out for public trial after the Passover. But while Peter was in prison, the church prayed very earnestly for him.

The night before Peter was to be placed on trial, he was asleep, fastened with two chains between two soldiers. Others stood guard at the prison gate. Suddenly, there was a bright light in the cell, and an angel of the Lord stood before Peter. The angel struck him on the side to awaken him and said, "Quick! Get up!" And the chains fell off his wrists. Then the angel told him, "Get dressed and put on your sandals." And he did. "Now put on your coat and follow me," the angel ordered.

So Peter left the cell, following the angel. But all the time he thought it was a vision. . . . They passed the first and second guard posts and came to the iron gate leading to the city, and this opened for them all by itself. So they passed through and started walking down the street, and then the angel suddenly left him.

Peter finally came to his senses. "It's really true!" he said. "The Lord has sent his angel and saved me from Herod and from what the Jewish leaders had planned to do to me!"

When he realized this, he went to the home of Mary, the mother of John Mark, where many were gathered for prayer. He knocked at the door in the gate, and a servant girl named Rhoda came to open it. When she recognized Peter's voice, she was so overjoyed that, instead of opening the door, she ran back inside and told everyone, "Peter is standing at the door!"

"You're out of your mind!" they said. When she insisted, they decided, "It must be his angel."

Meanwhile, Peter continued knocking. When they finally opened the door and saw him, they were amazed. He motioned for them to quiet down and told them how the Lord had led him out of prison. "Tell James and the other brothers what happened," he said. And then he went to another place. . . .

Empowered

315

The word of God continued to spread, and there were many new believers.

When Barnabas and Saul had finished their mission to Jerusalem, they returned, taking John Mark with them.

REFLECT

Here we see another example of God's supernatural intervention to ensure the continual growth of the church. In fact, Luke made a point of ending this dramatic story with these words: "The word of God continued to spread" (verse 24). So from that perspective, we see hope. But in the midst of this hope, there was great sorrow. Although God saved Peter, John's brother (James) was beheaded. How must this have felt to James's family and close friends? Peter was saved; James was not. When we feel unfairly treated—someone else's prayer for healing was answered, while ours was not—envy or anger may be the emotion that arises in us first. We refuse to express joy for the way another has been blessed. But how our hearts might be changed if, even as we suffer or struggle, we could truly rejoice with those who rejoice.

- Read this passage again. What word or phrase stands out to you? Sit quietly, reminding yourself that you are in God's loving presence, and ask him to show you how that word or phrase connects to your life.

- Reflect on an experience you've had in which you felt as though God treated you unfairly (perhaps healing came to someone else but not to you, or an opportunity opened for someone else but not for you). What do you feel as you think about that experience? What do you hear God saying to you as you reflect on that time?

- Imagine what it would be like to rejoice with the person who was blessed in the way you wanted to be but weren't. What would that be like for you? What would be hard?

RESPOND

Father, thank you for the ways you intervene supernaturally to preserve your church. I pray that I would be someone who rejoices with those who rejoice and mourns with those who mourn. Remove any resentment and anger I feel toward you or others when someone is blessed in certain ways and I am not. I pray that you would heal my hurts and disappointments. Continue to help me surrender every desire and longing to your will and to trust you with every aspect of my life—in the good times and in the difficult times. Amen.

THE PRACTICE OF LISTENING

a prayer to open

Holy Spirit, come. Center my heart.
Fill my mind. Guide my steps.

READ ACTS 13:1-12

One day as [the prophets and teachers of the church at Antioch] were worshiping the Lord and fasting, the Holy Spirit said, "Appoint Barnabas and Saul for the special work to which I have called them." So after more fasting and prayer, the men laid their hands on them and sent them on their way.

So Barnabas and Saul were sent out by the Holy Spirit. They went down to the seaport of Seleucia and then sailed for the island of Cyprus. There, in the town of Salamis, they went to the Jewish synagogues and preached the word of God. John Mark went with them as their assistant.

Afterward they traveled from town to town across the entire island until finally they reached Paphos, where they met a Jewish sorcerer, a false prophet named Bar-Jesus. He had attached himself to the governor, Sergius Paulus, who was an intelligent man. The governor invited Barnabas and Saul to visit him, for he wanted to hear the word of God.

But Elymas, the sorcerer (as his name means in Greek), interfered and urged the governor to pay no attention to what Barnabas and Saul said. He was trying to keep the governor from believing.

Saul, also known as Paul, was filled with the Holy Spirit, and he looked the sorcerer in the eye. Then he said, "You son of the devil, full of every sort of deceit and fraud, and enemy of all that is good! Will you never stop perverting the true ways of the Lord? Watch now, for the Lord has laid his hand of punishment upon you, and you will be struck blind. You will not see the sunlight for some time." Instantly mist and darkness came over the man's eyes, and he began groping around begging for someone to take his hand and lead him.

When the governor saw what had happened, he became a believer, for he was astonished at the teaching about the Lord.

REFLECT

Before Barnabas and Saul were sent off by their friends and the Holy Spirit to begin a journey that would last the rest of Saul's life (with intermittent returns to Jerusalem), they were together worshiping, praying, and fasting. We aren't told how long they had been engaged in these particular practices or whether they had approached God with a specific request. What we know is that in the midst of these practices, they heard the Holy Spirit, who then filled them anew and directed their path. We move so fast in nearly every area of our lives that we fail to stop, gather together in community, and turn our minds and hearts to God. But it is in these moments that we experience God's Spirit and hear how he seeks to guide, correct, and encourage us.

- Read this passage again. What word or phrase stands out to you? Sit quietly, reminding yourself that you are in God's loving presence, and ask him to show you how that word or phrase connects to your life.

- In what area of your life do you feel stuck or as though your faith is stagnant? What would being filled with the Holy Spirit anew in that area bring about (joy, progress, change, increased confidence, power)?

- What spiritual disciplines do you practice in community with other believers?

Empowered

What practices do you sense God might be calling you into (worship, prayer, fasting)? Who could you ask to join you in these practices?

RESPOND

Father, thank you that you speak through your Holy Spirit. I want to have ears to hear, though I know at times busyness, exhaustion, and my own choices close my ears to your voice and movement. Help me open spaces in my calendar and in my heart and mind to really listen to you. I ask that you would direct my path just as you did Paul's and that I would have the awareness and courage to go wherever you send me. Amen.

DAY 25

LISTEN TO ME!

a prayer to open

Holy Spirit, come. Center my heart.
Fill my mind. Guide my steps.

READ ACTS 13:13-41

Paul and his companions then left Paphos by ship for Pamphylia, landing at the port town of Perga. There John Mark left them and returned to Jerusalem. But Paul and Barnabas traveled inland to Antioch of Pisidia.

On the Sabbath they went to the synagogue for the services. After the usual readings from the books of Moses and the prophets, those in charge of the service sent them this message: "Brothers, if you have any word of encouragement for the people, come and give it."

So Paul stood, lifted his hand to quiet them, and started speaking. "Men of Israel," he said, "and you God-fearing Gentiles, listen to me.

"The God of this nation of Israel chose our ancestors and made them multiply and grow strong during their stay in Egypt. Then with a powerful arm he led them out of their slavery. He put up with them through forty years of wandering in the wilderness. Then he destroyed seven nations in Canaan and gave their land to Israel as an inheritance. All this took about 450 years.

"After that, God gave them judges to rule until the time of Samuel the prophet. Then the people begged for a king, and God gave them Saul . . . who reigned for forty years. But God removed Saul and replaced him with David, a man about whom God said, 'I have found David son of Jesse, a man after my own heart. He will do everything I want him to do.'

"And it is one of King David's descendants, Jesus, who is God's promised Savior of Israel! Before he came, John the Baptist preached that all the people of Israel needed to repent of their sins and turn to God and be baptized. As John was finishing his ministry he asked, 'Do you think I am the Messiah? No, I am not! But he is coming soon—and I'm not even worthy to be his slave and untie the sandals on his feet.'

"Brothers—you sons of Abraham, and also you God-fearing Gentiles—this message of salvation has been sent to us! The people in Jerusalem and their leaders did not recognize Jesus as the one the prophets had spoken about. Instead, they condemned him, and in doing this they fulfilled the prophets' words that are read every Sabbath. They found no legal reason to execute him, but they asked Pilate to have him killed anyway.

"When they had done all that the prophecies said about him, they took him down from the cross and placed him in a tomb. But God raised him from the dead! And over a period of many days he appeared to those who had gone with him from Galilee to Jerusalem. They are now his witnesses to the people of Israel.

"And now we are here to bring you this Good News. The promise was made to our ancestors, and God has now fulfilled it for us, their descendants, by raising Jesus. This is what the second psalm says about Jesus:

'You are my Son.
    Today I have become your Father.'

For God had promised to raise him from the dead, not leaving him to rot in the grave. He said, 'I will give you the sacred blessings I promised to David.' Another psalm explains it more fully: 'You will not allow your Holy One to rot in the grave.' This is not a reference to David, for after David had done the will of God in his own generation, he died and was buried with his ancestors, and his body decayed. No, it was a reference to someone else—someone whom God raised and whose body did not decay.

"Brothers, listen! We are here to proclaim that through this man Jesus there is forgiveness for your sins. Everyone who believes in him is made right in God's sight—something the law of Moses could never do. Be careful! Don't let the prophets' words apply to you. For they said,

'Look, you mockers,
be amazed and die!
For I am doing something in your own day,
something you wouldn't believe
even if someone told you about it.'"

REFLECT

Paul was obviously aware of his audience as he stood to speak to the attenders of the Pisidian Antioch synagogue. When he shared the good news about Jesus, he didn't just barrel ahead without concern for who was before him; he started with *their* story. We can picture his audience leaning forward in their chairs to hear his words because of how deeply Paul tapped into their long-held beliefs and desires for restoration and salvation. We all have this same desire—we long for restoration and salvation—even if we can't quite identify it with words. And when the story of Jesus touches that deep desire in us, we can't help but lean in and listen.

• Read this passage again. What word or phrase stands out to you? Sit quietly, reminding yourself that you are in God's loving presence, and ask him to show you how that word or phrase connects to your life.

• With what part of your story does the Jesus story resonate? What pains, wounds, and long-held beliefs and desires does Jesus touch in you?

• With whom would you like to share the gospel? What are their stories? What pain have they experienced? What do they seem content with, frustrated about, worried about in their families or everyday lives? Ask God to help you know how to share the gospel with those people in light of their stories.

RESPOND

Father, thank you for putting people in my path who knew how to share Jesus with me in a way that would resonate in light of my story and how you made me. I want to be someone who will listen to the stories of others to understand, even if only in part, what their hearts desire and how their pasts, pain, and problems might affect how they respond to you. Help me see each person through your eyes: as beloved, chosen, and cherished. Amen.

THE TRUTH OF GOD REVEALED

a prayer to open

Holy Spirit, come. Center my heart.
Fill my mind. Guide my steps.

READ ACTS 13:42-52

As Paul and Barnabas left the synagogue that day, the people begged them to speak about these things again the next week. Many Jews and devout converts to Judaism followed Paul and Barnabas, and the two men urged them to continue to rely on the grace of God.

The following week almost the entire city turned out to hear them preach the word of the Lord. But when some of the Jews saw the crowds, they were jealous; so they slandered Paul and argued against whatever he said.

Then Paul and Barnabas spoke out boldly and declared, "It was necessary that we first preach the word of God to you Jews. But since you have rejected it and judged yourselves unworthy of eternal life, we will offer it to the Gentiles. For the Lord gave us this command when he said,

'I have made you a light to the Gentiles,
to bring salvation to the farthest corners of the earth.'"

When the Gentiles heard this, they were very glad and thanked the Lord for his message; and all who were chosen for eternal life became believers. So the Lord's message spread throughout that region.

Then the Jews stirred up the influential religious women and the leaders of the city, and they incited a mob against Paul and Barnabas and ran them out of town. So they shook the dust from their feet as a sign of rejection and went to the town of Iconium. And the believers were filled with joy and with the Holy Spirit.

REFLECT

Paul's teaching influenced his listeners so much that they invited him and Barnabas back the next week, and apparently word spread like wildfire, because nearly the entire city gathered to listen. What was so powerful in what Paul said? Luke gave a clue by referring to "the word of the Lord" or "word of God" or "the Lord's message" four different times in just a few sentences. Paul simply shared the truth God had revealed through Jesus. In other words, he didn't rely on his oratory skills, his influence with the community, or a perceived openness in the crowd; he trusted entirely in the Holy Spirit and the power of the Word of God itself.

- Read this passage again. What word or phrase stands out to you? Sit quietly, reminding yourself that you are in God's loving presence, and ask him to show you how that word or phrase connects to your life.

- What truths drew you to Jesus originally? What truths help you remain faithful? What truths bring you hope?

- In what ways do you help the Word of God spread in your workplace and community, whether by your words or your actions? In what ways do you hinder the spreading of the Word of God?

Father, I want to be someone who helps spread your truth and acts in a way that people take notice of because of the obvious presence of your Spirit in me. Help me share your truth with my words and by my actions. Show me how I hinder the spreading of your word, and give me the discipline and ability to change. Use other people to point out where my life is not aligned with truth, and guide me back to you. May I be someone who encourages others in the ways they use their gifts to make you known. Amen.

OFFENDED BY THE GOSPEL

a prayer to open

Holy Spirit, come. Center my heart.
Fill my mind. Guide my steps.

READ ACTS 14:1-20

The same thing happened in Iconium. Paul and Barnabas went to the Jewish synagogue and preached with such power that a great number of both Jews and Greeks became believers. Some of the Jews, however, spurned God's message and poisoned the minds of the Gentiles against Paul and Barnabas. But the apostles stayed there a long time, preaching boldly about the grace of the Lord. And the Lord proved their message was true by giving them power to do miraculous signs and wonders. But the people of the town were divided in their opinion about them. Some sided with the Jews, and some with the apostles.

Then a mob of Gentiles and Jews, along with their leaders, decided to attack and stone them. When the apostles learned of it, they fled to the region of Lycaonia. . . . And there they preached the Good News.

While they were at Lystra, Paul and Barnabas came upon a man with crippled feet. He had been that way from birth, so he had never walked. He was sitting and listening as Paul preached. Looking straight at him, Paul realized he had faith to be healed. So Paul called to him in a loud voice, "Stand up!" And the man jumped to his feet and started walking.

When the crowd saw what Paul had done, they shouted in their local dialect, "These men are gods in human form!" They decided that Barnabas was the Greek god Zeus and that Paul was Hermes, since he was the chief speaker. Now the temple of Zeus was located just outside the town. So the priest of the temple and the crowd brought bulls and wreaths of flowers to the town gates, and they prepared to offer sacrifices to the apostles.

But when the apostles Barnabas and Paul heard what was happening, they tore their clothing in dismay and ran out among the people, shouting, "Friends, why are you doing this? We are merely human beings—just like you! We have come to bring you the Good News that you should turn from these worthless things and turn to the living God, who made heaven and earth, the sea, and everything in them. In the past he permitted all the nations to go their own ways, but he never left them without evidence of himself and his goodness. For instance, he sends you rain and good crops and gives you food and joyful hearts." But even with these words, Paul and Barnabas could scarcely restrain the people from sacrificing to them.

Then some Jews arrived from Antioch and Iconium and won the crowds to their side. They stoned Paul and dragged him out of town, thinking he was dead. But as the believers gathered around him, he got up and went back into the town. The next day he left with Barnabas for Derbe.

A common theme begins to emerge as we follow Paul and Barnabas in their Holy Spirit–guided journey to share the gospel "to the ends of the earth" (13:47, NIV): They were repeatedly embraced and then chased away under persecution and threat of death. In each new place they found themselves, they received initial favor as they shared the Good News and demonstrated the power of Jesus. But inevitably they offended one group or another because what they shared undermined those in power. Paul and Barnabas's message resonated deeply with some (who we are told believed) and offended others so much that Paul and Barnabas had to run for their lives.

- Read this passage again. What word or phrase stands out to you? Sit quietly, reminding yourself that you are in God's loving presence, and ask him to show you how that word or phrase connects to your life.

- Reflect on the parts of the gospel that were the hardest for you to hear (needing to repent; needing to receive the gift of grace, as opposed to earning salvation; turning away from certain behaviors; believing in the supernatural). Why were those parts hard for you to hear and receive?

- Are there parts of the gospel that you still haven't fully embraced or that you continue to struggle with? Which parts? Why? What long-held beliefs or sensibilities are being offended or challenged?

RESPOND

Father, thank you for the truth of the gospel. Thank you for the gift of repentance and forgiveness. Thank you that I don't have to work to earn salvation or your love; I am already fully and unfailingly loved. Thank you that you have promised to redeem my sin and pain and bad choices and that you want to transform me and restore me to wholeness. Help me release every part of my mind, heart, and body to you for healing and to be used for good. Amen.

DAY 28

ALL THAT GOD HAS DONE

a prayer to open

Holy Spirit, come. Center my heart.
Fill my mind. Guide my steps.

READ ACTS 14:21-28

After preaching the Good News in Derbe and making many disciples, Paul and Barnabas returned to Lystra, Iconium, and Antioch of Pisidia, where they strengthened the believers. They encouraged them to continue in the faith, reminding them that we must suffer many hardships to enter the Kingdom of God. Paul and Barnabas also appointed elders in every church. With prayer and fasting, they turned the elders over to the care of the Lord, in whom they had put their trust. Then they traveled back through Pisidia to Pamphylia. They preached the word in Perga, then went down to Attalia.

Finally, they returned by ship to Antioch of Syria, where their journey had begun. The believers there had entrusted them to the grace of God to do the work they had now completed. Upon arriving in Antioch, they called the church together and reported everything God had done through them and how he had opened the door of faith to the Gentiles, too. And they stayed there with the believers for a long time.

REFLECT

In this passage, we see Paul and Barnabas return to the church in Antioch after checking in on the new disciples in Iconium, Lystra, and Derbe (where they fled or had been chased away), providing encouragement and setting up a leadership structure for the new churches. Upon returning to Antioch, they focused not on their hardships but on all that God had done through them and on the doors he had opened for the Gentiles. This reporting back and reflection on God's work emboldened the church and reminded them of his presence, power, and faithfulness.

• Read this passage again. What word or phrase stands out to you? Sit quietly, reminding yourself that you are in God's loving presence, and ask him to show you how that word or phrase connects to your life.

• Reflect on your past week. Where was God's presence, power, or faithfulness evident? Where did the Holy Spirit guide you, open a door, provide comfort, or convict your heart of wrongdoing? How could you build this kind of reflecting into your daily routine?

• Reflect on a time someone shared something God had done in his or her life that emboldened your faith or encouraged you in some way. How could you build this practice of hearing how God is at work in a friend or family member into your weekly or monthly routine?

RESPOND

Father, thank you for your presence, power, and faithfulness in my life and in the world. I want to notice more and reflect more on all the ways you work in my moments, days, weeks, and months. Help me develop the discipline of reflecting on a regular basis and reporting to others all that you do so I can be encouraged and be an encouragement. May I have eyes to see evidence of your goodness and grace each day. Amen.

GRACE FOR ALL

a prayer to open

Holy Spirit, come. Center my heart.
Fill my mind. Guide my steps.

READ ACTS 15:1-21

While Paul and Barnabas were at Antioch of Syria, some men from Judea arrived and began to teach the believers: "Unless you are circumcised as required by the law of Moses, you cannot be saved." Paul and Barnabas disagreed with them, arguing vehemently. Finally, the church decided to send Paul and Barnabas to Jerusalem, accompanied by some local believers, to talk to the apostles and elders about this question. . . . They stopped along the way in Phoenicia and Samaria to visit the believers. They told them—much to everyone's joy—that the Gentiles, too, were being converted.

When they arrived in Jerusalem, Barnabas and Paul were welcomed by the whole church, including the apostles and elders. They reported everything God had done through them. But then some of the believers who belonged to the sect of the Pharisees stood up and insisted, "The Gentile converts must be circumcised and required to follow the law of Moses."

So the apostles and elders met together to resolve this issue. At the meeting, after a long discussion, Peter stood and addressed them as follows: "Brothers, you all know that God chose me from among you some time ago to preach to the Gentiles so that they could hear the Good News and believe. God knows people's hearts, and he confirmed that he accepts Gentiles by giving them the Holy Spirit, just as he did to us. He made no distinction between us and them, for he cleansed their hearts through faith. So why are you now challenging God by burdening the Gentile believers with a yoke that neither we nor our ancestors were able to bear? We believe that we are all saved the same way, by the undeserved grace of the Lord Jesus."

Everyone listened quietly as Barnabas and Paul told about the miraculous signs and wonders God had done through them among the Gentiles.

When they had finished, James stood and said, "Brothers, listen to me. Peter has told you about the time God first visited the Gentiles to take from them a people for himself. And this conversion of Gentiles is exactly what the prophets predicted. As it is written:

'Afterward I will return
and restore the fallen house of David.
I will rebuild its ruins
and restore it,
so that the rest of humanity might seek the
LORD,
including the Gentiles—
all those I have called to be mine.
The LORD has spoken—
he who made these things known so long ago.'

"And so my judgment is that we should not make it difficult for the Gentiles who are turning to God. Instead, we should write and tell them to abstain from eating food offered to idols, from sexual immorality, from eating the meat of strangled animals, and from consuming blood. For these laws of Moses have been preached in Jewish synagogues in every city on every Sabbath for many generations."

REFLECT

Chapter 15 of Acts reports a critical moment in the church. The apostles gathered together in Jerusalem to resolve a dispute over whether Gentiles were required to be circumcised and obey Mosaic law in order to be saved. Up to this point, none of the apostles had imposed such requirements on Gentiles. But apparently certain Pharisees who converted grew to resent the ease with which a Gentile could be saved. They grew to resent grace. Ultimately, the apostles affirmed that it is by grace alone—not works, circumcision, or the law—that *all* are saved.

- Read this passage again. What word or phrase stands out to you? Sit quietly, reminding yourself that you are in God's loving presence, and ask him to show you how that word or phrase connects to your life.

- Reflect on whether you have ever resented the extension of God's grace to someone. What triggered your resentment?

- Have you ever heard anyone say that grace is too good to be true? How did you (or how might you) respond to such an assertion?

RESPOND

Father, thank you for grace. Thank you that it is by grace alone that I am saved. Keep this truth at the center of my heart and mind, and make it the lens through which I see others. Remove any sense of superiority or resentment in my heart. Remind me of how far you have brought me and how far I have to go to look like Jesus. Allow me to be a messenger of your grace, and let my life showcase the need and beauty of your grace. Amen.

DAY 30

A SENSITIVE HEART

a prayer to open

Holy Spirit, come. Center my heart.
Fill my mind. Guide my steps.

READ ACTS 15:22-41

The apostles and elders together with the whole church in Jerusalem chose delegates, and they sent them to Antioch of Syria with Paul and Barnabas to report on this decision. The men chosen were two of the church leaders—Judas (also called Barsabbas) and Silas. This is the letter they took with them:

"This letter is from the apostles and elders, your brothers in Jerusalem. It is written to the Gentile believers in Antioch, Syria, and Cilicia. Greetings!

"We understand that some men from here have troubled you and upset you with their teaching, but we did not send them! So we decided, having come to complete agreement, to send you official representatives, along with our beloved Barnabas and Paul, who have risked their lives for the name of our Lord Jesus Christ. We are sending Judas and Silas to confirm what we have decided concerning your question.

"For it seemed good to the Holy Spirit and to us to lay no greater burden on you than these few requirements: You must abstain from eating food offered to idols, from consuming blood or the meat of strangled animals, and from sexual immorality. If you do this, you will do well. Farewell."

The messengers went at once to Antioch, where they called a general meeting of the believers and delivered the letter. And there was great joy throughout the church that day as they read this encouraging message.

Then Judas and Silas, both being prophets, spoke at length to the believers, encouraging and strengthening their faith. They stayed for a while, and then the believers sent them back to the church in Jerusalem with a blessing of peace. Paul and Barnabas stayed in Antioch. They and many others taught and preached the word of the Lord there.

After some time Paul said to Barnabas, "Let's go back and visit each city where we previously preached the word of the Lord, to see how the new believers are doing." Barnabas agreed and wanted to take along John Mark. But Paul disagreed strongly, since John Mark had deserted them in

Pamphylia and had not continued with them in their work. Their disagreement was so sharp that they separated. Barnabas took John Mark with him and sailed for Cyprus. Paul chose Silas, and as he left, the believers entrusted him to the Lord's gracious care. Then he traveled throughout Syria and Cilicia, strengthening the churches there.

REFLECT

The Jerusalem church leaders' letter addressing the dispute over Gentiles and circumcision is less clear than one might think it should be. It didn't address the issue head on and stated only that the Gentiles should not be burdened with anything other than a few food requirements and abstaining from sexual immorality. Scholars agree that obedience to these rules was not intended to be a prerequisite to salvation and have generally concluded that the food restrictions were included to encourage sensitivity among the diverse body of believers. As for the seemingly obvious prohibition against sexual immorality, scholars believe that the elders sought to warn new believers against conduct that had been normalized in the culture surrounding their churches. The key question for us seems to be, What cultural influences, even if not unmistakably immoral, might be inhibiting our ability to love others and honor God above all else?

- Read this passage again. What word or phrase stands out to you? Sit quietly, reminding yourself that you are in God's loving presence, and ask him to show you how that word or phrase connects to your life.

- What kinds of conduct have become normalized in our culture that we need to be aware of and careful to avoid as followers of Jesus because of the way they inhibit our ability to love others or honor God? Which of these behaviors is tempting to you? What practices help you remain faithful?

- How sensitive are you to the impact your words and actions might have on the faith of other believers? Who do you know currently struggling with their faith? How could you be more sensitive in the midst of that person's difficulties and doubts?

RESPOND

Father, thank you for the freedom Christ provided: freedom from being captive to sin, freedom from the eternal consequences of sin, freedom from the law. Help me use this freedom wisely and honor you—to follow you more closely, build up others in their faith, and be sensitive to what would make others stumble. Show me where I am weak and might stumble, and help me know what boundaries to draw and how to remain faithful. May my life be a testament to the life you offer. Amen.

WALKING IN CONFUSION

a prayer to open

Holy Spirit, come. Center my heart.
Fill my mind. Guide my steps.

READ ACTS 16:1-24

Paul went first to Derbe and then to Lystra, where there was a young disciple named Timothy. His mother was a Jewish believer, but his father was a Greek. Timothy was well thought of by the believers in Lystra and Iconium, so Paul wanted him to join them on their journey. In deference to the Jews of the area, he arranged for Timothy to be circumcised before they left, for everyone knew that his father was a Greek. Then they went from town to town, instructing the believers to follow the decisions made by the apostles and elders in Jerusalem. So the churches were strengthened in their faith and grew larger every day.

Next Paul and Silas traveled through the area of Phrygia and Galatia, because the Holy Spirit had prevented them from preaching the word in the province of Asia at that time. Then coming to the borders of Mysia, they headed north for the province of Bithynia, but again the Spirit of Jesus did not allow them to go there. So instead, they went on through Mysia to the seaport of Troas.

That night Paul had a vision: A man from Macedonia in northern Greece was standing there, pleading with him, "Come over to Macedonia and help us!" So we decided to leave for Macedonia at once, having concluded that God was calling us to preach the Good News there.

We boarded a boat at Troas and sailed straight across to the island of Samothrace, and the next day we landed at Neapolis. From there we reached Philippi, a major city of that district of Macedonia and a Roman colony. And we stayed there several days.

On the Sabbath we went a little way outside the city to a riverbank, where we thought people would be meeting for prayer, and we sat down to speak with some women who had gathered there. One of them was Lydia from Thyatira, a merchant of expensive purple cloth, who worshiped God. As she listened to us, the Lord opened her heart, and she accepted what Paul was saying. She and her household were baptized, and she asked us to be her guests. "If you agree that I am a true believer in the Lord," she said, "come and stay at my home." And she urged us until we agreed.

One day as we were going down to the place of prayer, we met a slave girl who had a spirit that enabled her to tell the future. She earned a lot of money for her masters by telling fortunes. She followed Paul and the rest of us, shouting, "These men are servants of the Most High God, and they have come to tell you how to be saved."

This went on day after day until Paul got so exasperated that he turned and said to the demon within her, "I command you in the name of Jesus Christ to come out of her." And instantly it left her.

Her masters' hopes of wealth were now shattered, so they grabbed Paul and Silas and dragged them before the authorities at the marketplace. "The whole city is in an uproar because of these Jews!" they shouted to the city officials. "They are teaching customs that are illegal for us Romans to practice."

A mob quickly formed against Paul and Silas, and the city officials ordered them stripped and beaten with wooden rods. They were severely beaten, and then they were thrown into prison. The jailer was ordered to make sure they didn't escape. So the jailer put them into the inner dungeon and clamped their feet in the stocks.

REFLECT

The partnership between Paul and Barnabas came to an end because of an argument over John Mark (see 15:36-41). The men went their separate ways, and Paul took Silas from the church in Jerusalem with him. As they reached Derbe (Paul's third time there), a disciple named Timothy joined them. From there, confusion and uncertainty set in. Where were they supposed to go? Asia? No. Bithynia? No. Scholars believe that Paul and his colleagues traveled hundreds of miles over several weeks during this period of uncertainty. Finally, based on Paul's vision, the men

Empowered

•

327

concluded that they were to go to Macedonia, a Roman province north of Greece. Once there, the theme that had played out in other Roman cities returned: Some opened their hearts to God's Word, and some were so protective of power and the status quo that they resisted the message and attacked the messengers.

- Read this passage again. What word or phrase stands out to you? Sit quietly, reminding yourself that you are in God's loving presence, and ask him to show you how that word or phrase connects to your life.

- Reflect on a time when you have felt confused about where God was leading you. What were the circumstances? Did you ever find clarity? How did that experience influence your faith?

- Who in your life is in the midst of a time of confusion, not knowing where God is leading or feeling unsure about a decision that needs to be made? What is one way you can be present with or encouraging to that person?

RESPOND

Father, thank you for the way you call me to walk by faith, listen for your voice, and discern with wise friends the way to go. So often I want clarity that doesn't come. Grow my faith and give me the ability to trust each step you set before me even if I don't see the whole picture. Grant me wise, compassionate friends who will pray and walk with me. Allow me to know your presence when the path is unclear. Amen.

DAY 32

THE POWER TO SING

a prayer to open

Holy Spirit, come. Center my heart.
Fill my mind. Guide my steps.

READ ACTS 16:25-40

Around midnight Paul and Silas were praying and singing hymns to God, and the other prisoners were listening. Suddenly, there was a massive earthquake, and the prison was shaken to its foundations. All the doors immediately flew open, and the chains of every prisoner fell off! The jailer woke up to see the prison doors wide open. He assumed the prisoners had escaped, so he drew his sword to kill himself. But Paul shouted to him, "Stop! Don't kill yourself! We are all here!"

The jailer called for lights and ran to the dungeon and fell down trembling before Paul and Silas. Then

he brought them out and asked, "Sirs, what must I do to be saved?"

They replied, "Believe in the Lord Jesus and you will be saved, along with everyone in your household." And they shared the word of the Lord with him and with all who lived in his household. Even at that hour of the night, the jailer cared for them and washed their wounds. Then he and everyone in his household were immediately baptized. . . . He and his entire household rejoiced because they all believed in God.

The next morning the city officials sent the police

to tell the jailer, "Let those men go!" So the jailer told Paul, "The city officials have said you and Silas are free to leave. Go in peace."

But Paul replied, "They have publicly beaten us without a trial and put us in prison—and we are Roman citizens. So now they want us to leave secretly? Certainly not! Let them come themselves to release us!"

When the police reported this, the city officials were alarmed to learn that Paul and Silas were Roman citizens. So they came to the jail and apologized to them. Then they brought them out and begged them to leave the city. When Paul and Silas left the prison, they returned to the home of Lydia. There they met with the believers and encouraged them once more. Then they left town.

REFLECT

The story of Paul and Silas in prison is filled with supernatural happenings. First, Paul and Silas—after having been stripped, beaten with rods, and fastened to a prison cell floor—prayed and sang hymns to God. Where did they find the courage, strength, and hope to do this other than by the presence of the Holy Spirit? Second, a violent earthquake shook the prison and caused the doors to open and the shackles to release. How did this happen other than by the power of the Holy Spirit? Third, the jailer and his entire family believed in Jesus upon hearing the word of the Lord. Who could have turned a Roman jailer's heart to Christ other than the Holy Spirit?

- Read this passage again. What word or phrase stands out to you? Sit quietly, reminding yourself that you are in God's loving presence, and ask him to show you how that word or phrase connects to your life.

- In what areas do you need the courage and strength to sing hymns to God? What hymn or song could capture your sorrow and pain or help remind you of who God is and how he has acted in the past?

- Is there anything holding you in shackles—a relationship, an addiction, a temptation, pain, something else? Invite the Holy Spirit's power into that situation. What is your role in breaking free?

RESPOND

Father, thank you for the presence and power of your Holy Spirit. I pray that I would be aware of the areas in which I need each of these and be able to call out to you for help. I want to be able to sing hymns and songs to you with courage and hope, even in my darkest moments. I want to be freed from everything that keeps me from loving and serving you and others fully. And I want to be guided each and every moment into the life you offer. I open my heart to you anew. Amen.

GROWING IN HUMILITY

a prayer to open

Holy Spirit, come. Center my heart.
Fill my mind. Guide my steps.

READ ACTS 17:1-15 _____

Paul and Silas then traveled through the towns of Amphipolis and Apollonia and came to Thessalonica, where there was a Jewish synagogue. As was Paul's custom, he went to the synagogue service, and for three Sabbaths in a row he used the Scriptures to reason with the people. He explained the prophecies and proved that the Messiah must suffer and rise from the dead. He said, "This Jesus I'm telling you about is the Messiah." Some of the Jews who listened were persuaded and joined Paul and Silas, along with many God-fearing Greek men and quite a few prominent women.

But some of the Jews were jealous, so they gathered some troublemakers from the marketplace to form a mob and start a riot. They attacked the home of Jason, searching for Paul and Silas so they could drag them out to the crowd. Not finding them there, they dragged out Jason and some of the other believers instead and took them before the city council. "Paul and Silas have caused trouble all over the world," they shouted, "and now they are here disturbing our city, too. And Jason has welcomed them into his home. They are all guilty of treason against Caesar, for they profess allegiance to another king, named Jesus."

The people of the city, as well as the city council, were thrown into turmoil by these reports. So the officials forced Jason and the other believers to post bond, and then they released them.

That very night the believers sent Paul and Silas to Berea. When they arrived there, they went to the Jewish synagogue. And the people of Berea were more open-minded than those in Thessalonica, and they listened eagerly to Paul's message. They searched the Scriptures day after day to see if Paul and Silas were teaching the truth. As a result, many Jews believed, as did many of the prominent Greek women and men.

But when some Jews in Thessalonica learned that Paul was preaching the word of God in Berea, they went there and stirred up trouble. The believers acted at once, sending Paul on to the coast, while Silas and Timothy remained behind. Those escorting Paul went with him all the way to Athens; then they returned to Berea with instructions for Silas and Timothy to hurry and join him.

REFLECT _____

When Paul and Silas were released from prison in Philippi, they moved on to Thessalonica, the capital of Macedonia, to share the gospel. As usual, they started in the synagogue and were met with a mixture of acceptance and rejection, openness and resistance. Luke contrasted the people in the next city, Berea, with those in Thessalonica, calling them "more open-minded" (verse 11) because of their eagerness and willingness to examine the Scriptures. When confronted with new ideas, the humble hearted seek to understand, learn, and listen to what God might want to teach them.

- Read this passage again. What word or phrase stands out to you? Sit quietly, reminding yourself that you are in God's loving presence, and ask him to show you how that word or phrase connects to your life.

- Is there any area of your faith in which you have doubts or lack clarity (Jesus' divinity, sexual issues, conflict resolution, how to engage with an enemy, forgiveness)? Have you examined the Scriptures carefully on the topic or topics you identified? What do you sense God leading you to do to resolve this or learn more?

- What issues (political, social, economic, relational) do you have very strong views about? How would you rate your level of humility and eagerness to learn about other viewpoints on those particular issues? What is one way you could move toward humility on those issues?

RESPOND

Father, thank you for the gift of the Scriptures and for giving your followers a way to know you more. And thank you for Jesus, the ultimate model of humility and grace. Help me, by your Spirit, study Scripture to understand and learn in the areas about which I feel confused or uncertain. Guide me into humility to listen to viewpoints that contradict my own and to increase my love and understanding for others, whatever their viewpoints. Keep what is true clear for me in the process, and may I follow you with every part of my being. Amen.

DAY 34

WHAT IS TRUE

a prayer to open

Holy Spirit, come. Center my heart.
Fill my mind. Guide my steps.

READ ACTS 17:16-34

While Paul was waiting for them in Athens, he was deeply troubled by all the idols he saw everywhere in the city. He went to the synagogue to reason with the Jews and the God-fearing Gentiles, and he spoke daily in the public square to all who happened to be there.

He also had a debate with some of the Epicurean and Stoic philosophers. When he told them about Jesus and his resurrection, they said, "What's this babbler trying to say with these strange ideas he's picked up?" Others said, "He seems to be preaching about some foreign gods."

Then they took him to the high council of the city. "Come and tell us about this new teaching," they said. "You are saying some rather strange things, and we want to know what it's all about." . . .

So Paul, standing before the council, addressed them as follows: "Men of Athens, I notice that you are very religious in every way, for as I was walking along I saw your many shrines. And one of your altars had this inscription on it: 'To an Unknown God.' This God, whom you worship without knowing, is the one I'm telling you about.

"He is the God who made the world and everything in it. Since he is Lord of heaven and earth, he doesn't live in man-made temples, and human hands can't serve his needs—for he has no needs. He himself gives life and breath to everything, and he satisfies every need. From one man he created all the nations throughout the whole earth. He decided beforehand when they should rise and fall, and he determined their boundaries.

"His purpose was for the nations to seek after God and perhaps feel their way toward him and find him—though he is not far from any one of us. For in him we live and move and exist. As some of your own poets have said, 'We are his offspring.' And since this is true, we shouldn't think of God as an idol designed by craftsmen from gold or silver or stone.

"God overlooked people's ignorance about these things in earlier times, but now he commands everyone everywhere to repent of their sins and turn to him. For he has set a day for judging the world with justice by the man he has appointed,

Empowered

•

331

and he proved to everyone who this is by raising him from the dead."

When they heard Paul speak about the resurrection of the dead, some laughed in contempt, but others said, "We want to hear more about this later." That ended Paul's discussion with them, but some joined him and became believers. Among them were Dionysius, a member of the council, a woman named Damaris, and others with them.

REFLECT

In this passage, Paul stated three beautiful truths about who God is and how he relates to us: He gives everyone life and breath and everything else, he is not far from any one of us, and in him we live and move and have our being.

- Read this passage again. What word or phrase stands out to you? Sit quietly, reminding yourself that you are in God's loving presence, and ask him to show you how that word or phrase connects to your life.
- As you read these truths, what emotions arise in you? Which one is hardest to really internalize and believe? Why?
- Who in your life needs to hear these truths? How might you share them with that person in a loving way (a card, phone call, sticky note, text)?

RESPOND

Father, thank you for life and the breath in my lungs. Thank you for every good gift you have provided me. Thank you for your nearness and the truth that you are not far off, distant, or uncaring but are close and compassionate. And thank you that no part of me exists or operates outside your loving, good presence. Help me remember these truths when I'm on the mountaintop and when I'm in the valley. It is in you that I live and move and have my being. Amen.

DAY 35

I AM WITH YOU

a prayer to open

Holy Spirit, come. Center my heart. Fill my mind. Guide my steps.

READ ACTS 18:1-16

Then Paul left Athens and went to Corinth. There he became acquainted with a Jew named Aquila, ... who had recently arrived from Italy with his wife, Priscilla. . . . Paul lived and worked with them, for they were tentmakers just as he was.

Each Sabbath found Paul at the synagogue, trying to convince the Jews and Greeks alike. And after Silas and Timothy came down from Macedonia, Paul spent all his time preaching the word. He testified to the Jews that Jesus was the Messiah. But when they opposed and insulted him, Paul shook the dust from his clothes and said, "Your blood is upon your own heads—I am innocent. From now on I will go preach to the Gentiles."

Then he left and went to the home of Titius Justus, a Gentile who worshiped God and lived next door to the synagogue. Crispus, the leader of the synagogue, and everyone in his household believed in the Lord. Many others in Corinth also heard Paul, became believers, and were baptized.

One night the Lord spoke to Paul in a vision and told him, "Don't be afraid! Speak out! Don't be silent! For I am with you, and no one will attack and harm you, for many people in this city belong to me." So Paul stayed there for the next year and a half, teaching the word of God.

But when Gallio became governor of Achaia, some Jews rose up together against Paul and brought him before the governor for judgment. They accused Paul of "persuading people to worship God in ways that are contrary to our law."

But just as Paul started to make his defense, Gallio turned to Paul's accusers and said, "Listen, you Jews, if this were a case involving some wrongdoing or a serious crime, I would have a reason to accept your case. But since it is merely a question of words and names and your Jewish law, take care of it yourselves. I refuse to judge such matters." And he threw them out of the courtroom.

REFLECT

Paul's stay in Corinth lasted a year and a half, and we know from two letters (1 and 2 Corinthians) that the church he planted there was a significant challenge. So God's words to him—"Don't be afraid. . . . I am with you" (verses 9-10)—must have been something he continually came back to as a reminder. Though these were words specific to Paul, we find them and others that convey the same meaning throughout Scripture. God has consistently provided similar reminders and comfort to believers throughout history.

- Read this passage again. What word or phrase stands out to you? Sit quietly, reminding yourself that you are in God's loving presence, and ask him to show you how that word or phrase connects to your life.

- In what areas are you currently experiencing fear? What exactly are you afraid of and why? How are you experiencing God in the midst of that fear? What resistance do you feel when you read his words "Don't be afraid" and "I am with you"?

- Is there someone in your life who tends to be afraid or is going through a time of fear? How might you be able to communicate or demonstrate God's presence to that person?

RESPOND

Father, thank you for your presence. I pray that I would remember that you are with me. So often I forget and act as if I am on my own. Remind me when I forget. Help me know your presence when I am overwhelmed. And when fear creeps in or overtakes me, turn my heart to you. Allow your words to come into my mind and fill me with courage to be and act in the ways in which you are calling me. Amen.

MAKE DISCIPLES

a prayer to open

Holy Spirit, come. Center my heart.
Fill my mind. Guide my steps.

READ ACTS 18:18-28

Paul stayed in Corinth for some time after that, then said good-bye to the brothers and sisters and went to nearby Cenchrea. There he shaved his head according to Jewish custom, marking the end of a vow. Then he set sail for Syria, taking Priscilla and Aquila with him.

They stopped first at the port of Ephesus, where Paul left the others behind. While he was there, he went to the synagogue to reason with the Jews. They asked him to stay longer, but he declined. As he left, however, he said, "I will come back later, God willing." Then he set sail from Ephesus. The next stop was at the port of Caesarea. From there he went up and visited the church at Jerusalem and then went back to Antioch.

After spending some time in Antioch, Paul went back through Galatia and Phrygia, visiting and strengthening all the believers.

Meanwhile, a Jew named Apollos, an eloquent speaker who knew the Scriptures well, had arrived in Ephesus from Alexandria in Egypt. He had been taught the way of the Lord, and he taught others about Jesus with an enthusiastic spirit and with accuracy. However, he knew only about John's baptism. When Priscilla and Aquila heard him preaching boldly in the synagogue, they took him aside and explained the way of God even more accurately.

Apollos had been thinking about going to Achaia, and the brothers and sisters in Ephesus encouraged him to go. They wrote to the believers in Achaia, asking them to welcome him. When he arrived there, he proved to be of great benefit to those who, by God's grace, had believed. He refuted the Jews with powerful arguments in public debate. Using the Scriptures, he explained to them that Jesus was the Messiah.

REFLECT

Among Jesus' last words to his disciples were "Go and make disciples of all nations, baptizing them in the name of the Father and of the Son and of the Holy Spirit, and teaching them to obey everything I have commanded you" (Matthew 28:19-20, NIV). Paul, Priscilla, and Aquila were among those in the early church to act in obedience to this command. Paul returned to the churches he had planted to help the disciples there grow in their knowledge and love of God and people. Meanwhile, Priscilla and Aquila took Apollos—the devoted, knowledgeable, and passionate preacher—into their home for further teaching. We see the fruit of this discipleship later: Paul's churches thrived and outlasted him, and Apollos's ability to teach the gospel and disciple others grew to be on par with Paul's (see 1 Corinthians 1:10-12).

- Read this passage again. What word or phrase stands out to you? Sit quietly, reminding yourself that you are in God's loving presence, and ask him to show you how that word or phrase connects to your life.

- Who are you helping grow in their knowledge and understanding of Jesus' love and commands? What prevents you from helping others in this way (feeling inadequate, inexperience, lack of knowledge, fear, lack of clarity, not knowing how to begin, busyness)? Given the knowledge and experience you *do* have, who could you help grow? What is one thing you could do to help them (share passages of Scripture, give them books to read, suggest a class or workshop, lead a small group, study God's Word with a small group)?

- Who is helping you grow in your knowledge and understanding of Jesus and his ways? Who could help you? What next step do you sense God asking you to take?

RESPOND

Father, thank you for the body of Christ and that there are believers ahead of me and behind me when it comes to knowledge and maturity of faith. Thank you that I can learn from both types of believers and that you've given me the ability and command to help others grow. Give me the courage to point someone else to a resource or person for additional growth, and open my eyes to someone who can help me grow. I want to know you more and follow you more closely. May it be so.

LEAD ME INTO RIGHTEOUSNESS

a prayer to open

Holy Spirit, come. Center my heart.
Fill my mind. Guide my steps.

READ ACTS 19:1-20

While Apollos was in Corinth, Paul traveled through the interior regions until he reached Ephesus, on the coast, where he found several believers. "Did you receive the Holy Spirit when you believed?" he asked them.

"No," they replied, "we haven't even heard that there is a Holy Spirit."

"Then what baptism did you experience?" he asked.

And they replied, "The baptism of John."

Paul said, "John's baptism called for repentance from sin. But John himself told the people to believe in the one who would come later, meaning Jesus."

As soon as they heard this, they were baptized in the name of the Lord Jesus. Then when Paul laid his hands on them, the Holy Spirit came on them, and they spoke in other tongues and prophesied. . . .

Then Paul went to the synagogue and preached boldly for the next three months, arguing persuasively about the Kingdom of God. But some became stubborn, rejecting his message and

publicly speaking against the Way. So Paul left the synagogue and took the believers with him. Then he held daily discussions at the lecture hall of Tyrannus. This went on for the next two years, so that people throughout the province of Asia—both Jews and Greeks—heard the word of the Lord.

God gave Paul the power to perform unusual miracles. When handkerchiefs or aprons that had merely touched his skin were placed on sick people, they were healed of their diseases, and evil spirits were expelled.

A group of Jews was traveling from town to town casting out evil spirits. They tried to use the name of the Lord Jesus in their incantation, saying, "I command you in the name of Jesus, whom Paul preaches, to come out!" . . . But one time when they tried it, the evil spirit replied, "I know Jesus, and I know Paul, but who are you?" Then the man with the evil spirit leaped on them, overpowered them, and attacked them with such violence that they fled from the house, naked and battered.

Empowered •

The story of what happened spread quickly all through Ephesus, to Jews and Greeks alike. A solemn fear descended on the city, and the name of the Lord Jesus was greatly honored. Many who became believers confessed their sinful practices. A number of them who had been practicing sorcery brought their incantation books and burned them at a public bonfire. The value of the books was several million dollars. So the message about the Lord spread widely and had a powerful effect.

REFLECT

Paul's next stop on his third missionary journey was Ephesus, a commercial hub on the Mediterranean Sea where the worship of Artemis formed a critical part of the culture. Paul stayed longer in Ephesus than anywhere else on his previous journeys and again encountered both acceptance and great resistance from Jews and Gentiles alike. This passage ends with a profound public display in which a group of magicians turned to the true living God and away from the sorcery they had practiced, confessing their sin and burning the tools of their trade. They took a dramatic step out of their old lives to embrace their new lives in Christ. Do we have the courage to do the same?

- Read this passage again. What word or phrase stands out to you? Sit quietly, reminding yourself that you are in God's loving presence, and ask him to show you how that word or phrase connects to your life.

- What part of your "old life" do you need to metaphorically burn or totally walk away from in order to embrace your new life in Christ? What is one step you need to take? Ask God for the grace and strength you need to do that.

- In 1 John 1:9, John wrote, "If we confess our sins, he is faithful and just and will forgive us our sins and purify us from all unrighteousness" (NIV). Is there anything you need to confess to God? In what area of your life do you want him to lead you into righteousness?

RESPOND

Father, thank you for receiving me with open arms when I turn to you. Thank you for enabling and empowering me to turn away from my sin and the things in my life that distract me from all you're calling me to do and be. Please guide me, by your Holy Spirit, into all righteousness found in Christ. May my thoughts, words, and actions increasingly reflect my new life in you. Mold me into Christ's image so that I can align with what you're doing to redeem and restore the world. Amen.

A GREAT DISTURBANCE

a prayer to open

Holy Spirit, come. Center my heart.
Fill my mind. Guide my steps.

READ ACTS 19:21-41

Afterward Paul felt compelled by the Spirit to go over to Macedonia and Achaia before going to Jerusalem. "And after that," he said, "I must go on to Rome!" He sent his two assistants, Timothy and Erastus, ahead to Macedonia. . . .

About that time, serious trouble developed in Ephesus concerning the Way. It began with Demetrius, a silversmith who had a large business manufacturing silver shrines of the Greek goddess Artemis. He kept many craftsmen busy. He called them together, along with others employed in similar trades, and addressed them as follows:

"Gentlemen, you know that our wealth comes from this business. But as you have seen and heard, this man Paul has persuaded many people that handmade gods aren't really gods at all. And he's done this not only here in Ephesus but throughout the entire province! Of course, I'm not just talking about the loss of public respect for our business. I'm also concerned that the temple of the great goddess Artemis will lose its influence and that Artemis . . . will be robbed of her great prestige!"

At this their anger boiled, and they began shouting, "Great is Artemis of the Ephesians!" Soon the whole city was filled with confusion. Everyone rushed to the amphitheater, dragging along Gaius and Aristarchus, who were Paul's traveling companions from Macedonia. Paul wanted to go in, too, but the believers wouldn't let him. Some of the officials of the province, friends of Paul, also sent a message to him, begging him not to risk his life by entering the amphitheater.

Inside, the people were all shouting, some one thing and some another. Everything was in confusion. In fact, most of them didn't even know why they were there. The Jews in the crowd pushed Alexander forward and told him to explain the situation. He motioned for silence and tried to speak. But when the crowd realized he was a Jew, they started shouting again and kept it up for about two hours: "Great is Artemis of the Ephesians! Great is Artemis of the Ephesians!"

At last the mayor was able to quiet them down enough to speak. "Citizens of Ephesus," he said. "Everyone knows that Ephesus is the official guardian of the temple of the great Artemis, whose image fell down to us from heaven. Since this is an undeniable fact, you should stay calm and not do anything rash. You have brought these men here, but they have stolen nothing from the temple and have not spoken against our goddess.

"If Demetrius and the craftsmen have a case against them, the courts are in session and the officials can hear the case at once. Let them make formal charges. And if there are complaints about other matters, they can be settled in a legal assembly. I am afraid we are in danger of being charged with rioting by the Roman government, since there is no cause for all this commotion. And if Rome demands an explanation, we won't know what to say." Then he dismissed them, and they dispersed.

REFLECT

It should come as no surprise that shortly after the word of the Lord "spread widely and grew in power" (verse 20, NIV), a riot broke out in Ephesus. After all, the word had started to disturb and threaten economic power and established religious structures. We too tend to react that way to hearing from God. Simply reading the Bible or praying is one thing, but once we hear him calling us out of old patterns of thought and behavior, something in us feels threatened and disturbed. We resist making actual changes in the way we spend our money, make decisions, and use our time.

Empowered

•

- Read this passage again. What word or phrase stands out to you? Sit quietly, reminding yourself that you are in God's loving presence, and ask him to show you how that word or phrase connects to your life.

- Reflect on the most significant change you have made based on a desire to align with God's ways. What resistance did you experience as you sought to make that change?

- What are the one or two attitudes or behaviors God is working in you to change? What resistance are you experiencing? What can you draw on from your prior experiences to give you hope or courage to take the next step?

RESPOND

Father, thank you for all the ways you have transformed me, moving me from my old life into a new one. Thank you for the ways you continue to lead and move and stir my desire to be more like Christ. Please keep working in me; overcome my resistance. Give me the courage to take one step toward transformation today. Be gentle with me and surround me with friends who will encourage and inspire me to draw closer to you. Amen.

FROM DESPAIR TO HOPE

a prayer to open

Holy Spirit, come. Center my heart.
Fill my mind. Guide my steps.

READ ACTS 20:1-16

When the uproar was over, Paul sent for the believers and encouraged them. Then he said good-bye and left for Macedonia. While there, he encouraged the believers in all the towns he passed through. Then he traveled down to Greece, where he stayed for three months. He was preparing to sail back to Syria when he discovered a plot by some Jews against his life, so he decided to return through Macedonia.

Several men were traveling with him. . . . They went on ahead and waited for us at Troas. After the Passover ended, we boarded a ship at Philippi in Macedonia and five days later joined them in Troas, where we stayed a week.

On the first day of the week, we gathered with the local believers to share in the Lord's Supper. Paul was preaching to them, and since he was leaving the next day, he kept talking until midnight. The upstairs room where we met was lighted with many flickering lamps. As Paul spoke on and on, a young man named Eutychus, sitting on the windowsill, became very drowsy. Finally, he fell sound asleep and dropped three stories to his death below. Paul went down, bent over him, and took him into his arms. "Don't worry," he said, "he's alive!" Then they all went back upstairs, shared in the Lord's Supper, and ate together. Paul continued talking to them until dawn, and then he left. Meanwhile, the young man was taken home alive and well, and everyone was greatly relieved.

Paul went by land to Assos, where he had arranged for us to join him, while we traveled by ship. He joined us there, and we sailed together to Mitylene. The next day we sailed past the island of Kios. The following day we crossed to the island of Samos, and a day later we arrived at Miletus.

Paul had decided to sail on past Ephesus, for he didn't want to spend any more time in the province of Asia. He was hurrying to get to Jerusalem, if possible, in time for the Festival of Pentecost.

While Paul and his companions traveled from Ephesus to Macedonia (where Philippi, Thessalonica, and Berea were), through Corinth, and then back through Asia, Paul wrote his second letter to the Corinthians (as well as his letter to the Romans). He shared just how intense and difficult his time in Ephesus really was: "We were under great pressure, far beyond our ability to endure, so that we despaired of life itself. Indeed, we felt we had received the sentence of death" (2 Corinthians 1:8-9, NIV). Paul attributed his survival to God's deliverance and the prayers of other believers, which enabled him to move from despair to hope.

- Read this passage again. What word or phrase stands out to you? Sit quietly, reminding yourself that you are in God's loving presence, and ask him to show you how that word or phrase connects to your life.

- What other believers do you or could you pray for on a regular basis? Do you know someone in the midst of difficult circumstances? Commit to praying for that person for a defined period of time.

- Do you have a prayer partner, a spiritual friend, or someone you could connect with once a week or once a month to pray? If not, who could you ask?

RESPOND

Father, thank you for hearing my prayers. I confess that I don't understand prayer: It's such a mystery in so many ways. But I am grateful that I can lift my voice and thoughts, present my unspoken needs, and bring others to you in prayer. Illuminate for me someone who needs prayer and support, and help me have the discipline to pray for that person. Please bring me to someone else's mind for prayer. Thank you for hearing me. Amen.

DAY 40

A SINGLE AIM

a prayer to open

Holy Spirit, come. Center my heart.
Fill my mind. Guide my steps.

READ ACTS 20:17-38

But when we landed at Miletus, he sent a message to the elders of the church at Ephesus, asking them to come and meet him.

When they arrived he declared, "You know that from the day I set foot in the province of Asia until now I have done the Lord's work humbly and with many tears. I have endured the trials that came to me from the plots of the Jews. I never shrank back from telling you what you needed to hear, either publicly or in your homes. I have had one message for Jews and Greeks alike—the necessity of repenting from sin and turning to God, and of having faith in our Lord Jesus.

"And now I am bound by the Spirit to go to

Empowered

339

Jerusalem. I don't know what awaits me, except that the Holy Spirit tells me in city after city that jail and suffering lie ahead. But my life is worth nothing to me unless I use it for finishing the work assigned me by the Lord Jesus—the work of telling others the Good News about the wonderful grace of God.

"And now I know that none of you to whom I have preached the Kingdom will ever see me again. I declare today that I have been faithful. If anyone suffers eternal death, it's not my fault, for I didn't shrink from declaring all that God wants you to know.

"So guard yourselves and God's people. Feed and shepherd God's flock—his church, purchased with his own blood—over which the Holy Spirit has appointed you as leaders. I know that false teachers, like vicious wolves, will come in among you after I leave, not sparing the flock. Even some men from your own group will rise up and distort the truth in order to draw a following. Watch out! Remember the three years I was with you—my constant watch and care over you night and day, and my many tears for you.

"And now I entrust you to God and the message of his grace that is able to build you up and give you an inheritance with all those he has set apart for himself.

"I have never coveted anyone's silver or gold or fine clothes. You know that these hands of mine have worked to supply my own needs and even the needs of those who were with me. And I have been a constant example of how you can help those in need by working hard. You should remember the words of the Lord Jesus: 'It is more blessed to give than to receive.'"

When he had finished speaking, he knelt and prayed with them. They all cried as they embraced and kissed him good-bye. They were sad most of all because he had said that they would never see him again.

REFLECT _____

How did Paul endure so much suffering, persecution, and pain? How did he continue to go from place to place, knowing that prison and hardship awaited him? How did he face such severe testing with humility and without losing hope or faith? In Paul's farewell speech to the Ephesian church elders, we learn that what kept him going was clarity about what God had called him to do. His "only aim" (verse 24, NIV) was to complete that task.

- Read this passage again. What word or phrase stands out to you? Sit quietly, reminding yourself that you are in God's loving presence, and ask him to show you how that word or phrase connects to your life.

- What has God called you to do in this season of your life? If you don't have clarity, pray for guidance, asking him to make it clear. Also, ask people who know you well where they see you most alive and connected to God.

- Busyness and multitasking are often the "hardships" (verse 23, NIV) that distract us from God's calling on our lives today. What tasks, errands, hobbies, and other activities—though they may themselves be good—keep you from what God has called you to do? What is he inviting you to do to regain your focus?

RESPOND _____

Father, thank you for the reminder that you have called me to love and extend your grace into the world in a unique way. You have given me gifts, skills, and a sphere of influence. Help me step into all you're asking of me and know what to continue and what to release so I can focus on my Kingdom assignment. Grant me the faith and courage to end the activities that distract me. My life is yours. Use me for your purposes. Amen.

THE LORD'S WILL BE DONE

a prayer to open   Holy Spirit, come. Center my heart.
Fill my mind. Guide my steps.

READ ACTS 21:1-16

After saying farewell to the Ephesian elders, we sailed straight to the island of Cos. The next day we reached Rhodes and then went to Patara. There we boarded a ship sailing for Phoenicia . . . and landed at the harbor of Tyre, in Syria, where the ship was to unload its cargo.

We went ashore, found the local believers, and stayed with them a week. These believers prophesied through the Holy Spirit that Paul should not go on to Jerusalem. When we returned to the ship at the end of the week, the entire congregation . . . left the city and came down to the shore with us. There we knelt, prayed, and said our farewells. Then we went aboard, and they returned home.

The next stop after leaving Tyre was Ptolemais, where we greeted the brothers and sisters and stayed for one day. The next day we went on to Caesarea and stayed at the home of Philip the Evangelist, one of the seven men who had been chosen to distribute food. He had four unmarried daughters who had the gift of prophecy.

Several days later a man named Agabus, who also had the gift of prophecy, arrived from Judea. He came over, took Paul's belt, and bound his own feet and hands with it. Then he said, "The Holy Spirit declares, 'So shall the owner of this belt be bound by the Jewish leaders in Jerusalem and turned over to the Gentiles.'" When we heard this, we and the local believers all begged Paul not to go on to Jerusalem.

But he said, "Why all this weeping? You are breaking my heart! I am ready not only to be jailed at Jerusalem but even to die for the sake of the Lord Jesus." When it was clear that we couldn't persuade him, we gave up and said, "The Lord's will be done."

After this we packed our things and left for Jerusalem.

REFLECT

This passage of Scripture feels a bit like a death march: Paul was on his final tour to say good-bye to those he discipled and loved. In each successive place, he was warned again of the suffering that awaited him in Jerusalem. In fact, we begin to feel as we did reading Luke's account of Jesus' final journey to Jerusalem (see Luke 18:31-34). Paul believed that his life would end as Jesus' did, yet he was confident that he was to go to Jerusalem anyway. In the end, Paul's friends, who believed he was making the wrong decision, relented and released him to God's care, trusting and praying that God's will would be done. When we're able to see God at work in another person's life, can we release our expectations and desires to bless them on their journey?

- Read this passage again. What word or phrase stands out to you? Sit quietly, reminding yourself that you are in God's loving presence, and ask him to show you how that word or phrase connects to your life.

- Reflect on a situation or decision you are currently facing in which you don't know the right way to go. How would you describe your feelings as you think about that situation or decision? Try praying each time the situation or decision comes to mind, just as the disciples did when they decided to release Paul: Make your desire known, and then ask that the Lord's will be done.

Empowered

•

- Is there someone in your life about to make a bad decision (maybe it's destructive, the timing is wrong, or the decision doesn't make sense)? What is your concern? Practice entrusting that person to God's care, and even if he or she makes the "bad" decision, pray that the Lord's will would be done.

RESPOND

Father, the hardest prayer to pray is that your will would be done. A battle rages in my heart and mind because of my own desires. Help me pray over my life, decisions, and relationships, "May your will be done." And help me pray this same prayer over the lives and decisions of the people I love. Increase my trust in you and grow my faith. May your will be done. Amen.

DAY 42

TO WIN AS MANY AS POSSIBLE

a prayer to open

Holy Spirit, come. Center my heart.
Fill my mind. Guide my steps.

READ ACTS 21:17-36

When we arrived, the brothers and sisters in Jerusalem welcomed us warmly.

The next day Paul went with us to meet with James, and all the elders of the Jerusalem church were present. After greeting them, Paul gave a detailed account of the things God had accomplished among the Gentiles through his ministry.

After hearing this, they praised God. And then they said, "You know, dear brother, how many thousands of Jews have also believed, and they all follow the law of Moses very seriously. But the Jewish believers here in Jerusalem have been told that you are teaching all the Jews who live among the Gentiles to turn their backs on the laws of Moses. They've heard that you teach them not to circumcise their children or follow other Jewish customs. What should we do? They will certainly hear that you have come.

"Here's what we want you to do. We have four men here who have completed their vow. Go with them to the Temple and join them in the purification ceremony, paying for them to have their heads ritually shaved. Then everyone will know that the rumors are all false and that you yourself observe the Jewish laws.

"As for the Gentile believers, they should do what we already told them in a letter: They should abstain from eating food offered to idols, from consuming blood or the meat of strangled animals, and from sexual immorality."

So Paul went to the Temple the next day with the other men. They had already started the purification ritual, so he publicly announced the date when their vows would end and sacrifices would be offered for each of them.

The seven days were almost ended when some Jews from the province of Asia saw Paul in the Temple and roused a mob against him. They grabbed him, yelling, "Men of Israel, help us! This is the man who preaches against our people everywhere and tells everybody to disobey the Jewish laws. He speaks against the Temple—and even defiles this holy place by bringing in Gentiles." (For earlier that day they had seen him in the city with Trophimus, a Gentile from Ephesus, and they assumed Paul had taken him into the Temple.)

The whole city was rocked by these accusations, and a great riot followed. Paul was grabbed and dragged out of the Temple, and immediately the gates were closed behind him. As they were trying to kill him, word reached the commander of the Roman regiment that all Jerusalem was in an uproar. He immediately called out his soldiers and officers and ran down among the crowd. When the mob saw the commander and the troops coming, they stopped beating Paul.

Then the commander arrested him and ordered him bound with two chains. He asked the crowd who he was and what he had done. Some shouted one thing and some another. Since he couldn't find out the truth in all the uproar and confusion, he ordered that Paul be taken to the fortress. As Paul reached the stairs, the mob grew so violent the soldiers had to lift him to their shoulders to protect him. And the crowd followed behind, shouting, "Kill him, kill him!"

REFLECT

In his first letter to the church he planted in Corinth, Paul wrote, "Though I am free and belong to no one, I have made myself a slave to everyone, to win as many as possible. To the Jews I became like a Jew, to win the Jews. To those under the law I became like one under the law (though I myself am not under the law), so as to win those under the law" (1 Corinthians 9:19-20, NIV). We see these words played out in Acts 21: Paul submitted to certain Jewish purification rituals even though he did not consider himself bound by them anymore. The church elders wanted him to do this to save his life, and Paul presumably agreed in order to "win" those who accused him of speaking against the law and the Temple. How far out of your comfort zone are you really willing to go to tell people about the love and grace of Jesus?

- Read this passage again. What word or phrase stands out to you? Sit quietly, reminding yourself that you are in God's loving presence, and ask him to show you how that word or phrase connects to your life.

- Are there people you refuse to engage with because they hold different beliefs or act in ways that disturb you? Who are those people? What are you afraid might happen if you engaged with them?

- How might God be inviting you to engage with those who are different from you in order to share his love and grace? What resistance do you feel to that invitation?

RESPOND

Father, thank you for the people in my life who took a step toward me to share your love. Thank you for those who took a risk on me and introduced me to the life and redemption you offer. Help me to be someone who reaches across divides of all kinds and engages with people who look, behave, and believe differently from me. Remind me of who I am in you, and then send me out to be whatever I need to be to spread your love and to share the gospel with words and actions. Dispel my fear and embolden my spirit. Amen.

Empowered

•

343

LISTEN NOW TO MY DEFENSE

a prayer to open

Holy Spirit, come. Center my heart.
Fill my mind. Guide my steps.

READ ACTS 21:37–22:22

As Paul was about to be taken inside, he said to the commander, "May I have a word with you?"

"Do you know Greek?" the commander asked, surprised. "Aren't you the Egyptian who led a rebellion some time ago and took 4,000 members of the Assassins out into the desert?"

"No," Paul replied, "I am a Jew and a citizen of Tarsus in Cilicia, which is an important city. Please, let me talk to these people." The commander agreed, so Paul stood on the stairs and motioned to the people to be quiet. Soon a deep silence enveloped the crowd, and he addressed them in their own language, Aramaic.

"Brothers and esteemed fathers," Paul said, "listen to me as I offer my defense." When they heard him speaking in their own language, the silence was even greater.

Then Paul said, "I am a Jew, born in Tarsus, a city in Cilicia, and I was brought up and educated here in Jerusalem under Gamaliel. As his student, I was carefully trained in our Jewish laws and customs. I became very zealous to honor God in everything I did, just like all of you today. And I persecuted the followers of the Way, hounding some to death, arresting both men and women and throwing them in prison. The high priest and the whole council of elders can testify that this is so. For I received letters from them to our Jewish brothers in Damascus, authorizing me to bring the followers of the Way from there to Jerusalem, in chains, to be punished.

"As I was on the road, approaching Damascus about noon, a very bright light from heaven suddenly shone down around me. I fell to the ground and heard a voice saying to me, 'Saul, Saul, why are you persecuting me?'

"'Who are you, lord?' I asked.

"And the voice replied, 'I am Jesus the Nazarene, the one you are persecuting.' The people with me saw the light but didn't understand the voice speaking to me.

"I asked, 'What should I do, Lord?'

"And the Lord told me, 'Get up and go into Damascus, and there you will be told everything you are to do.'

"I was blinded by the intense light and had to be led by the hand to Damascus by my companions. A man named Ananias lived there. He was a godly man, deeply devoted to the law, and well regarded by all the Jews of Damascus. He came and stood beside me and said, 'Brother Saul, regain your sight.' And that very moment I could see him!

"Then he told me, 'The God of our ancestors has chosen you to know his will and to see the Righteous One and hear him speak. For you are to be his witness, telling everyone what you have seen and heard. What are you waiting for? Get up and be baptized. Have your sins washed away by calling on the name of the Lord.'

"After I returned to Jerusalem, I was praying in the Temple and fell into a trance. I saw a vision of Jesus saying to me, 'Hurry! Leave Jerusalem, for the people here won't accept your testimony about me.'

"'But Lord,' I argued, 'they certainly know that in every synagogue I imprisoned and beat those who believed in you. And I was in complete agreement when your witness Stephen was killed. I stood by and kept the coats they took off when they stoned him.'

"But the Lord said to me, 'Go, for I will send you far away to the Gentiles!'"

The crowd listened until Paul said that word. Then they all began to shout, "Away with such a fellow! He isn't fit to live!"

REFLECT

Paul has one last chance to show his people—the Jews in Jerusalem—that Jesus was the fulfillment of the laws they held in such high regard. But instead of giving a theological explanation, he just shared what happened to him: who he'd been, his encounter with Jesus, his transformation, and what Jesus called him to do. The crowd was appalled by the notion that Gentiles would be brought into the family of God, as they had historically been the enemy or oppressor. Could God's grace really extend so far?

- Read this passage again. What word or phrase stands out to you? Sit quietly, reminding yourself that you are in God's loving presence, and ask him to show you how that word or phrase connects to your life.

- How would you describe yourself before you first encountered the saving love of Jesus? What were you like? Where did your loyalties lie? On what did you spend your time, money, and thoughts?

- How would you describe yourself now that you have encountered the saving love of Jesus? What's different about you? How have your priorities changed? How do you spend your time, money, and thoughts now? What remains the same? What do you want to change?

RESPOND

Father, thank you for the transformation you have brought in my life through Christ. Thank you for changing and rearranging my heart, mind, and actions. Please keep working in me, rooting out old patterns of wrongdoing and destructive behaviors, calling me into your ways of love, and empowering me to extend grace and compassion into this world. Let me be a force for good. Amen.

DAY 44

THE LORD STOOD NEAR

a prayer to open

Holy Spirit, come. Center my heart. Fill my mind. Guide my steps.

READ ACTS 22:23–23:11

They yelled, threw off their coats, and tossed handfuls of dust into the air.

The commander brought Paul inside and ordered him lashed with whips to make him confess his crime. He wanted to find out why the crowd had become so furious. When they tied Paul down to lash him, Paul said to the officer standing there, "Is it legal for you to whip a Roman citizen who hasn't even been tried?"

When the officer heard this, he went to the commander and asked, "What are you doing? This man is a Roman citizen!"

So the commander went over and asked Paul, "Tell me, are you a Roman citizen?"

"Yes, I certainly am," Paul replied.

"I am, too," the commander muttered, "and it cost me plenty!"

Paul answered, "But I am a citizen by birth!"

The soldiers who were about to interrogate Paul quickly withdrew when they heard he was a Roman citizen, and the commander was frightened because he had ordered him bound and whipped.

The next day the commander ordered the leading priests into session with the Jewish high council. He wanted to find out what the trouble was all about, so he released Paul to have him stand before them.

Gazing intently at the high council, Paul began: "Brothers, I have always lived before God with a clear conscience!"

Instantly Ananias the high priest commanded

those close to Paul to slap him on the mouth. But Paul said to him, "God will slap you, you corrupt hypocrite! What kind of judge are you to break the law yourself by ordering me struck like that?"

Those standing near Paul said to him, "Do you dare to insult God's high priest?"

"I'm sorry, brothers. I didn't realize he was the high priest," Paul replied, "for the Scriptures say, 'You must not speak evil of any of your rulers.'"

Paul realized that some members of the high council were Sadducees and some were Pharisees, so he shouted, "Brothers, I am a Pharisee, as were my ancestors! And I am on trial because my hope is in the resurrection of the dead!"

This divided the council—the Pharisees against the Sadducees—for the Sadducees say there is no resurrection or angels or spirits, but the Pharisees believe in all of these. So there was a great uproar. Some of the teachers of religious law who were Pharisees jumped up and began to argue forcefully. "We see nothing wrong with him," they shouted. "Perhaps a spirit or an angel spoke to him." As the conflict grew more violent, the commander was afraid they would tear Paul apart. So he ordered his soldiers to go and rescue him by force and take him back to the fortress.

That night the Lord appeared to Paul and said, "Be encouraged, Paul. Just as you have been a witness to me here in Jerusalem, you must preach the Good News in Rome as well."

REFLECT

After nearly being killed by his people and then stretched out for flogging by the Romans, Paul was released to stand trial before the Sanhedrin. He found little relief there, of course, and was accused of blasphemy and carried off by the Romans for his own safety. Although he felt compelled by the Holy Spirit to go to Jerusalem, this series of events must have tested his strength and conviction. Imagine what must have happened in Paul's heart when in the midst of this trial, Jesus came and "stood near" (23:11, NIV) him as an act of compassion and love. Jesus spoke words of encouragement and affirmation to him, assuring him that he would live to share his testimony in Rome, the very center of the civilized world at the time. Today, by his Spirit, Jesus is with us, guiding, encouraging, and giving us strength. Our part is to believe he is with us and ask him to open our eyes to the ways he stands near in our most significant struggles.

- Read this passage again. What word or phrase stands out to you? Sit quietly, reminding yourself that you are in God's loving presence, and ask him to show you how that word or phrase connects to your life.

- Reflect on your most trying time so far. As you look back on that time, who stood near you? What acts of compassion and love were directed toward you? In what ways did God come near you during that time?

- The apostle John wrote, "This is how love is made complete among us so that we will have confidence on the day of judgment: In this world we are like Jesus" (1 John 4:17, NIV). Who in your life is going through a trial? Ask God how you can be Jesus to that person, standing near and speaking encouragement and affirmation to them.

RESPOND

Father, thank you for the gift of your presence, whether by your Spirit or in and through others. Thank you for the ways you have stood near me in my past trials and for the assurance of your presence in all future trials and triumphs. I want to be Jesus to those around me—those going through great difficulty and trial. Open my eyes to those in need, and fill me with your compassion so I will have the desire and strength to stand with them. May your love prevail on earth as it does in heaven. Amen.

DAY 45

THE PROVIDENCE OF GOD

a prayer to open

Holy Spirit, come. Center my heart.
Fill my mind. Guide my steps.

READ ACTS 23:12-33

The next morning a group of Jews got together and bound themselves with an oath not to eat or drink until they had killed Paul. . . . They went to the leading priests and elders and told them, "We have bound ourselves with an oath to eat nothing until we have killed Paul. So you and the high council should ask the commander to bring Paul back to the council again. Pretend you want to examine his case more fully. We will kill him on the way."

But Paul's nephew . . . heard of their plan and went to the fortress and told Paul. Paul called for one of the Roman officers and said, "Take this young man to the commander. He has something important to tell him."

So the officer did, explaining, "Paul, the prisoner, called me over and asked me to bring this young man to you because he has something to tell you."

The commander took his hand, led him aside, and asked, "What is it you want to tell me?"

Paul's nephew told him, "Some Jews are going to ask you to bring Paul before the high council tomorrow, pretending they want to get some more information. But don't do it! There are more than forty men hiding along the way ready to ambush him. They have vowed not to eat or drink anything until they have killed him. They are ready now, just waiting for your consent."

"Don't let anyone know you told me this," the commander warned the young man.

Then the commander called two of his officers and ordered, "Get 200 soldiers ready to leave for Caesarea at nine o'clock tonight. Also take 200 spearmen and 70 mounted troops. Provide horses for Paul to ride, and get him safely to Governor Felix." Then he wrote this letter to the governor:

"From Claudius Lysias, to his Excellency, Governor Felix: Greetings!

"This man was seized by some Jews, and they were about to kill him when I arrived with the troops. When I learned that he was a Roman citizen, I removed him to safety. Then I took him to their high council to try to learn the basis of the accusations against him. I soon discovered the charge was something regarding their religious law—certainly nothing worthy of imprisonment or death. But when I was informed of a plot to kill him, I immediately sent him on to you. I have told his accusers to bring their charges before you."

So that night, as ordered, the soldiers took Paul as far as Antipatris. They returned to the fortress the next morning, while the mounted troops took him on to Caesarea. When they arrived in Caesarea, they presented Paul and the letter to Governor Felix.

REFLECT

Some would call the fact that Paul's nephew heard about the plot to kill Paul a coincidence: He just happened to be in the right place at the right time. But given that he overheard news of the plot the morning after Jesus told Paul he would testify in Rome, it seems more like providence: a special orchestration of events

Empowered

by God that resulted in Paul being transported out of Jerusalem and one step closer to Rome. Paul must have shaken his head with wonder when his nephew reported what he'd heard. Do we see all the ways God protects and provides for us? Are our eyes open to his movement?

- Read this passage again. What word or phrase stands out to you? Sit quietly, reminding yourself that you are in God's loving presence, and ask him to show you how that word or phrase connects to your life.

- Reflect on a time when you experienced a stunning coincidence. What happened? How did that experience make you feel?

- How open do you think you are to seeing God's movement and presence in your everyday life? What things catch your attention as evidence of him? How do you respond to those things when you see them?

RESPOND

Father, thank you that you are active in my life and in this world even when I am not aware or fail to notice. I want to be able to recognize when you are at work and align with what you're doing. Give me eyes to see where you orchestrate events for your purposes. Give me hands that respond when you call me to act, and a heart that is open and willing to follow you even when it's hard and I don't see the path ahead. Amen.

I WILL GIVE YOU WORDS AND WISDOM

a prayer to open

Holy Spirit, come. Center my heart.
Fill my mind. Guide my steps.

READ ACTS 24:1-21

Five days later Ananias, the high priest, arrived with some of the Jewish elders and the lawyer Tertullus, to present their case against Paul to the governor. When Paul was called in, Tertullus presented the charges against Paul in the following address to the governor:

"You have provided a long period of peace for us Jews and with foresight have enacted reforms for us. For all of this, Your Excellency, we are very grateful to you. But I don't want to bore you, so please give me your attention for only a moment. We have found this man to be a troublemaker who is constantly stirring up riots among the Jews all over the world. He is a ringleader of the cult known as the Nazarenes. Furthermore, he was trying to desecrate the Temple when we arrested him. You can find out the truth of our accusations by examining him yourself." Then the other Jews chimed in, declaring that everything Tertullus said was true.

The governor then motioned for Paul to speak. Paul said, "I know, sir, that you have been a judge of Jewish affairs for many years, so I gladly present my defense before you. You can quickly discover that I arrived in Jerusalem no more than twelve days ago to worship at the Temple. My accusers never found me arguing with anyone in the Temple, nor stirring up a riot in any synagogue or on the streets of the city. These men cannot prove the things they accuse me of doing.

"But I admit that I follow the Way, which they call a cult. I worship the God of our ancestors, and I firmly believe the Jewish law and everything written in the prophets. I have the same hope in God that these men have, that he will raise both the righteous and the unrighteous. Because of this, I always try to maintain a clear conscience before God and all people.

"After several years away, I returned to Jerusalem with money to aid my people and to offer sacrifices to God. My accusers saw me in the Temple as I was completing a purification ceremony. There was no crowd around me and no rioting. But some Jews from the province of Asia were there—and they ought to be here to bring charges if they have anything against me! Ask these men here what crime the Jewish high council found me guilty of, except for the one time I shouted out, 'I am on trial before you today because I believe in the resurrection of the dead!'"

REFLECT

Once the Roman army had removed Paul from Jerusalem and settled him in Herod's palace in Caesarea, he had five days before being called before the governor, Antonius Felix. As Paul responded to the charges brought by the high priest's lawyer, he was unreasonably calm. He methodically and clearly set forth the facts with little apparent emotion or fear. How was this possible? Perhaps Luke, during his time traveling with Paul, had shared these words of Jesus: "Make up your mind not to worry beforehand how you will defend yourselves. For I will give you words and wisdom that none of your adversaries will be able to resist or contradict" (Luke 21:14-15, NIV).

- Read today's Scripture again. What word or phrase stands out to you? Sit quietly, reminding yourself that you are in God's loving presence, and ask him to show you how that word or phrase connects to your life.

- What do you worry about most? Why? What is the insecurity or fear underneath the worry?

- How do you cope with your worry when it arises? What brings comfort? What perpetuates the worry? What do you want to say to God about your worry and whatever underlies it? Write out a prayer and ask him for what you desire and for relief from your worry.

RESPOND

Father, your Word is filled with passages about your peace and your presence in the midst of hardship, pain, and sickness, yet I don't always feel or access your peace. I worry about the unknown, what my future holds, and those I love. Remind me that all these things are in your hands, you love me, and my future is secure in you in heaven. Help me to release my grip on those I love and to entrust them to you. I want to be free of all worry and anxiety. Lead me. Amen.

IN SOMEONE ELSE'S HANDS

a prayer to open

Holy Spirit, come. Center my heart.
Fill my mind. Guide my steps.

READ ACTS 24:22-27

At that point Felix, who was quite familiar with the Way, adjourned the hearing and said, "Wait until Lysias, the garrison commander, arrives. Then I will decide the case." He ordered an officer to keep Paul in custody but to give him some freedom and allow his friends to visit him and take care of his needs.

A few days later Felix came back with his wife, Drusilla, who was Jewish. Sending for Paul, they listened as he told them about faith in Christ Jesus. As he reasoned with them about righteousness and self-control and the coming day of judgment, Felix became frightened. "Go away for now," he replied. "When it is more convenient, I'll call for you again." He also hoped that Paul would bribe him, so he sent for him quite often and talked with him.

After two years went by in this way, Felix was succeeded by Porcius Festus. And because Felix wanted to gain favor with the Jewish people, he left Paul in prison.

REFLECT

Governor Antonius Felix was in a tough spot. If he convicted Paul on the paltry charges presented by the Jewish high priest, he could get in trouble with the Roman higher-ups for treating a Roman citizen unjustly. But setting Paul free certainly would have resulted in a riot and Paul's death. Felix's answer? Stall. He adjourned the proceedings, extended Paul some freedom and the ability to see his friends, tried to get Paul to bribe him so he'd be off the hook, and then did nothing at all for *two years*. After that, Paul became the next governor's problem. Paul sat in the Caesarean prison for two years with no idea when or whether he would be freed. What must he have thought, felt, and done in those years? Did his faith falter?

• Read this passage again. What word or phrase stands out to you? Sit quietly, reminding yourself that you are in God's loving presence, and ask him to show you how that word or phrase connects to your life.

• Reflect on a time in which your life or some part of it was in someone else's hands. What did that feel like? What frustrated you or angered you about that? How did you experience God during that time?

• Are you in any way holding someone else's life or freedom in your hands? (Perhaps you are holding a grudge, are withholding love or forgiveness, or have some positional or personal leverage over another person.) What's motivating you? What do you sense God inviting you to do in that situation?

RESPOND

Father, thank you for freedom in Christ and that your promises are true even when I don't see how they could be under the circumstances. I pray for greater freedom in my heart and mind. I pray that whatever my circumstances, I remain faith filled and hopeful. Show me if I am negatively affecting the freedom of someone else by my words or actions. Help me release that person, and forgive me for inhibiting or controlling them. May your peace cover me, and may I walk in love and trust. Amen.

AN APPEAL TO CAESAR

a prayer to open

Holy Spirit, come. Center my heart.
Fill my mind. Guide my steps.

READ ACTS 25:1-12

Three days after Festus arrived in Caesarea to take over his new responsibilities, he left for Jerusalem, where the leading priests and other Jewish leaders met with him and made their accusations against Paul. They asked Festus as a favor to transfer Paul to Jerusalem (planning to ambush and kill him on the way). But Festus replied that Paul was at Caesarea and he himself would be returning there soon. So he said, "Those of you in authority can return with me. If Paul has done anything wrong, you can make your accusations."

About eight or ten days later Festus returned to Caesarea, and on the following day he took his seat in court and ordered that Paul be brought in. When Paul arrived, the Jewish leaders from Jerusalem gathered around and made many serious accusations they couldn't prove.

Paul denied the charges. "I am not guilty of any crime against the Jewish laws or the Temple or the Roman government," he said.

Then Festus, wanting to please the Jews, asked him, "Are you willing to go to Jerusalem and stand trial before me there?"

But Paul replied, "No! This is the official Roman court, so I ought to be tried right here. You know very well I am not guilty of harming the Jews. If I have done something worthy of death, I don't refuse to die. But if I am innocent, no one has a right to turn me over to these men to kill me. I appeal to Caesar!"

Festus conferred with his advisers and then replied, "Very well! You have appealed to Caesar, and to Caesar you will go!"

REFLECT

We don't know what motivated Paul when he appeared before the new governor, Festus, to appeal to Caesar. Did he hope for real justice and an acquittal? Was he seeking to live out Jesus' promise to him that he would testify in Rome? Was it a little bit of both? We do know from Paul's letters that he had respect for the rule of law: He encouraged followers of Jesus to obey the law (see Romans 13:1-7) and pray for governmental leaders (see 1 Timothy 2:1-2). In our divisive political climate, we can be tempted to dishonor our leaders with our words. Most of us hardly think about praying for them, especially if we disagree with their policies and causes. Paul offered us a different way.

- Read this passage again. What word or phrase stands out to you? Sit quietly, reminding yourself that you are in God's loving presence, and ask him to show you how that word or phrase connects to your life.

- Reflect on the words you use with friends, family, and colleagues and on social media about current or would-be government leaders. What attitudes do your words reflect? How well do you do at respecting these leaders and seeing them as human beings made in God's image?

- Do you regularly pray for governmental leaders, even those you disagree with? Why or why not?

RESPOND_____

Father, thank you for the leaders who have stepped into government to bring order to society and ensure peace and justice. Help me see these leaders with your eyes—eyes of love and compassion. Forgive me for things I have said that have diminished leaders or when I've failed to extend them grace and mercy in their human frailty. I pray that my words would be used to build people up, not tear them down. Guide me in honoring you and in my role as an ambassador of Christ in this world. Amen.

DAY 49

THE SCANDAL OF THE RESURRECTION

a prayer to open   Holy Spirit, come. Center my heart.
                                      Fill my mind. Guide my steps.

READ ACTS 25:13-27 _____

A few days later King Agrippa arrived with his sister, Bernice, to pay their respects to Festus. During their stay of several days, Festus discussed Paul's case with the king. "There is a prisoner here," he told him, "whose case was left for me by Felix. When I was in Jerusalem, the leading priests and Jewish elders pressed charges against him and asked me to condemn him. I pointed out to them that Roman law does not convict people without a trial. They must be given an opportunity to confront their accusers and defend themselves.

"When his accusers came here for the trial, I didn't delay. I called the case the very next day and ordered Paul brought in. But the accusations made against him weren't any of the crimes I expected. Instead, it was something about their religion and a dead man named Jesus, who Paul insists is alive. I was at a loss to know how to investigate these things, so I asked him whether he would be willing to stand trial on these charges in Jerusalem. But Paul appealed to have his case decided by the emperor. So I ordered

that he be held in custody until I could arrange to send him to Caesar."

"I'd like to hear the man myself," Agrippa said.

And Festus replied, "You will—tomorrow!"

So the next day Agrippa and Bernice arrived at the auditorium with great pomp, accompanied by military officers and prominent men of the city. Festus ordered that Paul be brought in. Then Festus said, "King Agrippa and all who are here, this is the man whose death is demanded by all the Jews, both here and in Jerusalem. But in my opinion he has done nothing deserving death. However, since he appealed his case to the emperor, I have decided to send him to Rome.

"But what shall I write the emperor? For there is no clear charge against him. So I have brought him before all of you, and especially you, King Agrippa, so that after we examine him, I might have something to write. For it makes no sense to send a prisoner to the emperor without specifying the charges against him!"

In this passage, we again see striking parallels to Jesus' arrest and trials. Paul was brought before Herod Agrippa II, the grandson of Herod Antipas, before whom Jesus appeared. And Festus and Agrippa seemed just as befuddled by the charges against Paul as their predecessors were by the charges against Jesus. At the heart of the charges against Paul, as Festus understood them, was the objection certain Jewish leaders had to Paul's assertion that Jesus was alive—whether the Resurrection had actually happened. The idea was then—as it is now—a powerful and controversial one. The Roman leaders must have been curious. Consider the masses of people who don't attend church all year but find their way there on Easter Sunday. Something draws them. Could someone really have been raised from the dead? And what does it mean if he was?

- Read this passage again. What word or phrase stands out to you? Sit quietly, reminding yourself that you are in God's loving presence, and ask him to show you how that word or phrase connects to your life.

- Take a moment to reflect on the Resurrection. Read Luke 24:1-12 or John 20:1-18 to refresh your memory. What would it have been like to be present to see the resurrected Jesus? What emotions do you think would have been triggered in you?

- Reflect on what impact the Resurrection has on the way you live. How does it influence your decisions?

RESPOND

Father, thank you that the Resurrection is true, that Jesus is alive, and that in him, eternal life is available to me. This is hard to comprehend, but I pray that you would help me understand the true weight of it. When I am sad or feel discouraged, I want to remember the Resurrection. When I feel alone, I want to remember that Jesus said he would always be with those who follow him. Give me an eternal perspective as I make decisions today, and help me get out of myself to serve others. Amen.

DAY 50

THE REASON FOR HOPE

a prayer to open
Holy Spirit, come. Center my heart.
Fill my mind. Guide my steps.

Empowered

•

Then Agrippa said to Paul, "You may speak in your defense."

So Paul, gesturing with his hand, started his defense: "I am fortunate, King Agrippa, that you are the one hearing my defense today against all these accusations made by the Jewish leaders, for I know you are an expert on all Jewish customs and controversies. Now please listen to me patiently!

"As the Jewish leaders are well aware, I was given a thorough Jewish training from my earliest childhood among my own people and in Jerusalem. If they would admit it, they know that I have been a member of the Pharisees, the strictest sect of our religion. Now I am on trial because of my hope in the fulfillment of God's promise made to our ancestors.

In fact, that is why the twelve tribes of Israel zealously worship God night and day, and they share the same hope I have. Yet, Your Majesty, they accuse me for having this hope! Why does it seem incredible to any of you that God can raise the dead?

"I used to believe that I ought to do everything I could to oppose the very name of Jesus the Nazarene. Indeed, I did just that in Jerusalem. Authorized by the leading priests, I caused many believers there to be sent to prison. And I cast my vote against them when they were condemned to death. Many times I had them punished in the synagogues to get them to curse Jesus. I was so violently opposed to them that I even chased them down in foreign cities."

REFLECT

To defend against the accusations, Paul reframed the dispute so those present could have a better understanding. It was not just the Resurrection or Paul's assertion of its truth that got him in trouble; it was what the Resurrection meant, both about who Jesus was and what was to come for those who believed in him. What led to Paul's trial was his hope—or confidence—that Jesus was the one to whom the law and the prophets pointed as the Savior and Messiah and that all people—Jews and Gentiles alike—could have eternal life through him. This was a dangerous hope, though. As we see in Paul's letters in the rest of the New Testament, the gospel undermined social-status structures, cultural norms, and boundaries that kept Jews and Gentiles separated.

- Read this passage again. What word or phrase stands out to you? Sit quietly, reminding yourself that you are in God's loving presence, and ask him to show you how that word or phrase connects to your life.

- The apostle Peter said, "Always be prepared to give an answer to everyone who asks you to give the reason for the hope that you have" (1 Peter 3:15, NIV). How would you answer a friend who asked, "Why do you have hope in Jesus?"

- What activities and disciplines tend to fill you with hope? What activities and environments tend to discourage you or leave you filled with doubt?

RESPOND

Father, thank you for Jesus. Thank you that all things point to him and that my eternity is secure in him. I want my life to be a testimony to the hope I have in him. Fill me with your Spirit anew each day and remind me of your love and presence. When someone asks me about my life, my journey, or my hope, give me the words to share clearly and courageously. And when I fall into despair, please bring along a friend to encourage me and remind me of the hope I have in you. Amen.

WHAT I AM IN CHRIST

a prayer to open

Holy Spirit, come. Center my heart.
Fill my mind. Guide my steps.

READ ACTS 26:12-32

"One day I was on such a mission to Damascus, armed with the authority and commission of the leading priests. About noon, Your Majesty, as I was on the road, a light from heaven brighter than the sun shone down on me and my companions. We all fell down, and I heard a voice saying to me in Aramaic, 'Saul, Saul, why are you persecuting me? It is useless for you to fight against my will.'

"'Who are you, lord?' I asked.

"And the Lord replied, 'I am Jesus, the one you are persecuting. Now get to your feet! For I have appeared to you to appoint you as my servant and witness. Tell people that you have seen me, and tell them what I will show you in the future. And I will rescue you from both your own people and the Gentiles. Yes, I am sending you to the Gentiles to open their eyes, so they may turn from darkness to light and from the power of Satan to God. Then they will receive forgiveness for their sins and be given a place among God's people, who are set apart by faith in me.'

"And so, King Agrippa, I obeyed that vision from heaven. I preached first to those in Damascus, then in Jerusalem and throughout all Judea, and also to the Gentiles, that all must repent of their sins and turn to God—and prove they have changed by the good things they do. Some Jews arrested me in the Temple for preaching this, and they tried to kill me.

But God has protected me right up to this present time so I can testify to everyone, from the least to the greatest. I teach nothing except what the prophets and Moses said would happen—that the Messiah would suffer and be the first to rise from the dead, and in this way announce God's light to Jews and Gentiles alike."

Suddenly, Festus shouted, "Paul, you are insane. Too much study has made you crazy!"

But Paul replied, "I am not insane, Most Excellent Festus. What I am saying is the sober truth. And King Agrippa knows about these things. I speak boldly, for I am sure these events are all familiar to him, for they were not done in a corner! King Agrippa, do you believe the prophets? I know you do—"

Agrippa interrupted him. "Do you think you can persuade me to become a Christian so quickly?"

Paul replied, "Whether quickly or not, I pray to God that both you and everyone here in this audience might become the same as I am, except for these chains."

Then the king, the governor, Bernice, and all the others stood and left. As they went out, they talked it over and agreed, "This man hasn't done anything to deserve death or imprisonment."

And Agrippa said to Festus, "He could have been set free if he hadn't appealed to Caesar."

REFLECT

Paul's defense before King Agrippa and Governor Festus was compelling, courageous, and convicting. And even in the face of the governor calling him "insane," Paul spoke his desire that everyone in his hearing would become what he is. What did Paul say he was in Christ? Elsewhere, he wrote that those in Christ are children of God (see Galatians 3:26), unfailingly loved (see Romans 8:37-39), temples of the Holy Spirit (see 1 Corinthians 6:19), free from the control and ultimate consequence of sin (see Galatians 5:1), overcomers (see Romans 8:37-39), and Christ's ambassadors in the world (see 2 Corinthians 5:20).

• Read this passage again. What word or phrase stands out to you? Sit quietly, reminding yourself that you are in God's loving presence, and ask him to show you how that word or phrase connects to your life.

Empowered •

- Which of the truths about who you are in Christ resonates with you the most? Why?

- Which of the truths about who you are in Christ is hardest for you to believe and receive? Why?

RESPOND

Father, thank you for the ability to turn to you in repentance. Thank you for taking me in and calling me your beloved child. Thank you for your presence within me and freeing me from the control that sin once had over me. Help me to be a humble, loving, grace-giving ambassador of your goodness and forgiveness. Give me words that are compelling, courageous, and convicting to others so they too can share this identity in Christ. Help me to be bold with the gospel and to open the opportunity for others to experience the truth of your grace. Amen.

IMPENDING DISASTER

a prayer to open

Holy Spirit, come. Center my heart.
Fill my mind. Guide my steps.

READ ACTS 27:1-12

When the time came, we set sail for Italy. Paul and several other prisoners were placed in the custody of a Roman officer named Julius, a captain of the Imperial Regiment. Aristarchus, a Macedonian from Thessalonica, was also with us. . . .

The next day when we docked at Sidon, Julius was very kind to Paul and let him go ashore to visit with friends so they could provide for his needs. Putting out to sea from there, we encountered strong headwinds that made it difficult to keep the ship on course, so we sailed north of Cyprus between the island and the mainland. Keeping to the open sea, we passed along the coast of Cilicia and Pamphylia, landing at Myra, in the province of Lycia. There the commanding officer found an Egyptian ship from Alexandria that was bound for Italy, and he put us on board.

We had several days of slow sailing, and after great difficulty we finally neared Cnidus. But the wind was against us, so we sailed across to Crete and along the sheltered coast of the island, past the cape of Salmone. We struggled along the coast with great difficulty and finally arrived at Fair Havens, near the town of Lasea. We had lost a lot of time. The weather was becoming dangerous for sea travel because it was so late in the fall, and Paul spoke to the ship's officers about it.

"Men," he said, "I believe there is trouble ahead if we go on—shipwreck, loss of cargo, and danger to our lives as well." But the officer in charge of the prisoners listened more to the ship's captain and the owner than to Paul. And since Fair Havens was an exposed harbor—a poor place to spend the winter— most of the crew wanted to go on to Phoenix, farther up the coast of Crete, and spend the winter there. Phoenix was a good harbor with only a southwest and northwest exposure.

REFLECT

This first segment of Paul's journey from Caesarea to Rome is difficult to read because of the looming danger we feel in Luke's words. The winds were high, it was nearly winter, progress was slow, and Paul himself warned of an impending disaster. He had experienced three shipwrecks before this (see 2 Corinthians 11:25), so he knew how hard that things could get. How must he have prepared his heart for what was coming?

- Read this passage again. What word or phrase stands out to you? Sit quietly, reminding yourself that you are in God's loving presence, and ask him to show you how that word or phrase connects to your life.

- Reflect on a time when disaster was looming and you had no ability to stop it. How did you prepare yourself? How would you prepare yourself differently today if faced with a similar problem?

- Who in your life is facing an impending storm (a death, a job or home loss, a divorce, a surgery)? How can you care for and encourage them in advance of that storm? What would serve them?

RESPOND _____

Father, I pray for your provision in and protection from impending storms. In your mercy and love, spare me and fill me with hope. Surround me with what I need in order to weather whatever might come and to remember your promises. May I be someone who draws close to those who have hard times ahead. Show me who will need a friend to walk with, and give me the strength and stamina to be that friend. Amen.

DAY 53

IN THE MIDST OF A STORM

a prayer to open   Holy Spirit, come. Center my heart.
                                       Fill my mind. Guide my steps.

READ ACTS 27:13-26 _____

When a light wind began blowing from the south, the sailors thought they could make it. So they pulled up anchor and sailed close to the shore of Crete. But the weather changed abruptly, and a wind of typhoon strength . . . burst across the island and blew us out to sea. The sailors couldn't turn the ship into the wind, so they gave up and let it run before the gale.

We sailed along the sheltered side of a small island named Cauda, where with great difficulty we hoisted aboard the lifeboat being towed behind us. Then the sailors bound ropes around the hull of the ship to strengthen it. They were afraid of being driven across to the sandbars of Syrtis off the African coast, so they lowered the sea anchor to slow the ship and were driven before the wind.

The next day, as gale-force winds continued to batter the ship, the crew began throwing the cargo overboard. The following day they even took some of the ship's gear and threw it overboard. The terrible storm raged for many days, blotting out the sun and the stars, until at last all hope was gone.

No one had eaten for a long time. Finally, Paul called the crew together and said, "Men, you should

Empowered

•

357

have listened to me in the first place and not left Crete. You would have avoided all this damage and loss. But take courage! None of you will lose your lives, even though the ship will go down. For last night an angel of the God to whom I belong and whom I serve stood beside me, and he said, 'Don't be afraid, Paul, for you will surely stand trial before Caesar! What's more, God in his goodness has granted safety to everyone sailing with you.' So take courage! For I believe God. It will be just as he said. But we will be shipwrecked on an island."

REFLECT _____

Paul and his shipmates found themselves in the midst of a devastating storm. They could not control their ship, the winds were hurricane strength, and eventually they gave up all hope. And then an angel of God stood beside Paul to reassure him and breathe hope and promise into despair. This supernatural intervention was light in the darkness and enabled Paul to provide encouragement in a seemingly hopeless situation. Oh that God would intervene in our darkest moments to grant us a sense of his presence, a word of encouragement, or a reminder of his promises.

- Read this passage again. What word or phrase stands out to you? Sit quietly, reminding yourself that you are in God's loving presence, and ask him to show you how that word or phrase connects to your life.

- Reflect on a time when you found yourself in the "midst of a storm." How did you feel during that time (defeated, discouraged, hopeless, confused)? What helped you continue to hold on to hope, or what brought you back to a place of hope?

- What storm are you in now, whether because of external circumstances or an internal battle? Who are you sharing your struggle with so you aren't alone? How do you sense God's presence and care in the midst of your struggle? What promises from Scripture might help you remember hope?

RESPOND_____

Father, sometimes pain seems to come in a constant stream with one thing after another creating more difficulty. Thank you for the good things in the midst of the storms. Help me see them, and turn my heart toward you in gratitude and faith. Remind me of your promises. Bring to mind someone I can share my experience with so I can know I am not alone, and give me the courage to invite them into my story. Have mercy on me and grant me your peace. Amen.

SURVIVAL

a prayer to open

Holy Spirit, come. Center my heart.
Fill my mind. Guide my steps.

READ ACTS 27:27-44

About midnight on the fourteenth night of the storm, . . . the sailors sensed land was near. They dropped a weighted line and found that the water was 120 feet deep. But a little later they measured again and found it was only 90 feet deep. At this rate they were afraid we would soon be driven against the rocks along the shore, so they threw out four anchors from the back of the ship and prayed for daylight.

Then the sailors tried to abandon the ship; they lowered the lifeboat as though they were going to put out anchors from the front of the ship. But Paul said to the commanding officer and the soldiers, "You will all die unless the sailors stay aboard." So the soldiers cut the ropes to the lifeboat and let it drift away.

Just as day was dawning, Paul urged everyone to eat. "You have been so worried that you haven't touched food for two weeks," he said. "Please eat something now for your own good. For not a hair of your heads will perish." Then he took some bread, gave thanks to God before them all, and broke off

a piece and ate it. Then everyone was encouraged and began to eat—all 276 of us who were on board. After eating, the crew lightened the ship further by throwing the cargo of wheat overboard.

When morning dawned, they didn't recognize the coastline, but they saw a bay with a beach and wondered if they could get to shore by running the ship aground. So they cut off the anchors and left them in the sea. Then they lowered the rudders, raised the foresail, and headed toward shore. But they hit a shoal and ran the ship aground too soon. The bow of the ship stuck fast, while the stern was repeatedly smashed by the force of the waves and began to break apart.

The soldiers wanted to kill the prisoners to make sure they didn't swim ashore and escape. But the commanding officer wanted to spare Paul, so he didn't let them carry out their plan. Then he ordered all who could swim to jump overboard first and make for land. The others held on to planks or debris from the broken ship. So everyone escaped safely to shore.

REFLECT

In the midst of pounding waves, darkness, and guaranteed shipwreck, Paul urged his shipmates to eat. He took bread, thanked God, broke the bread, and then gave it to all 276 people aboard to eat. Of course, as we read this passage and wonder what the sailors, prisoners, and Roman officials must have thought as Paul did this, we can't help but think of the Last Supper. They couldn't have known the significance, and we don't know what might have happened in their hearts as they participated. Paul knew that this sustenance—both spiritual and physical—would give them the strength and courage to survive. And when a new day dawned, all were saved.

- Read this passage again. What word or phrase stands out to you? Sit quietly, reminding yourself that you are in God's loving presence, and ask him to show you how that word or phrase connects to your life.

- Reflect on the rhythms of work and rest that you practice. Do you see any signs of exhaustion, an inability to be present, restlessness, or anxiety? What disciplines (rest, exercise, sleep, prayer, something else) do you need to

Empowered

incorporate more so you don't burn out or get sick in body or soul? What keeps you from doing these things?

- Who in your life is running themselves ragged? How could you encourage them to do what they need to do to prevent burnout and illness? What would get their attention and catalyze change?

RESPOND_____

Father, thank you for the reminder to take care of my body and soul, especially in seasons of stress, busyness, and pain. Help me to grow in the discipline of rest and to care for myself so I can live a long life and serve you until my last breath. I want to measure my life by the love I give, not by the number of hours I work or the amount of money I make. Renew in me a fire for what matters, and enable me to turn my time and attention toward those things. May you be seen in and through me. Amen.

STRENGTH IN WEAKNESS

a prayer to open   Holy Spirit, come. Center my heart.
                                       Fill my mind. Guide my steps.

READ ACTS 28:1-16 _____

Once we were safe on shore, we learned that we were on the island of Malta. The people of the island were very kind to us. It was cold and rainy, so they built a fire on the shore to welcome us.

As Paul gathered an armful of sticks and was laying them on the fire, a poisonous snake, driven out by the heat, bit him on the hand. The people of the island saw it hanging from his hand and said to each other, "A murderer, no doubt! Though he escaped the sea, justice will not permit him to live." But Paul shook off the snake into the fire and was unharmed. The people waited for him to swell up or suddenly drop dead. But when they had waited a long time and saw that he wasn't harmed, they changed their minds and decided he was a god.

Near the shore where we landed was an estate belonging to Publius, the chief official of the island. He welcomed us and treated us kindly for three days. As it happened, Publius's father was ill with fever and dysentery. Paul went in and prayed for him,

and laying his hands on him, he healed him. Then all the other sick people on the island came and were healed. As a result we were showered with honors, and when the time came to sail, people supplied us with everything we would need for the trip.

It was three months after the shipwreck that we set sail on another ship that had wintered at the island. . . . Our first stop was Syracuse, where we stayed three days. From there we sailed across to Rhegium. A day later a south wind began blowing, so the following day we sailed up the coast to Puteoli. There we found some believers, who invited us to spend a week with them. And so we came to Rome.

The brothers and sisters in Rome had heard we were coming, and they came to meet us. . . . When Paul saw them, he was encouraged and thanked God.

When we arrived in Rome, Paul was permitted to have his own private lodging, though he was guarded by a soldier.

How was Paul still standing when he reached the shores of Malta? He had been through so many trials: "Five times I received from the Jews the forty lashes minus one. Three times I was beaten with rods, once I was pelted with stones, three times I was shipwrecked, I spent a night and a day in the open sea, I have been constantly on the move. . . . I have known hunger and thirst and have often gone without food; I have been cold and naked" (2 Corinthians 11:24-27, NIV). Of course, he'd also been in prison multiple times and dragged in chains before various officials to defend himself. And then he was bitten by a snake! How did he have the energy to heal every sick person on the island? As we see later in 2 Corinthians 12:9-10, Paul discovered that in his weakness, he found God's power—and that power was unmatched and unending.

- Read this passage again. What word or phrase stands out to you? Then sit quietly, reminding yourself that you are in God's loving presence, and ask him to show you how that word or phrase connects to your life.

- Reflect on a time you felt God's strength in your weakness. How would you describe to a friend what you experienced?

- In what area of your life do you need God's strength because you have reached a point of weakness? What would be one way to invite him into that area?

RESPOND

Father, thank you that you are always strong and offering your strength to me. I know I tend to rely on my own ability and skill in certain areas and miss inviting you into those places, and I can forget to turn myself over to you in times of weakness, too. I want to live with the expectancy of experiencing your supernatural power. Amen.

DAY 56

WITH ALL BOLDNESS AND WITHOUT HINDRANCE

a prayer to open

Holy Spirit, come. Center my heart.
Fill my mind. Guide my steps.

READ ACTS 28:17-31

Three days after Paul's arrival, he called together the local Jewish leaders. He said to them, "Brothers,

I was arrested in Jerusalem and handed over to the Roman government, even though I had done nothing against our people or the customs of our ancestors. The Romans tried me and wanted to release me, because they found no cause for the death sentence. But when the Jewish leaders protested the decision, I felt it necessary to appeal to Caesar, even though I had no desire to press charges against my own people. I asked you to come here today so we could get acquainted and so I could explain to you that I am bound with this chain because I believe that the hope of Israel—the Messiah—has already come."

They replied, "We have had no letters from Judea or reports against you from anyone who has come here. But we want to hear what you believe, for the only thing we know about this movement is that it is denounced everywhere."

So a time was set, and on that day a large number of people came to Paul's lodging. He explained and testified about the Kingdom of God and tried to persuade them about Jesus from the Scriptures. Using the law of Moses and the books of the prophets, he spoke to them from morning until evening. Some were persuaded by the things he said, but others did not believe. And after they had argued back and forth among themselves, they left with this final word from Paul: "The Holy Spirit was right when he said to your ancestors through Isaiah the prophet,

'Go and say to this people:
When you hear what I say,
    you will not understand.
When you see what I do,
    you will not comprehend.
For the hearts of these people are hardened,
    and their ears cannot hear,
    and they have closed their eyes—
so their eyes cannot see,
    and their ears cannot hear,
    and their hearts cannot understand,
    and they cannot turn to me
    and let me heal them.'

So I want you to know that this salvation from God has also been offered to the Gentiles, and they will accept it."

For the next two years, Paul lived in Rome at his own expense. He welcomed all who visited him, boldly proclaiming the Kingdom of God and teaching about the Lord Jesus Christ. And no one tried to stop him.

REFLECT

The book of Acts ends without resolution. What happened to Paul? Why didn't Luke tell us? We don't have clear answers to either of these questions. It is fitting that this book, which started with Jesus' statement that the disciples would be his "witnesses in Jerusalem, and in all Judea and Samaria, and to the ends of the earth" (1:8, NIV), would end in Rome, with Paul preaching about the Kingdom of God and the Lord Jesus Christ with boldness and without hindrance. In his second letter to Timothy, his protégé, just before Paul's death (scholars believe he was martyred between AD 64 and 67), he said,

I have fought the good fight, I have finished the race, I have kept the faith. Now there is in store for me the crown of righteousness, which the Lord, the righteous Judge, will award to me on that day—and not only to me, but also to all who have longed for his appearing.   2 TIMOTHY 4:7-8, NIV

- Read Acts 28:17-31 again. What word or phrase stands out to you? Then sit quietly, reminding yourself that you are in God's loving presence, and ask him to show you how that word or phrase connects to your life.

- What are one or two insights God has granted you about the Holy Spirit during the past fifty-six days?

- What have you discovered to be true of God as you've read and reflected on the book of Acts? What have you discovered to be true of you?

Father, thank you for the book of Acts. Thank you for the rich history of your church and all the demonstrations of your power, provision, and love. Fill me with your Holy Spirit anew. Give me the courage and strength to open to your abiding presence and follow all that you call me to be and do. May I finish well the race you have marked out for me and always share about your Kingdom and the Lord Jesus Christ with boldness and without hindrance. Amen.

Heard

Lamenting Your Pain and the Pain of the World

I GOT MARRIED in 2017, after having been single for nearly fifteen years. And when I think about the process leading up to my marriage and then the day of our wedding and the days that have followed, the words that come to mind are *healing, redemptive, bonding, filling,* and *restorative.* God has used my husband, Steve, to heal and redeem some very long-standing wounds and insecurities in me (and continues to use him in this way). I had never been loved as fully before, and I've never known anyone so committed to growing and loving me well.

But when people ask me how married life is, there is only one completely genuine thought that comes to mind: *I'm tired of facing myself so much.* It turns out that when you allow yourself to be known and open yourself up to someone else, the biggest challenge is having to face your own brokenness and flaws: the ways you respond when you get hurt, when previously unknown triggers get touched, when your expectations aren't met, when unexpressed needs go unnoticed, and when problems beyond anyone's control arise. Of course, this explains all of life in some ways, but I have to say, when you're single and you've decided—consciously or subconsciously—not to let anyone get too close, this isn't stuff you need to deal with very much. No one is there to say, "When you respond that way, it hurts me."

So, in a funny kind of way, it was with my marriage that my first true encounter with lament began. The good news, though, is that it is also with my marriage that my first true encounter with hope began: the hope of redemption and resurrection and restoration in and through Christ.

To explain what I mean, I need to tell a personal and painful story. Early in our marriage, my husband and I were out to dinner with some friends of his. He had been friends with them for many years, well before I was in the picture. I felt a little bit left out of the conversation at different points, when old times or old shared acquaintances came up, but tried to stay engaged by asking questions and releasing the internal tension I felt. Later we went home to my husband's house, where the furniture and walls and air felt and tasted of a whole life that was lived before I came along. As we got ready to go to bed, I began to feel a barrier slowly but unmistakably building inside me. In retrospect, I can identify this barrier as a way I was trying to protect myself from some perceived potential emotional harm.

But in the moment, it felt like anger and disconnection, and it seemed as though it were happening in slow motion. I was withdrawing from my husband emotionally and had neither the ability nor the desire to stay connected. Some hurt deep inside me was so powerfully trying to protect itself that I had no capacity to stop it.

Lying there that night with an insurmountable wall around my heart toward the one person I knew was committed to me and loved me, I came face to face with all the broken pieces within me. The thoughts circled around in my head, one after another: *What if he wants his old life back? What if what was—his life before me—was better and he secretly longs for what he had instead of what we have together? I am not good enough. He doesn't really want me. He will leave me. I deserve to be left. I don't deserve to be loved. I'm not worth it.* Writing these words even now causes a tight ball to form in my gut, and my breathing to become shallow, so painful and deeply felt are these ideas. That night tears ran down my face and I begged God for his help. I couldn't see a way forward. I felt embarrassed and ashamed. If this wall was going to, seemingly without my permission, erect itself with such speed and effectiveness, what could I possibly do? I wouldn't be able to love my husband the way I desired to, the way I promised him I would. I could do nothing except cry out to God in sadness and pain.

Over the next few days, still raw from having faced myself so fully, I noticed that a sense of hope began to replace the despair I was feeling. I knew for certain I could not heal myself. There was no number of thought exercises I could do or books I could read that could come close to helping me. I needed to surrender myself anew to God's care. I believed I had done this before, but the gut-wrenching truth was that I still hadn't given myself fully over. I had held back, whether knowingly or not. Now God was asking me to open the deepest part of me, the most hurt part, and let him heal me. As my soul said yes, my mind filled with God's promises: "My grace is sufficient for you. I began this work in you, and I will finish it. I am with you. I will not leave you. I will strengthen you and uphold you. I will meet your need according to the riches of my glory in Christ Jesus. I am making all things new."[7]

I don't know your experience—whether you've faced your brokenness in this heart-wrenching, soul-disturbing way. Not everyone's journey to and through lament is the same. I do wish this for you, though, as cruel as it may sound. Lament over what has been broken in you because of either what someone else did to you or what you've done to yourself—or some combination—opens space for the hope of Christ to break in and heal you and make you whole again. So I pray this for you: I pray that God would give you eyes to see your desperate need for him to heal you and bring you into your full, whole self—your restored, resurrected self.

Reading through the Scriptures might not actually trigger lament in you. But my prayer is that as you read the prayers of lament over the next fifteen days, whether personal prayers or prayers for the world, God would slowly open you to seeing the places where you feel triggered and lash out, withdraw, or seek out coping strategies to avoid pain. Whether we are lamenting our own brokenness or the brokenness of the world, the desire is the same: that God might lead us into the hope we have in Jesus Christ, the redeemer and healer of all things.

PERSONAL LAMENT

IF WE'RE PAYING attention, we will have daily opportunities to face our own flaws and weaknesses. Whether it's in relationship with our spouses, children, friends, or coworkers, we will lash out, harbor resentment, or feel wounded by even a slight offense. Some seasons are worse than others for various reasons, but at times we may feel exhausted by our own brokenness and inability to act rightly toward those we love. In those moments, God invites us to cry out to him and share with him the shame and pain we feel. Our temptation is to close down and hide, and we might even excuse ourselves by saying that God already knows everything. Although this is true, expressing our hearts to him and speaking honestly about both our wounds and our sin allows healing to begin.

In addition, we have been hurt and continue to be pressed on all sides because of the brokenness of the world and those around us. Things are not as they should be. We desire relationships and experiences that do not fall within God's will for us, and the gap between our desires and his grows painful and obvious. Scripture teaches us that we can express our desires, heartache, and missed expectations to God. He listens and mourns with us. And he doesn't leave us there but rather moves us toward hope by reminding us of his love for us, his desire that we would be whole and healed, and his unrelenting faithfulness to bring us into the fullness of Christ.

Let us name and grieve the personal pain and despair we feel over our own flaws and failures and simultaneously open ourselves, as much as possible, to what God may have for us as we explore and lament our brokenness, sin, unmet desires, and inability to pray what Jesus prayed in the garden of Gethsemane: "Not my will, but yours be done" (Luke 22:42, NIV). God will point us toward the hope of Christ to redeem, heal, and restore. May we be open to this hope.

I AM WORN OUT FROM SOBBING

a prayer to open

In the midst of my pain, Lord, I cry out to you.
When darkness sets in and I can't see the light,
lead me in the way of hope, and fill my heart with joy.

READ PSALM 6 _____

O LORD, don't rebuke me in your anger
  or discipline me in your rage.
Have compassion on me, LORD, for I am weak.
  Heal me, LORD, for my bones are in agony.
I am sick at heart.
  How long, O LORD, until you restore me?
Return, O LORD, and rescue me.
  Save me because of your unfailing love.
For the dead do not remember you.
  Who can praise you from the grave?
I am worn out from sobbing.

All night I flood my bed with weeping,
  drenching it with my tears.
My vision is blurred by grief;
  my eyes are worn out because of all my
  enemies.
Go away, all you who do evil,
  for the LORD has heard my weeping.
The LORD has heard my plea;
  the LORD will answer my prayer.
May all my enemies be disgraced and terrified.
  May they suddenly turn back in shame.

REFLECT _____

When we are overwhelmed by our own brokenness or weakness, we can tend to think that God has turned away from us, left us to suffer on our own. We must rely on what we know to be true instead of what we are feeling in the moment: God is near, sustaining and allowing for every breath; his ear is bent toward us even as we imagine him leaning away.

- Review the opening verses of today's psalm. Where are you feeling weak and in need of God's compassion? Where do you need his healing and restoration?

- Now review the next verses and remember God's unfailing love for you. What is true about him? Consider simply repeating the prayer we prayed each day in the "Rooted" section: "I am loved. I am known. I belong to you."

- Finally, review the closing verses. What negative and untrue thoughts plague you in your weakness and seek to turn you away from God or cause you to doubt his love for you? Ask the Holy Spirit to help you see the lies you are believing and empower you to rest in what's true.

RESPOND _____

Have compassion on me, Lord, for I am weak.
Heal me, Lord, for my bones are in agony.
Restore me, Lord, so my heart will be whole.

SIN HAS DRAINED MY STRENGTH

a prayer to open

In the midst of my pain, Lord, I cry out to you.
When darkness sets in and I can't see the light,
lead me in the way of hope, and fill my heart with joy.

READ PSALM 31:9-15

Have mercy on me, LORD, for I am in distress.
Tears blur my eyes.
My body and soul are withering away.
I am dying from grief;
my years are shortened by sadness.
Sin has drained my strength;
I am wasting away from within.
I am scorned by all my enemies
and despised by my neighbors—
even my friends are afraid to come near me.
When they see me on the street,
they run the other way.

I am ignored as if I were dead,
as if I were a broken pot.
I have heard the many rumors about me,
and I am surrounded by terror.
My enemies conspire against me,
plotting to take my life.
But I am trusting you, O LORD,
saying, "You are my God!"
My future is in your hands.
Rescue me from those who hunt me down
relentlessly.

REFLECT

Facing our own sinfulness can be one of the most painful experiences of our lives. Often we ignore or justify. Sometimes we repent and deal with our sin in a healthy way that acknowledges our wrongdoing and God's grace. Other times—and it's usually when we find ourselves sinning in the same way over and over—we are laid low. We see our sin and simply cannot seem to act differently. We see the consequences and cannot get ourselves to change. In these moments, we must remember what's true: God is faithful to forgive.

- Review the first verses of today's reading. Reflect on whether any sin—past or present—is affecting your strength and ability to fully embrace the life Christ offers. What do you need to confess? Over what sin do you need the assurance of forgiveness?

- Now review the next verses. What consequences of your own sin are you experiencing in your life right now?

- Finally, review the last verses. In what ways are you tempted to doubt God's forgiveness and grace? Ask the Holy Spirit to help you grow in trusting God so you may turn to him with full confidence that your sin has been forgiven.

RESPOND

My life is in your hands, O Lord.
Rescue, forgive, and redeem me.
My trust is in you alone.

Heard

•

HOW LONG WILL YOU FORGET ME?

a prayer to open

In the midst of my pain, Lord, I cry out to you.
When darkness sets in and I can't see the light,
lead me in the way of hope, and fill my heart with joy.

READ PSALM 13

O LORD, how long will you forget me? Forever?
How long will you look the other way?
How long must I struggle with anguish in my soul,
with sorrow in my heart every day?
How long will my enemy have the upper hand?
Turn and answer me, O LORD my God!

Restore the sparkle to my eyes, or I will die.
Don't let my enemies gloat, saying, "We have defeated him!"
Don't let them rejoice at my downfall.
But I trust in your unfailing love.
I will rejoice because you have rescued me.
I will sing to the LORD
because he is good to me.

REFLECT

We all long to hear from God; we ask him to guide us, speak words of love and assurance to us, help us in our decisions, lead us in his ways. And there are times when the Scriptures seem to resonate so deeply and specifically or the sermons we hear seem meant by God for us alone. The way the sun alights on the water can be his personalized gift to us at times. But sometimes nothing seems to get in; we sense only his silence or absence. We grow anxious, doubtful, and shaken. The psalmist reminds us of what's true: God's love does not fail and he is good.

- Review the opening verses of today's psalm. In what area of your life are you longing to hear from God but hear only silence? What fears or anxieties does that unmet longing give rise to in you?

- Now review the next verses. What do you need in order to restore your confidence in God's love for you and constant presence with you? Ask him for what you need.

- Finally, review the closing verses. What are five to ten ways God has been good to you in your life? Allow whatever you identified to remind you of his goodness and faithfulness.

RESPOND

Answer my prayer and plea, O Lord my God.
Help me trust in your unfailing love and
rejoice because you have rescued me.
You have been good to me.

WHY HAVE YOU ABANDONED ME?

a prayer to open

In the midst of my pain, Lord, I cry out to you.
When darkness sets in and I can't see the light,
lead me in the way of hope, and fill my heart with joy.

READ PSALM 22:1-11

My God, my God, why have you abandoned
me?
Why are you so far away when I groan for
help?
Every day I call to you, my God, but you do not
answer.
Every night I lift my voice, but I find no relief.
Yet you are holy,
enthroned on the praises of Israel.
Our ancestors trusted in you,
and you rescued them.
They cried out to you and were saved.
They trusted in you and were never disgraced.
But I am a worm and not a man.
I am scorned and despised by all!

Everyone who sees me mocks me.
They sneer and shake their heads, saying,
"Is this the one who relies on the LORD?
Then let the LORD save him!
If the LORD loves him so much,
let the LORD rescue him!"
Yet you brought me safely from my mother's
womb
and led me to trust you at my mother's breast.
I was thrust into your arms at my birth.
You have been my God from the moment I
was born.
Do not stay so far from me,
for trouble is near,
and no one else can help me.

REFLECT

Jesus uttered the first line of this psalm on the cross. Having only ever experienced full communion with the Father and the Spirit, Jesus felt forsaken and alone. Though he suffered physically, emotionally, and relationally as he made his way to the cross, this sense of abandonment by the Father and Spirit must have been the darkest, most terrifying moment. And yet, for us, this is the beginning of restoration and hope. By overcoming darkness and death, Jesus gave us light and life. When we feel alone and abandoned, we must remember what's true: Because of Jesus, we are not far from God. In fact, as Paul said, our very lives are "hidden with Christ in God" (Colossians 3:3).

- Review the first verses of today's reading. In what area of your life do you feel most alone? What would not being alone look like?

- Now review the next verses. What do you know to be true of God and how he has acted throughout history and in your life?

- Finally, review the last verses. How are you longing to experience God right now? Express your desire to him, remembering that you are in his loving presence whether you sense it or not.

Heard

•

371

Do not stay so far from me, loving God.
Draw near; come close.
No one else can help me.
You have been my God from my beginning.

DAY 5

I HAVE SO MANY ENEMIES

a prayer to open

In the midst of my pain, Lord, I cry out to you.
When darkness sets in and I can't see the light,
lead me in the way of hope, and fill my heart with joy.

READ PSALM 3

O LORD, I have so many enemies;
  so many are against me.
So many are saying,
  "God will never rescue him!"
But you, O LORD, are a shield around me;
  you are my glory, the one who holds my head
    high.
I cried out to the LORD,
  and he answered me from his holy mountain.
I lay down and slept,

yet I woke up in safety,
  for the LORD was watching over me.
I am not afraid of ten thousand enemies
  who surround me on every side.
Arise, O LORD!
  Rescue me, my God!
Slap all my enemies in the face!
  Shatter the teeth of the wicked!
Victory comes from you, O LORD.
  May you bless your people.

REFLECT

The English language is full of idioms that describe that feeling we all get from time to time of being surrounded on all sides—when nothing is going our way. Just to name a few: "when it rains, it pours," "waiting for the other shoe to drop," "the hits just keep on coming," and "I can't catch a break." How do we keep our heads up in these seasons? How do we remain hopeful? We remember what's true: God sustains; God shields; God saves.

- Review the opening verses of today's psalm. In what area of your life do you feel you are being attacked, whether by people, by your own thoughts, or on a spiritual level?

- Now review the next verses. Read them slowly, reflecting on whatever came to mind in response to the first question. What is God saying to you through these verses?

- Finally, review the closing verses. What would rescue from your enemies or attackers look like? What are you longing for God to do? What do you sense him calling you to do?

SACRED QUESTIONS

Lord, I have so many enemies.
Rescue me. Give me strength.
Be my shield and my hope all the days of my life.

MY BODY IS SICK

a prayer to open

In the midst of my pain, Lord, I cry out to you.
When darkness sets in and I can't see the light,
lead me in the way of hope, and fill my heart with joy.

READ PSALM 38

O LORD, don't rebuke me in your anger
  or discipline me in your rage!
Your arrows have struck deep,
  and your blows are crushing me.
Because of your anger, my whole body is sick;
  my health is broken because of my sins.
My guilt overwhelms me—
  it is a burden too heavy to bear.
My wounds fester and stink
  because of my foolish sins.
I am bent over and racked with pain.
  All day long I walk around filled with grief.
A raging fever burns within me,
  and my health is broken.
I am exhausted and completely crushed.
  My groans come from an anguished heart.
You know what I long for, Lord;
  you hear my every sigh.
My heart beats wildly, my strength fails,
  and I am going blind.
My loved ones and friends stay away, fearing
    my disease.
  Even my own family stands at a distance.
Meanwhile, my enemies lay traps to kill me.

Those who wish me harm make plans to ruin
    me.
  All day long they plan their treachery.
But I am deaf to all their threats.
  I am silent before them as one who cannot
    speak.
I choose to hear nothing,
  and I make no reply.
For I am waiting for you, O LORD.
  You must answer for me, O Lord my God.
I prayed, "Don't let my enemies gloat over me
  or rejoice at my downfall."
I am on the verge of collapse,
  facing constant pain.
But I confess my sins;
  I am deeply sorry for what I have done.
I have many aggressive enemies;
  they hate me without reason.
They repay me evil for good
  and oppose me for pursuing good.
Do not abandon me, O LORD.
  Do not stand at a distance, my God.
Come quickly to help me,
  O Lord my savior.

REFLECT

The psalmist's words are extreme and attribute his physical illness to sin. Although sickness and disease might not be attributable to a particular sin, these things are the product of sin in the world. Sin and death are the precise maladies Jesus came to save us from, and he is even now working to bring healing and wholeness to all things, including our bodies. But before our full restoration, our bodies hurt,

Heard

•

weaken, and ultimately fail. To face this truth is often the most difficult thing we do in our lives, yet the truth is that we will receive new, glorified, everlasting bodies (see 1 Corinthians 15:35-58). Until then, we must rely on God's promises and presence to sustain us.

- Review the opening verses of today's psalm. What pain, sickness, or disease in your body are you longing for God to heal? What frustration do you need to express to him about that bodily suffering?

- Now review the next verses. In what ways do you feel as if your family and friends are lacking in empathy and sympathy for the pain you are suffering in your body? How might your experience inform the way you empathize with others experiencing physical suffering? Who comes to mind as someone who's suffering physically?

- Finally, review the closing verses. What is your plea to God in the midst of the pain you are experiencing? What is your hope?

RESPOND_____

Answer my prayer, Lord.
Heal my pain and suffering.
Don't abandon me or leave me alone.
Come quickly to help me, my healer.

DAY 7

I B U R S T I N T O T E A R S

a prayer to open

In the midst of my pain, Lord, I cry out to you.
When darkness sets in and I can't see the light,
lead me in the way of hope, and fill my heart with joy.

READ GENESIS 21:8-20_____

When Isaac grew up and was about to be weaned, Abraham prepared a huge feast to celebrate the occasion. But Sarah saw Ishmael—the son of Abraham and her Egyptian servant Hagar—making fun of her son, Isaac. So she turned to Abraham and demanded, "Get rid of that slave woman and her son. He is not going to share the inheritance with my son, Isaac. I won't have it!"

This upset Abraham very much because Ishmael was his son. But God told Abraham, "Do not be upset over the boy and your servant. Do whatever

Sarah tells you, for Isaac is the son through whom your descendants will be counted. But I will also make a nation of the descendants of Hagar's son because he is your son, too."

So Abraham got up early the next morning, prepared food and a container of water, and strapped them on Hagar's shoulders. Then he sent her away with their son, and she wandered aimlessly in the wilderness. . . .

When the water was gone, she put the boy in the shade of a bush. Then she went and sat down by herself about a hundred yards away. "I don't want to watch the boy die," she said, as she burst into tears.

But God heard the boy crying, and the angel of God called to Hagar from heaven, "Hagar, what's wrong? Do not be afraid! God has heard the boy crying as he lies there. Go to him and comfort him, for I will make a great nation from his descendants."

Then God opened Hagar's eyes, and she saw a well full of water. She quickly filled her water container and gave the boy a drink.

And God was with the boy as he grew up in the wilderness.

REFLECT

There are times when all we can do is burst into tears out of despair and distress. Hagar's experience as told in this passage from Genesis certainly falls into that category. What more could she do? She had no ability to change her circumstances, and all she could see in her future were a dead son, a lifetime of begging, and everything else a dismissed slave woman would face. She was without hope and could do nothing more than cry tears of anguish. In the midst of her agony, though, God acted to relieve her suffering and filled her with hope and life again.

- Reflect on a time when you were in utter despair and could do nothing more than burst into tears. What do you remember about God's presence during that time? How did he restore you to hope and life?

- What loss or experience might you need to grieve that you've previously avoided or suppressed? What fears do you have about lamenting that experience or loss?

- In what area of your life are you longing for renewed hope and life? What is your prayer?

RESPOND

Open my eyes to your presence, Lord.
Heal what's broken.
Fill me with hope and life again.

TAKE THIS CUP FROM ME

a prayer to open

In the midst of my pain, Lord, I cry out to you.
When darkness sets in and I can't see the light,
lead me in the way of hope, and fill my heart with joy.

READ LUKE 22:39-46

Accompanied by the disciples, Jesus left the upstairs room and went as usual to the Mount of Olives. There he told them, "Pray that you will not give in to temptation."

Heard

375

He walked away . . . and knelt down and prayed, "Father, if you are willing, please take this cup of suffering away from me. Yet I want your will to be done, not mine." Then an angel from heaven appeared and strengthened him. He prayed more fervently, and he was in such agony of spirit that his sweat fell to the ground like great drops of blood.

At last he stood up again and returned to the disciples, only to find them asleep, exhausted from grief. "Why are you sleeping?" he asked them. "Get up and pray, so that you will not give in to temptation."

REFLECT

Jesus' experience in the garden of Gethsemane just before he would be crucified is a painful, agonizing picture of a desire for things to be other than they were. Jesus prayed that the Father would find another way for humanity to be saved and redeemed. His despair was so deep that his body bled and his soul was in anguish. But he didn't allow the pain he felt to overcome his trust in the Father. He didn't allow his desire to be relieved of his calling to overtake his desire to do God's will. Rather, he opened himself to the Spirit to be strengthened and prepared to resist the temptation to exert his own will: "Not my will, but yours be done" (verse 42, NIV).

- In what area of your life do you see a gap between your own desire and God's desire for you? What does lamenting that gap look like if you use Jesus as your model?

- In what ways do you need the Holy Spirit to strengthen you and prepare you to resist the temptation to exert your will rather than trust God's will?

- Jesus invited his closest friends to go with him and pray. Who can you invite into your deepest struggle right now? In light of what is reflected in today's passage, how might you invite them to pray?

RESPOND

Father, if you are willing, take this cup from me; yet not my will, but yours be done.
Not my will, but yours be done.
May your will be done.

LAMENT FOR THE WORLD

It is easy to look out into the world and see what's wrong. Wars rage, disease and hunger run rampant, corruption reigns, natural disasters strike unsuspecting people and places without restraint. We call out to God to rescue us from this earth that seems to be filled with sin and disorder. Is it okay to wonder where he is and ask why so much suffering has to take place? Can it really be true that God loves the world? Can we believe that he is redeeming and restoring and working to make all things new? The Bible is rife with examples of the psalmists and prophets calling out to God with their questions, fears, and even demands for justice to be done; for the unrighteous to be punished; and for evil to be defeated. In our day, living in the tension between the Kingdom as it is present now and as it is yet to come, we know the outcome and see glimpses of what's coming, but we still live in a time of such brokenness and sin. But something has been revealed to us that the prophets and psalmists did not know: that in Jesus Christ, God has acted and revealed his plan and purposes that he's had since the foundation of the earth. In Christ, sin and death have been defeated and are on their way out, never to be seen again. Life has entered, resurrection is coming, and eternal life in God's presence and light is our future.

Let us authentically and fully lament the state of the world and yet still hold on to the hope we have in Christ. We'll open our eyes to the ways God is already working to right all wrongs and allow our sadness over the current state of things to lead us to a place of hope and action. May we be open to this hope.

HOW LONG WILL YOU DELAY?

a prayer to open   In the midst of the pain in the world, Lord, I cry out to you.
When darkness overwhelms and the light has faded,
lead me in the way of hope, and grant me eyes to see your goodness.

READ PSALM 90:13-17

O LORD, come back to us!
How long will you delay?
Take pity on your servants!
Satisfy us each morning with your unfailing
love,
so we may sing for joy to the end of our lives.
Give us gladness in proportion to our former
misery!

Replace the evil years with good.
Let us, your servants, see you work
again;
let our children see your glory.
And may the Lord our God show us his
approval
and make our efforts successful.
Yes, make our efforts successful!

REFLECT

Don't you ever want to scream out, "Enough! Relent! We give up! We give in! No more!" This is the psalmist's impulse. He has seen the pain and suffering in the world and begs God for compassion and mercy. At times this is our only option. When bad things happen, we want to act and relieve suffering, and of course God calls us to do this. There are situations, though, when we simply cannot relieve suffering; no action we take and no solution we bring can heal. Knowing that the world is plagued by sin, we can ask for God's small mercies and for him to show us glimpses of the Kingdom in our midst and yet to come.

Heard

•

- As you read today's lament, what world issue or problem came to mind? If you feel the Holy Spirit leading you to do so, spend time personalizing this lament. Pray the words as your own.

- As you consider more closely whatever world issue or problem came to mind for you as you read, where do you see good, compassion, or glimpses of God at work even in the midst of that problem?

- How is God calling you to participate in what he's doing to restore and redeem people and the rest of creation in the problem or issue you have identified?

RESPOND⎯⎯⎯⎯⎯⎯⎯⎯⎯⎯⎯⎯⎯⎯⎯⎯⎯⎯⎯⎯⎯⎯⎯⎯

God, remind us of your unfailing love and fill us with your Spirit. Give us gladness of heart. Let us see you at work in our world today, and don't delay. Let our children see you at work. Don't give up on us! Come, Lord Jesus.

DAY 10

WHY DO YOU IGNORE OUR SUFFERING?

a prayer to open   In the midst of the pain in the world, Lord, I cry out to you.
When darkness overwhelms and the light has faded,
lead me in the way of hope, and grant me eyes to see your goodness.

READ PSALM 44:23-26 ⎯⎯⎯⎯⎯⎯⎯⎯⎯⎯⎯⎯⎯⎯⎯⎯⎯⎯⎯⎯

Wake up, O Lord! Why do you sleep?
  Get up! Do not reject us forever.
Why do you look the other way?
  Why do you ignore our suffering and
    oppression?

We collapse in the dust,
  lying face down in the dirt.
Rise up! Help us!
  Ransom us because of your
    unfailing love.

REFLECT ⎯⎯⎯⎯⎯⎯⎯⎯⎯⎯⎯⎯⎯⎯⎯⎯⎯⎯⎯⎯⎯⎯⎯

Suffering is universal, but some people and places in the world suffer without relief. Their hurting never abates. Generation after generation is ravaged by hunger or war or oppression or disease. If you've been to any of these places rife with suffering, you know that many people in seemingly dark and desperate situations are still filled with joy, find great purpose in their circumstances, and feel loved by God. How is this possible? What can be learned from this?

- As you read today's lament, what people group or place came to mind? If you feel the Holy Spirit leading you in this direction, spend time simply making this lament on behalf of that people or place. Pray the words as your own.

- As you consider more closely whatever people group or place came to mind for you as you read, where do you see good, compassion, or glimpses of God at work even in the midst of such difficult circumstances?

- How is God calling you to participate in what he's doing to restore and redeem the people or place you have identified?

RESPOND

God, we are longing for your return and full restoration. Come quickly! Help us! Don't let us be crushed under the weight of the sinfulness and brokenness of this world. Come, Lord Jesus.

WHO CAN HEAL US?

a prayer to open In the midst of the pain in the world, Lord, I cry out to you. When darkness overwhelms and the light has faded, lead me in the way of hope, and grant me eyes to see your goodness.

READ LAMENTATIONS 2:11-22

I have cried until the tears no longer come;
  my heart is broken.
My spirit is poured out in agony
  as I see the desperate plight of my people.
Little children and tiny babies
  are fainting and dying in the streets.
They cry out to their mothers,
  "We need food and drink!"
Their lives ebb away in the streets
  like the life of a warrior wounded in battle.
They gasp for life
  as they collapse in their mothers' arms.
What can I say about you?
  Who has ever seen such sorrow?
O daughter of Jerusalem,
  to what can I compare your anguish?
O virgin daughter of Zion,
  how can I comfort you?
For your wound is as deep as the sea.
  Who can heal you?
Your prophets have said
  so many foolish things, false to the core.
They did not save you from exile
  by pointing out your sins.
Instead, they painted false pictures,
  filling you with false hope. . . .
All your enemies mock you.

They scoff and snarl and say,
  "We have destroyed her at last!
We have long waited for this day,
  and it is finally here!"
But it is the LORD who did just as he
    planned.
  He has fulfilled the promises of disaster
  he made long ago.
He has destroyed Jerusalem without mercy.
  He has caused her enemies to gloat over her
  and has given them power over her.
Cry aloud before the Lord,
  O walls of beautiful Jerusalem!
Let your tears flow like a river
  day and night.
Give yourselves no rest;
  give your eyes no relief.
Rise during the night and cry out.
  Pour out your hearts like water to the Lord.
Lift up your hands to him in prayer. . . .
"O LORD, think about this!
  Should you treat your own people this way?
Should mothers eat their own children,
  those they once bounced on their knees?
Should priests and prophets be killed
  within the Lord's Temple?
See them lying in the streets . . .

Heard

•

379

killed by the swords of the enemy.
You have killed them in your anger,
slaughtering them without mercy.
You have invited terrors from all around. . . .

In the day of the LORD's anger,
no one has escaped or survived.
The enemy has killed all the children
whom I carried and raised."

REFLECT _____

Jeremiah, the author of Lamentations, wept for the torment his people experienced. But he also suffered along with them. He didn't cry out to God from afar; he got close and identified personally with their pain and suffering. As followers of Jesus, we have the Holy Spirit within us and can be ambassadors of Christ's presence and comfort. But do we get close enough?

- As you read today's lament, who came to mind? Is there a group of people near you who suffer from a particular kind of pain? If you feel the Holy Spirit leading you to do so, spend time making Jeremiah's lament on behalf of the people you thought of. Pray the words as your own.

- As you consider more closely the suffering of those who came to mind for you as you read, how might you get close enough to be an ambassador of Christ?

- How is God calling you to participate in what he's doing to restore and redeem the suffering of the people you have identified?

RESPOND _____

God, we are crying out to you with broken hearts and anguished souls. We see the suffering all around us: starving children, dying parents, endless oppression. Save us! Come, Lord Jesus.

DAY 12

HOW LONG WILL THE WICKED BE ALLOWED TO GLOAT?

a prayer to open

In the midst of my pain, Lord, I cry out to you.
When darkness overwhelms and the light has faded,
lead me in the way of hope, and grant me eyes to see your goodness.

READ PSALM 94:1-15 _____

O LORD, the God of vengeance,
　O God of vengeance, let your glorious justice
　　shine forth!
Arise, O Judge of the earth.
　Give the proud what they deserve.

How long, O LORD?
　How long will the wicked be allowed to gloat?
How long will they speak with arrogance?
　How long will these evil people boast?
They crush your people, LORD,

hurting those you claim as your own.
They kill widows and foreigners
and murder orphans.
"The LORD isn't looking," they say,
"and besides, the God of Israel doesn't care."
Think again, you fools!
When will you finally catch on?
Is he deaf—the one who made your ears?
Is he blind—the one who formed your eyes?
He punishes the nations—won't he also
punish you?
He knows everything—doesn't he also know
what you are doing?

The LORD knows people's thoughts;
he knows they are worthless!
Joyful are those you discipline, LORD,
those you teach with your instructions.
You give them relief from troubled times
until a pit is dug to capture the wicked.
The LORD will not reject his people;
he will not abandon his special
possession.
Judgment will again be founded on justice,
and those with virtuous hearts will pursue it.

REFLECT _____

We see victims of suffering, hardship, oppression, and injustice. What about the oppressors and perpetrators? They too are something we can lament. So often it seems as if the unjust, bullies, and oppressors are holding their heads high and being lifted up for their evil acts. Psalm 94 teaches us to call out to God in the face of evil and ask *him* to make things right. As for us, we are not to repay evil with evil or take revenge but rather to overcome evil with good (see Romans 12:19-21).

• As you read today's lament, who came to mind? Pray the words as your own.

• As you consider more closely the perpetrators of hurt, oppression, and injustice in our day, what vengeful or vindictive thoughts or actions (even if minor) do you need to confess or seek forgiveness for?

• How is God calling you to participate in what he's doing to restore and redeem even the oppressors and perpetrators of harm in our world?

RESPOND _____

God, grant us relief from the wicked. Disempower people who oppress, demean, and enslave. Look upon us with compassion and grace. Let your justice reign! Restore us all! Come, Lord Jesus.

DAY 13

HOW LONG WILL YOU BE ANGRY WITH OUR PRAYERS?

a prayer to open
In the midst of the pain in the world, Lord, I cry out to you.
When darkness overwhelms and the light has faded,
lead me in the way of hope, and grant me eyes to see your goodness.

Heard

•

Please listen, O Shepherd of Israel,
  you who lead Joseph's descendants like a
    flock.
O God, enthroned above the cherubim,
  display your radiant glory
  to Ephraim, Benjamin, and Manasseh.
Show us your mighty power.
  Come to rescue us!
Turn us again to yourself, O God.
  Make your face shine down upon us.
  Only then will we be saved.

O LORD God of Heaven's Armies,
  how long will you be angry with our prayers?
You have fed us with sorrow
  and made us drink tears by the bucketful.
You have made us the scorn of neighboring
    nations.
  Our enemies treat us as a joke.
Turn us again to yourself, O God of Heaven's
    Armies.
  Make your face shine down upon us.
  Only then will we be saved.

REFLECT _____

What does it mean when our prayers go unanswered? Has God turned away from us because of something we've done? Has he closed his ears to our voices so he can no longer hear? Is he angry at all of humanity and deciding to take a break? Seemingly unanswered or ignored requests are among the most difficult things for us to understand and come to grips with. From our vantage point, there are prayers we say that God couldn't possibly ignore or deny, yet we do not see the outcome we desire: A disaster strikes, war breaks out, masses of people are displaced. As John did in Revelation, we can only cry out to Jesus, "Come!" (Revelation 22:17). He responds, "Yes, I am coming soon" (verse 20).

- As you read today's lament, what suffering that you've prayed against came to mind? If you feel the Holy Spirit leading you to do so, spend time simply making this lament specific to the prayers you've prayed. Pray the words as your own.

- As you consider more closely whatever area of suffering you have prayed against, where do you see good, compassion, or glimpses of God at work even in the midst of that suffering?

- How is God calling you to participate in what he's doing to restore and redeem our suffering world even as your specific prayers aren't resulting in the outcome you desire?

RESPOND _____

God, bend your ear to us. Don't allow our sorrow to swallow us whole. Make your face shine down upon us. Turn us again to yourself. Come and rescue us! Come, Lord Jesus.

WHERE IS YOUR JUSTICE?

a prayer to open

In the midst of the pain in the world, Lord, I cry out to you.
When darkness overwhelms and the light has faded,
lead me in the way of hope, and grant me eyes to see your goodness.

READ PSALM 58

Justice—do you rulers know the meaning of the
word?
Do you judge the people fairly?
No! You plot injustice in your hearts.
You spread violence throughout the land.
These wicked people are born sinners;
even from birth they have lied and gone their
own way.
They spit venom like deadly snakes;
they are like cobras that refuse to listen,
ignoring the tunes of the snake charmers,
no matter how skillfully they play.
Break off their fangs, O God!
Smash the jaws of these lions, O LORD!
May they disappear like water into thirsty
ground.

Make their weapons useless in their hands.
May they be like snails that dissolve into slime,
like a stillborn child who will never see
the sun.
God will sweep them away, both young and
old,
faster than a pot heats over burning thorns.
The godly will rejoice when they see injustice
avenged.
They will wash their feet in the blood of the
wicked.
Then at last everyone will say,
"There truly is a reward for those who live for
God;
surely there is a God who judges justly here
on earth."

REFLECT

Our world needs kind, humble, and strong leaders who maintain order, empower
and encourage people to be and do their best for the common good, and ensure
that systems and infrastructures work and don't act as tools of oppression. So
often we experience just the opposite: government, business, community, and
even church leaders whose hunger for power, self-interest, and greed incapacitates
them from leading well and ends in hurt, violence, mismanagement, or all three.
We can hardly imagine, most of us, being led by loving, wise, and Christ-centered
women and men. We see so few examples. As we await the arrival of our true King,
may God give us more leaders after his own heart.

- As you read today's lament, what leader came to mind? If you feel the Holy
  Spirit leading you to do so, spend time simply making this lament on behalf
  of whomever that leader leads. Pray the words as your own.

- As you consider more closely the leader that came to mind for you as you
  read, where do you see God at work even in the midst of that leader's
  deficiencies or brokenness?

- How is God calling you to participate in drawing out goodness and equity
  from our leaders?

Heard

God, we long for your justice in this world. Save us from injustice and unfair rulers and governors. Make what is wrong right again. Restore goodness and righteousness. Come, Lord Jesus.

DO YOU NOT LISTEN?

a prayer to open

In the midst of the pain in the world, Lord, I cry out to you.
When darkness overwhelms and the light has faded,
lead me in the way of hope, and grant me eyes to see your goodness.

READ HABAKKUK 1:1-4

This is the message that the prophet Habakkuk received in a vision.

How long, O LORD, must I call for help?
 But you do not listen!
"Violence is everywhere!" I cry,
 but you do not come to save.
Must I forever see these evil deeds?
 Why must I watch all this misery?

Wherever I look,
 I see destruction and violence.
I am surrounded by people
 who love to argue and fight.
The law has become paralyzed,
 and there is no justice in the courts.
The wicked far outnumber the righteous,
 so that justice has become perverted.

REFLECT

It is no stretch to feel the pain of Habakkuk's complaint about violence and conflict in his world. Ours is rife with the same things that made him cry out to God. But something—someone—has happened since Habakkuk's time: Jesus! The Kingdom of God has arrived, albeit not fully. We see evidence of the Kingdom that Habakkuk could not have seen. Jesus—the long-awaited, anticipated Messiah and King—has overcome sin and death and now reigns. So although certain things in this world may look similar, a coup has occurred and all things are being made new. We might not always have eyes to see what God is doing, but we can follow Habakkuk's lead: "I will rejoice in the LORD, I will be joyful in God my Savior" (Habakkuk 3:18, NIV).

- As you read today's lament, what violent situation or injustice in the world came to mind? Pray the words as your own.

- As you consider more closely whatever violent situation or injustice came to mind for you as you read, where do you see evidence that God's Kingdom is breaking in and that love is more powerful than evil?

- How is God calling you to participate in what he's doing to restore and redeem this world even as violence and injustice persist?

RESPOND_____

God, we are calling out to you! Let us see your glory, love, and saving arm. Do not allow the destruction and wrongdoing of the wicked to overtake the world. Let us see your goodness! Come, Lord Jesus.

Amazed

Worshiping God for the Beauty of Creation

I REDISCOVERED THE beauty of nature a few years ago when I found myself out for a walk that was intended to clear my head after a full afternoon of writing. I needed some air, but I would never want to waste a moment, so as I walked out the door, I scrolled through available podcasts to find a thirty-minute talk. This way I could learn something as I walked. Thirty minutes would amount to four laps around the neighborhood pond at a good pace. About three minutes in, I did something I'd never done: I veered off the paved path into the damp grass and down to the reeds lining the water. From a distance the pond seemed choked by dull browns and harbingers of winter, my least favorite season. But as I got closer I discovered movement and breath and life. My eyes could not hold it all in a single glance. Every little detail demanded my attention: Cottony puffs sprouted out of large seed pockets, tiny flowers peeked from seemingly dead stalks, golden grasses bent in the wind, a dotted beetle tiptoed across a tree stump, and wispy snowflake blossoms bathed themselves in sunlight.

I couldn't help but touch these fall textures, and as I kneeled to run my fingers along a prickly shoot, a grasshopper leaped across my hand, startling me to laughter. In that moment, I realized how long it had been since I'd been out wandering, without a plan or stopwatch. I'd forgotten to be a stroller, or (as the French would say) a *flâneur*: someone who wanders to notice the small and hidden wonders. Instead, I'd been walking on the path, trying not to get my shoes muddy. I'd been on a schedule, accomplishing things. I started to consider what else I might have missed: in my daughter's eyes, in a friend's voice, or within my soul.

What I know for sure is that God's glorious and intricate creation does not impose itself on us very often. Sure, there is the harvest moon that practically takes your breath away as it floats at the horizon. Autumn trees showing off their dazzling reds might as well yell out for attention as you pass. But for the most part, nature is subtle and quiet, waiting for us to come out and wander around. Creation beckons us, but only as a whisper or a soft lullaby. There is just so much to see and take in, from the veins running along the smallest leaf to the bees hovering above blossoms in the sun to complex root systems of countless trees finding their way to drink and be nourished. It is a feast for the soul and the senses. Even the invisible can stop us in our tracks—consider the wind and the smell of pine trees or the briny ocean.

Beauty surrounds us, whether in the songs of birds, the stars of the night sky, the giggles of children on the playground, or the eyes of a friend. It is easy to get caught up in our day-to-day lives—our to-do lists, agendas, and appointments—and forget that each landscape, animal, and person we encounter reveals the creativity and love of God. In this fifteen-day section, we open our eyes to the wonder of God, the Creator, and allow our hearts to worship him for the beauty of the world. We're going to be using a practice called *visio divina* (holy seeing). As author Adele Ahlberg Calhoun has said, this holy seeing enables us to "behold created beauty" and leads us to pray—and indeed, I would add, to worship.[8] Each day, we will open our time by reading Psalm 104, a stunning tribute and testimonial to creation. Then we will go outside and spend time reflecting on a particular aspect of nature as a way of allowing our senses and selves to be awakened to the wonder of our Creator and Sustainer.

May we not forget to go out wandering to delight in the small and hidden wonders. Not one of them came into being apart from the divine hand.

DAY 1

DAYLIGHT

READ PSALM 104

Let all that I am praise the LORD.
O LORD my God, how great you are!
  You are robed with honor and majesty.
  You are dressed in a robe of light.
You stretch out the starry curtain of the
    heavens;
  you lay out the rafters of your home in the rain
    clouds.
You make the clouds your chariot;
  you ride upon the wings of the wind.
The winds are your messengers;
  flames of fire are your servants.
You placed the world on its foundation
  so it would never be moved.
You clothed the earth with floods of water,

water that covered even the mountains.
At your command, the water fled;
  at the sound of your thunder, it hurried away.
Mountains rose and valleys sank
  to the levels you decreed.
Then you set a firm boundary for the seas,
  so they would never again cover the earth.
You make springs pour water into the ravines,
  so streams gush down from the mountains.
They provide water for all the animals,
  and the wild donkeys quench their thirst.
The birds nest beside the streams
  and sing among the branches of the trees.
You send rain on the mountains from your
    heavenly home,

and you fill the earth with the fruit of your
labor.
You cause grass to grow for the livestock
and plants for people to use.
You allow them to produce food from the
earth—
wine to make them glad,
olive oil to soothe their skin,
and bread to give them strength.
The trees of the LORD are well cared for—
the cedars of Lebanon that he planted.
There the birds make their nests,
and the storks make their homes in the
cypresses.
High in the mountains live the wild goats,
and the rocks form a refuge for the hyraxes.
You made the moon to mark the seasons,
and the sun knows when to set.
You send the darkness, and it becomes night,
when all the forest animals prowl about.
Then the young lions roar for their prey,
stalking the food provided by God.
At dawn they slink back
into their dens to rest.
Then people go off to their work,
where they labor until evening.
O LORD, what a variety of things you have
made!
In wisdom you have made them all.

The earth is full of your creatures.
Here is the ocean, vast and wide,
teeming with life of every kind,
both large and small.
See the ships sailing along,
and Leviathan, which you made to play in
the sea.
They all depend on you
to give them food as they need it.
When you supply it, they gather it.
You open your hand to feed them,
and they are richly satisfied.
But if you turn away from them, they panic.
When you take away their breath,
they die and turn again to dust.
When you give them your breath, life is created,
and you renew the face of the earth.
May the glory of the LORD continue forever!
The LORD takes pleasure in all he has made!
The earth trembles at his glance;
the mountains smoke at his touch.
I will sing to the LORD as long as I live.
I will praise my God to my last breath!
May all my thoughts be pleasing to him,
for I rejoice in the LORD.
Let all sinners vanish from the face of the earth;
let the wicked disappear forever.
Let all that I am praise the LORD.
Praise the LORD!

REFLECT_____

Movement #1

Go outside and find a place where you can stop and notice the daylight, whether
it's just casting out the darkness, at its peak for the day, or fading into night. For
about a minute, fix your gaze on one object illuminated by the daylight.

• What colors, shapes, and textures do you see? What do you smell as you
breathe deeply? What do you hear around you as you stand still?

• What emotions are stirred in you as you gaze at the object that has been
illuminated by the daylight?

Movement #2

Now allow your eyes to take in everything surrounding the one object you had
been focused on, noticing how that object fits into or compares to the whole.
Reflect on the whole for a moment.

- What is wondrous about the daylight today?
- What does focusing on the daylight lead you to pray? What do you want to say to God, the Creator?

A PRAYER TO CLOSE_____

I will sing to you, Lord, as long as I live. I will praise you to my last breath!
May all my thoughts be pleasing to you, for I rejoice in you, Lord, the Creator.

CLOUDS

a prayer to open

Awaken my senses to you, Lord.
Clear all distractions that rob me of your presence.
Remind me that you are the Creator and Sustainer of all things.
And may my heart be filled with wonder. Amen.

READ PSALM 104 (see pages 388–389)

REFLECT_____

Movement #1

Go outside and find a place where you can stop and stare up at the clouds, whether they are thick and billowy, dark and low hanging, or wispy across the sky. For about a minute, fix your gaze on one cloud.

- What colors, shapes, and textures do you see? What do you smell as you breathe deeply? What do you hear around you as you stand still?
- What emotions are stirred in you as you gaze at that particular cloud?

Movement #2

Now allow your eyes to take in as many clouds as you can see, noticing how the cloud you initially focused on fits into or compares to the whole. Reflect on the whole sky for a moment.

- What is wondrous about the clouds as you take them in today?
- What does focusing on the clouds lead you to pray? What do you want to say to God, the Creator?

A PRAYER TO CLOSE

I will sing to you, Lord, as long as I live. I will praise you to my last breath!
May all my thoughts be pleasing to you, for I rejoice in you, Lord, the Creator.

DAY 3

WATER

a prayer to open

Awaken my senses to you, Lord.
Clear all distractions that rob me of your presence.
Remind me that you are the Creator and Sustainer of all things.
And may my heart be filled with wonder. Amen.

READ PSALM 104 (see pages 388–389)

REFLECT

Movement #1

Go outside and find a place where you can stop and see water, whether it's a body of water, a rain puddle, or even water coming from a sprinkler or fountain. For about a minute, fix your gaze on one aspect of that water.

- What colors, shapes, and textures do you see? What do you smell as you breathe deeply? What do you hear around you as you stand still?

- What emotions are stirred in you as you gaze at that part of the water?

Movement #2

Now allow your eyes to take in as much of the water as you can see, noticing how the aspect of the water you initially focused on fits into or compares to the whole. Reflect on the whole collection of water for a moment.

- What is wondrous about this water that you see today?

- What does focusing on the water lead you to pray? What do you want to say to God, the Creator?

A PRAYER TO CLOSE

I will sing to you, Lord, as long as I live. I will praise you to my last breath!
May all my thoughts be pleasing to you, for I rejoice in you, Lord, the Creator.

Amazed

•

391

TREES

Awaken my senses to you, Lord.
Clear all distractions that rob me of your presence.
Remind me that you are the Creator and Sustainer of all things.
And may my heart be filled with wonder. Amen.

READ PSALM 104 (see pages 388–389)

REFLECT_____

Movement #1

Go outside and find a place where you can stop and examine a tree, whether it's in full blossom, beginning to change colors, bare for the winter, or springing to life. For about a minute, fix your gaze on one part of that tree.

- What colors, shapes, and textures do you see? What do you smell as you breathe deeply? What do you hear around you as you stand still?

- What emotions are stirred in you as you gaze at that particular part of the tree?

Movement #2

Now allow your eyes to take in the entire tree, noticing how the part you initially focused on fits into or compares to the whole. Reflect on the entire tree for a moment.

- What is wondrous about this tree that stands before you today?

- What does focusing on this tree lead you to pray? What do you want to say to God, the Creator?

A PRAYER TO CLOSE_____

I will sing to you, Lord, as long as I live. I will praise you to my last breath!
May all my thoughts be pleasing to you, for I rejoice in you, Lord, the Creator.

ANIMALS

*a prayer to open*Awaken my senses to you, Lord.
Clear all distractions that rob me of your presence.
Remind me that you are the Creator and Sustainer of all things.
And may my heart be filled with wonder. Amen.

READ PSALM 104 (see pages 388–389)

REFLECT_____

Movement #1

Go outside and find a place where you can see an animal of any kind, whether a farm animal, a squirrel, or your own dog. For about a minute, fix your gaze on one part of that animal.

• What colors, shapes, and textures do you see? What do you smell as you breathe deeply? What do you hear around you as you stand still?

• What emotions are stirred in you as you gaze at that particular part of the animal?

Movement #2

Now allow your eyes to take in the entire animal and its environment, noticing how the part you initially focused on fits into or compares to the whole. Reflect on the entire animal for a moment.

• What is wondrous about this animal before you today?

• What does focusing on this animal lead you to pray? What do you want to say to God, the Creator?

A PRAYER TO CLOSE_____

I will sing to you, Lord, as long as I live. I will praise you to my last breath!
May all my thoughts be pleasing to you, for I rejoice in you, Lord, the Creator.

BIRDS

a prayer to open

Awaken my senses to you, Lord.
Clear all distractions that rob me of your presence.
Remind me that you are the Creator and Sustainer of all things.
And may my heart be filled with wonder. Amen.

READ PSALM 104 (see pages 388–389)

REFLECT

Movement #1

Go outside and find a place where you can catch a glimpse of a bird of any kind, whether a sparrow foraging for seeds, a duck floating in the water, or a woodpecker, blue jay, or cardinal hiding in a tree. For as much time as is possible, fix your gaze on one part of the bird.

- What colors, shapes, and textures do you see? What do you smell as you breathe deeply? What do you hear around you as you stand still?

- What emotions are stirred in you as you gaze at that particular part of the bird?

Movement #2

Now allow your eyes to take in the entire bird and its environment, noticing how the part you initially focused on fits into or compares to the whole. Reflect on the entire bird for a moment.

- What is wondrous about this bird that crossed your path today?

- What does focusing on this bird lead you to pray? What do you want to say to God, the Creator?

A PRAYER TO CLOSE

I will sing to you, Lord, as long as I live. I will praise you to my last breath!
May all my thoughts be pleasing to you, for I rejoice in you, Lord, the Creator.

SACRED QUESTIONS

FOOD FROM THE EARTH

a prayer to open

Awaken my senses to you, Lord.
Clear all distractions that rob me of your presence.
Remind me that you are the Creator and Sustainer of all things.
And may my heart be filled with wonder. Amen.

READ PSALM 104 (see pages 388–389)

REFLECT_____

Movement #1

Go outside and find a place where you can see growing fruits, vegetables, or grains, whether in a home garden, at a local farm, or in a nearby field. For about a minute, fix your gaze on one part of that garden, farm, or field.

- What colors, shapes, and textures do you see? What do you smell as you breathe deeply? What do you hear around you as you stand still?

- What emotions are stirred in you as you gaze at that particular part of the garden, farm, or field?

Movement #2

Now allow your eyes to take in the entire garden, farm, or field, noticing how the part you initially focused on fits into or compares to the whole. Reflect on the entire garden, farm, or field for a moment.

- What is wondrous about the garden, farm, or field before you today?

- What does focusing on these spaces lead you to pray? What do you want to say to God, the Creator?

A PRAYER TO CLOSE_____

I will sing to you, Lord, as long as I live. I will praise you to my last breath!
May all my thoughts be pleasing to you, for I rejoice in you, Lord, the Creator.

MOON AND STARS

a prayer to open

Awaken my senses to you, Lord.
Clear all distractions that rob me of your presence.
Remind me that you are the Creator and Sustainer of all things.
And may my heart be filled with wonder. Amen.

READ PSALM 104 (see pages 388–389)

REFLECT

Movement #1

Go outside in the evening and find a place where you can stop and stare up at the moon or the stars, whether you can see a million stars or a single one, whether the moon is waxing or waning. For about a minute and as much as is possible, fix your gaze on one star or the moon alone.

- What colors, shapes, and textures do you see? What do you smell as you breathe deeply? What do you hear around you as you stand still?

- What emotions are stirred in you as you gaze at the moon or the star?

Movement #2

Now allow your eyes to take in as much of the moon and stars as you can see, noticing how the moon or the star you initially focused on fits into or compares to the whole sky. Reflect on the moon and stars as a whole for a moment.

- What is wondrous about the moon and stars as you take them in today?

- What does focusing on the moon and stars lead you to pray? What do you want to say to God, the Creator?

A PRAYER TO CLOSE

I will sing to you, Lord, as long as I live. I will praise you to my last breath!
May all my thoughts be pleasing to you, for I rejoice in you, Lord, the Creator.

SEASONS

a prayer to open

READ PSALM 104 (see pages 388–389)

REFLECT _____

Movement #1

Go outside and find a place where you can take in the beauty of the season you are currently experiencing, whether it's the hottest day of summer; a color-studded fall evening; a barren, whitewashed winter morning; or a burgeoning spring night. For about a minute, fix your gaze on one object that characterizes the season you're experiencing now.

- What colors, shapes, and textures do you see? What do you smell as you breathe deeply? What do you hear around you as you stand still?

- What emotions are stirred in you as you gaze at the object you chose?

Movement #2

Now allow your eyes to take in as much of the environment around you as you can see, noticing how the object you initially focused on fits into or compares to the whole landscape. Reflect on the season as a whole for a moment.

- What is wondrous about the season you are currently experiencing as you notice its characteristics today?

- What does focusing on the season lead you to pray? What do you want to say to God, the Creator?

A PRAYER TO CLOSE _____

I will sing to you, Lord, as long as I live. I will praise you to my last breath!
May all my thoughts be pleasing to you, for I rejoice in you, Lord, the Creator.

GROUND

a prayer to open   Awaken my senses to you, Lord.
Clear all distractions that rob me of your presence.
Remind me that you are the Creator and Sustainer of all things.
And may my heart be filled with wonder. Amen.

READ PSALM 104 (see pages 388–389)

REFLECT_____

Movement #1

Go outside and find a place where you can get close to the ground, whether it's covered in green grass, dirt and rocks, fallen leaves, or white snow. For about a minute, fix your gaze on one part of the ground.

• What colors, shapes, and textures do you see? What do you smell as you breathe deeply? What do you hear around you as you stand still?

• What emotions are stirred in you as you gaze at that particular part of the ground?

Movement #2

Now allow your eyes to take in the ground all around you, noticing how the part you initially focused on fits into or compares to the whole. Reflect on the ground that surrounds you for a moment.

• What is wondrous about the ground upon which your feet are planted today?

• What does focusing on the ground lead you to pray? What do you want to say to God, the Creator?

A PRAYER TO CLOSE_____

I will sing to you, Lord, as long as I live. I will praise you to my last breath!
May all my thoughts be pleasing to you, for I rejoice in you, Lord, the Creator.

SACRED QUESTIONS

FLOWERS AND PLANTS

a prayer to open

Awaken my senses to you, Lord.
Clear all distractions that rob me of your presence.
Remind me that you are the Creator and Sustainer of all things.
And may my heart be filled with wonder. Amen.

READ PSALM 104 (see pages 388–389)

REFLECT _____

Movement #1

Go outside and find a place where you can stop and examine flowers or plants, whether they're growing wildly in a field, lining your neighbor's yard, or sprucing up a local restaurant's landscaping. For about a minute, fix your gaze on one part of a flower or plant.

- What colors, shapes, and textures do you see? What do you smell as you breathe deeply? What do you hear around you as you stand still?

- What emotions are stirred in you as you gaze at that particular part of the flower or plant?

Movement #2

Now allow your eyes to take in the entire flower or plant, noticing how the part you initially focused on fits into or compares to the whole. Reflect on the whole for a moment.

- What is wondrous about this flower or plant that decorates the scenery in which you find yourself today?

- What does focusing on this flower or plant lead you to pray? What do you want to say to God, the Creator?

A PRAYER TO CLOSE _____

I will sing to you, Lord, as long as I live. I will praise you to my last breath!
May all my thoughts be pleasing to you, for I rejoice in you, Lord, the Creator.

WIND

a prayer to open

Awaken my senses to you, Lord.
Clear all distractions that rob me of your presence.
Remind me that you are the Creator and Sustainer of all things.
And may my heart be filled with wonder. Amen.

READ PSALM 104 (see pages 388–389)

REFLECT

Movement #1

Go outside and find a place where you will notice the wind, whether it's barely rustling the leaves, violently kicking up dirt or waves, or nearly absent. For about a minute, fix your gaze on one object that is being moved by the wind.

· What colors, shapes, and textures do you see? What do you smell as you breathe deeply? What do you hear around you as you stand still?

· What emotions are stirred in you as you see the way the wind moves the object on which you're focused?

Movement #2

Now allow your eyes to take in everything surrounding the one object you had been focused on, noticing how that object fits into or compares to the whole. Reflect on the whole for a moment.

· What is wondrous about the wind today?

· What does focusing on the wind lead you to pray? What do you want to say to God, the Creator?

A PRAYER TO CLOSE

I will sing to you, Lord, as long as I live. I will praise you to my last breath!
May all my thoughts be pleasing to you, for I rejoice in you, Lord, the Creator.

WEATHER

a prayer to open

Awaken my senses to you, Lord.
Clear all distractions that rob me of your presence.
Remind me that you are the Creator and Sustainer of all things.
And may my heart be filled with wonder. Amen.

READ PSALM 104 (see pages 388–389)

REFLECT_____

Movement #1

Go outside and find a place where you can take notice of the weather: the temperature, precipitation, wind, and humidity. For about a minute, fix your gaze on any object that grabs your attention.

- What colors, shapes, and textures do you see? What do you smell as you breathe deeply? What do you hear around you as you stand still?

- What emotions are stirred in you as you consider the way the weather affects the object on which you're focused?

Movement #2

Now allow your eyes to take in everything surrounding the one object you had been focused on, noticing how that object fits into or compares to the whole. Reflect on the whole for a moment.

- What is wondrous about the weather today?

- What does focusing on the weather lead you to pray? What do you want to say to God, the Creator?

A PRAYER TO CLOSE_____

I will sing to you, Lord, as long as I live. I will praise you to my last breath!
May all my thoughts be pleasing to you, for I rejoice in you, Lord, the Creator.

INSECTS

a prayer to open

Awaken my senses to you, Lord.
Clear all distractions that rob me of your presence.
Remind me that you are the Creator and Sustainer of all things.
And may my heart be filled with wonder. Amen.

READ PSALM 104 (see pages 388–389)

REFLECT

Movement #1

Go outside and find a place where you can catch a glimpse of an insect of any kind, whether a bumblebee searching for nectar, a spider spinning its web, or an ant hauling a grain of sand. For as much time as is possible, fix your gaze on the insect.

- What colors, shapes, and textures do you see? What do you smell as you breathe deeply? What do you hear around you as you stand still?
- What emotions are stirred in you as you gaze at the insect?

Movement #2

Now allow your eyes to take in the insect and its environment, noticing how the creature fits into or compares to the whole. Reflect on the insect for a moment.

- What is wondrous about this insect and its environment that you perhaps strained to notice today?
- What does focusing on this insect and its environment lead you to pray? What do you want to say to God, the Creator?

A PRAYER TO CLOSE

I will sing to you, Lord, as long as I live. I will praise you to my last breath!
May all my thoughts be pleasing to you, for I rejoice in you, Lord, the Creator.

PEOPLE

a prayer to open

Awaken my senses to you, Lord.
Clear all distractions that rob me of your presence.
Remind me that you are the Creator and Sustainer of all things.
And may my heart be filled with wonder. Amen.

READ PSALM 104 (see pages 388–389)

REFLECT_____

Movement #1

Go outside and find a place where you can see people gathered together, whether at a park, on the beach, at a restaurant, or on the street. For about a minute, as unobtrusively as possible, fix your gaze on one particular person, remembering they were made in God's very image.

- What colors, shapes, and textures do you see? What do you smell as you breathe deeply? What do you hear around you as you stand still?

- What emotions are stirred in you as you gaze at that particular person?

Movement #2

Now allow your eyes to take in the entire group of people, noticing how the person you initially focused on fits into or compares to the whole. Reflect on the entire group of people for a moment.

- What is wondrous about the people before you today?

- What does focusing on people lead you to pray? What do you want to say to God, the Creator?

A PRAYER TO CLOSE_____

I will sing to you, Lord, as long as I live. I will praise you to my last breath!
May all my thoughts be pleasing to you, for I rejoice in you, Lord, the Creator.

For the Sake of Others

Reaching Out to Serve

ALTHOUGH IN OUR day most Christians would say that we are called to love and serve one another because that's what Jesus taught, the idea that we are saved and transformed for the sake of others originates from well before he walked the earth. Most of us know of the Creation story, and most of us know about the fall of humanity into sin. But many of us, whether consciously or not, think of Scripture in that short progression: Creation, the Fall, Jesus! We skip over or diminish all that happened between the Fall and Jesus, and in doing so, we miss the depth, breadth, and beauty not only of God's redemption but also of our role in it.

To really understand our purpose and our mission, we need to look at Abraham, way back in Genesis 12 (where he was called Abram). As we do that, we also need to keep the backdrop of that Scripture in mind. In Genesis 3–11, we read story after story of sinfulness and rebellion. But then in Genesis 12:1-4, we read,

And YHWH said to Abram,
Get yourself up and go
   from your land, and from your kindred, and
      from your father's house,
   to the land that I will show you.
     And I will make you into a great nation;
     and I will bless you;

    and I will make your name great.
  And be a blessing,
   And I will bless those who bless you;
   whereas the one who belittles you, I will curse;
   and in you will be blessed all kinship groups
     on the earth.
  And Abram went just as YHWH said to him.[9]

So here we find the pivotal moment in God's story. He made Abram several promises and gave him two commands: He told him to "go," and he told him to "be a blessing." And God promised that through Abram, God would bless all the nations, by which he meant all the people of the earth. So central is this promise that the apostle Paul described it as the gospel in advance. In his letter to the Galatians, Paul said, "Scripture foresaw that God would justify the Gentiles by faith, and announced the gospel in advance to Abraham: 'All nations will be blessed through you'" (3:8, NIV).

In God's promise to Abram, we see God's mission: that his Good News was to bless the nations—to bless the whole world. We hear echoes of this promise to Abraham in John's announcement of the gospel in John 3:16: "God so loved the world . . ." Perhaps even more amazing is that God called Abram (and his descendants) to partner with him to actually carry out this mission. In other words, God said he would bless all the nations, but he depends on human beings—their faithfulness and obedience—to actually accomplish that mission. He didn't form a people and choose them for their own sake; rather, he formed and chose Israel (Abraham's descendants) for the sake of the whole world.

What we see, then, for the rest of the Old Testament is the story of God carrying out his mission and Israel seeking to be faithful to its mission to be a blessing. First God formed a people (Israel) and then preserved them from famine and settled them in Egypt. Later God redeemed them from slavery in Egypt and brought them into the land he'd promised. In the process, he gave them the law so they would know how to live and so could be a light to the nations around them. In other words, he equipped them to show the world around them what a community under God's care and law looks like—how it can flourish and thrive. Israel's mission was about being a light.

But then, of course, along the way we see God's people fail in their obedience and faithfulness. Instead of being a blessing to the nations, and despite calls to return to God and their mission by the prophets, God's people ended up being just like the other nations. Yet there was hope. The prophets told of a future day when God would gather and renew his people to carry out his mission to completion.

And then God acted. He came to earth in Jesus and fulfilled Israel's mission. Jesus fulfilled the law, acting with righteousness, humility, mercy, and justice. He not only acted to redeem us and usher in the Kingdom but also showed us what it is to be a light to the nations—the light of the world. Jesus' message was this: *In me, find life, forgiveness, and salvation and then bring it to everyone else! Go into the world and be the light, as I have shown you.* So in Jesus, God has reestablished his people and empowered them with his Spirit to reach the world with his redemption and restoration. All the while, he himself is continuing to act. And this is where we come in. We bless and love and share the story of Jesus because we have been invited into this historic, compelling story of God's redemption of all things. We get to be part of the mission! We are blessed and saved to bring blessing to the world. We are brought in not for our sake but for the sake of others—for the sake of the world. We are actually participating in God's restoration.

When we walk with Jesus through the Gospels, as we did in the "Revealed" section, we see a life that confers blessing, not only in the ultimate sense of inviting a person to know and follow Jesus—to share with them the good news of forgiveness and salvation and the Kingdom—but also in the sense of showing everyday kindness, compassion, and sacrifice.

The question for us is this: How do we do this—carry out God's mission in the world? If you find yourself in this part of the book, you've already begun:

You've received and responded to Jesus' invitations to you, and you've opened yourself to God's transformation of your heart, mind, and hands. Now the call is to step into the service of others. And, of course, this call happens along the way because we are always learning to live more fully into Jesus' invitations. Our transformation is a lifelong process.

For the next thirty-five days, we will follow this journey: first, seeing Jesus as our example and our King (days 1–3); second, allowing our lives to speak and reflect our relationships with Jesus (days 4–13); third, doing good in the world with the Holy Spirit's direction and help (days 14–25); fourth, inviting others into the life Jesus has granted us (days 26–28); and, finally, praying for the world so we don't grow weary (days 29–35). Each of these parts of the journey depends upon all the others. What we need most to carry out and participate in God's mission is to be transformed. After all, without the Holy Spirit, we are no different from the Israelites. We need God's eyes and his heart. To be people out of whom the love of Christ flows naturally, we need to be transformed. To be transformed, we need to love and serve others, so we do both.

JESUS, OUR EXAMPLE AND KING

DAY 1

I HAVE COME

a prayer to open

Father in heaven, hallowed be your name.
May your Kingdom come, may your will be done
on earth as it is in heaven.

READ LUKE 4:14-21

Then Jesus returned to Galilee, filled with the Holy Spirit's power. Reports about him spread quickly through the whole region. He taught regularly in their synagogues and was praised by everyone.

When he came to the village of Nazareth, his boyhood home, he went as usual to the synagogue on the Sabbath and stood up to read the Scriptures. The scroll of Isaiah the prophet was handed to him. He unrolled the scroll and found the place where this was written:

"The Spirit of the LORD is upon me,
for he has anointed me to bring Good News
to the poor.

He has sent me to proclaim that captives will
be released,
that the blind will see,
that the oppressed will be set free,
and that the time of the LORD's favor has
come."

He rolled up the scroll, handed it back to the attendant, and sat down. All eyes in the synagogue looked at him intently. Then he began to speak to them. "The Scripture you've just heard has been fulfilled this very day!"

When asked why Jesus came to the world, Christians usually answer with something like "To save me from my sins." Of course, it is true that Jesus did and does this. But the gospel is so much bigger and broader and deeper! Jesus came to bring good news to the poor: that God's favor had come, that the Kingdom of God had arrived, and that, as a result, captives would be released, the blind would see, and the oppressed would be set free. God had intervened! The course of human history had changed. Jesus is Lord and King, reigning over all things. Not only that, but he invites us, the church, to participate in his Kingdom now, doing the very things for others that he did when he walked the earth. In other words, we have been saved from our sins and are being transformed from the inside out for the sake of others so they might know that Jesus is Lord and be saved, healed, freed, and made whole.

- What emotions are evoked when you hear the words of Jesus reflected in Luke's Gospel?

- How has your understanding of Jesus' purpose in coming to earth as a human changed over time? What accounts for the changes you see?

- Take a few minutes to reflect on the robustness of the gospel you currently share or believe. Where do you need God to expand your understanding? How is he calling you to participate in his Kingdom?

RESPOND

Father, forgive me for the ways I have reduced your Good News to an individual salvation plan. I am so thankful to be saved and in relationship with you, but you are doing so much more! Open my eyes to the ways you are redeeming and healing the whole world, pursuing every person, engaging every heart, and building a people—the church—to carry the Good News of Jesus' reign and your Kingdom. Let me be an agent of healing, freedom, and justice here and now. Let me live for the sake of others. Amen.

DAY 2

AS I HAVE LOVED YOU

a prayer to open

Father in heaven, hallowed be your name.
May your Kingdom come, may your will be done
on earth as it is in heaven.

I have loved you even as the Father has loved me. Remain in my love. When you obey my commandments, you remain in my love, just as I obey my Father's commandments and remain in his love. I have told you these things so that you will be filled with my joy. Yes, your joy will overflow! This is my commandment: Love each other in the same way I have loved you. There is no greater love than to lay down one's life for one's friends. You are my friends if you do what I command. I no longer call you slaves, because a master doesn't confide in his slaves. Now you are my friends, since I have told you everything the Father told me. You didn't choose me. I chose you. I appointed you to go and produce lasting fruit, so that the Father will give you whatever you ask for, using my name. This is my command: Love each other.

REFLECT _____

Jesus is our example of how to live for the sake of others. He shows us how to love—how to forgive, extend mercy, demonstrate compassion, be gracious and truthful. But sacrificial love like Jesus' can be difficult for us. The only way we can become people who love naturally, sacrificially, and unselfishly is by abiding in his love. Unless we stay close to him, remembering we are beloved and safe, we will be unable to love others in the way he calls us. We will run out of capacity and reach the end of ourselves. With his love filling and fueling us, though, our eyes are opened to the lonely and hurting, our patience levels grow and we can be present to those who test our ability to love, and we become less focused on ourselves, putting others first.

- What images come to mind as you think about remaining in Jesus' love?

- What attitudes, thoughts, and behaviors arise in you when you aren't spending time in Jesus' presence and being reminded of his abiding love for you? In other words, what helps you realize you've distanced yourself from him?

- Where are you low on capacity to love right now? Is there a particular person you're struggling to love well? Are you losing patience with your family? Take a couple of minutes in God's loving presence and ask him to center you on his love, remind you of your belovedness, and fill you with the love of Jesus.

RESPOND _____

Father, thank you for the love you've poured out for me in and through Jesus. Help me to stay close, to continually receive that love. I know that when I stay close to you, I am filled and able to love others well, yet I allow busyness and day-to-day tasks to steal my time. I allow worries to overwhelm me and doubt to crash over me. In your mercy, call me back to you; nudge my heart toward you again. Expand my capacity and patience so I can love others the way Jesus loves the world. Amen.

For the Sake of Others

LIVE LIKE JESUS HERE

a prayer to open
Father in heaven, hallowed be your name.
May your Kingdom come, may your will be done
on earth as it is in heaven.

READ 1 JOHN 4:13-19

And God has given us his Spirit as proof that we live in him and he in us. Furthermore, we have seen with our own eyes and now testify that the Father sent his Son to be the Savior of the world. All who declare that Jesus is the Son of God have God living in them, and they live in God. We know how much God loves us, and we have put our trust in his love.

God is love, and all who live in love live in God, and God lives in them. And as we live in God, our love grows more perfect. So we will not be afraid on the day of judgment, but we can face him with confidence because we live like Jesus here in this world.

Such love has no fear, because perfect love expels all fear. If we are afraid, it is for fear of punishment, and this shows that we have not fully experienced his perfect love. We love each other because he loved us first.

REFLECT

God's love is perfected, or made complete, not when we receive it but when, after receiving it, we express it to others. Holding it within us, being stingy in handing it out, stunts God's love. But if we instead pour it out freely and fully to others— even when it costs us, hurts us, and inconveniences us—we live like Jesus here in the world. He is our best example and our most perfect model. His way is the way we live for the sake of others and participate in what he is doing in the world.

- Reflect on what you know of Jesus' life and how he loved. How would you describe his love to a friend?

- Consider whether there has been a time when you have hoarded God's love, seeking to keep it to yourself instead of expressing it fully to others. What impact did that have on you?

- As you consider fully living and loving for the sake of others, what fears and self-centered desires arise within you? How might those fears and desires act as barriers to modeling Jesus' life?

RESPOND

Father, fill me to overflowing with your love. Give me the courage and faith to extend whatever you've given me to others freely and fully, knowing that your love is unending. For the times I have been stingy with love or hoarded your love, forgive me. I want to be like Jesus in this world. Transform whatever needs to change so that I can be. And break down the barriers—the fears and desires—that will get in the way. Amen.

FRUIT OF THE SPIRIT

a prayer to open

Father in heaven, hallowed be your name.
May your Kingdom come, may your will be done
on earth as it is in heaven.

READ GALATIANS 5:13-26

For you have been called to live in freedom, my brothers and sisters. But don't use your freedom to satisfy your sinful nature. Instead, use your freedom to serve one another in love. For the whole law can be summed up in this one command: "Love your neighbor as yourself." But if you are always biting and devouring one another, watch out! Beware of destroying one another.

So I say, let the Holy Spirit guide your lives. Then you won't be doing what your sinful nature craves. The sinful nature wants to do evil, which is just the opposite of what the Spirit wants. And the Spirit gives us desires that are the opposite of what the sinful nature desires. These two forces are constantly fighting each other, so you are not free to carry out your good intentions. But when you are directed by the Spirit, you are not under obligation to the law of Moses.

When you follow the desires of your sinful nature, the results are very clear: sexual immorality, impurity, lustful pleasures, idolatry, sorcery, hostility, quarreling, jealousy, outbursts of anger, selfish ambition, dissension, division, envy, drunkenness, wild parties, and other sins like these. Let me tell you again, as I have before, that anyone living that sort of life will not inherit the Kingdom of God.

But the Holy Spirit produces this kind of fruit in our lives: love, joy, peace, patience, kindness, goodness, faithfulness, gentleness, and self-control. There is no law against these things!

Those who belong to Christ Jesus have nailed the passions and desires of their sinful nature to his cross and crucified them there. Since we are living by the Spirit, let us follow the Spirit's leading in every part of our lives. Let us not become conceited, or provoke one another, or be jealous of one another.

REFLECT

Paul spent the bulk of his letter to the Galatians sharing the gospel and encouraging his listeners to find freedom in Christ rather than become enslaved to either the law (a set of rules to abide by) or the flesh (selfish desires that lead to destruction instead of life). Instead, he said, we are to live by the Spirit, and the Spirit provides freedom. But the freedom of the Spirit doesn't lead us to do whatever we want, to indulge or satisfy our every desire; rather, the freedom of the Spirit leads us to serve one another in love. We have been given freedom to live for the sake of others, and there is no mistaking a life lived in the Spirit. We will see obvious evidence: the "fruit." When we see love, joy, peace, patience, kindness, goodness, faithfulness, gentleness, and self-control in our lives (or, perhaps better put, when others see these in our lives), we know we are living by the Spirit. When we are living by the Spirit, our lives will speak of the one we follow.

• Take a few minutes to do some inventory. How are you doing in living the

For the Sake of Others

fruit of the spirit? Consider asking a family member or close friend what they see in you.

- When are you susceptible to self-indulgence or self-centered actions? What practices help you cultivate fruit of the Spirit?

- Where would you like to see growth in yourself when it comes to the fruit of the Spirit? What is your prayer?

RESPOND

Father, I come before you as best as I know how to open my heart to your transforming work. I long to live in complete freedom, displaying the fruit of your Spirit in every part of my life. Show me the ways I am still enslaved to rules or my own selfish desires. In the areas I need to grow, give me opportunities and humility so I can more fully live out the freedom I have in Christ by loving others as you do. Amen.

DAY 5

HOW TO BE FRUITFUL

a prayer to open

Father in heaven, hallowed be your name.
May your Kingdom come, may your will be done
on earth as it is in heaven.

READ JOHN 15:1-8

I am the true grapevine, and my Father is the gardener. He cuts off every branch of mine that doesn't produce fruit, and he prunes the branches that do bear fruit so they will produce even more. You have already been pruned and purified by the message I have given you. Remain in me, and I will remain in you. For a branch cannot produce fruit if it is severed from the vine, and you cannot be fruitful unless you remain in me.

Yes, I am the vine; you are the branches. Those who remain in me, and I in them, will produce much fruit. For apart from me you can do nothing. Anyone who does not remain in me is thrown away like a useless branch and withers. Such branches are gathered into a pile to be burned. But if you remain in me and my words remain in you, you may ask for anything you want, and it will be granted! When you produce much fruit, you are my true disciples. This brings great glory to my Father.

REFLECT

Yesterday we read about the fruit of the Spirit, but how do we actually cultivate that fruit? Do we just try really hard—wake up each morning and declare, "I will be joyful today"? We all know pure determination doesn't work—or at least, doesn't last. So how do we grow fruit? The words of Jesus in today's passage tell us that we stay connected to him. It's the only way. In fact, for most of us, if we looked back at the times we lashed out in anger, gave in to temptation, or acted in our own best interests instead of serving someone else over the last week, we likely could identify a feeling of disconnection from Christ during those times. When our intimacy with Christ increases, our fruitfulness increases.

- What stands out to you as you read the words of Jesus in today's passage? What invitation do you sense he is extending to you through this Scripture?

- How is your connection with Jesus during this particular season of your life?

- What circumstances, relationships, and practices are getting in the way? What practices and relationships help you stay connected?

RESPOND

Father, thank you for the invitation to remain connected to you in and through Jesus. I long for that constant connection, in which I am aware of your presence, your love, and your power. Show me the ways I block my connection with you or try to do things in my own strength. Guide me into relationships that foster and encourage my ability to remain in you. Amen.

DAY 6

FILLED WITH LOVE

a prayer to open

Father in heaven, hallowed be your name. May your Kingdom come, may your will be done on earth as it is in heaven.

READ 1 CORINTHIANS 13

If I could speak all the languages of earth and of angels, but didn't love others, I would only be a noisy gong or a clanging cymbal. If I had the gift of prophecy, and if I understood all of God's secret plans and possessed all knowledge, and if I had such faith that I could move mountains, but didn't love others, I would be nothing. If I gave everything I have to the poor and even sacrificed my body, I could boast about it; but if I didn't love others, I would have gained nothing.

Love is patient and kind. Love is not jealous or boastful or proud or rude. It does not demand its own way. It is not irritable, and it keeps no record of being wronged. It does not rejoice about injustice but rejoices whenever the truth wins out. Love never gives up, never loses faith, is always hopeful, and endures through every circumstance.

Prophecy and speaking in unknown languages and special knowledge will become useless. But love will last forever! Now our knowledge is partial and incomplete, and even the gift of prophecy reveals only part of the whole picture! But when the time of perfection comes, these partial things will become useless.

When I was a child, I spoke and thought and reasoned as a child. But when I grew up, I put away childish things. Now we see things imperfectly, like puzzling reflections in a mirror, but then we will see everything with perfect clarity. All that I know now is partial and incomplete, but then I will know everything completely, just as God now knows me completely.

Three things will last forever—faith, hope, and love—and the greatest of these is love.

Love has become one of the most ubiquitous words in the English language. Most often we associate love with a feeling, an emotion we experience. It's something we fall into—we can't control it! The love we see in the Bible is something quite different. As theologian Scot McKnight says, "Love is about the rugged commitment" to be with, for, and unto another person.[10] This is what we see in Jesus: a covenant love that is inconvenient and disruptive and calls us to be in proximity and seek the best for the other. We are largely incapable of this love—that is, unless we allow the Holy Spirit to fill, lead, and guide us.

- Where do you see the love described in today's passage reflected in your life? In what areas are you struggling to demonstrate this kind of love?

- What is your life saying about your commitment and desire to love, whether to those who know you or to those who simply observe you?

- Take a few minutes in prayer, asking God to show you where you need to grow when it comes to the love that pours out of you to others. What did he illuminate for you?

RESPOND

Father, I want to love like you. I want to go out of my way, be inconvenienced, be disrupted, and love with abandon. Help me to release my grip on my own agenda, allow space to love, and slow down and see when and how to love those whose paths I cross. Transform my self-centeredness and grow my heart's capacity to love. Amen.

DAY 7

FILLED WITH JOY

a prayer to open

Father in heaven, hallowed be your name. May your Kingdom come, may your will be done on earth as it is in heaven.

READ ACTS 3:1-11

Peter and John went to the Temple one afternoon to take part in the three o'clock prayer service. As they approached the Temple, a man lame from birth was being carried in. Each day he was put beside the Temple gate, the one called the Beautiful Gate, so he could beg from the people going into the Temple. When he saw Peter and John about to enter, he asked them for some money.

Peter and John looked at him intently, and Peter said, "Look at us!" The lame man looked at them eagerly, expecting some money. But Peter said, "I don't have any silver or gold for you. But I'll give you what I have. In the name of Jesus Christ the Nazarene, get up and walk!"

Then Peter took the lame man by the right hand and helped him up. And as he did, the man's feet and ankles were instantly healed and strengthened. He jumped up, stood on his feet, and began to walk! Then, walking, leaping, and praising God, he went into the Temple with them.

All the people saw him walking and heard him praising God. When they realized he was the lame beggar they had seen so often at the Beautiful Gate, they were absolutely astounded! They all rushed out in amazement to Solomon's Colonnade, where the man was holding tightly to Peter and John.

REFLECT

A lack of true, deep joy means we've lost our perspective—we've turned our attention to the things of this world and put our hope in temporary things. This is no surprise! The world can wear us down and turn us away from what's true. When we're able to see with eternal eyes—remembering what Jesus has done, that we are secure in him, and that God is right now at work to redeem, restore, and renew—we can live in joy. Of course, we can do this only as we remain connected to Jesus and cultivate our relationship with him.

- Where in your life do you see the kind of joy the paralyzed man showed after he was healed? In what areas of your life are you struggling to demonstrate this kind of joy?

- What is your life saying about the joy you have, whether to those who know you or to those who simply observe you?

- Take a few minutes in prayer, asking God to show you where you need to grow when it comes to the joy that naturally comes from his salvation. What did he illuminate for you?

RESPOND

Father, I long for an eternal perspective—one in which I can focus on what really matters and not get sidetracked by the insignificant and temporary. Give me eyes to see what to focus on in my life, my neighborhood, and the world. Fill me with your joy so I can, regardless of my circumstances, rejoice in you, knowing I am fully and forever loved and secure as your child. Amen.

FILLED WITH PEACE

a prayer to open

Father in heaven, hallowed be your name.
May your Kingdom come, may your will be done
on earth as it is in heaven.

READ PSALM 23

The LORD is my shepherd;
I have all that I need.

He lets me rest in green meadows;
he leads me beside peaceful streams.

He renews my strength.
He guides me along right paths,
 bringing honor to his name.
Even when I walk
 through the darkest valley,
I will not be afraid,
 for you are close beside me.
Your rod and your staff
 protect and comfort me.

You prepare a feast for me
 in the presence of my enemies.
You honor me by anointing my head with oil.
 My cup overflows with blessings.
Surely your goodness and unfailing love will
 pursue me
 all the days of my life,
and I will live in the house of the LORD
 forever.

REFLECT

Peace in a violent, frantic, accelerating world can be hard to find. We wonder what peace even looks like. Although we may worry about big tragedies and fear significant loss, usually it's our own habits and routines that rob us of peace. We layer task upon task, activity upon activity. And those things may be great fun and exhilarating, but our nonstop pace makes our souls rushed and unsettled. We're constantly moving, continuously connected. We can hardly be shocked that we have no peace. As we open space, say no to busyness, and rest in Jesus' love, we will know peace.

- Where in your life do you see the kind of peace that emanates from Psalm 23? In what areas are you struggling to live with this sense of peace?

- What is your life saying about the peace within your soul, whether to those who know you or to those who simply observe you?

- Take a few minutes in prayer, asking God to show you where you need to grow when it comes to embracing the peace he offers. What did he illuminate for you?

RESPOND

Father, I long for deep peace in my heart, mind, and soul. Please open me to the peace and wholeness you offer instead of the frantic, busy exhaustion I often fight against. Help me see the ways my routines and practices contribute to a lack of peace and contentment. Grow my trust in you so I can rest, break the hold that technology can have on me, and continue to open space for me to be transformed and healed by your love. Amen.

DAY 9

FILLED WITH PATIENCE

a prayer to open

Father in heaven, hallowed be your name.
May your Kingdom come, may your will be done
on earth as it is in heaven.

Dear brothers and sisters, be patient as you wait for the Lord's return. Consider the farmers who patiently wait for the rains in the fall and in the spring. They eagerly look for the valuable harvest to ripen. You, too, must be patient. Take courage, for the coming of the Lord is near.

Don't grumble about each other, brothers and sisters, or you will be judged. For look—the Judge is standing at the door!

For examples of patience in suffering, dear brothers and sisters, look at the prophets who spoke in the name of the Lord. We give great honor to those who endure under suffering. For instance, you know about Job, a man of great endurance. You can see how the Lord was kind to him at the end, for the Lord is full of tenderness and mercy.

REFLECT

We generally think of patience when we're waiting in line at the grocery store or when the person driving in front of us is going twenty below the speed limit. But patience as a fruit of the Spirit is more like not losing heart in the midst of difficult and trying circumstances. When you are tempted to despair, believe the worst, or doubt God's goodness, be patient: Do not lose heart. Remember what's true: Jesus is returning. The Kingdom has come. The Kingdom is coming! You are forgiven and saved. Do not lose heart.

- Where in your life do you see the kind of patience James described? In what areas are you struggling to live with this sense of patience?

- What is your life saying about your patience level, whether to those who know you or to those who simply observe you?

- Take a few minutes in prayer, asking God to show you where you need to grow when it comes to patience. What did he illuminate for you?

RESPOND

Father, help me model patience wherever I am. Give me the grace to wear it throughout the day and practice it in situations in which I might otherwise be tempted to despair. When I am tired, under stress, worried, or afraid, grant me your perspective, wisdom, and energy. Help me go beyond myself and act in step with your Spirit. Amen.

DAY 10

FILLED WITH KINDNESS AND GOODNESS

a prayer to open

Father in heaven, hallowed be your name. May your Kingdom come, may your will be done on earth as it is in heaven.

Then Elimelech died, and Naomi was left with her two sons. The two sons married Moabite women. One married a woman named Orpah, and the other a woman named Ruth. But about ten years later, both Mahlon and Kilion died. This left Naomi alone, without her two sons or her husband.

Then Naomi heard in Moab that the LORD had blessed his people in Judah by giving them good crops again. So Naomi and her daughters-in-law got ready to leave Moab to return to her homeland. With her two daughters-in-law she set out from the place where she had been living, and they took the road that would lead them back to Judah.

But on the way, Naomi said to her two daughters-in-law, "Go back to your mothers' homes. And may the LORD reward you for your kindness to your husbands and to me. May the LORD bless you with the security of another marriage." Then she kissed them good-bye, and they all broke down and wept.

"No," they said. "We want to go with you to your people."

But Naomi replied, "Why should you go on with me? Can I still give birth to other sons who could grow up to be your husbands? No, my daughters, return to your parents' homes, for I am too old to marry again. And even if it were possible, and I were to get married tonight and bear sons, then what? Would you wait for them to grow up and refuse to marry someone else? No, of course not, my daughters! Things are far more bitter for me than for you, because the LORD himself has raised his fist against me."

And again they wept together, and Orpah kissed her mother-in-law good-bye. But Ruth clung tightly to Naomi. "Look," Naomi said to her, "your sister-in-law has gone back to her people and to her gods. You should do the same."

But Ruth replied, "Don't ask me to leave you and turn back. Wherever you go, I will go; wherever you live, I will live. Your people will be my people, and your God will be my God. Wherever you die, I will die, and there I will be buried. May the LORD punish me severely if I allow anything but death to separate us!" When Naomi saw that Ruth was determined to go with her, she said nothing more.

We know kindness and goodness when we see them—or it might be more accurate to say that we sense these qualities in people. Think of people you know who are kind. There's more to it than just acts of kindness: It's something in their eyes, in their body language, in their spirit. And when these kind people act, we experience them more fully somehow. Jerry Bridges, author of *The Fruitful Life*, said it this way:

> Kindness is the inner disposition, created by the Holy Spirit, that causes us to be sensitive to the needs of others, whether physical, emotional, or spiritual. Goodness is kindness in action—words and deeds.[11]

- Where in your life do you see the type of kindness and goodness Ruth displayed? In what areas are you struggling to live with this sense of kindness and goodness?

- What is your life saying about your kindness and goodness, whether to those who know you or to those who simply observe you?

- Take a few minutes in prayer, asking God to show you where you need to grow when it comes to kindness and goodness. What did he illuminate for you?

Father, I long to demonstrate kindness to those I know and strangers alike. Build kindness in me, and allow it to come out in action as goodness toward others. Help me do what is good, what serves others, even when it costs me, and let it flow not from a desire to look good but from a desire to love like you. Amen.

FILLED WITH FAITHFULNESS

a prayer to open

Father in heaven, hallowed be your name. May your Kingdom come, may your will be done on earth as it is in heaven.

READ MATTHEW 25:14-30

Again, the Kingdom of Heaven can be illustrated by the story of a man going on a long trip. He called together his servants and entrusted his money to them while he was gone. He gave five bags of silver to one, two bags of silver to another, and one bag of silver to the last—dividing it in proportion to their abilities. He then left on his trip.

The servant who received the five bags of silver began to invest the money and earned five more. The servant with two bags of silver also went to work and earned two more. But the servant who received the one bag of silver dug a hole in the ground and hid the master's money.

After a long time their master returned from his trip and called them to give an account of how they had used his money. The servant to whom he had entrusted the five bags of silver came forward with five more and said, "Master, you gave me five bags of silver to invest, and I have earned five more."

The master was full of praise. "Well done, my good and faithful servant. You have been faithful in handling this small amount, so now I will give you many more responsibilities. Let's celebrate together!"

The servant who had received the two bags of silver came forward and said, "Master, you gave me two bags of silver to invest, and I have earned two more."

The master said, "Well done, my good and faithful servant. You have been faithful in handling this small amount, so now I will give you many more responsibilities. Let's celebrate together!"

Then the servant with the one bag of silver came and said, "Master, I knew you were a harsh man, harvesting crops you didn't plant and gathering crops you didn't cultivate. I was afraid I would lose your money, so I hid it in the earth. Look, here is your money back."

But the master replied, "You wicked and lazy servant! If you knew I harvested crops I didn't plant and gathered crops I didn't cultivate, why didn't you deposit my money in the bank? At least I could have gotten some interest on it."

Then he ordered, "Take the money from this servant, and give it to the one with the ten bags of silver. To those who use well what they are given, even more will be given, and they will have an abundance. But from those who do nothing, even what little they have will be taken away. Now throw this useless servant into outer darkness, where there will be weeping and gnashing of teeth."

REFLECT

To examine our faithfulness, we must look at the ways we spend our time, money, and talents. To whom or what would someone looking at our calendars and bank accounts think we're devoted? No matter our words, our actions speak louder. But saying yes to God and demonstrating our faithfulness by our actions means saying no to lots of values and idols our culture says we should want and will fulfill us. Only the Spirit can guide us into faithfulness and single-minded devotion to God in the face of such strong cultural pulls.

- Where in your life do you see the kind of faithfulness shown by the two servants in this parable? In what areas are you struggling to be faithful with what God has given you?

- What is your life saying about your faithfulness to God, whether to those who know you or to those who simply observe you?

- Take a few minutes in prayer, asking God to show you where you need to grow when it comes to your faithfulness to him. What did he illuminate for you?

RESPOND

Father, my deepest desire is to be faithful to you—fully devoted, completely loyal, totally obedient—yet other things pull at me, pull me away from you. Help me be faithful. Show me where my loyalty is divided. Lead me in the way of faithfulness because I cannot be faithful to you and your commands by my own power and strength. Grant me your mercy when I fail. Amen.

FILLED WITH GENTLENESS

a prayer to open

Father in heaven, hallowed be your name.
May your Kingdom come, may your will be done
on earth as it is in heaven.

READ PROVERBS 15:1-4

A gentle answer deflects anger,
but harsh words make tempers flare.
The tongue of the wise makes knowledge
appealing,
but the mouth of a fool belches out
foolishness.

The LORD is watching everywhere,
keeping his eye on both the evil and the good.
Gentle words are a tree of life;
a deceitful tongue crushes the spirit.

REFLECT

When we are rushed, anxious, afraid, angry, sad, or tired, gentleness is often the first thing to go. We spit out a harsh word or shoot off a harsh text or email. Or maybe we act pridefully and refuse help when we obviously need it. With gentleness, we can tend to the story and pain of others. We can empathize and seek to understand. We can accept the love of those around us. We can lead others to the heart of Jesus.

- Where in your life do you see gentleness? In what areas are you struggling to demonstrate gentleness with your words and actions?
- What is your life saying about your gentle spirit, whether to those who know you or to those who simply observe you?
- Take a few minutes in prayer, asking God to show you where you need to grow when it comes to gentleness in words and actions. What did he illuminate for you?

RESPOND_____

Father, help me be aware of the words I use and how I use them. I want only to build people up, encourage them, and bring gentleness and respect to conversations. Guide me in knowing when I am apt to respond harshly, and convict my heart when I run afoul of gentleness with my words. May I be a person others see as a gentle presence: gentle in words and in spirit. Amen.

DAY 13

FILLED WITH SELF-CONTROL

a prayer to open

Father in heaven, hallowed be your name. May your Kingdom come, may your will be done on earth as it is in heaven.

READ MATTHEW 4:1-11 _____

Then Jesus was led by the Spirit into the wilderness to be tempted there by the devil. For forty days and forty nights he fasted and became very hungry.

During that time the devil came and said to him, "If you are the Son of God, tell these stones to become loaves of bread."

But Jesus told him, "No! The Scriptures say,

'People do not live by bread alone,
  but by every word that comes from the
    mouth of God.'"

Then the devil took him to the holy city, Jerusalem, to the highest point of the Temple, and said, "If you are the Son of God, jump off! For the Scriptures say,

'He will order his angels to protect you.
And they will hold you up with their hands

so you won't even hurt your foot on a
    stone.'"

Jesus responded, "The Scriptures also say, 'You must not test the LORD your God.'"

Next the devil took him to the peak of a very high mountain and showed him all the kingdoms of the world and their glory. "I will give it all to you," he said, "if you will kneel down and worship me."

"Get out of here, Satan," Jesus told him. "For the Scriptures say,

'You must worship the LORD your God
    and serve only him.'"

Then the devil went away, and angels came and took care of Jesus.

For the Sake of Others •

We may confuse self-control and self-mastery; none of us can master ourselves completely. We've all tried it. We've all failed. But we can surrender ourselves to the control of the Holy Spirit and allow God to transform our disordered desires and sinful thoughts and actions. Where we are weak, God gives us supernatural strength. Where we are tempted, he gives us courage to turn away. Where we are broken, he heals us. When we fail, he can forgive us. We need only open ourselves and say yes to what God will give, and there our selves will be controlled by the Spirit.

- Where in your life do you see the kind of self-control Jesus displayed? In what areas are you struggling to exercise self-control?

- What is your life saying about your self-control, whether to those who know you or to those who simply observe you?

- Take a few minutes in prayer, asking God to show you where you need to grow when it comes to self-control. What did he illuminate for you?

RESPOND

Father, give me insight into myself in moments when I'm tired, triggered, or anxious. Help me see where I am weak and needing to protect against saying or doing something I'll regret. Give me the strength to stay alert and stand firm so as not to give in to whatever Satan might tempt me to consider. Fill my mind with thoughts of you, and turn my heart toward you in times of weakness. Amen.

DOING GOOD THROUGH THE SPIRIT

WITH THE HELP
OF THE HOLY SPIRIT

a prayer to open

Father in heaven, hallowed be your name.
May your Kingdom come, may your will be done
on earth as it is in heaven.

READ JOHN 14:25-29

I am telling you these things now while I am still with you. But when the Father sends the Advocate as my representative—that is, the Holy Spirit—he will teach you everything and will remind you of everything I have told you.

I am leaving you with a gift—peace of mind and heart. And the peace I give is a gift the world cannot give. So don't be troubled or afraid. Remember what I told you: I am going away, but I will come back to you again. If you really loved me, you would be happy that I am going to the Father, who is greater than I am. I have told you these things before they happen so that when they do happen, you will believe.

If we were left to our own strength and desires, Jesus' instructions about how to be and love in the world would be impossible to follow. Only with the help of the Holy Spirit do we have any chance of loving like Jesus. The Holy Spirit is our guide, our teacher, and our reminder. He is our power and our strength. Without him, we would be utterly incapable. But as we are empowered by him and transformed over time, and as we practice what Jesus taught, we become capable of extending love, grace, and forgiveness in the ways Jesus did.

- Where are you lacking strength and courage to love?
- Where has fear overtaken you?
- Where is self-centeredness or perceived busyness overwhelming you?

RESPOND

God, fill me anew with your Holy Spirit. Give me an open heart and mind to all that your Spirit longs to transform in me, and grant me the strength I need as I seek to live for the sake of others. Amen.

DAY 15

THE SPIRIT WILL GUIDE YOU

a prayer to open

Father in heaven, hallowed be your name.
May your Kingdom come, may your will be done
on earth as it is in heaven.

READ JOHN 16:12-15

There is so much more I want to tell you, but you can't bear it now. When the Spirit of truth comes, he will guide you into all truth. He will not speak on his own but will tell you what he has heard. He will tell you about the future. He will bring me glory by telling you whatever he receives from me. All that belongs to the Father is mine; this is why I said, "The Spirit will tell you whatever he receives from me."

REFLECT

Jesus' disciples were very concerned when he told them he was leaving them. After all, he was the most significant part of their lives, and they had given up everything to follow him. He sought to comfort them by telling them that he would ascend to be King and then the Holy Spirit would come to guide them. Jesus made good on this promise, as we know, and not long after he went to be with the Father and was enthroned as King, the Holy Spirit came upon all the believers. Today when

For the Sake of Others

we put our faith in Jesus, he sends the Holy Spirit to us, too, to guide and direct us into truth and help us love others.

- Where do you long for truth in your life?
- How would you articulate that longing to God?
- What is the truth the Spirit leads us to?

God, fill me anew with your Holy Spirit. Give me an open heart and mind to all that your Spirit longs to transform in me, and grant me the strength I need as I seek to live for the sake of others. Amen.

DAY 16

YOU ARE THE LIGHT OF THE WORLD

a prayer to open

Father in heaven, hallowed be your name. May your Kingdom come, may your will be done on earth as it is in heaven.

READ MATTHEW 5:13-16

You are the salt of the earth. But what good is salt if it has lost its flavor? Can you make it salty again? It will be thrown out and trampled underfoot as worthless.

You are the light of the world—like a city on a hilltop that cannot be hidden. No one lights a lamp and then puts it under a basket. Instead, a lamp is placed on a stand, where it gives light to everyone in the house. In the same way, let your good deeds shine out for all to see, so that everyone will praise your heavenly Father.

REFLECT

Jesus identified his disciples—those he called and set apart—as "the salt of the earth" (verse 13) and "the light of the world" (verse 14). In other words, as followers of Jesus, we have received not only eternal life but also a purpose for this life.

Close your eyes and imagine yourself sitting in a favorite, familiar spot. Get comfortable there, listening for sounds, seeing what is around you. Then imagine Jesus next to you or across from you, looking into your eyes and saying the words he said to the disciples: "You are the salt of the earth. You are the light of the world. Let your light shine before others, that they may see your good deeds and glorify your Father in heaven."

- What would you do today if you allowed Jesus' words to guide you? What would you stop doing today if you allowed his words to guide you?

SACRED QUESTIONS

- What doubts arise in you as you think about being the light of the world and the salt of the earth? What fears or worries arise in you when you consider Jesus' words applying to you?

- Are there ways you are hiding your light "under a basket" or not allowing others to know that you follow Jesus? Take a few moments to ask God to show you if there are certain areas of life in which you are hiding your light.

RESPOND

Father, you have called me the salt of the earth and the light of the world. May it be so! Teach me how to be this. I don't fully understand how these powerful words could apply to me. You have seen my deeds and heard my thoughts. I hide my light to avoid controversy and questions and criticism, or I seek my own glory, my own accolades by my good deeds. I want my life to illuminate the darkness. Let it encourage others in your ways so they find freedom and life that is truly life. Here I stand. May I be the light of the world. Amen.

LOVE YOUR NEIGHBOR AS YOURSELF

a prayer to open

Father in heaven, hallowed be your name.
May your Kingdom come, may your will be done
on earth as it is in heaven.

READ LUKE 10:25-37

One day an expert in religious law stood up to test Jesus by asking him this question: "Teacher, what should I do to inherit eternal life?"

Jesus replied, "What does the law of Moses say? How do you read it?"

The man answered, "'You must love the Lord your God with all your heart, all your soul, all your strength, and all your mind.' And, 'Love your neighbor as yourself.'"

"Right!" Jesus told him. "Do this and you will live!"

The man wanted to justify his actions, so he asked Jesus, "And who is my neighbor?"

Jesus replied with a story: "A Jewish man was traveling from Jerusalem down to Jericho, and he was attacked by bandits. They stripped him of his clothes, beat him up, and left him half dead beside the road.

"By chance a priest came along. But when he saw the man lying there, he crossed to the other side of the road and passed him by. A Temple assistant walked over and looked at him lying there, but he also passed by on the other side.

"Then a despised Samaritan came along, and when he saw the man, he felt compassion for him. Going over to him, the Samaritan soothed his wounds with olive oil and wine and bandaged them. Then he put the man on his own donkey and took him to an inn, where he took care of him. The next day he handed the innkeeper two silver coins, telling him, 'Take care of this man. If his bill runs higher than this, I'll pay you the next time I'm here.'

"Now which of these three would you say was a neighbor to the man who was attacked by bandits?" Jesus asked.

The man replied, "The one who showed him mercy."

Then Jesus said, "Yes, now go and do the same."

For the Sake of Others

425

Jesus told his disciples in no uncertain terms to go and show tangible, actionable, costly mercy the way the Samaritan did for the stranger on the side of the road.

Close your eyes and imagine yourself sitting in a favorite, familiar spot. Get comfortable there, listening for sounds, seeing what is around you. Then imagine Jesus next to you or across from you, looking into your eyes, telling you the story of the Samaritan, and then saying these words: "Now go and do the same."

- What would you do today if you allowed Jesus' words to guide you? What would you stop doing today if you allowed his words to guide you?

- What doubts arise in you as you think about showing mercy the way the Samaritan did? What fears or worries arise in you when you consider Jesus' words applying to you?

- Are there ways in which you are assessing people and determining whether they are worthy of your time and attention? Take a few moments to ask God to show you if there are certain areas of life in which you are withholding mercy because it would be uncomfortable or costly.

RESPOND

Father, thank you for your mercy and grace. Thank you for granting me the ability to be a carrier of that mercy and grace in the world. I want to model the Samaritan in this story—to do good to those who need help, regardless of the inconvenience it might cause me, the price I might have to pay in time or money, or whether the person in need looks like someone "worthy" of my help. Grow me in humility and give me eyes to see every person through your loving gaze. And may I act to love my neighbor as myself. Amen.

DAY 18

WHAT'S MORE IMPORTANT

a prayer to open

Father in heaven, hallowed be your name. May your Kingdom come, may your will be done on earth as it is in heaven.

READ MATTHEW 23:23-24

What sorrow awaits you teachers of religious law and you Pharisees. Hypocrites! For you are careful to tithe even the tiniest income from your herb gardens, but you ignore the more important aspects of the law—justice, mercy, and faith. You should tithe, yes, but do not neglect the more important things. Blind guides! You strain your water so you won't accidentally swallow a gnat, but you swallow a camel!

Jesus cares about what's in our hearts. In his day, the Pharisees held themselves in high regard because of their compliance with the minutiae of the Jewish law, even giving a tenth of their mint, dill, and cumin to the Temple as part of their tithe. But Jesus could see that despite their compliance with the technical parts of the law, they were not acting in love, the most important aspect of the law; they were not acting justly, with mercy, or in faith.

Close your eyes and imagine yourself sitting in a favorite, familiar spot. Get comfortable there, listening for sounds, seeing what is around you. Then imagine Jesus next to you or across from you, looking into your eyes and then saying these words: "Do not neglect the most important things: to extend justice and mercy and exercise faith!"

- What would you do today if you allowed Jesus' words to guide you? What would you stop doing today if you allowed his words to guide you?

- What doubts arise in you as you think about your ability to extend justice and mercy and to exercise faith as Jesus is calling you? What fears or worries arise in you when you consider his words applying to you?

- What aspects of extending justice and mercy are difficult for you? Take a few moments to ask God to show you if there are ways in which you need to grow in extending justice and mercy and exercising faith in him.

RESPOND

Father, I want my heart and actions to align. I can sit silently in the face of injustice at times because of fear or complacency. I can fail to extend mercy because of busyness or a simple lack of compassion. I need your help and your heart. Give me opportunities to speak out for justice, and the courage to act as you call me. May my eyes be on the lookout for people who need mercy, and may my hands be ready to serve. May I focus on the most important things. Amen.

WHEN YOU GIVE TO THE NEEDY

a prayer to open

Father in heaven, hallowed be your name. May your Kingdom come, may your will be done on earth as it is in heaven.

READ MATTHEW 6:1-4

Watch out! Don't do your good deeds publicly, to be admired by others, for you will lose the reward from your Father in heaven. When you give to someone in need, don't do as the hypocrites do—blowing

For the Sake of Others

trumpets in the synagogues and streets to call attention to their acts of charity! I tell you the truth, they have received all the reward they will ever get. But when you give to someone in need, don't let your left hand know what your right hand is doing. Give your gifts in private, and your Father, who sees everything, will reward you.

REFLECT _____

Giving to those in need was not a new concept to the Jews of Jesus' day. Doing so had been part of what God first commanded them when he formed them as a people (see Exodus 23:6-11). Based on Jesus' words, though, giving had apparently become somewhat of a show in which people sought recognition for their charity. So he very clearly directed his followers to give in private, not for fanfare.

Close your eyes and imagine yourself sitting in a favorite, familiar spot. Get comfortable there, listening for sounds, seeing what is around you. Then imagine Jesus next to you or across from you, looking into your eyes and then saying the words he said to his first followers: "Don't do your good deeds publicly, to be admired by others, but give your gifts in private."

- What would you do today if you allowed Jesus' words to guide you? What would you stop doing today if you allowed his words to guide you?

- What doubts arise in you as you think about giving to the needy in the way Jesus instructed his disciples? What fears or worries arise in you when you consider his words applying to you?

- What characteristics and virtues form in you when you give to the needy without fanfare or recognition? Take a few moments to ask God to show you if there are certain areas of life in which you are giving in order to draw attention to yourself.

RESPOND _____

Father, thank you for your goodness and the way you provide for me. I know I have given to people in need just to be recognized or feel good about myself. Shape my heart so it desires to give whether I get something out of it or not. Purify my motivations so I give as you give. May I be attuned to the needs of others, my mind and heart always looking to serve and give. Amen.

DAY 20

THE LEAST OF THESE

a prayer to open

Father in heaven, hallowed be your name.
May your Kingdom come, may your will be done
on earth as it is in heaven.

But when the Son of Man comes in his glory, and all the angels with him, then he will sit upon his glorious throne. All the nations will be gathered in his presence, and he will separate the people as a shepherd separates the sheep from the goats. He will place the sheep at his right hand and the goats at his left.

Then the King will say to those on his right, "Come, you who are blessed by my Father, inherit the Kingdom prepared for you from the creation of the world. For I was hungry, and you fed me. I was thirsty, and you gave me a drink. I was a stranger, and you invited me into your home. I was naked, and you gave me clothing. I was sick, and you cared for me. I was in prison, and you visited me."

Then these righteous ones will reply, "Lord, when did we ever see you hungry and feed you? Or thirsty and give you something to drink? Or a stranger and show you hospitality? Or naked and give you clothing? When did we ever see you sick or in prison and visit you?"

And the King will say, "I tell you the truth, when you did it to one of the least of these my brothers and sisters, you were doing it to me!"

Then the King will turn to those on the left and say, "Away with you, you cursed ones, into the eternal fire prepared for the devil and his demons. For I was hungry, and you didn't feed me. I was thirsty, and you didn't give me a drink. I was a stranger, and you didn't invite me into your home. I was naked, and you didn't give me clothing. I was sick and in prison, and you didn't visit me."

Then they will reply, "Lord, when did we ever see you hungry or thirsty or a stranger or naked or sick or in prison, and not help you?"

And he will answer, "I tell you the truth, when you refused to help the least of these my brothers and sisters, you were refusing to help me."

And they will go away into eternal punishment, but the righteous will go into eternal life.

REFLECT

Jesus told a story that invited his followers to picture a world where every person— and particularly those who are at the margins of society—is treated with the dignity and honor of a king. But not just any king: King Jesus. If we saw King Jesus hungry, we wouldn't look down our noses and refuse him food for whatever reasons we might conjure in our own minds.

Close your eyes and imagine yourself sitting in a favorite, familiar spot. Get comfortable there, listening for sounds, seeing what is around you. Then imagine Jesus next to you or across from you, looking into your eyes and then saying these words: "When you see the vulnerable and most dishonored in society, see me, and treat them with the dignity and care you would extend to me."

- What would you do today if you allowed Jesus' words to guide you? What would you stop doing today if you allowed his words to guide you?

- What doubts arise in you as you think about serving the "least of these" (verse 40) in the ways Jesus instructed his disciples? What fears or worries arise in you when you consider his words applying to you?

- When you don't care for vulnerable or discarded people when you encounter them, what stops you? Take a few moments to ask God to show you if there are ways in which you need to grow in your attitudes and actions toward the outcasts in our society.

For the Sake of Others

Father, give me eyes to see the least of these and come to their aid whenever necessary and whatever the cost. I don't want to view some as lower than others, some deserving of less dignity. Help me see Jesus in those who are hungry or thirsty, in those who are homeless and ragged. Give me eyes to see the King in those who have come from a different land or are suffering with sickness or are imprisoned. Build in me a spirit that says, "Of course I will help. Of course I will serve. Of course I will love." May it be so.

TO DO GOOD

a prayer to open

Father in heaven, hallowed be your name.
May your Kingdom come, may your will be done
on earth as it is in heaven.

READ MARK 3:1-6

Jesus went into the synagogue again and noticed a man with a deformed hand. Since it was the Sabbath, Jesus' enemies watched him closely. If he healed the man's hand, they planned to accuse him of working on the Sabbath.

Jesus said to the man with the deformed hand, "Come and stand in front of everyone." Then he turned to his critics and asked, "Does the law permit good deeds on the Sabbath, or is it a day for doing evil? Is this a day to save life or to destroy it?" But they wouldn't answer him.

He looked around at them angrily and was deeply saddened by their hard hearts. Then he said to the man, "Hold out your hand." So the man held out his hand, and it was restored! At once the Pharisees went away and met with the supporters of Herod to plot how to kill Jesus.

REFLECT

The experts in Jewish law and leaders of the synagogue consistently sought to trick Jesus into breaking the laws by which they lived. These were laws they held sacred and believed were God-ordained, yet these leaders were so unbending that they valued compliance with the law over compassion toward people. Jesus valued both.

Close your eyes and imagine yourself sitting in a favorite, familiar spot. Get comfortable there, listening for sounds, seeing what is around you. Then imagine Jesus next to you or across from you, looking into your eyes and then saying these words: "Is this a day to love and build someone else up, or to judge and speak or act harshly?"

- What would you do today if you allowed Jesus' words to guide you? What would you stop doing today if you allowed his words to guide you?

- What doubts arise in you as you think about allowing compassion to trump compliance with what you believe is right under the law? What fears or worries arise in you when you consider Jesus' words applying to you?

- From whom have you withheld compassion because you don't agree with their choices, are angry with them, or disapprove of their behavior or attitudes? Take a few moments to ask God to show you how Jesus would show compassion to those people.

RESPOND

Father, forgive me for the times I have withheld love and compassion and chosen to be unnecessarily rigid in my thinking. Help me to always choose to do good. Grant me a spirit that seeks your truth and extends your grace. When I become legalistic, show me, and lead me to ask the right questions to seek to understand what is happening in my own heart and mind. Lead me in every way. Amen.

BLESS YOUR ENEMIES

a prayer to open

Father in heaven, hallowed be your name.
May your Kingdom come, may your will be done
on earth as it is in heaven.

READ LUKE 6:27-36

But to you who are willing to listen, I say, love your enemies! Do good to those who hate you. Bless those who curse you. Pray for those who hurt you. If someone slaps you on one cheek, offer the other cheek also. If someone demands your coat, offer your shirt also. Give to anyone who asks; and when things are taken away from you, don't try to get them back. Do to others as you would like them to do to you.

If you love only those who love you, why should you get credit for that? Even sinners love those who love them! And if you do good only to those who do good to you, why should you get credit? Even sinners do that much! And if you lend money only to those who can repay you, why should you get credit? Even sinners will lend to other sinners for a full return.

Love your enemies! Do good to them. Lend to them without expecting to be repaid. Then your reward from heaven will be very great, and you will truly be acting as children of the Most High, for he is kind to those who are unthankful and wicked. You must be compassionate, just as your Father is compassionate.

REFLECT

Are we sure Jesus didn't mix up the words *enemies* and *friends*? To our friends—love, do good, bless, pray, offer our coats and shirts, give, and lend—of course! But to our enemies? To those who hurt, persecute, humiliate, slander, betray, and judge us or the people we love? Jesus is not calling us to something he was unwilling to do: "Since our friendship with God was restored by the death of his Son while we were still his enemies, we will certainly be saved through the life of his Son. So now we can rejoice in our wonderful new relationship with God because our

Lord Jesus Christ has made us friends of God" (Romans 5:10-11). Jesus is calling us to love as he does.

Close your eyes and imagine yourself sitting in a favorite, familiar spot. Get comfortable there, listening for sounds, seeing what is around you. Then imagine Jesus next to you or across from you, looking into your eyes and then saying these words: "Bless, do good to, and love your enemies. Yes, that person, the one who just came to mind."

- What would you do today if you allowed Jesus' words to guide you? What would you stop doing today if you allowed his words to guide you?

- What doubts arise as you think about doing good to someone who has hurt you in some way? What fears or worries surface when you consider Jesus' words applying to you?

- Who is an enemy you can barely tolerate, let alone imagine loving, blessing, or directing good toward? Take a few moments to ask God to show you how Jesus would love that person.

RESPOND

Father, Jesus' words here seem impossible to obey. How can I do this? How can I want the best for someone who has hurt me or someone I love? Help me. Mold and shape my heart so I can do this. To start, I offer you this prayer for [insert the name of an enemy you have identified]: "May you bless [name], keep [name], and make your face to shine upon [name] on this day. Amen."

WELCOME THE STRANGER

a prayer to open

Father in heaven, hallowed be your name. May your Kingdom come, may your will be done on earth as it is in heaven.

READ HEBREWS 13:1-3

Keep on loving each other as brothers and sisters. Don't forget to show hospitality to strangers, for some who have done this have entertained angels without realizing it! Remember those in prison, as if you were there yourself. Remember also those being mistreated, as if you felt their pain in your own bodies.

REFLECT

In our world today, strangers are considered dangerous, or at least suspect. We are to avoid and distance ourselves from them for fear of what harm they could bring. But strangers held a special place in Jesus' heart. In Matthew 25, we read these words of Jesus: "I was a stranger, and you invited me into your home" (verse 35). The author of Hebrews picked up on this teaching, highlighting the importance of welcoming strangers and showing compassion and care for those who are isolated and alone because the place in which they find themselves is not their home.

Close your eyes and imagine yourself sitting in a favorite, familiar spot. Get comfortable there, listening for sounds, seeing what is around you. Then imagine Jesus next to you or across from you, looking into your eyes and then saying these words: "Consider those around you who are strangers here. Reach out to them. Welcome them."

- What would you do today if you allowed Jesus' words in Matthew 25:35 to guide you? What would you stop doing today if you allowed his words to guide you?

- What doubts arise as you think about reaching out to a stranger or welcoming one into your home? What fears or worries surface when you consider Jesus' words applying to you?

- Who are the "strangers" in your city or town? Under what circumstances does your path cross theirs? Take a few moments to ask God to show you how to express compassion and care toward those who feel isolated or at least unfamiliar with the places in which they find themselves.

RESPOND

Father, soften my heart toward those who find themselves in strange places. Give me insight into how they might be feeling and the confusion or discomfort they may be experiencing in a new environment. Dispel any fears in me that arise from differentness or strangeness, and help me extend the love of Jesus to those people. Show me how to welcome the strangers to my table in the same way you welcomed me to your table. Amen.

DAY 24

VISIT THE PRISONER

a prayer to open

Father in heaven, hallowed be your name.
May your Kingdom come, may your will be done
on earth as it is in heaven.

READ HEBREWS 13:1-3

Keep on loving each other as brothers and sisters. Don't forget to show hospitality to strangers, for some who have done this have entertained angels without realizing it! Remember those in prison, as if you were there yourself. Remember also those being mistreated, as if you felt their pain in your own bodies.

Prisoners are a group our society pushes away or places in cells, throwing away the key. They are deemed the bottom of the barrel when it comes to humans in a culture. After all, they are in prison for bad behavior, sometimes murderous and violent conduct. Yet in Jesus' view, they are worthy of love and care and compassion. They, like the rest of us, can be redeemed, made whole, made clean by Jesus. They are not to be forgotten but remembered and visited. In Jesus' parable about the final judgment, he says of those destined for eternal life, "I was in prison, and you visited me" (Matthew 25:36).

Close your eyes and imagine yourself sitting in a favorite, familiar spot. Get comfortable there, listening for sounds, seeing what is around you. Then imagine Jesus next to you or across from you, looking into your eyes and then saying these words: "Remember those in prison. How would you want to be treated if you were there? Make a visit."

- What would you do today if you allowed Jesus' words in Matthew 25:36 to guide you? What would you stop doing today if you allowed his words to guide you?

- What doubts arise as you think about visiting a prisoner? What fears or worries surface when you consider Jesus' words applying to you?

- Who do you know in prison or who has a family member in prison? Take a few moments to ask God to show you what he's calling you to as far as remembering and visiting the prisoner.

RESPOND

Father, I can't imagine the pain and suffering of those in prison. Soften my heart so I can empathize with the deep hurt that must sit within them as they live behind bars and face whatever wrongs they have committed. I pray for their healing and wholeness. Open a door for me to visit someone in prison, and help me be a peaceful and loving presence. Amen.

DAY 25

DO NOT GET TIRED OF DOING GOOD

a prayer to open

Father in heaven, hallowed be your name.
May your Kingdom come, may your will be done
on earth as it is in heaven.

Don't be misled—you cannot mock the justice of God. You will always harvest what you plant. Those who live only to satisfy their own sinful nature will harvest decay and death from that sinful nature. But those who live to please the Spirit will harvest everlasting life from the Spirit. So let's not get tired of doing what is good. At just the right time we will reap a harvest of blessing if we don't give up. Therefore, whenever we have the opportunity, we should do good to everyone—especially to those in the family of faith.

REFLECT

If we seek to do good by our own strength, we will get tired. We might get resentful of God or of others. If we seek to save the world instead of joining with God in his saving of the world, we will get worn out because the job's too big, beyond our ability. But if we align with the Spirit, we will feel full and alive. This is not to say we don't need rest for our bodies and minds and souls. In fact, we can build rhythms of rest into our life. God made us to need these rhythms. When we refuse them, we can be sure we have disconnected from him and are going it alone. Jesus says, "Come to me, all of you who are weary and carry heavy burdens, and I will give you rest" (Matthew 11:28).

Close your eyes and imagine yourself sitting in a favorite, familiar spot. Get comfortable there, listening for sounds, seeing what is around you. Then imagine Jesus next to you or across from you, looking into your eyes and then saying these words: "Why are you so tired? What have you taken on that isn't yours? Come and rest."

- What would you do today if you allowed Jesus' words in Matthew 11:28 to guide you? What would you stop doing today if you allowed his words to guide you?

- What doubts arise as you think about building rhythms of rest into your life? What fears or worries surface when you consider Jesus' words applying to you?

- What rhythms of rest do you need to build into your days, weeks, months, and years? Take a few moments to ask God to help you put into practice the rest you need so you do not grow tired of doing good.

RESPOND

Father, you have called me to so much. You have called me to love beyond what I am capable of. I look through all you ask and almost wither under the weight. But this is me attempting to go it alone. This is me seeing you as a distant God who has left the world spinning without you. Remind me of your presence here by your Spirit. Remind me that I need only align with what you are already doing and be guided along in the work of love. Give me the courage to trust you and to rest regularly. Amen.

For the Sake of Others

GO AND MAKE DISCIPLES

a prayer to open

Father in heaven, hallowed be your name.
May your Kingdom come, may your will be done
on earth as it is in heaven.

READ MATTHEW 28:1-20

Early on Sunday morning, as the new day was dawning, Mary Magdalene and the other Mary went out to visit the tomb.

Suddenly there was a great earthquake! For an angel of the Lord came down from heaven, rolled aside the stone, and sat on it. His face shone like lightning, and his clothing was as white as snow. The guards shook with fear when they saw him, and they fell into a dead faint.

Then the angel spoke to the women. "Don't be afraid!" he said. "I know you are looking for Jesus, who was crucified. He isn't here! He is risen from the dead, just as he said would happen. Come, see where his body was lying. And now, go quickly and tell his disciples that he has risen from the dead, and he is going ahead of you to Galilee. You will see him there. Remember what I have told you."

The women ran quickly from the tomb. They were very frightened but also filled with great joy, and they rushed to give the disciples the angel's message. And as they went, Jesus met them and greeted them. And they ran to him, grasped his feet, and worshiped him. Then Jesus said to them, "Don't be afraid! Go tell my brothers to leave for Galilee, and they will see me there."

As the women were on their way, some of the guards went into the city and told the leading priests what had happened. A meeting with the elders was called, and they decided to give the soldiers a large bribe. They told the soldiers, "You must say, 'Jesus' disciples came during the night while we were sleeping, and they stole his body.' If the governor hears about it, we'll stand up for you so you won't get in trouble." So the guards accepted the bribe and said what they were told to say. Their story spread widely among the Jews, and they still tell it today.

Then the eleven disciples left for Galilee, going to the mountain where Jesus had told them to go. When they saw him, they worshiped him—but some of them doubted!

Jesus came and told his disciples, "I have been given all authority in heaven and on earth. Therefore, go and make disciples of all the nations, baptizing them in the name of the Father and the Son and the Holy Spirit. Teach these new disciples to obey all the commands I have given you. And be sure of this: I am with you always, even to the end of the age."

REFLECT

Jesus' last command to his disciples was "Go tell others! Invite them in! Share with them what I've taught you!" (see verses 19-20). How the early disciples did this is what we see in the book of Acts and the rest of the New Testament. But there can be no doubt that extending the invitation to others continues to be Jesus' command to us. The real question is, why would they listen to us? They won't if our lives look just like everyone else's. But if our lives speak love, joy, peace, patience, kindness, goodness, faithfulness, gentleness, and self-control; if we love those the world discards or hates; if we show mercy and forgiveness beyond what is expected; and if we live for the sake of others, those who come across our paths won't be able to turn away. They will listen because our lives say what we believe: that Jesus is Lord and we follow him alone.

- What does your life say?
- How likely is someone to listen to you if you tell them about the life Jesus offers?
- Spend a few minutes remembering you are in God's loving presence, looking at what others see when you're at work, church, or home, or in your community stores, restaurants, or public spaces.

RESPOND

Pray out of whatever surfaced in your time of reflection.

DAY 27

THE GOSPEL

a prayer to open

Father in heaven, hallowed be your name.
May your Kingdom come, may your will be done
on earth as it is in heaven.

READ ACTS 10:34-48

Then Peter replied, "I see very clearly that God shows no favoritism. In every nation he accepts those who fear him and do what is right. This is the message of Good News for the people of Israel—that there is peace with God through Jesus Christ, who is Lord of all. You know what happened throughout Judea, beginning in Galilee, after John began preaching his message of baptism. And you know that God anointed Jesus of Nazareth with the Holy Spirit and with power. Then Jesus went around doing good and healing all who were oppressed by the devil, for God was with him.

"And we apostles are witnesses of all he did throughout Judea and in Jerusalem. They put him to death by hanging him on a cross, but God raised him to life on the third day. Then God allowed him to appear, not to the general public, but to us whom God had chosen in advance to be his witnesses. We were those who ate and drank with him after he rose from the dead. And he ordered us to preach everywhere and to testify that Jesus is the one appointed by God to be the judge of all—the living and the dead. He is the one all the prophets testified about, saying that everyone who believes in him will have their sins forgiven through his name."

Even as Peter was saying these things, the Holy Spirit fell upon all who were listening to the message. The Jewish believers who came with Peter were amazed that the gift of the Holy Spirit had been poured out on the Gentiles, too. For they heard them speaking in other tongues and praising God.

Then Peter asked, "Can anyone object to their being baptized, now that they have received the Holy Spirit just as we did?" So he gave orders for them to be baptized in the name of Jesus Christ. Afterward Cornelius asked him to stay with them for several days.

In Peter's speech, we have one of the earliest tellings of the gospel. Peter walked with Jesus for three years and was one of the three disciples who had the closest relationship with him. Notice what he deemed critical to share and what he left out. Notice his invitation at the end of his presentation. Notice the arrival of the Holy Spirit in the midst of Peter's speech. For those listening, there could be no response but to be baptized and then learn the ways of Jesus.

- What are the elements of the Good News Peter shares in this passage?

- How does what Peter shared compare with the gospel you have heard or have shared with others?

- Spend a few minutes remembering you are in God's loving presence, reflecting on how you might share the gospel with others as you keep Peter's example in mind.

RESPOND

Pray out of whatever surfaced in your time of reflection.

DAY 28

BE GENTLE AND SHOW TRUE HUMILITY

a prayer to open

Father in heaven, hallowed be your name. May your Kingdom come, may your will be done on earth as it is in heaven.

READ TITUS 3:1-8

Remind the believers to submit to the government and its officers. They should be obedient, always ready to do what is good. They must not slander anyone and must avoid quarreling. Instead, they should be gentle and show true humility to everyone.

Once we, too, were foolish and disobedient. We were misled and became slaves to many lusts and pleasures. Our lives were full of evil and envy, and we hated each other. But—

When God our Savior revealed his kindness and love, he saved us, not because of the righteous things we had done, but because of his mercy. He washed away our sins, giving us a new birth and new life through the Holy Spirit. He generously poured out the Spirit upon us through Jesus Christ our Savior. Because of his grace he made us right in his sight and gave us confidence that we will inherit eternal life.

This is a trustworthy saying, and I want you to insist on these teachings so that all who trust in God will devote themselves to doing good. These teachings are good and beneficial for everyone.

Being invited to a party is far different from being forced to attend a meeting with your boss. Both could be equally good in the end, but there is something powerful about having a choice. The gospel presents us with an invitation. Jesus never forced himself on us but instead invited us to see and experience him. If we turn around and offer this same invitation to others—to see and experience Jesus—we are following in the way of Jesus. On the other hand, if we threaten or use scare tactics, we alienate and close off opportunities for further conversation. Indeed, being pushy or coming across as self-righteous in our words and actions typically acts as a barrier to the gospel. This is why we must be humble and gentle, remembering where we came from and how Jesus met us there.

- What would sharing the gospel humbly and gently look like for you?
- When have you applied pressure or used fear in sharing Jesus' invitation?
- Spend a few minutes remembering that you are in God's loving presence, reflecting on how you might share the gospel gently and with humility.

RESPOND

Pray out of whatever surfaced in your time of reflection.

PRAYING FOR THE WORLD

DAY 29

PRAYER FOR PEACE

REFLECT

War. Gun violence. Conflict. Name-calling. Hate speech. These words describe the events of our time, our political discourse, and what happens in our communities and homes. Unfortunately, even as Christ followers, we can get pulled into these things, allowing judgment, fear, and anger to overtake grace, kindness, and humility. In writing to the church in Colossae, the apostle Paul reminded the Christians there that once they became followers of Jesus, their lives were hidden with Christ in God:

As God's chosen people, . . . clothe yourselves with compassion, kindness, humility, gentleness and patience. Bear with each other and forgive one another if any of you has a grievance against someone. Forgive as the Lord forgave you. And over all these virtues put on love, which binds them all together in perfect unity.

Let the peace of Christ rule in your hearts, since as

For the Sake of Others

members of one body you were called to peace. And be thankful. Let the message of Christ dwell among you richly as you teach and admonish one another with all wisdom through psalms, hymns, and songs from the Spirit, singing to God with gratitude in your hearts. And whatever you do, whether in word or deed, do it all in the name of the Lord Jesus, giving thanks to God the Father through him.

COLOSSIANS 3:12-17, NIV

- Spend a few minutes now praying for peace—in our world, in your country, in your community, in your church, and in your family.

- What reconciliation would be necessary for peace to prevail in these places? What transformation of hearts and minds would be required? Pray for those things to happen.

- Ask God to show you where and how you can be a peacemaker.

A PRAYER TO CLOSE

May your Kingdom come, may your will be done on earth as it is in heaven.

PRAYER FOR LEADERS

REFLECT

Our leaders—church leaders, governmental leaders, private-sector leaders, school leaders, and community leaders—need wisdom, insight, humility, and creativity to lead well in this complex, global world. We are practiced in criticizing our leaders and holding them to high standards, but they also need our prayers. The author of the book of Hebrews wrote this, speaking of early church leaders:

Have confidence in your leaders and submit to their authority, because they keep watch over you as those who must give an account. Do this so that their work will be a joy, not a burden, for that would be of no benefit to you. Pray for us. We are sure that we have a clear conscience and desire to live honorably in every way. I particularly urge you to pray so that I may be restored to you soon.

HEBREWS 13:17-19, NIV

Many of our leaders have big jobs, manage many layers of stress and expectations, and have people looking to them for answers. All of them are imperfect and fail our expectations often or from time to time. And all of them—from the honorable to the dishonorable, and everyone in between—were made in God's image and are loved so deeply that God gave his Son, Jesus, that they might have eternal life.

- Spend a few minutes now praying for leaders, from world leaders to the leaders you specifically report to or are led by.

- What would they need in order to lead from a healthy heart? What wisdom and insight might they need for carrying out their responsibilities? What might they need to remember about who God is and who they are in his sight to lead well?

- Pray as God leads you, and ask him to show you how you can be a light and blessing to the leaders you know.

A PRAYER TO CLOSE

May your Kingdom come, may your will be done
on earth as it is in heaven.

DAY 31

PRAYER FOR ENEMIES

REFLECT

Among the most challenging of Jesus' words are these:

To you who are listening I say: Love your enemies, do good to those who hate you, bless those who curse you, pray for those who mistreat you. If someone slaps you on one cheek, turn to them the other also. If someone takes your coat, do not withhold your shirt from them. Give to everyone who asks you, and if anyone takes what belongs to you, do not demand it back. Do to others as you would have them do to you.

If you love those who love you, what credit is that to you? Even sinners love those who love them. And if you do good to those who are good to you, what credit is that to you? Even sinners do that. And if you lend to those from whom you expect repayment, what credit is that to you? Even sinners lend to sinners, expecting to be repaid in full. But love your enemies, do good to them, and lend to them without expecting to get anything back. Then your reward will be great, and you will be children of the Most High, because he is kind to the ungrateful and wicked. Be merciful, just as your Father is merciful.

LUKE 6:27-36, NIV

To pray for our enemies—to love them, bless them, and do good to them is—for most of us, the most difficult calling we can imagine. In fact, we are skilled at coming up with ways to avoid doing precisely what Jesus instructed. We commit to not seeking revenge or to tolerating our enemies, but doing actual good to them and praying that God would bless them? No way. He couldn't have meant that we should bless and do good to "those people" or "that person." But there is no hesitation, no hedging in Jesus' words. Though everything in us resists, this is the call of Christ—to pray for, love, bless, and do good to our enemies.

- Spend a few minutes now praying for your enemies. Bring to mind first a global enemy. What feelings arise as you bring that person or those people to mind? Speak those feelings to God as honestly as you know how. Ask him to fill you with his Spirit, to give you his eyes and heart, and then pray for that enemy.

- Now bring to mind a personal enemy. What feelings surface as you bring that person to mind? Speak those feelings to God as honestly as you can. Ask him to fill you with his Spirit, to give you his eyes and heart, and then pray for that enemy.

- What would God need to transform in the heart of each person you identified to turn him or her toward his love? What wounds would need to be healed?

A PRAYER TO CLOSE

May your Kingdom come, may your will be done
on earth as it is in heaven.

DAY 32

PRAYER FOR REFUGEES

REFLECT

There are more than sixty-five million refugees and internally displaced people in the world today as a result of war and persecution, according to the United Nations High Commissioner for Refugees. That is one in every 113 people. Children make up almost half of the refugee population.[12] We know from Scripture God's heart for refugees and foreigners and his call to us as his followers. Here is just one example from the mouth of Moses:

Circumcise your hearts, therefore, and do not be stiff-necked any longer. For the LORD your God is God of gods and Lord of lords, the great God, mighty and awesome, who shows no partiality and accepts no bribes. He defends the cause of the fatherless and the widow, and loves the foreigner residing among you, giving them food and clothing. And you are to love those who are foreigners, for you yourselves were foreigners in Egypt.

DEUTERONOMY 10:16-19, NIV

Consider your home and all the things that make you feel safe, at ease, and comfortable there. So many people in our world lack the comfort and security a home provides. Refugees live running from place to place, in tents meant to be temporary, or within fences and camps that fail to provide for even basic needs. Most live in fear and in a constant state of uncertainty.

- Spend a few minutes now praying for the refugees of the world.

- What must it be like to live in constant fear and without a home or place to return to? What must the hearts and minds of the refugees long for or look toward for hope?

- Pray for the individual bodies, hearts, minds, and souls of the men, women, and children—all loved so deeply by God—who have been displaced and seek refuge from war and persecution. Pray that God would show you what he's inviting you to do to love the foreigners and refugees where you live.

A PRAYER TO CLOSE

May your Kingdom come, may your will be done
on earth as it is in heaven.

PRAYER FOR THE HURTING

REFLECT

Everyone we encounter is hurting in one way or another. There are millions of people who don't have enough to eat. There are those who suffer from disease and sickness. Others have been deeply wounded and abused. Still others are plagued by mental illness. And then there are the heartbroken, the lonely, and the abandoned. Suffering is a central element of the human experience and will be until the restoration of all things. In the meantime, in the midst, we hope, we wait, and we join in God's Kingdom work. As Paul wrote to the church in Rome,

I consider that our present sufferings are not worth comparing with the glory that will be revealed in us. For the creation waits in eager expectation for the children of God to be revealed. For the creation was subjected to frustration, not by its own choice, but by the will of the one who subjected it, in hope that the creation itself will be liberated from its bondage to decay and brought into the freedom and glory of the children of God.

We know that the whole creation has been groaning as in the pains of childbirth right up to the present time. Not only so, but we ourselves, who have the firstfruits of the Spirit, groan inwardly as we wait eagerly for our adoption to sonship, the redemption of our bodies. For in this hope we were saved. But hope that is seen is no hope at all. Who hopes for what they already have? But if we hope for what we do not yet have, we wait for it patiently.

In the same way, the Spirit helps us in our weakness. We do not know what we ought to pray for, but the Spirit himself intercedes for us through wordless groans. And he who searches our hearts knows the mind of the Spirit, because the Spirit intercedes for God's people in accordance with the will of God.

ROMANS 8:18-27, NIV

- Spend a few minutes now praying for the hurting. Perhaps there is a specific group of people God brings to mind: those who are hungry, lonely, or sick. As you consider the way that group suffers, what emotions, doubts, fears, and pain would that suffering cause? With your words, bring those people before God and ask him to intervene, heal, and make his presence known.

- Ask God to show you what he's inviting you to do for that group as a way of participating in his plans.

- Pray also for particular people you know who are suffering right now. What do they need? How is God inviting you to love and serve them?

A PRAYER TO CLOSE

May your Kingdom come, may your will be done on earth as it is in heaven.

DAY 34

PRAYER FOR THE SEARCHING

REFLECT

There are people all over the world—from those in penthouses in the largest cities to those in huts in the most remote villages—searching for God. Some are actively searching by asking questions, attending church, or maybe reading the Bible. Others are trying to fill their lives with things they think will satisfy the deep desires within them. Often once our eyes are opened to the fact that Christ is the only one who can satisfy our deepest longings, we turn a blind eye toward or even look down on those who are still searching.

When the Pharisees and teachers of the Jewish law questioned why Jesus welcomed tax collectors and sinners to eat with him, Jesus told these two parables:

Suppose one of you has a hundred sheep and loses one of them. Doesn't he leave the ninety-nine in the open country and go after the lost sheep until he finds it? And when he finds it, he joyfully puts it on his shoulders and goes home. Then he calls his friends and neighbors together and says, "Rejoice with me; I have found my lost sheep." I tell you that in the same way there will be more rejoicing in heaven over one sinner who repents than over ninety-nine righteous persons who do not need to repent.

Or suppose a woman has ten silver coins and loses one. Doesn't she light a lamp, sweep the house and search carefully until she finds it? And when she finds it, she calls her friends and neighbors together and says, "Rejoice with me; I have found my lost coin." In the same way, I tell you, there is rejoicing in the presence of the angels of God over one sinner who repents.

LUKE 15:4-10, NIV

God pursues the lost—the people who are searching, the people caught in sin, and the people who think they don't need him. And as followers of Jesus, we are called to be his ambassadors, pursuers of those who are still searching.

- Spend a few minutes now praying for the people all over our world who are lost and searching for God.

- What comes to mind as you think about what they might be feeling and what they might need to know?

- Ask God to bring to mind specific people he is inviting you to reach out to so they might come to know his goodness and love. Pray for those individual people, and pray that God would show you the best next step to take with each one.

A PRAYER TO CLOSE

May your Kingdom come, may your will be done on earth as it is in heaven.

PRAYER FOR THE CHURCH

REFLECT

When Christ followers join together and demonstrate the love of God to the world by sharing the gospel, serving the poor, seeking justice and peace, and making disciples, this body (the church) is an unstoppable force for good in the world. The church can, however, get caught up in the things of the world: the divisiveness, insults, cynicism, and fear that mark our culture today. The church can grow insular and unwelcoming instead of being a light in the darkness. As Jesus neared his death, he prayed these words for the church:

My prayer is not for them alone. I pray also for those who will believe in me through their message, that all of them may be one, Father, just as you are in me and I am in you. May they also be in us so that the world may believe that you have sent me. I have given them the glory that you gave me, that they may be one as we are one—I in them and you in me—so that they may be brought to complete unity. Then the world will know that you sent me and have loved them even as you have loved me.

Father, I want those you have given me to be with me where I am, and to see my glory, the glory you have given me because you loved me before the creation of the world.

Righteous Father, though the world does not know you, I know you, and they know that you have sent me. I have made you known to them, and will continue to make you known in order that the love you have for me may be in them and that I myself may be in them. **JOHN 17:20-26, NIV**

- Spend a few minutes now praying for the church—the worldwide body of Christ. Join in Jesus' prayer that the church would be united and hold to its mission to proclaim and demonstrate God's love.

- What are the things creating division in the church? Pray for the reconciliation and resolution of those things. Pray that the church would be a light to the lost and the searching—a place that welcomes and invites people to come to know Jesus.

- Now pray for your particular church. What needs exist? What could use strengthening? Pray that God would open your eyes to the role you are to play in your church and provide you with a next step for contributing.

A PRAYER TO CLOSE

May your Kingdom come, may your will be done
on earth as it is in heaven.

Christmas

Waiting for the Coming Christ

EVERY CHRISTMAS FOR at least the past fifteen years, my friend Becky has been organizing an event on the south side of Chicago for kids who live in a shelter that houses battered and abused women and their children. Most of the children are younger than ten years old and have already suffered enough for a lifetime. But on this day, Becky, along with a group of volunteers of which I have been a part for nearly all of those fifteen years, brings hearty home-cooked food and a gift for every one of the fifty to sixty kids there. Because of the coordination Becky does in advance, each present is handpicked for the particular child, and the gifts include both a toy or fun item and a winter coat or other practical item.

From the outside, this event may look like any other event that occurs around Christmastime, with no tie to Jesus himself or the meaning of Christmas. It might appear to be locked into the cultural imagination of Christmas as a consumeristic extravaganza. But if you could be present at the events, you would detect something utterly different going on under the surface. You see, after we eat (the volunteers serve the women and children), each child is called up by name near the Christmas tree. For years Marcus, a volunteer, would call out, "Tyler! Come on up! Merry Christmas. Let's all give a clap for Tyler!" All those gathered in the shelter would clap and cheer, as if to say, "We see you, Tyler! We love and value you!" Child after child would be called up to receive a gift and a cheer. Each one would turn back to his or her mom with joy and delight.

Christmas is God's "I see you! I love and value you!" to humanity. Historically, Christmas was the beginning—from our perspective—of the revelation that "all of God's promises have been fulfilled in Christ with a resounding 'Yes!'" (2 Corinthians 1:20). Now Christmas is the day we celebrate the actual historical event in which the eternal Word of God came to earth in a human body to be with his creation and experience what it means to live in a vulnerable, aging, limited body. In other words, he didn't seek to help us from afar; he came close. God became flesh and "moved into the neighborhood," as Eugene Peterson would say (John 1:14, MSG), in order to show us how to live, to suffer alongside us by going through all that we experience in a body, and then to redeem and restore us. This was God's promise and purpose all along. Now we are waiting for Christ to return and finally and fully bring God's Kingdom on earth.

But we are not simply idle during this time, waiting out our hours on earth so we can make it somewhere else. We actually get to participate in what God is doing to redeem and restore the world. We get to say to Tyler and all the little boys and girls like him, "I see you! I love and value you!" because we have been given the Holy Spirit to guide and empower us to be like Jesus in the world. Each time I think of this, it astounds me. Of course, we get to say way more than even just "I see you! I love and value you!" We get to say that the Creator of all things loves and sees each individual person around us, so much so that he acted in a spectacular way—through Jesus Christ—to bring them into new life to be with him, living in light and power and love. We wait for Christ to return, and as we do, we get to join in God's work: "Through Christ, our 'Amen' (which means 'Yes') ascends to God for his glory" (2 Corinthians 1:20).

This fifteen-day section will focus on the truth that God came to be with us—to say yes to us—in a body. This body started as a helpless baby and then grew into a toddler, then a young prepubescent boy, then a teenager, and finally a man. The invitation in this section is to open ourselves to discovering what it means for us that God was embodied in Jesus of Nazareth, especially in a season marked so deeply by consumerism and non-Christian tradition.

A SON IN A MOTHER'S WOMB

Begin by taking a few breaths and paying attention to the air moving in and out of your lungs and mouth. Notice where you feel tension or discomfort in your body. To the extent you are able, try to relax, let the chair you are sitting in fully support your body, and release the tension as you breathe deeply.

a prayer to open

Here I am, Lord, in my tired, aging, hurting, wondrous body. Open my heart to you now. You are my High Priest who knows.

READ LUKE 1:26-38

In the sixth month of Elizabeth's pregnancy, God sent the angel Gabriel to Nazareth, a village in Galilee, to a virgin named Mary. She was engaged to be married to a man named Joseph, a descendant of King David. Gabriel appeared to her and said, "Greetings, favored woman! The Lord is with you!"

Confused and disturbed, Mary tried to think what the angel could mean. "Don't be afraid, Mary," the angel told her, "for you have found favor with God! You will conceive and give birth to a son, and you will name him Jesus. He will be very great and will be called the Son of the Most High. The Lord God will give him the throne of his ancestor David. And he will reign over Israel forever; his Kingdom will never end!"

Mary asked the angel, "But how can this happen? I am a virgin."

The angel replied, "The Holy Spirit will come upon you, and the power of the Most High will overshadow you. So the baby to be born will be holy, and he will be called the Son of God. What's more, your relative Elizabeth has become pregnant in her old age! People used to say she was barren, but she has conceived a son and is now in her sixth month. For the word of God will never fail."

Mary responded, "I am the Lord's servant. May everything you have said about me come true." And then the angel left her.

REFLECT

One of the hardest realities for us to grasp is that God made himself nothing and took on the form of a human. And he didn't start as a strong young man in his twenties. He started where we all start: helpless in his mother's womb. The story of Christmas begins with the story of a baby in a womb.

- What words and images come to mind when you think of a human baby growing within a woman's womb?

- Reflect on the reality that God came to be with us by being grown and nourished in a woman's womb, just as all human babies are. What does this truth reveal to you about his love?

- How does the fact that Jesus was formed in Mary's womb reveal the sacredness God sees and the value he places on the human body?

RESPOND

Jesus Christ—
Wonderful Counselor, Mighty God, Everlasting Father, and Prince of Peace;
the one through whom and for whom all things were made; and
the one in whom I live and move and have my being—
you became flesh and made your dwelling among us.
And nothing—neither death nor life, angels nor demons, the present nor the future; not any powers, height nor depth, nor anything else in all creation—can separate me from the love of our God, which is in you, Jesus Christ my Lord.

DAY 2

JESUS, WHOSE MOTHER WAS MARY

Begin by taking a few breaths and paying attention to the air moving in and out of your lungs and mouth. Notice where you feel tension or discomfort in your body. To the extent you are able, try to relax, let the chair you are sitting in fully support your body, and release the tension as you breathe deeply.

READ MATTHEW 1:1-17

This is a record of the ancestors of Jesus the Messiah, a descendant of David and of Abraham:

Abraham was the father of Isaac.
Isaac was the father of Jacob.
Jacob was the father of Judah and his brothers.
Judah was the father of Perez and Zerah (whose mother was Tamar).
Perez was the father of Hezron.
Hezron was the father of Ram.
Ram was the father of Amminadab.
Amminadab was the father of Nahshon.
Nahshon was the father of Salmon.
Salmon was the father of Boaz (whose mother was Rahab).
Boaz was the father of Obed (whose mother was Ruth).
Obed was the father of Jesse.
Jesse was the father of King David.
David was the father of Solomon (whose mother was Bathsheba, the widow of Uriah).
Solomon was the father of Rehoboam.
Rehoboam was the father of Abijah.
Abijah was the father of Asa.
Asa was the father of Jehoshaphat.
Jehoshaphat was the father of Jehoram.
Jehoram was the father of Uzziah.
Uzziah was the father of Jotham.

Jotham was the father of Ahaz.
Ahaz was the father of Hezekiah.
Hezekiah was the father of Manasseh.
Manasseh was the father of Amon.
Amon was the father of Josiah.
Josiah was the father of Jehoiachin and his brothers (born at the time of the exile to Babylon).

After the Babylonian exile:
Jehoiachin was the father of Shealtiel.
Shealtiel was the father of Zerubbabel.
Zerubbabel was the father of Abiud.
Abiud was the father of Eliakim.
Eliakim was the father of Azor.
Azor was the father of Zadok.
Zadok was the father of Akim.
Akim was the father of Eliud.
Eliud was the father of Eleazar.
Eleazar was the father of Matthan.
Matthan was the father of Jacob.
Jacob was the father of Joseph, the husband of Mary.
Mary gave birth to Jesus, who is called the Messiah.

All those listed above include fourteen generations from Abraham to David, fourteen from David to the Babylonian exile, and fourteen from the Babylonian exile to the Messiah.

REFLECT

In this genealogy, Matthew makes clear that Jesus was born into a line of human beings—some we can read about in Scripture and some who are never mentioned. Jesus had a mother, and Jesus' mother's husband (Joseph) was in the line of David. Jesus' father is, of course, Father God, the Creator. But what we rarely think about is whether Jesus looked like Mary, his mother. What attributes of hers did he have? What mannerisms? Might they have had the same laugh, the same hands?

• What attributes and mannerisms do you share with your mother? If you are a parent, what attributes and mannerisms of yours do you see in your children? How do you feel when you consider the fact that you carry attributes of your mother and that your children carry attributes of yours?

• Reflect on the reality that Jesus has a body like yours—with eyes, a nose, ears, a mouth, smile lines, hands, and feet. What does this reveal to you about God's love?

- What does the truth that Jesus has a body like yours reveal to you about the care we are to give our bodies and the respect which we are to extend to others' bodies?

RESPOND

Jesus Christ—
Wonderful Counselor, Mighty God, Everlasting Father, and Prince of Peace;
the one through whom and for whom all things were made; and
the one in whom I live and move and have my being—
you became flesh and made your dwelling among us.
And nothing—neither death nor life, angels nor demons, the present nor the future; not any powers, height nor depth, nor anything else in all creation—can separate me from the love of our God, which is in you, Jesus Christ my Lord.

DAY 3

A BABY LYING IN THE MANGER

Begin by taking a few breaths and paying attention to the air moving in and out of your lungs and mouth. Notice where you feel tension or discomfort in your body. To the extent you are able, try to relax, let the chair you are sitting in fully support your body, and release the tension as you breathe deeply.

a prayer to open

Here I am, Lord, in my tired, aging, hurting, wondrous body. Open my heart to you now. You are my High Priest who knows.

READ LUKE 2:1-21

At that time the Roman emperor, Augustus, decreed that a census should be taken throughout the Roman Empire. . . . All returned to their own ancestral towns to register for this census. And because Joseph was a descendant of King David, he had to go to Bethlehem in Judea. . . . He took with him Mary, to whom he was engaged, who was now expecting a child.

And while they were there, the time came for her baby to be born. She gave birth to her firstborn son. She wrapped him snugly in strips of cloth and laid him in a manger, because there was no lodging available for them.

That night there were shepherds staying in the fields nearby, guarding their flocks of sheep. Suddenly, an angel of the Lord appeared among them, and the radiance of the Lord's glory surrounded them. They were terrified, but the angel reassured them. "Don't be afraid!" he said. "I bring you good news that will bring great joy to all people.

The Savior—yes, the Messiah, the Lord—has been born today in Bethlehem, the city of David! And you will recognize him by this sign: You will find a baby wrapped snugly in strips of cloth, lying in a manger."

Suddenly, the angel was joined by a vast host of others—the armies of heaven—praising God and saying,

"Glory to God in highest heaven,
and peace on earth to those with whom
God is pleased."

When the angels had returned to heaven, the shepherds said to each other, "Let's go to Bethlehem! Let's see this thing that has happened, which the Lord has told us about."

They hurried to the village and found Mary and Joseph. And there was the baby, lying in the manger. After seeing him, the shepherds told everyone what had happened. . . . All who heard the shepherds' story were astonished, but Mary kept all these things in her heart and thought about them often. The

Christmas

shepherds went back to their flocks, glorifying and praising God for all they had heard and seen. It was just as the angel had told them.

Eight days later, when the baby was circumcised, he was named Jesus, the name given him by the angel even before he was conceived.

REFLECT_____

Mary gave birth to Jesus—to God with us. We have no reason to believe that the birthing process was unique or less painful than any other birth. And as was required under the Jewish law, Jesus was circumcised on the eighth day of his life, as any other male baby would have been circumcised. How rare it is for us to think of Jesus this way: as a little baby, with little baby parts, treated like any other Jewish boy of his time.

- What words and images come to mind when you think of a human baby having just been born?

- Why do you think it was important for Jesus to have come to us this way instead of simply having appeared as an adult?

- Reflect on the reality that God came to be with us through the normal human birthing process, was vulnerable and crying, and was born with a penis, as every other human boy has been born. What does this truth reveal to you about God's love? What does it reveal about Jesus' ability to identify with you?

RESPOND_____

Jesus Christ—
Wonderful Counselor, Mighty God, Everlasting Father, and Prince of Peace;
the one through whom and for whom all things were made; and
the one in whom I live and move and have my being—
you became flesh and made your dwelling among us.
And nothing—neither death nor life, angels nor demons, the present nor the future; not any powers, height nor depth, nor anything else in all creation—can separate me from the love of our God, which is in you, Jesus Christ my Lord.

DAY 4

THE CHILD GREW
AND BECAME STRONG

Begin by taking a few breaths and paying attention to the air moving in and out of your lungs and mouth. Notice where you feel tension or discomfort in your body. To the extent you are able, try to relax, let the chair you are sitting in fully support your body, and release the tension as you breathe deeply.

READ LUKE 2:25-40

At that time there was a man in Jerusalem named Simeon. He was righteous and devout and was eagerly waiting for the Messiah to come and rescue Israel. The Holy Spirit was upon him and had revealed to him that he would not die until he had seen the Lord's Messiah. That day the Spirit led him to the Temple. So when Mary and Joseph came to present the baby Jesus to the Lord as the law required, Simeon was there. He took the child in his arms and praised God, saying,

"Sovereign Lord, now let your servant die in peace,
  as you have promised.
I have seen your salvation,
  which you have prepared for all people.
He is a light to reveal God to the nations,
  and he is the glory of your people Israel!"

Jesus' parents were amazed at what was being said about him. Then Simeon blessed them, and he said to Mary, the baby's mother, "This child is destined to cause many in Israel to fall, and many others to rise. He has been sent as a sign from God, but many will oppose him. As a result, the deepest thoughts of many hearts will be revealed. And a sword will pierce your very soul."

Anna, a prophet, was also there in the Temple. She was the daughter of Phanuel from the tribe of Asher, and she was very old. Her husband died when they had been married only seven years. Then she lived as a widow to the age of eighty-four. She never left the Temple but stayed there day and night, worshiping God with fasting and prayer. She came along just as Simeon was talking with Mary and Joseph, and she began praising God. She talked about the child to everyone who had been waiting expectantly for God to rescue Jerusalem.

When Jesus' parents had fulfilled all the requirements of the law of the Lord, they returned home to Nazareth in Galilee. There the child grew up healthy and strong. He was filled with wisdom, and God's favor was on him.

REFLECT

Jesus was so small that he was held in the arms of his parents and relatives and elders in the Temple. Jesus teethed; his body grew; his muscles got strong. How often do we think about the fact that Jesus did not instantly go from a baby to a man?

• What words, images, and attributes come to mind when you think of a young boy? What do you see? What is his bodily experience?

• Reflect on the reality that God came to be with us first through the body and mind of a little boy who had parents and siblings and friends. What does this truth reveal to you about God's love? What does it reveal about Jesus' ability to identify with you?

• Reflect on the children in your family and community. How does knowing that Jesus went through similar experiences as those children in growing up shape your love toward them?

Jesus Christ—
Wonderful Counselor, Mighty God, Everlasting Father, and Prince of Peace;
the one through whom and for whom all things were made; and
the one in whom I live and move and have my being—
you became flesh and made your dwelling among us.
And nothing—neither death nor life, angels nor demons, the present nor the future; not any powers, height nor depth, nor anything else in all creation—can separate me from the love of our God,
which is in you, Jesus Christ my Lord.

HE BECAME VERY HUNGRY

Begin by taking a few breaths and paying attention to the air moving in and out of your lungs and mouth. Notice where you feel tension or discomfort in your body. To the extent you are able, try to relax, let the chair you are sitting in fully support your body, and release the tension as you breathe deeply.

a prayer to open   Here I am, Lord, in my tired, aging, hurting, wondrous body.
Open my heart to you now.   You are my High Priest who knows.

READ MATTHEW 3:13–4:11

Then Jesus went from Galilee to the Jordan River to be baptized by John. But John tried to talk him out of it. "I am the one who needs to be baptized by you," he said, "so why are you coming to me?"

But Jesus said, "It should be done, for we must carry out all that God requires." So John agreed to baptize him.

After his baptism, as Jesus came up out of the water, the heavens were opened and he saw the Spirit of God descending like a dove and settling on him. And a voice from heaven said, "This is my dearly loved Son, who brings me great joy."

Then Jesus was led by the Spirit into the wilderness to be tempted there by the devil. For forty days and forty nights he fasted and became very hungry.

During that time the devil came and said to him, "If you are the Son of God, tell these stones to become loaves of bread."

But Jesus told him, "No! The Scriptures say,

'People do not live by bread alone,
    but by every word that comes from the
        mouth of God.'"

Then the devil took him to the holy city, Jerusalem, to the highest point of the Temple, and said, "If you are the Son of God, jump off! For the Scriptures say,

'He will order his angels to protect you.
And they will hold you up with their hands
    so you won't even hurt your foot on a
        stone.'"

Jesus responded, "The Scriptures also say, 'You must not test the LORD your God.'"

Next the devil took him to the peak of a very high mountain and showed him all the kingdoms of the world and their glory. "I will give it all to you," he said, "if you will kneel down and worship me."

"Get out of here, Satan," Jesus told him. "For the Scriptures say,

'You must worship the LORD your God
    and serve only him.'"

Then the devil went away, and angels came and took care of Jesus.

In Jesus' baptism, we see one of the most stunning moments of all time: the Father's acknowledgment of Jesus as his Son, his beloved, and the affirmation of this truth by his voice and the presence of the Holy Spirit. Immediately afterward, Jesus' body and mind are tested. He is hungry and thirsty and presumably very tired from not having eaten in forty days. He is alone. He is outside in the wilderness. The one who created all things and holds all things together is humbled by a limited human body.

- What do you think Jesus was feeling in his body during his time in the wilderness? Consider his hunger, the temperature, his aloneness, and where and how he slept.

- Reflect on the reality that God came to be with us in a body that would hunger and hurt and be uncomfortable and tired. What does this truth reveal to you about his love? What does it reveal about Jesus' ability to identify with you?

- Reflect on the times you have been hurt, uncomfortable, or exhausted. How might your experience help you identify with and serve someone you know who is going through something similar?

RESPOND

Jesus Christ—
Wonderful Counselor, Mighty God, Everlasting Father, and Prince of Peace;
the one through whom and for whom all things were made; and
the one in whom I live and move and have my being—
you became flesh and made your dwelling among us.
And nothing—neither death nor life, angels nor demons, the present nor the future; not any powers, height nor depth, nor anything else in all creation—can separate me from the love of our God, which is in you, Jesus Christ my Lord.

DAY 6

JESUS WAS SLEEPING

Begin by taking a few breaths and paying attention to the air moving in and out of your lungs and mouth. Notice where you feel tension or discomfort in your body. To the extent you are able, try to relax, let the chair you are sitting in fully support your body, and release the tension as you breathe deeply.

Here I am, Lord, in my tired, aging, hurting, wondrous body.
Open my heart to you now. You are my High Priest who knows.

READ MATTHEW 8:23-27

Then Jesus got into the boat and started across the lake with his disciples. Suddenly, a fierce storm struck the lake, with waves breaking into the boat. But Jesus was sleeping. The disciples went and woke him up, shouting, "Lord, save us! We're going to drown!"

Jesus responded, "Why are you afraid? You have so little faith!" Then he got up and rebuked the wind and waves, and suddenly there was a great calm. The disciples were amazed. "Who is this man?" they asked. "Even the winds and waves obey him!"

REFLECT

Many of us have read this passage a number of times. Our focus, rightly, has likely always been on Jesus' power to calm the wind and waves. What we often miss in this miraculous scene is that Jesus was sleeping just moments before—through a pretty bad storm. How exhausted must he have been to have curled up on a wooden boat and fallen asleep?

• What do you think Jesus was feeling in his body when he climbed into the boat with his disciples? As best you can, picture him—his body—finding a place to curl up and fall asleep. What do you see?

• Reflect on the reality that God came to be with us in a body that needed sleep and at times grew exhausted. What does this truth reveal to you about his love? What does it reveal about Jesus' ability to identify with you?

• Reflect on the times you have been exhausted and desperately in need of sleep. How might your experience help you identify with and serve someone you know who is sleep deprived?

RESPOND

Jesus Christ—
Wonderful Counselor, Mighty God, Everlasting Father, and Prince of Peace;
the one through whom and for whom all things were made; and
the one in whom I live and move and have my being—
you became flesh and made your dwelling among us.
And nothing—neither death nor life, angels nor demons, the present nor the future; not any powers, height nor depth, nor anything else in all creation—can separate me from the love of our God, which is in you, Jesus Christ my Lord.

JESUS WEPT

Begin by taking a few breaths and paying attention to the air moving in and out of your lungs and mouth. Notice where you feel tension or discomfort in your body. To the extent you are able, try to relax, let the chair you are sitting in fully support your body, and release the tension as you breathe deeply.

a prayer to open   Here I am, Lord, in my tired, aging, hurting, wondrous body. Open my heart to you now. You are my High Priest who knows.

READ JOHN 11:17-35

When Jesus arrived at Bethany, he was told that Lazarus had already been in his grave for four days. Bethany was only a few miles down the road from Jerusalem, and many of the people had come to console Martha and Mary in their loss. When Martha got word that Jesus was coming, she went to meet him. But Mary stayed in the house. Martha said to Jesus, "Lord, if only you had been here, my brother would not have died. But even now I know that God will give you whatever you ask."

Jesus told her, "Your brother will rise again."

"Yes," Martha said, "he will rise when everyone else rises, at the last day."

Jesus told her, "I am the resurrection and the life. Anyone who believes in me will live, even after dying. Everyone who lives in me and believes in me will never ever die. Do you believe this, Martha?"

"Yes, Lord," she told him. "I have always believed you are the Messiah, the Son of God, the one who has come into the world from God." Then she returned to Mary. She called Mary aside from the mourners and told her, "The Teacher is here and wants to see you." So Mary immediately went to him.

Jesus had stayed outside the village, at the place where Martha met him. When the people who were at the house consoling Mary saw her leave so hastily, they assumed she was going to Lazarus's grave to weep. So they followed her there. When Mary arrived and saw Jesus, she fell at his feet and said, "Lord, if only you had been here, my brother would not have died."

When Jesus saw her weeping and saw the other people wailing with her, a deep anger welled up within him, and he was deeply troubled. "Where have you put him?" he asked them.

They told him, "Lord, come and see." Then Jesus wept.

REFLECT

Jesus wept. John does not say that Jesus got choked up or looked sad; he wept with the grief and sorrow that death brings.

- What comes to mind when you think of someone weeping? What does it look like? Sound like? What is the body doing as it weeps?

- Reflect on the reality that God came to be with us in a body that wept with grief in the face of death. What does this truth reveal to you about his love? What does it reveal about Jesus' ability to identify with you?

- Reflect on a time you have experienced deep grief. How might your experience help you identify with and serve someone you know who is grieving?

Jesus Christ—
Wonderful Counselor, Mighty God, Everlasting Father, and Prince of Peace;
the one through whom and for whom all things were made; and
the one in whom I live and move and have my being—
you became flesh and made your dwelling among us.
And nothing—neither death nor life, angels nor demons, the present nor the future; not any powers, height nor depth, nor anything else in all creation—can separate me from the love of our God, which is in you, Jesus Christ my Lord.

DAY 8

JESUS ATE

Begin by taking a few breaths and paying attention to the air moving in and out of your lungs and mouth. Notice where you feel tension or discomfort in your body. To the extent you are able, try to relax, let the chair you are sitting in fully support your body, and release the tension as you breathe deeply.

a prayer to open

Here I am, Lord, in my tired, aging, hurting, wondrous body.
Open my heart to you now.   You are my High Priest who knows.

READ MARK 2:13-17

Then Jesus went out to the lakeshore again and taught the crowds that were coming to him. As he walked along, he saw Levi son of Alphaeus sitting at his tax collector's booth. "Follow me and be my disciple," Jesus said to him. So Levi got up and followed him.

Later, Levi invited Jesus and his disciples to his home as dinner guests, along with many tax collectors and other disreputable sinners. (There were many people of this kind among Jesus' followers.) But when the teachers of religious law who were Pharisees saw him eating with tax collectors and other sinners, they asked his disciples, "Why does he eat with such scum?"

When Jesus heard this, he told them, "Healthy people don't need a doctor—sick people do. I have come to call not those who think they are righteous, but those who know they are sinners."

REFLECT

Of great controversy during Jesus' life were the kinds of people with whom he ate. Consider, though, that he ate. He drank wine, shared conversation over fresh fish and vegetables. Maybe food got stuck in his teeth, he burped, and his stomach squealed as it digested his food.

- What comes to mind as you think about the fact that Jesus ate and drank and his body processed foods just as ours do?

- Reflect on the reality that God came to be with us in a body and took in food and digested it in a typical human way. What does this truth reveal to you about his love? What does it reveal about Jesus' ability to identify with you?

- How might your view of your body—and all its weird sounds and responses to food or lack of it—be influenced as you consider that Jesus' body worked just the same way?

RESPOND

Jesus Christ—
Wonderful Counselor, Mighty God, Everlasting Father, and Prince of Peace;
the one through whom and for whom all things were made; and
the one in whom I live and move and have my being—
you became flesh and made your dwelling among us.
And nothing—neither death nor life, angels nor demons, the present nor the future; not any powers, height nor depth, nor anything else in all creation—can separate me from the love of our God, which is in you, Jesus Christ my Lord.

DAY 9

JESUS SWEAT

Begin by taking a few breaths and paying attention to the air moving in and out of your lungs and mouth. Notice where you feel tension or discomfort in your body. To the extent you are able, try to relax, let the chair you are sitting in fully support your body, and release the tension as you breathe deeply.

a prayer to open   Here I am, Lord, in my tired, aging, hurting, wondrous body.
Open my heart to you now. You are my High Priest who knows.

READ LUKE 22:39-46

Then, accompanied by the disciples, Jesus left the upstairs room and went as usual to the Mount of Olives. There he told them, "Pray that you will not give in to temptation."

He walked away, about a stone's throw, and knelt down and prayed, "Father, if you are willing, please take this cup of suffering away from me. Yet I want your will to be done, not mine." Then an angel from heaven appeared and strengthened him. He prayed more fervently, and he was in such agony of spirit that his sweat fell to the ground like great drops of blood.

At last he stood up again and returned to the disciples, only to find them asleep, exhausted from grief. "Why are you sleeping?" he asked them. "Get up and pray, so that you will not give in to temptation."

REFLECT

Jesus' anxiety and anguish about his upcoming gruesome death was so severe that his sweat fell to the ground like great drops of blood. His body ached and fought, so desperate was his human will to escape what he had been called to do on earth for us.

Christmas

•

- Close your eyes and reflect on Jesus in the garden of Gethsemane just hours before he would be put to death by crucifixion. How must his body have been responding? What other sensations besides what we are told can you imagine him experiencing in his body?

- Reflect on the reality that God came to be with us in a body that hurt and responded as our bodies do to pain and anguish. What does this truth reveal to you about his love? What does it reveal about Jesus' ability to identify with you?

- Reflect on the times you have been in physical pain. How might your experience help you identify with and serve someone you know who is currently suffering physical pain?

RESPOND

Jesus Christ—
Wonderful Counselor, Mighty God, Everlasting Father, and Prince of Peace;
the one through whom and for whom all things were made; and
the one in whom I live and move and have my being—
you became flesh and made your dwelling among us.
And nothing—neither death nor life, angels nor demons, the present nor the future; not any powers, height nor depth, nor anything else in all creation—can separate me from the love of our God, which is in you, Jesus Christ my Lord.

DAY 10

THEY NAILED HIM TO THE CROSS

Begin by taking a few breaths and paying attention to the air moving in and out of your lungs and mouth. Notice where you feel tension or discomfort in your body. To the extent you are able, try to relax, let the chair you are sitting in fully support your body, and release the tension as you breathe deeply.

a prayer to open

Here I am, Lord, in my tired, aging, hurting, wondrous body.
Open my heart to you now. You are my High Priest who knows.

READ MATTHEW 27:32-50

Along the way, they came across a man named Simon, who was from Cyrene, and the soldiers forced him to carry Jesus' cross. And they went out to a place called Golgotha (which means "Place of the Skull"). The soldiers gave Jesus wine mixed with bitter gall, but when he had tasted it, he refused to drink it.

After they had nailed him to the cross, the soldiers gambled for his clothes by throwing dice. Then they sat around and kept guard as he hung there. A sign was fastened above Jesus' head, announcing the charge against him. It read: "This is Jesus, the King of the Jews." Two revolutionaries were crucified with him, one on his right and one on his left.

The people passing by shouted abuse, shaking their heads in mockery. "Look at you now!" they yelled at him. "You said you were going to destroy the Temple and rebuild it in three days. Well then, if you are the Son of God, save yourself and come down from the cross!"

The leading priests, the teachers of religious law, and the elders also mocked Jesus. "He saved others," they scoffed, "but he can't save himself! So he is the King of Israel, is he? Let him come down from the cross right now, and we will believe in him! He trusted God, so let God rescue him now if he wants him! For he said, 'I am the Son of God.'" Even the revolutionaries who were crucified with him ridiculed him in the same way.

At noon, darkness fell across the whole land until three o'clock. At about three o'clock, Jesus called out with a loud voice, *"Eli, Eli, lema sabachthani?"* which means "My God, my God, why have you abandoned me?"

Some of the bystanders misunderstood and thought he was calling for the prophet Elijah. One of them ran and filled a sponge with sour wine, holding it up to him on a reed stick so he could drink. But the rest said, "Wait! Let's see whether Elijah comes to save him."

Then Jesus shouted out again, and he released his spirit.

REFLECT

Jesus' body was brutalized by the Roman soldiers. How did he endure such suffering?

- Close your eyes and reflect on Jesus as he walked to the cross and then was beaten, spit upon, stripped, and then crucified. How must his body have been responding? What other sensations besides what we are told can you imagine him experiencing in his body?

- What is the most painful experience your body has endured? As you think of that experience, what comes to mind? What do you remember? How did you endure?

- Reflect on the reality that Jesus submitted his body—his real, human, feeling body—to be beaten, spit upon, nailed through, and hung for your sake and the sake of the world. What does this truth reveal to you about God's love? What does it reveal about Jesus' ability to identify with you?

RESPOND

Jesus Christ—
Wonderful Counselor, Mighty God, Everlasting Father, and Prince of Peace;
the one through whom and for whom all things were made; and
the one in whom I live and move and have my being—
you became flesh and made your dwelling among us.
And nothing—neither death nor life, angels nor demons, the present nor the future; not any powers, height nor depth, nor anything else in all creation—can separate me from the love of our God, which is in you, Jesus Christ my Lord.

PUT YOUR HAND INTO THE WOUND IN MY SIDE

Begin by taking a few breaths and paying attention to the air moving in and out of your lungs and mouth. Notice where you feel tension or discomfort in your body. To the extent you are able, try to relax, let the chair you are sitting in fully support your body, and release the tension as you breathe deeply.

a prayer to open
Here I am, Lord, in my tired, aging, hurting, wondrous body. Open my heart to you now. You are my High Priest who knows.

READ JOHN 20:24-29

One of the twelve disciples, Thomas . . . , was not with the others when Jesus came. They told him, "We have seen the Lord!"

But he replied, "I won't believe it unless I see the nail wounds in his hands, put my fingers into them, and place my hand into the wound in his side."

Eight days later the disciples were together again, and this time Thomas was with them. The doors were locked; but suddenly, as before, Jesus was standing among them. "Peace be with you," he said. Then he said to Thomas, "Put your finger here, and look at my hands. Put your hand into the wound in my side. Don't be faithless any longer. Believe!"

"My Lord and my God!" Thomas exclaimed.

Then Jesus told him, "You believe because you have seen me. Blessed are those who believe without seeing me."

REFLECT

When Jesus rose from the dead, he rose in his body, glorious and new though it was. He could touch, eat, speak, and see, and he carried the wounds of the crucifixion still. He was no ghost or spirit. He remained and remains embodied.

- Why do you think Jesus wanted Thomas to touch his wounds? Why does it matter that when Jesus rose, he remained—and remains—embodied?

- In what ways have you unintentionally disembodied Jesus—thought of him as only a spirit—in your faith journey? How has that affected you?

- Reflect on the reality that Jesus rose from the dead and still has his body. What does this truth reveal to you about God's love? What does it reveal about Jesus' ability to identify with you?

RESPOND

Jesus Christ—
Wonderful Counselor, Mighty God, Everlasting Father, and Prince of Peace;
the one through whom and for whom all things were made; and
the one in whom I live and move and have my being—
you became flesh and made your dwelling among us.

SACRED QUESTIONS

And nothing—neither death nor life, angels nor demons, the present nor the future; not any powers, height nor depth, nor anything else in all creation—can separate me from the love of our God, which is in you, Jesus Christ my Lord.

HE UNDERSTANDS OUR WEAKNESSES

Begin by taking a few breaths and paying attention to the air moving in and out of your lungs and mouth. Notice where you feel tension or discomfort in your body. To the extent you are able, try to relax, let the chair you are sitting in fully support your body, and release the tension as you breathe deeply.

a prayer to open

Here I am, Lord, in my tired, aging, hurting, wondrous body. Open my heart to you now. You are my High Priest who knows.

READ HEBREWS 4:15-16

This High Priest of ours understands our weaknesses, for he faced all of the same testings we do, yet he did not sin. So let us come boldly to the throne of our gracious God. There we will receive his mercy, and we will find grace to help us when we need it most.

REFLECT

Having followed Jesus' life and identified some of his bodily experiences, we can't help but more fully grasp what the author of Hebrews says in this passage. It is not the case that Jesus understands because he knows all things or can imagine how we feel. He knows from personal experience: He has known vulnerability, pain, suffering, temptation, exhaustion, hunger, grief. He knows the weakness it is to be in a body as a human being.

• Consider the weaknesses of your body. What does it mean to you as you pray and persevere that Jesus knows your weaknesses?

• Reflect on the reality that one who mediates and stands before God on your behalf knows the weaknesses of being human from firsthand, actual experience. What does this truth reveal to you about God's love? What does it reveal about Jesus' ability to identify with you?

• How might coming to terms with the weaknesses and vulnerabilities of your body help you understand and serve those you tend to view as weak or less capable?

Christmas

Jesus Christ—
Wonderful Counselor, Mighty God, Everlasting Father, and Prince of Peace;
the one through whom and for whom all things were made; and
the one in whom I live and move and have my being—
you became flesh and made your dwelling among us.
And nothing—neither death nor life, angels nor demons, the present nor the future; not any powers, height nor depth, nor anything else in all creation—can separate me from the love of our God, which is in you, Jesus Christ my Lord.

DAY 13

BODIES THAT WILL NEVER DIE

Begin by taking a few breaths and paying attention to the air moving in and out of your lungs and mouth. Notice where you feel tension or discomfort in your body. To the extent you are able, try to relax, let the chair you are sitting in fully support your body, and release the tension as you breathe deeply.

a prayer to open

Here I am, Lord, in my tired, aging, hurting, wondrous body.
Open my heart to you now. You are my High Priest who knows.

READ 1 CORINTHIANS 15:35-54

But someone may ask, "How will the dead be raised? What kind of bodies will they have?" What a foolish question! When you put a seed into the ground, it doesn't grow into a plant unless it dies first. And what you put in the ground is not the plant that will grow, but only a bare seed of wheat or whatever you are planting. Then God gives it the new body he wants it to have. A different plant grows from each kind of seed. Similarly there are different kinds of flesh—one kind for humans, another for animals, another for birds, and another for fish.

There are also bodies in the heavens and bodies on the earth. The glory of the heavenly bodies is different from the glory of the earthly bodies. The sun has one kind of glory, while the moon and stars each have another kind. And even the stars differ from each other in their glory.

It is the same way with the resurrection of the dead. Our earthly bodies are planted in the ground when we die, but they will be raised to live forever. Our bodies are buried in brokenness, but they will be raised in glory. They are buried in weakness, but they will be raised in strength. They are buried as natural human bodies, but they will be raised as spiritual bodies. For just as there are natural bodies, there are also spiritual bodies.

The Scriptures tell us, "The first man, Adam, became a living person." But the last Adam—that is, Christ—is a life-giving Spirit. What comes first is the natural body, then the spiritual body comes later. Adam, the first man, was made from the dust of the earth, while Christ, the second man, came from heaven. Earthly people are like the earthly man, and heavenly people are like the heavenly man. Just as we are now like the earthly man, we will someday be like the heavenly man.

What I am saying, dear brothers and sisters, is that our physical bodies cannot inherit the Kingdom of God. These dying bodies cannot inherit what will last forever.

But let me reveal to you a wonderful secret. We will not all die, but we will all be transformed! It will happen in a moment, in the blink of an eye, when the last trumpet is blown. For when the trumpet sounds, those who have died will be raised to live forever. And we who are living will also be transformed. For our dying bodies must be transformed into bodies that will never die; our mortal bodies must be transformed into immortal bodies.

Then, when our dying bodies have been transformed into bodies that will never die, this Scripture will be fulfilled:

"Death is swallowed up in victory."

REFLECT

The fact that Jesus conquered death in his body and rose again in his body means that we too will rise after death. We will live again, but not as spirits or disembodied souls: We will have glorious new bodies that will never die.

- What confusion, emotions, or concerns arise in you when you read today's passage?

- In what parts of your body are you longing for healing and restoration? What would full restoration look like for that part of your body?

- Reflect on the reality that because Jesus rose from the dead, conquering death, we who are in Christ will also rise from the dead and receive new, eternal bodies. What does this truth reveal to you about God's love? What does it reveal about Jesus' ability to identify with you?

RESPOND

Jesus Christ—
Wonderful Counselor, Mighty God, Everlasting Father, and Prince of Peace;
the one through whom and for whom all things were made; and
the one in whom I live and move and have my being—
you became flesh and made your dwelling among us.
And nothing—neither death nor life, angels nor demons, the present nor the future; not any powers, height nor depth, nor anything else in all creation—can separate me from the love of our God, which is in you, Jesus Christ my Lord.

I AM MAKING EVERYTHING NEW!

Begin by taking a few breaths and paying attention to the air moving in and out of your lungs and mouth. Notice where you feel tension or discomfort in your body. To the extent you are able, try to relax, let the chair you are sitting in fully support your body, and release the tension as you breathe deeply.

a prayer to open   Here I am, Lord, in my tired, aging, hurting, wondrous body.
Open my heart to you now. You are my High Priest who knows.

Then I saw a new heaven and a new earth, for the old heaven and the old earth had disappeared. And the sea was also gone. And I saw the holy city, the new Jerusalem, coming down from God out of heaven like a bride beautifully dressed for her husband.

I heard a loud shout from the throne, saying, "Look, God's home is now among his people! He will live with them, and they will be his people. God himself will be with them. He will wipe every tear from their eyes, and there will be no more death or sorrow or crying or pain. All these things are gone forever."

And the one sitting on the throne said, "Look, I am making everything new!" And then he said to me, "Write this down, for what I tell you is trustworthy and true." And he also said, "It is finished! I am the Alpha and the Omega—the Beginning and the End. To all who are thirsty I will give freely from the springs of the water of life. All who are victorious will inherit all these blessings, and I will be their God, and they will be my children."

REFLECT

The most poignant reality about being embodied is the suffering and pain our bodies must endure, whether in the bumps and bruises of growing up or in our vulnerability to external dangers, sickness and disease, aging, and death. God's promise is to relieve those sufferings. He is making all things new, including our bodies, and there is a day coming when there will be no more pain or suffering or death.

- Imagine getting to live in your body without ever feeling pain because you are no longer at risk for being hurt. What do you imagine that being like?

- Reflect on God's promise that your body will be healed and whole. What would it look like to live in that truth? How might your courage be affected?

- Reflect on the reality that in and through Jesus, the embodied one, God is making all things new and will remove all possibility of pain and suffering and death. What does this truth reveal to you about God's love? What does it reveal about Jesus' ability to identify with you?

RESPOND

Jesus Christ—
Wonderful Counselor, Mighty God, Everlasting Father, and Prince of Peace;
the one through whom and for whom all things were made; and
the one in whom I live and move and have my being—
you became flesh and made your dwelling among us.
And nothing—neither death nor life, angels nor demons, the present nor the future; not any powers, height nor depth, nor anything else in all creation—can separate me from the love of our God, which is in you, Jesus Christ my Lord.

SACRED QUESTIONS

WORD BECAME FLESH

a prayer to open   Here I am, Lord, in my tired, aging, hurting, wondrous body.
Open my heart to you now. You are my High Priest who knows.

READ JOHN 1:1-14

In the beginning the Word already existed.
The Word was with God,
and the Word was God.
He existed in the beginning with God.
God created everything through him,
and nothing was created except through
him.
The Word gave life to everything that was
created,
and his life brought light to everyone.
The light shines in the darkness,
and the darkness can never extinguish it.

God sent a man, John the Baptist, to tell about
the light so that everyone might believe because
of his testimony. John himself was not the light; he
was simply a witness to tell about the light. The one
who is the true light, who gives light to everyone,
was coming into the world.

He came into the very world he created, but the
world didn't recognize him. He came to his own
people, and even they rejected him. But to all who
believed him and accepted him, he gave the right
to become children of God. They are reborn—not
with a physical birth resulting from human passion
or plan, but a birth that comes from God.

So the Word became human and made his
home among us. He was full of unfailing love and
faithfulness. And we have seen his glory, the glory
of the Father's one and only Son.

REFLECT

The eternal Son of God, in communion with the Father and the Spirit forever, lowered himself, humbled himself, and embodied himself in order to save us. Oh that we could remember this truth when we relate to, call on, live in, and share Jesus. If we could somehow prevent ourselves from thinking of him as a disembodied spirit who is far from us and unable to know all the pain and joy we experience in our bodies, how might our images of our own bodies change? How might we better care for ourselves? How might we grow in respect for the bodies of others, seeing them as sacred and specially made by God instead of things to be used or abused, as is so often the case? May we always remember that God came in the flesh, in a body, and to this very moment Jesus has a body.

- Having spent the past fifteen days focusing on the truth of God's coming in the flesh to be with us, what happens in you when you read this rich, well-known announcement about Jesus Christ?

- How have these fifteen days influenced your view and understanding of your own body?

- Reflect on the reality that the Word—the eternal Son of God—became flesh and made his dwelling among us. What does this truth reveal to you about God's love? What does it reveal about Jesus' ability to identify with you?

Christmas

•

467

Jesus Christ—
Wonderful Counselor, Mighty God, Everlasting Father, and Prince of Peace;
the one through whom and for whom all things were made; and
the one in whom I live and move and have my being—
you became flesh and made your dwelling among us.
And nothing—neither death nor life, angels nor demons, the present nor the future; not any powers, height nor depth, nor anything else in all creation—can separate me from the love of our God,
which is in you, Jesus Christ my Lord.

Easter

Experiencing Jesus' Last Days and Resurrection

THE RESURRECTION OF Jesus stands at the center of the Christian faith. Without the Resurrection, there is no hope. How did the most miraculous event in all of history turn into a story about pastels, bunnies, and colored eggs? Many of us spend more time dyeing eggs with our children than we do contemplating and expressing gratitude for all that Jesus suffered so we may live forever. And once church service ends on Resurrection Sunday (or whatever day we attend service), most of us go back to life as usual. Somehow the resurrection of Jesus has become another date on our calendar, a historical event that we celebrate, but it doesn't affect our day-to-day life. As Paul said in Romans 8:11, "If the Spirit of him who raised Jesus from the dead is living in you, he who raised Christ from the dead will also give life to your mortal bodies because of his Spirit who lives in you" (NIV).

The problem we have is that we can't force ourselves to live in the resurrection power of Christ. We can't will it. Rather, we need to surrender to God's Spirit in us and allow him to live through us as we live in him. As a way to open ourselves to all that God seeks to do in and through us by his resurrection power, we will spend the seven days leading up to Resurrection Sunday using a spiritual practice called imaginative prayer as we read about Jesus' last days.

Before we dive in, let me give you an example of how an imaginative-prayer experience might draw us into deeper relationship with and knowledge of God.

One night at a contemplative church service I helped lead at Willow Creek, a guest speaker we'd invited to teach led us through an imaginative-prayer exercise featuring the story of Jesus (and then Peter) walking on the water (see Matthew 14:22-33). First the speaker read the story to familiarize us again with what had happened. Then he asked us to close our eyes. He began reading again, but this time as he read, he asked us to imagine ourselves there in the boat with Peter and the other disciples. He asked what we saw, smelled, heard. He asked us to pay attention to who was with us and what we were doing. Then he simply left us in silence to encounter Jesus.

I was in the small boat and it was storming. Darkness drowned out all the light. Waves crashed into the boat, and my shoes filled with water. People I didn't know surrounded me, and next to me, huddled under my arm, was my daughter, Jamie. We both cried out with fear because it was clear we wouldn't survive.

Then I heard a voice calling to me: "Come! Don't be afraid! Come!" I looked up and my eyes met Jesus' eyes. They were compassionate and calm. He held out his hand to me from where he stood, outside the boat, but upon what I could not tell. Everything in me wanted to put my hand in his and be pulled to safety. But Jamie was with me, grasping on to me with the full force of her body. In order to be rescued, I would have to let go of her. I turned my eyes back to Jesus and said, "I can't. I can't leave her." He said, "I will save her, too, but you need to go first." I couldn't do it. I wrapped my arms even tighter around Jamie, and Jesus moved on to the person beside me in the boat.

I opened my eyes and realized I was sitting in the Willow Creek chapel. I was safe, in a chair, on the land. Jamie was at a friend's house babysitting.

This was my first experience with imaginative prayer. I have rarely heard from God more clearly. I did not trust him, not completely, not fully. I did not trust him with my Jamie. Although with my words I would surely affirm that God loves my daughter more than I ever could—after all, he's God and his love is unending and eternal, not to mention never sidetracked by distraction, exhaustion, or the myriad of other human things that impede my love—this experience of imaginative prayer, in which I had to act, revealed that, when it came down to it, I didn't believe he could love and care for her better than I. Through this experience, God had identified something I did not know and called me to deeper trust and relationship with him.

Many stories in Scripture can be more fully entered into through our God-given imaginations, but often this practice can be an even greater gift when it comes to the stories we have known our whole lives in one form or another. The familiarity most of us have with the Scriptures describing what happened to Jesus the week before his resurrection makes these the perfect stories for us to seek to enter more fully. We will journey through the last days of Jesus' time on earth, including his crucifixion and resurrection, and see what God might show us about how we are relating to him, how we can more closely identify with Jesus, and anything else he might use to draw us closer to himself so that we may live with resurrection power, trusting him fully.

KING JESUS

a prayer to open   Help me experience your presence. Lead me to deeper levels of trust.
Give me the courage to put my hands in yours.

READ LUKE 19:28-44

As [Jesus] came to the towns of Bethphage and Bethany . . . he sent two disciples ahead. "Go into that village over there," he told them. "As you enter it, you will see a young donkey tied there that no one has ever ridden. Untie it and bring it here. If anyone asks, 'Why are you untying that colt?' just say, 'The Lord needs it.'"

So they went and found the colt, just as Jesus had said. And sure enough, as they were untying it, the owners asked them, "Why are you untying that colt?"

And the disciples simply replied, "The Lord needs it." So they brought the colt to Jesus and threw their garments over it for him to ride on.

As he rode along, the crowds spread out their garments on the road ahead of him. . . . All of his followers began to shout and sing as they walked along, praising God for all the wonderful miracles they had seen.

"Blessings on the King who comes in the name of the LORD!
Peace in heaven, and glory in highest heaven!"

But some of the Pharisees among the crowd said, "Teacher, rebuke your followers for saying things like that!"

He replied, "If they kept quiet, the stones along the road would burst into cheers!"

But as he came closer to Jerusalem and saw the city ahead, he began to weep. "How I wish today that you of all people would understand the way to peace. But now it is too late, and peace is hidden from your eyes. Before long your enemies will build ramparts against your walls and encircle you and close in on you from every side. They will crush you into the ground, and your children with you. Your enemies will not leave a single stone in place, because you did not recognize it when God visited you."

REFLECT

- Use your imagination to enter into this passage of Scripture. Close your eyes and picture yourself there with Jesus. Where do you find yourself? Are you on the sidelines or at the center of the action? What do you see, hear, smell? What do you notice about Jesus?

- How did you experience Jesus in this imaginative time?

- Read Zechariah 9:9-13. What does this Old Testament prophecy illuminate about Jesus' kingship? *complete   gentle yet powerful   timeless*

RESPOND

Lord Jesus, you are King of all things—
the things on earth and the things in heaven.
May my eyes see you as King.
May my body honor you as King.
May my heart revere you as King.

BROKEN JESUS

a prayer to open   Help me experience your presence. Lead me to deeper levels of trust. Give me the courage to put my hands in yours.

READ MARK 14:12-26

On the first day of the Festival of Unleavened Bread, when the Passover lamb is sacrificed, Jesus' disciples asked him, "Where do you want us to go to prepare the Passover meal for you?"

So Jesus sent two of them into Jerusalem with these instructions: "As you go into the city, a man carrying a pitcher of water will meet you. Follow him. At the house he enters, say to the owner, 'The Teacher asks: Where is the guest room where I can eat the Passover meal with my disciples?' He will take you upstairs to a large room that is already set up. That is where you should prepare our meal." So the two disciples went into the city and found everything just as Jesus had said, and they prepared the Passover meal there.

In the evening Jesus arrived with the Twelve. As they were at the table eating, Jesus said, "I tell you the truth, one of you eating with me here will betray me."

Greatly distressed, each one asked in turn, "Am I the one?"

He replied, "It is one of you twelve who is eating from this bowl with me. For the Son of Man must die, as the Scriptures declared long ago. But how terrible it will be for the one who betrays him. It would be far better for that man if he had never been born!"

As they were eating, Jesus took some bread and blessed it. Then he broke it in pieces and gave it to the disciples, saying, "Take it, for this is my body."

And he took a cup of wine and gave thanks to God for it. He gave it to them, and they all drank from it. And he said to them, "This is my blood, which confirms the covenant between God and his people. It is poured out as a sacrifice for many. I tell you the truth, I will not drink wine again until the day I drink it new in the Kingdom of God."

Then they sang a hymn and went out to the Mount of Olives.

REFLECT

• Use your imagination to enter into this passage of Scripture. Close your eyes and picture yourself there with Jesus. Where do you find yourself? Are you on the sidelines or at the center of the action? What do you see, hear, smell? What do you notice about Jesus?

• How did you experience Jesus in this imaginative time?

• Read Exodus 12:1-30. What does this story of the original Passover illuminate about Jesus' mission?

RESPOND

Lord Jesus, your body was broken for my sake
and for the sake of the world.
May your brokenness piece me back together.
May your brokenness heal me.
May your brokenness heal the whole world.

WEEPING JESUS

a prayer to open   Help me experience your presence. Lead me to deeper levels of trust.
Give me the courage to put my hands in yours.

READ MATTHEW 26:36-46

Then Jesus went with them to the olive grove called Gethsemane, and he said, "Sit here while I go over there to pray." He took Peter and Zebedee's two sons, James and John, and he became anguished and distressed. He told them, "My soul is crushed with grief to the point of death. Stay here and keep watch with me."

He went on a little farther and bowed with his face to the ground, praying, "My Father! If it is possible, let this cup of suffering be taken away from me. Yet I want your will to be done, not mine."

Then he returned to the disciples and found them asleep. He said to Peter, "Couldn't you watch with me even one hour? Keep watch and pray, so that you will not give in to temptation. For the spirit is willing, but the body is weak!"

Then Jesus left them a second time and prayed, "My Father! If this cup cannot be taken away unless I drink it, your will be done." When he returned to them again, he found them sleeping, for they couldn't keep their eyes open.

So he went to pray a third time, saying the same things again. Then he came to the disciples and said, "Go ahead and sleep. Have your rest. But look—the time has come. The Son of Man is betrayed into the hands of sinners. Up, let's be going. Look, my betrayer is here!"

REFLECT

• Use your imagination to enter into this passage of Scripture. Close your eyes and picture yourself there with Jesus. Where do you find yourself? Are you on the sidelines or at the center of the action? What do you see, hear, smell? What do you notice about Jesus?

• How did you experience Jesus in this imaginative time?

• Read Isaiah 51:17-23. What does Isaiah's prophecy illuminate about Jesus' experience in the garden of Gethsemane?

RESPOND

Lord Jesus, you wept and grieved as you drank
down the dregs of my sin and the sin of the world.
May I feel the weight of your grief.
May I know the pain of your weeping.
May I sense your presence in the darkness.

CONVICTED JESUS

a prayer to open   Help me experience your presence. Lead me to deeper levels of trust.

Give me the courage to put my hands in yours.

READ MARK 14:60-72

Then the high priest stood up before the others and asked Jesus, "Well, aren't you going to answer these charges? What do you have to say for yourself?" But Jesus was silent and made no reply. Then the high priest asked him, "Are you the Messiah, the Son of the Blessed One?"

Jesus said, "I AM. And you will see the Son of Man seated in the place of power at God's right hand and coming on the clouds of heaven."

Then the high priest tore his clothing to show his horror and said, "Why do we need other witnesses? You have all heard his blasphemy. What is your verdict?"

"Guilty!" they all cried. "He deserves to die!"

Then some of them began to spit at him, and they blindfolded him and beat him with their fists. "Prophesy to us," they jeered. And the guards slapped him as they took him away.

Meanwhile, Peter was in the courtyard below. One of the servant girls who worked for the high priest came by and noticed Peter warming himself at the fire. She looked at him closely and said, "You were one of those with Jesus of Nazareth."

But Peter denied it. "I don't know what you're talking about," he said, and he went out into the entryway. Just then, a rooster crowed.

When the servant girl saw him standing there, she began telling the others, "This man is definitely one of them!" But Peter denied it again.

A little later some of the other bystanders confronted Peter and said, "You must be one of them, because you are a Galilean."

Peter swore, "A curse on me if I'm lying—I don't know this man you're talking about!" And immediately the rooster crowed the second time.

Suddenly, Jesus' words flashed through Peter's mind: "Before the rooster crows twice, you will deny three times that you even know me." And he broke down and wept.

REFLECT

• Use your imagination to enter into this passage of Scripture. Close your eyes and picture yourself there with Jesus. Where do you find yourself? Are you on the sidelines or at the center of the action? What do you see, hear, smell? What do you notice about Jesus?

• How did you experience Jesus in this imaginative time?

• Read Mark 14:27-31 and John 21:15-19. What does Jesus' prediction of Peter's denial and Jesus' gracious reinstatement of Peter back into relationship illuminate about God's forgiveness?

RESPOND

Lord Jesus, though you were innocent,
you were accused and convicted of the world's sin.
Though you were faithful, you were betrayed.
Though you were true, you were denied.
May I claim your innocence.
May I model your faithfulness.
May I stand in your truth.

SUFFERING JESUS

a prayer to open   Help me experience your presence. Lead me to deeper levels of trust.
Give me the courage to put my hands in yours.

READ LUKE 23:32-46

Two others, both criminals, were led out to be executed with him. When they came to a place called The Skull, they nailed him to the cross. And the criminals were also crucified—one on his right and one on his left.

Jesus said, "Father, forgive them, for they don't know what they are doing." And the soldiers gambled for his clothes by throwing dice.

The crowd watched and the leaders scoffed. "He saved others," they said, "let him save himself if he is really God's Messiah, the Chosen One." The soldiers mocked him, too, by offering him a drink of sour wine. They called out to him, "If you are the King of the Jews, save yourself!" A sign was fastened above him with these words: "This is the King of the Jews."

One of the criminals hanging beside him scoffed, "So you're the Messiah, are you? Prove it by saving yourself—and us, too, while you're at it!"

But the other criminal protested, "Don't you fear God even when you have been sentenced to die? We deserve to die for our crimes, but this man hasn't done anything wrong." Then he said, "Jesus, remember me when you come into your Kingdom."

And Jesus replied, "I assure you, today you will be with me in paradise."

By this time it was about noon, and darkness fell across the whole land until three o'clock. The light from the sun was gone. And suddenly, the curtain in the sanctuary of the Temple was torn down the middle. Then Jesus shouted, "Father, I entrust my spirit into your hands!" And with those words he breathed his last.

REFLECT

- Use your imagination to enter into this passage of Scripture. Close your eyes and picture yourself there with Jesus. Where do you find yourself? Are you on the sidelines or at the center of the action? What do you see, hear, smell? What do you notice about Jesus?

- How did you experience Jesus in this imaginative time?

- Read Isaiah 53:1-12. What does Isaiah's prediction about how the coming Messiah would suffer for the sake of all humanity illuminate about Jesus' suffering?

RESPOND

Lord Jesus, you suffered humiliation, separation, and death
to offer forgiveness, reconciliation, and life.
May I forgive as you forgave.
May I reconcile as you reconciled.
May I live as you lived.

UNSEEN JESUS

a prayer to open   Help me experience your presence. Lead me to deeper levels of trust. Give me the courage to put my hands in yours.

READ LUKE 24:13-32

That same day two of Jesus' followers were walking to the village of Emmaus.... As they walked along they were talking about everything that had happened.... Jesus himself suddenly came and began walking with them. But God kept them from recognizing him.

He asked them, "What are you discussing so intently as you walk along?"

They stopped short, sadness written across their faces. Then one of them, Cleopas, replied, "You must be the only person in Jerusalem who hasn't heard about all the things that have happened there the last few days."

"What things?" Jesus asked.

"The things that happened to Jesus, the man from Nazareth," they said. "He was a prophet who did powerful miracles, and he was a mighty teacher in the eyes of God and all the people. But our leading priests and other religious leaders handed him over to be condemned to death, and they crucified him. We had hoped he was the Messiah who had come to rescue Israel. This all happened three days ago.

"Then some women from our group of his followers were at his tomb early this morning, and they came back with an amazing report. They said his body was missing, and they had seen angels who told them Jesus is alive! Some of our men ran out to see, and sure enough, his body was gone." ...

Then Jesus said to them, "You foolish people! You find it so hard to believe all that the prophets wrote in the Scriptures. Wasn't it clearly predicted that the Messiah would have to suffer all these things before entering his glory?" Then Jesus took them through the writings of Moses and all the prophets, explaining from all the Scriptures the things concerning himself.

By this time they were nearing Emmaus.... They begged him, "Stay the night with us, since it is getting late." So he went home with them. As they sat down to eat, he took the bread and blessed it. Then he broke it and gave it to them. Suddenly, their eyes were opened, and they recognized him. And at that moment he disappeared!

They said to each other, "Didn't our hearts burn within us as he talked with us on the road and explained the Scriptures to us?"

REFLECT

- Use your imagination to enter into this passage of Scripture. Close your eyes and picture yourself there with Jesus. Where do you find yourself? Are you on the sidelines or at the center of the action? What do you see, hear, smell? What do you notice about Jesus?

- How did you experience Jesus in this imaginative time?

- Read Psalm 22. What does the fact that Jesus quoted this psalm with his last breaths reveal about his experience on the cross?

RESPOND

Lord Jesus, I have failed to believe,
fallen into despair, and
closed my eyes to your presence.
May I walk in faith.
May I live in hope.
May my soul be awakened.

RISEN JESUS

a prayer to open   Help me experience your presence. Lead me to deeper levels of trust. Give me the courage to put my hands in yours.

READ JOHN 20:11-18

Mary was standing outside the tomb crying, and as she wept, she stooped and looked in. She saw two white-robed angels, one sitting at the head and the other at the foot of the place where the body of Jesus had been lying. "Dear woman, why are you crying?" the angels asked her.

"Because they have taken away my Lord," she replied, "and I don't know where they have put him."

She turned to leave and saw someone standing there. It was Jesus, but she didn't recognize him. "Dear woman, why are you crying?" Jesus asked her. "Who are you looking for?"

She thought he was the gardener. "Sir," she said, "if you have taken him away, tell me where you have put him, and I will go and get him."

"Mary!" Jesus said.

She turned to him and cried out, "Rabboni!" (which is Hebrew for "Teacher").

"Don't cling to me," Jesus said, "for I haven't yet ascended to the Father. But go find my brothers and tell them, 'I am ascending to my Father and your Father, to my God and your God.'"

Mary Magdalene found the disciples and told them, "I have seen the Lord!" Then she gave them his message.

REFLECT

- Use your imagination to enter into this passage of Scripture. Close your eyes and picture yourself there with Jesus. Where do you find yourself? Are you on the sidelines or at the center of the action? What do you see, hear, smell? What do you notice about Jesus?

- How did you experience Jesus in this imaginative time?

- Read Psalm 24. What does this hope-filled psalm reveal to you about God's power, particularly as you read it in the context of Jesus' resurrection?

RESPOND

Lord Jesus, you are risen! You are alive!
You are present! You know my name!
May I hear your call.
May I turn to your love.
May I live in your presence.

Acknowledgments

THIS BOOK would not have been but for the presence, support, and love of my family, friends, and mentors. I am forever grateful to each of you.

Becky Sankey: You introduced me to Jesus through your life, your love, and your sacrifice. Your consistent faithfulness continues to stun and compel me.

Michael Freeborn: You convinced me that grace is real, taught me how to tell a story, and put me on a path that changed my life and eternity.

Steven Berg: You showed me faithfulness in the midst of trial, tragedy, and pain. You revealed the heart of Christ to me.

Amy Radeck: You showed me how to receive the love of Jesus. Our hours on your couch with Beth Moore, A. W. Tozer, and Brother Lawrence are carved into my heart and soul.

Michael Fox: You have been a faithful and devoted mentor and friend in all things writing and faith. Our phone prayers, visits, and lively theological debates have fed my soul and heart.

Lawrence and Martha Temfwe: Your steadfast, sacrificial, and prayerful lives reveal God's Kingdom on earth. You have taught me how to worship God with my life, surrender to God's purposes, and love others with God's reckless love.

Stella Kasirye: My prophetic, gifted sister in Christ. How different life would be without our yearly car prayers! So many of my major decisions have been made with your counsel, prayer, and support.

Ed Ramsami: You have encouraged me, affirmed my calling to write and teach, and been a faithful friend.

Aaron Niequist: Few people have had a greater impact on my spiritual growth. You opened my eyes to the Kingdom of God, the importance of spiritual practices, and the expansiveness of God's love for our world.

Josie, Sue, and Nicole: Your impact on my life is indelible. We have done some amazing ministry and life together. You have encouraged me, supported me, and loved me. Our friendship is a reflection of God's goodness in my life.

Dan Lovaglia: You gave me more opportunities than I ever deserved and believed in me beyond what I could have imagined.

John and Jenna Perrine: My dear, wise pastoral friends. You have filled my soul, been present in my best and worst days, and taught me so much about what it means to follow Christ.

Steve Carter: Thank you for always encouraging me and convincing me that my gifts are valuable and needed in the church.

Willow Creek congregation: Thank you for your engagement with the daily devotionals, encouraging me, and sharing the way God has used the devotionals in your life. You'll never know how much your words have meant.

September Vaudrey and Christine Anderson: Thank you for reading my proposal and giving me such thoughtful and helpful comments. Thank you Chris Ferebee, Angela Scheff, and Don Pape for taking a chance on me. Thank you Caitlyn Carlson for your awesome editing, knowing my heart, and making the book better.

Mom, Dorsey, Dad, Anna, Tracey, and Kendall: Thank you for your lifelong love, support, and care. You have always believed in me.

Joy, Sandra, Lori, and Rhianna: My fellow travelers and dearest friends—I don't think I'll know the true impact and depth of your friendship and love for years to come. You have been my place of refuge and soul care. You have shown me Christ and true community.

Steve, my love and husband: You are the love of my life. You see me like no one ever has and love me in ways I didn't think anyone ever could. Your support and encouragement means everything. And we've just gotten started!

Jamie, my daughter: There are no words sufficient to describe the impact you have had on my life, my writing, and my faith. You bring out the best in me and show me what love is. I can't wait to see the woman you become. You are a demonstration of God's goodness, faithfulness, love, and grace. You are my honey bunches of oats.

God, thank you for bringing each person on this list into my life and showing me more of who you are and who I am through each one. You are my loving Father, King, Rescuer, Refuge, and Guide. You found me and keep pursuing every part of my heart so that I may be transformed for your glory and for the sake of others.

Notes

1. Emphasis added.
2. Emphasis added.
3. Emphasis added.
4. Emphasis added.
5. Yinong Chong, Cheryl D. Fryar, and Qiuping Gu, "Prescription Sleep Aid Use Among Adults: United States, 2005–2010," NCHS Data Brief No. 127 (August 2013): 5, https://www.cdc.gov/nchs/data/databriefs/db127.pdf.
6. Elizabeth Barrett Browning, *Aurora Leigh*, ed. Kerry McSweeney (Oxford: Oxford University, 2008), 246.
7. See 2 Corinthians 12:9; Philippians 1:6; Matthew 28:20; Colossians 1:10-14; Revelation 21:5.
8. Adele Ahlberg Calhoun, *Spiritual Disciplines Handbook: Practices That Transform Us* (Downers Grove, IL: IVP, 2015), 47.
9. Christopher J. H. Wright, *The Mission of God: Unlocking the Bible's Grand Narrative* (Downers Grove, IL: IVP, 2006), 200, author's translation.
10. Scot McKnight, *A Fellowship of Differents: Showing the World God's Design for Life Together* (Grand Rapids, MI: Zondervan, 2016), 54.
11. Jerry Bridges, *The Fruitful Life* (Colorado Springs, CO: NavPress, 2006), 99.
12. "Figures at a Glance," United Nations Human Rights Commission (UNHRC), http://www.unhcr.org/en-us/figures-at-a-glance.html.

Topical Index